personal money management

PRENTICE-HALL, INC., Englewood Cliffs, New Jersey

GALE E. HURLEY
Cañada College
Redwood City, California

personal money management

A CONSUMER GUIDE

Library of Congress Cataloging in Publication Data

HURLEY, GALE E (date)
Personal money management.

1. Finance, Personal. I. Title.
HG179.H87 332'.024 75-35884
ISBN 0-13-657650-8

Printed in the United States of America

10 9 8 7 6 5 4 3

Prentice-Hall International Inc., *London*
Prentice-Hall of Australia Pty. Limited, *Sydney*
Prentice-Hall of Canada, Ltd., *Toronto*
Prentice-Hall of India Private Limited, *New Delhi*
Prentice-Hall of Japan, Inc., *Tokyo*
Prentice-Hall of Southeast Asia Pte. Ltd., *Singapore*

contents

People have always been interested in their personal finances, but in our inflationary era the reasons for their interest are especially apparent. People are being financially squeezed not only by general price level increases, but also by higher taxes, increased and costly leisure-time pursuits, a proliferation of goods and services that generate increased consumer desire, and even by longer life-spans, which create a need for more generous retirement funds. Students are filling personal money management classes that offer useful information on planning and management of personal resources. This book will also provide valuable background reading for courses in business, economics, home economics, and sociology. It is directed primarily toward persons who recognize the need to plan for and review their correct expenditures and their future goals.

This book suggests that the reader plan for his goals and reach them by proper management of his time, energy, and money. The reader should think for himself and not automatically accept traditional concepts of consuming, saving, insurance, investment, and housing; many of these concepts are fostered by business interests that stand to benefit if the consumer acts in a traditional manner. However, some traditional methods of personal money management *do* work. Therefore, the reader should consider all the alternatives and then decide for himself.

This text is divided into three major parts which correspond to a typical personal financial cycle. First, the individual sets his financial goals and priorities and attempts to manage his daily financial life including saving, purchasing, and borrowing. Second, he considers the consequences of catastrophe, the need for security, and the cost of insuring against certain hazards. Finally, the individual takes a long-term view of his financial status and considers home ownership and other investments for a more secure future.

Part 1 offers suggestions and techniques to help you allocate your financial resources reasonably in everyday life. Once you have defined your goals and priorities and balanced your budget, you need to know how to avoid faulty purchase, credit, and savings decisions. A consumer armed with accurate knowledge of the many alternatives available in our economy is much more likely to decide a purchase or financial matter satisfactorily.

Part 2 describes various insurance programs and asks you to consider the risks involved in each and the implications inherent in a particular risk. Is the secure feeling provided by a certain insurance protection worth the premiums? Why, when,

preface

and how much insurance to purchase are important decisions that will face you at all stages of life. Part 2 closes with a discussion of retirement planning and the disposition of property through wills, trusts, and gifts.

Part 3 details the many long-term investment possibilities open to you. It discusses income tax and encourages you to prepare your own return, which will help you recognize the tax ramifications of wages and other short-term income as compared to long-term capital gains. A separate chapter covers housing, one of the most important financial commitments made by a family or an individual. Other real estate investments are fully explored, both as companions to and as alternatives to home ownership. Several chapters describe security investment from the viewpoint of the small investor, covering such topics as common stock, bonds, and mutual funds. A final chapter offers suggestions on other types of investment opportunities.

Acknowledgment is given to the many government agencies, industry associations, and professional groups whose pamphlets and statistical information have proven invaluable. Special thanks also to the many students and colleagues who listened, read, and criticized the material in the book, especially Don Pewthers of New York Life Insurance Company and Jeff Anderson of Merrill Lynch, Pierce, Fenner and Smith, Inc. Alexander Pappas, at the College of Alameda, Alameda, California, also deserves special mention for his incisive review of the manuscript and his many suggestions about insurance. And special thanks to Patricia Hill for her efforts and understanding. Without Pat's insistence and encouragement, this text would not have been written.

personal money management

one

Before you can intelligently invest for the future, you must learn to cope with everyday financial affairs. Part one deals with the everyday financial considerations that all consumers must understand.

You must plan for your personal financial and consumer goals. You may not need to "keep up with the Joneses," but you should keep up with your own plans and goals. Individual and family groups often use differing techniques to reach their goals. We will examine the techniques people use to purchase goods and services. We will also examine the techniques of money accumulation needed to purchase items in the consumer market place. We will question the use of credit instead of savings. We will examine the effects of credit and determine whether it can be controlled effectively.

Part one should help you to reflect on the basics of financial planning. It will make you a much more informed consumer if you consider all the details and complications of what appears to be the simple everyday life.

financial planning for daily living

plan ahead

Almost everyone has important personal goals. Few people lack at least some partly defined goal based upon their own system of values. Few are completely happy-go-lucky and dependent upon friends or fate. Most people need personal goals to provide some self-realization for their value systems. Let us assume, therefore, that you have some goals or thoughts about what you want to accomplish. For example, do you want the "good life" for yourself and family? Do you want the simpler and less material things in life so that you will not have to strive so hard to reach a monetary goal? Do you want to help others through economic, political, and social reform? Do you want to retire early and enjoy the fruits of your labor and investment?

Whatever your general goals, it is wise to spend some time thinking about and evaluating them. You should, in general terms, have reachable goals. Your goals should reflect your values and those of your family to the greatest degree possible. Second, they should reflect those of friends, acquaintances, and society. Daydreams and pie-in-the-sky will not suffice for either personal or financial goals. Any goal is best programmed in a series of steps: short-term, intermediate-term, and long-term goals. By this sequential device you reinforce your personal long-term goal, which is presumably what your life is all about. A goal is not reached by sheer luck or secret wishes, but rather by design. Start with a careful self-appraisal of your strengths and weaknesses. In doing so you will be more realistic in setting all your goals, personal and financial.

SELF-APPRAISAL

List your accomplishments and failures and, even more important, *why* you succeeded or failed in various tasks in your personal and business life. Next, consider what you can do to insure continued success in your accomplishments and to rectify past failures. This self-appraisal should help you understand your potential and help you decide if the goals you set are reachable.

CHOOSING AMONG ALTERNATIVES

Planning to reach your goals is most important. You may aspire to materialistic goals or to altruistic goals, but your success in reaching either of them is much more likely with proper planning. A well-balanced life-plan should include planning for recreation, personal development, vocational development, education, and financial security. As you will probably note, there is a persistent theme of time and money in a life-plan. Your life-style and personal values will probably tip the balance in favor of either time or money. Your particular priorities and values influence your course of action throughout your lifetime. For example, you may choose a career that offers managerial and financial opportunities if you want authority, power, and economic freedom. You may choose a social-service career to "help others," even though the financial rewards may not be as great. You may also choose a career or life-style that allows you to leave your work problems on the job, not bring them home with you; or you may live for your work.

A person must plan to manage his time and money concurrently in order to reach his particular goals. Time should be carefully planned; this valuable resource becomes money if it is diligently utilized. Consider time as a vast deposit from which you can withdraw but never replace; hence it is a limited resource that becomes more valuable as the supply becomes more limited. Time, as both a personal and financial resource, is limited by your productive income periods. For example, a person cannot always devote enough time to business and social pursuits during his working years. You may have to decide which is more important to you, time or money.

Money, while it cannot become or create time, can and does finance leisure and recreation activities, so if you produce sufficient income in a relatively short period of time, you may be able to enjoy longer leisure time periods.

We can now label our time and money planning by the more appropriate title of financial planning, the process whereby an individual determines his values and priorities and attempts to find the most financially and personally rewarding method of reaching his goals. One must discover as many alternatives as possible during this planning process, because a person's strengths and weaknesses are not always readily apparent. He then chooses one or more plans from the many available and begins the journey toward his goal. Reaching your financial goal requires some discipline and much looking ahead. It does not have to be complicated if you first construct plans to reach your short and intermediate goals.

Financial planning is only the beginning. A person must implement his plans. This requires a fair amount of initiative. Then he must review his accomplishments regularly to insure that he is still on the path toward his financial goal. Money management is the process of implementing or carrying out and reviewing the financial plans that one has set. Generally, it is wise to stick to your original financial plan until your circumstances change; then you should revise your plan to meet the new circumstances.

LONG-TERM AND SHORT-TERM FINANCIAL GOALS

Your personal goals will determine your budget and will change as your circumstances change. Financial experts and sociologists have long noted that the individual's and family's goals tend to change at various periods of the life cycle. Table 1–1 illustrates this and may cause you to consider further your own goals. Remember that your goals, your life-style, and your budget are a reflection of your values and as such must be considered personal.

The goals listed in Table 1–1 are just a few of the many goals people have at any stage in life. They represent the major in-

Table 1–1 Short-term goals in relation to the life cycle

Life-Cycle Period	Goals
Youth	Recreation
Young adults	Recreation/Education/Occupation
Family—small children	Housing/Sufficient income
Family—older children	Education/High standard of living
Mature—no children at home	Recreation/Investment for retirement
Retirement	Enjoyment of life/Health

terests and financial goals of most people. Even if you are not aware of it, the family budget tends to revolve around these goals.

RECORD KEEPING A MUST

It is important that you have a personal record-keeping system for filing information in a place where it can be retrieved as it is needed. Have you ever filed something important away and then not been able to find it? We all have. This frustrating experience does not have to happen if you organize your personal records. Usually a large accordion file-folder, some envelopes, and a safety-deposit box are all that are required. Actually, if you are willing to accept the risk of fire or theft, you do not need to rent the safety-deposit box.

The main advantage of a record-keeping system is that valuable information is not so easily forgotten or lost. A good record-keeping system will allow a review of information whenever desired. A regular review of your personal records will provide pertinent information to assist you in reaching your goals.

Contents of a Personal File System

What belongs in your personal record-keeping system? Whatever you want in it and consider important to your goals. Polling in my classes over a number of years has led to the following suggested major classifications: Banking, Education, Income Tax, Insurance, Investment, Medical Records, Personal Records, Purchases, Real Estate, and Miscellaneous.

Each of these classifications can be subdivided under whatever headings are comfortable to you for easy filing and retrieval of papers and assorted items. For instance, you might subdivide the classification of "Banking" into blank checks, cancelled checks, and savings passbooks or certificates. A reference file-folder for pamphlets, news clippings, and articles on banking and its subdivisions might save you money, especially when you are hunting for a depository for your funds at the highest possible rate of interest.

A reference file-folder on each major classification will be useful and will help you in money matters. Each classification deserves to be subdivided. "Education" might contain folders of transcripts, honors received, athletic awards, student loans, and applications that you have made. "Income Tax" should contain your returns for the last six years, envelopes for supporting documents, and any information and receipts needed to support next year's return. "Insurance" will be a rather thick portfolio if you keep your policies at home. Each type of insurance policy should have a separate folder to keep receipts, riders, billings, and assorted papers in some order. Staple all papers with a common policy number together. "Investment" probably will be a rather thin folder for a young person. However, now is the time to gather articles on the subject, keep business cards of investment analysts and generally start toward your financial goals. "Medical Records" is an example of your personalized record-keeping system. Immunization and dental records would certainly be deposited under this classification, as could various insurance and information booklets. Medical bills paid during the calendar year might also be filed in one place for major-medical and tax purposes.

The "Personal Records" file is one of the most important. It should contain such items as birth certificates, marriage licenses, religious records, passports, visas, military records and discharge papers, Veterans Administration records, social security records, and the like. A "Purchases" file could be subdivided into contracts, receipts, guarantees and warranties, and parts and repair catalogs. A "Real Estate" file would have legal documents for each piece of property owned as well as receipts and memos to account for any improvements made to the properties. The latter information is needed to establish an adjusted cost for the property whenever you sell. Each property should have a separate file. Correspondence with tenants, finance agencies, and government agencies could be filed by the property address.

Finally, a "Miscellaneous" file is a must for papers that do not fit elsewhere. Your personal record-keeping system will probably contain other classifications of interest to you such as travel brochures, maps, and small-business enterprises. The important thing is to file information logically in order to retrieve it as needed. Since your personal life cannot be segmented and filed as simply as business papers, your records should be thoroughly reviewed at least once a year for income tax purposes and to ascertain if you really are meeting the goals you have established for yourself.

YOUR NET WORTH

Earlier in the chapter, you made a self-appraisal of your strengths and weaknesses to assist in setting realistic personal goals. You must do the same thing for financial goals. The first step in sound financial management is to determine your present worth so that you may base future financial planning on current resources available to you. This is accomplished by determining your net worth.

Net worth is found by subtracting liabilities from assets: $A - L = NW$. In accounting, the equation is shown on a balance sheet as follows: assets equal liabilities plus net worth, $A = L + NW$. Basically, you are attempting to determine your true financial worth at a particular moment. Assets consists of all the things that you own. You estimate their dollar value. Liabilities are debts that you owe; they are claims against your assets. The difference is what you truly own, or your net worth.

You should prepare a balance sheet because it is a very informative tool to help you plan and review your money management. Many lenders require you to list assets and liabilities to determine your net worth for long-term loans. Bankers are interested in the amount of equity you have in your assets, and therefore you should also be interested. Equity is your ownership portion in any asset that is being purchased on credit. It is the present value of the asset less a creditor's claim against it. It will be heartening to note that just about everyone, students included, has a positive net worth. Frankly, it takes an unreasonable amount of bad luck or extremely poor money management to have your liabilities exceed your assets.

Balance Sheet

Table 1–2 is an example of a simplified family balance sheet. Note that it does not detail small assets that are consumed in everyday living. While these items may have cost a considerable dollar amount, they generally have little resale or borrowing

Table 1–2 Able family balance sheet for year ending December 31, 1975

Assets			
CURRENT ASSETS			
Cash			
Average checkbook balance	$300		
Savings accounts			
Bank	100		
Savings and Loan Association	500		
Credit Union	500		
Total current assets			$1,400
FIXED ASSETS			
Housewares and clothing	$1,000		
Furniture	4,000		
Boat	2,000		
Automobile	5,000		
Total personal property		$12,000	
Home		40,000	
Total fixed assets			52,000
TOTAL ASSETS			$53,400
Liabilities			
CONTINUOUS LIABILITIES			
Average balance on credit accounts			
Service accounts	$100		
Revolving accounts	200		
Total continuous liabilities		$300	
LONG-TERM LIABILITIES			
Installment accounts	$ 1,100		
Credit union loans	3,000		
Mortgage on home	18,000		
Total long-term liabilities		22,100	
TOTAL LIABILITIES			$22,400
NET WORTH			31,000
TOTAL LIABILITIES AND NET WORTH			$53,400

value. Such items as clothing, food supplies, household utensils and supplies, household soft goods, and small tools and hardware fall into this category. Hopefully these items have been purchased out of current income and do not constitute a liability or claim against your more noteworthy assets and therefore are not listed as an asset or liability on a simplified balance sheet.

Assets should be valued at market value or cost, whichever is lower. In this manner you will not overstate your net worth and give yourself a false sense of security. Not all possible assets and liabilities have been listed above. We have used only those that tend to be owned by a typical family.

Increasing Net Worth

This book is based upon the concept of informing you of how to increase your assets and (in the long run) to decrease your liabilities, thereby improving your net-worth position. Informed selection among the many consumer purchase choices and the many savings, investment, and insurance choices will do just that: cut costs and increase your asset equity position. The balance sheet lets you know your present financial standing, while the budget sheet indicates your monthly cash flow and ability to work toward your goal of improved net-worth position.

Balance sheet information should be put to work as part of your current planning and ultimate goal planning. Most likely you will not be satisfied with your net worth and will probably desire to increase it. This, you know, can be accomplished by increasing assets or decreasing liabilities. It can also be done (hopefully) by increasing liabilities, which can then be used to generate additional assets through income production or appreciation in the value of the purchased asset. For example, business people often borrow money (increase their liabilities) in order to purchase inventory or equipment (assets) for their business.

YOUR BUDGET

Preparing an individual or family budget can be a very rewarding or a very frustrating experience. In either case it will be a very personal experience. You and your family have your own life-style and preferred standard of living. In addition, you have short-term, intermediate-term, and long-term aspirations. You have unlimited current and future desires and rather limited income and resources to satisfy these desires. The problem, therefore, is to satisfy as many current desires and obligations as possible, save for future goals, and hopefully increase your net worth through expansion of your income and appreciation-producing assets. Your budget is a flexible guideline that helps you plan and implement the action necessary to accomplish all of these.

Certain considerations must be taken to insure the preparation of an adequate budget. First, know the general principles of money management. Second, gather all necessary financial data for budget planning. Third, balance income and outgo. And finally, review, adjust, and use your budget.

General Principles of Money Management

1. Live within your income by controlling your expenses. Do not attempt to keep up with the Joneses unless you can afford to do so.
2. Keep adequate records, including a budget. Life will be easier if you have records

available when you need them. You cannot possibly commit every piece of information to memory.

3. Be aware of your checkbook balance. Add the latest stub entry to your checkbook immediately. Keep it current and correctly balanced with the latest bank statement.
4. Be honest with yourself when preparing a budget. Develop guidelines that have reality and flexibility. You will be able to stay within such guidelines much more easily.
5. Compare your budget with national averages if you are interested in doing so. Remember that your life-style will be somewhat different from others'. Averages should be used only to satisfy your curiosity and to verify that you are reasonably close to a normal spending pattern.
6. Set up a budget period that is comfortable for you and that adequately accounts for all income and expenses. A monthly accounting period will probably prove to be the easiest and most satisfactory period, especially since most accounts are billed to you monthly. Budgets using other time periods such as weeks, quarters, or years have been used with varying degrees of success.

Financial Data for Budget Planning

We will assume a monthly budget period for the purposes of budget preparation.

1. Estimate your income from all sources. Use net income after withholding taxes, insurance, and other deductions. The idea is to record on a cash take-home basis for simplicity. Your estimations should be compiled on a monthly basis including prorated annual expenses. Include only guaranteed income.
2. Establish expense groupings. Your past expenditure patterns will assist you with this task. Many financial and educational organizations have prepared budget sheet formats with expense groupings already delineated for the use of their clients.
3. Determine your past spending patterns. You will definitely see the need for written records when you attempt to remember all this information. Be honest with yourself.
4. Spread out your lump-sum payments. Budget a portion of income each month for quarterly, semiannual, and annual obligations. A major problem faced by most people is the financial hardship engendered by lump-sum payments due for taxes and insurance premiums. You will save on finance charges when you save in advance for these outlays.
5. Assign responsibility for certain expenditures to different members of your family. This is usually accomplished by granting an allowance for each member of the family, who is then expected to pay these expenses. Detailed accounting should not be required from each family member unless there is a chronic imbalance in his expenditures.
6. Agree on major purchases. If husbands and wives disagree on major expenditures, there will almost certainly be a deterioration of the budget program.

Balancing Your Budget

Balancing is undoubtedly the hardest part of budgeting. Your priorities must be constantly considered. If your income exceeds your outgo, the process becomes quite easy. The major decision becomes, How much should I save for future needs and desires? Unfortunately, most people barely balance, or even more likely, they have a deficit balance. This is the moment of truth. You must do some trading of desires to make your outgo match your income. Here is where cooperation and understanding are needed by all family members. What priorities are truly important?

Table 1–3 Your budget is your whole spending plan. (This budget was worked out using an example of $10,000 annual take-home pay. Write your own plan into the blanks below the figures in the example.)

Category	Weekly	Monthly	Yearly	Percent
Savings	$9.62	$41.67	$500.00	5%
Housing	48.08	208.33	2,500.00	25
Food	48.08	208.33	2,500.00	25
Transportation	23.08	100.00	1,200.00	12
Clothing	19.23	83.33	1,000.00	10
Medical	13.46	58.33	700.00	7
Furnishings	7.69	33.33	400.00	4
Recreation	7.69	33.33	400.00	4
Personal	7.69	33.33	400.00	4
Miscellaneous	7.69	33.33	400.00	4
Spending Total	$192.31	$833.31	$10,000.00	100%

Review, Adjust, and Use Your Budget

You must be honest with yourself and have sufficient willpower to stick to your plans. If they are unrealistic, change them. If you regularly have surplus funds, your budget may be too loose. When this happens, you may be able to advance your planned timetable of major purchases or start your investment portfolio at an earlier date. In any case, regular reviews of your budget performance are necessary to insure current and future financial stability.

As you prepare your own budget work sheet, you will note that many expenses are fixed while some are more flexible. Obviously, the more fixed your outgo, the more rigid the allocation of the balance of your income. You may not have enough "give" in your budget to allow for trading off one want for another. Actually, whenever your budget does not balance, you have three alternatives: decrease your outgo, increase your income, or compromise between the two.

DECREASED OUTGO?

Does your budget balance? Is there enough income to cover fixed expenses, to provide sufficient money for everyday living expenses and still have something left for savings? If so, you are indeed fortunate. A majority of people are not so fortunate and must begin the process of determining what to do about it. A hard fact of financial and everyday life is that a person's desires and wants are almost unlimited, while his income is generally much more limited.

Cutting Back

Your first alternative is to decrease outgo. Giving up something is always hard on the morale, but it is far better to do so than to worry constantly about where you will get more money to pay for excessive expenditures. Another idea would be to review your budget at the beginning of the year and plan your monthly expenses. Make these plans fit into your limited income and you will not have to cut back on the standard of living to which you have become accustomed.

During periods of continuous inflation, cutting back is a very sensible procedure. Lessened demand has a curtailing effect on price increases. Unfortunately, demands on lower-priced goods often bring about a price increase on these items. Often the net effect on you as a consumer is that you hold your expenditures at their present level but receive lower-quality products. The alternative is to pay the higher price, imbalance your budget, and feed inflation.

Changing Priorities

As mentioned previously, things do not have to be eliminated entirely. You must consider your priorities and wants; what is important to you? Basically your priorities help you determine your budget. Averages make good guidelines; your personal priorities make your personal budget.

Your daily expenses involve many short-term decisions. Often you can trade off one want for another to provide yourself and family with those things that you value most dearly. You may purchase less-expensive cuts of meat, eat out less often, purchase fewer fashionable clothes in exchange for a vacation or some new furniture. Consider the total cost of such a trade-off in terms of dollars and in terms of time. Remember that time has value. Also, is it worth foregoing many small wants for a rather long period of time for one large want?

INCREASED INCOME?

The second alternative is to increase income. This may be just as distasteful as decreasing outgo. A decision is necessary; you cannot continue deficit spending indefinitely. It costs too much in money and worry.

Sound planning often requires the planner to give up immediate pleasures for future rewards. Increasing your income may demand that you do the same. Basically you forego time and money with their respective pleasures in order to increase income immediately or sometime in the future. Some methods used to increase income include overtime work, second jobs, operating a small business, having both spouses work, and getting more education for a better job. We will look at each of these in turn.

All the methods of increasing income require an investment of time, which takes you or your spouse away from the pleasures of family, friends, rest, and relaxation. Perhaps this is the true measure of the value of time and its management.

Overtime

Overtime is a good source of extra income when it is available. The wage scale is especially attractive at time-and-a-half or double time. However, do not count on it.

Fellow employees are also aware that overtime pay rates are attractive. Seniority and various rotation schemes may affect your chances of regularly scheduled overtime. Furthermore, businesses are also aware that it is costly to them and attractive to workers. During periods of lessened economic activity, overtime is the first item cut from the business budget.

Use discretion with overtime pay, and you will have an opportunity to supplement, but not balance, your budget. Separate and save your overtime pay until you have gathered the extra amount of money needed to purchase the product or service that you desire. In this manner you will be able to fulfill some of your desires without imbalancing or stretching your budget. Furthermore, you will not have to rely on overtime pay that may never materialize. Always consider overtime pay as something extra, not a part of your income, for budget purposes.

Second Jobs

Second jobs are another method of increasing income. These may be of a temporary or seasonal nature and should therefore be treated as one would treat overtime income. Permanent second jobs may be considered as part of your regular income for budget purposes. Generally, second jobs do not pay as well as your regular job, or you would most likely switch jobs. They normally do not provide the fringe benefits available on the first job, because you are usually a part-time employee. Also, as a part-time employee, you seldom work enough hours to qualify for overtime pay. Second jobs do have some advantages. The change of pace associated with working at a different set of tasks is much more helpful to your physical and mental well being than working extra hours at the same tasks performed in your regular job. Second, it may be to your advantage to have a second income you can rely upon to help you balance your budget, save some cash, or purchase the extra things that you have desired but could not afford.

Owning Your Own Small Business

Operating a small business is yet another method that an individual can use to provide extra income. The small business can either be a service or product-oriented operation. It might have its origins in your hobby, in which case you get the added benefit of enjoyment and relaxation. Certain tax advantages accrue to you when you operate your own business or profession. Chapters 11 and 15 will discuss the problems and opportunities afforded the small-business person. For budget purposes, the major disadvantage is that you cannot count on a certain level of income unless you expend a great deal of time and energy on your business.

Notice that all methods of securing extra income create problems for family and social life. This is particularly true because of the time element and the development of interests outside the home, which are necessary for any added endeavor. The cooperation and understanding of family members is vital to any such undertaking. It is perhaps even more crucial that the family plan together and agree to either of the last two methods of increasing income: having both spouses work and getting more education for a better job.

Working Spouses

When both spouses work the family obviously has a greater guaranteed income. But is it really worth it in terms of family disruptions, actual net income, and the interests and aspirations of the working/homemaking spouse? Each part of the question must be answered in terms of the whole family. There is no acceptable answer for society as a whole. Therefore, your family must determine if it is really worth it. Do not rely upon "keeping up with the Joneses," since they too may be wondering if it is really worth it.

Many family frustrations and inconveniences can be overcome through thoughtful time management. The use of convenience items in housekeeping and food preparation is a must when the homemaking spouse is working. Housekeeping becomes much more a family affair with voluntary and involuntary chores required of ali household members. Work-saving appliances and utensils become more necessary.

A desire for an increase in net family income is the usual reason a wife goes to work either full-time or part-time. Unfortunately, there is often a difference between the desire for, and the actuality of, the increase. Part-time work for a part-time salary often does not return a net increase in cash flow if all the hidden costs are considered. Full-time employment is more likely to return a "profit," but it would depend upon such directly related items as specific hours worked, rate of pay, union dues, commuting costs, child-care costs, and direct outlay for lunches.

In addition to direct work-related costs, there are often many hidden costs paid by a working spouse. These take the form of extra clothes or uniforms, depending on the job. Possibly an extra automobile will be needed, involving the many added costs of insurance, maintenance, and repairs over and above the purchase price. More expensive convenience foods, work-saving appliances, "conscience" money to provide for the children's entertainment, added dining out and entertainment for the entire family in order to relax and be together, and finally a more luxurious vacation to recuperate after working all year may well be the result of having both spouses work.

Family disruptions and less net income than expected are negative considerations in determining whether a wife should work outside the home. The interests and aspirations of the wife are positive considerations and must receive paramount attention. Many women seek socioeconomic and professional fulfillment outside the home. They should not be expected to act as family caretakers. Each spouse should be allowed to develop his or her interests with the understanding and cooperation of the other. Time-honored traditions such as "a woman's place is in the home" should be laid to rest. Our social concepts are changing as rapidly as our technology. A man should defer to the work preferences of his wife, especially if their marriage is to last in a world of social equality and mutual respect.

More Education for a Better Job

Government agencies, educators, and business people often state that the more responsible and better-paying positions go to people with a baccalaureate degree or higher graduate degree. Occupations requiring managerial skills or professional knowledge require a certain amount of time and education. Educators may be somewhat suspect in their motives for such statements, but the other two representatives of our employing society reflect the labor market and its compensation policies.

Numerous studies conclude that a male student who completes high school should earn approximately $500,000 during his work career. This average male student may expect to increase his income by 50 percent if he completes a college degree. Therefore, an investment of four years of time and study might yield a return of about $62,500 for each year of college.

Many studies find that more education results in more income. The U.S. Department of Labor reports an increase in paraprofessional occupations. These positions are technical in nature and are designed to relieve professional people, such as doctors, engineers, teachers, and social workers, from much of the detail in their daily jobs. The skills and knowledge for these positions usually require a two-year associate-in-arts degree involving a specific vocational program at a community college.

In the final analysis, financial planning must include a consideration of the amount of resource input you wish to make available to reach your long-term financial goals. Education, which requires the outlay of time, money, and effort, is an important resource tool that will help you reach your goals. In fact, you may not really have much choice in the matter. Job technology and employers desiring or requiring a more educated person are already exerting subtle pressures to establish the two-year college degree as the new norm in education. If you do not invest in a college education, you may find yourself less in demand in the labor market. It would be enjoyable to choose whether you wish to increase your income through a college education, but you may count on a continuing trend to require some college education just to secure an entrance-level job in the business world.

You and your family must weigh the sacrifices needed to prepare for the future as compared to enjoying the present. Increased income in the future may result from investing in a college education in the present. Unfortunately, income in the future does not balance a budget in the present. Perhaps the best solution to your budget problem lies in decreasing present outgo by controlled spending and by preparing to increase future income through higher education. Your solution, of course, must be acceptable to other members of your family.

Vocabulary and Concepts

Assets	Liabilities
Balance sheet	Life cycle
Budget plan	Net worth
Expenditure pattern	

Questions for Discussion

1. Why is self-appraisal so necessary to reach your goals?
2. What are the significant advantages available to young people for long-range financial planning?
3. Should a number of alternative methods for reaching your self-established goals be considered? Why or why not?
4. Explain how short-term goals must be used as stepping stones to reach long-term goals.
5. Discuss how you can increase your net worth. What alternatives are available?
6. What information is needed to plan a budget properly?
7. What are the alternatives available to people unable to balance their budget?

Projects

1. Review your personal record-keeping system. Are your papers and documents arranged so that you can find any item needed?
2. Determine your net worth. Prepare a balance sheet in the process. Be sure to include the fair market value or replace-

ment value of all your noncash possessions, and list all current and long-term debt.

3. Analyze your monthly cash flow. Start recording all your expenditures to determine where your money is really being spent.
4. Prepare a weekly, monthly, and annual budget for yourself or your family.

Case Problem

Arthur and Barbara Able are in their mid-twenties and have a two-year-old daughter. They own their home in the suburbs. Their balance sheet is illustrated in Table 1–2. Most of their net worth has accrued because of rising real estate values. Art has a take-home pay of $10,000 per year, but this amount no longer is adequate because of rising prices. An example of their current budget is illustrated in Table 1–3.

Barbara is considering part-time employment as a secretary at $2.50 per hour for a four-hour, five-day-per-week position. Barbara's job would be located ten miles from home. Consider all the expenses involved in the possibility of Barbara working part-time to help with the family's finances. Calculate all the expenses and determine if it is financially feasible for Barbara to work part-time. What other alternatives are available to the Able family?

2

We are in the age of consumerism. Ever since men and women began to produce goods and services for barter or purchase, we have been consumers, but we live now in an age of consumer awareness. Evidence of consumerism abounds in the imposing number of consumer protection agencies and consumer advocacy groups. You read and hear about consumerism constantly. The media tell you what to buy, on the one hand, and offer "Hot Line" redress on the other. One practices consumerism by purchasing a product or a service and weighing the value received from the purchase. The odds of consumer satisfaction differ greatly with the type of purchase. Figure 2–1 illustrates a recent survey of consumer appraisals of value received on various consumer items.

According to the Conference Board survey reported in 1974, consumers' appraisal of value received differed widely by product category. Recreation (78.5 percent), home furnishings (73.6 percent), and foods (71.7 percent) received the highest average of better ratings. Least favorable ratings went to home maintenance and utilities (53.0 percent), apparel (57.6 percent), and finance (61.5 percent). Since inflation has continued at a high rate since 1974, a newer survey would probably change the value-received scale within the category groupings.

The age of consumer awareness is just beginning. True protection for the consumer is not yet available, despite the many laws that attempt to regulate business practices and protect the consumer. The consumer is not king; at best he is a citizen who must protect his rights in the market place. The consumer is the largest unorganized majority in the country, even though everyone is a consumer. Unfortunately, your best interests are not always first in the arenas of government and business. Consumers tend to act individually rather than by group action and are therefore not as noticeable as business and labor interests, which have lobbyists that garner the attention of government in an organized and articulate fashion.

Caveat emptor (let the buyer beware) is still a mandate for today's consumer. You are still in a defensive position. Anything you can do to elect and advise consumer-responsive legislators will assist the consumer movement and yourself. This advocacy will not destroy our economic system or the free enterprise concept. It simply will make businesses more responsible for the goods and services they produce and sell. We have heard many protestations of consumer sovereignty from all three branches of government and from organized business. Perhaps we will be sovereign if government and business cooperate in a "Consumer Bill of Rights."

consumerism

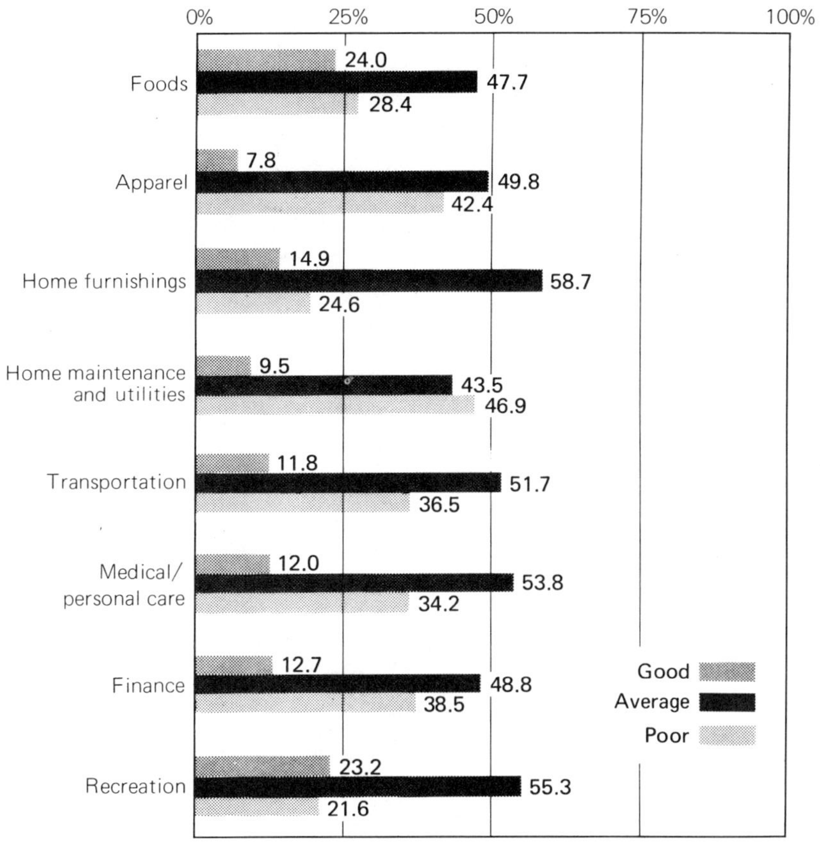

Figure 2–1 Consumer Appraisal of Value Received for Money Spent, by Product Category (Average Percent Distribution of Responses). *(The Conference Board, National Consumer Finance Association)*

CONSUMER BILL OF RIGHTS

There is nothing new about consumer rights. President John F. Kennedy proclaimed four basic consumer rights in 1962: (1) the right to safety, (2) the right to be informed, (3) the right to choose, and (4) the right to be heard. Presidents Johnson, Nixon, and Ford, along with many members of Congress, have reiterated the concept of consumer rights (however, not necessarily with the same vigor). Numerous consumer rights laws have been advocated and legislated in some degree over the last decade. Unfortunately, the law that finally evolves is often too little and too late.

Government and business should form a bill of rights agreeing that all products purchased should provide the following basic consumer information:

1. A permanent label, with the name and mailing address of the manufacturer, for consumer complaints.

2. The product name, model number, serial number, and manufacturing date must be permanently visible on all products.
3. A "good until" date must be listed on all products with perishable characteristics.
4. Foods, drugs, and textiles must be labeled with a percentage list of ingredients in descending order.
5. A warning of known harmful effects of any ingredient.
6. Instructions for normal use with an express warranty as to intended use and product life.
7. Warning as to hazards of normal use and abnormal use.
8. A highly visible notice, if the product must be used in conjunction with another product.
9. A booklet of repair instructions with a list of specifications and repair service locations.
10. A parts list with current prices and the address from which they can be ordered by mail.
11. Retail sales prices should be posted conspicuously in single-unit prices.
12. Products packaged in multiple sizes must also be priced by unit of measurement.

These are the *minimum* rights that a consumer should expect. Availability of competing models and prices would be informative, but hard to maintain. The quality of the ingredients and the workmanship that make up a final product are hard to determine objectively. However, efforts to develop informational standards of this sort should be endorsed.

You cannot wait for the "Consumer Bill of Rights" to happen. You must take steps to protect yourself now. Be aware of consumer motivation and the selling process. Know the selling strategies of those products and services that you are likely to purchase. And finally, know how to use the remedies available to you if you are a dissatisfied consumer. Personal money management is a continuous process.

CONSUMER MOTIVATION

An overall view of what motivates a person to behave in a certain way or purchase a particular product or service will help you better understand consumerism and all its implications. Buying behavior is triggered by a series of stimulus-response and problem-solution actions initiated by the buyer or the seller. The process creates tension, which continues to build on a conscious or unconscious level until a consumer takes some action. The heart of consumer motivation lies in relieving a need or a want. A salesperson knows this.

Needs and Wants

Behavioral scientists have established two major classifications of desires upon which most needs and wants are based: physiological/biological desires and social/psychological desires. The former relate to the function of the human body, while the latter and more controversial desires are related to the individual's self-fulfillment and his relations with others. Needs are considered something that cannot be left unfilled. They often operate on an unconscious level. Wants are generally categorized as desires that should be fulfilled if possible. Professional salespeople are trained in need and want recognition. They will often understand why a buyer is motivated, although the real reason is lost on the buyer himself. Buyers feel they must justify their motives and often state apparent reasons for their actions rather than their real reasons. According to one theory, researchers can categorize motivation as an external or internal force.

External Motivation

Your social environment provides much of your buying motivation. Such external factors as age, race, religion, and occupation have an effect on what you buy. Your income and education also affect your desires to buy. These are called socioeconomic factors. The items purchased must be socially and culturally acceptable to you, persons you know, and your general social class.

The product itself, its price, and the effect of advertising provide more external motivation to induce you to buy. These factors generally influence you only when an item or class of items is socially acceptable. Advertising particularly attempts to make products, services, and business socially acceptable. It attempts to influence the public to purchase a particular type or brand of merchandise. It attempts to relate directly to you if at all possible by stressing the social benefits to you. When this occurs, it unleashes the internal forces that motivate each of us.

Internal Motivation

Your psychological characteristics determine the strength of your internal motivations. Behavioral scientists do not agree on exactly what these are and to what degree they affect individual buying behavior. In any case, you are induced to purchase a product or service directly by a salesperson or indirectly by advertising on the basis of either a rational or emotional appeal to which you respond. Probably part of any motivation is external and part is internal.

Rational motivation factors include price, durability, intended use, and total benefit. These factors lead to a more objective and considered approach to purchasing. Salespersons and advertising use this approach whenever the product or service attributes are most outstanding.

Emotional motivation factors are essentially those that are other than rational. They create a subjective, introspective approach to purchasing. A list of emotional reasons why people buy is endless and is as varied as the number of psychologists and marketing researchers involved. Consider these emotional reasons in light of your desires and motivations.

1. *Safety* This motivation covers the need for protection against loss or fear of loss. Safety and alleviation of fear may be purchased by insurance, door locks, savings bonds, adequate lighting, and health products. Security becomes more important as people grow older.
2. *Power and social adequacy* Superiority to compete with others and social adequacy may be purchased. Any item or service that shows superiority or at least adequacy has a ready market. Books, education, cultural activities, and athletics could fit into this category. Keeping up with the Joneses tends to fit this category also.
3. *Profit* Increasing income, decreasing expenses, savings, and getting a bargain are well-known motivations to purchase an item. The purchase of tools, books, securities, savings bonds, resale merchandise, employment-agency services, and sale items may be motivated by desire for personal profit.
4. *Comfort and pleasure* People like to be physically comfortable. They like to play and relax. Labor-saving devices, luxury goods, sports, and recreation are representative of this category.

5. *Love and romance* A sense of duty to family pervades the former, while attention to the opposite sex prevails in the latter motivation. Numerous products and services are sold for these reasons.
6. *Adventure* People like new places, new things, and new experiences. The word *new* is widely used to sell all sorts of products and services, such as travel, automobiles, toothpaste, and fashions. Many impulse purchases are made for this reason.

Note that there is an overlap in these buying motivations. This is because they cannot really be categorized. There is also an overlap between rational and emotional buying reasons. Consumers often confuse impulse buying with emotional buying when what they are really doing is unplanned buying. An impulse purchase may be rational as well as emotional. Most likely it will be the latter.

GENERAL SHOPPING PRINCIPLES

Once you decide you need (want) something, your best protection is to evaluate carefully the product or service that you wish to purchase. Obviously, the less valuable the purchase, the less time and evaluation effort you will give to the purchase. The amount of time you spend considering a purchase will be minimal, regardless of value, if you know your merchandise. As we will discuss later in the chapter, you can keep well informed about merchandise by maintaining records of past purchases and your appraisal of them. Failing this, you can become currently informed if the time and effort are worth it. Finally, you can at least base your choice on some general shopping principles, if you have nothing else to rely on.

Merchandise Classified

Consumer merchandise is usually classified by the extent of purchase activity needed by the buyer. The traditional classifications are convenience goods, shopping goods, and specialty goods. These are not mutually exclusive; there is considerable overlap. Few consumers verbally categorize merchandise in this manner; their method of purchase classifies the merchandise for them. What is considered a convenience item to one consumer may be a shopping or specialty item to another. What, how, when, and where you purchase something will have an effect on the price you pay and the quality you get.

Convenience goods These items are generally of low price and are available through many retail outlets. The consumer is not as interested in brand as he is in convenience. He will substitute brands, the store he usually patronizes, and sometimes even the type of product in preference to convenience. One might say that he does not care what he buys or where he buys it, as long as it serves his purpose.

Shopping goods The terminology implies that a consumer will compare the price and quality of this type of merchandise. Since a large portion of consumer products are branded, shopping will entail a brand comparison, although shopping goods have been categorized traditionally as nonbranded products that require some comparison for price and quality. Shopping goods tend to be more expensive than convenience goods. Draperies, hardware, furniture, yardage, and building materials usually fit the traditional category. Services and branded merchandise also fit this category if the consumer does comparison shopping.

Specialty goods These products have

a patronage because of a brand name, a unique product, or a particular retail store. A unique product has no exact substitute. A specialty store specializes in one or more special lines of merchandise. How unique the specialty happens to be depends on the number of competitors. A specialty item is defined as any item that causes a consumer to inconvenience himself to purchase it. Chain stores, discount stores, and other mass merchandisers carry a limited assortment of specialty items. These retailers usually feature private and off brands.

Brand-name merchandise The superiority of brand names is not universal. However, a well-known brand usually has a proven reputation for past performance. A well-known brand may also be just a well-promoted brand. The brand identification may be the only thing that identifies it and separates it from competitors. Since a manufacturer places his reputation on a brand name, he is more likely to attempt to maintain its performance or durability if at all possible. Few businesses care to "lose a good thing" or advertise something that is likely to fail.

Private-brand merchandise Private-label merchandise may be broadly interpreted as either unknown-brand or store-brand merchandise. *Unknown* or *off brands* are usually manufactured by small companies or imported from overseas. Since they do not have the production capacity, distribution system, or marketing and advertising budgets necessary to compete with the nationally known brands, the manufacturers usually sell these products at lower prices. Most likely the quality will match the price, because there is no reputation to maintain.

Private-brand merchandise features the retailer's label. The retailer is staking his reputation on the merchandise. Larger retailers such as Sears, Penney's, or Macy's order merchandise to their own specifications. It may be superior, inferior, or equal to name-brand merchandise. Often the goods are manufactured in the factory of a nationally advertised company. The merchandise may also be manufactured by a factory owned and operated by the retailer, as is the policy with Sears. Merchandise may also be contracted to a small producer. Private brands simply mean retailer specifications and retailer reputations.

Buying Guidelines

Many consumers think that the purchase of the most expensive or the least expensive merchandise is the simple solution to the consumer value quandary. This could not be further from the truth. As mentioned earlier, you must take the time and energy to analyze your purchases, consistent with their cost and usefulness. The following are general guides to informed consumerism. Note that some of these guides are diametrically opposed to each other. They are generally for use by persons with very few funds left in their budget. Your particular life-style, priorities, and discretionary income will help you choose which of these guidelines to follow in a particular situation:

1. Compare values. Check the quality and design of competing products in relation to the price. Never buy in haste.
2. Buy quality based on intended use. In some situations appearance and quality are not needed, especially if the item is an integral part of something you are making or building.
3. Select basic styles. Whether in clothes or equipment, the "basics" will remain

functionally and socially acceptable for longer periods of time. Stay away from fads.

4. Compare private brands with national brands. Both have a reputation to maintain. *If* the quality is the same, the private brand should be less expensive.
5. Buy the middle of the line. Investigate the usual three levels of quality. Base your decision on guidelines 1, 2, and 3. "Good, Better, and Best" are often featured in mail-order catalogs and chain stores. Good is often minimal quality while Best may be overpriced because of extra unneeded features.
6. Don't overpay for convenience. You pay extra for the shopping convenience of neighborhood and quick-stop stores. You pay extra for prepared, frozen, and specially packaged goods. You also pay extra for special services. Before relying on others, do it yourself.
7. Buy the large economy size—if you can use it! It works especially well for nonperishable staples. The price per ounce or other measure declines considerably in larger packages.
8. Take advantage of sales—if you can use the item! Table 2–1 indicates the usual months when many retailers offer sales on selected merchandise. There is no reason why you cannot plan ahead.
9. Don't shop too often. Each time you enter a store you are likely to purchase more than you intended. Retailers thrive on impulse and emotional buying. Bring a list and stick to it.
10. Pool your buying. This suggestion can bring a lot of trouble. You must join a cooperative or work closely with friends and neighbors. Quantity discounts on food and beverages are available in this manner. Partnerships and memberships are available in travel clubs, flying clubs, and resorts. Expensive recreational equipment and vacation homes may be purchased in partnership. However, choose your partners with care.
11. Rent rather than buy. There are many occasions when renting for a short period is more practical than purchase. Rental rather than purchase of seldom used recreational items and tools should definitely be considered.
12. Pay cash. Sometimes discounts are available to the cash buyer. Buying immediately consumed services and vacations on the installment plan is like paying for a dead horse. Credit of any kind may lead to overextension of your budget.
13. Use credit. This is a good device to assure that you receive proper satisfaction from your purchase. If it has not been paid for, you have bargaining power in any dispute.
14. Choose your retailers with care. Merchandise, service, and pleasant atmosphere are important. Dealer reputation for personal satisfaction is most important.
15. Do not sign any contract until you read and understand it. Never sign a contract with blank spaces or unitemized charges.
16. Do not become a victim of advertised specials. Watch for "bait and switch" tactics. Ask for "rain checks" on out-of-stock specials.
17. Ask and you may receive. When in doubt about performance, guaranty, warranty, or refund, ask. If you want a particular service, ask. If you have a complaint, ask for redress. Ask and you may receive. Don't ask and nothing will be volunteered.

These guidelines are not absolute rules. They must be flexible. It is possible to carry them to the extreme when such tactics are not required. When your money supply is tight, the guidelines can be tightened. They can be loosened when you can afford it.

You can apply these general guidelines to the purchase of just about anything including food, clothing, and automobiles,

Table 2–1 Bargain calendar

Item Bargain Calendar	Monthly Sale Calendar
Air conditioner—February, March, August	*January*—Appliances, bedding, bicycles, coats, furniture, housewares and small appliances, radio, stereo, sportswear, toiletries, toys, white goods
Appliances—January, March, July, October	*February*—Air conditioners, carpets, drapes, stationery
Automobiles—September, December	*March*—Air conditioners, appliances, luggage, ski equipment, television sets
Bedding—January, August	*April*—Cleaning aids, clothing
Bicycles—January, September	*May*—Cleaning aids, paints, television sets, tires, white goods
Building materials—June	*June*—Building materials, carpets, fabrics, furniture
Carpets—February–Summer	*July*—Appliances, carpets, fabrics, furniture, sportswear, toiletries and notions
Cleaning aids—April, May	*August*—Air conditioners, bedding, carpets, clothing, coats, drapes, fabrics, furniture, gardening supplies, paints, tires, white goods
Clothing—April, August, September	*September*—Automobiles, clothing, gardening supplies
Coats—January, August, December	*October*—Appliances, fishing equipment, luggage, paints, stationery
Drapes—February, August	*November*—Ski equipment, tires, toys
Fabrics—Summer	*December*—Automobiles, coats
Fishing equipment—April, October	
Furniture—January, Summer	
Gardening supplies—August, September	
Houseware and small appliances—January, September	
Luggage—March, October	
Paints—May, August, October	
Radio and stereo—January, May	
Ski equipment—March, November	
Sportswear—January, July	
Stationery—February, October	
Television sets—Spring	
Tires—May, August, November	
Toiletries and notions—January, July	
Toys—January, November	
White goods—January, May, August	

which we will discuss in greater detail. A knowledge of retail pricing strategies will also help you resist buying goods that appear to be bargains. If you understand the pricing strategy, you may reevaluate the bargain.

Retail Pricing Strategy

Attention to the buying guidelines still leaves a customer with a purchase decision. The final question you ask yourself must be, "Is the price right?" Retailers are aware of this and attempt to make prices as psychologically pleasing as possible. Remember, you can't get something for nothing. A merchant can usually set any retail price he wishes on the merchandise he sells. He will attempt to price goods to return the highest profit either through single unit sales or total volume sales. Your awareness of the following tactics may have a savings impact on your buying decisions. Here are some typical pricing strategies:

1. *Odd pricing* A $4.99 price has the psychological connotation of a $4 price. You tend to drop the odd cents—a round-off syndrome.
2. *Multiple pricing* The "two for" pric-

ing method may not save you money. It can be a method of disguising price increases. If you need only one item, the price will be rounded upward.

3. *Discount pricing* Discounted from what? What is the list price? Is the list price inflated to start with? Many manufacturers print higher prices on labels and tags to allow a discount or markdown.
4. *Trade-in pricing* Dealers must maintain a profit margin. They are interested in the difference between the trade-in allowance and the selling price quoted. You must be also. The same dealer margin may be calculated by either raising the selling price or lowering the trade-in allowance.
5. *Volume and size discount* Economies may be available if you can use more product without waste. Calculate the price per unit of measure to be sure you are getting a bargain. Sometimes larger sizes will cost you more!
6. *Loss-leader pricing* Generally dealers must sell above their cost. The low prices on selected items build store traffic. Dealers hope you will purchase other merchandise at the regular or perhaps inflated price to make up for their "loss." Take advantage of bargains, but control your impulses.
7. *Wholesale pricing* There are no standards for what represents wholesale. Most "wholesaling" by retailers is a form of discounting. Theoretically, a retail store cannot sell wholesale in most localities. A true wholesale price is a *trade discount* available from a distributor who sells to the trade or to other resellers.

All of these price strategies are designed to induce you to buy. The underlying tone is that a consumer can be confused by bargain prices. You can! Become informed and keep informed. If you do not know the general price level of the merchandise, how can you spot a true bargain or even a reasonable price?

Fair-trade prices A number of states have fair-trade pricing laws. These allow the manufacturer to set the retail price of the goods they sell to retailers. Generally a contract with one retailer in the state binds all other retailers to that price if they wish to sell that manufacturer's brand. This process allows manufacturers to control prices and maintain a quality image if they so desire. It also allows small retailers to compete with large retailers on a price basis because they cannot be undersold.

Fair-trade contracts are known as price-maintenance agreements. They usually set a floor on retail prices to discourage discounting. However, there is usually nothing in the agreement to stop a retailer from charging a higher price. This is often the case in small towns and tourist areas. Price-maintenance agreements are only "fair" to businesses that gain advantage from this, primarily the noncompetitive small business. These agreements are certainly not "fair" to the consumer.

We will now take a look at food, clothing, and automobile purchases in greater depth, because these represent a large portion of your consumer dollar. A wide array of information is available on all these subjects. Continually check your daily newspaper for consumer information items. Local programming on radio and television often provides consumer buying suggestions. Women's and consumer magazines constantly offer suggestions on the purchase, operation, and home management of these important products.

BUYING FOOD

Food prices are skyrocketing. Inflation plus supply and demand factors are increasing the costs of food at an accelerated pace. In

1971 the U.S. Department of Agriculture (USDA) figured that the average family spent approximately 25 percent of its family budget on food and related items. At that time surveys by the food industry indicated that the food budget represented somewhat less than 20 percent of expenditures. Both sources did agree that their percentages were below the worldwide averages of 30 to 35 percent. We have been "spoiled" by higher incomes and lower food prices than were available in most other countries. Unfortunately this advantage is now coming to an end. USDA forecasts say that American consumers can expect to use well over 25 percent of their budget for food in the near future.

Food Cost Factors

Many items affect the price that a family pays for its food. Basically, your life-style influences your food costs. The quality, quantity, and where you purchase your foods are reflected in the prices you pay. You can still have a well-balanced, low-cost diet by judicious planning, shopping, and substitution.

Life-style The recent trend of having both spouses in a family work has had a significant impact upon American food-purchasing habits. U.S. Department of Labor statistics indicate that over 32 million women are employed. Several surveys point out that these women are still responsible for the food shopping and food preparation in their households. This trend leads to the consumption of more commercially prepared foods and convenience items because of the time factor involved and the availability of higher family income.

A second life-style factor results from less physical effort expended on the job. This should lead to less food and calorie intake, which does not always happen in our society. Instead, there has been a noticeable increase in dietary food purchases to compensate for the increased weight of many people.

Quality Processed food is reasonably safe because of federal and local health regulations. The U.S. Department of Agriculture (USDA) is charged with inspecting meats, poultry, and their products when they are shipped in interstate commerce. This involves inspection before and after slaughter and during the packing process. The Federal Food and Drug Administration (FDA) is charged with preventing the sale of all contaminated foods in interstate commerce. State and local agencies police food processing within the states.

However, some foods are unsafe because of processing, packing, or storage problems. The regulatory agencies and food distributors attempt to monitor food safety but do not always succeed because of understaffing, ineffective laws, and some negligence. This means that you must protect yourself, which is the message throughout this text. Watch for damaged packages and cans. Look for shelf-life and use dates. Smell the food and look for discoloration. If in doubt, it is better to return the item to the store where it was purchased.

Over one hundred foods are graded for quality by the USDA, the states, trade associations, and individual processors. You should know the various grading standards, although different grades of a food are equally safe for human consumption and are about equal in nutritive value.

Descriptive terms may help identify products, but they are not a very reliable guide to quality or to accuracy. Food retailers are not required to standardize descriptive labels. For example, Idaho potatoes should be from Idaho, but the term does not offer a grade standard. London broil and bar-b-cue are terms used to describe steaks, but what kind and what grade of meat?

Quantity The size and age of your family has a decided effect on food costs. Figure 2–2 illustrates weekly food costs of a family based on size and age. No one can arbitrarily set a food budget for the average family. As you can plainly see, it depends on who is in the family.

Place of purchase Where you buy groceries also has a great effect on your total grocery bill. You are probably aware of the price differences between "mom-and-pop" stores, convenience quick-stop stores, and independent markets, cooperatives, and chain supermarkets. There is an overlap in categories, but prices probably descend in the order listed. Supermarkets tend to have the lowest prices, especially if they feature "discount." Cooperatives *may* be the lowest priced stores if you become a member. You should investigate their prices, services, and past annual membership refunds. Your choice of store should reflect the time, convenience, price level, and quality involved in an individual purchase. Regular grocery shopping should be confined to a few stores that seem to offer the best total prices. Decide on one store for most purchases and use the others for their specials. Sometimes you can find all your grocery and nonfood items in a one-stop supermarket and discount store.

To find the store that consistently offers the total lowest prices in your shopping area, you must conduct your own personal survey. Base the survey on approximately twenty-five products that you regularly purchase.

Money-Saving Tips

Consumer advocates, home economists, and government specialists are constantly offering suggestions for saving on food costs. The list is endless. Before buying everything in sight, stop and consider some of the following suggestions:

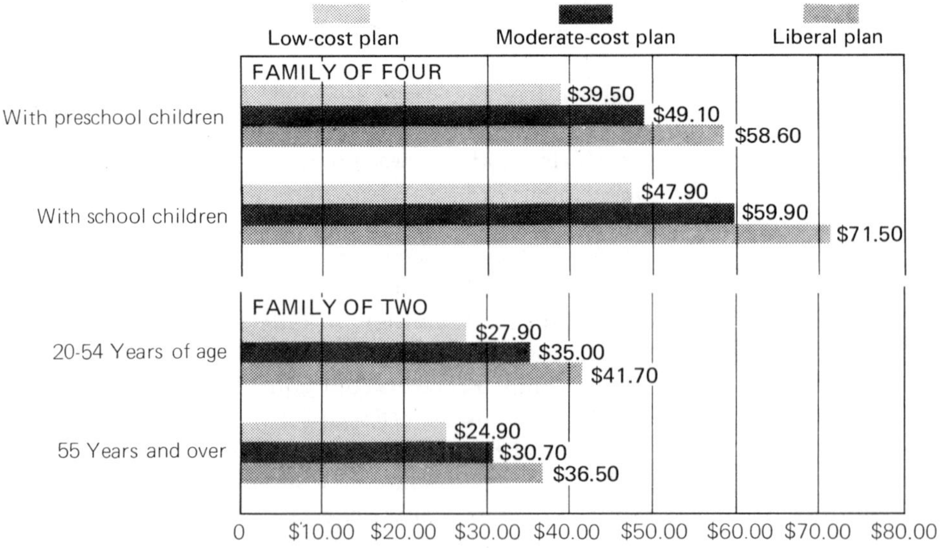

Figure 2–2 Weekly Food Costs and Family Size, December 1974. *(U.S. Department of Agriculture)*

1. Keep a shopping list in a convenient place. Add to it as you use an item.
2. Bring your shopping list to the store and *stick to it.*
3. Plan your meals around advertised specials.
4. Plan your shopping trip to visit at least two stores.
5. Shop once a week. Leave the store as soon as possible.
6. Shop on a full stomach. If you are hungry, you will overbuy.
7. Buy in quantity or larger size only if the items can be stored and used conveniently. Small-size packages cost more. You pay for the packaging.
8. Know your prices.

There are many other money-saving ideas available if you stop and think. Calculate price per ounce or other measurement to determine comparative value. Substitute lower priced food types and brands whenever possible. Buy on the basis of intended use. For example, no one needs to know what is in a stew or a punch. Buy seasonally to take advantage of supply and prices.

You should also watch the check-out clerk; he can easily misread a price or punch the wrong key. Use the "cents-off" coupons if you plan to purchase these items. Return poor-quality or spoiled food products; be sure to bring your cash register receipt. Ask for rain checks on out-of-stock advertised items. Remember that specialized bakery, delicatessen, gourmet, and boutique department items are usually more expensive than ordinary items. They may add to your total food cost even if you do not purchase them because of increased costs. Extra services such as carry-out, delivery, give-aways, and trading stamps also add to your food cost.

Convenience foods, such as sliced lunch meat and cheese, individually wrapped items, and no deposit–no return containers, are usually more expensive. Check the ingredients carefully, because some mixes and frozen foods are less expensive and more convenient than buying all the components separately. Eliminate unnecessary snack foods. Drink water; you will really save money! Control impulse buying, and shop alone if possible.

BUYING CLOTHING

Many people believe there is less emphasis on clothing today because of the trend toward casual wear and the decline in using clothes as a status or prestige symbol. Perhaps the average dollar amount spent for clothing has not increased as rapidly as it has for transportation and food items, but this is rather hard to believe when looking at the upgraded quality and prices of new clothes. We do have more flexibility in style today than we have had in the past, but fashion is still very much with us. You can be in fashion and yet save money by planning your complete wardrobe in advance.

Planning Your Wardrobe

The clothing budget must be a part of the family budget. If you spend less for clothes, you will have money for something else. Many people tend to spend more for clothing because of a real or imagined need for clothing. New clothes give you a psychological uplift. When you need to improve your self-image or impress someone else, you may overextend your clothing budget. By proper planning of your family's wardrobe, however, you may continually have a positive self-image and save money, too!

Make an inventory Part of objectively determining a family's clothing needs requires finding out what is already possessed. Conduct an inventory, and then prepare a "model stock." This is how retailers determine their merchandise needs for resale. The inventory should be taken twice a year, in the early spring and early fall, to provide ample time to purchase for the upcoming summer and winter seasons.

Once you have taken stock of your clothing, you can determine your current clothing needs. Provide yourself with a well-balanced wardrobe. The only way to do this is to make up a "balance sheet": write down the number and types of clothing owned and wearable by each family member. Do this by groupings such as sweaters, shirts, pants, and so on. Then fill in the gaps by purchasing new items according to your priorities and what will apparently remain in fashion for some time.

Some people will prefer to maintain a "perpetual inventory." According to this retailing procedure, you replace clothing as it wears out rather than waiting for a twice-a-year inventory. It works quite well with basic items such as shoes, socks, underwear, dresses, pants, shorts, and blouses. Even so, some items are still seasonal. Most people should use both systems to be comfortably dressed and fashionable, and yet save money.

How much clothing each family should have is up to the individuals in the family. Obviously, income and number of family members will have a great bearing on quantity. Life-styles and personal preferences may have to be compromised if money is a limiting factor, as it tends to be with young families.

Merchandise quality Quality clothes look right, feel right, and wear right. How do you tell quality? You want clothes that are wearable and easy to care for. You look for quality features in the fabric, construction, fit, durability, color, and style. You are most likely to find quality in brand-name clothing because the manufacturer must maintain his reputation. Brand-name apparel companies test their products for durability, washability, and fit. Therefore, you are reasonably certain of the quality of the merchandise.

There are industry size-standards, but because of various construction features, sizes in clothing tend to differ by brand. You must really work at getting quality merchandise at a reasonable price. Less than two-thirds of all consumers were satisfied with the value of their clothing purchases, according to the survey mentioned at the beginning of the chapter.

Seasonal merchandise Retailers are placing seasonal merchandise on their shelves earlier every year—bathing suits in January and winter coats in July. This is done to get a jump on competitors (who do the same thing), to have a longer selling season, and to allow time to reorder "best sellers." You will have a wider selection earlier in the season. Shop a number of stores to learn what will be in fashion. Your seasonal clothing choices should be made on the same quality basis as your basic wearing apparel.

A growing number of quality retailers carry seasonal merchandise all year long to accommodate the mobile American. "Winter in the sun" and "skiing in July" are becoming more popular. If you can afford these vacations but cannot find the out-of-season merchandise, you will have to purchase your vacation clothing at high-priced resort shops. However, if you plan ahead, you can purchase travel and vacation items during the prior season, when the needed items, in good supply, are probably priced lower than at the resorts.

The Clothing Budget

There is no hard and fast rule on how much money to allow for annual clothing purchases. Money for clothing should be divided by seasons and by individual needs. Budgets can be stretched in large families by using hand-me-downs or an exchange plan among children and other family members. A few extra dollars spent on a well-fitting, well-constructed item of high quality may be a bargain if it can last through a number of children.

According to 1974 surveys by the Bureau of Labor Statistics, the average family of four spends about 10 percent of its income on clothing. This amounts to about $300 per person per year and makes clothing the number four item in a budget. Probably you do not fit into this "average family," so you should develop your own flexible budget. Be aware of the characteristic spending patterns that are common to all families:

1. The amount spent on family clothing increases with the size and age of the children, peaking when the children are in their mid-teens.
2. Individual expenditures for clothing seem to taper off somewhat when a person reaches his late twenties.
3. As family income increases, the dollar amount spent increases, but the percentage of income spent decreases.
4. Money spent for clothing in most families is consistently greater for female members.

Evaluating sales and specials Retailers have had clothing sales for years. Their purpose is to rid the store of overstocked and undersold merchandise and to make room for new items. Occasionally, popular items will be "on sale" if a line has been discontinued. Soiled items and customer returns are often placed on sale. Remember that a retailer is in business to make a profit. He will generally not reduce his prices unless he has a good reason to do so. Look for that reason; it may save you from making a mistake.

The exceptions to leftover sales seem to be the good buys available in the seasonal promotional sales as listed in table 2–1. Often such sales are offered with the support of the manufacturers, so that real price reductions from regularly stocked merchandise are available. A good sale will have some regular merchandise available at reduced prices in order to make the sale look respectable. These are where you find the real bargains. If a coat is regularly priced at $100 but is reduced to $75 for the sale, you will realize a savings of 25 percent. This is much better than you can get from any investment, providing you need and will use the coat. Be sure clothing will remain in style. It is a doubtful saving if you purchase any clothing item just because it is on sale and then use it sparingly because you do not enjoy wearing it. Follow your wardrobe planning even when taking advantage of sales. If you don't need it, don't buy it.

All too often a retailer will offer "special purchases." These are lower priced and usually lower quality items that are used as traffic builders. The retailer has purchased merchandise at a lower price and is just passing a part of his savings on to you. Good brand names occasionally may be offered in this manner. This occurs when a manufacturer must also move his merchandise at a lower price because it is not selling for some reason. Watch for fit, fabric, and construction when buying a "special." Often the reason for the sale—the defect—will not show up until the item has been worn and subsequently cleaned.

Choosing Your Retailer

There are many places to buy clothing—department stores, specialty shops, chain stores, discount stores, and variety, drug, and supermarket outlets. The first two types tend to carry name-brand and exclusive-label merchandise. Chain stores carry their own private brand. The others tend to carry off-brand merchandise.

Other sources available include mail order and direct door-to-door sales. Used clothing is available from thrift stores, rummage sales, and garage sales. Often good used merchandise is available. This can be helpful to a growing family. When ordering clothing by mail pay close attention to the description in the catalog. The convenience of ordering by mail or telephone may be outweighed by your inability to check construction and fit until you receive the merchandise. If it is unsatisfactory, you have the added problem of wrapping and returning. Catalog prices are not necessarily inexpensive by the time you add the freight charges. New catalog merchandise prices may be higher or lower than retail competition because the company buyer must forecast and set his prices months in advance. He can misprice in either direction, although there is a tendency to overprice because of the inflation factor. On the other hand, if inflation is causing rapid retail price rises, catalog prices may be a bargain, especially during the later stages of the catalog's life.

Whenever you shop, you will wish to get your money's worth. It is up to you to compare values. Brand-name merchandise is usually no more expensive in an exclusive store than it is in a full-line department store, specialty shop, or boutique. However, exclusive-label merchandise is likely to be considerably more expensive in boutiques and exclusive specialty stores. Also, because it is exclusive, you cannot make an adequate price comparison. Your decision as to where to buy clothing should be based first on the general quality you wish and second on the type of extra services offered by the store. You must determine how much extra you are willing to pay for "service."

Money-Saving Tips

Clothing is one of the most varied personal-consumption items that must be purchased. Because of this problem, it is very easy to overspend your budget and still end up with an unsatisfactory wardrobe. Following these guidelines may help you to get more clothing satisfaction for your money:

1. It is better to have fewer high-quality clothes than more cheaper clothes.
2. Have a general awareness of prices and quality in different types of clothes.
3. Shop several stores to compare quality, price, style, and fit.
4. Look at more than one level of quality so you can better compare.
5. Read the hangtags and labels to know what you are buying.
6. Know your fabrics. Know how much care each fabric requires in the way of washing, drying, and dry cleaning.
7. Watch for workmanship in stitching, buttons, zippers, and reinforced areas.
8. Make sure stripes, checks, and plaids match at seams and openings, especially in sale merchandise.
9. Build your wardrobe around a few coordinated colors for better use.
10. Purchase basic items like socks in multiple units. You will not need to throw away an entire pair if one sock gets a hole that cannot be mended.

11. Keep records of brand performance.
12. Retain all labels and sales slips.
13. Don't buy "fad" items. Control your family's impulse spending.
14. Avoid "bargains" you don't need, but shop the "good" seasonal sales.

AUTOMOBILES AND BUYING TRANSPORTATION

Buying transportation means buying an automobile to most people. Automobiles are usually the most convenient means of transportation between any two points within a few hundred miles. They are also the most expensive! The average family spends between 10 and 15 percent of its budget on transportation (automobiles). It is usually the third largest budget item. For a young man it is often the largest budgetary item.

Public Transportation

Before immediately deciding you *must* have an automobile you should consider public transportation. If you live in a large city or suburb with reasonably good transit service, at least try it out. A slight inconvenience may save you a considerable amount of money. Obviously this arrangement works best in cities. However, suburban consumers may be able to retain the status of a one-car family and save money by commuting to work.

Intercity travel for one or two persons is generally less expensive by air, train, or bus if an auto is not needed at your destination. As mentioned earlier in the chapter, it is often less expensive to rent if you have only an occasional need for an item. Public transportation and a one-day auto rental at your destination could be the answer.

Before You Buy an Automobile

An automobile is likely to be the second largest purchase you will make in your lifetime. Therefore, give it plenty of thought before you venture into the market. You cannot conceivably look at every make and model of new cars, much less look at all the used vehicles.

You probably have some general preference as to the type of car you would like to have. At least five factors should influence you as a car buyer. These will differ in order of your personal priorities: (1) purchase price, (2) operating costs, (3) use pattern, (4) past experience, and (5) pure desire. The last of these may cost you a lot of money if you forsake rational decision making for your emotions.

Size and body style The size and type of automobile you purchase should provide for your family's needs and use pattern. There is a rather big spread in operating costs based on automobile size. The size and type of auto create all sorts of psychological stumbling blocks. At one time, one measured status by the size and price of a car. The reverse is almost true today, due to the frustrations of owning and operating a car. Either way, you may not buy an auto that fits your needs. Think about your prejudices and *why* you have them. For instance, do you really want a big car because it is convenient? Because it is comfortable? Because you look successful? Figures 2–3 and 2–4 may offer you some perspective on car sizes and body styles. The Ford Motor Company has a free annual publication, *Car Buying Made Easier,* that provides general information on auto selection and specific information on Ford products.

Attempt to narrow your choice down somewhat by reading the various reports on new automobile test performance ratings.

Consumer Reports, Consumer Research, Motor Trend, Popular Mechanics, Popular Science, and *Road and Track* all provide test performance and customer complaint information. The first two magazines do not carry advertising and therefore do not tend to pull any punches. New-car data can sometimes be used to make inferences about older models of the same make. In fact, you can research through old editions of these magazines once you narrow a used car choice to a few alternatives. By limiting your choice you will know the merchandise better. This should help your bargaining position for either new or used automobiles.

Optional accessories and replacement parts Emotion again plays a big part in dressing up your car. Auto salespeople have

CAR SIZE EXAMPLES AND SPECIAL MODELS

Wheelbase	Base Models	Special Models
About 94″ to 101″ 	**Subcompact** Ford Pinto, AMC Gremlin, Chevrolet Vega, VW Beetle	**Luxury/Sport** Ford Mustang II, Mercury's Capri, Pontiac Astre
About 102″ to 111″ 	**Compact** Ford Maverick, Mercury Comet, Buick Apollo, Plymouth Duster, AMC Hornet	**Practical Luxury** Ford Granada, Mercury Monarch, Mercedes 280
About 112″ to 118″ 	**Intermediate** Ford Torino, Mercury Montego, Chevrolet Chevelle, Dodge Coronet	**Personal Luxury** Ford Elite, Mercury Cougar, Chevrolet Monte Carlo, Chrysler Cordoba
119″ UP 	**Standard** Ford LTD, Chevrolet Impala, Plymouth Gran Fury, Mercury Marquis, Buick Le Sabre, Oldsmobile Ninety Eight, Pontiac Grand Ville, Chrysler New Yorker	**Personal Luxury** Thunderbird, Continental Mark IV, Buick Riviera, Oldsmobile Toronado **Luxury Standard** Lincoln Continental, Cadillac

OTHERS include specialty cars, small van/buses and trucks. Wheelbase figures are not "hard-and-fast" figures necessarily approved or accepted by all manufacturers.

What are the advantages, disadvantages, and seating accommodations of the sizes? Generally:

Size	Advantages	Disadvantages	Seats
Subcompact Wheelbase About 94″ to 101″	Lowest cost available in U.S. Extremely easy to handle, park, garage. Excellent fuel mileage.* Low operating, maintenance costs. Uncomplicated engines, usually 4-cylinder. Good second, or son-and-daughter car.	Slightly stiffer ride, usually because of short wheelbase and light weight. Limited space for passengers, cargo. Luxury interiors and some optional equipment not available on all models.	Two, front somewhat crowded. Two rear, crowded.

Figure 2–3 *(Ford Motor Company, Dearborn, Michigan)*

Advantages, disadvantages, and seating accommodations of the sizes. Generally: (Continued)

Size	Advantages	Disadvantages	Seats
Compact **Wheelbase About 102″ to 111″**	Low initial cost. Low operating, maintenance cost. Good fuel mileage.* Easy to handle, park, garage. Fair cross-country car. Excellent for commuting. Good size for family of two adults, two small children.	Less-smooth ride than next sizes up.† Less comfortable than larger cars for frequent long trips.† Passenger and cargo space somewhat limited.† Instruments, option choices somewhat limited.†	Two to three, front. Two to three, rear.
Intermediate **Wheelbase About 112″ to 118″**	Good room and comfort at low cost. Not as bulky as full-size cars. Easy to handle in traffic, to park, to garage. Relatively low-cost operation and maintenance. Well balanced for long-trip road car; gives good ride. Adequate passenger and cargo space. Good choice of engines, options, etc. Fairly good on fuel mileage.*	Not as spacious for big families or those with lots of luggage. Not as well suited for heavy loads or heavy-duty trailer towing. May need V-8 engine for hill-country operation.	For normal trips: Three, front. Three, rear. For long trips: Two, front. Two, rear (or three children).
Standard Size **Wheelbase 119″ UP**	Most stability and riding comfort. Widest choice of options and equipment. Best long-trip car. Hauls heavy loads. Tows trailers easiest. Excellent for bigger families. Provides most space for passengers, cargo. Ideal for car pooling.	Costs more to buy, operate, maintain. Lower fuel mileage.* A bigger size to handle, park, garage. More complicated and heavier.	Three, front (bench seats). Three, rear in comfort.

BODY STYLES

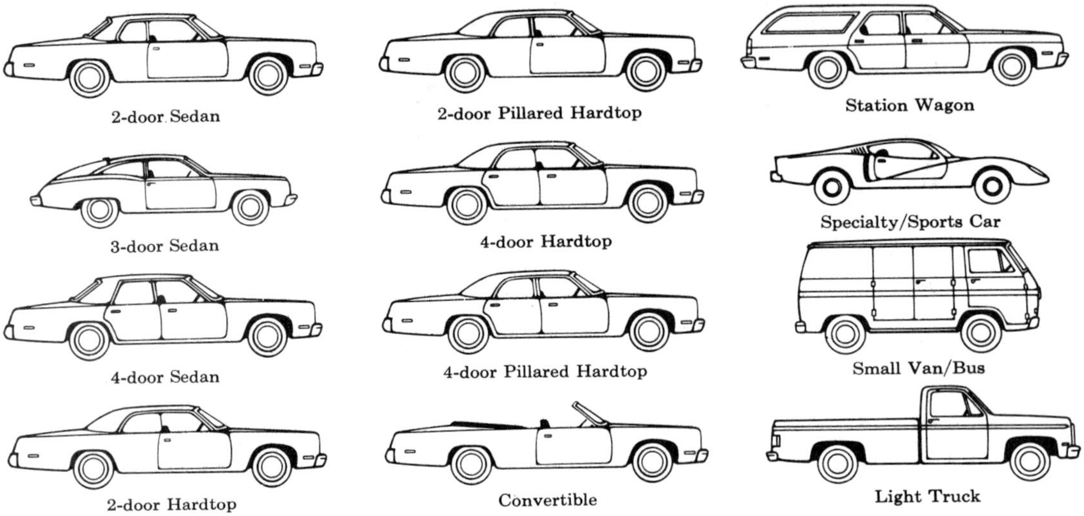

Body Style	Advantages	Disadvantages
Sedan, 2-door	Lowest-cost in a given line. Good family car for those with small children (no doors in rear). Sturdy, least subject to body squeaks as it ages. Rigid body-and-pillar design.	Awkward getting in and out of, or loading rear seat. Wider doors make it somewhat more difficult to get in and out of car in tight parking places.
Sedan, 3-door	Combines benefits of sedan and station wagon. Rear seat can be folded down to provide cargo area approaching that of a station wagon while retaining the body lines of a sedan. Often comes with "sporty" fittings and trim as standard.	Approximately the same as 2-door sedans. Usually available only in intermediate, compact, and subcompact sizes.

Figure 2–4 *(Ford Motor Company, Dearborn, Michigan)*

two chances to get you—on the basic purchase price or on the numerous accessories that you "need." Salespeople are not averse to selling you an inexpensive automobile and loading it with extras. It might be less expensive for you to purchase a luxury model by the time you are finished. Optional equipment can easily boost the car price by another $1,000. Generally, accessories cost more on the smaller models than on standard size cars. Does this tell you something? By deciding on any options before you shop or negotiate, you may be able to control your impulses.

Consider the cost of *replacement parts* when evaluating a new or used car purchase. These parts are often needed to operate your car; they are not optional accessories. Replacement part costs generally increase with the size of the domestic automobile. Foreign parts are expensive because of import and supply costs.

Body Style (continued)	Advantages	Disadvantages
Sedan, 4-door	Good family car; 4 doors make easy entrance and exit to both front and rear, especially for older people. Sturdy because it has between-side-windows pillars. Narrower doors make it somewhat easier for you to get in and out of car in tight parking places.	More doors may subject car to more squeaks, drafts, as it ages. More doors and windows to lock for secure parking. Children in rear have access to rear-door locks and handles.
Hardtops, 2- and 4-door	Side views unobstructed by body pillars, with all side windows down. Hold resale value better than sedans.	Least rigid structure of all the metal-roof cars. Cost more. In 4-door models, children in rear have access to rear-door locks and handles.
Pillared Hardtops, 2- and 4-door	Stronger roof structure than conventional hardtop. Better alignment and seal of windows against wind and water.	In 4-door models, children in rear have access to rear-door locks and handles.
Convertible	Unique design, compared to metal-roof cars—"different." Provides full open-air-and-sunshine driving. Usually has heavier, lower-center-of-gravity construction to compensate for lack of metal-roof rigidity and bracing.	Least rigid roof structure of all cars. Upkeep of fabric roof and raise-lower mechanism required. More subject to theft and vandalism by slashing roof. Depending on design, rearward visibility limited with top up. Most squeaks and rattles, as car ages. Few models available.
Station Wagon	Highly useful all-purpose vehicle. Carries most passengers and cargo of all car-line vehicles Versatile, rugged, adaptable. Has good resale value.	Slightly noisier than sedans. Larger interior with big window area takes longer to heat in cold weather, or cool in hot weather. Subject to more rattles and squeaks than sedans, as it ages. Higher-priced than sedans.
Specialty/ sports cars	Unique styling. Options offered in wide range. Usually has more horsepower per pound of vehicle to give greater performance.	Higher-priced, compared to more conventional models. Higher-cost insurance probable if it has a high-powered engine. Limited number of passengers, up to four, with crowded rear seat. More subject to theft.
Vans/ buses	Most space enclosed in least amount of body. Versatile, all-purpose passenger and cargo carriers. Low-cost operation, maintenance. Good forward visibility.	Noisier than passenger cars. More subject to wind forces. Subject to rattles, squeaks and drafts, as they age. Not the best road performers. Require care to guard from overloading.
Light trucks	Versatile, multiple-purpose design. Good rural-area type of transportation. Good stability and performance with loads. Good "second car" for rural-area family. Good commercial vehicle for contractors, others who work from job-site to job-site.	Usually limited to three passengers, in cab. Commercial or farm licensing normally required. Open-box type exposes uncovered cargo to all weather. No cargo security when parked and left unattended.

Operating Costs

If you buy a new automobile you may be purchasing a $15,000 machine! This is what you will initially spend for your new car plus its operating costs over a period of ten years. Costs of owning and operating an automobile vary widely from person to person and model to model. The original cost and the annual mileage are important in determining your operating costs, which are usually figured on a cost-per-mile basis. Prices for gasoline, oil, tires, and batteries also tend to increase with the size of the automobile. Figure 2–5 illustrates the operating costs per mile for 1974 subcompact, compact, and standard-size cars. You will spend about 15.89¢ a mile to drive and maintain a 1974 standard size car for ten years, which is $15,892.36 for the estimated

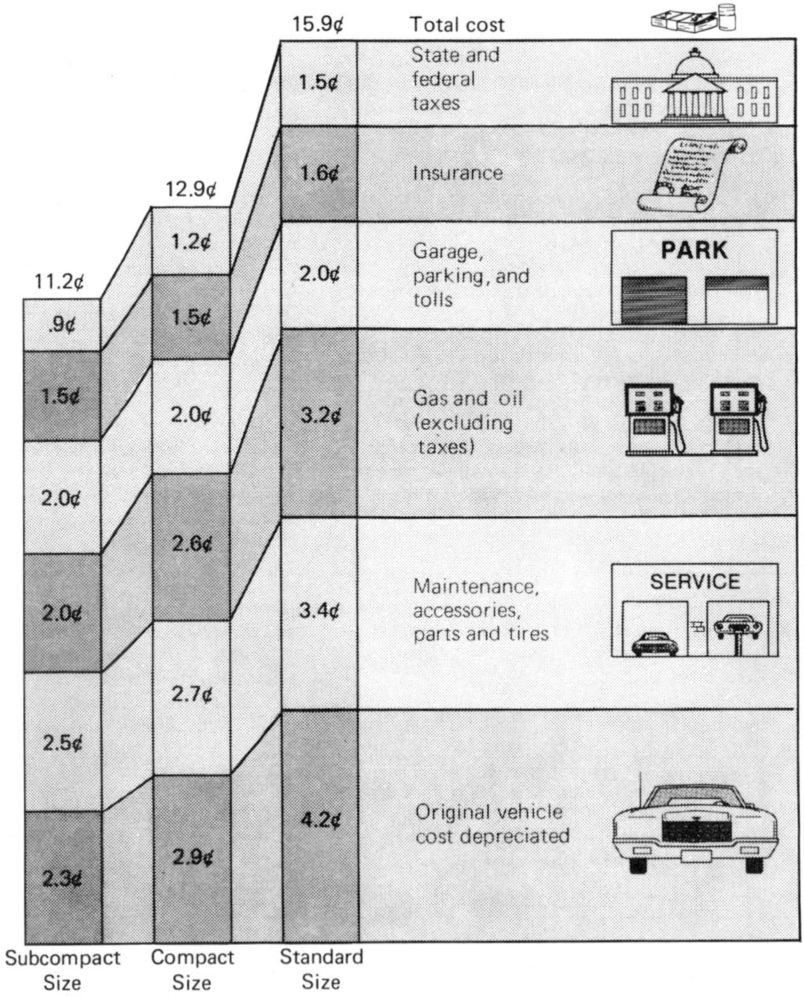

Figure 2–5 Cost of Operating an Automobile (Cents per Mile). *(U.S. Department of Transportation)*

life of the car. If you have a 1974 compact, you will spend about 12.88¢ a mile, or $12,879.53 for using the car ten years. If you have a subcompact, you can count on spending 11.15¢ a mile, or $11,153.10 for using the subcompact for ten years.

The purchase price is only the first in a long line of costs that must be paid in operating your standard-size car during its approximate 100,000-mile, ten-year trip from the assembly line to the junkyard. Depreciation of $4,201 is by far the greatest single cost. Other major costs for a ten-year period are: (1) $4,032 for some 7,700 gallons of gasoline, (2) $2,940 for maintenance and repairs; (3) $1,618 for insurance; and (4) $1,960 for garaging, parking, and tolls.

The U.S. Department of Transportation conducts annual surveys on automobile operating costs. Detailed information on this subject, gasoline mileage comparison by make and model, and selected safety tests are available from the U.S. Department of Transportation, Washington, D.C. 20590.

Ownership and operating costs are technically two different things, but you should think of them as one because they come out of the same pocket—yours! Ownership costs are fixed costs, those that change little regardless of how much or how little driving you do during the year. Operating costs are variable costs that increase directly with the mileage driven. Total automobile costs are the sum of fixed and variable costs. The following list divides the two groups and should remind you of the many expenses associated with an automobile.

Some fixed costs are determined at purchase time; others change from year to year. Depreciation is the decline in value of the car from year to year. It is greatest during the first two years of ownership. Higher mileage tends to increase the rate of depreciation. We will discuss depreciation for tax and business purposes later in the text. For now, remember that depreciation is the difference between the original drive-out price and what the car is worth when traded or resold. Invariably you never get as much as you would like. An estimated depreciation rate for a standard-size car would be somewhere in the following ranges:

Fixed Costs	Variable Costs
Depreciation	Gasoline and oil
Insurance	Maintenance service
Sales tax	Repairs
Licenses and fees	Bridge and road tolls
Garage	Parking fees
Interest on loan	Traffic fines

First year:	30 to 40 percent
Second year:	15 to 25 percent
Third year:	10 to 15 percent
Fourth year:	10 percent

Variable costs per mile tend to increase with the age of the car. Your car will tend to use slightly more gas and oil and use up batteries and tires more often as it begins to wear out. Repairs, of course, begin to proliferate.

New-Car Purchases

There is no set selling price for a new car. The *sticker* price that must be placed on all new cars is strictly a *manufacturer's suggested list* price. It provides a beginning point for negotiation if you know the markup on the different sizes of automobiles. By subtracting the markup you get the dealer's invoice, which is what he paid for the car. Markups differ by car size. They are approximately as follows:

Subcompact:	10 to 15 percent
Compact:	15 to 17 percent
Intermediate:	18 to 20 percent
Standard:	20 to 22 percent
Luxury:	22 to 25 percent

Never pay the sticker price for an automobile. To figure how much you should offer, add a dealer's profit of anywhere from $150 to 10 percent of his invoice plus freight charges and dealer preparation charges to the price of the basic automobile. Now add about 50 percent of the cost of those "needed" accessories. (Accessories have a much higher markup.) This is probably the lowest price you can expect to pay. If you are buying during a slack period, the dealer will bargain. At other times, expect to pay a higher price. Taxes and license are added after negotiation of the purchase price.

Used-Car Purchases

It is harder to shop for a used car than for a new one because there are so many more possible problems. The main question any prospective used car buyer should ask is "What's wrong with it? Why did the previous owner sell it?" This is not to say that you cannot get a good used automobile at a reasonable price, or that the previous owner or the dealer is not honest. It's just that not many cars are traded when they are problem-free. The main reason you would buy a used car is to save money, and if you put too much into repairs, you haven't saved anything.

When buying a used car stick to the simpler models; there will be less to go wrong. Do not be fooled by good-looking lines and a shiny appearance. The tires will be recaps or third-line quality in many cases. Paint, wax, and water will do wonders for most used cars. However, these things do not improve the mechanical performance. First, you must *thoroughly inspect* the car for wear and tear and possibly for accident damage. Second, take it for a *test drive*. Listen for strange noises, watch brake and steering performance, notice smoky exhaust, overheating, and pick-up action. Finally, if it passes these tests, take it to a *mechanic* or *diagnostic center*. If you really like the car, the $15 to $25 charge will be a bargain.

Automobile Financing and Insurance

We will discuss automobile financing and insurance in much greater detail in chapters three and eight, respectively. These are relatively fixed costs, which greatly add to the cost of ownership. It is not unusual to pay an extra $600 for interest on a thirty-six-month auto loan. By shopping for your credit, however, you can almost certainly get lower-cost financing than would be available through the auto dealer. Auto insurance is another area in which a cautious buyer can save money by selecting his own insurance agent and insurance company. This cost does not stop after a few years; it continues in varying degrees as long as you have your car. Insurance for the young driver is exceedingly expensive, as you well know.

Shopping Tips

Before purchasing an automobile read about the different models and makes available. Know your merchandise. Know your prices, especially if you are buying a used car or have a trade-in. The *Red Book* published quarterly by the National Automobile Dealers Association or the *Blue Book* published quarterly by the Kelley Organization contain both wholesale and retail used car prices. The *Annual Buying Guide* issue of *Consumer Reports* also has both new and used price quotations.

You can find numerous money-saving tips on auto purchases in many periodicals. Read them before shopping for any automobile. In addition, you should be aware of the following information and suggestions:

1. Year-end new car price reductions do not cover the 30 percent to 40 percent depreciation loss. Model clearance prices are bargains only if you expect to keep the car for more than three years.
2. Make a comparison work sheet when shopping for automobiles. Know how much you can afford to pay.
3. Contact your credit union, employee group, or consumer group about possible fleet purchase prices for new cars.
4. Get a written warranty whenever possible. Know the term and warranty conditions. Know what parts and what labor are included.
5. Clean and refurbish your trade-in. Attempt to sell it yourself before trading it.
6. Learn to do minor auto maintenance yourself.
7. Use good driving habits and proper routine maintenance. They will increase the life of your automobile and reduce your costs.

Should You Lease a Car?

There has been a great increase in automobile leasing transactions in the last few years. Leasing companies and dealers offer a wide variety of leasing terms. Basically there are only two types of leases, the closed-end and the open-end.

The *closed-end lease* provides for a fixed monthly cost with no adjustments at the end of the contract term. The lessor sets his rate based on type of car, expected mileage and depreciation factors, and his profit. Any change in the forecasted depreciation at the end of the lease is the problem of the lessor. The lessee walks away from the lease without obligation. Closed-end leases are more expensive because the leasing company must attempt to cover for any unanticipated problems.

The *open-end lease* is approximately $20 per month less than the closed-end variety. Terms are the same *except* the lessee agrees to settle the contract at the market value of the car at the end of the lease. This means if the car depreciates more rapidly than forecast, you will have a balloon payment at the end of the lease to make up for any non-amortized depreciation. Presumably, if the car is worth more, you would get a refund. The latter seldom happens. Extreme caution is required in an open-end lease because of the tendency for lessors to underestimate depreciation and set the monthly payments rather low to sell you on the lease.

The actual monthly payments on any lease will differ because of the make, model, and type of lease. In addition to this, you must pay separately, or add to the contract, the following items: (1) tax and license, (2) routine maintenance, and (3) insurance. Taxes and licenses are usually included in the contract. Maintenance and insurance are probably available at lower cost elsewhere but will be included in the lease at correspondingly higher lease rates.

The small print often makes the difference between two leasing contracts. For example, you should determine in advance exactly what are the limitations on wear and tear. When does a scratch become body work? Is there a tire replacement clause? What are the mileage charges for excess mileage? What penalties are there for early lease termination?

Cost comparison Lessors purchase their autos at fleet prices. To this they add the cost of their financing and overhead, plus their profit. The result will be a price similar to that for which you could purchase and finance your own car. A lease simply guarantees to take an automobile off your hands at a certain time for a "guaranteed" price. Any cost comparison will have to be based on the particular details of a comparable proposed purchase and proposed lease. The more services you get in a lease transaction, the more it will cost. For a person who trades automobiles every one or two years, there will probably be little difference in cost. However, for longer periods of time, the purchase of an automobile should be less expensive. After thirty-six months you will own a three-year-old auto that may have potential maintenance problems. With a lease, you start paying all over again, but you will have a new automobile that should have fewer maintenance problems.

The real difference between buying and leasing lies in the convenience of leasing. There is little bargaining to do, you know what your ownership cost will be (especially in a closed-end lease), and the low deposit requirements keep your capital free for other uses. Leasing is an ideal arrangement for businesspeople. Leasing is not likely to benefit a consumer as much, because he can probably lower the cost of financing and insurance by shopping around. In fact, a consumer often loses the income-tax deduction that is available for finance charges.

CONSUMER PROTECTION

As a result of the immense interest caused by the consumer movement, federal, state, and industry agencies and groups have begun to inform the consumer and to protect him from gross inequities. This is only the beginning. There has been and always will be a time lag between the formulation of a grievance and the beginning of remedial action by industry or government. This is because of the lobbying pressure-groups, the cumbersome legislative machinery of any organization, and the real fear of possible loss of freedom. Questions continually arise as to how much protection consumers should have to provide for their health, safety, and economic well-being. For instance, there are current controversies over vitamins, health insurance, auto insurance, auto seat-belt devices, pension plans, labeling of products, and pollution and environmental protection. Often health and safety legislation causes economic hardship to industries. The industries then pass any higher costs on to the consumer, who pays higher prices.

Sources of Protection

The best possible consumer protection is your own common sense. Do not put yourself in a position where you need to seek redress. Know your rights and responsibilities as a consumer. When in doubt over any transaction, seek information and advice before committing yourself. Deal only with a reputable business concern.

Government protection Some federal protection is available for almost every facet of consumerism that involves interstate commerce. The Food and Drug Administration (FDA), the Office of Consumer Affairs, the Health, Education, and Welfare Department (HEW), and the Federal Trade Commission (FTC) are among the federal agencies regulating industry and protecting the consumer to varying degrees.

Numerous state agencies also provide consumer protection. Each state has developed its own forms of protection with differing degrees of enforcement. The State Attorney General's office is charged with consumer protection in most states, while nine states have recognizable Consumer Affairs offices.

County and local consumer councils are beginning to proliferate. Help is at hand on the local level: if you need any information or have a complaint that you feel government can assist with, telephone for help. *Hot lines* have been established in some communities to assist consumers in contacting specific agencies that can best help them with their problems. As a citizen and taxpayer, you should have the benefit of some local centralized office that can direct you. Look in the white pages of your telephone directory for one of the following listings that can act as your starting point:

1. Consumer Assistance
2. Consumer Complaints
3. Consumer Protection
4. Attorney General
5. District Attorney

The first three may be under their own headings or under the U.S. Government, State, County, or City lists, as would be the latter two.

Private protection Most private protection takes the form of information rather than regulation, even though some industry and professional groups do have enforcement powers over their members. Consumer organizations such as Consumers Research, Inc., and Consumers Union are used by many people to secure information about product quality and reliability. Action groups such as "Nader's Raiders," Consumer Alliance, Inc., Common Cause, the Sierra Club, and the American Civil Liberties Union provide varying degrees of assistance to consumers. The Better Business Bureau maintains files on complaints against businesses. It attempts to provide a reasonably objective atmosphere for complaints between businesses and customers. BBBs are sponsored by local businesspeople, whose aim is to rid their communities of unscrupulous dealers.

Suggested Complaint Sequences

Different consumer problems require different courses of action to get redress. Generally it is best to start on a local basis and work your way to the top. Keep calm, and express your complaint in a dignified and intelligent manner.

Start with your local merchant if your complaint relates to a product or service rendered by him. Go to the particular department where you purchased the merchandise. Second, contact the manufacturer by telephone or letter. An increasing number of major manufacturers provide toll-free telephone service to settle customer complaints. If you write, keep a duplicate copy in case you need to refer to the original complaint. Address complaints to the manager of customer relations. If this does not bring a satisfactory response, do not be afraid to write directly to the president of the company. At this point, if you have been unsuccessful in solving the problem, you should turn to outside help.

It is usually wise to advise the business to whom you are complaining that you intend to seek outside help. Companies seldom care to have consumer complaints registered with government regulatory agencies. Often they will offer a compromise settlement that is satisfactory to everyone concerned. Whenever you write to any consumer help agency, send a carbon copy to the company involved. Whether you should write to a federal, state, or local agency is the real problem. Telephone your nearest consumer agency listed in the telephone directory for advice on this matter.

Simultaneous complaints to various agencies and to the Better Business Bureau may help. Another increasingly popular method of securing action is to contact your local media. Radio, television, and newspapers often have programs, news personalities, or columnists that provide "hot line" results. The power of negative publicity may soften a business organization. Sometimes these media intercedings bring the problem to the attention of the right person in the organization. Even with our modern communications and technology, businesses often have problems with internal communication. Reaching the right person at the beginning can keep a small problem small.

A final course of action may be to seek a legal remedy by bringing suit against the business with which you have a complaint. Your local Legal Aid Society or Lawyers' Reference Service can often advise you whether to proceed. The first organization will generally offer free basic legal advice, while the latter will put you in contact with a member who will offer this advice for a reduced fee. If you decide on legal action with an attorney, the customary professional fees would be charged.

An alternative to using a lawyer is to proceed as your own counsel in *small claims court.* All states have some form of court system to deal with claims involving relatively small amounts of money. You will have to check with your county court clerk for details. These courts often have different names such as people's courts or justice courts. The rules and jurisdiction of these courts differ greatly, but the common denominator seems to be that only laymen can plead cases; lawyers are not allowed to represent either party. Dollar claims generally cannot exceed $500. Often large and small businesses use these courts as a form of collection agency to get payment on defaulted debts. You should be able to do the same thing if you have been damaged in a business transaction.

You can circumvent the whole complaint process by not getting yourself into a problem situation to start with. Recognize that all business sales transactions involve making a contract that is enforceable in a court of law. Each party to a contract obtains certain rights and assumes certain duties and obligations. The buyer's rights are the seller's duties and vice versa. Your main *right* is that in the case of the sale of goods, the article purchased will measure up to a certain standard or will operate in a certain manner. This is called an implied warranty of fitness for normal use. Your main duty is to pay for the goods. You must pay for goods and services that meet the terms of your contract. Start any purchase by carefully deciding if you want the article or service being purchased. Make certain that it is satisfactory before you pay.

Vocabulary and Concepts

Better Business Bureau	Fair-trade pricing
Buying motivation	Fixed costs
Caveat emptor	Impulse buying
Closed-end lease	Open-end lease
Consumer protection	Shopping goods
Consumer sovereignty	Socioeconomic factors
Convenience goods	Special purchase
Depreciation	Specialty goods
	Variable costs

Questions for Discussion

1. Explain the difference between a need and a want.
2. Why do people buy?
3. Examine buying behavior in its relationship with the types of goods offered for sale. Do you agree with these classifications? What generalizations can you make about the classifications?
4. Convenience can be less expensive, or it can be more expensive. How do you explain this statement?
5. Which of the retail pricing strategies listed in this chapter are beneficial to the consumer?
6. What is meant by descriptive-terms food labeling? How does this affect the consumer?
7. Why should you go to the bother of inventorying the family clothing?
8. List a possible sequence of actions that you could take in a consumer complaint involving a clock-radio that fails to operate correctly after six months.
9. Which auto leasing arrangement is best, the open-end or the closed-end lease? Why?

Projects

1. Review the Consumer Bill of Rights. Can you add any other rights that would benefit the consumer, yet not be an unreasonable imposition upon business?
2. Develop a grocery shopping list that is fairly standard for your family. Compare the prices at three stores. This can be transformed into a permanent check-off list.
3. Develop your own set of buying guidelines. You may wish to rephrase some of those listed in this chapter.
4. Organize a neighborhood grocery buying cooperative. Visit wholesale produce terminals and staple goods warehouses.
5. Make a calendar of your personal expected purchases. This can be integrated with a personal record-keeping system with important due dates specifically marked.
6. Visit your local small claims court. Find out the costs, time, and effort needed to file a claim.

Case Problem

Art and Barbara Able have decided to review their present automobile expenses before purchasing a used car for Barbara. Help them calculate the true cost of owning and operating their present automobile. They have a one-year-old standard-size auto, which cost $5000. Depreciation was not considered in their balance sheet as illustrated in table 1–2. Helpful information to solve this problem is available in chapters 1, 2, and 11. You may assume that the Ables travel 15,000 miles per year, including Art's commute. You may use averages or local costs in your calculations.

3

People have different viewpoints about credit. Some people think credit is "good," others say it is "bad." Credit is neither good nor bad by itself. It assumes these adjectives only when you use it either properly or improperly. Since this text concerns consumer credit rather than commercial credit, the term *credit* will mean consumer credit. Real estate and home mortgage credit will not be included in our discussion of consumer credit. They will be treated in a later chapter.

Credit can best be described as a medium of exchange involving trust. It is a medium of exchange in that goods, services, and monies pass from one party to another in exchange for a promise to pay for these goods, services, and monies at some time in the future. The creditors, who grant the credit, must decide whether they trust the would-be debtor. Will the debtor fulfill his promise and make the needed payment or series of payments?

Credit is not a right. Individuals and businesses do not have to grant credit to anyone. They do so only when there is reasonable expectation of being paid. The Fair Credit Reporting Act of 1971, however, does require that business inform a credit applicant why he is being refused credit. Credit generally cannot be refused on the discriminatory basis of sex, religion, or age. This is a reasonable requirement and is a legal right of the applicant.

USES OF CREDIT

Credit is an economic phenomenon permeating all facets of American society. Rich and poor, young and old, all use credit to some extent. As we discuss the different types of credit, you will readily see how credit in some way touches everyone, and everyone should learn to understand it and use it to his advantage.

At the end of January 1975, there was a total of $187.1 billion in outstanding consumer credit according to figures released by the Federal Reserve Board. Given a population of about 220 million people, this would amount to over $850 for every man, woman, and child in the United States. Making the further assumption that the average household consists of three people, each household would have consumer credit obligations in excess of $2,550. This figure is neither good nor bad. Again, the individual's debt ratio and his reasons for using credit determine whether it is good or bad.

Consumers are extended credit and granted loans for almost any reason. Credit unions, for example, usually state that they grant loans for any provident reason. Borrowers can always seem to find a provident

consumer credit

reason for borrowing and lenders, including credit unions, always seem to vie for their business. Sellers extend credit and lenders offer money for such diverse things as vacations, everyday living expenses, family emergencies, clothing, education, dining out, medical treatment, taxes, and funeral services. Practically anything can be purchased on credit. The American consumer has definitely decided that it is worth the added cost to purchase on credit and to borrow against his future income to enjoy the present use of goods and services.

ADVANTAGES AND DISADVANTAGES OF CREDIT

As previously stated, the good or bad in the use of credit is relative. Lending institutions and other credit grantors have issued many pamphlets and brochures detailing the advantages of credit and providing a series of do's and don'ts. Usually these free items are available at the nearest branch of a finance company or bank. Household Finance Corporation deserves special mention for its *Money Management Series* as does Wells Fargo Bank for its *Dollar and Cent Guides.*

Advantages to the Consumer

The following advantages are generally recognized by consumers and creditors as being useful to the individual. Of course, not all people will need the specific advantages enumerated below:

1. *Convenience and safety* Credit cards provide a personal medium of exchange usable only by the cardholder, who needs to carry less currency.
2. *Convenient purchase records* The monthly billing cycle from department stores, oil companies, doctors, and others allows the consumer to keep better records of his purchases. Hopefully he can maintain control of his budget in this manner.
3. *Earlier enjoyment of goods and services* Borrowing against future income to enjoy a purchase today is a personal money management decision.
4. *Special sale offers* A wise use of credit can be the purchase of sale items at reduced prices if you really need the item. Reduced prices should offset any interest charge to the consumer. Many department stores have special presale promotions especially for their credit customers.
5. *Income-tax deduction* Taxpayers who itemize their income-tax returns can claim interest charges as a deduction. You are not really getting interest completely free because only a portion of the interest charges is offset through tax procedures. The extent of this advantage depends upon your tax bracket.
6. *Inflationary trends* The purchase of goods and services on credit is billed at current-value dollars. The extended credit terms over a long period of time, thirty-six months, for example, will be paid in future-value dollars that have less purchasing power. A consumer theoretically will save on the difference involving deflated dollars and inflated prices.
7. *Anticipated shortage of goods* Buy now for the best selection: that may be good advice. If you are currently short of funds, credit can solve your dilemma of when to purchase goods and services that may be in short supply.
8. *Ease of returning goods* If the goods have not been paid for, you might get a little more sympathy and satisfaction from the seller if you desire to return merchandise. If he has your money, you risk a possible runaround or a flat rejection.

9. *No charge for credit* If you pay for your purchases within the credit-billing period, there normally will not be a finance charge.

Disadvantages to the Consumer

There are always counterforces in our society; therefore we can expect to find some disadvantages to consumer use of credit.

1. *Credit may be costly.* Borrowing money or using extended credit will create an annual interest charge somewhere between 6 and 36 percent. A full discussion of this topic will be presented later in the chapter.
2. *Credit may create insecurity.* Some people worry over their debts. They do not rest easy while they owe anyone.
3. *Credit may lead to fiscal irresponsibility.* Too many fixed obligations may lead to an overextension of your ability to pay your bills. A constant balancing act takes place. If you pay only selected bills, you become a credit captive, shopping only those stores where you have paid your bill.
4. *Credit is easy to get, but hard to pay back.* Once you are granted credit, it is overly easy to expand the sources of credit available to you.
5. *Credit purchasers spend more per unit, more often.* Sales reports of most department stores indicate that credit customers are their best source of revenue. You more closely identify with a store if you have its credit card. Furthermore, you receive its sales circulars and are likely to shop more often. The unit value of merchandise purchased by credit customers is approximately 20 percent higher than that of cash customers.

Social Desirability of Credit

Credit is not only an economic phenomenon, it is a sociological happening. Customers today attach little social stigma to being in debt. If anything, the reverse is true. Society as a whole has benefited from the rewards of credit through an expanded economy and a higher standard of living. The individual generally has the option of using credit to his advantage or disadvantage depending upon his income, understanding of credit practices, and his willpower in purchasing goods and services. His standard of living can go up or down, at least temporarily, depending on his decisions.

Free choice in our society is important. However, many people are unable to exercise a free choice in their use or non-use of credit. These consumers usually are the unemployed, the welfare recipient, the retired person, the less educated and less knowledgeable person, and the minority person. Many of these people have regular income from public or other sources. They are often denied credit because of historical practices based upon group behavior. If they have the ability to pay, perhaps they should be allowed a limited amount of credit. Montgomery Ward, the large Chicago-based retailer, is experimenting with just such a plan.

The National Commission on Consumer Finance, established by the Consumer Protection Act of 1968—the Truth-in-Lending Act—is looking into the various problems of credit associated with low-income groups. A few of the research projects currently under way include: (1) development of a credit scoring system for lenders who extend credit to low-income borrowers; (2) research into whether educational and counseling programs are needed to supplement truth-in-lending; (3) comparisons of credit availability based upon residence areas; (4) studies of what happens to applicants rejected for credit at large retailers; (5) research on the effect of abolishment of the holder-in-due-course doctrine on credit practices; (6) study of interest-rate structures on a state by state basis; (7) investigation of the effect of low interest rates on the price of retail goods; and (8) an evaluation of experimental credit-granting programs now in operation in the United States.

The Commission's finding and recommendations will have an effect on all consumers, and you should keep informed of current legislative proposals on both state and national levels. Transmit your ideas and thoughts to your representatives so that they have some idea of how the individual consumer sees these problems. Organized lobbies from the credit industry and from consumer advocates will surely make their wishes known; you should do likewise.

AVAILABLE CREDIT PLANS

Part of the problem with credit is the wide variety of plans available from many different sources at varying rates of interest. We will first identify the important features of credit by type of credit plan and then compare approximate interest rates by source of lender or credit grantor.

Cash-Loan Credit

The borrowing of money is considered cash-loan credit. The lender offers you money in return for your promise to pay it back with a stated interest charge. Cash-loan credit usually precedes the purchase of goods or services. Instead of arranging for retail credit to be granted, the borrower secures the money first and then does his shopping. Debt consolidation, the lumping of all bills into one payment, may be considered a cash loan following the procurement of goods and services. Commercial banks, consumer-finance companies, and credit unions are the most important sources of cash loans. Relatives, industrial banks, home-finance companies, insurance companies, and "loan sharks" are other notable sources of various types of cash loans.

Service Credit

The term *service credit* refers to credit generally offered by service and professional establishments. It is a form of retail credit granted to almost everyone. Until recently service organizations did not require the formalities of a credit application; they just billed the customer at the end of each month for services rendered.

Today, one must complete credit forms before any service starts. Fewer establishments wait until the end of the month to bill you. Firms often send out billings immediately upon completion of the service if the service is of an occasional nature. Also they often make billings through banks or other professional collection services, indicating their ardent desire for quick payment. Doctors, dentists, and repair services follow this procedure because there is a tendency for the hard-pressed consumer to put off paying these particular bills. Telephone companies and other public utilities use monthly cycle billing directly from their own computer centers because of the continuing nature of their services. Many intermittent-service and continuous-service companies require deposits in order to receive their services on credit.

Charge Accounts

The retail charge account is one of the oldest forms of credit. While it is decreasing in importance compared to revolving credit, it is still noteworthy. This type of credit is usually "free." In order to obtain a thirty-day charge account, one must either be well known by the manager-proprietor or else complete a short credit application. Purchases made at the retail establishment are recorded and then billed to the customer at the end of the month. The customer then has thirty days to make payment in full but is expected to pay within ten days.

In practice the retailer can expect the thirty-day account to stretch beyond this period. For this reason mass retailers have abandoned this type of account, which ties up operating capital. The small-town store and the neighborhood retailer with a well-known clientele are virtually the only stores offering this type of account. They must do so for competitive reasons. Luxury-goods retailers and supper clubs often provide this service for their regular customers while offering other types of credit to their occasional customers.

Department stores, furniture stores, and jewelers promote thirty-sixty-ninety-day accounts for expensive durable goods as a convenience to their customers and as an inducement to purchase. The plan may differ slightly among stores. In one case, the purchase is billed on a declining balance basis with a finance charge added to the declining balance. The interest is forgiven upon payment of the total balance within a ninety-day period. In the second case, the sale is arranged in one, two, or three installments without billing for the finance charges.

Revolving Credit

There are basically four different types of revolving credit, each sponsored by a different kind of retail or credit organization. None of the types are mutually exclusive; there is an overlap in contractual agreements, purchasing privileges, and in the businesses and consumers that either accept or use these forms of credit. The four types of revolving credit are: retail revolving credit, bank-card credit, oil-company credit, and travel and expense credit.

The usual contractual agreement for all types of revolving credit contains the following basic provisions:

1. Establishment of a limited dollar amount of credit
2. Purchases to be enumerated, summarized, and billed once a month
3. No finance charge if customers pay in full within the billing period
4. A legal finance charge as a percentage of the unpaid balance to be added to the next billing
5. Customer option of paying all or any part of his obligation subject to a minimum payment
6. Evidence of contractual agreement and customer identification established by issuance of a plastic credit card with embossed customer account number
7. Collateral or downpayment normally not required

Retail revolving credit Department stores were the first organizations to use revolving credit. The success of their system brought about the other credit cards. Revolving credit has a simple concept: make it easy for the customer to purchase by having him simply sign the sales receipt. The open contract allows continuous purchasing without visiting the credit department. Customers who pay within the billing period get free use of the credit, while those who take longer to pay face interest charges. It is at the customer's option to make full or time payments. Customers who make delayed payments help to pay for the operation of the credit department and may actually contribute toward a profit for the credit grantor. This system makes everyone happy.

As mentioned earlier, department stores promote credit because it brings in repeat customers who buy in greater dollar amounts per sale than cash customers. A holder of one of these credit cards becomes a somewhat loyal reader of the store's advertisements. Most important, if you once use credit at a given store while on a relatively tight budget, you become their credit captive. Opening new accounts elsewhere would spread your payments unwisely, so you concentrate your credit purchases at the first store. In this manner you can keep payments as low as the minimum monthly charge. Figure 3–1 illustrates the billing statement of a large retailer.

Bank-card credit Small retailers were unable to compete with the credit terms

JCPenney Charge Account Statement
P. O. Box 1587, Oakland, CA 94604
Telephone (415) 834-1400

Account Number	Billing Date
000-000-000-0-0	01-02-75

Notice: See reverse side and accompanying statements for important information.

Previous Balance	–Payments	–Credits
165.40	10.00	22.50
+FINANCE CHARGE	+Purchases	+Ins. Premium
2.04	16.88	
= New Balance	Amount Due	Next Billing Date
157.44	10.00	02-02-75

To avoid **FINANCE CHARGE** pay New Balance by ▲

Balances	Periodic Rates	ANNUAL PERCENTAGE RATE
Up to $1000	1.50%	18.0%
Over $1000	1.00%	12.0%
MINIMUM CHARGE	.50	

FINANCE CHARGE is computed on $ 136.13, the AVERAGE DAILY **BALANCE** (See Reverse Side for explanation)

J. C. Penney Company, Inc.
P. O. Box 1587, Oakland, CA 94604
Telephone (415) 834-1400
When paying in person, present entire statement at your Penney Store.

000-000-000-0-0

JANE A. CONSUMER
946 PLEASANT PLACE
PINE VALLEY, CALIF. XXXXX

Please return this part with your payment.

You may at any time pay all or any part of your balance.

Transactions after the billing date will appear on next month's statement.

Amount Paid $ ______

New Balance	Minimum Amount Due	Next Billing Date
131.55	10.00	02-02-75

DP 6196G (Rev. 1/74) Payment must reach us on or before ↗

DP 6196G (Rev. 1/74)

Explanation of Balances upon which **FINANCE CHARGE** Computed*

Average Daily Balance. The previous balance less insurance premiums due, unpaid **FINANCE CHARGES** and credit relating to purchases previously billed is adjusted on a daily basis by subtracting payments after being first applied to insurance premiums and unpaid **FINANCE CHARGES** previously billed. The sum of these daily balances divided by the number of days in the billing period is the Average Daily Balance.

Adjusted Balance. The previous balance less insurance premiums due and unpaid **FINANCE CHARGES** is adjusted by subtracting payments and credits after being first applied to insurance premiums and unpaid **FINANCE CHARGES**.

The **FINANCE CHARGE** amount includes 4% General Excise Tax on **FINANCE CHARGES** for Hawaii accounts.

*Each of these computations exclude purchases not previously billed.

Figure 3–1 Retail Store Billing Statement. *(J. C. Penney Company, Inc., New York)* offered by the large department and chain stores. The banking industry stepped in and developed a multi-store charge card with a bank rather than the retailer acting as the supplier of capital for credit purchases. Two major bank-card systems emerged. The trend seems to be toward the assimilation of smaller bank-card systems into the major ones—the BankAmericard and Master Charge systems. Both major systems have extended their credit card acceptance to many foreign countries to compete directly with the travel and expense credit cards.

The bank acts as a middleman who contracts separately with the consumer and the retailer. The consumer, allowed a certain revolving credit limit, may charge goods and services to his bank-card account at the merchants who honor his particular bank card. The merchant contracts with one or more banks to accept their bank cards as payment for goods and services. He then discounts his credit sales-receipts at the bank for ready cash. The retailer does not need a credit department nor does he have capital funds tied up in accounts receivable. The cost to the retailer ranges from 1½ to 5 percent of credit sales depending upon volume and type of business.

The major advantage to the consumer is that he receives only one monthly billing yet still retains his shopping independence. He may become a captive of his bank card if he allows a continuing balance to develop.

Bank cards offer other useful credit services, such as a form of cash loan with a basic lending fee of 2 percent ($1.00 minimum) plus any finance charges incurred by an unpaid balance on the monthly billing. Figues 3–2 and 3–3 are examples of the application or authorization forms sent to consumers in their monthly billings enticing them to use these special bank-card services. The more popular services are enumerated below.

1. *Cash advances* Cash loans are available by presenting your bank card to the cashier at a participating bank.
2. *Cash by mail* The bank will mail you a check or deposit the loan in your checking account (fig. 3–2).

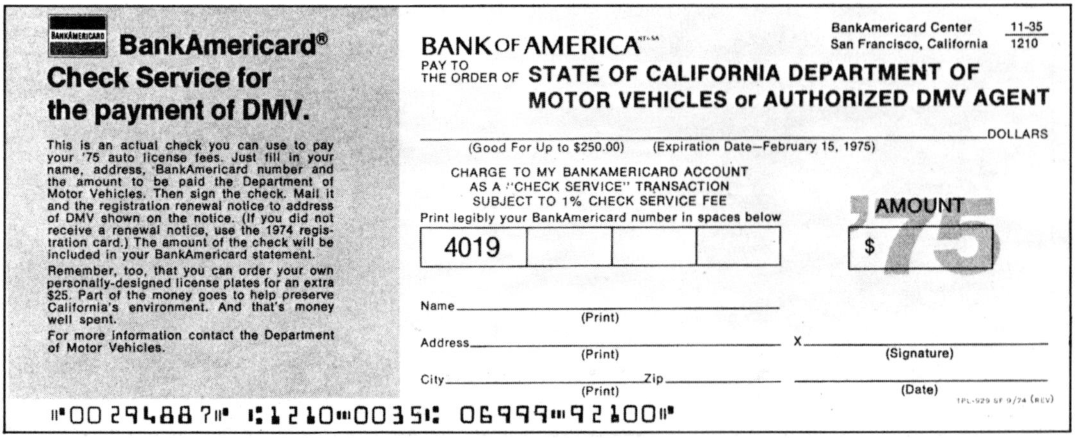
BankAmericard® Check Service for the payment of DMV.

This is an actual check you can use to pay your '75 auto license fees. Just fill in your name, address, BankAmericard number and the amount to be paid the Department of Motor Vehicles. Then sign the check. Mail it and the registration renewal notice to address of DMV shown on the notice. (If you did not receive a renewal notice, use the 1974 registration card.) The amount of the check will be included in your BankAmericard statement.

Remember, too, that you can order your own personally-designed license plates for an extra $25. Part of the money goes to help preserve California's environment. And that's money well spent.

For more information contact the Department of Motor Vehicles.

BANK OF AMERICA N.T.&S.A.

BankAmericard Center, San Francisco, California — 11-35 / 1210

PAY TO THE ORDER OF STATE OF CALIFORNIA DEPARTMENT OF MOTOR VEHICLES or AUTHORIZED DMV AGENT

DOLLARS

(Good For Up to $250.00) (Expiration Date—February 15, 1975)

CHARGE TO MY BANKAMERICARD ACCOUNT AS A "CHECK SERVICE" TRANSACTION SUBJECT TO 1% CHECK SERVICE FEE

Print legibly your BankAmericard number in spaces below

4019

AMOUNT '75

$

Name (Print)

Address (Print)

City (Print) Zip

X (Signature)

(Date)

TPL-929 SF 9/74 (REV)

⑈0029488 7⑈ ⑆1210⑉0035⑆ 06999⑉92100⑈

Figure 3–2 Cash Advance Credit Card Loan. *(Bank of America N.T. & S.A., San Francisco)*

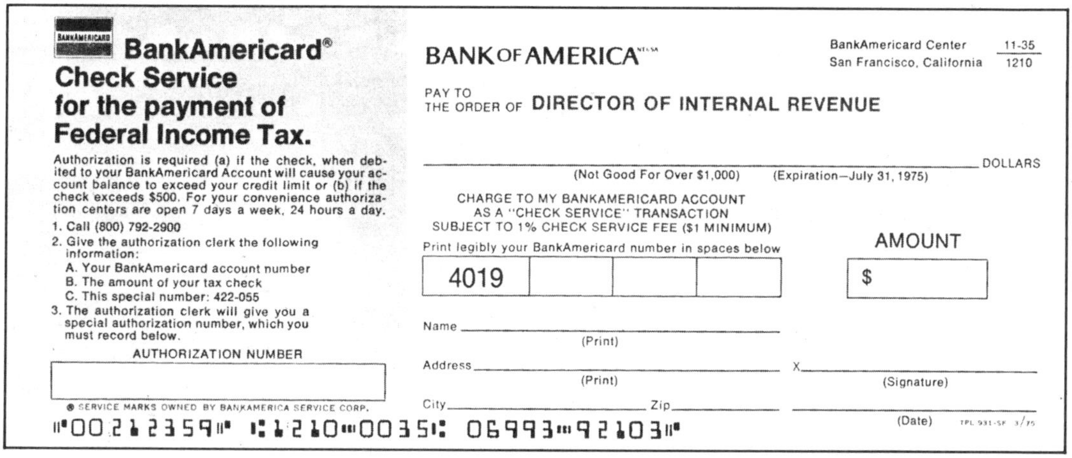
BankAmericard®
Check Service
for the payment of
Federal Income Tax.

Authorization is required (a) if the check, when debited to your BankAmericard Account will cause your account balance to exceed your credit limit or (b) if the check exceeds $500. For your convenience authorization centers are open 7 days a week, 24 hours a day.

1. Call (800) 792-2900
2. Give the authorization clerk the following information:
   A. Your BankAmericard account number
   B. The amount of your tax check
   C. This special number: 422-055
3. The authorization clerk will give you a special authorization number, which you must record below.

AUTHORIZATION NUMBER

® SERVICE MARKS OWNED BY BANKAMERICA SERVICE CORP.

BANK OF AMERICA

BankAmericard Center 11-35/1210
San Francisco, California

PAY TO THE ORDER OF DIRECTOR OF INTERNAL REVENUE

______ DOLLARS
(Not Good For Over $1,000) (Expiration—July 31, 1975)

CHARGE TO MY BANKAMERICARD ACCOUNT
AS A "CHECK SERVICE" TRANSACTION
SUBJECT TO 1% CHECK SERVICE FEE ($1 MINIMUM)

Print legibly your BankAmericard number in spaces below

4019

AMOUNT
$

Name ______ (Print)
Address ______ (Print)
City ______ Zip ______
X ______ (Signature)
______ (Date)

Figure 3–3 BankAmericard Check Service. *(Bank of America N.T. & S.A., San Francisco)*

3. *Reserve checking account* By prior arrangement you may overdraft your checking account, and an automatic cash advance will be charged against your bank card.
4. *Federal, state, and city income tax payments* Signing the check service application form makes it a check payable to the tax authority (fig. 3–3).
5. *Property tax payment* Operates on the same principles as above.
6. *Auto license fees* Same as above.

The latter services fulfill a timely need for many consumers. The first three services should provide cash for any other contingency that might arise. You should appreciate the convenience of bank-card services, but be aware that they do cost extra regardless of whether you pay in full when billed.

Oil-company credit Oil-company revolving credit differs from the other major types of revolving credit in the length of the "free" credit period. The other systems offer a twenty-five to thirty-day period in which to pay in full, whereas many major oil companies allow a fifty-five-day period, or two billing cycles, before assessing a finance charge as low as 10 percent APR.

Auto repairs and accessories up to a certain dollar amount may be charged with oil credit cards. Some companies have a card interchange agreement with noncompeting regional oil companies to allow their motorist customers a nationwide credit system. In addition, many companies have credit-card agreements with selected motel and hotel chains as a convenience for their cardholders. Some of the additional services available with oil credit cards were curtailed during the gasoline shortage and are only now being revived.

Travel and expense credit The name of this category implies who uses these cards: "T and E" cards have been used by businesspeople and travelers since the early 1950s. American Express, Carte Blanche, and Diners Club are most prominent in this field.

Customers use T and E cards for airline travel, restaurants, hotels and motels, rent-a-car services, and gift and specialty shop purchases. T and E cards provide the customer with a monthly billing, which is expected to be paid in full within thirty days. Extended terms are available, but they are not used by many cardholders. Businesses often procure cards for their executives and salespeople.

An annual fee of approximately $15 is charged by T and E card companies to help defray the costs of billing. This charge tends to eliminate the casual use of the card and provides a certain amount of status to the cardholder. Normally, one must have a minimum income of $10,000 per year to acquire a T and E card. Discounts on merchant credit card sales provide the main source of revenue for these companies. International travelers make extensive use of the American Express card because of this firm's reputation and extensive network of international branches. Most businesses that honor T and E cards also honor bank-cards. Why pay for status?

Installment credit Consumer installment credit claims the largest slice of outstanding consumer debt. Separate contracts for each purchase or each loan differentiate installment accounts from revolving accounts. The consumer completes a separate application and has his credit investigated each time he desires to purchase on the installment plan. Retail outlets, commercial banks, finance companies, and credit unions provide the bulk of installment credit. Figure 3–4 shows the amount and source of installment credit in January 1975.

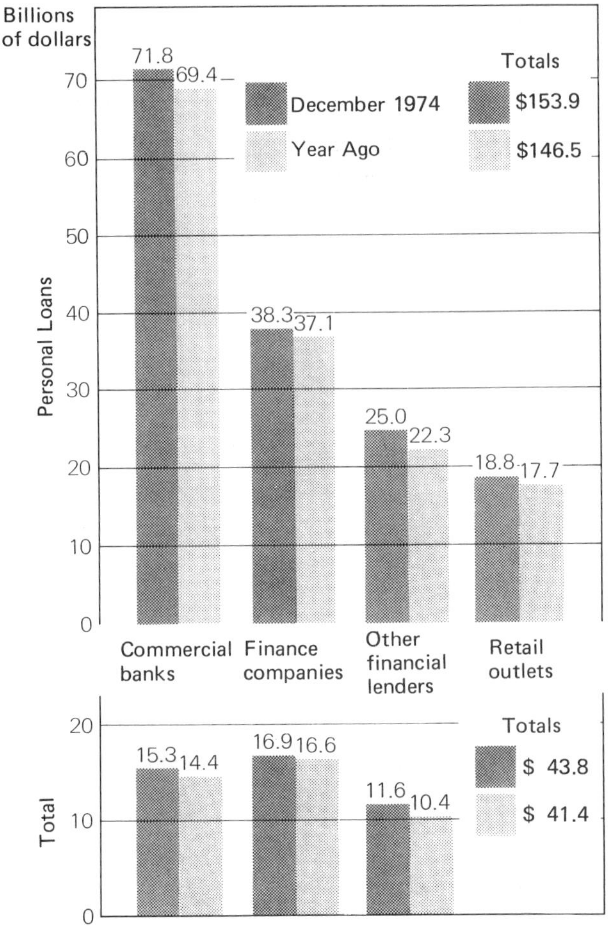

Figure 3–4 Consumer Installment Credit Outstanding, January 1975.

Certain other characteristics also typify installment contracts. They are:

1. Consumers usually purchase durable or "big ticket" items by installment. One rarely pays for goods of this sort out of current income; they are either saved for in advance or purchased by time payment.
2. It is usually necessary to make down payments on durable goods purchases. This creates an equity position for the purchaser so that he will continue payment until the debt is retired.
3. It is often necessary to provide collateral, liens, or chattel mortgages. If goods are purchased, the item itself serves as security. Failure of the buyer to complete payment allows the seller or lender to claim or re-

possess the collateral. This threat and a down payment usually suffice to insure payment.

4. Except in the case of special 90-day purchase accounts, merchants add a finance charge to the amount borrowed or the unpaid balance.
5. The purchaser makes equal monthly payments (installments) for a given number of months.
6. Prepayment penalties may be assessed for full payment of the installment contract in advance of the agreed-upon date. It is not always advantageous to pay off an installment contract in advance, as we shall see later in this chapter.

Financing one's expensive purchases by use of installment has become an American way of life. It is the only way many people can afford these purchases if they are unable or unwilling to save in advance. Smaller purchases can also be financed under the installment plan through the use of coupon booklets. Macy's, Gimbel's, and others offer booklets with coupons valued at varying amounts. The customer spends these like cash in the issuing company's stores after signing an installment contract agreeing to pay for the total value of the coupon booklet plus interest over a stated period of time. The plan allows flexible purchasing of many items with repayment on a fixed installment basis.

Seventy-five percent of all automobiles are purchased on installment credit. The purchaser may arrange for credit through the dealer or with a financing institution. Auto dealers usually have at least one bank and one sales finance company available to provide the necessary credit. If a consumer with a good credit record and ability to pay deals directly with a bank or credit union, he will most likely get a more favorable interest rate.

THE COST OF CREDIT

Just about everything costs money. Borrowing money is no exception. Receiving credit is basically the same as borrowing money. Credit grantors charge an additional fee beyond the cash price of the goods or services purchased. This added fee may be called a "service charge," a "finance charge," or a "carrying charge." It is really an interest charge for the use of someone else's money.

You can determine the cost of credit in two ways: (1) in terms of dollars and cents, and (2) in terms of an annual percentage rate.

Dollar Cost

In terms of dollars and cents, the consumer can immediately see his out-of-pocket expense for the use of credit. But can he tell whether it is a fair charge for credit? Interest in dollar amounts is calculated on the basis of principal times rate times time: $I = P \times R \times T$. The question still persists: Is it a fair charge?

Many organizations offering installment credit use precomputed installment repayment tables. These tables allow equal repayment amounts for differing periods. Because these tables often set the principal amount at an odd figure, not the exact amount you care to borrow, you still will not know if the dollar cost is a good deal in comparison with another installment plan.

Annual Percentage Rate

Figuring the cost of credit in terms of an annual percentage rate (APR) solves the problem of comparing different plans. The APR is the simple-interest rate established for the use of a given amount of money (principal) for a period of one year. As mentioned earlier, the interest charge is based on principal times rate times time. The APR, however, acts as a common denominator to all plans. By use of a constant-ratio formula, you can convert the dollar cost of credit into the annual percentage rate. You take the amount of money borrowed (principal), the interest charges in dollars, and the number of installments, and then expand or contract the time period through the constant-ratio formula to come up with an annual percentage. The consumer can then compare the APR for each credit offer to determine which has an acceptable rate of interest.

Any installment contract can be analyzed to determine the annual percentage rate using the constant-ratio formula as follows:

$$APR = \frac{2\,MI}{P(N+1)}$$

Formula terms defined:

APR = Annual percentage rate
M = Number of payments in one year
I = Interest charge in dollars
P = Principal amount borrowed
N = Total number of payments in the contract

Annual percentage rate

Banks often quote their interest rates in terms of dollars of interest per hundred dollars. Other lenders quote in terms of dollars per payment. This can lead to confusion. Which of the following quotes offers the best deal?

A. The First National Bank will lend at the rate of $7 per $100 on a new car purchase if you put one-fourth down. Therefore, if you buy a $4,000 automobile you will finance $3,000 over a three-year period with carrying charges amounting to $630 ($7 × 30 [hundreds] × 3 [years]). You will make equal monthly payments of $100.83 for thirty-six months.

B. The Second National Bank will lend $3,500 on the same car. You must pay $90 per month for forty-eight months.

The calculations follow:

Example A $$APR = \frac{2 \times 12 \times 630}{3000\ (36+1)} = 13.6\%$$

Example B $$APR = \frac{2 \times 12 \times 820}{3500\ (48+1)} = 11.5\%$$

In example B it was necessary to multiply $90 × 48 months to arrive at a total time cost of $4,320. By subtracting the principal of $3,500, we were able to figure the interest expense of $820.

The consumer can choose between a larger down-payment and higher monthly payments, or a smaller down-payment and smaller monthly payments for a longer period of time. Without the APR, you would not be able to determine the "best deal." One pays less interest in dollars in example A, but one also borrows less money.

Truth in Lending

The Truth-in-Lending Act requires that the APR be shown in any written credit transaction, and any credit advertisement that quotes rates or dollar finance charges must also quote the APR. Salespeople are also required to quote the APR rather than any of the misleading rates or dollars per hundred that they have historically used to confuse the consumer. It is up to the consumer to understand the importance of the APR and to use it for comparison purposes. In brief, the lower the annual percentage rate, the lower the dollar cost of a given amount of credit (principal) for a one-year period.

What simpler comparison can a person make? Before any major purchase or borrowing on credit the consumer should compare various sources of loan funds to determine the APR. We will present approximate ranges of the annual percentage rate for various lending and credit-granting institutions later in the chapter.

The APR can also be determined on interest charges based upon unpaid balances. Multiply the rate quoted for a particular period of time by the number of periods in a year. Most rates are quoted on the monthly unpaid balance, so you should multiply by twelve. Many bank cards and department stores charge interest of $1\frac{1}{2}$ percent per month on the unpaid balance, thereby charging an annual rate of 18 percent ($1\frac{1}{2} \times 12$).

Other Factors Affecting the Cost of Credit

As mentioned earlier, the cost of credit is based on principal times rate times time ($P \times R \times T = I$). The lender's terms of repayment of the loan will determine the amount borrowed and the length of time the principal is held. The earlier bank examples figured the interest on the original amount borrowed rather than on the declining balance. This changed the annual interest rate to 13.6 percent from what apparently was a 7 percent loan. Therefore, we have a rule of thumb: installment accounts quoted as dollars per hundred or percent per hundred will be approximately twice the quoted rate.

Term and amortization loans This doubling of the interest rate occurs because the funds lent are not held by the borrower for the entire period of the loan. He pays an equal portion back each period (month). The borrower has the entire loan at the beginning of the loan, half of it mid-term during the period, and nothing left at the end of the loan. On the average, he has the use of only half of what he has borrowed. Table 3–1 and the following examples explain how the length of time borrowed funds are held by the borrower affects the annual percentage rate.

According to example A, $100 borrowed for one year at 8 percent will cost $8 interest or 8 percent (APR). You keep the $100 for one year and pay it back as a lump-sum of $108. This is considered a term loan, money borrowed for a specific term and then repaid. In example B, $100 borrowed for one year at 8 percent will cost $8 interest or 14.8 percent APR. You repay the $100 plus $8 in twelve equal installments of $9. The APR is almost double because on the average you have the *use* of $50, not $100, and are paying $8 for this privilege. This is an installment or amortized loan. In equal installment loans creditors usually apply more of the first installment payments toward interest charges than in later payments. This lowers the APR to somewhat less than 16 percent (double the nominal rate of 8 percent). Table 3–3 shows how this is accomplished.

Most consumer lending institutions use the installment method because consumers are more likely to be able to make relatively small installments as compared to one lump-sum payment. Installments set up a habit for the consumer. There is no "out-of-sight, out-of-mind" problem for the bank. Of course lenders do not mind getting approximately half their principal returned by the middle of the contract. They can lend it out again!

Banks especially, but other lending sources too, offer term loans upon request. They must have reasonable proof that you will be able to pay off the loan in one lump-

Table 3–1 Effect of time on funds held by borrower on annual percentage rate. Nominal rate 8%, interest charge $8.

Example A Term Loan*		Example B Installment Loan†	
Elapsed Time	*Loan Fund Balance*	*Elapsed Time*	*Loan Fund Balance*
Beginning	$100.00	Beginning	$100.00
1 month	100.00	1 month	91.67
2 month	100.00	2 month	83.33
3 month	100.00	3 month	75.00
4 month	100.00	4 month	66.67
5 month	100.00	5 month	58.33
6 month	100.00	6 month	50.00
7 month	100.00	7 month	41.67
8 month	100.00	8 month	33.33
9 month	100.00	9 month	25.00
10 month	100.00	10 month	16.67
11 month	100.00	11 month	8.33
12 month	0.00	12 month	0.00

* $100.00 principal and $8.00 interest repaid at expiration of loan. Borrower has use of $100.00 for one year at 8% APR.

† $100.00 principal and $8.00 actually repaid in 12 monthly installments of $9. Loan fund balance represents repayment of principal only. Borrower has use of $50 (on the average) during the year at 14.8% APR.

sum payment when it is due. Term loans are usually made for business reasons because there is some productive income resulting from the loan. Term loans against savings and securities may be allowed because the collateral can be used for security or for repayment. Most consumer loans are amortized not only because of the repayment ability factor, but because the goods or services purchased by consumer credit are literally consumed. Even when collateral is used for security, it usually declines in value as the installment payments are made. All too often, the consumer still owes more than the current value of the goods purchased.

Add-on and discount loans Lenders affect the APR by means of adding the interest charge to the loan principal or by discounting the interest charge from the loan principal. If you are offered a choice of an add-on or discount loan, which would you choose? It would appear that a "discount" would be a good deal because we all know that a discount means a cut rate. After all, many retailers advertise discounts which mean lower prices.

It does not work that way in finance. In the add-on method the finance or interest charge is added to the principal for repayment. The examples shown earlier all used this method. In the discount method, the interest charge is subtracted from the loan principal. The loan proceeds after interest would be less than originally requested. The interest, in effect, has been paid in advance by being discounted from the principal. The original principal amount borrowed is the amount repaid. Add-on and discount loans may be amortized (installment-payment)

Table 3–2 Dollar amount and APR differentiated by add-on or discount interest. Principal of $1,000 at nominal rate of 8%.

Add-on Term		Add-on Installment	
1 Payment at Year End		*12 Monthly Payments*	
Interest charge:	$80	Interest charge:	$80
You get:	$1,000	You get:	$1,000
APR:	8%	APR:	14.8%
Discount Term		**Discount Installment**	
1 Payment at Year End		*12 Monthly Payments*	
Interest charge:	$80	Interest charge:	$80
You get:	$920	You get:	$920
APR:	8.7%	APR:	16.1%

The APR can be calculated by using the formula:

$$APR = \frac{2MI}{P(N + 1)}$$

loans or they may be term (lump-sum payment) loans. One thousand dollars borrowed for one year at 8 percent ($8 per hundred) would cost $80 under each of these possibilities. The APR would differ as shown in table 3–2.

The basic difference between add-on and discount loans is that under the discount method you get less money for the same finance charge. Therefore, you pay a higher annual interest *rate*.

When borrowing money, ask for an add-on loan. In fact, make it a term add-on loan if you are capable of paying the loan in one lump-sum. Generally, term loans are granted on a discount basis, while installment contracts are based on the add-on method.

Costly Contract Terms to Watch For

Credit contracts are invariably drawn by the lending institution, since they are in the business and prepare many contracts daily. The forms are preprinted and usually contain clauses favorable to the lender. Professional lenders must abide by the lending regulations of the states in which they operate, so these clauses are most likely legal. The federal government and many state governments are investigating many of these credit terms in view of the current consumer awareness and because many contract provisions are not in the public interest. This should not stop you from shopping the different lenders for more favorable terms with fewer restrictive clauses.

Balloon payment This type of contract offers low monthly installments to make it look inviting. The last installment, however, is a large amount to make up for the low monthly installments. Many consumers are unable to make the final installment and thereby default the payment. In some states the debtor loses his collateral and winds up with a deficiency judgment against him.

Acceleration clause Lenders often insert an acceleration clause into a contract. This allows the lender to accelerate or speed up repayment of the installment at his option. Such a requirement could create a financial burden for the borrower.

Default clause Most contracts have a form of acceleration clause in them: if the buyer or borrower is in default, the remaining balance is due and payable. Default is defined differently in different states. Generally, default is taken to mean nonpayment or part-payment of a scheduled installment. Most states have a grace period of ten days past the due date before this clause can be enforced However, consumers should be aware of the credit sales and small-loan laws of their state and not rely on this generalization.

Confession-of-judgment clauses The borrower waives his right to defend his reason for nonpayment. Fortunately, this type clause is not recognized by many courts. Usually as part of the clause, the borrower agrees to pay all court costs and the "reasonable" attorney fees of the lender who takes legal action to enforce collection. Courts automatically grant the lender his legal costs in attempting collection if the borrower fails to appear in court or if he loses the case. In some states this clause is extended to provide for automatic wage assignments as part of the confession of judgment.

Late-payment penalty Such a penalty goes hand in hand with acceleration and default clauses. Lenders use the late-payment penalty as a club to encourage on-time payment. This extra charge will usually pacify lenders to the extent that they will not invoke the acceleration or default clauses. The amount of the penalty varies among the states, with 10 percent being in favor among mortgage lenders.

Consumer advocates are beginning to question the legality of the late charge. Ten percent amounts to extreme usury if a payment is made ten days into the late period. The APR in such a case would amount to 360 percent.

Prepayment penalty It is bad enough to pay a late charge, but should you have to pay an early charge? Real estate mortgage lenders usually charge the next six months interest as a prepayment penalty. Prepayment penalties on durable goods and auto installment contracts vary among the states; up to a $25 fee is allowed. The California Automobile Sales Finance Act allows the lender to deduct $25 from the interest refund whenever an auto installment contract is paid off in advance while no penalty is allowed the creditor on other retail installment sales. Each state has its own laws regarding prepayment penalties.

Formal prepayment procedures differ from state to state and company to company. There are two main methods of paying off a precomputed installment contract prior to maturity. First, have the lender compute a payoff figure and pay that amount. Second, send in payment for all the remaining installments and then receive a refund of the remainder of the finance charge. Both plans have the same mathematical result: a hopefully lower finance charge than was originally agreed to in the written installment contract. It may turn out that because of prepayment penalty charges, the borrower will not save anything by paying off the contract earlier than previously agreed.

Let us assume while we determine how installment interest refunds are computed that there is no prepayment penalty. The amount of interest the lender earns and the amount of interest the borrower is refunded are based upon how much money is outstanding (loaned) for how long. Since you are paying back the loan in installments, there would be a greater unpaid balance during the first months of the loan than during subsequent months. When your monthly payments are equal, a greater portion of each payment goes to interest during the first few months and a lesser portion during the last few months.

This brings us to the most commonly used method of interest allocation on installment accounts. It is called the "sum-of-the-digits" method, more commonly the "Rule of 78." The digits for *all* the months in a contract are added, and this sum becomes the denominator to determine fractionally how much interest to allocate to each month. This method can be applied to any length contract using appropriate figures: If someone borrowed $1,000 for one year at $8 per hundred, it would cost him $80. How is it earned? Is 1/12 of the interest earned each month, or is a greater portion earned when the unpaid balance of the loan is still high? Using the sum-of-the-digits method we add 12 months, 11 months, 10 months, etc. and find the sum of the months (digits), which in this case is 78. Ergo, the "Rule of 78." Ratio analysis or prorating shows that 12/78 of the $80 interest is earned during the first month, 11/78 is earned during the second month, and the interest continues to decline until 1/78 is earned during the final month of the loan contract.

At this point you may think, "If I pay off early I should get a proportionate refund. If I pay off the loan in three months (a quarter-year), I should get back three-fourths of the interest, in this case $60." Unfortunately that is not how interest is proportioned. You would get whatever is left of the $80 after the lender has deducted whatever portion of the $80 he has earned. In this example the lender has earned 12/78, 11/78, and 10/78 for a total of 33/78 of the $80 during the three-month period. This amounts to $33.84, or 42.3 percent, of the $80. The borrower does not get the $60 he has dreamed of saving; instead he gets $46.16 ($80 – 33.84), about $15 less than anticipated. Table 3–3 is a graphic illustration of this concept.

A thorough understanding of credit charges will make you more aware of the costs of credit. In the case of installment refunds, we can say two things with relative certainty: (1) the sum-of-the-digits method of allocating earned interest is a legitimate method of determining interest, and (2) you will not save as much as you think by paying off installment accounts in advance.

It is still wise to pay off loans early, because any interest charge is still a cost to you unless you can earn a greater return than the APR payable on your installment contract. One exception to this suggestion would be that the added cost of a prepayment penalty may nullify any savings you make by the advance payment.

Declining-balance installment accounts operate on the basis of equal principal installments plus interest added to each month's payment. The total payment amount declines somewhat each month because as the balance declines, so does the interest computed on the unpaid balance. The declining balance method does not require a precomputation of interest, so there is no refund to figure. But you do end up paying the same dollar amount of interest as in a precomputed equal installment loan if both have the same terms and annual percentage rate.

Credit life insurance The Truth-in-Lending Act made credit life insurance an option rather than a requirement for the borrower. The purpose of credit life insurance is to cover the risk of the debtor being unable to pay the loan due to death or serious injury. The creditor becomes the beneficiary of the term policy, which remains in force for the duration of the installment contract. The premium rates

Table 3–3 "Rule of 78"

Contract Month	$1,000 Loan for One Year		Installments Being Used	
1	× × × × × × × × × × × ×		12	
2	× × × × × × × × × × ×		11	
3	× × × × × × × × × ×		10	
4	× × × × × × × × ×		9	
5	× × × × × × × ×		8	
6	× × × × × × ×	(73%)	7	57
7	× × × × × ×		6	
8	× × × × ×		5	
9	× × × ×		4	
10	× × ×		3	
11	× ×		2	
12	×	(100%)	1	78
78			78	

Each × stands for $83.33 of a finance company's money used by a customer during a particular month. By the end of the sixth month, 57/78 (73 percent) of the finance charges and loan amount have been used. If a customer pays off a loan before maturity, the computation of the payoff amount or refund on finance charges will be based on the loan amount used up to payoff time.

differ among lenders because of varying rates offered by insurance companies cooperating with them. The rates usually are based on a group term policy, and in many states law determines rate maximums. Interest costs are high enough without the added costs of an "insurance" policy. It is apparent that credit life insurance is simply a method of passing a business risk onto the unwary consumer.

Credit-card liability Recent federal legislation has reduced a cardholder's liability for loss, theft, or unauthorized use of a credit card. Cardholders are liable only for a maximum of $50 in unauthorized charges if they give notification of loss to the credit card issuer. The required notification is to allow the issuer to blacklist the card account number, hopefully reducing losses.

Cardholders should protect themselves by notifying the issuing company immediately by telephone and then following up with a written letter by certified mail. This procedure would preclude any later disagreement as to notification. Other devices for consumer credit-card liability protection include (1) making a list of all credit-card numbers and the notification addresses, (2) eliminating seldom-used credit cards, and (3) knowing the whereabouts of all your credit cards. The $50 liability limit has practically eliminated the need for credit-card insurance.

APPROXIMATE RATES BY TYPE OF LENDER

State law governs the interest rates that individuals and most lending institutions may charge. It would be futile to list the interest rates for each state by the type of lender because of the almost infinite possibilities for change. Therefore this text will give approximate ranges for interest charges. The idea is to form an overview of interest-rate ranges, services, regulations, and credit acceptances by type of lender. Each reader should comparison shop his local credit-granting institutions to determine the rates offered in his locale. The following list is in rough ascending order by annual percentage rate. Persons with extremely good credit ratings, income, and net worth will probably be able to secure better interest rates than those enumerated. Follow the old adage, "Ask and you shall receive."

Relatives (0–6 percent)

Students often think of parents and other relatives as a source of free money. This source seldom materializes. However, if you are sincere and businesslike, you may be able to arrange a mutually beneficial loan contract. Offer terms in writing to your parents and relatives that provide a better rate of interest than they can receive from their savings accounts. Chances are the rate you agree to pay will be better than you can get at a commercial lending institution.

Do not fail to pay the money back as agreed. This low-cost source of money will no longer be available to you if you default.

Individuals (10 percent)

Individual lenders usually operate in the second-mortgage market or in business-opportunities markets. Most states have some legal maximum rate for individual lenders in order to attempt to control loan-shark practices and provide protection to the consumer. These rates are usually part of the state usury laws.

Insurance Companies (6 percent)

Life-insurance customers who own cash value policies may borrow against their policy once there is a sufficient reserve fund established. You would borrow at a rate 1 or 2 percent above the interest rate paid to you by the insurance company. After a few years contribution on your part, there is a sufficient amount of money in the savings portion of the insurance policy to borrow against. If you should die before paying the money back to the insurance company, the borrowed amount is deducted from the proceeds payable to your beneficiaries. Also, if you should terminate the policy, the cash surrender value is reduced by the amount of the loan.

Credit Unions (9–12 percent)

A credit union is a cooperative of savers and borrowers brought together by a common bond. These nonprofit organizations are organized by members of unions, churches, and employees of a business. The vast majority of credit unions are owned and operated by employees of business organizations. The more affluent members purchase shares (save) in the credit union. Those members who need to borrow do so at rather favorable rates.

The 9 percent rate usually applies to loans backed by collateral, like autos or credit-union shares, while the 12 percent rate is applicable to all other borrowing purposes. The rates are low because the cost of operating a credit union is usually low. The credit committee itself is often a volunteer group leaving the need for only a few salaried employees. Offices are often subleased to the credit union by the sponsoring agency. A select clientele and cautious lending policies keep losses to a minimum. Payroll deduction is an important method of collection payment, thereby reducing losses.

Homeowner Loan Companies (13 percent average)

Homeowner loans are usually available through finance companies, their affiliates, or through specialized second-mortgage companies. The rates average about 13 percent and are lower than many banks and personal finance companies because of the specialized nature of these large loans. Rates normally start at 24 percent and decline as the total amount borrowed increases. Terms are usually for three to five years.

Advertisements by these companies stress the borrowing of money to consolidate the borrower's outstanding debts. In loans of this type, the borrower's home is used for collateral. Default on loans of this type often results in the loss of your home to the second-mortgage holder.

Commercial Banks (15 percent average)

Banks do not have regulated interest rates on cash loans. They are simply governed by the laws of supply and demand. Competition tends to keep these loan rates within reason. Rates average 12 percent on new automobile contracts, depending on the down-payment offered; 12–22 percent on used automobile contracts, and 18 percent on durable-goods installment contracts and personal installment loans.

Revolving Charge Accounts (18 percent average)

Bank cards, travel-expense cards, oil-company cards, and department-store credit cards are all regulated as to interest rates and contract procedures by the individual states. Most states allow 18 percent per year. Rates are normally quoted as so much per month, usually 1½ percent per month. On account balances over $1,000 the rate drops, usually to 1 percent per month on that portion over $1,000.

Industrial Loan Companies (24 percent average)

These organizations are also known as industrial banks. The Morris Plan typifies this type of lender, who offers both secured and unsecured loans plus passbook loans on clients' savings accounts. Rates and types of loans differ from state to state but may start at 36 percent and decline to 12 percent on balances over $2,500.

Personal-Finance Companies (24 percent average)

These companies are also known as consumer-finance companies or small-loan companies. They average about 24 percent (APR) on their contracts for the lending of money. They quote their rates on the unpaid balance even though they precompute most installment-contract payments from payback tables to allow for equal monthly payments.

Personal-finance company rates are higher than commercial banks because of the usually smaller amounts loaned per transaction and the greater risk of default by their customers. They tend to grant credit more readily and with greater convenience and speed to all types of borrowers. Rates start at approximately 36 percent per month on the first $100 borrowed and decrease as the amount borrowed becomes larger. The less expensive money is programmed to be repaid last; as the unpaid balance declines the remaining balance is charged interest at the appropriate scale.

Pawnbrokers (24 percent average)

Pawnshops serve the useful function of providing loans to persons who leave resaleable articles at the pawnshop as security. Credit ratings are of little importance. What matters is the title to the pawned articles and the resale value of the article if it is not redeemed.

Customers usually have one year to redeem their pawned articles by paying back the loan amount and interest charges. The rates go down on a graduated scale similar to those of personal-finance companies, i.e., 36 percent on the first $100 borrowed. Failure to redeem the article allows the pawnbroker to sell it at whatever price he can secure. Most borrowers receive no more than approximately 50 percent of the market value for the pawned items because of the risks inherent in the resale of used consumer goods.

Loan Sharks (No Limit)

The unfortunate person who borrows from a "loan shark," "business acquaintance," or "friend" will soon discover really high finance charges. Many people laugh at the thought of loan sharks, but they are still prevalent in our society. Large industrial organizations seem to spawn this type of lender; the loan shark seems to know when the less knowledgeable person needs a quick loan. The ease with which money is loaned often beguiles the unsuspecting borrower. The loan is made without question and without any contract. This is because the rates are always usurious and definitely unenforceable in a court of law.

Table 3–4, which shows the maximum credit rates under California law, typifies state regulation of consumer credit interest rates. Again, each state has its own set of rates and regulations.

OBTAINING CREDIT

One of the questions foremost in the minds of students is, "How can I obtain credit?" Students want access to the "horn of plenty." They feel that no store wants to be the first to grant them credit and they want to know what to do about it. These questions resolve themselves with time. However, you may not have the time to wait or may wish to have some control over who will grant you credit and when they will grant it. The easiest way to establish credit is to borrow against your savings account, which will be used as collateral for repayment. This procedure will establish a credit rating in your name.

What Can You Afford?

Eventually someone will grant you credit. Then the question you should ask is, "Can I really afford it?" Competition among cash lenders and especially among retail stores often results in the granting of a line of credit or a cash loan in excess of your ability to repay it comfortably.

It would be wise to reconsider your credit needs and ask only for an amount that you can pay back with ease. In a few words, do not ask what you can easily get or need; ask for the amount that you can repay. This is extremely important because you have only a limited amount of income available for repayment of debts. After-tax income is disposable income, money available to the consumer for spending or saving. Consumers must commit much of their disposable in-

Table 3–4 Maximum credit rates under California law

	Maximum Rate Under the Law	APR
CREDIT PURCHASES		
Revolving charge account	On outstanding monthly balance*	
	To \$1,000—1½% per month	18%
	Over \$1,000—1% per month	12%*
Auto installment contract	On unpaid balance†	
	1% per month	22.2%†
Other installment contracts	On unpaid balance†	
	To \$1,000—⅚ of 1% per month	18.5%†
	Over \$1,000—⅔ of 1% per month	14.8%†
LOANS		
Individual lender	On unpaid balance	
	10% per year	10%
Credit union	On unpaid balance	
	1% per month	12%
Bank	No maximum	No maximum
Savings and loan association	No maximum	No maximum
Finance company:		
Personal property broker	On unpaid balance	
	To \$225—2½% per month	30%
	\$225 to \$625—2% per month	24%
	\$625 to \$1,650—1½% per month	18%
	Over \$1,650—1% per month	12%
	Over \$10,000	No maximum
Industrial loan company	On unpaid balance	
	To \$700—2% per month	24%
	Over \$700—1% per month	12%
	(Any size to 1½% per month avg.)	18%
Pawnbroker	On unpaid balance‡	
	To \$100—2½% per month	30%‡
	\$100 to \$500—2% per month	24%‡
	Over \$500—1% per month	12%‡

* Because the law does not define outstanding balance, retailers may apply credit charges in such a manner as to exceed 18 percent per year.
† The credit charge is added to the total amount owing at the start of the contract rather than on the unpaid balance each month, hence almost doubling the apparent rate for one year. Two- and three-year contracts using the add-on method will be slightly higher.
‡ A flat dollar charge of \$1 to \$10 for the first 90 days is applied to loans under \$150; hence all loans will exceed the stated rate.

come to fixed or semi-fixed expenditures such as rent, food, and transportation. What is left after these expenditures is discretionary income, money to be spent at the whim of its owner. As we all know well, there is often little money left for us to use at our discretion.

At this point, it is necessary to consider the consequences of transferring part of your discretionary spending to fixed expenditures because you have contracted for installment or revolving credit. You have put yourself in a corner and can no longer choose how to spend your money, because it is already committed. Life becomes less enjoyable and much more frustrating. To avoid this corner adopt a conservative approach to credit. A consumer tends to be overoptimistic about his ability to pay installment and revolving accounts. It would be wise to follow the advice of many consumer money-management experts: do not commit more than 10 percent of your monthly disposable income to installment contracts. Allow yourself financial flexibility and extra cash for those expenses and needs that always seem to crop up.

Credit Rating

Your ability to secure the amount of money you want or need will be based on your credit rating. Your credit rating may also stop you from securing a specific job or from obtaining needed insurance. Your credit rating is simply a file of your credit history that is maintained by local and regional organizations who specialize in credit reporting to any merchant, financial institution, or business desiring such information. Your local credit bureau, the Retail Credit Company, and TRW-Credit Data Corporation are examples of such organizations. Each supplies its clients with information about consumer bill-paying habits, defaults, court judgments, changes of residence, divorces, and payment disputes. They cull their information from clients, public records, and newspaper reports. Usually the credit-reporting agency does not rate the consumer; it just reports all pertinent information and lets the client-creditor make the decision whether to grant the credit. At one time, credit bureaus did rate consumers, but abuses, errors, and misunderstandings arose as to interpretation and use of the rating report.

The Fair Credit Reporting Act allows a consumer to examine his credit file to learn what information has been recorded about him, what sources supplied the information, and the names of the recipients of this information. The consumer may insert written rebuttal to disputed information on file. Credit-reporting agencies must notify their clients upon request of the consumer if there is faulty information in the file. The Fair Credit Reporting Act generally limits information on file to the last seven years. This limitation was imposed because some agencies had kept adverse information on file indefinitely, restricting credit for some consumers who had incurred credit problems sometime in the distant past.

Shopping for Credit

Since you usually pay for credit, you should shop for it like any other commodity. The time to do so is before you have an actual need or emergency. By shopping in advance your credit application will be shown in the best possible light. If you do not need credit, your income will cover your current expenses. If you are able to save money from your income, this will also prove that you do not need credit. You will be able to establish credit at an organization that offers reasonable interest rates because you will not be in a hurry to take whatever is available. Since you are not financially strapped, you will be able to compare the interest rates offered.

Credit Application

Each credit grantor has its own credit application upon which it considers your credit worthiness. The final decision is based upon the "four C's of credit": Character, Capacity, Capital, and Collateral. Character is considered your willingness to pay under adverse conditions. You may be willing and able to pay under normally prosperous conditions, but would you continue to make good on your obligation if your prospects became bleak? Your credit history may be a clue to your character. Capacity is your financial ability to pay the loan or credit purchase out of income. Do you have sufficient discretionary income to pay the installment or revolving account and still have something left to do with as you please? Capital is considered your assets other than income, which can be used either to pay the obligation or act as collateral as needed. Collateral is a legal pledge of assets that may be appropriated by the lender if the debtor defaults. It is normally used only as backup security on cash loans or big installment contracts. A co-signer or co-maker may be used as a security device by some lenders. The co-signer becomes legally liable for payment if the debtor fails to pay for any reason. Obviously, it is not a good idea to co-sign for anyone.

The weight applied to each of the "three C's" will differ with the lending institution or credit-granting institution. Generally they will emphasize character and capacity, and they will investigate the stability factor of the applicant in depth. Lenders have developed rating systems based upon the information supplied by the applicant and credit-reporting agencies. Figures 3–5 and 3–6 are contrasting credit applications. Note that the Master Charge application allows the applicant to rate himself. This is really a public-relations ploy as the bank still secures added information and makes the final credit decision.

The specific credit criteria may differ between lenders, but the type of information asked for is essentially the same on all application forms. Applicants can expect to be asked questions relating to income, employment, residence, marital status, age, credit outstanding, references, and assets. The questions are designed to allow a credit manager to decide intelligently whether to grant the credit request. Obviously the questions also provide a basis for locating the debtor if payment is not made.

An interesting rule of thumb seems to apply to credit-granting institutions: the looser the credit granting, the tighter the payment collection; the tighter the credit granting, the looser the payment collection. This means if the lender or grantor allows easy credit, he will not hesitate to contact you if you are late in paying; conversely, if you are thoroughly screened for credit worthiness, the store or lender will not risk losing your patronage by confronting you immediately if you are late.

TOO MUCH CREDIT

"You can have too much of a good thing," in matters of credit as well as with many other pleasantries of life. Too much credit may lead to personal disaster and bankruptcy. It is not terribly hard for an individual to reach the point where bankruptcy is the only way out. And bankruptcy is often not the "out" that people expect it to be. Let us see how a person gets himself into a financial bind that is insurmountable.

A consumer expects too much. He often expects to be able to buy all the goods and services advertised on television, in magazines, and in other media. He expects to receive more income in the near future to help pay for these goods and services. He expects to be able to balance his bills by "robbing Peter to pay Paul." He expects to engage in deficit spending for a short period of time only. He expects to exercise his willpower starting tomorrow. His expectations get the best of him!

1 **Circle** the number on each line that describes you and **write** it in the code box to the right.

2 **Add** your scores plus bonus points. Enter your total score.

3 If you have scored 19 points or more **complete** the additional information, seal and **mail** today

							CODE BOX
A	AGE	21-25 1	26-35 2	36-45 2	46-64 2	65 & OVER 1	
B	MARITAL STATUS	SINGLE 1	SEPARATED 1	DIVORCED 1	WIDOWED 1	MARRIED 2	
C	DEPENDENTS (include yourself)	ONE 2	TWO 2	THREE 2	FOUR 1	FIVE OR MORE 1	
D	LIVING FACILITIES	WITH PARENTS 1	RENT: FURN. 1	RENT: UNFURN. 2	OWN-MTG. 4	OWN-NO MTG. 5	
E	YEARS AT PRESENT ADDRESS	UNDER 1 YR. 1	1-2 YRS. 1	3-5 YRS. 2	6-10 YRS. 2	OVER 10 YRS. 3	
F	YEARS AT PREVIOUS ADDRESS	UNDER 1 YR. 1	1-2 YRS. 1	3-5 YRS. 2	6-10 YRS. 2	OVER 10 YRS. 3	
G	TOTAL MONTHLY INCOME	UNDER $400 1	$400-600 1	$601-800 3	$801-1000 5	OVER $1000 7	
H	YEARS WITH PRESENT EMPLOYER	UNDER 1 YR. 1	1-3 YRS. 2	4-6 YRS. 3	7-10 YRS. 4	OVER 10 YRS. 5	
I	TOTAL MONTHLY OBLIGATIONS (include rent or mortgage payment)	UNDER $75 2	$75-125 2	$126-200 2	$201-300 1	OVER $300 1	
J	OCCUPATION	PART-TIME 1	UNSKILLED 2	SKILLED or EQUIV. 3	EXEC. OR SUPER 4	PROFESSIONAL 4	

BONUS POINTS

ADD **2** POINTS IF YOU HAVE A TELEPHONE LISTED IN YOUR NAME

ADD **5** POINTS IF YOU HAVE ANY LOAN EXPERIENCE AT THIS BANK

ADD **3** POINTS FOR LOAN EXPERIENCE AT OTHER BANK OR FINANCE CO.

ADD **2** POINTS IF YOU HAVE A CHECKING OR SAVING ACCT. AT THIS BANK

IF YOU SCORE 19 POINTS OR MORE MAIL TODAY . . . IF LESS THAN 19, LET'S TALK!

TOTAL SCORE

The right of final credit approval is reserved by this bank.

Figure 3–5 Master Charge Rate Yourself Credit Application. *(Motivational Systems Inc., New York)*

BankAmericard®/Instant Cash Student Account Application

FOR BANK USE ONLY # ___ TYPE 1 3 5 7 / 2 4 6 8 — C.L. 1 3 5 / 2 4 — # 1 2 / 2 4 — LOCATION CODE — OFFICE REC STATUS CODE

PT SCR — SOLICITATION CODE — DATE 1 2 3 4 5 6 7 8 9 0 — APPROVED BY

OFFICE NUMBER

☐ BAC ONLY
☐ I/C ONLY } EXISTING CARDHOLDER
☐ BAC & I/C

1. APPLICANT:

LAST NAME	FIRST NAME	INITIAL	DATE OF BIRTH	DRIVERS LIC. NO.	SOC. SEC. NO
ENROLLMENT STATUS ☐ PART TIME ☐ FULL TIME	SPOUSE'S FIRST NAME	INITIAL	DATE OF BIRTH	DRIVERS LIC. NO.	SOC. SEC. NO.
COLLEGE RESIDENCE ADDRESS	CITY	STATE	ZIP	PHONE (COLLEGE RESIDENCE)	
PERMANENT RESIDENCE PHONE	☐ RENT ______ $ PER MONTH YOU PAY ☐ LIVE WITH PARENTS ☐ OWN	NAME OF COLLEGE		NO. OF DEPENDENTS	
PERMANENT RESIDENCE ADDRESS	CITY	STATE	HOW LONG YRS. MOS.	U. S. CITIZEN ☐ YES ☐ NO	
☐ FRESH ☐ SOPH ☐ JR ☐ SR ☐ GRAD SCHOOL	DEGREE SOUGHT ______ DATE OF GRADUATION ______	NAME AND ADDRESS OF NEAREST RELATIVE		PHONE #	

2. EMPLOYMENT & INCOME:

EMPLOYED BY	PHONE	POSITION		YEARS	MONTHS
EMPLOYER'S ADDRESS	CITY	STATE	ZIP	MONTHLY INCOME	
PREVIOUSLY EMPLOYED BY	ADDRESS	CITY	STATE	YRS.	MOS.
SPOUSE EMPLOYED BY	PHONE	POSITION		YEARS	MONTHS
EMPLOYER'S ADDRESS	CITY	STATE	ZIP	MONTHLY INCOME	
PREVIOUSLY EMPLOYED BY	ADDRESS	CITY	STATE	YRS.	MOS.

OTHER INCOME (GRANTS, SCHOLARSHIPS, PARENTS' ALLOWANCES, ETC.) DESIGNATE SOURCE AND ADDRESS

3. DEPOSITS: Name of Banks, Savings & Loan Associations & Credit Unions

BANK	OFFICE	☐ CHECKING ☐ SAVINGS
SAVINGS & LOAN	OFFICE & LOCATION	
CREDIT UNION	OFFICE & LOCATION	

4. CREDIT REFERENCES: List other loans and charge accounts: (Banks, Finance Co.'s, Credit Unions, Stores, etc.) Attach separate sheet if necessary.

			LOAN #	BAL. DUE	MO. PYMTS.
HOME MORTGAGED TO AND ADDRESS				$	$
AUTO MAKE	YEAR	FINANCED BY AND ADDRESS		$	$
AUTO MAKE	YEAR	FINANCED BY AND ADDRESS		$	$
PAYMENTS BEING MADE TO (NAME & ADDRESS) 1.				$	$
2.				$	$
3.				$	$
4.				$	$
			TOTALS		

BankAmericard Agreement

Each of the undersigned jointly and severally agrees: (1) To assume responsibility for credit extended by Bank of America National Trust and Savings Association (BANK) to any of the undersigned from the BANKAMERICARD Account or to anyone authorized by any of the undersigned to use any BANKAMERICARD credit card ("credit card") issued to any of the undersigned; (2) To pay, at such place as BANK designates, obligations evidencing such credit, and finance and other charges where applicable, including reasonable attorney's fees in the event of suit, in accordance with such terms and conditions as BANK may adopt from time to time; (3) To notify BANK promptly in writing of loss of the credit card; (4) The credit card is the property of BANK and may be cancelled by BANK at any time; (5) To surrender the credit card upon demand; (6) To the extent permitted by law, to waive and release BANK from all defenses, rights and claims the undersigned may have against any merchant or company receiving payment from the BANKAMERICARD Account; (7) Any claim of BANK against the undersigned shall, at BANK's option, become immediately due and payable, without prior notice, if the undersigned fails to perform any of the terms hereof or make payments as otherwise agreed or if any one of the undersigned dies, becomes insolvent, commits an act of bankruptcy, fails to pay, when due, any other indebtedness owed to BANK or any other person or if any writ of attachment, execution, garnishment or other legal process is issued against any property of any of the undersigned.

Authorization

I (We) authorize you to obtain such information as you may require from whatever sources you may deem necessary and agree that the application shall remain your property, whether it is approved or not. I (We) hereby certify that all statements furnished by me (us) are true and complete and are made for the purpose of obtaining credit. I (We) agree to notify you of any material change in the information as set forth and that information shall be construed by you to be a continuing statement of the condition of the undersigned(s) until written notice to the contrary is received by you. I (We) further agree to submit such additional information concerning my (our) financial status as you may request.

Please issue the BankAmericard credit cards in the following names. Please fill in title (Mr., Mrs., Miss, Ms., or Dr.) only if you desire it printed on cards.

Date ______

TITLE · PRINT NAME (1) — TITLE · PRINT NAME (2)

SIGNATURE OF APPLICANT (1) — SIGNATURE OF APPLICANT (2)

☐ BANKAMERICARD ONLY
☐ INSTANT CASH ONLY
☐ BANKAMERICARD & INSTANT CASH
CURRENT BANKAMERICARD ACCOUNT #

COMPLETE REVERSE SIDE FOR INSTANT CASH

Please deliver completed application to nearest Bank of America Office. (DO NOT MAIL)

Figure 3–6 Bank Americard/Instant Cash Student Account Application. *(Bank of America N.T. & S.A., San Francisco)*

Overextension

The first step toward financial ruin is the opening of too many revolving charge accounts along with a few installment accounts. If continuing balances develop in revolving accounts, they assume the characteristics of installment accounts, only worse. They can continue to increase in size of monthly payment and in the absolute amount of the obligation because no one is available to counsel the consumer until he begins to miss payments.

Consumers can easily open ten or more revolving accounts once credit has been established. It is so convenient to have a credit card for each store to give a wide assortment of goods and services to choose from. At first he charges only a little here and a little there and pays in full each month. Then one month he fails to pay the account or accounts in full. This gives him more spending money. It's so easy!

Naturally he does not want any one account to get too large, so he carefully spreads his spending over a number of stores. Eventually all of his revolving charge accounts are beginning to creep upward. It does not seem like too much money is involved. He continues to pay on all the accounts, but he also keeps on buying more goods on credit than the payments cover each month. He is going deeper into debt with his eyes open.

Assuming our customer makes \$10 payments each month to ten different stores, he pays only \$100 a month toward the charge accounts. If he continues this deficit spending, each account could easily rise to a \$100 continuous balance, making a total debt of \$1,000. Furthermore, a $1\frac{1}{2}$ percent finance charge each month on these accounts amounts to \$15 interest. Therefore, the \$100 that he pays toward the accounts amounts to only \$85. You can see it is not easy to reduce what you owe. If you continue purchasing you will continue to accrue interest charges and never get your accounts paid in full.

Perhaps the average consumer could continue the balancing act necessary to maintain his credit rating by paying the minimum amounts requested on revolving accounts. Usually he has other installment accounts for purchases such as furniture, automobiles, and recreational and entertainment equipment. When this is the case, there is no flexibility in his budget. Desires continue to plague this consumer; his ability to pay does not continue at the same pace as his ability to desire and his ability to purchase.

Debt Consolidation

Hopefully, somewhere along the line our consumer realizes he has gotten in over his head. He no longer has the ability to pay all of his monthly obligations. At this point, he becomes aware of debt-consolidation loans. A loan of this sort pays off all the outstanding revolving accounts, installment accounts, and other bills (medical, dental, etc.) he may have. Placing all debt into one loan allows the debtor to lengthen the time of repayments and lower the monthly outlay. The average interest rates may decline somewhat because of the size of the consolidated debt. The lower rate is not too likely, because our consumer is now becoming a credit risk. He will probably have to secure his loan from a personal-finance company or a homeowner-loan company.

A finance company that makes a debt-consolidation loan almost invariably requires some sort of security. This is necessary because of the large loan and the risk involved. Using the prior example, our consumer can easily owe $3,000 on an automobile at $100 per month, $1,500 on furniture at $50 per month, $1,500 on other durables at $50 per month, and $1,000 in various medical, dental, vacation, and small-loan obligations, payable at $100 a month, plus the $1,000 owed on the revolving accounts at a minimum of $100 per month. His total obligations, therefore, are $8,000, with monthly payments approximating $400. He is indeed a prime candidate for debt consolidation.

The greater the amount of the loan, the longer the repayment period one will need. He will generally have a choice of repayment terms. Security choices are available, too. Loans under $5,000 use automobiles, boats, trailers, furniture, and cosigners for security. Loans over $5,000 usually require use of your home, paid for or not, as security. Cautious lenders in some states attempt to use both personal and real property as security.

Our consumer will offer his home as collateral. He can secure a fully amortized $8,000 loan for a period of 8 1/6 years. His monthly payments would be $120.

What has he done? Our consumer has mortgaged his future. He has assumed monthly payments of $120 per month for 8 1/6 years in exchange for obligations maturing in one to three years. This debt will seem to last an eternity. It is over and above normal living expenses. Our consumer has reduced his monthly payments by $280. Assuming that his deficit spending was $130, he would now have about $150 discretionary spending money.

If our consumer is now accustomed to high living, it will be hard to keep within the bounds of his discretionary spending money. He will have to destroy his credit cards and purchase on a cash basis. He will not be able to finance anything on the installment plan during the next 8 1/6 years unless his income increases or he forgoes his discretionary spending money and again becomes boxed in. If he could not control credit and spending the first time, can he control it for the next 8 1/6 years? What do you think his chances are?

Composition of Creditors

Sometimes a person does not have sufficient collateral to protect a lender who would grant a debt-consolidation loan. In such situations the consumer will not get the loan and will be harassed by his creditors for payments he can not afford to make. The end of financial responsibility is in sight. The debtor apparently has no future. But he does have a chance if he can prove to himself and to his creditors that he can exercise willpower and repay his obligations. It takes the understanding and patience of all concerned.

The debtor may take any one of three approaches to this problem. He may contact his creditors individually, work through a credit counselor, or work through the courts in a Chapter XIII bankruptcy proceeding. All three choices accomplish somewhat the same thing: to allow the debtor to pay his obligations over a prolonged period of time. We will look at each choice.

Individual contacts between debtors and creditors are least likely to work because of the tendency of a creditor to look out for himself and not believe the debtor, who has probably already promised to make payments by a certain time and has failed to do so. Besides, he bought too much before, so he might do so again—before paying off his debts. If the creditors are few and the amounts are not extensive, a debtor can arrange to spread his payments over a longer period of time. The debtor must be candid in his approach to his creditors and honest as to his intentions. Threats by either party usually do not accomplish anything.

Using the services of a credit counselor may offer an acceptable alternative to the debtor's individual effort to mollify his creditors. Credit counselors are persons or organizations that arrange moratoriums and elongated pay-backs between debtors and creditors. Sometimes known as commercial proraters, they receive approximately 10 percent of the monies handled as their fee. Their fee is one more cost of going too deep in debt.

A number of states have outlawed commercial proraters and replaced them with government agencies that accomplish the same thing. While the author is not in complete approval of all credit-counseling operations, they do accomplish an important service. They have the necessary reputation among creditors to get the creditor's permission to proceed with a repayment plan that has a good possibility of working.

Credit counselors contact all creditors on behalf of the debtor and make new arrangements for repayment. They arrange with the employer to send the debtor's paycheck directly to the counselor for disbursement. Needless to say, the debtor must agree to this arrangement and must also agree to live on a spartan allowance until the bulk of the obligations is paid off. Whether the counseling organization is a cooperative sponsored by the local retailers' association or a completely private organization, the fee is something the debtor could have saved if he had had enough sense to stop purchasing before he was obliged to use the services of a prorater or credit counselor.

The third choice available to our debtor-consumer is to file bankruptcy under Chapter XIII of the bankruptcy laws. To do so, a debtor must be deeply in debt to the point of insolvency: when his liabilities exceed his assets.

Certain advantages accrue to a debtor desiring to repay under Chapter XIII proceedings: (1) If one-half of his creditors agree to such proceedings, all are bound. Creditors would generally tend to agree to elongated repayment if the alternative is straight bankruptcy and repayment of only a small part of the obligation, which would come from the prorated distribution of the debtor's liquidated assets. (2) Interest charges stop accumulating, a big help in reducing the outstanding debt. (3) Administrative costs tend to be lower than the fee of approximately 10 percent taken by commercial proraters.

Secured creditors and priority creditors are less likely to agree to Chapter XIII proceedings because they are first in line for payment. The major disadvantages of Chapter XIII proceedings are that a person may not again file for bankruptcy within six years, and creditors may not want to give up the interest which would accrue under the first two plans. Chapter XIII procedures are similar to those of commercial proraters, but in bankruptcy proceedings the court administers the repayment money through a trustee agreed to by the creditors.

Repossession

Sometimes overextension of installment credit can lead to the repossession of a durable good that has some resale value. A creditor would use either a seller's lien or a chattel mortgage to retain an interest in the item. Loan or credit laws in most states allow the creditor contractual repossession rights either automatically or by notification to some government agency if the debtor defaults. The debtor's only protections in such repossessions may be a ten-day waiting period before the repossessed good may be sold, having the first chance to redeem the item, or, better yet, having the option of not making further payments on the item if he has any doubt about his ability to continue the installments over the balance of the contract.

Many consumers believe that their debt worries are over if the durable good is repossessed. Do not believe it. The costs associated with repossession are added to the debt, the item is often resold at a terrific discount, and any deficit balance is usually still owed by the debtor: the debt does not go away. A few states disallow deficit balances after repossession, but the consumer must look to his own state laws on this subject. California, for example, allows deficiency judgments on automobile repossessions while disallowing them on other durables purchased on credit.

It would be better for a debtor to sell his auto or other durable good himself and apply the proceeds to the debt, rather than voluntarily or involuntarily returning the good to the seller or lender if a deficiency balance must be paid by court judgment. The reason is simply that the debtor will attempt to secure a reasonable price for the good while the repossessor will wholesale it at a lower price, knowing that he can secure the balance from the debtor. Also there will not be any repossession costs if the debtor sells the item himself and applies the proceeds to the debt. Finally, there is the possibility of salvaging one's credit rating by voluntarily disposing of an item and applying the proceeds to the debt, since repossession action will appear on the consumer's credit rating.

Court Judgments

Creditors often pursue debtors into court to secure payment of debts. Confession-of-judgment clauses in credit contracts automatically secure a court order for the debtor to pay. This allows the creditor to pursue legally, but not to harass, the debtor. If the debtor still does not cooperate by paying his debt, the creditor may petition the courts for an attachment of his assets or a garnishment of his salary.

In attachment proceedings, the court responds to a petition of the creditor, determines that the creditor's attempts to collect a legal debt have been fruitless, and then orders the sheriff to attach sufficient assets of the debtor to pay the debt in full. The assets may be bank accounts or other property that is usually sold at auction to settle the debt. In garnishment proceedings, the creditor petitions the court to garnish a portion of the debtor's salary for as long a period of time as is necessary to pay the debt. Recent changes in federal law limit a garnishment to 25 percent of a person's take-home pay and protect the debtor from being fired by his employer because of one garnishment incident. Employers generally take a rather dim view of garnishment procedures because of the added administrative costs they entail, not to mention the potential loss of productivity on the part of the employee who believes he is working for less wages.

You can see that creditors use the laws and the courts to their advantage. Many consumer advocates have been working to mitigate the advantages given to the creditor over the years. The consumer, however, cannot rely on immediate changes in the law or on the goodwill of the creditor. His only real protection is in controlling his credit impulses; otherwise, the final step is bankruptcy.

Bankruptcy

The vast majority of bankruptcies in the United States are personal bankruptcies of wage earners and salaried employees. They are not caused by business failures. Overextension of credit is the main cause, and underlying medical, marital, and unemployment difficulties trigger the downfall of the consumer.

Bankruptcy laws, federal in origin, are administered by the individual states. Bankruptcy results will differ somewhat in each state because personal exemptions differ. A petitioner for bankruptcy may generally withhold certain personal and real property from the bankruptcy proceedings. Creditors are not allowed to liquidate such property to satisfy the debts owed by the bankrupt.

The concept behind bankruptcy is to forgive the overburdened debtor and allow him to return to a productive economic life because he will lose all incentive to work if he sees no way out of debt. He does not have to make restitution beyond his assets after his personal exemptions under state law have been deducted.

Bankruptcy proceedings call for all assets and debts of the would-be bankrupt to be listed with the court. After deduction of exemptions, there is an auction of the balance of saleable assets to retire as much of the debt as possible. Taxes, legal costs of bankruptcy, some wages, and some rents receive priority payment along with secured debts. Most secured debts are covered only to the extent of the security, and any deficit balance is treated as a general creditor debt. General creditors receive the balance of monies from liquidated assets—if any—on a prorated basis of their claim to the total claims left to be paid.

The end result of bankruptcy is mixed. The bankrupt keeps his exempted property such as the tools of his trade, some furniture, some livestock, a small equity in an automobile and up to $20,000 equity in a homesteaded residence, depending upon state law. The creditors sometimes get a small portion of what is owed rather than losing everything. The debtor is forgiven any balance owed to general creditors. However, he does not get off completely free: any debt incurred through fraud is not forgiven. Frankly, if a creditor desires to pursue a given debt, he most likely can prove fraud or deception in the credit application, especially since debtors habitually hide or "forget" a few obligations when formally requesting credit. In addition, taxes, bankruptcy legal costs, two-months employee wages, personal injury judgments, and alimony are not forgiven. Finally, a debtor cannot petition again for bankruptcy for seven years, thereby giving any new creditors ample time to collect their debts.

In summary, there is no easy way out of debt. Bankruptcy is not a particularly good solution. Commercial prorating is expensive. Continuing finance charges are expensive for most types of consumer debt. The only rational solution is to use credit wisely, which means use it with moderation.

Vocabulary and Concepts

Add-on interest
Amortized loan
Annual percentage rate
Bankruptcy
Collateral
Credit
Deficiency judgment
Discounted interest

Fair Credit Reporting Act	Repossession
Finance charge	Revolving credit
Installment credit	Rule of 78
Maturity	Security
Principal	Term loan
	Truth-in-Lending Act

Questions for Discussion

1. What are the advantages of credit? What are the disadvantages?
2. Explain the concept and procedures of service credit.
3. Are there any kind of charge accounts that do not require payment of finance charges? Explain.
4. What are the usual contractual agreements contained in revolving credit accounts?
5. How do bank credit cards differ from retail store credit cards? Why?
6. What are the main characteristics of installment credit contracts?
7. Explain the concepts of the dollar cost of credit and the annual percentage rate (APR). Why is the APR needed?
8. In what ways do term loans and installment loans differ?
9. Explain the difference between an add-on loan and a discount loan. Which gives the better deal to the debtor?
10. How would you describe the sequence of events leading to the overextension of credit? What undesirable results occur from such an overextension? How much credit can you afford?

Projects

1. Find out the maximum rates of interest for lending institutions in your state.
2. Complete a credit application for a department store. Arrange for credit before you need it. Compare this with a rate-yourself bank-card application.
3. If you are refused credit, find out why. Ask to see your credit file at your local credit bureau. This is allowed under the Fair Credit Reporting Act.
4. Check the different types of credit life insurances available in your state. Are any of these required?
5. Visit a credit counseling agency or the federal bankruptcy court in your area. Compare the differences in philosophy and procedure.

Case Problem

Bartholomew Baker is a very precise person who wishes to double-check the accuracy of the Annual Percentage Rate quoted by an automobile dealer. The sales price of the auto including options, dealer preparation, and destination charges is $4,000. Bart is to pay 25 percent down in the form of a trade-in. Sales tax and license fees are $240 and $100, to be paid separately. Monthly payments will be $110 per month for thirty-six months. What is Bart's cash flow (out-of-pocket expense) in this transaction? What is the APR? The actual finance charge? Can you suggest a commercial lender that is less expensive?

4 a planned savings program

Saving is best described as putting aside a portion of your current income for a future purpose. A person is much more likely to save for future use if he has a goal. The added incentive of trying to reach a specific goal is often the difference between a spender and a saver. While spending is a rather enjoyable pastime, saving can be just as enjoyable and certainly more satisfying in the future if you have accumulated funds available.

A person must first convince himself that saving is a worthwhile experience before it can become a habit. Look around; notice that there are people who appear to have spending-money and yet are able to purchase some of the more expensive consumer items without constantly going into debt. Obviously, some of the people have higher incomes than yours, but many are in your wage bracket and some earn even less than you. Ask them how they managed to accumulate their money, or, better yet, figure it out for yourself. If you really want something, you will make the necessary effort to get it. Saving is an effort because you must forgo today's spending for a future reward. You must look ahead to that future reward; otherwise saving will have little meaning. We will look at the four main reasons for saving: personal goals, emergency funds, future spending, and long-term investment.

PERSONAL GOALS

Any reason is a good reason to save; however, personal improvement and personal wants probably account for a good portion of the young saver's accumulation. Older savers tend to be more interested in investment and retirement. Personal-improvement savings may be for college, travel, automóbiles, furniture, clothing, and leisure-time equipment, among other things. It is not important to differentiate between personal improvement and personal wants for savings purposes. The main point is that the would-be saver should have a great desire to reach a personal goal that requires an expenditure of a significant amount of money, more than can be taken easily from current income.

EMERGENCY SAVINGS

Too many people consider emergency savings a luxury they cannot afford. Perhaps they have considered the consequences, perhaps not. Serious thought should be given to the concept of emergency savings.

Is it a luxury to have emergency savings? The American Bankers Association has recommended that appròximately three months' salary be saved for emergency purposes. With the average American family income approaching $12,000 annually, is $3,000 in savings a luxury? It all depends upon how you look at it! Before resolving the dilemma, let us look further into the concept of emergency savings.

A person may feel that he never has an emergency and does not expect any and therefore has no need for such a fund. However, unusually large medical and dental bills, car repairs, and house and appliance repairs do happen to just about everyone. It is almost a matter of how often these emergencies occur and how much they cost each time they happen. If you pay for these happenings out of current income, chances are they are either "small" emergencies or you have a very adequate salary. If you have been fortunate up to this point, consider the possibility of a business decline or loss of your job. The law of averages works against you the longer you go without some emergency happening. Emergency savings may be considered a form of self-insurance and must be included as part of one's overall financial planning.

Three months' salary may be too much to put aside if you have a good credit rating and are not in debt. Perhaps it is wise to have your emergency fund do double duty as a personal-goal fund. Your goal can be delayed or dismissed in case of a major emergency.

SAVING FOR FUTURE SPENDING

Saving, by its very definition, is a method used to accumulate a lump-sum of money for future spending. How much money to amass and how soon to amass it are considerations determined by your personal goals. No matter what your personal goals, good reasons to save for future spending for all periods of time are readily apparent.

You will need short-term savings to balance your budget and pay your monthly living expenses. You receive income in weekly, biweekly, or monthly increments, but you spend at different times and in different amounts. Savings, held in checking accounts, help to smooth out this flow of money. An extra amount over and above your current outgo will provide a comfortable buffer and sense of financial security. It will be available for those extra purchases that occasionally become desirable and will save you money in checking-account charges if you maintain the prescribed minimum balances required by your bank.

Intermediate-term and long-term savings are necessary to gather up the lump-sums of money to buy the many consumer products and services that you cannot purchase with current income because they are too expensive. Without planning for future wants, the average consumer would either buy on credit, thereby cutting down on current discretionary spending, or else do without. Neither of these alternatives is desirable.

A thorough look at your spending history will probably reveal a leakage of funds. If you can find a way to plug these budget gaps, this money can be saved for future spending. Consider the alternatives: bits of money squandered on disposable and often unneeded goods and services, or the purchase of a more expensive and durable good or a desirable and enjoyable service. Which would you prefer: a lot of little things or a new dining-room set, a few movies and dinners or a week-end mini-vacation? The choice will invariably be predicated on a person's life-style. It is simply more enjoyable to spend large sums of money than it is to spend smaller sums. It is usually much easier to enjoy the big purchase than to remember where the small amounts of money went and wonder why you cannot afford the big purchase.

Future spending is indeed a very important reason to save, provided that inflation does not erode your purchasing power too greatly. The thrift institutions should pay the saver sufficient interest to cover the annual increase in the cost of living. The interest rate should allow a saver to retain his relative financial position as his capital grows. Thrift institutions should pay a higher rate of interest to further induce people to save and better their financial position. A negative interest, or a form of dis-saving, takes place whenever the inflation rate is greater than savings interest. Current consumption could replace the savings inclination of the individual if the inflation rate should weaken his financial position.

For example, the inflation rate for 1974–75 was in the neighborhood of 15 percent. At this rate, a dis-saving takes place if savings are deposited at the rate of $7\frac{1}{2}$ percent. A saver would be financially ahead if he purchases goods that he will need in the near future now, rather than saves at $7\frac{1}{2}$ percent and then pays an extra 15 percent for the item during the next year, suffering a $7\frac{1}{2}$ percent dis-saving, or loss.

SAVING FOR LONG-TERM INVESTMENT

The more sophisticated and future-oriented saver will set a goal of asset accumulation. You have probably read about young people who have become self-made millionaires through a combination of talent, savings, and investing. You probably know an older person who is now saving for retirement and estate purposes. Both the young and the old have one thing in common: the saving of capital for investment. The difference lies in when they started saving for capital accumulation and why they started at a particular time in life. Personal goals played a major consideration in the reasons why they saved, when they saved, and at what rate they saved. Income, desire, ability, life-style, and life cycle all play important roles in their long-term investment plans.

The main reason for saving over the long term is to provide security. Security means different things to different people. Housing, capital accumulation, and retirement are usually high on everyone's list of security needs.

Housing is usually an expense and an investment. It is an expense because it must be purchased. It is an investment because it might appreciate in value. There will be some return on the cost as compared to renting if you can accumulate the necessary down payment. Most people do not really have enough money saved to cover all the expenses of down-payment, closing costs, moving, and decorating and furnishing a home. Home purchase is a good reason to save in rather large increments for the first investment of a family.

Saving is an important component of capital accumulation—investment—and retirement because without savings the would-be investor or retiree has nothing to work with. Most American workers rely on Social Security and company pensions for retirement and do not consider the possibilities of savings and investment programs until their children are grown and they are nearing retirement. Again, the life-cycle and personal wants are often determining factors in this decision.

THE DIFFERENT OBJECTIVES OF SAVING AND INVESTING

Savers accumulate funds using different instruments and institutions of saving or investing. Savings or investment instruments include passbooks, certificates of deposit, stocks, bonds, notes, mutual-fund shares, and other lesser-known devices. Savings and investing institutions include such organizations as banks, savings and loan associations, credit unions, government units, insurance companies, investment companies, and securities brokers. No one instrument or institution completely meets the specific objectives of the saver in terms of rate of return on investment, degree of safety for the savings capital, liquidity, and long-term appreciation. These objectives in saving are often diametrically opposed to each other. A saver cannot expect a high rate of return without some risk, so he must forgo safety of his capital. If he prefers safety of capital or certainty of income, he cannot expect a high yield or rate of return. If he desires liquidity—ease of securing cash—he cannot expect long-term appreciation. We will analyze savings and investment institutions that pay a relatively fixed interest for their usefulness in meeting specific objectives later in this chapter. Those institutions that offer a variable return on investments will be discussed in chapters 13, 14, 15, and 16.

HOW MUCH SHOULD YOU SAVE?

Personal Goals and Budgets

Savings must come from your current income. Unfortunately, so must your current living expenses. A conflict can easily develop over priorities if income is insufficient to cover adequately both savings and living. It might be wise to list your financial goals and reasons for saving to be sure that you are doing what you want. Budgeting practices and the ease with which you can stay within a budget must also be taken into consideration.

The amount you set aside for savings goals may be too much or too little. A person can become discouraged if he cannot maintain his desired savings rate. Likewise, if it takes too long to accumulate money toward a particular goal, a person may become discouraged. In the final analysis, the amount you save is most likely going to be a compromise between your goal-oriented desire to save a large amount of money in a short period of time and the amount you can comfortably set aside in your budget. The actual amount will lean one way or the other based upon what is more important to you.

National Savings Patterns

The percentage of income committed to savings differs widely from family to family and from year to year. This is primarily because of the relationship among income, age, education, savings, and the national economic outlook. We can make an interesting yearly comparison of aggregate savings as a percentage of disposable personal income. The saving ratio tends to change with the national economic outlook. Savings rose during 1960–67, a period of somewhat noninflationary economic growth. Economic recession then forced a turnabout in personal savings in 1968–69. The population as a whole will save during good times and bad. There is, however, a tendency to look into alternate investments during good times and to refrain from purchasing during economic recession, thereby affecting the percentage of personal savings. Figure 4–1, Indexes of Consumer Financial Be-

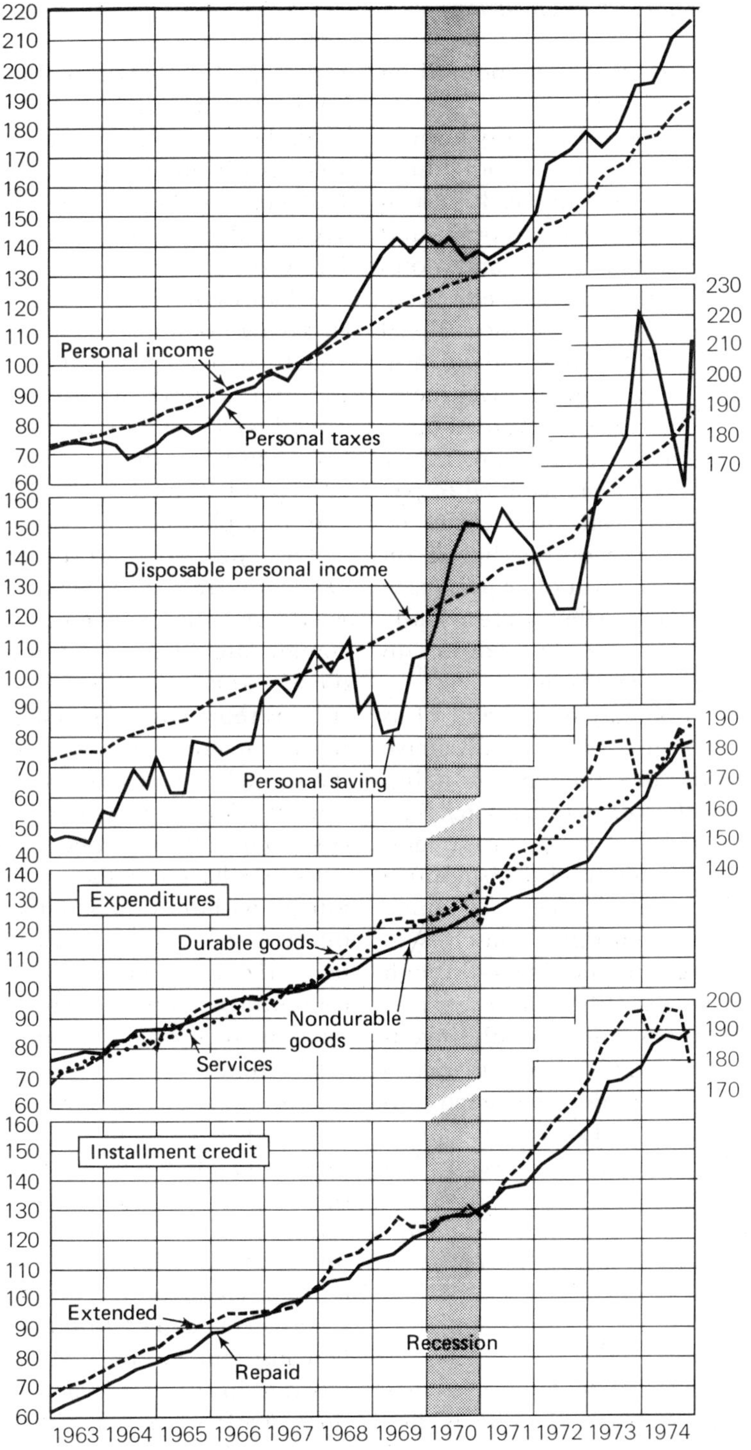

Figure 4–1 Indexes of Consumer Financial Behavior.

havior, substantiates the rise and fall of personal savings.

Personal savings are not the only form of liquid assets owned by many individuals and families. Investors can readily turn promissory notes, corporate stocks and bonds, and government bonds and notes to cash; these investments are therefore considered investment-type liquid assets. Fixed assets, items not readily converted to cash, are accumulated as a form of investment, savings, and consumption. Automobiles, homes, and household durables are rather expensive assets, but the money used to pay for them must have been saved either by setting aside income, or by purchasing on the installment plan, a form of negative saving or contract saving. Homes are usually considered an investment, in addition to being a consumer expenditure.

Basically everyone may be thought of as a saver. Some individuals and families have well-defined goals and the savings habit, while others must be forced into saving. The savings can be deposit savings, investment-type savings, or durable-goods consumptive savings. Most people practice a combination of the two, committing themselves to contractual future-oriented savings—through mortgage payments, life-insurance premiums, pension plans, and monthly investment plans in securities—and also purchasing fixed-asset durable goods to maintain a high standard of living. Family savings are probably more consumption oriented than in prior decades because of reliance on Social Security, pension plans, and welfare to take care of the future.

Systematic Savings Plans

People cannot accumulate money savings needed to reach their goals as easily as they might like. Unforeseen expenditures arise and offer a good excuse for not having saved the targeted sum within a given period of time. Careful analysis will often reveal that your wants got in the way of your savings goals because the unforeseen expenditures were really unnecessary, or that you have budgeted too large an amount for monthly savings. Both of these savings problems can be overcome with a little planning.

Chances are that if you have a problem in saving your surplus money it is because you treat it as just that, something that is left over, a quirk of fate. You are using the *Spend Now–Save Later* nonplan. A plan to save is just as important as a plan to budget and spend. Change your thinking and priorities to a plan of *Save Now–Spend Later.*

Owe yourself. Plan on it. Fit a savings "expenditure" into your budget. Adjust whatever other expenses you have to accommodate savings. You must place savings on an equal footing with other expenses such as rent. You must not only budget savings; you must budget a realistic amount. Too much savings will result in a deficit budget. You then will dip into savings to cover current expenses. Most savings institutions have a withdrawal charge for too much withdrawal activity in any one quarter, so too large a savings budget may be costly. It is better to start your savings commitments on the low side and gradually increase them as you gain economic confidence.

One method of saving is to open a Vacation or Christmas Club account. This procedure often gives the saver added incentive to put aside the amount intended for saving. Where and how you save will often have an effect on the success or failure of your savings effort. Try saving where it is most convenient to do so. You may not be consistent in saving if you must go to a separate institution to deposit savings. Consider mail deposits to improve your consistency of savings. Better yet, try saving through payroll deduction. You do not get your hands on this money and therefore

Example: $\$50 \times 1/4 = \$12.50$ or

$$\$1{,}000 \times .05 \times \frac{90}{360} = \$12.50$$

A $1,000 principal earns $12.50 interest at 5 percent for a period of ninety days or one-quarter year.

The actual dollar amount of interest earned in a fixed-rate savings account depends not only on the rate of interest but on other factors as well. The method used to determine the amount of interest to be paid is one factor. Financial institutions, which are profit-making concerns, usually compute interest in a manner favorable to them. If you borrow money, the interest charge may be calculated on the beginning balance for the life of the loan; but if you deposit money, the interest may be computed on the basis of the actual time your money was on deposit, or perhaps on an even shorter period. Financial institutions must charge more interest than they pay out if they desire to stay in business. They must also offer depositors competitive interest rates for savings deposits because savers attempt to maximize the return on their money to accumulate funds as rapidly as possible. One method of increasing the effective interest rate is to compute the effects of compound interest. Figure 4–2 illustrates how this is advertised in a savings and loan company brochure.

The Effect of Compounding

Compound interest is the interest calculated on the original principal plus any unpaid interest accruing to the principal. Using the formula, principal times rate equals simple interest, the interest is left in the savings account to form a larger principal.

Example: $\$1{,}050 \times 5\% = \$52.50$

The $50 interest from the earlier example was left to accumulate interest with the original principal, $1,000. In the above example, the new larger principal amount of $1,050 yielded a higher dollar return of $52.50 through compounding, rather than $50 at simple interest. At the end of the second year there would be $1,102.50 principal and interest in the account.

The process is a continuing one called compounding as interest stays in the account to generate more interest. Interest may be added to interest at any time according to the deposit agreement. Compounding by financial institutions is usually done annually, semiannually, quarterly, monthly, or daily. Some institutions have actually advertised *continuous* compounding.

Table 4–1 indicates how the value of $1 deposited will increase through annual compounding over a number of years at different rates of interest. For example, 5 percent compounding for a two-year period will yield $1.1025 per dollar deposited. We have already calculated this to be $1,102.50 on a $1,000 principal. For ten years, one dollar would yield $1.629, or $1,629 principal and interest on a $1,000 principal. Semiannual or quarterly compounding can be determined by halving or quartering the rate and doubling or quadrupling the time period. More complete compound interest tables may be found in your local library.

CRITERIA FOR SELECTING A SAVINGS INSTITUTION

Since the benefits of saving are so many and so obvious, most consumers eventually open a savings account at one of the many savings institutions vying for their money. How can you determine which of these institutions gives you the greatest yield for

Table 4–1 Compound-interest rates on one dollar

Periods (Years)	1%	2%	3%	4%	5%	6%	Periods (Years)
1	1.0100000	1.0200000	1.0300000	1.0400000	1.0500000	1.0600000	1
2	1.0201000	1.0404000	1.0609000	1.0816000	1.1025000	1.1236000	2
3	1.0303010	1.0612080	1.0927270	1.1248640	1.1576250	1.1910160	3
4	1.0406040	1.0824322	1.1255088	1.1698586	1.2155062	1.2624770	4
5	1.0510100	1.1040808	1.1592741	1.2166529	1.2762816	1.3382256	5
6	1.0615202	1.1261624	1.1940523	1.2653190	1.3400956	1.4185191	6
7	1.0721354	1.1486857	1.2298739	1.3159318	1.4071004	1.5036303	7
8	1.0828567	1.1716594	1.2667701	1.3685690	1.4774554	1.5938481	8
9	1.0936853	1.1950926	1.3047732	1.4233118	1.5513282	1.6894790	9
10	1.1046221	1.2189944	1.3439164	1.4802443	1.6288946	1.7908477	10
11	1.1156684	1.2433743	1.3842339	1.5394541	1.7103394	1.8982986	11
12	1.1268250	1.2682418	1.4257609	1.6010322	1.7958563	2.0121965	12
13	1.1380933	1.2936066	1.4685337	1.6650735	1.8856491	2.1329283	13
14	1.1494742	1.3194788	1.5125897	1.7316764	1.9799316	2.2609040	14
15	1.1609690	1.3458683	1.5579674	1.8009435	2.0789282	2.3965582	15
16	1.1725786	1.3727857	1.6047064	1.8729812	2.1828746	2.5403517	16
17	1.1843044	1.4002414	1.6528476	1.9479005	2.2920183	2.6927728	17
18	1.1961475	1.4282462	1.7024331	2.0258165	2.4066192	2.8543392	18
19	1.2081090	1.4568112	1.7535061	2.1068492	2.5269502	3.0255995	19
20	1.2201900	1.4859474	1.8061112	2.1911231	2.6532977	3.2071355	20
21	1.2323919	1.5156663	1.8602946	2.2787681	2.7859626	3.3995636	21
22	1.2447159	1.5459797	1.9161034	2.3699188	2.9252607	3.6035374	22
23	1.2571630	1.5768993	1.9735865	2.4647155	3.0715238	3.8197497	23
24	1.2697346	1.6084372	2.0327941	2.5633042	3.2250999	4.0489346	24
25	1.2824320	1.6406060	2.0937779	2.6658363	3.3863549	4.2918707	25

your savings deposit? Major considerations that will help you in your selection of a savings institution are: interest rates, safety, compound interval, interest-earning period, interest-payment times, withdrawal procedures, and convenience, services, and gifts. We will analyze each of these in this order even though different individuals will weight each criterion with a different degree of importance.

Interest Rates

Usually the higher the quoted interest rate, the greater will be the interest received from the savings institution. Compare the rates of interest offered by each type of savings institution. Within a given geographic area, all commercial banks will generally offer the same rate of interest. So will mutual banks, industrial banks, and savings and loan associations. These organizations will differ in other criteria within their industry, but usually all will offer the highest nominal interest rate permitted by law. Agencies of the federal government usually set the interest rates for the institutions that they regulate or insure. Federal or state limitations control excessive rate competition, which could prove detrimental to the savings institutions and create all sorts of monetary problems.

To earn higher interest rates, you must deposit larger amounts of money for longer periods of time. Savings institutions are willing to pay higher rates of interest to savers who invest in certificates of deposit, which are long-term deposits in comparison to short-term passbook accounts. Figure 4–2 shows the different yields of larger deposits for longer periods of time.

Savings deposits are known as time deposits in the financial community. By leaving money on deposit with a savings institution, the depositor allows the organization to use his money for mortgages, loans, and other investments with a long-term lending commitment.

Safety

Safety is of more importance to most savers than it is to most investors. Savers wish to be assured of getting back at least the same amount of money as they originally deposited. Investors would also like to be assured of the safety of their capital, but they, by the nature of investment, are willing to risk their capital in hopes of receiving a higher return on their investment. Growth and income are more important to the investor than is safety of capital.

Savings-deposit insurance is automatically available to savers in the vast majority of savings institutions. A federal agency insures individual savings accounts to $40,000 if an insured savings institution should fail. Decals and placards normally proclaim this added safety feature at each entrance to the insured establishment. While very few banks and savings institutions do fail, a saver should make certain he is protected since there is no added cost to him.

The $40,000 protection limit applies to any single depositor regardless of the number of individual accounts he may have in any one savings institution. All branches of a company are considered to be one company for purposes of deposit insurance. Federal law does not prohibit placing deposits in different savings companies as a hedge against the $40,000 limit. The law also does not prohibit separate insured accounts for each member of a family, nor does it prohibit joint-tenancy accounts and trust accounts, thereby giving a much greater deposit insurance protection to families wishing to deposit large sums of money with safety. Figure 4–3 is an advertisement from a savings and loan association brochure describing how this can be accomplished.

Compound Interval

The more often that interest is added to your principal, the greater will be the base upon which more interest is computed. Savings institutions will compound the interest on your account at intervals ranging from annually to daily. Widespread use of computers has made daily interest computation feasible.

The interval between compounding has generally been lessened by savings institutions as they compete for the savers' deposits. Government regulations often control the maximum nominal interest rate that can be paid to savers but normally do not determine the compound interval. The individual savings organizations do that.

Interest-Earning Period

If all other criteria are about equal, the account that pays retroactive interest offers the best return. Interest earnings can be affected by the date that the interest begins and the date when the interest ends.

FOR A FAMILY OF TWO □ UP TO $200,000 INSURED

EXAMPLE How husband and wife may have insured accounts totaling $200,000.

Individual Accounts	
Husband	$40,000
Wife	$40,000
Joint Account	
Husband and Wife	$40,000
Revocable Trusts	
Husband as Trustee for Wife	$40,000
Wife as Trustee for Husband	$40,000
	$200,000

EXAMPLE How one parent and one child may have insured accounts totaling $160,000. (Or, this same grouping of accounts can be arranged for one grandparent and one grandchild.)

Individual Accounts	
Parent	$40,000
Child	$40,000
Joint Account	
Parent and Child	$40,000
Revocable Trust	
Parent as Trustee for Child	$40,000
	$160,000

FEDERAL SAVINGS AND LOAN INSURANCE CORPORATION · SAFETY OF YOUR SAVINGS · INSURED UP TO $40,000

This is the official seal of the Federal Savings and Loan Insurance Corporation. You will find it prominently displayed at all Great Western Savings offices. Only qualified, member associations may display this seal.

FOR A FAMILY OF THREE □ UP TO $400,000 INSURED

EXAMPLE How a husband, wife and one child may have insured accounts totaling $400,000. (Or, this same grouping of insured accounts can be arranged for grandfather, grandmother and one grandchild.)

Individual Accounts	
Husband	$40,000
Wife	$40,000
Child	$40,000
Joint Accounts	
Husband and Wife	$40,000
Husband and Child	$40,000
Wife and Child	$40,000
Revocable Trusts	
Husband as Trustee for Wife	$40,000
Husband as Trustee for Child	$40,000
Wife as Trustee for Husband	$40,000
Wife as Trustee for Child	$40,000
	$400,000

EXAMPLE How one grandparent and two grandchildren may have insured accounts totaling $320,000. (Or, this same grouping of insured accounts can be arranged for one parent with two children.)

Individual Accounts	
Grandparent	$40,000
Grandchild Number One	$40,000
Grandchild Number Two	$40,000
Joint Accounts	
Grandparent and Grandchild Number One	$40,000
Grandparent and Grandchild Number Two	$40,000
Child Number One and Child Number Two	$40,000
Revocable Trust Accounts	
Grandparent as Trustee for Grandchild Number One	$40,000
Grandparent as Trustee for Grandchild Number Two	$40,000
	$320,000

FOR A FAMILY OF FOUR □ UP TO $560,000 INSURED

EXAMPLE How husband, wife and two children may have insured accounts totaling $560,000. (Or, this same grouping of insured accounts can be arranged for grandfather, grandmother and two grandchildren.)

Individual Accounts	
Husband	$40,000
Wife	$40,000
Child Number One	$40,000
Child Number Two	$40,000
Joint Accounts	
Husband and Wife	$40,000
Husband and Child Number One	$40,000
Wife and Child Number Two	$40,000
Child Number One and Child Number Two	$40,000
Revocable Trust Accounts	
Husband as Trustee for Wife	$40,000
Husband as Trustee for Child Number One	$40,000
Husband as Trustee for Child Number Two	$40,000
Wife as Trustee for Husband	$40,000
Wife as Trustee for Child Number One	$40,000
Wife as Trustee for Child Number Two	$40,000
	$560,000

Any family group is entitled to increased amounts of insurance for their savings through multiple accounts. If the examples shown do not fit your needs, our Savings Counselors will welcome the opportunity of helping you select the arrangement of insured accounts that is right for your family. Remember, at Great Western Savings, you earn the highest interest available anywhere with the complete safety of insured savings.

Figure 4–3 Methods of Increasing Deposit Insurance. *(Great Western Savings & Loan Association, Beverly Hills, California)*

Different savings institutions use different periods to calculate when a depositor's savings may earn interest. You naturally want the longest possible period for earning interest. The basic formula for calculating interest reflects this concept: $P \times R \times T = I$; principal times rate times time equals interest.

At the beginning of the deposit or reinvestment period, a saver may find any of the following conditions applicable by shopping the various savings organizations:

1. Earn from date of deposit.
2. Deposit by the tenth of the month, earn from the first.
3. Deposit by the twenty-fifth of the quarter, earn from the first.
4. Deposit after the first of the month, earn from the first of the following month.
5. Deposit after the first of the quarter, earn from the first of the following quarter.

Points 2 and 3 provide for retroactive earning of interest. The savings institution does not have your deposit for its use but is willing to pay interest on it if you deposit within a reasonable period. This is really quite an inducement to begin saving after the earning period has already started, or to switch your deposit from a competitor without losing any interest.

When interest earnings stop is also important because this affects the amount of interest. We will discuss termination of interest under withdrawal procedures.

Interest-Payment Times

Interest may be compounded daily and may accumulate over a fairly long period of time, but all is for nothing if the interest is not credited to your account for payment before you withdraw it. The payment-time concept is important simply because you must be a depositor of record when interest is paid, or you do not receive any of the interest that your deposit has earned. Earned interest may be paid by crediting your savings balance or by mailing a check for the interest. Company policy on maximum balances often determines whether an account is credited or paid by check.

Payments to accounts are usually made quarterly, semiannually, or annually. A few institutions pay or credit your account on a monthly basis. Some organizations pay all interest that you have earned up to date of withdrawal. Quarterly payments, however, are the most widely used term for payment of earned interest. This procedure acts as a deterent to "in and out" savers by penalizing them or forcing them to maintain their account until the payment date. The shorter the period between interest payments, the more flexibility the saver has in the withdrawal of his money. Often it will benefit a saver to borrow against his own savings for a short period rather than withdraw them and forfeit all interest earned since the last payment date.

Interest paid to date of withdrawal would not necessitate the use of interim borrowing. Unfortunately, savings organizations are more interested in holding down their costs than in paying the saver for the actual use of his money. Savers must look out for themselves and attempt to maintain as high a rate of return as possible by looking at all possible withdrawal alternatives. First, plan ahead; hold off using your savings until date of payment, then withdraw them for use. Second, calculate the amount of interest you would lose by early withdrawal. Third, calculate the interest cost of a savings-secured loan for the number of days until the interest payment is made on the savings account. Now, choose your course of action based upon the out-of-pocket loss to you plus the inconvenience involved in the loan application paper work or the inconvenience of waiting until the interest-payment date.

Withdrawal Procedures

Of all the criteria for selecting a savings institution, withdrawal procedures are perhaps the most important, the least publicized, and the most confusing. We have differentiated between earning interest and being paid the earned interest. The question now arises, what happens if the saver wishes to withdraw funds at a time other than at the specified payment date? When this occurs, which funds are withdrawn from an active account, those newly deposited or those on deposit since the last interest payment? Upon what balance is interest earned *and* paid?

To understand clearly the method of treating withdrawals, it is beneficial to look at two extremes in calculating interest in an active savings account: FIFO (first in–first out) and LIFO (last in–first out). Under FIFO, the savings institution assumes that any withdrawal is the money that has been on deposit the longest period of time. Interest is then paid on short-term deposit money, which is less costly to the savings institution. Under LIFO, the savings institution assumes that any withdrawal is the money most recently deposited to the account. Interest is then paid on longer-term deposits, which provide more interest to the saver. The basic formula for calculating interest, $P \times R \times T = I$, principal times rate times time equals interest, should help clarify the difference between FIFO and LIFO.

An example involving a systematic savings plan paying 5 percent compounded and paid semiannually should further clarify the difference. Assume you have a beginning balance of $1,000 and deposit $100 on the first of each month. Your activity pattern would be that in the table below.

A. Under FIFO, the $500 withdrawal would be subtracted from the beginning balance for purposes of interest calculation as follows:

Balance	$500 at 5% for 6 months =	$12.50
January	$100 at 5% for 6 months =	2.50
February	$100 at 5% for 5 months =	2.08
March	$100 at 5% for 4 months =	1.67
April	$100 at 5% for 3 months =	1.25
May	$100 at 5% for 2 months =	.83
June	$100 at 5% for 1 month =	.42
Total FIFO interest on ending balance =		$21.25

B. Under LIFO, the $500 withdrawal would be subtracted from the last five $100 deposits, leaving:

Balance	$1,000 at 5% for 6 months =	$25.00
January	$100 at 5% for 6 months =	2.50
Total LIFO interest on ending balance =		$27.50

A more accurate method is DD–DW (date of deposit–date of withdrawal). Under this system interest is calculated and paid up to date of withdrawal regardless of when the usual date for crediting and paying interest happens to fall. DD–DW could be either the FIFO or LIFO method without an early-withdrawal penalty. Banks and other savings institutions use this method only when it is competitively necessary.

C. Under DD–DW using the FIFO method, the prior example could be calculated as follows:

Balance	$500 at 5% for 6 months =	$12.50
Balance	$500 at 5% for 5½ months =	11.46

Date	Withdrawal	Deposit	Interest	Balance
January 1				$1,000
January 1		$100		$1,100
February 1		$100		$1,200
March 1		$100		$1,300
April 1		$100		$1,400
May 1		$100		$1,500
June 1		$100		$1,600
June 15	$500			$1,100
July 1		$100	paid	$1,200 plus interest

January	\$100 at 5% for 6 months =	2.50
February	\$100 at 5% for 5 months =	2.08
March	\$100 at 5% for 4 months =	1.67
April	\$100 at 5% for 3 months =	1.25
May	\$100 at 5% for 2 months =	.83
June	\$100 at 5% for 1 month =	.42
Total DD–DW FIFO interest		\$32.71

D. Under DD–DW using the LIFO method, the prior example could be calculated as follows:

Balance	\$1,000 at 5% for 6 months =	\$25.00
January	\$100 at 5% for 6 months =	2.50
February	\$100 at 5% for 4½ months =	1.88
March	\$100 at 5% for 3½ months =	1.46
April	\$100 at 5% for 2½ months =	1.04
May	\$100 at 5% for 1½ months =	.63
June	\$100 at 5% for ½ month =	.21
Total DD–DW LIFO interest		\$33.12

These examples point out that while banks and savings institutions can advertise the same interest rate, they might not pay the same dollar amount. The nominal rate often varies from the true or effective rate of interest. Various mathematical formulas may be used to calculate the true interest rate. The text examples have been computed to the nearest cent on the basis of a 360-day year divided into 12 months of 30 days each. While this does not give the exact interest calculated on a 365-day year, it is the most convenient and commonly used method. Fortunately, interest tables and computers are now used to calculate earnings.

If you cannot locate a savings institution that credits you with interest until date of withdrawal, consider borrowing against your savings until the interest on your account is paid. By leaving your money on deposit, you do not have to consider FIFO and LIFO. Your interest on the original balance and subsequent monthly deposits will amount to \$33.75, considerably more than under examples A and B. You must, however, subtract the cost of borrowing the \$500 from June 15 to July 1. Often the interest charged on a loan secured by a savings account is only 1 percent above the savings interest rate. However, even at 8 percent loan rate the cost would be only \$1.67 if your particular depository does not have a minimum loan fee or some other charge to raise the cost of the fifteen-day loan.

The net yield to you would be \$32.08 in this case. In example A, if the total cost of a fifteen-day loan is less than \$12.50 (\$33.75 – \$21.25), and example B, if the total cost is less than \$6.25 (\$33.75 – \$27.50), you would do well to leave your savings on deposit and borrow against them until the interest is paid to your account.

Since you receive interest to the date of withdrawal under examples C and D, you would not consider borrowing at 8 percent to save 5 percent. \$32.71 and \$32.72 respectively are greater than a net yield of \$32.08.

Of minor importance in withdrawal procedures is the activity charge, if any, required by many savings institutions for transacting too many withdrawals in a given period of time, usually a quarter of a year. The activity charge usually is fifty cents per withdrawal after two "free" withdrawals during the three-month period. Savings institutions discourage excess account activity and cut their costs by imposing this charge. You, as a saver, will probably do better with a checking account rather than a savings account to smooth out your income and outgo cash flow. You should figure the costs and convenience of having both a checking account and a savings account. Chapter 5 will provide information on the use of checking accounts.

Convenience, Service, and Gifts

The somewhat intangible criteria of convenience, service, and gifts must be considered, especially within the industry grouping of any one type of savings institution. Generally all companies within the same segment of the savings industry offer the same rate of interest, earning period, and payment times; provide insured savings; and have approximately the same withdrawal procedures. Therefore, you actually select the type of institution you wish on the above criteria and then select the individual company based on convenience, service, and other personal factors.

Convenience may be the location or the banking hours available. It may be postage-paid transactions by mail or the uncrowded conditions and short wait at the bank.

Service competition may include such items as simple courtesy or a single waiting line, free safe-deposit boxes, free checking accounts, money orders, traveler's checks, financial counseling services, notary services, and trust deed collection. It may be low-cost insurance, travel tours, or other bargains.

Gifts are usually inducements to open savings accounts and should be considered only if all other criteria tend to be equal. Savings institutions in various parts of the country have been known to give away clocks, radios, encyclopedias, weekends for two, and other gifts to secure your business. Federal regulatory agencies have discouraged this practice to a degree, but new business campaigns by savings institutions do provide an occasional opportunity to receive a "free" gift.

SAVINGS INSTITUTIONS

Knowing what to compare in savings institutions will help you mathematically determine which is the best yield for you. Knowing the purpose and general operating characteristics of savings institutions together with the specific criteria of convenience, safety and liquidity, and yield will help you determine which type of institution will help you reach your savings goal. We will look at commercial banks, mutual savings banks, savings and loan associations, credit unions, industrial banks, United States government bonds, and life-insurance companies as savings institutions you should compare before selecting one or more for your use.

Commercial Banks

The term *all-purpose financial institution* best describes the commercial bank because a complete line of financial services is usually available under one roof. Students often think that banks are the only savings, lending, and checking-account institutions available and that these functions are the banks' only services. Chapter 5 will delve into the various services available at most commercial banks.

There are more commercial banks than any other single type of savings institution. They operate under federal supervision. All banks must also operate within the banking and finance codes of the states in which they are located.

Convenience The sheer number of commercial banks, especially in states that allow branch banking, makes convenience an especially good selling point for banks. They perform so many different functions that a strong demand for commercial banks becomes readily apparent. Because the demand for commercial banks is satisfied by allowing a large number of bank locations, the use of bank savings services becomes very convenient.

Safety and liquidity The average depositor does not need to worry about bank safety. His deposits are insured to $40,000 per individual depositor. Any number of accounts, savings and checking, belonging to one individual are insured up to a total of $40,000. The depositor desiring greater safety through deposit insurance will have to deposit excess sums in competing banks, start a joint account, or place funds in the name of a relative. Figure 4–3 illustrated the concept of plural accounts in one savings institution.

The Federal Deposit Insurance Corporation, FDIC, was established in 1933 to protect the small saver by providing deposit insurance for all national banks and any state bank that desired to provide its customers with this added protection. The cost of this protection is absorbed by the banks and not passed directly on to the depositor. Only a few banks are not covered, and these are mostly small state-chartered banks in rural areas.

It is wise to make sure that your deposit is insured. While very few banks become insolvent, it does happen. Bankers sometimes pay too high an interest rate to large depositors to get the use of their money and then overextend the bank resources with a few large loans that might be considered very risky.

Liquidity is a prime feature of bank savings deposits. Theoretically savings are time deposits, to remain in the hands of the bank until proper notice is given. By law, commercial banks may retain your passbook savings for thirty days after a withdrawal request. In practice, this is never done. It remains, however, a legal right of the bank to do so. The only time this right would be exercised is if there were a run on the bank, if many depositors asked for their funds at the same time. The legal right to delay withdrawals is to provide the banks with sufficient time to change some of their long-term investments to cash if necessary. Normally banks would borrow needed funds from the Federal Reserve Bank and not liquidate their investments.

Since the withdrawal notice is waived, all that the saver must do is complete a withdrawal slip and present his passbook. Also, banks normally do not ask for advance notice on certificates of deposit, the long-term savings certificate. However, if you withdraw your funds prior to maturity, you are penalized ninety days passbook interest, and your account interest rate declines to the passbook interest rate as required by federal regulations.

Yield The amount of interest paid on your savings account at a commercial bank will change from time to time because of national and local economic conditions. If the banks need more money because of strong demand for loans, they will have to entice you to save by raising their interest rates. Other types of savings institutions will do the same; therefore the Federal Reserve Board of Governors will regulate the interest rate for the various savings industry institutions to maintain competition and proper balance between the competitors. If banks do not have a great demand for loans, they will lower their savings interest rates to maintain their profit margin.

Banks generally pay a lower rate of interest on passbook accounts and savings certificates than do other types of deposito-

Combine a high interest certificate of deposit or Investors Passbook with a Bank of America regular savings account. Then you have both high yield and flexibility working for you. You've tied up top bank interest and still have money handy.

With a regular savings account you can take your money out any time. If there's an emergency, just withdraw funds from your regular savings. That way you won't have to touch your higher interest, fixed maturity account. You've got the early withdrawal penalty licked. Your high yield account goes on working undisturbed at Bank of America.

What sounder investment can you make than one that promises high yield, complete flexibility and bank safety? With a regular savings account plus a certificate of deposit or Investors Passbook, you have it all. Visit your nearest Bank of America. We'll show you how our Personal Choice Savings plans can help you meet your goals.

7¼%	annual interest 4-10 year Certificate of Deposit. $1000 minimum.
6½%	annual interest Investors Passbook. $500 minimum. 2-1/2 year maturity. (10 calendar quarters) Add $100 or more anytime.
6%	annual interest Investors Passbook. $500 minimum. 1 year maturity. (4 calendar quarters) Add $100 or more anytime.
5½%	annual interest Investors Passbook. $500 minimum. 90 day maturity. (1 calendar quarter) Add $100 or more anytime.
4½%	Regular savings account. Start with as little as $2. Put your money in. Take it out, anytime.

On certificates of deposit and Investors Passbook accounts opened after July 5, 1973, Federal law prohibits withdrawal prior to maturity unless three months of the interest thereon is forfeited and interest on the amount withdrawn is reduced to the regular savings rate.

Figure 4–4 Typical Bank Interest Rates. *(Bank of America N.T. & S.A., San Francisco)*

ries. Commercial banks remain competitive and continue to hold more dollar savings than other savings institutions because of their convenience. Most customers like the concept of one-stop banking.

The specific rates of interest will differ from area to area within the country based upon loan demand and the amount of savings on deposit. The rates will also differ by type of account within the banks. The lower rates of interest apply to passbook accounts allowing deposits and withdrawals at any time. Higher rates of interest apply to certificates of deposit held to maturity for terms varying from ninety days to six years. Figure 4–4 indicates the annual interest rates offered at one bank. The lower minimum deposits required by commercial banks as compared to other savings institutions offer the small saver a chance to earn higher rates of interest on his deposit. This competitive factor along with the financial supermarket concept of convenience is probably why banks still maintain a rather large segment of the public's savings.

Mutual Savings Banks

Mutual savings banks are state-chartered savings depositories owned by the depositor. No stock is issued or available as an investment. These banks pay dividends on the savings of depositors based upon the profits from the banks' investment portfolios of real estate mortgages and corporate securities.

The 490 mutual savings banks are concentrated in the New England and Middle Atlantic region of the United States. States containing the greatest number of savings banks are Massachusetts, New York, Connecticut, Maine, and New Hampshire.* Well over 50 percent of the dollar deposits are located in New York.

Convenience Many savings banks have branch locations for easy access by the depositor. Transactions by mail help make deposits and withdrawals relatively easy. The limited service offered by savings banks is most often a result of the restrictions placed on their operations by the state in which they operate. As their name implies, saving is their prime banking function, and real-estate lending is their major source of income. While they do not offer checking accounts or trust services, some banks are authorized to sell savings-bank life insurance. This coverage is available in only a few states, but it is a good buy because this low-cost insurance is sold over the counter without commission. Mutual savings banks offer their customers group rates for all the various types of life insurance.

Safety and liquidity All but 1 of the 490 savings banks are insured. The FDIC insures 327 of them, and state insurance funds cover the balance. The FDIC provides account insurance, on the same basis as commercial banks, up to $40,000 per individual account. State insurance funds may differ as to coverage.

Since mutual savings banks are state-regulated, the ease of withdrawing money may differ among the states. A depositor may demand his passbook savings account at any time without wait, even though savings banks may legally require thirty to ninety days notice. Time deposits of ninety days or more may be withdrawn prior to maturity but will be subject to an interest forfeiture penalty.

It is more necessary for savings banks to have the notice clause available because of the nature of their investments. Real-estate mortgages comprise about 70 percent of mutual savings-bank portfolios, and this type of asset generally takes time to liquidate. Needless to say, few savings banks have ever had to resort to this procedure. Normally a bank would borrow needed funds from the Federal Home Loan Bank system until its liquidity had been restored.

Yield The average rate of return paid on time deposits in all mutual savings banks is slightly less than the rate paid by savings and loan associations but higher than the rates paid by commercial banks for the same type of savings account. Mutual savings banks generally pay the highest interest rates permitted by law for their particular type of savings depository because they must be competitive to attract the savings dollar.

Savings and Loan Associations

Savings and loan associations constitute the second largest depository of savers' funds after commercial banks. These savings institutions are located in all fifty states and

* Mutual savings banks are located in Alaska, Connecticut, Delaware, Indiana, Maine, Maryland, Massachusetts, Minnesota, New Hampshire, New Jersey, New York, Ohio, Oregon, Pennsylvania, Puerto Rico, Rhode Island, Vermont, Washington, and Wisconsin.

compete effectively with commercial banks for savings deposits. They are sometimes known as building and loan associations, cooperative banks, and homestead associations in the various states, but the most common identifying term is savings and loan association.

Approximately two-thirds of all associations are federally chartered, with the balance state chartered. All operate under some form of local, state, and federal regulations as to customer services, rates of interest allowable for savings, and cash reserve requirements. Despite some differing services among the several states, all savings and loans are primarily committed to loan money on home first mortgages. Eighty-five percent of the total savings and loan portfolio is in mortgage loans. Funds to lend come from the various types of savings on deposit with the associations.

Convenience Since savings and loan associations specialize in savings, they have a number of different savings plans available. This choice of savings plans is perhaps the most important consideration for savers. Part of the choice of plans consists of selecting interest rates offered for different deposit periods, minimum deposits, and free services that go with minimum deposits. Figure 4–2 indicated the different plans available at one savings and loan association.

Because savings and loan associations do not and cannot legally offer a complete set of banking services, they attempt to make it as easy as possible for their clients to do business with them. They often provide deposits and withdrawals by mail, free gifts to those who open new accounts, free safety deposit boxes, free traveler's checks, and free checking accounts through nearby banks. Savings and loan associations are presently seeking legislation to allow them to provide checking accounts through their own offices. Branches are located throughout a given area to promote business, thereby making it more convenient for people to do business.

Safety and liquidity The Federal Savings and Loan Insurance Corporation (FSLIC) provides insurance on savings deposits up to $40,000. It operates in a manner similar to the Federal Deposit Insurance Corporation (FDIC), which insures bank deposits: each insured account is reimbursed as soon as possible in cash, or it is transferred to a solvent association in the same geographical area. Sometimes, the "as soon as possible" clause allows the FSLIC to take extra time to liquidate accounts to pay back depositors. Usually a rotation plan is put into effect to return a portion of the insured's deposit immediately. As money becomes available more is paid to each depositor when his name comes up on rotation. While not all savings and loans are insured, the vast majority are. Federal associations must be insured, and state associations are invited to participate.

The individual depositor has good liquidity if his funds are in a savings and loan association. The time deposit he chooses may vary from passbook accounts, which feature no-wait, in-and-out savings accounts, to the certificates of deposit (CDs), whose terms vary from ninety days to ten years. While savings and loan associations may require thirty to ninety days notice on a withdrawal, they seldom, if ever, exercise this privilege. They redeem CDs before maturity upon demand, but at a reduced interest rate: interest earned since last payment is reduced to the passbook rate and ninety days interest is deducted at the passbook rate. This penalty reduces the number of withdrawals on long-term accounts but still allows liquidity if the depositor needs his funds.

Yield Figure 4–2 earlier illustrated the rate of return offered to savings depositors by a typical savings and loan association. Historically savings and loan associations offer a higher interest return than commercial banks. They usually are ½ to 1 percent higher on passbook accounts and ¼ percent higher on long-term certificates of deposit.

Credit Unions

A credit union is a nonprofit cooperative organization of people who save their money, which is used to make consumer loans to each other. All members of the credit union are bound by a common association, such as working for the same employer or belonging to the same fraternity, union, or church. Most credit unions are organized around employers because of the greater ease of setting up payroll savings and loans and because both employer and employee find the credit union advantageous.

There are more credit unions than any other specific type of savings institution. Approximately twenty-four thousand credit unions serve over 22 million members, about 10 percent of the United States population. The typical credit union is rather small, having fewer than one thousand members and assets of less than $750,000. Membership limitations account for the typically small size. To become a member, a person must purchase at least one share in the credit union. Shares are savings deposits, usually in $5 increments.

Credit unions may be either federally or state chartered. At present there are approximately thirteen thousand credit unions under federal charter. Any group of seven or more people bound by a common association may organize a credit union if they meet the criteria of the chartering agency. Officials of most small credit unions are volunteers. Clerical help is normally salaried, to provide adequate and continuous service to members.

Convenience Systematic saving is the big convenience factor for credit union savers. Small monthly deposits are encouraged to form the thrift habit. Payroll deduction is the usual method employed to promote saving, but direct cash deposits are also accepted.

Many employers provide office space on company premises for an employee credit union. The proximity to work areas allows employees to use a credit union's facilities during the working day, a definite member convenience. Those employees not near the credit union facility are often allowed the use of company telephones and mail services to carry out their savings and loan transactions. A common disadvantage of small credit unions is the limited business hours because much of the help is voluntary or part-time.

Consumer loans represent most of the loan business of a credit union, and it is often through seeking a loan that a person becomes a saver. He borrows from the credit union because of favorable loan rates and after repaying the loan continues payroll deduction of the loan installment amount as his savings deposit amount. The ease of maintaining one of each type of account is an inducement to prospective members.

Safety and liquidity Since credit unions are usually organized around one employer, the business success of the employer will affect the credit union's ability to be a viable financial institution. If the employer is growing, new members needing loans or depositing savings are constantly added. However, if the employer is laying off employees, membership drops, savings of terminated employees are withdrawn, and loans owed by the terminated employees often go unpaid. Fortunately, there is a much stronger bond between a credit union member and the credit union than with other savings institutions, so that this safety of assets problem is not as great as it appears.

In the normal course of business, payroll deduction accounts for almost 100 percent payback, thereby eliminating the risk of loan default. In addition, savings accounts may now be insured up to $40,000 by the National Credit Union Administration (NCUA), provided the federal- or state-chartered credit union applies to the NCUA and meets certain standards. This insurance cost is borne by the credit union in much the same manner as by banks and savings and loan associations.

State and federal laws allow credit unions the right to demand notice before withdrawals are made. This right is seldom exercised because the credit union would lose the confidence of its members and lose its savings business to competitive depositories. Dividends are usually paid twice yearly, allowing savers access to their funds semiannually without loss of interest. Most other savings institutions pay dividends quarterly.

Yield The dividend rate on shares in credit unions is historically higher than the interest rate paid by banks and savings and loan associations for short-term deposits. While credit unions charge comparatively low loan rates, they also have relatively low operating costs, permitting them to return most excess monies to the saving members.

Federally chartered credit unions have been legally limited to a 6 percent return to all members. This is on passbook-type accounts, normally the only type of savings offered. State-chartered credit unions may or may not have dividend limitations. With good management, a conservative lending policy, and no dividend limitations, a credit union may pay an exceedingly good dividend rate. As an example: United Air Lines Employees' Credit Union, Inc., a state-chartered company, has paid up to a 7½ percent dividend rate on savings.

Industrial Banks and Thrift Companies

Industrial banks and thrift companies operate in approximately one-half of the states. These organizations are chartered by the states in which they operate to provide loans from $50 to $15,000 at regulated rates of interest to businesses and consumers. They secure a portion of their lendable funds from the saving public by offering passbook and time-certificate savings accounts at favorable rates of interest.

Convenience Since industrial banks and thrift companies are usually restricted to small loans and savings accounts by the various state regulatory agencies, they cannot offer the many financial services people expect. Location of the office and the ease of deposit and withdrawal are their only convenience factors.

Safety and liquidity There is no federal agency to insure the deposits in either industrial banks or thrift companies because they are not federally chartered or regulated. Insurance is sometimes offered by a cooperative insurance effort of the industry within an individual state. In California the Thrift Guarantee Corporation "guarantees" deposits to $10,000. Each member bank or thrift company may pledge a portion of its reserves to a central fund as a form of mutual insurance, or each may purchase deposit insurance from a commercial insurance company. Either option is usually voluntary, so the individual depositor should definitely investigate the safety of these institutions.

The liquidity of industrial banks and thrift companies ranks with other banks and savings depositories. They may demand written notice of withdrawal in most states, but they seldom do because of competitive pressures. Since they deal in relatively short-term loans, industrial banks and thrift companies are constantly liquidating outstanding loans and thereby have funds available for withdrawal.

Yield Interest rates offered to savers by industrial banks and thrift companies are usually higher than those offered to the general public by competing institutions. The lack of a public image and a lack of awareness on the part of savers together with the slightly greater risk of privately placed deposit insurance has caused savers to be hesitant in taking advantage of the higher interest rates.

A typical thrift company return is 6 percent on passbook accounts and $6\frac{1}{2}$ to $7\frac{1}{2}$ percent on certificates of deposit, depending on the company's need for lendable funds and on the maximum rates allowable in each state.

U.S. Government Savings Bonds

The federal government finances its operations through taxation of individuals and corporations. Revenues from these sources do not come into the Treasury at the same time that expenditures must be made; therefore, the federal government borrows to meet its current expenses and the deficit that it often incurs. Treasury bills, notes, and bonds, and government savings bonds are the major forms of borrowing used. Bills and notes are short-term government borrowings of less than five years, while bonds are long-term obligations of the government, usually of more than five years in length. We will explain Treasury paper in chapter 16. Government savings bonds are in smaller denominations and are designed for the small saver and investor. Two types of savings bonds, Series E and Series H, are presently available.

The Series E bond has proven to be the most popular savings bond. It is an appreciation or discount bond. Savers purchase them at a 25 percent discount from the face value denomination, such as $18.75 on $25, $75 on $100, and $750 on $1,000.

The Series H bond is a current-income bond, which the saver purchases at full face value. He then receives interest paid by check semiannually. The Series H bond is presently offered in $1,000 denominations.

Convenience U.S. government savings bonds may be purchased at most commercial banks, at many post offices, and at Treasury offices. The greatest number, however, are sold through payroll savings plans at your place of employment. This arrangement allows you to save systematically and without effort.

The interest earned on government savings bonds must be reported for federal income-tax purposes, much the same as any other savings. Series E bond interest need not be reported until the bond is redeemed, thereby allowing the saver the option of the accrual or the cash basis for tax purposes.

Safety and liquidity The very fact that savings bonds are the guaranteed debt of the United States probably makes them as safe an investment as you can find. They are actually safer than cash because they are registered to the purchaser-saver and are nonnegotiable (not salable to a third party). The Bureau of the Public Debt will issue new savings bonds if the original ones are lost or stolen. It would be a good idea to keep the serial numbers of any savings bonds in a safe place separate from the bonds themselves. The Treasury Department will actually keep your bonds for you if you make the necessary application through your post office or bank.

A savings bond may be redeemed by the Treasury Department, a bank, or a post office beginning six months from the date of purchase.

Yield A set redemption price is scheduled for all Series E and H bonds. The saver can determine his yield by dollar amount and percentage by the length of time he holds the bonds. Series E bonds now mature in five years and ten months, while Series H bonds mature in ten years.

If held to maturity, both will yield about 6 percent interest per year, which is competitive with commercial depositories. If they are redeemed in the first two years after purchase, they yield 4½ percent. Generally the saver is encouraged to hold his savings bonds because the redemption schedule for E bonds and the interest schedule for H bonds goes up dramatically after the half-way-to-maturity mark.

Life-Insurance Savings

Another choice of savings for the consumer is his present life-insurance policy. Almost 21 percent of all individual savings are in cash-value life-insurance policies.

Convenience Life insurance is as convenient a way to save as any other method. Since there is a psychological need for security and protection, the consumer is *forced* to save when paying for his protection. This feature is a definite advantage for the would-be saver who cannot seem to put money away in any other manner. Transactions can be made at nearby branches, by mail, or even by personal visits from an insurance agent.

The savings feature of a permanent life policy can be considered an investment that requires little attention. Minimum guaranteed yields set a base amount known as the cash value of the policy. If the life-insurance policy is a participating one, dividends over and above the guarantee may be credited or paid to the policy holder. If these dividends are left with the company, they, too, earn interest and do not require much attention.

Safety and liquidity Historically life insurance companies have an enviable record of solvency. They have tremendous assets: the industry total is in excess of $240 billion. With such assets available they are able to diversify their investments and choose relatively safe and conservative investments. In addition, their underwriting usually covers all claims and contributes to an increase in assets. If they underestimate claims, they can always increase premiums or improve their risk-selection.

The saver has access to his life-insurance savings through the loan provisions of his policy. He may borrow the accumulated cash value at an interest rate of 6 to 8 percent. He may also terminate his policy at any time and receive the cash value of his policy. If he chooses the second option, his life-insurance protection lapses. In both options, the insurance company normally has the right to demand ninety days to six months notice as a form of delay. This option is similar to that enjoyed by other savings institutions and is seldom exercised because of competition.

Liquidity is *not* as readily available in life-insurance policies as it is in other savings media, because the idea is to make the saving as compulsory as possible by attaching it to the protection feature of the policy. It *costs* the policy holder an interest charge for borrowing against his insurance or his entire life insurance protection if he wishes to liquidate his life-insurance savings. Other savings media provide semiannual or quarterly interest payment dates, at which time the saver's withdrawal does not lose accumulated interest. This is not so with life-insurance savings.

Yield The interest rate paid by permanent life insurance policies differs with the type of policy protection coverage, length of term, premium, company investment policy, claims record, and overhead cost of each company. The saver can count only on the *minimum guaranteed* dollar cash value stipulated in his policy. Sales literature and agent representatives suggest that greater returns through dividends are available if your policy is a participating one. This is essentially true because life insurance company guarantees are usually a rather conservative 2 to 3 percent. If the company has a good earnings year or if the premium was too high for the claims paid by a mutual insurance company, the policyholder can expect another 1 to 2 percent yield. Further explanation of life insurance as a form of savings or investment will be given in chapter 6.

An extra increase in yield in insurance savings is available to the policy holder because cash value accumulation is not currently taxable and will never be taxable if the cash value does not exceed total premium payments at surrender. Assuming you surrender your permanent insurance at age sixty-five when you retire, accumulated interest will most likely be at a lower rate because of your now-limited income.

Where Should You Save?

All savings institutions have some advantages and disadvantages. Choose the depository that best satisfies your particular savings needs. If you can allow your savings to remain on deposit for three months or more, you should think in terms of time deposits that pay higher rates of interest. (See figures 4–2 and 4–4.)

Probably an insured credit union that pays interest every six months will give the best combination of safety, liquidity, and yield if you are eligible for membership and the interest payment dates are reasonably akin to your needs. Otherwise, consider industrial banks or thrift companies for high interest and liquidity. For larger sums and longer periods, savings and loan associations and mutual savings banks offer good yields. For smaller saving amounts with a good yield but with longer periods of time necessary to get the good yield, consider buying government savings bonds by payroll deduction. Finally, for convenience on short-term deposits, and smaller minimum time certificates, consider commercial banks. Life insurance performs a protection function rather than a true savings function.

Vocabulary and Concepts

Appreciation	Liquidity
Capital accumulation	Safety of capital
Compound interest	Simple interest
Depositor's insurance	Withdrawal procedures
Emergency savings	Yield
Inflation	

Questions for Discussion

1. What effect does inflation have on savings? What can be done to counteract this effect?
2. Savings and investment have offered different yet similar objectives. Explain.
3. How does the stage of the life cycle affect your savings pattern? Where do savings come from?
4. In the narrow sense, what types of savings assets are there? In a broader sense, what constitutes a form of savings?

5. What is the philosophical difference between a "save now–spend later" plan and a "spend now–save later" plan?
6. What are the criteria for selecting a savings institution? What priority do you give the different criteria?
7. Explain how it may be less expensive to borrow money than to withdraw the same amount from your savings.
8. Why is it beneficial to have more than one savings account or certificate of deposit?
9. Compare the features of the Series E and Series H U.S. savings bonds.
10. List the main advantages of each major type of savings institution.

Projects

1. Make an objective list of reasons to save, then make a personal, subjective list. Now make a list of reasons why you should *not* save. Compare the pros and cons of saving for your particular life-style.
2. Investigate the various forms of systematic savings plans available to you. What sort of payroll deductions are available through your employer? What plans are offered by commercial institutions to create a systematic saving habit?
3. Set a long-term savings goal for yourself based on what you would like to have on deposit at the end of five years. Determine what interest rates and systematic deposit amounts are necessary to reach this goal. Compound-interest tables for periodic deposits will be helpful.
4. Examine the withdrawal features, interest rates, and payment periods for passbook savings accounts in your area. Check a representative commercial bank, savings bank, savings and loan association, credit union, and thrift company.
5. Make a diagram comparing the deposit premiums, interest rates, and term-of-deposit requirements for all savings institutions and media available in your area.

Case Problem

Before purchasing a new car, Bart Baker desires to find out how much money he will save on the car purchase if he saves $100 monthly to pay cash rather than finance the car. Assume he makes monthly deposits for thirty months at 6 percent annual interest compounded monthly. Calculations may be made using compound-interest tables allowing for periodic deposits. Assume that new car prices do not increase and that his trade-in does not depreciate. At the moment, he has a $1,000 trade-in and $340 for the tax and license.

As a separate calculation, determine how long Bart will have to save if his trade-in will depreciate $200 per year and the new car will increase in price by $200 per year.

5 using bank services

The commercial bank is the one institution that has the facilities and services to handle your day-to-day financial transactions. You could shop around and divide your business among a number of institutions, but your actions would result in inefficiency and inconvenience and would probably cost you more money. The *financial supermarket* concept has been fully promoted by the American Bankers Association. By federal and state regulations, other financial institutions are not allowed to provide commercial or checking accounts or many other of the financial services rendered by a full-service bank.

The number of services offered by each bank will differ with its size and location. As a consumer you should be aware of the different services available in a commercial bank and know how they are used.

TYPES OF BANKS

Not all banks are commercial banks, and not all commercial banks are full-service banks. However, by the American Bankers Association's definition, a full-service bank is any commercial bank, because only commercial banks offer checking accounts in addition to the savings and loan services.

Financial institutions other than commercial banks are really specialized savings and loan institutions. They accept your long-term and short-term savings deposits and then lend or invest the money. Government regulations limit rates of interest, dollar amounts, length of term, and types of savings, loans, and investments that these institutions can offer. Chapters 3 and 4 explained the various loan and savings features of different financial institutions.

When using the term *bank,* we will mean one of the fourteen thousand commercial banks in the United States.

THE FEDERAL RESERVE SYSTEM

The function of the Federal Reserve System is to foster a flow of credit and money throughout the banking system that will facilitate an orderly economic growth and a stable dollar. The "Fed," as it is commonly called, accomplishes its functions through reserve banking by purchasing and selling U.S. government securities on the open market, lending to member banks, and changing the reserve requirements of member banks as needed. It is a banker's bank and does not do business directly with the public, except for the sale of government securities.

All national banks and many state banks are members of the Federal Reserve System.

Approximately half of the banks in the country belong to it, but they hold over 80 percent of the total bank deposits. Furthermore, member banks hold about 90 percent of the country's demand, or checking account, deposits. To become a member, a bank must purchase capital stock in the nearest Reserve Bank in the amount of 3 percent of its capital and surplus and maintain another 3 percent subject to requisition by the Reserve Bank.

Banks that become members of the Federal Reserve System must assume several important obligations. They must maintain legal reserves on deposit without interest at the Reserve Bank, remit for payment checks drawn against them when presented by a Reserve Bank, and comply with various federal laws, regulations, and conditions of membership regarding the adequacy of capital, mergers with other banking institutions, establishment of branches, relations with holding-company affiliates, loan and investment limitations, and other matters. If the member bank is chartered by a state, it must be subject to general supervision and examination by the Federal Reserve.

In return for assuming the above obligations, member banks are entitled to the following privileges: (1) to borrow from the Federal Reserve Banks, subject to discounting, when temporarily in need of additional funds; (2) to use Federal Reserve facilities for collecting checks, settling clearing balances, and transferring funds to other cities; (3) to obtain currency whenever required; (4) to share in the informational facilities provided by the system; (5) to participate in the election of six of the nine directors of the Federal Reserve Bank for their district; and (6) to receive a cumulative statutory dividend of 6 percent on the paid-in capital stock of the Federal Reserve Bank.

TYPES OF SERVICES

Banks offer a wide variety of services under such different designations as Time Plan Loan, Master Charge Card, Check Reserve Account, The Bank Package, and Tenplan Account, which are respectively an installment loan, a bank credit card, a reserve-credit checking account, a specially priced group of bank services, and a special checking account. You should know what basic financial services banks offer regardless of what your bank may wish to call them.

Deposit and transfer services occupy most of the operational time and facilities of the typical bank. Cash flow for the bank comes from monies deposited to time accounts (savings) and demand accounts (checking). As noted previously, certain portions of the money must be kept in reserve to insure the safety and liquidity of the bank. Checking accounts, which allow the transfer of personal funds on demand, are the unique service rendered by banks. In fact, this is the differentiating feature of commercial banks.

Besides savings accounts and checking accounts, other services usually offered by banks include consumer loans of all types, business loans, real-estate loans, drafts, other negotiable instruments, and letters of credit. Business services such as accounting, billing, payroll, and collections are often rendered by the larger banks. Investment management, securities transactions, escrow transactions, and trust functions are performed by large and small banks. Often the complete corporate name of a bank is something like First National Bank and Trust Company, to indicate its fiduciary (trust) services. Finally, many banks have international departments. We will look at these bank services in greater detail so that you may use them to your advantage.

CHOOSING YOUR BANK

It is the business of all banks to provide professional financial services. How each bank accomplishes these tasks should determine which bank you choose. Intangible criteria such as courtesy and personal interest in your financial transactions may be the deciding factors if competing banks offer essentially the same services. Ask yourself personal questions such as: Do I feel welcome here? Is it a comfortable place to do business? Can I get advice on how to handle money?

Customer Convenience

Assuming that courtesy and a feeling of welcome rank high at the bank you are considering, you will still want to look at other important service criteria.

Waiting in line Some banks have inaugurated one master waiting line, which feeds to all teller windows. No more guessing which is the fastest individual line! Other banks may have express tellers, drive-in windows, and walk-up windows. Which would you prefer?

Banking hours 10:00 a.m. to 3:00 p.m., Monday through Thursday, and 10:00 a.m. to 6.00 p.m. on Friday may be the usual banking hours, but this is often an inconvenience to the customer. Some banks have now inaugurated extended hours. Other banks keep their drive-in and walk-up windows open beyond 3:00 p.m. A new trend is automated banking by means of deposit and credit-card loans available through automated tellers or money machines located outside regular bank offices or in unmanned branches. These usually have daily twenty-four-hour service.

Branch banking Convenient location to your home or place of employment will probably be important to you. Find a bank with branches at both places, and you will be able to transact most of your business at your personal convenience. If you choose a bank with numerous branches, perhaps statewide, you will always find it convenient to cash a check or transact other banking business no matter where you are.

Mail Many banks offer deposit and loan service by mail. If your bank does not have convenient branches or if you cannot find the time or do not have the inclination to visit your bank, try banking by mail.

College student services A growing number of banks offer special services to persons going to college to acquaint the student with bank services and hopefully secure his future banking business. Often these services are offered only at branches near a college campus and include such things as low-cost checking accounts, limited-credit bank cards, small loans without parental guarantees, and government-insured student education loans repayable after graduation.

Opening the Checking Account

New accounts are normally opened by the bank's receptionist or new-accounts clerk rather than by a regular teller. In this manner the bank can take extra time to explain its procedures and charges and make you feel welcome.

The steps involved are relatively simple:

1. Select the type of checking account that meets your needs.
2. Complete an information card and a signature verification card for the bank's record.
3. Receive an account number.
4. Make an initial deposit.

5. Receive a supply of checks, a register, and deposit slips.
6. Choose style and color of checkbook if a choice is available.

A number of these steps will be elaborated upon later in the chapter.

Joint Accounts

Before selecting the type of checking account, you must decide if you wish an individual or joint account. It is generally beneficial for married couples and partners in a small business to have a joint account so that each person may write checks against the account. Each person entitled to write checks against an account must have his or her signature on file with the bank.

Having a joint account provides two big advantages to the co-owners. First, bank service charges will probably be lower because there is only one account. Second, a joint account normally provides for right of survivorship in case of the death of one of the joint owners of the account. This right provides access to the account by the survivor, so that everyday living and business expenses can be met without waiting for the results of long-drawn-out court proceedings. Have your bank explain the procedures used in your state to assure immediate access by the survivor.

PERSONAL CHECKING ACCOUNTS

A checking account makes it possible to transfer funds without carrying large sums of cash. It simplifies payments by mail and provides a record and receipt for any payment transaction. Choosing the check plan best suited for your needs requires some forecasting. How many checks do you expect to issue on a monthly basis? Can you keep a minimum balance in your account without spending it? After answering these questions you can choose among at least three alternatives: regular checking accounts, special checking accounts, and reserve-credit checking accounts. Most banks now provide all three plans, with minor variations. Each bank labels the plans differently, so you will have to investigate the various plans offered to find the features you desire.

Regular Checking Accounts

Regular checking accounts are also known as commercial accounts. A monthly service charge is computed on the number of checks you write and the minimum balance you maintain in your account. This basic plan has been the most popular over the years. A pamphlet showing the schedule of charges is normally published by each bank so that a customer can plan or verify his checking account costs.

A variation of the basic plan is being implemented by more and more banks. It provides for unlimited check writing at a flat fee based on the minimum balance maintained in the checking account. The big advantage here is that the customer always knows what the service charge on his account is going to be; he does not have to resort to a published graduated schedule of fees. More important, he can write as many or as few checks as he wishes without incurring changing fees. The flat-fee plan is often known as the Three/Two/One or the Two/One/Free plan.

A statement showing the deposits and the checks that have been paid against your account is mailed to you monthly. The service charge from either the basic plan or the flat-fee plan is automatically deducted from your balance.

Special Checking Accounts

If you plan to write only a few checks each month, a special checking account will be less costly. This plan will generally prove to be less expensive if you keep a small minimum balance in your account. It will be necessary for you to calculate the cost involved to keep your expense to a minimum with a special checking account.

Most banks charge a fee of fifteen cents per check on the special account. The fee is deducted from your balance in multiples of $1.50 for each ten checks cleared by the bank. A maintenance fee of fifty cents may be charged each ninety days when statements are mailed if the balance drops below $100.

The Bank of America offers a promotional deal on their special checking account, which they call a *Tenplan Account.* A tie-in with the Bank Americard credit card offers *Tenplan* users a rate of ten cents per check. Cardholders will probably write fewer checks because of bank-card purchases and thereby can benefit from a special checking account. Figure 5–1 is part of a brochure describing the various plans available at a large bank.

Reserve-Credit Checking Accounts

A built-in cash reserve or line of credit is available to checking-account customers at most banks. The basic idea is to allow the check writer to overdraw his account by receiving an automatic loan from the bank. To obtain this service you must complete a separate authorization, credit limit, and loan agreement. The reserve-credit plan normally operates through regular checking accounts and does not cost extra if it is not used. The big advantages are instant credit as needed and no overdraft charges.

You will be charged a loan fee by your bank when you do write a check for an amount greater than your checkbook balance. The amount will differ with the method and loan rates charged by your bank. Generally, one of two methods will be used, as noted below.

The more popular method is to tie the reserve-credit checking account to the bank's own bank-card system. Any check in excess of your account balance will be covered by a cash advance charged to your bank-card. The advance is normally in multiples of $50 automatically deposited to your checking account. The transfer fee will usually be from $2 to $4 per hundred, depending on the bank. No further charge is made unless the advance is not paid during the usual twenty-five-day billing period of the bank-card. After that time the 1 percent to $1\frac{1}{2}$ percent per month interest charge on unpaid balances becomes effective.

The other method employs a separate automatic-loan system. Whenever checks are written for more than you have in your account, an automatic deposit is made in multiples of $50 to $100 to cover the overdraft. A separate reserve-credit loan account is activated with interest computed at bank rates from the day of the loan to the day of repayment. Monthly statements are sent to show your loan status and to offer installment repayment of the loan if it is desired.

Checking-Account Costs

Only after World War II did banks begin charging for checking accounts. Banks have the use of your money while awaiting your demand (check) upon your account. Since the aggregate amount of all accounts is a vast sum for any bank, you can visualize the

Overdrafts.

One mishap that can occur when your records are not up to date is the overdraft. This happens when you write a check that's greater than the amount of money left in your account.

The normal procedure with an overdraft is for the bank to return the check, unpaid, to the payee. Because of the extra handling involved, you are charged $3.00 for each check that causes an overdraft or has to be returned. However, Bank of America's Instant Cash Service can help protect against overdrafts. It is explained in detail later.

When you deposit a check for credit to your account and for any reason it is not valid or cannot be paid by the bank on which it is drawn, the check will be sent back to you.

If this happens, a 30¢ handling charge may be applied to your account.

Four checking plans.

Bank of America has designed a wide range of Personal Choice Checking Plans for the convenience and economy of our many different customers. Whether you write a lot of checks or just a few, whether you like to keep a large balance or a small one, we have a plan that's just right for you. Check to see which one of the following best fits your needs:

1. All-in-One Checking Plan.

The All-in-One Checking Plan combines a number of our most useful services into one account and offers it for a flat fee of just $2.00 a month. Here is what you get: unlimited checkwriting with no minimum balance, free personalized checks, Check Guarantee Card, Instant Cash overdraft protection, Automatic Transfer Service (optional), the Timesaver Statement, BankAmericard® and unlimited Travelers Cheques, commission-free. One application handles it all at any Bank of America office.

2. Custom Checking Plan.

This convenient package includes many of the services most often asked for in a checking account: unlimited checkwriting with no minimum balance, free personalized checks, Timesaver Statement, commission-free Travelers Cheques and an optional Automatic Transfer Service—all for a flat monthly fee of $2.50. It's similar to the All-in-One Checking Plan without a BankAmericard, Instant Cash overdraft protection and the Check Guarantee Card.

3. Basic Checking Plan.

With the Basic Checking Plan, your service charges depend on both the number of checks you write and the balance you keep. If you maintain either a minimum balance of at least $300 or an average balance of at least $600, there's *no service charge* at all.

Minimum Balance

Number of Checks	Under $100	$100-199	$200-299	$300 or more
0	$ .80	$ .80	$ .50	
1	.89	.87	.57	Free.
2	.98	.94	.64	No
3	1.07	1.01	.71	Service
4	1.16	1.08	.78	Charge.
5	1.25	1.15	.85	
10	1.70	1.50	1.20	Unlimited
20	2.60	2.20	1.90	Number
30	3.50	2.90	2.60	of Checks.
Each Additional Check....	.09	.07	.07	

4. Tenplan.®

The Tenplan is for people who write just a few checks, so it's simple and uncomplicated. Statements are sent to you in January, April, July and October. You pay $1.50 service charge, deducted after the first, eleventh, twenty-first, etc. check paid. This averages 15¢ per check.

Figure 5–1 Typical Checking Plans Available, as Depicted in Bank Brochure. *(Bank of America N.T. & S.A., San Francisco)*

amount of interest-free money available to a bank. This money is called *float,* and banks use it for loans and investments. The bigger the bank, the bigger the float, especially since it is more likely that checks will be written to a payee who will deposit the funds to his account in another branch of the same bank. All that is done in such instances is transfer a deposit from one account to another, with the bank still getting the use of the money.

It is ironic that free checking accounts are still available from many small banks. These banks have less float and therefore less use of their customers' demand deposits. They normally offer free accounts to attract customers because they cannot compete with the convenience of branch banking.

Some customers have access to free personal checking accounts because they have business checking accounts at a bank. Others become "charter" members and are given free accounts as a promotional device when the bank first opens. Still others receive free checking accounts by maintaining large savings accounts at mutual savings banks, credit unions, or savings and loan associations. These institutions pay a bank to maintain your "free" checking account as a cost of securing your savings deposit business.

Figure 5–1 indicates the costs involved in using a checking account but certainly does not cover all the hidden costs. Some banks charge for imprinting your name, address, and telephone number on your check, i.e., for personalizing your checks. Also, there is normally a charge for *scenic* checks, where a picture image or unique design background is imprinted on standard check forms. When these checks first appeared on the market, they impressed the payee because they were different. This is no longer the case: almost all banks offer them, and people are no longer impressed. You can save the $2.50 charge for scenic checks by asking your bank for the standard or regular checks. On the check reorder form you may have to look very, very carefully for the appropriate box to order the standard checks.

Assuming that you write over ten checks a month, you can get a "free" checking account by maintaining a minimum balance in your account. By doing this you will save more money than if you put the same minimum balance amount in a passbook savings account. For example, if you maintain a minimum balance of $300, there will be no charge for the Two/One/Free plan, flat-fee checking account. You would be charged $2 per month if the account balance dropped to near zero, which is often the case. If your low-minimum-balance situation continues to exist month after month, the annual charge will be $24 ($2 × 12 months). If you put the $300 in a passbook savings account at 5 percent interest, you will receive interest of $15 ($300 × .05) per year.

Would you rather earn interest at $15 per year in a savings account and spend $24 for a checking account at a net loss of $9, or put the $300 into your checking account and not spend the $24 on service charges and thereby not have a loss of $9? Obviously the second alternative is better providing you do not go below the minimum balance and get charged for doing so. One way to insure that you do not drop below the minimum balance is to exclude the $300 from your check register—out of sight, out of mind. For people who write ten or more checks each month, the checking-account minimum balance should be their first form of savings.

Bank packages A number of banks are attempting to make the service charge for checks more palatable to the customer by including "extra" or "free" services as part of the service charge. The whole thing has become a competitive promotional scheme among banks and is wrapped up as a special bank package. The monthly service charge is usually $2 to $3.

A customer is enticed to buy the package for a set fee. He then gets a "free" unlimited checking account and some combination of the following:

1. Personalized name and address imprint on his checks.
2. Scenic checks.
3. Courtesy card to facilitate cashing checks.
4. Bank credit card.
5. Reserve-credit checking account.
6. Safety-deposit box (usually the smallest size).
7. No charge for the purchase of unlimited traveler's checks.
8. Passbook savings account. (Some banks start your account with a $5 balance; others require that you have an account in which you must deposit a $5 minimum.)

Be a wise consumer and compute the dollar cost of a bank package. Note that most of these services are already available without cost. Why pay for what you can get free or at lower cost? Probably the only time these packages are economically feasible is if you pay between $24 and $36 per year for safety-deposit boxes and/or traveler's checks. Even these are available without charge by maintaining a $1,000 savings account in many savings banks, savings and loan associations, and credit unions.

USING A CHECKING ACCOUNT

Upon opening an account the customer receives a temporary supply of checks and deposit slips with his account number. By mail he later receives his permanent supply of checks and deposit slips, which may also be personalized with his name and address. These will be encoded with his customer account number in MICR (Magnetic Ink Character Recognition) characters in the lower left corner of his checks.

Deposits

Unless you have established a reserve-credit checking account, you must have money on deposit before you can "demand" it. To deposit funds, banks suggest you use the deposit forms that accompany your checkbook. Figure 5–2 illustrates a typical deposit slip. You simply enter the date and the amounts of money you wish to deposit in currency, coin, and checks in the spaces provided. Checks should be listed by the A.B.A. (American Bankers Association) number located in the upper right-hand corner of all checks. Extra space is provided on the back of the deposit slip for recording more checks. The bank teller will record your deposit by making an entry in the *Record of Deposits* section of your check register. If you deposit by mail, the bank will send you a receipt by return mail.

Writing Checks

A check is a negotiable instrument transferring a sum of money from one party to another upon demand. It is necessary to follow prescribed procedures carefully. If you do not, your check may not be honored, or it might be altered and cashed for an amount greater than you wrote.

For your protection, examine every check you write. Use ink to preclude alterations. Fill in all spaces completely. Be sure that the figures and written amount agree and that the check is dated. Sign the check in the same manner as your signature

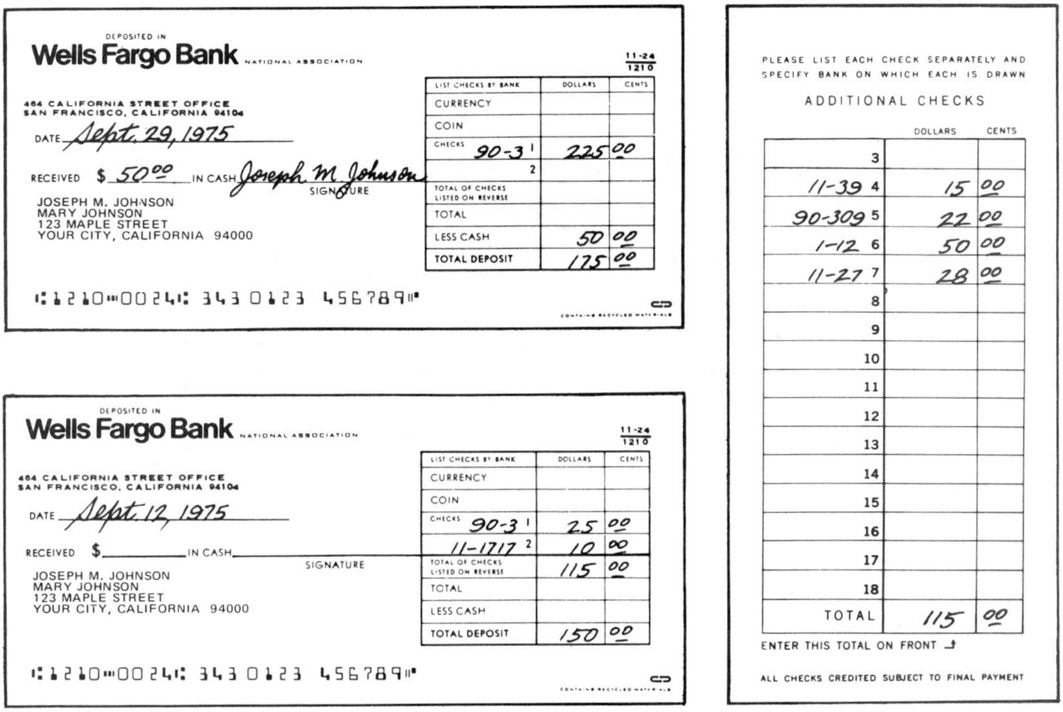

Figure 5–2 Deposit Slips Used in a Typical Checking Account. *(Wells Fargo Bank N.A.)*

card. If paying a bill due on a charge account, write the charge account number in the upper left corner of the check in case the bill stub gets separated from your payment check.

Figure 5–3 explains in detail the steps necessary in writing checks. If you make an error it is wise to destroy a check and write a new one. Each step is quite important:

1. *The check number* If your checks are not already numbered, be sure to number them. Write the number in your check register to help in balancing your statement.
2. *The date* Checks may be dated any day of the week. Do not write a future date, because banks are not authorized to pay checks with future dates.
3. *The payee* Checks should be made payable to a specific person or company. Checks payable to "order," "cash," or "bearer" may be cashed by anyone.
4. *The amount* Be sure the written and figure amounts agree. Banks normally will not honor checks that have differing amounts, even though the written amount is considered correct. To protect yourself against alterations enter the amount as far to the left as possible in both spaces. Make a line across unfilled space.
5. *The signature* Never sign a check in advance of use. Your signature should correspond exactly with that on file at the bank.

Keeping track of your balance is most

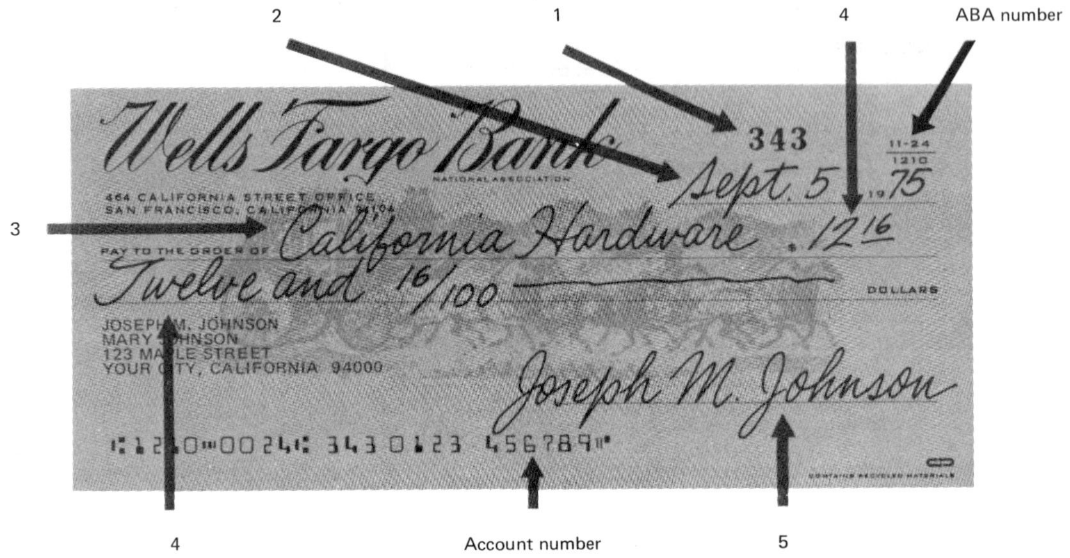

Figure 5–3 How to Write a Check. *(Wells Fargo Bank N.A.)*

important. Mathematical error and failure to record a check in your register are the two most common mistakes that show up on your monthly statement. Both of these mistakes can be overcome by following a simple procedure. Double-check your arithmetic each time you write a check or make a deposit and always complete the check stub or the check register before writing the check.

Figure 5–4 illustrates the two types of check-writing records in popular use. The stub record provides for easier addition and subtraction while the check register allows you to see easily what checks you have issued. If you have a choice, the latter method will probably give you better psychological control over your spending and aid in reconciling your bank statement.

A problem occurs whenever two people write checks on a joint account. The possibility of overdrafting becomes much greater if each has a separate checkbook. One solution is to have one person control the checkbook to keep the balance updated. The other person should operate on a cash basis, keeping two or three spare checks in his wallet for emergencies. Anytime the second person writes a check, he should record the issuing information on a piece of paper kept with the spare checks. As soon as possible, he should transfer the information to the master check register in exchange for a blank check. By keeping a constant number of checks in his wallet, he would always be reminded if he has issued a check.

Endorsing Checks

Before depositing a check or transferring it to another person, you (as payee) must endorse the check. This is done by signing your name (as shown on the payee line) on the back left end of the check. If your payee name is not the same as your correct signature on file at the bank, sign your authorized

CHECK NO	DATE	CHECK ISSUED TO	AMOUNT OF CHECK	✓	DATE OF DEP	AMOUNT OF DEPOSIT	BALANCE

PLEASE BE SURE TO DEDUCT ANY MAINTENANCE CHARGE THAT MAY AFFECT YOUR ACCOUNT...

CHECK NO.	DATE	CHECKS ISSUED TO OR DESCRIPTION OF DEPOSIT	AMOUNT OF CHECK	CHECK FEE IF ANY	AMOUNT OF DEPOSIT	BALANCE FORWARD	
		To				Check or Dep.	
						Bal.	
		To				Check or Dep.	
						Bal.	
		To				Check or Dep.	
						Bal.	
		To				Check or Dep.	
						Bal.	

NO. ____________ $ ____________

____________ 19 ____

TO ____________

FOR ____________

	DOLLARS	CENTS
BAL. BRO'T. FOR'D.		
AM'T. DEPOSITED		
TOTAL		
AM'T. THIS CHECK		
BAL. CAR'D. FOR'D.		

NOTICE: Make No Alteration or Change on Any Check.
If Error is Made Write New Check.

Figure 5–4 Checkbook Registers. *(Bank of America N.T. & S.A., San Francisco; Wells Fargo Bank N.A.)*

signature below the payee signature. In case of joint payees, both must endorse the check to negotiate or deposit it.

Whenever you endorse a check you become liable for payment of the check. The laws of negotiable instruments apply to check endorsements; you guarantee that the check is valid and that you have received value for it. You in turn may hold prior endorsers liable for payment of the check if the maker should default for any reason.

There are several types of endorsements: blank, special, restrictive, and qualified. Figure 5–5 shows examples of each.

A *blank* endorsement is simply the payee's signature. It transfers title to anyone holding it at the time. Since it can be cashed by anyone, you should not use a blank endorsement until you are actually giving the check to someone. A *special* endorsement names an endorsee, who is the person you are giving the check to and the next person who must endorse it. No one else can negotiate the check. A *restrictive* endorsement specifies what can be done with the check and restricts further endorsement. Deposits sent through the mail should have a restrictive endorsement as shown in figure 5–5. A *qualified* endorsement limits the liability of the endorser while transferring title to the check or other negotiable instrument. Essentially what the endorser is saying is, "I am giving you this check from someone else, but I will not be responsible for its payment." Qualified endorsements are most often used in business transactions where a check is made payable to an agent or representative to be given to a client or a principal. If the agent does not receive any value directly from the check, he may use the qualified endorsement. No one may use this type of endorsement as a way of getting out of paying his liabilities because normally you will have been given value such as a product or service and have given the check as return value (payment).

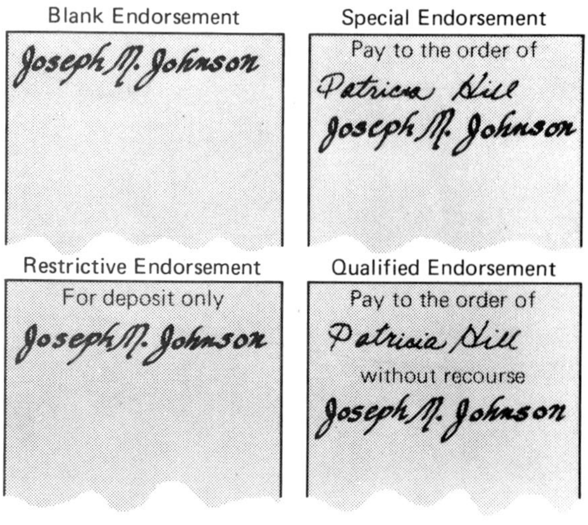

Figure 5–5 Check Endorsements.

Bank Statements

Each month or each quarter the bank sends you a statement of the debits and credits to your account since the last statement. Figure 5–6 illustrates a typical checking-account bank statement. Statements will differ with each bank. A new trend is to combine savings accounts, checking accounts, and even loan accounts on one statement. A bank statement gives you the opportunity to reconcile your checkbook balance with the bank's balance. The reconciliation should be done as soon as possible after receipt of the bank statement in order to deduct any service charges from your checkbook balance and to keep from magnifying any errors made by you or the bank. The best reason to balance your checkbook is simply to know the amount of money you have in your account.

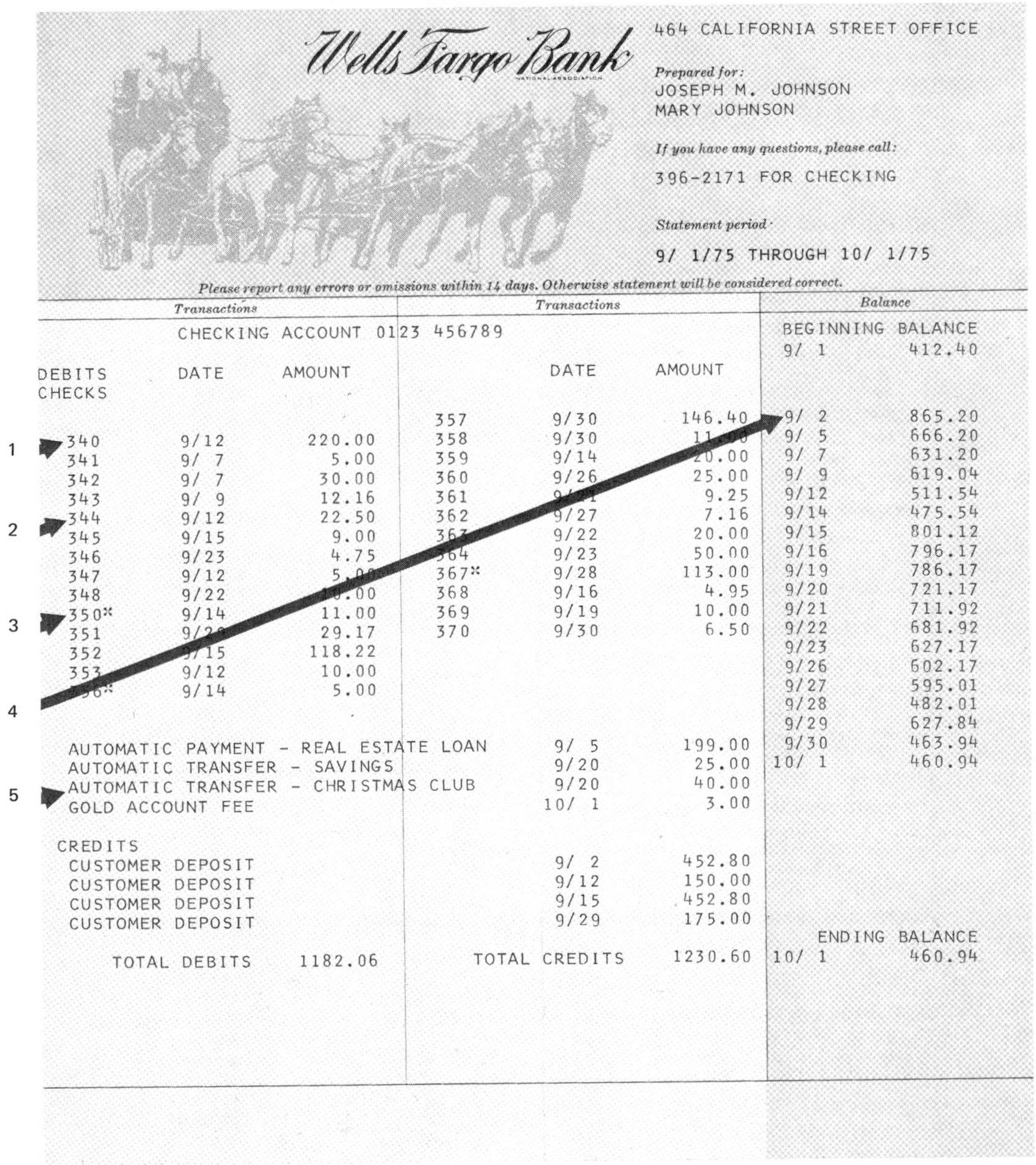

Wells Fargo Bank
NATIONAL ASSOCIATION

464 CALIFORNIA STREET OFFICE

Prepared for:
JOSEPH M. JOHNSON
MARY JOHNSON

If you have any questions, please call:
396-2171 FOR CHECKING

Statement period:
9/ 1/75 THROUGH 10/ 1/75

Please report any errors or omissions within 14 days. Otherwise statement will be considered correct.

Transactions | *Transactions* | *Balance*

CHECKING ACCOUNT 0123 456789

BEGINNING BALANCE 9/ 1 412.40

Marker	DEBITS CHECKS	DATE	AMOUNT		DATE	AMOUNT
				357	9/30	146.40
1	340	9/12	220.00	358	9/30	11.00
	341	9/ 7	5.00	359	9/14	20.00
	342	9/ 7	30.00	360	9/26	25.00
	343	9/ 9	12.16	361	9/27	9.25
2	344	9/12	22.50	362	9/27	7.16
	345	9/15	9.00	363	9/22	20.00
	346	9/23	4.75	364	9/23	50.00
	347	9/12	5.00	367*	9/28	113.00
	348	9/22	10.00	368	9/16	4.95
3	350*	9/14	11.00	369	9/19	10.00
	351	9/29	29.17	370	9/30	6.50
	352	9/15	118.22			
	353	9/12	10.00			
	356*	9/14	5.00			
4						

Marker	Item	DATE	AMOUNT
	AUTOMATIC PAYMENT - REAL ESTATE LOAN	9/ 5	199.00
	AUTOMATIC TRANSFER - SAVINGS	9/20	25.00
	AUTOMATIC TRANSFER - CHRISTMAS CLUB	9/20	40.00
5	GOLD ACCOUNT FEE	10/ 1	3.00
	CREDITS		
	CUSTOMER DEPOSIT	9/ 2	452.80
	CUSTOMER DEPOSIT	9/12	150.00
	CUSTOMER DEPOSIT	9/15	452.80
	CUSTOMER DEPOSIT	9/29	175.00

TOTAL DEBITS 1182.06 TOTAL CREDITS 1230.60

Balance date	Balance
9/ 2	865.20
9/ 5	666.20
9/ 7	631.20
9/ 9	619.04
9/12	511.54
9/14	475.54
9/15	801.12
9/16	796.17
9/19	786.17
9/20	721.17
9/21	711.92
9/22	681.92
9/23	627.17
9/26	602.17
9/27	595.01
9/28	482.01
9/29	627.84
9/30	463.94
10/ 1	460.94

ENDING BALANCE 10/ 1 460.94

Figure 5–6 Typical Checking Account Bank Statement. *(Wells Fargo Bank N.A.)*

The back of your bank statement often has a form with step-by-step instructions on how to reconcile your checkbook balance with the bank-statement balance. If it does not have a form, follow the steps listed:

Your Statement Balance		$274.25
1. Sort your checks numerically.		
2. Add any deposits made but not shown on your statement.	$40.00	$314.25
3. Any checks missing from the numerical sequence have not yet been paid by the bank. List them, total the amount, and subtract it from the line 2 figure.	$14.25	$300.00
Your Checkbook Balance		$317.85
4. Subtract any service charges.	$ 2.85	$315.00
5. Subtract the amounts of any automatic transfers shown on your statement.	$15.00	$300.00

If lines 3 and 5 agree, your checkbook balance is correct. At this time be sure to subtract any bank charges from your checkbook. If lines 3 and 5 do not agree, double-check each entry in your checkbook register for accuracy, and make certain that all checks have been entered in it. If you still cannot reconcile your statement, your bank should help you if it practices the "full service" concept.

Check Processing

Most checks are processed by computer. Checks drawn on the same bank as that of the payee are cleared by that bank's service center. Checks drawn on another bank in the same area are processed by a central clearing house, with the banks settling the net differences among them by one payment. Most checks will clear within twenty-four hours. Depositors should not attempt to use float or they will most likely be embarrassed! Be sure to deposit sufficient funds on the day you write a check; otherwise an overdraft may result.

Overdrafts

Banks do not have to honor checks drawn on accounts with insufficient funds. If they do so, it is because you are a good customer, and they do not wish to embarrass you or lose your future business. Extra handling is required every time an overdraft occurs, so banks generally charge $3 to $4 for this activity. An overdraft is really a loan without a formal agreement. If the overdraft amount is more than about $20, many banks will not honor your check. It is returned to the payee's bank marked "insufficient funds." The payee's bank then resubmits the check for payment or returns the check to him for collection. The payee will then contact you.

The best way to keep from being charged for overdrafts is to maintain a sufficient minimum balance to keep from paying the regular check service charge. This way you would save the overdraft charge and the monthly service charge. An alternative is to apply for a reserve-credit checking account. The cost of an overdraft would then run about $2 per $100 loaned.

Stop Payments

After you have written a check you can stop payment by notifying your bank before your check clears. Some banks will accept a temporary stop-payment order by telephone. All banks require a written order as a permanent record to limit their liability if a question should arise later as to payment or nonpayment. The stop-payment order needs information concerning the account number, date, payee, and the amount. There is normally a small charge of $1 or $2 for this service.

Since most banks are automated, the computer is programmed to deny clearance to any stop-order check by reading the account number and the amount. The tellers at the branch of issue are also notified to watch for the check in case it is physically presented for payment.

The usual reasons for stopping payment are lost or stolen checks. However, consumers often pay for goods and services by check only to find them unsatisfactory. In such cases, quick action is necessary to effect a stop payment on the check, because merchants normally make daily deposits to their banks.

Check Acceptance

If you follow all the prior suggestions on choosing the correct checking account, on recording the information in the check stub, and on completing the check itself, you will have just one more problem—getting someone to accept your check. Checks are not legal tender, so no one has to accept them, because they are not the currency of the country. Checks are simply a demand by you to your bank to pay someone (payee) your money.

Even banks will not accept checks that are not drawn on their own bank if you are not a depositor. In fact checks are a form of *draft* to be paid on demand at the place printed on the check, the specific branch or bank of deposit. If you are a depositor in the bank of demand, you can negotiate the check at any branch of the bank as a courtesy to you. If you are not a depositor, you must clear it through a branch of your bank. You may cash it at the specific branch listed on the check, if you have plenty of identification.

When accepting a check from someone, it is a good idea to secure at least two forms of identification. Usually a driver's license will have the person's signature and perhaps his photograph. Record his license number and address on the check for identification and possible track-down purposes. As a second form of identification, ask for a T and E (travel and expense) credit card or a bank credit card. Copy the identification information onto the back of the check. Make sure all the information you record is current and plausible. Remember, even if all the identification information is correct, the check may not be good because of insufficient funds. You still do not have to trust anyone by accepting his check. On the other hand, no one has to accept your check, either.

Collecting a dishonored check is time-consuming, expensive, and not always very successful. If you can find the check passer, you can sue if he refuses to pay. Merchants often display placards stating that there will be a charge for returned checks. They hope that this warning will discourage customers from giving them checks without sufficient funds. Actually, they have no authority to levy a charge for a returned check. They cannot get this extra money from a person without suing for damages, a very inconvenient process.

As a rule of thumb never take a *blank* check or a *two-party* check, as these are notoriously hard to collect if they are dishonored. A *blank* check, also known as a counter check, is on a standard form not imprinted by a bank and, of course, does not carry an account number. The blank-check forms are normally bought at stationery stores and are sometimes available at various merchants in case a customer forgets his or her checkbook. Blank checks are legal because the laws of negotiability do not require that the bank and account number be imprinted on checks. Actually, checks can be and have been written on just about every conceivable type of material. Cowhides, pieces of lumber, plastic, and even movie starlets have been negotiated as checks, usually for some promotional purpose. The risk is greater with blank checks because in addition to the great risk of identification and trustworthiness, you have the problem of bank, branch address, and account-number accuracy.

The *two-party* check is issued by one person to another who endorses it so that it might be cashed by a third person. In this situation the maker has time to stop payment on the check if he had a problem with the first payee. This situation will obviously create collection problems for you. Assuming you get plenty of identification from the endorser (second person), you still do not know anything about the original maker. It is much better to take the personal check of the second person rather than chance the extra risks involved in a two-party check.

Always cash or negotiate a check as soon as possible after accepting it. The longer you wait, the greater the possibility that the maker will change his mind about payment and place a stop-payment order with his bank, or that he will run out of funds in his account, or that you will misplace or lose the check. Banks do not have to honor a check that is not presented for payment within a "reasonable length of time." Generally banks will not honor checks more than six months old. Known as stale checks, these require the bank to contact the maker to find out if he wishes the payment to be made. Many business and government checks are stamped with the limitation, "not good after six months." The liability behind the check still stands, but it would be necessary to get a new check from the issuer, an inconvenience to everyone concerned.

Finally, never accept a postdated check, one that is dated for a future day. You have not accepted a check, but a time draft, a promise to pay to a payee a certain sum of money at a future time and place through a certain bank. Banks will not accept these postdated checks until the actual date arrives. About the only reason a maker would postdate a check is that he has insufficient funds on deposit when he writes the check and hopes to have enough in his account by the date on the check. The risk that the maker will not put money in his account is added to all the other risks discussed earlier when you accept a postdated check.

OTHER TRANSFER SERVICES

If you wish to transfer funds to another person, your personal check is probably the most convenient method if he will accept it. Mail-order merchants have to accept checks or go out of business. Often they delay sending you merchandise until your personal check has cleared. To speed a mail transaction, you can gain immediate acceptance of your order by sending a certified check or by purchasing a bank-issued check, draft, or money order, payable to whomever you wish. Most banks charge a small fee for these transfer services. The amount is often dependent upon whether the customer is a depositor of the bank.

Certified Checks

The payment of your personal check is guaranteed by your bank when you arrange for a certified check. The bank certifies that fact by stamping "Certified" across the check in special ink. Your payee recognizes that the check is guaranteed by the bank and will therefore more readily accept it. The bank can guarantee the check because it sets aside sufficient funds from your account to pay the check when presented. Since you must physically go to the bank to arrange for a certified check, there is no special advantage to be gained from this procedure.

Some banks give their select customers *courtesy* or *check-guarantee cards* valid for a given period. These cards can make your personal check more acceptable to merchants in a face-to-face transaction because the bank will guarantee to honor your check up to the amount stated on the card. For mail transactions it is probably better to purchase some form of draft that is more easily recognized as "guaranteed" by your prospective payee. The trend at most banks is away from certified checks and toward the use of cashier's checks.

Cashier's Checks

Depositors and nondepositors may use cashier's checks, which are drawn by a bank upon itself and therefore always good for payment. Customers purchase cashier's checks for whatever amount they wish and pay cash for them. A fee of about fifty cents per hundred dollars is charged for this service. When the check is cashed, the cancelled check remains at the bank.

A variation of the cashier's check is the *bank money order*, which contains the name of the purchaser. Money orders are usually for amounts under $300. Banks usually recommend the purchase of a *bank draft* for sending money out of your area. Bank drafts are three-party negotiable instruments. Your bank writes a check (draft) on a correspondent bank in the area where the payee lives by using funds it has on deposit in the other bank.

Traveler's Checks

Since it is not a good idea to carry large sums of money while traveling, and since most businesses will not accept out-of-area personal checks, it is convenient to purchase and use traveler's checks. Banks guarantee to replace them if they are lost or stolen. They are available in denominations of $10, $20, $50, $100, $500, and $1,000 at the cost of approximately $1 per $100. Certain large banks have their own traveler's checks, while smaller banks, savings and loan associations, and travel agencies act as agents for American Express Company, Bank of America, Thomas Cook & Son Limited, and the First National City Bank of New York, among others. Some checks are more readily recognized and accepted than others. Make certain that representative agencies are available in your area of travel. At the time of purchase, you sign each check and receive a numbered register to keep track of their use. The list of numbers should be kept separate from the checks in case they are lost or stolen. Denominations of $50 or $100 are more practical than $10s and $20s; otherwise you will get writer's cramp during purchase and spend too much time in line to cash small-denomination checks.

Retailers, hotels, airlines, gift shops, and other businesses throughout the world honor most traveler's checks. It is necessary to countersign the check so that the payee can compare your signature to the signature already on the check.

A letter of credit is available for use by persons who have a need for large amounts of money while traveling. It replaces traveler's checks to the extent that a letter of credit can be purchased in any amount, thereby saving the drudgery of signing and carrying a wad of traveler's checks. The bank furnishes the purchaser with a list of correspondent banks that will honor the letter by issuing local drafts against the letter of credit. As each bank issues a draft against the letter of credit, it endorses the letter, subtracting the amount of the draft issued from the credit-value balance. The letter of credit is especially useful when you are traveling through a number of foreign countries, but it can also be used domestically.

Miscellaneous Transfer Instruments

Some banks provide *wire-service money orders* among branches and to correspondent banks. This service speeds a transfer transaction by telegraphic or private wire order to issue a draft to a person in a different location. Better known methods of telegraphic fund transfers are Western Union in the United States and American Express for international fund transfers.

Automatic fund transfers are becoming commonplace in full-service banks. Various banks provide consumer bill-paying services by automatically sending checks or crediting the creditor company's bank accounts. Your own checking account is charged for the bills paid. Prior arrangements must be made to have your creditors send their bill to your bank. If your bank does not offer bill-paying services, it will probably offer automatic transfer of funds from your checking account to your savings account and to any loan account you may have at your bank.

SAVINGS ACCOUNTS

Bank savings accounts are widely used. The convenience of the one-stop financial supermarket insures that there will always be plenty of customers using the savings facilities of the commercial bank. Many customers use a bank passbook savings account to build up savings to a respectable balance and then transfer the funds to other institutions that pay higher rates of interest. This process is continually repeated so that they always have some savings in their local bank.

Special-purpose savings accounts are actively solicited by most banks. These include such short-term accounts as Christmas Club, Vacation Club, and School savings accounts. Long-term certificates of deposit are offered to large investors, as noted in chapter 4. Often banks will require that a portion of a long-term business loan be kept at the bank as a time deposit for a given period of time.

Banks not only offer various types of savings accounts; they also provide facilities to purchase U.S. savings bonds. Some banks offer their own savings or investment bonds backed by bank assets. Bank bonds provide savings and investing opportunities of five to fifteen years with investment amounts ranging from $100 to $1000. Bank bond interest rates are competitive with Series E and H government savings bonds and are available as either discount or interest-bearing bonds.

LOAN SERVICES

A wide variety of loans are available through a full-service bank. Small personal loans may be offered on an installment basis with separate repayment contracts, or they might be arranged through either a bank credit-card system or a reserve-credit checking account. If you are credit worthy, consumer installment loans are available for any good purpose that may require bank financing. Chapter 3 covers consumer lending and credit practices in detail.

Other lending services offered include financing of residential and commercial real estate, farm real estate, and such farm-related loans as crop-production term loans to farm-equipment installment loans. Business loans covering such diverse items as plant, equipment, inventory, and business operations are made regularly. Financing a small business or for that matter any business requires close cooperation between the businessperson and the banker.

BUSINESS SERVICES

The size of a bank, its assets, and number of branches affect, at least to a degree, the type of business services offered. A statewide bank can offer interbranch credit information, plant location service, collections, bill of lading freight-payment and many other services requiring on-the-spot representation. Smaller banks sometimes provide many of these services through correspondent banks and the use of a bank wire system.

On a more localized basis, a full-service bank may provide payroll accounting, billing service, employee deposit and loan systems, and community development service, including specialized research on small-business operation. Municipalities, other government bodies, and various nonprofit organizations also receive financial advice and banking services. Many banks provide free checking accounts without minimum balances to parent-teacher associations, scout groups, community service clubs, and other similar groups to promote community spirit and accomplishment.

TRUST SERVICES

Most banks are chartered as trust companies or have trust departments, meaning that they can act as administrators and managers of estates, trusts, and investment portfolios. Banks can be trustees under a will or under a living trust to manage any property, real or personal, for your own benefit, for your family, or for other designated beneficiaries.

In most states banks may be appointed executors or coexecutors through a will to carry out the wishes of the testator. This device allows your wishes to be carried out without interruption because a bank has a continuing existence, whereas a friend or a relative may be sick, may predecease you, or may not be able to handle the financial part of your will satisfactorily. Further information on trusts is provided in chapter 10.

OTHER SERVICES

Safe-Deposit Boxes

Banks and some savings and loan associations provide vault-room security for their customers' valuables. Fees for the service differ with the size of the box rented, generally from $6 for a 200-square-inch elongated drawer to hundreds of dollars per year for a file-cabinet-size deposit box. The small-size boxes are sometimes offered as a "free" service to customers who maintain a minimum savings deposit at the bank or savings and loan association. Security is provided by limited customer access to the vault and by requiring two separate sets of keys to open the box.

Safe-deposit boxes are fireproof and theftproof and therefore provide the perfect storage place for items that are expensive or difficult to replace. Access is reasonably convenient during banking hours. The bank provides individual cubicles to allow a customer privacy while working with the contents of the box. Safe-deposit boxes should be in joint ownership to allow both husband and wife access, and in case one dies, the survivor will be able to enter the box with minimal red tape.

Currency Service

The coin and currency of the United States are released to the public through the member banks of the Federal Reserve System. Your local bank will provide you with rolls of coin in any denomination and will exchange your rolled coins for currency. Smaller banks often allow local merchants the use of their coin-counters to facilitate this type of transaction. Currency in most denominations is also available for purchase or replacement as it becomes mutilated or worn out. Foreign exchange, coin and currency of other countries, is readily available in larger banks and upon order in smaller banks. Traveler's packets of popular foreign currencies are often prepared as a packaged item for use as tips and service payments upon arrival in a foreign country. Normally any bank that sells foreign currency will also purchase left over foreign currency upon your return.

Miscellaneous Services

Banking is a very competitive business. Banks rely on the use of depositors' money to make a profit. Anything that they can do to get your business is important to them. By offering a wide range of "full services" to individuals, to businesses, and to governments, they entice you into their bank. The bank's services then become familiar to you, and you become a customer primarily because of the conveniences offered. Only the more publicized and consumer-oriented services have been described in detail in this text. You should contact your bank for help in any financial transaction in which it is needed.

Vocabulary and Concepts

Commercial bank
Demand deposit
Dishonored check
Endorsement
Federal Reserve System
Fiduciary
Float
Joint account
Negotiation
Overdraft
Payee
Reconciliation
Reserve-credit
Stop payment
Time deposit
Trust services

Questions for Discussion

1. What are the most important services rendered by banks for their consumer customers? How would you rank their services in importance?
2. Explain how a reserve-credit checking account works. Why is it usually tied in with a bank credit card?
3. What is accomplished by endorsing a check? What methods of endorsement are available? What does each accomplish?
4. How does a person stop payment on a check? What are the consequences of such an action?
5. No one has to accept your check. Why? Even banks will usually not honor checks drawn on other branches if you are not a customer. Why?
6. Explain the differences between a certified check, a cashier's check and a traveler's check. What other types of negotiable instruments do banks usually have available?
7. Is a "bank package" a saving for the consumer? Explain.
8. What are the usual steps in reconciling a checking account?
9. What types of currency service are generally available in a bank?

Projects

1. Compare two local banks (one large and one small) as to hours of operation and services offered for consumers. Compare their charges for loans and other services.

2. Investigate college-oriented services offered by a local bank. Does the bank have a college representative? How much does a student ordinarily save by using the special college-student services?
3. Make a list of items and documents that you should place in a safe-deposit box. Rank each item in terms of value, ease of replacement, and how often the document or item must be reviewed during the year. How much will your safe-deposit box cost? Is ownership of a safe-deposit box worth the cost, effort, and security involved?
4. Investigate the APR and procedures involved in applying for the different types of loans available at your bank. Why do rates vary with the type of loan and type of applicant?

Case Problem

Art and Barbara Able know that the best way to save money is not to spend it. They figure that they can save more by keeping $300 in their checking account at all times. Perform the necessary calculations to prove or disprove the idea that your first "savings" should be in your checking account.

An innovation is the all-in-one bank package that provides a checking account without minimum balance requirements, a bank credit card, overdraft protection, and unlimited traveler's checks for $2 to $3 per month. Would this alternative be better if the Ables purchased $1,000 in traveler's checks annually? What if they didn't use traveler's checks?

two

risk and the need for insurance

Our lives are fraught with risk because we cannot forecast what uncertainties lie ahead. Perhaps this is what makes life interesting. It can definitely make life more expensive. Most of our daily risks are insignificant, but certain events—fire, accident, sickness, theft, and death—create serious economic loss.

Risk is really the chance of loss or exposure to harm. It is measured in terms of probability. A person tries to reduce his risks if he can. He will probably have four choices, not all of which may be acceptable:

1. Eliminate the risk or its cause.
2. Establish a fund to cover a possible loss.
3. Hedge the risk by having two or more of the items subject to loss.
4. Shift the risk by purchasing insurance.

Eliminating the risk is perhaps the most effective way of eliminating the chance of loss. Usually the risk cannot be eliminated, but it can be reduced. The catastrophes previously mentioned can be reduced by fireproofing, using safety precautions, and maintaining good health procedures.

Accumulating funds to cover the loss is another approach. This reserve may be called a form of self-insurance. This works well with smaller losses that can be overcome but does not help an individual with a catastrophic loss. Small losses can be covered by income, and medium-sized losses by the accumulated fund, but a large loss would not be covered. It would take a lifetime to cover certain losses; but if the chances of the catastrophe happening are very slight, it may be worth hedging against the risk through self-insurance.

A person may also hedge a risk by having two pieces of property. One would act as backup in case the first is lost for some accidental reason. You cannot have a second health or a second life, not to mention a second house or car for backup purposes. The first two are impossible, and the latter two are likely to be uneconomical.

Since the first three choices may be impractical under many circumstances, the consumer has insurance as a final choice. Insurance combines the risks of many people by collecting money from each person and paying it to the few who suffer losses, thereby eliminating the economic risk for all participants.

Insurance involves the law of large numbers and the principle of an insurable risk. Commercial insurance companies will not provide risk coverage (insurance) unless losses can be predicted by the application of the law of large numbers, which involves the use of averages. The larger the number of cases used, the greater the accuracy of the loss prediction in a given risk. Actuarial calculations use mortality tables based upon many thousands of deaths over a long period. Accident, fire, and theft losses are predicted in a similar manner using past records of loss.

No matter how large a number of cases is involved, someone seeking coverage must be economically insurable from the standpoint of the insurance company, or it will not provide the risk coverage. Insurable risks must involve the following conditions:

1. Any loss must be accidental.
2. Any loss must be measurable and classifiable.
3. Any loss must not be a universal or simultaneous hazard.
4. There must be a sufficient number of similar risks to measure for prediction and rate-setting purposes.

The consumer pays for all the losses in life, no matter which alternative method he uses to reduce his risk. Actually, he does not reduce the hazard, except on rare occasions; he just makes the catastrophe more economically bearable, providing the cost of reducing the risk is not worse than the risk of the loss itself. Of all the alternatives, insurance may be the least costly if the consumer properly assesses the odds of a catastrophe happening to him. You can be overinsured or underinsured as well as properly insured. Unfortunately, the why, when, and how much of insurance are highly emotional questions. The insured, the uninsured, and the insurance companies are all biased.

Few people can afford the amount of insurance they would need to be fully secure. Life would be rather dull and without the niceties of a good standard of living if the average consumer purchased every type of insurance offered or every type he felt he needed. He would forsake the present for a possible future happening that may or may not occur. The average consumer must compromise between security and expense, between the present and the unpredictable future. As a consumer, you should become well informed on all aspects of risk and insurance and then decide for yourself. Do not be pressured by what other people tell you is necessary.

Chapters 6, 7, and 8 deal with the risks and insurance that are associated with loss of earned income due to death and disability, the costs of illness and injury, and the loss of assets due to casualty or liability. Chapter 9 deals with the problems of providing income during retirement, while chapter 10 presents the methods of protecting and transferring one's estate at death.

Part two should be viewed in its entirety. Add up the cost of protecting yourself from economic catastrophe; you will be surprised at your monthly and yearly cash outlay for insurance. Even if you do not pay for all your insurances, include them since they are fringe benefits in lieu of cash wages. A middle-income family of four with two teen-agers can expect to pay approximately $1,600 per year or $133 per month for various insurances. When you include social security and other retirement insurance, these figures rise to approximately $2,400 per year or $200 per month. This estimate is based on annual payments of $300 for life insurance, $500 health insurance, $100 dental insurance, $500 auto insurance, $200 homeowner's insurance, and $800 social security. You can see why it is so important for a consumer to evaluate the needs and costs of insurance.

6 life insurance

Ask a number of persons what life insurance is, and you will get many answers. Some will say it is the sharing of a risk, or an economic protection, or a form of forced savings. Others will describe life insurance as a gamble or an emotional consideration. Actually, it is all these things and probably more.

A SHARING OF A RISK

Life insurance, like all other forms of insurance, involves sharing a risk among many people. Each person contributes a proportionate share—a premium—to a life-insurance company to provide some economic security to his beneficiaries. The risk is shared either to prorate or to reduce the economic catastrophe to each of the people insured. But what is the risk that is shared or passed on to the insurance company? It is not death—you do not reduce your chance of death. What you do reduce is the economic insecurity of the family if the insured dies.

Life insurance is an economic concept involving the probabilities of life and death. The risk that is shared is an economic one requiring you to explore fully all conceivable alternatives before choosing how you will divide the risk between your family and the insurance company. Your choice should be part of your total financial planning.

AN ECONOMIC PROTECTION

Life insurance provides economic protection —this is its prime function. The protection feature always includes a money settlement to the insured's beneficiaries or estate. The amount of the payment is known as the *death benefit* and is based upon the *face value* stated in the policy. It is paid by the insurance company even if only one premium payment has been made on a valid and current insurance policy. The face value becomes an immediate or instant estate. If an insurance company pays off, the insurance may be considered a good investment on the part of the now-deceased insured person. On the other hand, if the insured person survives, you may conclude that the protection was not a good investment. Your conclusion may be inaccurate because the protection was there if it was needed. It would be more accurate to conclude that life insurance is an investment in economic security. If the insured dies, the beneficiaries have the security of an instant estate. If the insured lives, the beneficiaries have the security of the breadwinner's income. Life insurance is really *income insurance,* since

Age	American Experience (1843-1858)		Commissioners 1941 Standard Ordinary (1930-1940)		Commissioners 1958 Standard Ordinary (1950-1954)		Annuity Table for 1949—Male (1939-1949)		United States Total Population (1959-1961)	
	Deaths Per 1,000	Expectation of Life (Years)	Deaths Per 1,000	Expectation of Life (Years)	Deaths Per 1,000	Expectation of Life (Years)	Deaths Per 1,000	Expectation of Life (Years)	Deaths Per 1,000	Expectation of Life (Years)
0	154.70	41.45	22.58	62.33	7.08	68.30	4.04	73.18	25.93	69.89
1	63.49	47.94	5.77	62.76	1.76	67.78	1.58	72.48	1.70	70.75
2	35.50	50.16	4.14	62.12	1.52	66.90	.89	71.59	1.04	69.87
3	23.91	50.98	3.38	61.37	1.46	66.00	.72	70.65	.80	68.94
4	17.70	51.22	2.99	60.58	1.40	65.10	.63	69.70	.67	67.99
5	13.60	51.13	2.76	59.76	1.35	64.19	.57	68.75	.59	67.04
6	11.37	50.83	2.61	58.92	1.30	63.27	.53	67.78	.52	66.08
7	9.75	50.41	2.47	58.08	1.26	62.35	.50	66.82	.47	65.11
8	8.63	49.90	2.31	57.22	1.23	61.43	.49	65.85	.43	64.14
9	7.90	49.33	2.12	56.35	1.21	60.51	.48	64.89	.39	63.17
10	7.49	48.72	1.97	55.47	1.21	59.58	.48	63.92	.37	62.19
11	7.52	48.08	1.91	54.58	1.23	58.65	.49	62.95	.37	61.22
12	7.54	47.45	1.92	53.68	1.26	57.72	.50	61.98	.40	60.24
13	7.57	46.80	1.98	52.78	1.32	56.80	.51	61.01	.48	59.26
14	7.60	46.16	2.07	51.89	1.39	55.87	.52	60.04	.59	58.29
15	7.63	45.50	2.15	50.99	1.46	54.95	.54	59.07	.71	57.33
16	7.66	44.85	2.19	50.10	1.54	54.03	.55	58.10	.82	56.37
17	7.69	44.19	2.25	49.21	1.62	53.11	.57	57.13	.93	55.41
18	7.73	43.53	2.30	48.32	1.69	52.19	.58	56.17	1.02	54.46
19	7.77	42.87	2.37	47.43	1.74	51.28	.60	55.20	1.08	53.52
20	7.80	42.20	2.43	46.54	1.79	50.37	.62	54.23	1.15	52.58
21	7.86	41.53	2.51	45.66	1.83	49.46	.65	53.27	1.22	51.64
22	7.91	40.85	2.59	44.77	1.86	48.55	.67	52.30	1.27	50.70
23	7.96	40.17	2.68	43.88	1.89	47.64	.70	51.33	1.28	49.76
24	8.01	39.49	2.77	43.00	1.91	46.73	.73	50.37	1.27	48.83
25	8.06	38.81	2.88	42.12	1.93	45.82	.77	49.41	1.26	47.89
26	8.13	38.12	2.99	41.24	1.96	44.90	.81	48.44	1.25	46.95
27	8.20	37.43	3.11	40.36	1.99	43.99	.85	47.48	1.26	46.00
28	8.26	36.73	3.25	39.49	2.03	43.08	.90	46.52	1.30	45.06
29	8.34	36.03	3.40	38.61	2.08	42.16	.95	45.56	1.36	44.12
30	8.43	35.33	3.56	37.74	2.13	41.25	1.00	44.61	1.43	43.18
31	8.51	34.63	3.73	36.88	2.19	40.34	1.07	43.65	1.51	42.24
32	8.61	33.92	3.92	36.01	2.25	39.43	1.14	42.70	1.60	41.30
33	8.72	33.21	4.12	35.15	2.32	38.51	1.21	41.75	1.70	40.37
34	8.83	32.50	4.35	34.29	2.40	37.60	1.30	40.80	1.81	39.44
35	8.95	31.78	4.59	33.44	2.51	36.69	1.39	39.85	1.94	38.51
36	9.09	31.07	4.86	32.59	2.64	35.78	1.49	38.90	2.09	37.58
37	9.23	30.35	5.15	31.75	2.80	34.88	1.61	37.96	2.28	36.66
38	9.41	29.62	5.46	30.91	3.01	33.97	1.73	37.02	2.49	35.74
39	9.59	28.90	5.81	30.08	3.25	33.07	1.87	36.08	2.73	34.83
40	9.79	28.18	6.18	29.25	3.53	32.18	2.03	35.15	3.00	33.92
41	10.01	27.45	6.59	28.43	3.84	31.29	2.22	34.22	3.30	33.02
42	10.25	26.72	7.03	27.62	4.17	30.41	2.48	33.30	3.62	32.13
43	10.52	26.00	7.51	26.81	4.53	29.54	2.80	32.38	3.97	31.25
44	10.83	25.27	8.04	26.01	4.92	28.67	3.19	31.47	4.35	30.37
45	11.16	24.54	8.61	25.21	5.35	27.81	3.63	30.57	4.76	29.50
46	11.56	23.81	9.23	24.43	5.83	26.95	4.12	29.68	5.21	28.64
47	12.00	23.08	9.91	23.65	6.36	26.11	4.66	28.80	5.73	27.79
48	12.51	22.36	10.64	22.88	6.95	25.27	5.25	27.93	6.33	26.94
49	13.11	21.63	11.45	22.12	7.60	24.45	5.88	27.07	7.00	26.11
50	13.78	20.91	12.32	21.37	8.32	23.63	6.56	26.23	7.74	25.29

Figure 6–1 Mortality Table. *(Institute of Life Insurance)*

Age	American Experience (1843-1858) Deaths Per 1,000	American Experience (1843-1858) Expectation of Life (Years)	Commissioners 1941 Standard Ordinary (1930-1940) Deaths Per 1,000	Commissioners 1941 Standard Ordinary (1930-1940) Expectation of Life (Years)	Commissioners 1958 Standard Ordinary (1950-1954) Deaths Per 1,000	Commissioners 1958 Standard Ordinary (1950-1954) Expectation of Life (Years)	Annuity Table for 1949—Male (1939-1949) Deaths Per 1,000	Annuity Table for 1949—Male (1939-1949) Expectation of Life (Years)	United States Total Population (1959-1961) Deaths Per 1,000	United States Total Population (1959-1961) Expectation of Life (Years)
51	14.54	20.20	13.27	20.64	9.11	22.82	7.28	25.40	8.52	24.49
52	15.39	19.49	14.30	19.91	9.96	22.03	8.04	24.58	9.29	23.69
53	16.33	18.79	15.43	19.19	10.89	21.25	8.84	23.78	10.05	22.91
54	17.40	18.09	16.65	18.48	11.90	20.47	9.68	22.99	10.82	22.14
55	18.57	17.40	17.98	17.78	13.00	19.71	10.56	22.20	11.61	21.37
56	19.89	16.72	19.43	17.10	14.21	18.97	11.49	21.44	12.49	20.62
57	21.34	16.05	21.00	16.43	15.54	18.23	12.46	20.68	13.52	19.87
58	22.94	15.39	22.71	15.77	17.00	17.51	13.48	19.93	14.73	19.14
59	24.72	14.74	24.57	15.13	18.59	16.81	14.54	19.20	16.11	18.42
60	26.69	14.10	26.59	14.50	20.34	16.12	15.66	18.48	17.61	17.71
61	28.88	13.47	28.78	13.88	22.24	15.44	16.87	17.76	19.17	17.02
62	31.29	12.86	31.18	13.27	24.31	14.78	18.20	17.06	20.82	16.34
63	33.94	12.26	33.76	12.69	26.57	14.14	19.67	16.37	22.52	15.68
64	36.87	11.67	36.58	12.11	29.04	13.51	21.28	15.68	24.31	15.03
65	40.13	11.10	39.64	11.55	31.75	12.90	23.07	15.01	26.22	14.39
66	43.71	10.54	42.96	11.01	34.74	12.31	25.03	14.36	28.28	13.76
67	47.65	10.00	46.56	10.48	38.04	11.73	27.19	13.71	30.53	13.15
68	52.00	9.47	50.46	9.97	41.68	11.17	29.58	13.08	33.01	12.55
69	56.76	8.97	54.70	9.47	45.61	10.64	32.20	12.46	35.73	11.96
70	61.99	8.48	59.30	8.99	49.79	10.12	35.09	11.86	38.66	11.38
71	67.67	8.00	64.27	8.52	54.15	9.63	38.27	11.28	41.82	10.82
72	73.73	7.55	69.66	8.08	58.65	9.15	41.77	10.71	45.30	10.27
73	80.18	7.11	75.50	7.64	63.26	8.69	45.62	10.15	49.15	9.74
74	87.03	6.68	81.81	7.23	68.12	8.24	49.85	9.61	53.42	9.21
75	94.37	6.27	88.64	6.82	73.37	7.81	54.50	9.09	57.99	8.71
76	102.31	5.88	96.02	6.44	79.18	7.39	59.61	8.58	62.96	8.21
77	111.06	5.49	103.99	6.07	85.70	6.98	65.22	8.10	68.67	7.73
78	120.83	5.11	112.59	5.72	93.06	6.59	71.37	7.63	75.35	7.26
79	131.73	4.74	121.86	5.38	101.19	6.21	78.11	7.17	83.02	6.81
80	144.47	4.39	131.85	5.06	109.98	5.85	85.50	6.74	92.08	6.39
81	158.60	4.05	142.60	4.75	119.35	5.51	93.59	6.32	102.19	5.98
82	174.30	3.71	154.16	4.46	129.17	5.19	102.44	5.92	112.44	5.61
83	191.56	3.39	166.57	4.18	139.38	4.89	112.11	5.54	121.95	5.25
84	211.36	3.08	179.88	3.91	150.01	4.60	122.67	5.18	130.67	4.91
85	235.55	2.77	194.13	3.66	161.14	4.32	134.18	4.84	143.80	4.58
86	265.68	2.47	209.37	3.42	172.82	4.06	146.71	4.51	158.16	4.26
87	303.02	2.18	225.63	3.19	185.13	3.80	160.33	4.20	173.55	3.97
88	346.69	1.91	243.00	2.98	198.25	3.55	175.12	3.90	190.32	3.70
89	395.86	1.66	261.44	2.77	212.46	3.31	191.15	3.62	208.35	3.45
90	454.55	1.42	280.99	2.58	228.14	3.06	208.49	3.36	227.09	3.22
91	532.47	1.19	301.73	2.39	245.77	2.82	227.19	3.12	245.98	3.02
92	634.26	.98	323.64	2.21	265.93	2.58	247.33	2.88	264.77	2.85
93	734.18	.80	346.66	2.03	289.30	2.33	268.96	2.67	282.84	2.69
94	857.14	.64	371.00	1.84	316.66	2.07	292.12	2.47	299.52	2.55
95	1,000.00	.50	396.21	1.63	351.24	1.80	316.83	2.28	314.16	2.43
96			447.19	1.37	400.56	1.51	343.12	2.10	329.15	2.32
97			548.26	1.08	488.42	1.18	370.97	1.94	344.50	2.21
98			724.67	.78	668.15	.83	400.35	1.79	360.18	2.10
99			1,000.00	.50	1,000.00	.50	431.20	1.65	376.16	2.01
100							463.41	1.52	392.42	1.91
101							496.87	1.40	408.91	1.83
102							531.39	1.29	425.62	1.75
103							566.76	1.20	442.50	1.67
104							602.71	1.10	459.51	1.60
105							638.96	1.02	476.62	1.53
106							675.14	.94	493.78	1.46
107							710.90	.86	510.95	1.40
108							745.82	.75	528.10	1.35
109							1,000.00	.50	545.19	1.29

it replaces income not earned because of the "premature" death of the breadwinner.

FORCED SAVINGS

Life insurance is often sold as a form of forced savings. The idea is that a consumer does not have sufficient foresight or willpower to provide himself with a savings or investment program that will leave him in good financial shape when he retires. While this is true of some people, it is not economically sound for a knowledgeable person to save in this manner. If you understand the basic concept of insurance as the sharing of risk or the seeking of economic protection from a risk, your insurance dollar should be allocated to the protection of the beneficiaries in case of the untimely death of the breadwinner. Your choice of insurance policies will determine your allocation. An intelligent choice of policies will provide you with a greater amount of protection for your dollar and allow you to use a portion of your available protection and savings dollars in higher-interest-paying savings or in growth investment programs.

A GAMBLE

Some people refer to life insurance as a gamble rather than as an investment. As mentioned in the introduction to part two, all insurance is based on the law of averages —so is gambling. In gambling you take a monetary risk by wagering on the outcome of an occurrence. Hopefully, you know the statistical odds in your gamble, but chances are you disregard them in favor of luck. This situation sounds similar to insurance, but there is a major difference. Gambling creates risk; when you gamble it is usually a voluntary act, because you can take the wager or leave it. It will not adversely affect your pocketbook if you do not gamble. This is not the case in life insurance, because it reduces an economic risk. The risk of economic insecurity caused by the death of the breadwinner is voluntary only to the extent of not being insured or not providing sufficient assets in an estate. The cause of the risk, namely premature death, is not usually voluntary. The risk of economic insecurity may be overcome by providing an adequate estate through normal asset buildup over the years. Young people have not had the time to build up these assets. Therefore they must provide an instant estate for their beneficiaries through life insurance. Any "gamble" in life insurance is guessing the probability of whether the insured will die in a given period. A decision can be made to purchase or forgo life-insurance protection based upon these probabilities.

Mortality tables are one basis for determining the probability of death in a given period. Life-insurance companies base their premiums partly on these tables. Figure 6–1 is a mortality table. Note that the number of deaths in any one year is not overly significant until the average person reaches middle age. Based on the concept of averages, the odds of your living to a relatively old age are quite good. Insurance companies recognize this by offering lower premiums to younger people.

AN EMOTIONAL CONSIDERATION

People often consider life insurance from a very emotional viewpoint. Insurance companies also view it from an emotional point of view, at least when advertising their product. Figure 6–2 is indicative of the emotionalism in life-insurance marketing.

Sometimes this emotionalism pervades the agent's sales presentation. In any case, it cannot be totally disregarded by the consumer or the insurance agent.

One indication of the emotional issue in life insurance is the name given to the protection offered—life insurance. Perhaps it would be more correct to call the protection death insurance, but who would buy it? Insurers argue that the term *life insurance* is descriptive because the insurance provides money for the beneficiaries of the insured to continue living, or it provides money for retirement if the insured survives. An even better name for life insurance would be income insurance. However, critics of life in-

I am an idea.
I am a promise.
I help men see visions, dream dreams, and achieve economic immortality.
I am education for the children.
I am savings.
I am also property that increases in value from year to year.
I lend money when you need it most—with no questions asked.
I pay off mortgages so that the family can remain together in its own home.
I assure fathers the daring to live and the moral right to die.
I create, manage, and distribute property.
I am the great emancipator from want.
I guarantee the continuity of business . . . I protect the jobs of employees . . . I conserve the employer's investment.
I am tangible evidence that a man is a good husband and father.
I am a declaration of financial independence, a charter of economic freedom.
I am the difference between an "old man" and an "elderly gentleman."
I provide cash if illness, injury, old age, or death cuts off the breadwinner's income.
I am the only thing that father can buy on the installment plan that mother doesn't have to finish paying for.
I am a certificate of character, an evidence of good citizenship, an unimpeachable title to the right of self-government.
I bring dignity, peace of mind, and security to the latter years of life.
I am a "great social compact that merges the individual into the mass and places behind the frailty of man, standing alone, the immeasurable strength of men, standing together."
I supply investment capital that makes the smoke go up the chimneys, wheels turn, and motors hum.
I guarantee that there "will always be Christmas—with tinsel, a happy fireside, and the laughter of children—even though father is not there."
I am the guardian angel of the home.
I AM YOUR LIFE INSURANCE POLICY.

Figure 6–2 I Am a Piece of Paper . . . But Even More . . . *(New York Life Insurance Company, New York)* surance still prefer to call it death insurance. All conclude that true insurance for beneficiaries, for clean-up expenses, or for taxes is based upon providing protection in case of an early death of the family breadwinner. Whatever you call life insurance, recognize that different types of policies provide for different goals. We will examine the functions of the various life-insurance policies later in the chapter.

REASONS FOR BUYING LIFE INSURANCE

People buy life insurance primarily to replace the earnings of the family breadwinner in case of an untimely death. A secondary reason for purchasing life insurance is to provide a savings fund for some reason, usually retirement. Liquidity of an estate and business ownership reasons are also important. We will look specifically at the first two reasons.

If we could know when we are to die, we could make definite plans. If we are sure to survive until age seventy-two, the average age of death, we could accumulate and use our assets according to plan. The uncertainty of the time of death is faced by people of all ages. It requires considerable thought about life insurance to be certain that a sufficient estate is available for the surviving family members.

The surviving family members are usually in a state of emotional shock and certainly do not need the specter of financial insecurity added to their grief. Two major money problems arise when the head of the household dies. These are where to get the necessary money to pay the immediate expenses associated with death and where to get money for the long-term living expenses of the surviving family members. The necessity of providing for these expenses reflects what is often called the needs approach to purchasing life insurance.

Immediate Expenses

Often people say they do not need life insurance because they do not have dependents. This is a somewhat fallacious argument, because everyone generates some expense when he dies. If you do not have an emergency savings fund or other usable asset, it might be appropriate to purchase life insurance. Let us look at the more notable immediate expenses:

Medical expenses Doctor bills, hospital bills, and other medical expenses can add up rapidly prior to death. An elongated sickness or serious accident, in which the patient lingers between life and death, is not unusual. Medical services are expensive by anyone's standards and costs appear to be increasing at an inflationary rate. If the deceased had good health and accident insurance, this economic problem would be substantially reduced or eliminated.

Burial expenses The cost of mortuary facilities, funerals, cemetery plots, mausoleums, and cremation procedures can run into thousands of dollars. Everyone must die sooner or later, so this expense transcends all age groups, sexes, marital states, and economic levels.

Unpaid bills Most people have a few unpaid bills at any given moment. Single persons often have a number of department-store accounts and probably automobile installments. Married persons are even more into credit accounts because of the added responsibilities of raising a family.

Legal expenses Expenses related to estate administration, taxes, court costs, and legal fees differ with the size of the assets of the deceased. If the deceased caused or was the victim of an accident, legal fees will be rather large. Even with liability and accident insurance, delays in payment may occur because overstrained court calendars may slow judicial decisions. Some of the legal expenses cannot be put off until final settlements are reached.

Family Protection

The standard of living of the surviving members of a family is of great importance to all concerned. Since the husband is usually the breadwinner and is statistically more likely to die at an early age than his wife, we will think in terms of protection for wives and children. Life insurance now becomes income insurance for the family. Each family may be in a slightly different state in the life cycle, but the economic needs are much the same with all families.

The readjustment period A husband is not only the breadwinner; he is also a consumer. He probably used a large slice of the family's discretionary income for hobbies, sports, and entertainment, in addition to his share of food, clothes, and medical expenses. The elimination of his personal expenses will help the family budget to a degree, but this can be offset by a compensating increase in household repair costs and family money-handling problems if the deceased was particularly adept at these things. Also, until the family settles into a new routine without the husband, its expenses will be higher than they should be. Among other things, the wife may hunt for a job, or the family may move to smaller quarters. The insurance industry normally considers the readjustment period to be six months.

The family period The younger the family, the longer the period until the children are on their own. The reduced income provided by a working mother will probably be insufficient to maintain the standard of living the family enjoyed from the income of the deceased father. As the children become teen-agers, the missing income will become even more important because of the money demands for special clothes and recreation so necessary to the teen-age sense of well-being. Theoretically the father would have provided for all these "necessities" through increased salary and job promotions. As we shall see later, Social Security will provide some income to the widow and children during this period.

The widow's gap Between the time that the children leave home and the time that a widow reaches age sixty to sixty-two and retirement, there is a period known as the widow's gap. Social Security does not provide any survivor's benefits during this period. The widow must work, live off assets, live off insurance, or survive on some combination of these three possibilities.

The widow's retirement years Retirement brings reduced income whether the husband is deceased or living. Widows must rely on partial Social Security benefits earned by their husbands or on benefits that they may have earned in their own name. Probably the benefits will not be very great in either case, because the husband will not have contributed very much to Social Security before his untimely death, and the widow's contributions to Social Security will not have been adequate because of her lower salary and relatively short period of employment.

Mortgage payoff One of the biggest expenses faced by a widow and children is the high cost of housing. It is usually less traumatic for the family to remain in its house upon the death of the husband and father. By eliminating the mortgage payment or the need for rental payments, the survivors will be in much better financial shape to carry on the business of living.

Education fund Parents want the best for their children. A fatherless family would be hard put financially to send one or more children to college or technical school. If the father were alive, current income plus savings could be used for this worthwhile cause. Life insurance can provide for this contingency.

A Savings Fund

Many people use life insurance as a method of accumulating a long-term savings fund. It can be argued that a savings fund is not an economical use of life-insurance premiums, but it can be equally argued that life-insurance savings provide protection against the risk of not having accumulated a fund for retirement, education, or other important reasons. Cash-value life insurance provides a return to the insured if he should live.

Retirement fund Social Security may be a good base upon which to build a retirement income. It is not enough to provide a reasonably good standard of living upon retirement. Extra income or extra assets are a must to overcome the risk of insufficient income during retirement years. Life insurance with a cash value provides a program of forced savings which can be used to supplement Social Security.

Emergency fund It is hard for people without much willpower to keep from dipping into emergency funds for nonemergency uses. A cash-value life-insurance policy may be used for such an emergency fund. It could still be cashed or borrowed against in nonemergencies, but this is less likely to happen because the basic protection feature would be destroyed. Cash-value life insurance can also be used to enhance one's credit position. It can be used as collateral for a loan from an outside source, thereby leaving the protection intact. Outside loans have to be paid back. One could have credit life insurance as part of the loan contract to maintain full protection.

Taxation If you anticipate accumulating a moderate estate for retirement or for transfer to heirs of life insurance with a cash buildup has great liquidity and can be used to pay income taxes and estate taxes. Life insurance proceeds payable to beneficiaries are income-tax free to them. Only the interest on money left with an insurance company under the various settlement options is taxable income.

The Value of Human Life

All the reasons given for purchasing life insurance are certainly worthwhile, but they may not apply in an individual case. Choose your good reasons with the assistance of your beneficiaries. If the idea is to provide protection for loved ones, their needs and desires should be considered. Discuss with them the present and future implications of living on a reduced income.

In addition to the needs approach to buying life insurance, the concept of the dollar value of human life might be considered in terms of lost income and lost services. Each member of the family—husband, wife, and children—has an economic value in terms of anticipated earnings and anticipated services. One cannot put a dollar value upon the loss of companionship of family members, because companionship cannot be adequately valued or replaced by money.

The value of a husband or wife as principal wage earner The dollar value of the principal wage earner is based primarily on the economic services he or she renders to the family. Earning capacity is affected by many factors such as training, experience, and type of job. Let us assume a twenty-five-year-old man has a salary of $1,000 per month, or $12,000 per year. He would earn $480,000 over his working life to age sixty-five. The figure of $480,000 earned over the next forty years would be highly inaccurate because we have not considered salary increases and inflation, which would raise his projected earnings, nor have we accounted for income taxes and the husband's direct expenses, which would decrease the take-home pay available for the rest of the family.

Let us assume that the husband will follow normal promotion and salary increases and end up with an average of $1,500 per month, or $18,000 per year. The husband's earning expectancy is now $720,000 over a forty-year period. Inflation at a conservative rate of 3 percent per year should be added to the earnings amount to give us a more accurate total earnings figure of $1,357,222 over the forty-year period. At a 3 percent inflation rate, $18,000 per year will amount to $57,006 in the fortieth year. If nothing else, this simple mathematical example should give you an idea of the high cost of inflation!

Now we must subtract taxes and expenses from our total. The early death of the husband would deprive the family of his expected income of over one and one-third of a million dollars, but even if he lives, the family would not get the use of this amount because of taxes and his personal expenses, which would include the purchase of life insurance. Probably 25 percent of his gross income will go to taxes, and another 15 percent will be spent on his personal expenses each year. Now we have $10,800 of usable family net income as the average annual value the husband contributes to his family. Crank in a 3 percent inflation factor on this average over forty years, and we have a total of $814,333 as the husband's contribution. Even after considering taxes and personal expenses, you can immediately see that the face amount of life insurance based strictly on human life value would be too expensive for the family to afford. The premiums would come to over $250 per month just for term life insurance!

Present worth In our example one does not need life insurance in the amount of $814,333 because there is a big difference between receiving $10,800 a year for forty years with a 3 percent inflation bonus and receiving $814,333 as a lump-sum now. The lump-sum could be invested at interest, thereby greatly increasing the income of the family, but as just noted the premium would be prohibitive. What we need to know is how much money is needed now to invest at a reasonable rate of interest to provide $10,800 per year for forty years. The use of present-value tables (see table 6–1) provides for the calculation of the present dollar amount needed to reach a specific sum at some future time. With a periodic income, we would use a present value of one per year table, to determine the lump-sum of money needed now to provide for a larger sum for a given period.

By using the table at a 5 percent interest rate, we see that the present value of $1 per year for forty years is $17.16 (rounded). We can therefore calculate the value of $10,800 per year for forty years at 5 percent as $185,328. This means that a husband's future salary expectations to retirement, less taxes and his personal expenses, could be "purchased" now for *only* $185,328, a far cry from the $1,357,222 we first thought was needed to replace his salary!

The value of a husband or wife as secondary wage earner The death of a

Table 6–1 Present value of annuity of $1 per period

n*	4%		5%		6%		n
1	0.9615	3846	0.9523	8095	0.9433	9623	1
2	1.8860	9467	1.8594	1043	1.8333	9267	2
3	2.7750	9103	2.7232	4803	2.6730	1195	3
4	3.6298	9522	3.5459	5050	3.4651	0561	4
5	4.4518	2233	4.3294	7667	4.2123	6379	5
6	5.2421	3686	5.0756	9206	4.9173	2433	6
7	6.0020	5467	5.7863	7340	5.5823	8144	7
8	6.7327	4487	6.4632	1276	6.2097	9381	8
9	7.4353	3161	7.1078	2168	6.8016	9227	9
10	8.1108	9578	7.7217	3493	7.3600	8705	10
11	8.7604	7671	8.3064	1422	7.8868	7458	11
12	9.3850	7376	8.8632	5164	8.3838	4394	12
13	9.9856	4785	9.3935	7299	8.8526	8296	13
14	10.5631	2293	9.8986	4094	9.2949	8393	14
15	11.1183	8743	10.3796	5804	9.7122	4899	15
16	11.6522	9561	10.8377	6956	10.1058	9527	16
17	12.1656	6885	11.2740	6625	10.4772	5969	17
18	12.6592	9697	11.6895	8690	10.8276	0348	18
19	13.1339	3940	12.0853	2086	11.1581	1649	19
20	13.5903	2634	12.4622	1034	11.4699	2122	20
21	14.0291	5995	12.8211	5271	11.7640	7662	21
22	14.4511	1533	13.1630	0258	12.0415	8172	22
23	14.8568	4167	13.4885	7388	12.3033	7898	23
24	15.2469	6314	13.7986	4179	12.5503	5753	24
25	15.6220	7994	14.0939	4457	12.7833	5616	25
26	15.9827	6918	14.3751	8530	13.0031	6619	26
27	16.3295	8575	14.6430	3362	13.2105	3414	27
28	16.6630	6322	14.8981	2726	13.4061	6428	28
29	16.9837	1463	15.1410	7358	13.5907	2102	29
30	17.2920	3330	15.3724	5103	13.7648	3115	30
31	17.5884	9356	15.5928	1050	13.9290	8599	31
32	17.8735	5150	15.8026	7667	14.0840	4339	32
33	18.1476	4567	16.0025	4921	14.2302	2961	33
34	18.4111	9776	16.1929	0401	14.3681	4114	34
35	18.6646	1323	16.3741	9429	14.4982	4636	35
36	18.9082	8195	16.5468	5171	14.6209	8713	36
37	19.1425	7880	16.7112	8734	14.7367	8031	37
38	19.3678	6423	16.8678	9271	14.8460	1916	38
39	19.5844	8484	17.0170	4067	14.9490	7468	39
40	19.7927	7388	17.1590	8635	15.0462	9687	40
41	19.9930	5181	17.2943	6796	15.1380	1592	41
42	20.1856	2674	17.4232	0758	15.2245	4332	42
43	20.3707	9494	17.5459	1198	15.3061	7294	43
44	20.5488	4129	17.6627	7331	15.3831	8202	44
45	20.7200	3970	17.7740	6982	15.4558	3209	45
46	20.8846	5356	17.8800	6650	15.5243	6990	46
47	21.0429	3612	17.9810	1571	15.5890	2821	47
48	21.1951	3088	18.0771	5782	15.6500	2661	48
49	21.3414	7200	18.1687	2173	15.7075	7227	49
50	21.4821	8462	18.2559	2546	15.7618	6064	50

* n = number of periods needed for periodic income.

husband or wife who was the secondary wage earner would cause a loss of income to the family. This amount is readily determinable. If the spouse were not employed, there would still be a considerable economic loss if it were necessary to hire a person to care for the children and perform various household tasks. This amount can be projected. The present worth of projected expenses caused by the loss of a working spouse and housekeeper would then be calculated in the same manner as the value of the principal wage earner.

The value of a child The concept of human value can be taken to the extreme by calculating the loss of services provided by children in the family. For our purposes we will assume that children's services have limited economic value. Later in the chapter we will look into who should be insured and for how much.

"Insurance Poor"

There are many reasons to buy life insurance. These may be based on the needs of the insured and the family, or on the replacement value of its members. In either case, if the family purchased all the life insurance needed to cover all contingencies or to replace the salary or services of a loved one, the family would indeed be "insurance poor." All the figures used in the example are projections, averages, and estimates. Your family will have its own set of figures to work with, but even these will be estimates. The most important thing to remember is that you and your family are living in the *present* and will have to forgo many of today's pleasures if you wish to be completely insured against all contingencies on a "need" or "value lost" basis. Is it really worth the financial strain of paying $100 or more per month to provide fully against a risk that has only a slight probability of happening during a specific period? Remember, insurance premium rates tend to reflect probability.

No one will dispute that some funds are needed to cover the "probability" of expenses when someone dies. Nor will he dispute that funds are needed to provide a reasonably comfortable living for the family survivors or that some funds are needed for retirement. The dispute arises in how these funds shall be accumulated. A *compromise solution* will find your family looking toward many different methods of securing funds rather than relying on insurance alone. You must consider your reasons for purchasing life insurance against your ability to pay insurance premiums for all these reasons. It is only good sense to insure against the greatest risks. It then becomes important to determine which are the greatest risks in order to relieve the financial strain of overpaying insurance premiums.

The Best Reasons Are the Biggest Economic Risks

According to statistics, the average person is not going to die until he or she is well into his or her retirement years. If you care to assume that you are average, you can provide protection where it is most needed. If you are not average, you may not be insurable. Look at it this way: if the insurance company agrees to insure you, you must be a reasonably good risk. Agree with their analysis and become a coinsurer of yourself, allowing the insurance company to insure you only for the most important economic losses. If they will not insure you, the whole question of insurance becomes academic.

When you look at all the reasons for buying life insurance, it becomes apparent that many of the reasons are really just whimsical. Other alternatives can be found to purchasing life insurance. The choice of insurance priorities must lie with the insured and his family, not with the insurance agent. Let us look into some of the alternatives.

Immediate expenses may include medical, burial, and legal expenses and unpaid bills. Hopefully, medical expenses will be covered by health and accident insurance. Unpaid bills are a normal part of living expenses and should be considered part of the survivor's living expenses. A decision could be made to return automobiles or other hard goods if it becomes necessary, or if it is economically feasible to do so. Legal expenses should not be too high if appropriate wills and joint-tenancy papers have been prepared. This leaves burial expenses. A special fund is really needed to cover burial expenses because of the high costs involved. The cost of burial arrangements can be lowered somewhat by preplanning low-cost services and specifying them in your will.

Family protection is probably uppermost in the minds of most husbands and wives. How much should be left, for what reasons, and for what periods of time? If sufficient assets have not been accumulated before the death of the husband, or if there is insufficient insurance, a widow must rely on Social Security, her own employment, remarriage, or some combination of these. Social Security provides a good base but is not sufficient in itself. For planning purposes, it might be best to consider her as a single person making her own way. Children will obviously complicate the alternatives and make it imperative that funds be available for a readjustment period and a reasonable time thereafter—at least until the youngest is in school.

During the school years, and until the children leave home, a widow has Social Security for the children and herself, which can be supplemented by employment. During the widow's gap, the only source of money will be her employment income. At retirement only a small Social Security benefit may be available. All these periods require some funds, but they can be partly planned for or adjusted to if the widow is not completely helpless. The only absolute necessity is to provide money for the family's readjustment period of one to five or more years, depending on your mutual decision.

It is desirable to have mortgage funds and educational funds, but these should be guaranteed by life insurance only after the basic family-protection coverage is calculated. Premium rates for these extra insurances should be compared with basic term life insurance. If the family did not own a home, would there be need for mortgage insurance? What if the children did not wish to go to college after you and your family sacrificed your present standard of living by putting money into premiums? These funds are not absolute necessities. Statistically, the husband will live to provide money for these items.

Savings funds for retirement, emergencies, and taxation may be accumulated by methods other than purchasing life insurance. Retirement funds can be garnered by savings, contributing to pension funds, and setting up an investment program. Chapter 9 will investigate Social Security and other retirement programs. The emergency fund is really another name for the family's readjustment fund, needed in case of the husband's untimely demise. Other types of emergency may be handled through a savings or borrowing plan. Most families do not need a taxation fund until late in their life cycle, and then only if the estate is fairly large.

We have narrowed somewhat the reasons for buying life insurance only because the average family cannot afford the luxury of purchasing all that it wants to replace the economic value of its members or to provide for all possible contingencies. Once you analyze your insurance needs, decide upon an insurance program that will not leave you either underinsured or "insurance poor."

TYPES OF INSURANCE POLICIES

The multitude of names given to life-insurance policies is designed to promote the idea that each company's policies are unique. They are not! Differing terminology is strictly a marketing plan to help the salesperson sell and to make it difficult to compare benefits and costs among competing policies.

There are basically two types of life-insurance policies: those that provide protection only and those that provide protection and a savings feature, or cash value. There are infinite variations and combinations available, but we can identify most policies as term, straight life, limited-payment life, and endowment insurance. We will delve into the main features and the advantages and disadvantages of each so that you may determine which type of policy best suits your insurance requirements. A series of charts near the end of this chapter enables you to compare the costs and insurance protection offered for the basic life-insurance policies and for the more popular special types of life-insurance policies. A clear definition of your insurance goals, combined with an understanding of your needs and a comparison of costs and protection, will assist you in your selection of life insurance.

Term Insurance

A term policy is a contract to provide a specified amount, the face value, of life-insurance protection for a specified period of time. It is called *term* because the protection is for a limited term, as compared to whole-life insurance, which is in force until the policy holder dies or cancels the policy. Terms range from one to twenty years or to a specific age, such as sixty-five or seventy.

The face value of insurance remains in force at the same premium level during the term. The longer the level term, the higher the premium rate. At the end of the term, insurance protection ceases, as do the premium payments. There is no cash value or savings feature in a true term-insurance policy. If continued protection is desired, it is necessary to renew the policy for a new term at a higher premium rate. The higher premium rate occurs because the mortality rate of your age group is greater than it was five years before. You are a greater risk. This concept is called a step-rate premium: the cost is directly related to the risk during the term.

Renewable term Many term policies contain a slight extra-cost option that allows the policyholder to renew his insurance protection for extra periods of time without evidence of insurability. Regardless of the health status of the policyholder, the insurance company would have a contractual obligation to renew his life insurance for another term. Usually the company limits the number of renewals allowed and the age at which a renewal can be made in order to keep its risks within reason.

Convertible term Usually a term policy that is renewable is also convertible. This option allows a policyholder to convert his temporary term insurance to a permanent type of insurance such as whole life without having to provide evidence of his insurability. The periods of convertibility are normally limited in this option. Many term policies require that the conversion to permanent insurance be made during the first two-thirds of the term, to minimize the uninsurability risk to the insurance company. As in the case of the renewable option, there is a natural tendency for those who have health problems to convert to a permanent insurance.

If and when a policyholder converts to a permanent-type insurance, he is faced with paying the higher premiums associated with such insurance. The term contract may specify either the *attained age* or the *original age* method of conversion. The policyholder may occasionally be given a choice. Under the attained-age method, the insured at the date of conversion simply pays the premium rates for his present age group as scheduled in his new policy. Under the original-age method, the insured's premium payments will be based on what the rate would have been on the new permanent policy had he purchased it originally rather than the term policy. To get this original premium rate the policyholder must make up the difference between the term payments and the permanent insurance payments over the entire period from the date of the original contract to the date of conversion. Some companies require only the reserve that would have accrued. This lump-sum payment attempts to put the insurance company in the same position as it would have been if the customer had bought permanent insurance.

Decreasing term A modification to the step-rate-premium concept of term insurance involves the purchase of decreasing-term life insurance. The insured purchases term insurance for a relatively long term, ten to twenty years, for a level premium but with a decreasing amount of protection. He can easily budget the premium cost as a fixed expense during the term of the contract. The idea behind decreasing term is to provide the greatest amount of protection during the period of greatest need for a relatively low premium payment. As the need decreases, so does the protection. This policy is especially recommended for families with young children, large mortgages, and few assets. During this period of greatest need, while paying a relatively low premium, the family should be saving and acquiring other assets to make up for the decrease in insurance protection.

Advantages of term insurance The big advantages of term are its low cost and its flexibility. You are paying for pure protection. The premium rates are between a sixth and a third of the premium rates for straight life insurance. The lowest rates will be for group term. As an alternative you can get temporary protection that is three to six times *greater* than that provided by a permanent (cash value) policy for the same premium rate. With term insurance you get the most protection for your premium dollar. Another advantage is that your beneficiaries get the full face value of a term policy if you should die. The insurance company pays the entire face-value amount from its reserves; there are no savings to be contributed from your cash value.

Term is flexible because of the renewal and conversion features. It can be purchased as a low-cost, temporary insurance with plans to convert when the family can better afford to do so. It can be purchased for almost any length of time and can be easily combined with permanent insurance to match protection with family need. Specialized types of term policies will be discussed later in the chapter.

Disadvantages of term insurance If you do not get something for your money, you may feel that you have been cheated. With term insurance you get temporary protection but no savings. You do not have a cash surrender value nor can you borrow against the term policy, since it does not have any cash value. Your low-cost payments only provide protection; the policy pays off only if you die. If you "buy term and invest the rest," the aforementioned disadvantage will not be noticeable because you will most likely have a greater cash return through other investments than through the purchase of a permanent-type life insurance. Unfortunately, very few people have the willpower to "invest the rest."

Another major disadvantage of term is the increasing premium rates charged each term upon renewal. The mortality rate established for the age of the purchaser determines the cost of temporary insurance. Finally, you will lose your insurance coverage if you cannot afford the higher premiums upon renewal, fail to pay within a grace period, or cancel the policy in order to invest your entire premium.

Straight-Life Insurance

Straight life, sometimes known as whole life, is a permanent-type policy providing lifetime insurance coverage in return for lifetime premium payments. The premiums, which remain the same throughout the life of the policy (level-premium basis), provide the least expensive means of obtaining permanent protection. The amount of the premium depends upon the age of the insured when the contract starts. The starting premium is always higher than term insurance because of the level-premium concept and cash value feature. It remains at the same rate until the insured dies or discontinues the policy. During the early years of the contract, the straight-life premium is more than what is needed to cover the cost of protection. This excess premium becomes a policy reserve that builds up a cash value as a form of savings and also allows the level-premium concept to operate. Life-insurance companies, in the main, are state regulated. Almost all states require that the cash value be equal to the reserve by the twentieth policy year. The more competitive companies usually reach this by the twelfth year. The reserves are partially used to offset the need for higher premiums in later years, when the mortality rate for a person's age group rises above the original rate. The level-premium concept is a simple actuarial averaging device.

Advantages of straight-life insurance Many people want straight life because it is a permanent insurance with a contractually guaranteed premium rate good for the lifetime of the insured. It provides "living" benefits as well as "death" benefits because of the cash-value buildup. It may be considered a form of forced savings because few policyholders would willingly discontinue the premium payments. If they did, the savings would be eroded and eventually eliminated along with the protection.

An important advantage is the possibility of borrowing against the cash-value feature. Borrowing against cash value can be for any reason. If the amount borrowed is not paid back with interest, the proceeds of the policy are reduced accordingly. Also, the cash value of a policy can be used to make premium payments whenever the insured cannot do so or forgets to do it.

Disadvantages of straight-life insurance Higher premium rates in the early years of the family life cycle make straight-life insurance unattractive to young married couples. They cannot get as much protection for their insurance dollar because a policy reserve must be established to level out the premium payments against the increasing risk of death and because the insurance company must build a reserve to pay off against the inevitable claim for either living or dying.

A second major disadvantage relates to the long-term nature of whole-life policies, including straight life. Inflation is a historical trend and may even be a national policy. In either case it eats into long-term savings and investments so that the cash surrender value from straight-life policies will actually return a diminished dollar-value amount. The face value of any life insurance policy also suffers from the same inflation malady. The low cash-value guarantee of 3 percent is another disadvantage if the insured considers the alternative investments available. The cash value is the amount stipulated in the insurance contract as being available upon surrender (termination) of the contract. It is similar to, but not considered, interest.

An often-unrecognized disadvantage is the face-value payoff on straight-life insurance upon the death of the insured. Straight life actually turns out to be a decreasing-term insurance with an increasing cash value to maintain the contractual face value of the policy. If you should die, the insurance company *pays* your beneficiaries the face value as per contract, but it *keeps* your *cash value* (savings). Another way of looking at it is that the company pays your beneficiaries your cash accumulation (cash value) and then pays the difference up to the face-value amount out of company funds. If you purchase straight-life insurance, you are a coinsurer (through the savings feature) but are probably not aware of it.

Limited-Payment Life Insurance

Limited-payment life insurance is a variation of straight life. The insured pays his premiums over a stipulated limited period and receives insurance coverage and a cash-value build-up over his lifetime. Premiums are usually paid over twenty or thirty years but may be as short as a single payment. An alternative is to pay to a specified age such as sixty-five, the normal retirement age.

The object of this system is to have lifetime (whole) insurance coverage while paying the premiums in a shorter period of time. The reserve of a limited policy accumulates more rapidly than a straight-life policy, because the level premiums must be higher for the policy to become "paid up" within the stipulated period.

Advantages of limited-payment life insurance The most apparent advantage of any limited-payment insurance is the elimination of the premium payments at completion of the contractually specified period. Persons in certain occupations, such as athletes, entertainers, and authors, who have either short careers or variable income potential, could make payments during their most productive income periods to take advantage of paid-up insurance protection and forced savings. Limited-payment insurance also has a loan value available to policyholders.

Disadvantages of limited-payment life insurance The premiums of limited-payment life insurance are even higher than straight-life premiums because the same coverage is paid for during a shorter period of time. This makes it even less desirable for the average young family in need of protection. Just as in straight-life insurance, inflation eats away at cash surrender values in a limited-payment policy. Since cash values (reserves) build up rapidly in limited-payment policies, any payoff in case of death would return even more of the deceased's money before the beneficiaries would receive any of the company's money.

Endowment Insurance

The main idea behind an endowment plan is the accumulation (saving) of funds for a specific period of time, usually ten or twenty years. At the end of the period the full face value of the policy is payable to the insured. Once the policy matures, it consists entirely of savings and interest; no insurance protection remains. If the insured dies prior to the end of the endowment period, the beneficiaries receive the full face value. To endow is to give, either to one's self or to one's beneficiaries.

In order to pay the face value at maturity, which must happen in all endowment policies, the insurance company must charge very high premium rates. The excess premiums over the cost of protection during the beginning years go into the policy reserve just as in straight and limited-payment insurance. The cash value builds up even more rapidly since the reserve must equal the face value at the end of the endowment period.

Advantages of endowment insurance Endowment policies serve as a method of forced savings to accumulate a specified sum of money in a specified period of time regardless of whether the insured lives or dies. The creation of education funds for the children and retirement funds for the insured and spouse are noteworthy reasons to use an endowment plan if the insured would not otherwise save the money.

Disadvantages of endowment insurance The disadvantages of endowment insurance are many. When the policy matures the insured is no longer insured; his beneficiaries no longer have any economic protection. The premium is extremely high in relation to the amount of protection offered and also extremely high in relation to other basic life-insurance policies. Since the goal of an endowment policy is to provide an insured savings program, the cash value increases rapidly, with the balance of savings soon surpassing the insurance protection balance. If the insured should die shortly before reaching the endowment maturity, his beneficiaries would receive the face value of the policy, but it would consist almost entirely of the insured's savings and very little of the insurance company's money.

Miscellaneous Policies

Most of the miscellaneous policies itemized in the following paragraphs are combinations of term insurance and some form of permanent life insurance. These special policies are attempts by life-insurance companies to provide special coverage for every conceivable situation.

Retirement-income policies Retirement-income policies are a form of endowment insurance that is to mature at age sixty-five or whatever other retirement age the insured specifies. The Internal Revenue Service has approved many retirement income policies for tax-sheltered Individual Retirement Accounts. Savings accumulate rapidly to provide a payback in a lump-sum upon retirement or to provide monthly installment payments through the purchase of an annuity. The cash value will generally exceed the face value by maturity in order to provide for a greater cash return. This dramatically lessens the insurance protection for the beneficiaries if the insured does not reach his retirement age; however, insurance protection is incidental to the forced savings program.

Modified life This policy is a combination of term and straight life that provides permanent insurance to young families who cannot afford the higher-cost permanent-insurance premiums. The premium rates charged are lower during the first years of the contract and then automatically increase as the term coverage converts automatically to straight life. This is a cash value policy.

Family plans There are three different types of life-insurance policies that have "family" in the name. All purport to help the family; however, basic term will provide the required protection at a lower cost. Be aware of the mechanics of each "family" policy. The *family maintenance policy* consists of a monthly income to the beneficiaries (usually $10 per $1,000 of face value) from the date of death to the contract maturity date, after which time no further payment is made. These policies are normally written for periods of five, ten, fifteen, and twenty years. If the insured survives he may continue the policy as a form of straight-life insurance. The *family income policy* differs from the family maintenance policy. It guarantees a monthly income for a specific period of time, not just for the remaining years in the contract. In both cases, the beneficiaries usually do not get the face value upon the death of the insured but must receive installment payments until the contract matures. This settlement arrangement can be changed by requesting the "commuted" value in a lump-sum.

Another policy is the *family policy*, which is not related to the aforementioned policies. It is a package protection plan involving various combinations of straight life and term on *all* members of the family. The policy usually consists of straight life on the husband in units of $5,000 and term insurance on the wife and children. The wife normally gets a half to a quarter the coverage of the husband, and there is a flat $500 to $1,000 coverage on each child. No extra premium is charged for children born after the contract is in effect. A family policy does not usually provide the greatest amount of protection where it is really needed—on the breadwinner.

Mortgage insurance A special decreasing-term insurance policy is available to a homeowner through his mortgage lender. The premium is usually based upon the age of the husband and is relatively low because the selling and administration costs are reduced by adding it to the monthly mortgage payments. The protection decreases as the mortgage principal decreases. It is advantageous if the family does not have access to other low-cost term insurance and if the family desires to own its home outright upon the death of the husband. Many life-insurance agents sell decreasing-term insurance directly to homeowners in the amount of the outstanding mortgage. A young family need not purchase this insurance immediately if it wishes to assume the economic risk of the husband's premature death, because many mortgage companies reoffer this insurance to their clients approximately once every year.

The chief disadvantages appear to be whether the family wants to be potentially "insurance poor" and possibly spend currently needed income on "extra" protection that might never be needed. Second, a finance charge may be levied directly or indirectly because the insurance premium is usually paid monthly. Third, the death benefit may force a payoff on a low interest rate mortgage that should be maintained.

Credit life insurance Another form of decreasing-term insurance is the credit life insurance payable to a creditor beneficiary.

The face value of the policy decreases as the outstanding loan decreases. The surviving family would not have to pay off any loans or credit obligations such as automobile and furniture contracts that are covered by this type of insurance. Generally this insurance is not warranted if sufficient basic life insurance is held by the family. Lenders can no longer require this insurance, even though they promote it vigorously. It is more expensive than most individual term policies.

Short-term travel life insurance The most common example of traveler's life insurance is found at the nation's airport insurance counters. Up to $300,000 of term insurance is available at the rate of $.25 per $7,500. This should be termed accident insurance. Death due to illness is not covered; only ground and air accidents involving commercial carriers during a *single* trip are covered if the result is accidental death or disability. The element of risk is statistically less great per mile traveled by air than by private automobile, but the catastrophe of an aircraft accident has created a demand for such insurance. This type insurance may be worthwhile if you have insufficient basic insurance and are a nervous traveler. The protection offered for the limited time makes it more expensive than purchasing a regular accident policy that is good for a year and covers all accidents.

Group insurance Group insurance consists of a master policy issued to a "group," of which individual members are insured by individual agreements within the terms of the master policy. Most groups consist of employees and members of unions or fraternal and professional associations.

Most group policies are term-insurance policies issued on the lives of employees of a single company. Often group life insurance is a "fringe benefit" available in varying amounts to all employees—union and nonunion, management and nonmanagement. It may be contributory or noncontributory, meaning that the employer and the employee each pay part of the premium or that the entire premium is absorbed by the employer. Medical examinations are usually not required because risk to the insurance company is spread over a great number of people. Medical questionnaires are occasionally used when individuals enroll late and/or the group is under ten in size.

Premiums are relatively low for both the employer and the employee because administrative costs are kept to a minimum, and because the employer usually collects the premium through payroll deduction if the plan is contributory. Well over one-third of all life-insurance coverage is under a group policy of some sort. Even though there is no cash value under most plans, group term insurance provides the greatest possible protection for the least premium. If you should quit the group, almost all contributory and noncontributory policies are convertible to permanent individual insurance at current premium rates. Generally you must convert to these higher-cost plans within thirty days of leaving the group.

Young people can often get as good a deal with individual term insurance as with group because the group rate is based on the average of all the ages in the group. Group premium rates are very often less than $4.00 per $1,000 per year, so it is still worthwhile discovering what groups you belong to.

DECISIONS IN PURCHASING LIFE INSURANCE

A number of major decisions must be made in the process of purchasing, cancelling, or renewing life-insurance policies. Among them are: For what reasons am I purchasing insurance? How much insurance should be carried? On whom? When should it be purchased? For how long a period? What is the net cost?

How Much Life Insurance Should a Family Have?

To determine the face value of life insurance that your family should have, it would be wise to consider carefully the reasons why *your family* desires life-insurance protection. We have discussed many reasons already; now you and your family must determine the face value needed for your situation. If you are purchasing insurance as a memorial to yourself or to impress yourself, you might be wise not to buy any! You will be remembered far longer (and bitterly) if you fail to provide insurance than if you provide an amount that takes good care of your family! Both husband and wife should share in deciding how much insurance to carry. After all, the wife is the likely beneficiary. Both of you, and the rest of the family as well, must give up something for the present to pay the premiums to cover a possible future happening. Your decision will probably be a compromise between what you would like and what you can afford.

Many companies recommend that at least 5 percent of family income be invested in life insurance, or that the total face value of your life insurance should equal four times your annual income. These are ridiculous statements designed to promote the sale of ordinary life insurance with a cash surrender value. The exact amount of insurance coverage needed for your family depends upon the number of your dependents, their ages, your outstanding debts, your family's standard of living, and the benefits available from Social Security, group life insurance, and any company pension plan. As mentioned earlier, you can attempt to cover every need, but the premiums would be prohibitive. The *minimum* amount of insurance necessary to cover the financial hardships caused by the death of a family breadwinner is the amount of money needed to pay the expenses for the family readjustment period of one to five years.

This amount will not provide a very big cushion for a young family, but if the family purchases extra term insurance during the periods of its greatest financial vulnerability, it can successfully insure itself. Once children begin school, a wife can seek employment. She may also remarry within a few years. These factors should be considered when you are trying to determine the amount of insurance needed to protect the family.

In most families there is no doubt that the husband's life should be insured. Until adequate insurance (more than the minimum) protects the breadwinner, it is a waste of needed premium money to insure the wife and children. Once adequate insurance covers the husband, the family might place some insurance on the wife if her death would create severe financial hardship for the family. The main reasons for insuring a wife are last expenses, potential child-care expenses, and the loss of a wife's income.

When and For How Long Should You Carry Life Insurance?

When to purchase life insurance is subject to much disagreement. Life-insurance companies generally recommend that you purchase it as early as possible, since the younger you are, the lower the premium rate. Moreover, early purchase preserves your insurability. An example of this is the so-called jumping juvenile policy taken out on young children. This policy allows each $1,000 face value to increase to $5,000 at the age of twenty-one. It costs more than a standard straight-life policy, but it provides a cash value that can be borrowed against, surrendered, or optioned to $5,000 of straight life or limited payment life to age sixty-five at a relatively low premium and without a physical examination.

While it is generally true that premium rates increase as you grow older, there is a period between the ages of eighteen and twenty-five when they generally remain the same with most companies. This means that you do not save any more on annual premiums by purchasing at age eighteen than by purchasing at age twenty-five. The earlier you purchase, the longer you pay. If you do not have any children, and if your wife is capable of self-support, there is little reason, other than insurability or a forced-savings program, to purchase before age twenty-five. The premium rate chart shown in table 6–2 indicates a rate of $3.50 per thousand for ages eighteen to twenty-five. If you purchased term insurance at age twenty in the amount of $25,000, you would pay $87.50 annually. Over the six-year period, age twenty through age twenty-five, you would pay $525.00 without having anything to show for it. Figure 6–1, in the first part of the chapter, illustrates the mortality tables used by life-insurance companies to determine deaths per thousand. They form the basis upon which premium rates are set. Note that 1.15 deaths per thousand actually occurred during the period 1959–61 in the twenty-year-old group. The rate increased to 1.26 per thousand in the twenty-five-year-old group. Putting the mortality table and the premiums together, we find that you would pay $525 for protection against the mortality rate of 7.45 per thousand over this six-year period. A ten-year renewable term would cost $875.00 from age twenty through age twenty-nine, using the same chart.

You must ask yourself if you wish term protection when it is not really needed. Do you wish to spend $525 without receiving any tangible return? This same concept can be carried to more mature ages. Why buy protection if it is not needed? If you want forced savings and reasonable protection, you should purchase straight-life insurance. With table 6–3 you can determine your premium rates and cash value in ten years, twenty years, and at age sixty-five. If at age twenty you purchase a $25,000 straight-life policy, it would cost you $9.71 per thousand with a waiver-of-premium clause. The annual charge would be $242.75, with $2,427.50 of premium payments over a ten-year period. The cash value in ten years, at age thirty, would be $1,480.75. The net cost to you would be the premium payments less the cash value, which in this case is $946.75 for the ten-year period. With both term and straight-life insurance you would pay close to $90 per year for protection during your twenties. If you held the straight-life policy for a longer period, the cash value would increase at a faster rate through compounding. Later in this chapter we will look at the cost of life insurance. Now it looks like you could save $90 a year by saving money in some manner other than life insurance, although your savings would not be forced, and you would not be insured for $25,000. However, if you do not need the protection, why buy it? The purchase of unneeded life insurance at an early age is similar to purchasing a sale item that you do not need! The odds of dying between ages twenty and thirty, based on the 1959–61 United States death experience as shown in figure 6–1, would be the sum of

Table 6–2 Typical annual premium rates for five-year term life

Age Last Birthday		$25,000–$49,999			$50,000–$99,999			$100,000 and Over			Waiver of Prem. per $1,000	ADB
M	*F*	*Annual Rate per $1,000*	*Annual $25,000*	*Annual $40,000*	*Annual Rate per $1,000*	*Annual $50,000*	*Annual $75,000*	*Annual Rate per $1,000*	*Annual $100,000*	*Annual $150,000*	*Female Rate* $1\frac{1}{2}$ × Male	per $1,000
20	23	$3.50	$87.50	$140.00	$3.22	$161.00	$241.50	$3.12	$312.00	$468.00	.13	.95
21	24	3.50	87.50	140.00	3.24	162.00	243.00	3.14	314.00	471.00	.13	.95
22	25	3.50	87.50	140.00	3.25	162.50	243.75	3.15	315.00	472.50	.13	95
23	26	3.50	87.50	140.00	3.27	163.50	245.25	3.17	317.00	475.50	.14	.95
24	27	3.50	87.50	140.00	3.28	164.00	246.00	3.18	318.00	477.00	.14	.95
25	28	3.50	87.50	140.00	3.30	165.00	247.50	3.20	320.00	480.00	.14	.95
26	29	3.51	87.75	140.40	3.32	166.00	249.00	3.22	322.00	483.00	.14	.95
27	30	3.56	89.00	142.40	3.34	167.00	250.50	3.24	324.00	486.00	.15	.95
28	31	3.61	90.25	144.40	3.36	168.00	252.00	3.26	326.00	489.00	.15	.95
29	32	3.68	92.00	147.20	3.38	169.00	253.50	3.28	328.00	492.00	.16	95
30	33	3.75	93.75	150.00	3.40	170.00	255.00	3.30	330.00	495.00	.16	.95
31	34	3.84	96.00	153.60	3.44	172.00	258.00	3.34	334.00	501.00	.17	.95
32	35	3.92	98.00	156.80	3.52	176.00	264.00	3.42	342.00	513.00	.17	.95
33	36	4.07	101.75	162.80	3.67	183.50	275.25	3.57	357.00	535.50	.18	.95
34	37	4.21	105.25	168.40	3.95	197.50	296.25	3.85	385.00	577.50	.18	.95
35	38	4.39	109.75	175.60	4.15	207.50	311.25	4.05	405.00	607.50	.19	.95
36	39	4.59	114.75	183.60	4.34	217.00	325.50	4.24	424.00	636.00	.19	.95
37	40	4.82	120.50	192.80	4.55	227.50	341.25	4.45	445.00	667.50	.20	.95
38	41	5.08	127.00	203.20	4.77	238.50	357.75	4.67	467.00	700.50	.21	.95
39	42	5.36	134.00	214.40	5.04	252.00	378.00	4.94	494.00	741.00	.21	.95
40	43	5.69	142.25	227.60	5.35	267.50	401.25	5.25	525.00	787.50	.22	.95
41	44	6.07	151.75	242.80	5.71	285.50	428.25	5.61	561.00	841.50	.23	.95
42	45	6.48	162.00	259.20	6.11	305.50	458.25	6.01	601.00	901.50	.24	.95
43	46	6.93	173.25	277.20	6.56	328.00	492.00	6.46	646.00	969.00	.25	.95
44	47	7.44	186.00	297.60	7.05	352.50	528.75	6.95	695.00	1042.50	.28	.95

Table 6–3 Typical annual premiums and guaranteed values for permanent life per $1,000

Age Last Birthday		10th Year Values			20th Year Values			At Age 65 Values			Annual Premiums per $1,000 (For $5,000–$9,999, add $1.00 per $1,000 to rate shown for $10,000–$24,999)			Accidental Death Benefit	Waiver of Premium (Female Rate $1\frac{1}{2}$ × male)	Average Annual Cost/Credit per $1,000 at Age 65		
M	*F*	*Paid Up*	*Cash Value*	*Extended Protect. to Age*	*Paid Up*	*Cash Value*	*Extended Protect. to Age*	*Paid Up*	*Cash Value*	*Extended Protect. to Age*	*$10,000-24,999*	*$25,000-49,999*	*$50,000 And Over*			*$10,000-24,999*	*$25,000-49,999*	*$50,000 And Over*
20	23	$220	$59.23	48	$488	$175.67	62	$850	$559.01	79	$10.15	$9.50	$8.50	.95	.21	$2.27 cr	$2.92 cr	$3.92 cr
21	24	225	62.50	49	494	182.93	63	845	555.74	79	10.48	9.83	8.83	.95	.22	2.15 cr	2.80 cr	3.80 cr
22	25	231	65.93	50	500	190.37	63	840	552.31	79	10.81	10.16	9.16	.95	.23	2.03 cr	2.68 cr	3.68 cr
23	26	236	69.52	50	505	197.98	64	835	548.71	79	11.17	10.52	9.52	.95	.25	1.89 cr	2.54 cr	3.54 cr
24	27	242	73.26	51	511	205.76	64	829	544.93	79	11.53	10.88	9.88	.95	.26	1.76 cr	2.41 cr	3.41 cr
25	28	247	77.13	52	517	213.71	65	823	540.95	79	11.92	11.27	10.27	.95	.28	1.60 cr	2.25 cr	3.25 cr
26	29	253	81.15	52	522	221.81	65	816	536.76	79	12.33	11.68	10.68	.95	.30	1.44 cr	2.08 cr	3.08 cr
27	30	258	85.29	53	527	230.06	65	810	532.35	78	12.76	12.11	11.11	.95	.32	1.25 cr	1.90 cr	2.90 cr
28	31	263	89.55	54	532	238.45	66	803	527.71	78	13.22	12.57	11.57	.95	.35	1.04 cr	1.69 cr	2.69 cr
29	32	268	93.91	54	537	246.97	66	795	522.81	78	13.69	13.04	12.04	.95	.37	.83 cr	1.48 cr	2.48 cr
30	33	273	98.35	55	542	255.61	67	787	517.65	78	14.20	13.55	12.55	.95	.38	.59 cr	1.24 cr	2.24 cr
31	34	278	102.86	55	547	264.36	67	779	512.21	78	14.73	14.08	13.08	.95	.40	.34 cr	.99 cr	1.99 cr
32	35	282	107.44	56	551	273.21	68	770	506.46	78	15.30	14.65	13.65	.95	.42	.05 cr	.70 cr	1.70 cr
33	36	286	112.09	56	555	282.16	68	761	500.39	77	15.89	15.24	14.24	.95	.45	.25	.40 cr	1.40 cr
34	37	290	116.81	57	560	291.18	69	751	493.96	77	16.51	15.86	14.86	.95	.47	.58	.07 cr	1.07 cr
35	38	294	121.60	58	564	300.30	69	741	487.18	77	17.15	16.50	15.50	.95	.50	.91	.26	.74 cr
36	39	298	126.46	58	568	309.49	69	730	480.00	77	17.81	17.16	16.16	.95	.53	1.26	.61	.39 cr
37	40	301	131.39	59	571	318.75	70	719	472.43	76	18.51	17.86	16.86	.96	.57	1.64	.99	.01 cr
38	41	305	136.41	59	575	328.09	70	706	464.43	76	19.23	18.58	17.58	.96	.60	2.03	1.38	.38
39	42	308	141.52	60	579	337.49	71	694	455.99	76	19.99	19.34	18.34	.97	.65	2.45	1.80	.80
40	43	311	146.72	60	583	346.95	71	680	447.09	76	20.80	20.15	19.15	.98	.70	2.92	2.27	1.27
41	44	315	152.02	61	586	356.47	72	666	437.71	75	21.68	21.03	20.03	.99	.75	3.44	2.79	1.79
42	45	318	157.40	62	590	366.01	72	651	427.81	75	22.60	21.95	20.95	1.00	.81	4.00	3.35	2.35
43	46	321	162.86	62	593	375.57	73	635	417.36	75	23.58	22.93	21.93	1.02	.87	4.61	3.96	2.96
44	47	324	168.41	63	597	385.12	74	618	406.31	74	24.64	23.99	22.99	1.04	.95	5.29	4.64	3.64
45	48	327	174.03	63	600	394.63	74	600	394.63	74	25.75	25.10	24.10	1.07	1.03	6.02	5.37	4.37
46	49	330	179.72	64	604	404.06	75	582	382.28	74	26.93	26.28	25.28	1.09	1.12	6.81	6.16	5.16
47	50	333	185.47	65	607	413.36	75	562	369.20	73	28.17	27.52	26.52	1.12	1.23	7.66	7.01	6.01
48	51	336	191.27	65	610	422.47	76	541	355.37	73	29.48	28.83	27.83	1.15	1.36	8.58	7.93	6.93
49	52	338	197.11	66	612	431.33	77	518	340.72	73	30.85	30.20	29.20	1.18	1.50	9.56	8.91	7.91

the deaths for each age, or 12.62 deaths per thousand over the ten-year span—pretty good odds to go without protection! Hopefully, the money not spent on insurance would be saved or invested, in which case there probably would be enough funds to cover your burial expenses, in case the odds went against you. This is self-insurance, but it could leave your beneficiaries without adequate cash.

If you need insurance, get it. If there is any doubt about your future insurability, purchase insurance at your first opportunity. If your job or your personal habits place an intangible but nonetheless greater risk of death upon you, you should not put off the purchase of life insurance. You may become uninsurable because of deteriorating health, serious injuries, or hazards associated with a job or hobby. Family histories often reveal illness and death tendencies that could affect descendants. Consider your personal traits and habits in the decision to purchase life insurance. Heavy drinkers, long-distance automobile commuters, people with quick tempers, and those who are considered careless are more likely to be exposed to danger and possible death than the average person. Insurance companies attempt to screen out as many potential risks as possible by use of questionnaires, applications, and physical examinations. False information may negate the claims of your beneficiaries, so answer all questions truthfully, even though there is an incontestable clause effective after two years.

Let us assume you purchase life insurance when you first need it. How long should you keep it in force? As long as you need the protection. Why keep it longer? It is wasted premium money if the policy is term insurance. If it is straight life, the savings feature is probably paramount in importance. Can you and your family continue to save in other ways if you should discontinue most of your coverage? If you can, investigate other institutions offering higher rates of return. Transfer your cash surrender value to another institution, and continue your plan of saving and investing. If you cannot save, keep your straight-life policy in force, and you will have a lump-sum of money (or alternate option) available when retirement comes.

The actual length of time when protection is needed for survivors will differ greatly among families; fifteen to twenty years may be all the protection that is needed. Situations that have a dramatic effect on the family's finances should be considered: When is the last child no longer dependent? Does the wife have skills to make her financially independent? Are there sufficient assets to cover a readjustment period? Is there a planned savings or investment program? Is a pension or Social Security program available for retirement? And above all, what is the present and potential health of the insured? The point to remember is that protection is not usually needed for a "lifetime," but you will need savings for that "lifetime," especially the retirement part.

Costs and Rewards of Life Insurance

Premium costs of life insurance are affected by many things. If you are easily overwhelmed by rate quotations from one insurance agent, just imagine what comparison shopping with three or four agents will do to you! Companies do charge different rates for the same coverage.

Companies charging higher rates may do so for various reasons: they may have higher overhead costs, higher marketing costs, less success in their investments, more deaths among their insured clients, or maybe they wish more profit. Competition and volume also affect the premium rates charged by the company.

The decisions of the insured will also affect the rate. These decisions can maximize your protection and savings goals and minimize your cost:

1. The type of policy
2. Your age upon application and acceptance
3. Added benefits available through extra-cost riders
4. Face value of policy
5. Frequency of premium payment

Frequent payments such as semiannual, quarterly, or monthly payments will add up to more than the annual rate because of handling costs and potential loss of investment income to the insurance company. Tables 6–2 and 6–3 are rate charts that illustrate the complexities of life insurance premium rating. Costs will vary from policy to policy and from company to company. Figure 6–3 portrays the industry average cost per $1,000 of coverage on various types of policies, while figure 6–4 indicates the amount of different types of insurance that an annual premium of $100 will purchase.

Cash Value

A permanent life insurance policy provides for savings in the form of cash value (often

What Various Policies Cost
Approximate Annual Premiums for $10,000 of Insurance*

Type of Policy	**Age At Which Policy is Issued**					
	20	21	22	23	24	25
Five Year Term (Renewable and Convertible)	$ 52.80	$ 52.90	$ 53.00	$ 53.10	$ 53.20	$ 53.50
Straight Life	115.00	118.70	122.20	125.70	129.50	133.50
Life Paid-Up-at-65	126.60	130.50	134.60	139.00	143.70	148.60
20-Payment Life	198.40	202.60	206.90	211.30	215.90	220.70
Retirement Income at 65	176.90	184.10	191.70	199.70	208.20	217.20
20-Year Endowment	425.50	425.70	426.00	426.20	426.60	426.90

*Rates shown are approximate premium rates for $10,000 of life insurance protection for men. Rates of "participating" policies would be higher, but the cost would be lowered by annual dividends. "Nonparticipating" policy premium rates would be somewhat lower than those shown and no dividends would be paid. Measured in cost per $1,000 of insurance, policies under $10,000 would be a little higher in premium rates and lower for $25,000 and over. Policies for women are at lower rates in recognition of their lower mortality rates.

Figure 6–3 Policy Costs on $10,000 Policy. *(Institute of Life Insurance, New York)*

What $100 a Year Will Buy (Approximate Amounts)

(Male Age 22)

	Amount of Insurance $100 a Year Will Buy*	Cash Value at Age 65 Per $100 Annual Premium
1. Term (5 year renewable & convertible)	$19,000	None
2. Straight Life	8,000	$4,660
3. Life-Paid-Up-at-65	7,200	4,986
4. Family Income (20 years)	7,700	4,504
5. Endowment at 65	5,700	5,700
6. 20-Payment Life	4,400	3,036
7. Retirement Income at 65	4,000	6,250
8. 20-Year Endowment	2,100	Matured (age 42)

*Most companies have minimum policy limits of $1,000, $3,000 or $5,000.

Figure 6–4 Approximate Protection Available for $100 per Year. *(Institute of Life Insurance, New York)*

known as the cash surrender value). It is the reason why so many people are either convinced or decide to purchase straight-life insurance. The cash value increases with the length of time the policy is held. During the first few years no savings accumulate in straight life and very little in endowments. Once the costs of selling the policy and the protection costs are covered by premium input, the cash value begins to accumulate rapidly through compounding. Cash-value life-insurance policies make an ideal savings medium for people who are not savers by nature.

When the policyholder terminates a straight-life policy he has a number of options regarding the cash surrender value. He may:

1. Take the cash value and cancel the policy.
2. Purchase a paid-up permanent policy with a reduced face value.
3. Purchase extended-term insurance at the original face value for a specific number of years.
4. Purchase an annuity.

The first three options are popularly known in the life-insurance trade as *non-forfeiture provisions.* Table 6–4 illustrates the value of these options at various ages when straight life is purchased at age twenty.

Dividends

The amount of your premium will depend upon whether your insurance company pays dividends. Companies that pay dividends

Table 6–4 Approximate non-forfeiture value per $10,000 of insurance for a straight-life insurance policy issued at age twenty

Permiums Paid to Age	Cash Value	Paid-up Insurance	Extended Term Insurance
25	$ 210	$ 810	6 yrs.–219 days
30	760	2,520	20 yrs.–106 days
40	2,180	5,370	24 yrs.–349 days
65	5,910	8,570	15 yrs.–348 days

Source: Institute of Life Insurance, New York

sell participating (par) policies, while those that do not pay dividends provide non-participating (nonpar) policies. The real difference lies in the marketing philosophy of the insurance companies. The nonpar companies tend to set lower premium rates than par companies. Nonpar companies determine the premium rates and then gain or lose on their claims and investment experience during the year. They keep any added profits and absorb any unexpected losses.

Par companies lure policyholders with the idea of providing dividends: policyholders get to participate in profits, or so it seems! The companies set their premium rates high enough to cover possible losses from unusually high claims. If contingencies do not develop, the extra money goes back to the policyholders. This returned money is erroneously called dividends; it is really a return of a premium overcharge.

In the final analysis, the net cost is about the same in par and nonpar policies. Usually, par companies sell the lowest-cost permanent policies, while nonpar companies sell the lowest-cost term policies. You choose a company whose plan appeals to you: do you wish a lower premium, or would you like to have added savings through dividends? However, the longer the term the better the par policy because the dividend can be used to lower the premium payments. Mutual insurance companies, owned by policyholders, sell only participating policies, while stock insurance companies, owned by stockholders, may sell either type or both.

Dividends are a return of excess premium, an overcharge. The amount of the dividend is not guaranteed by the company and will differ from year to year, based upon the year's experience with claims, costs, and investments. You can expect some dividend each year because the company has priced the premium high enough to exceed expected claims and expenses and earnings on reserves. The lure and reward of dividends lies in their potential uses:

1. Take the cash.
2. Reduce next year's premium.
3. Allow the dividends to accumulate at interest.
4. Buy additional paid-up insurance.
5. Buy term insurance to cover cash value.

Net Cost

Once you have determined the minimum amount of life-insurance coverage your family needs, you must choose the type of policy—cash-value or term. Figures 6–3 and

6–4 portray the cost of various life-insurance policies from two different points of view—the premium cost per $1,000 on a $10,000 policy and how much insurance an annual premium of $100 will buy. You can look at the cost of insurance in terms of getting the most protection for the least amount of premium or using a given annual amount of money to provide protection and possible savings. Perhaps several policies will provide the exact coverage you need when you need it. Several policies would provide the flexibility to add or drop coverage as needed, but they are likely to cost more because of fixed policy charges and higher rates and lower dividends on smaller policies. Insurance agents claim that net cost is the only basis for comparing accurately the cost among participating and nonparticipating policies and for comparing term insurance with straight-life insurance. This is true if the comparison is complete. Unfortunately there is a tendency to make biased comparisons in order to prove a point or sell cash value insurance.

The concept of net cost involves figuring the true cost of insurance as that amount left after subtracting dividends and cash value from the premiums paid over a given period of time. Actually financial experts disagree whether cash value should be subtracted from total premiums to find the net cost. Purists contend that only dividends (return of excess premiums) should be considered in determining net cost. Since many insurance agents attempt to sell straight-life insurance on a net-cost basis of subtracting cash value from premiums, in order to impress you with the "true" cost, we will also subtract cash value.

The premium rate charts in figures 6–3 and 6–4 can be used to illustrate net cost. A $25,000 straight-life policy can be purchased for an annual premium of $11.27 per thousand at age twenty-five. For one year the premiums would be $281.75, and in twenty years the premiums paid in would amount to $5,635. This would be your cost. You have accumulated a cash value of $213.71 per thousand over the twenty-year period as the savings feature of your straight-life policy. A $25,000 policy would accumulate a cash value of $5,342.75. Subtract the cash value from the paid-in premiums over the period to get your net cost: $292.25. Although you pay $281.75 each year, your *net cost* would amount to $14.61 a year. Straight-life insurance appears to be a very good deal when explained in this manner; by this calculation it is practically free.

Now let us see how much term costs. Figure 6–3 indicates that the annual premium rate for five-year term insurance is $3.50 per thousand at age twenty-five, $3.75 at age thirty, $4.39 at age thirty-five, and $5.69 at age forty. The premium cost for $25,000 of term would be as follows:

age 25–29	$ 87.50 per yr. × 5 yrs. =	$437.50
age 30–34	93.75 per yr. × 5 yrs. =	468.75
age 35–39	109.75 per yr. × 5 yrs. =	548.75
age 40–44	142.25 per yr. × 5 yrs. =	711.25
	Total cost =	$2,166.25

The *average* cost per year appears to be $108.31 for term insurance. This is less than $281.75, the annual premium for straight life, but much more than the *net cost* per year for straight life of only $14.61.

At this point we have only half the comparison. Our unequal comparison is between $25,000 term insurance (pure protection) at a "cost" of $108.31 per year and $25,000 straight life (protection *and* savings) at a "cost" of $14.61 per year. If you subtract savings from the premium costs of straight-life insurance, then the same principle should be applied to term life. Term life costs an average of $108.31 per year, while straight life costs $281.75 per year. This difference of $173.44 can be invested or saved each year over the twenty-year period to show a lower net cost for term. This concept is often called *buy term and invest the rest.*

Buy Term and Invest the Rest

For a true net cost comparison between term and straight-life insurance, it is necessary to use the same annual premium deposit to determine what rewards you would reap from the two alternatives. In the above example the *average difference* between term and straight annual premiums was $173.44. For a more accurate comparison, however, we should calculate the annual difference each year because of the step concept of term premium rates:

Each yr. age 25–29	$ 87.50 cost,	$194.25 difference
Each yr. age 30–34	93.75 cost,	188.00 difference
Each yr. age 35–39	109.75 cost,	172.00 difference
Each yr. age 40–44	142.25 cost,	139.50 difference

During the first five years you have $194.25 to invest each year; during the second five years you have $188.00 each year; and so on. You could invest this money in stocks, bonds, mutual funds, or any of the various forms of savings. Assuming a relatively conservative 6 percent per year compounded annually, the total money saved would amount to $7,000.91 (using compound interest tables to two places). By subtracting the savings/investment gain from the out-of-pocket cost for the term insurance over the twenty-year period, we will end up with a *net credit* of $4,834.66 rather than a *net cost* of $292.25, as with straight-life insurance.

The point of this comparison of "net cost" between straight-life and term insurance is to recognize that you must make an informed investment and protection comparison. In the case of straight life you buy protection and savings with one life-insurance contract; therefore, when comparing net cost with that of term insurance you should compare a similar dollar investment in life-insurance protection and in a savings program of your own. In straight-life insurance the plan is automatic; you do not need to administer your savings; the life-insurance company does it for you. This convenience costs you a lower return on the savings element of your straight-life insurance compared to other investments over short-term periods of up to twenty-five years. Beyond this period of time, straight life will return a greater cash yield if you desire continued protection and pay the excessive term premiums required at mature ages. (Higher premiums mean less money available to save or invest.)

In term insurance, however, you may not realize the big savings that you plan if you are unable or unwilling to invest or save the difference in premium between straight life and term. You must have willpower and dedication to your savings goal. Only you can decide which plan has the lowest net cost based on your ability to save.

Different Policies for Different Reasons

Since your family's life-insurance protection needs will change over the years, you may wish to add or drop coverage from time to time. The purchase of several term policies will give you more protection flexibility than will one large policy. Premium costs are usually a few cents less per thousand dollars of face value on large policies, but the flexibility is probably worth the difference. Any term policy should have renewable and convertible clauses in case your savings willpower turns out to be nonexistent.

By purchasing only the protection that you actually need, you should save on premium costs. Your basic coverage should be purchased through commercial insurance companies. Extra term policies can be added as your family grows and your needs for insurance increase. You might be able to buy such in the form of group insurance through your employer at costs even lower than those shown in the rate charts. If your family becomes smaller, and your insurance needs decrease, you can decrease your coverage.

Personal habits change, as do family relationships. Both have an effect on the amount of coverage desired or needed. We do not usually think that a person needs extra life insurance because he or she may be reckless, careless, or an excessive social drinker, but these are good reasons to have additional life-insurance policies. At the other extreme, approximately 40 percent of all marriages end in divorce. Term insurance seems to be the most appropriate solution to many situations.

POLICY FEATURES

An insurance policy is a contract between you and the insurance company. It contains the terms that have been agreed to and lists the benefits and protection that you are purchasing for your premium. It has been said that what the big print gives, the small print takes away, so read your policy carefully. Policies have different restrictions and benefits, so when comparing policies you should be aware of the major clauses, options, and riders listed in most contracts. The following *alphabetical* list of clauses, options, and riders will help you understand the coverage provided in most policies. Keep in mind that clauses describe benefits, options offer a choice to the insured, and riders are additional benefits available at extra cost.

Automatic premium-loan provision The insurance company automatically agrees to grant a loan by borrowing from the cash value to pay any overdue premium.

Beneficiary option The person named in the policy to receive the insurance money upon the death of the insured is called the beneficiary. The designation of a beneficiary is of prime importance. The insured should have the right to revoke or change beneficiaries. A contingent beneficiary is often designated to receive payment in the event of the death of both the insured and the primary beneficiary.

Cash value The money (savings) that a policyholder gets back upon surrendering his policy. It may be borrowed against for continuing protection.

Disability income rider This rider provides for a waiver of premium and for creation of a monthly income if the insured becomes totally and permanently disabled. This rider should be compared with income protection plans available through the various health and casualty insurances.

Dividend A return of premium in a participating insurance policy. Because it is a refund of excess premiums paid whenever the insurance company has better profits than expected, its amount is not guaranteed.

Double-indemnity rider An accidental-death-benefit clause that doubles the face value if death is caused by accident. Certain types of death are usually not covered. A clause usually requires that deaths resulting from an accident must occur within ninety days of the accident for this rider to be effective. The added premium is rather low, but this rider has the nature of a gamble rather than of true insurance.

Extended-term clause A cash-value policy will remain in force whenever premiums are not paid. The cash value is automatically used to maintain the policy at the original amount by buying term insurance until the cash value is exhausted.

Face value The sum stated on the face of the policy that is to be paid upon the death of the insured.

Grace period clause The period in which a policy will not lapse even though the premium payment has not been made. It is usually thirty-one days. This clause is extremely important in term policies, where there are no cash reserves to carry the policy until payment is made.

Incontestability clause A one-year or two-year period after which the insurance company is completely liable and cannot contest the validity of the policy. The time period is sufficient to allow the company to investigate the insured's application. Misrepresentation, concealment, and fraud generally cannot be used as defenses to disallow payment to beneficiaries.

Limitation-of-coverage clause Disallows payment of death benefits when death occurs under certain circumstances. The limitations are sometimes removed by extra premium payments. Accidental death benefits are seldom paid under these limitations even if the face-value payment is made. Some limitations or exclusions are:

1. Aviation clause—Pilots dying as a result of private aviation accidents may not be covered unless higher premiums are paid.
2. Suicide clause—Death by suicide is normally excluded for a period of two years. Only the premium is returned if death by suicide occurs during the two-year period.
3. War clause—Excludes payment for death connected with war or insurrection or sometimes any association with the military. This clause differs greatly among companies but is usually attached only to policies purchased during wartime periods.

Loan clauses Cash-value policies allow low-interest-rate (normally 6 to 8 percent) loans against the cash value. Interest is payable on loans at the premium date. The principal is subtracted from the face value if the insured should die or from the cash value if the insured lives and surrenders the policy. Loans may be paid at any time.

Misstatement-of-age clause This clause clarifies insurance company procedures if the age of the insured is misstated for any reason. If the insured's age is incorrect, the amount payable to the beneficiary will be adjusted to the amount of insurance that the premiums paid would actually purchase at his correct age. Age for insurance premium purposes is based upon the insured's *nearest* age. A 25½-year-old person would be considered 26 years old.

Nonforfeiture provisions These policy provisions protect the insured from inadvertent forfeiture of his insured status. Whenever a policyholder with a cash reserve policy cannot or does not wish to pay his premium, he can request the company to pay him cash value, purchase a reduced paid-up permanent life policy, or purchase extended-term insurance with the reserves. If the policyholder does not choose an option, the extended-term clause automatically becomes operable.

Reinstatement clause All policies set forth the conditions under which the policyholder can reinstate a lapsed policy. The usual requirements are that the policyholder must be currently insurable, pay up any delinquent premiums at 5 percent interest, and may have to pay off any loans against the policy. Companies usually set a time limit of five years for reinstatement.

Settlement options All insurance contracts outline the options available to the insured or his beneficiaries for settlement of the cash value or the face value. The cash-value settlement payable to the insured was previously noted. Face-value settlements payable to beneficiaries will be discussed later in the chapter. Settlement options allow the policy proceeds to be taken as a lump-sum or in monthly payments.

Waiver-of-premium rider For a nominal additional premium, a policyholder may protect himself against the need to pay premiums if he becomes totally and permanently disabled. Insurance companies may differ as to what constitutes disability, but courts have defined this status innumerable times. This rider is a good buy.

POLICY SETTLEMENTS AND CLAIMS

Beneficiaries

You have the right as policyholder to name the person or persons who will receive the face-value proceeds if you should die. These persons are called the beneficiaries of the policy.

A policyholder may opt for either a revocable or an irrevocable beneficiary. An irrevocable designation of beneficiary places a vested interest with the beneficiary. Changes cannot be made to the life-insurance policy without permission of an irrevocable beneficiary. In a community-property state a wife once designated as a beneficiary usually has an irrevocable status if she contests her removal. The main advantage of an irrevocable beneficiary designation is a reduction in federal taxes on estates valued at over $60,000 provided there is no incidence of the insured's ownership. This will be discussed in chapter 10. The advantage of a revocable designation is that changing circumstances might cause a policyholder to change his beneficiary. Without a beneficiary, the face value of a life-insurance policy is paid to the estate, where the money is not only subject to inheritance and estate taxes, but also comes into probate. As a general asset of the estate the face value could be subject to creditors' claims.

The *primary beneficiary* is designated to receive the face-value proceeds upon the death of the policyholder. Since the primary beneficiary is often the wife of the policyholder, it is wise to designate a *contingent beneficiary,* a person or persons who will receive payment if the primary beneficiary predeceases or dies simultaneously with the policyholder. Children are often contingent beneficiaries. A trustee should be designated contingent beneficiary to safeguard the money on behalf of minor children. More than one level of contingent beneficiary can be named.

Settlement Options

The welfare of your beneficiaries is most likely the main reason that you purchase life insurance. You must decide carefully how they are to receive the proceeds. You should consider whether the beneficiary is capable of safeguarding, saving, and investing a large sum of money. If your wife administers the family budget, have her take a lump-sum; if she has not had any practical money-handling experience, one of the partial-payment options may be in her best interest. A mutual decision should be made in this respect.

If the policyholder, or the beneficiary upon the death of the policyholder, has not chosen a specific settlement option, the policy proceeds will be paid in one lump-sum. The settlement options other than the lump-sum payment are designed to provide an income to the beneficiary. In some policies options may be arranged to allow the beneficiary the right to change the settlement form after a period of time has elapsed. A portion of the proceeds may be assigned to a specific option, with the balance paid in a lump-sum. The options available are spelled out in the policy. The following are the usual options:

Deposit option The insurance company holds the proceeds on deposit and pays monthly interest to the beneficiary at the rate stated in the policy, usually $2\frac{1}{2}$ to 3 percent. Actually the company may pay higher interest rates, but it guarantees the stated rate. Normally the length of time that the money is to remain on deposit is designated by the policyholder when he elects to use this option. This option safeguards the principal amount but does not provide the beneficiary sufficient living income on small policies.

Installment option for fixed period The life-insurance company makes equal monthly installments for a predetermined number of years. At the end of the period the principal has been exhausted. This option normally provides sufficient income during the payment period but does not safeguard the principal. Once the policyholder dies the beneficiary cannot change the time period to suit his or her needs. The installment schedule applicable to this option is usually tabulated in the policy.

Installment option for fixed amount This option is similar to the fixed-period option, except the payment amount is fixed. The predetermined monthly amount is paid until the principal is exhausted. Since the amount of income is of greater importance than the period of time over which it is paid, this option is of greater use to the beneficiary than the fixed-period option. Often the beneficiary is given the right to change the amount by the terms of the policy. The installment schedule applicable to this option is also tabulated in the policy.

Life-income option The company pays benefits according to a schedule of payments in the policy during the life of the beneficiary. A number of different payment plans and guarantees are available. Payments by the insurance company may be guaranteed for a given period even if the primary beneficiary dies. This option is an annuity, which will be discussed in more detail in chapter 9. The age and sex of the beneficiary determine the amount of the monthly payment in a life-income settlement option. The younger the beneficiary, the smaller the monthly payment amount.

Claims Procedure

Companies seldom use the incontestable clause or the misstatement-of-age clause to dishonor a beneficiary claim, but they scrutinize accidental-death claims very closely. Some companies attempt not to pay double indemnity if death arose from certain illegal acts such as drunk driving, possession or use of drugs, and so on. These cases are sure to go to court. Proof of death of the policyholder and the circumstances surrounding his demise must be given to the life-insurance company so that it may determine whether the policy covered the death circumstances. Beneficiaries are usually required to provide identity proof when they contact the life-insurance company. Each insurance company has different claims procedures. If the insured chose a reputable company and reputable insurance agent, the beneficiary will have few problems in making a claim.

SHOPPING FOR LIFE INSURANCE

When you shop for life insurance (and other insurance, too) a big problem is how to get accurate information in order to compare one policy with another. Hopefully the information in this chapter will make life insurance more understandable, but you must still contact an insurance company and its agent. You should contact two companies and two agents for a proper comparison. Contacting more than this will probably lead to confusion.

Insurance Company Selection

Not all insurance companies are alike. Although they are subject to the regulations of government agencies in states where they are licensed to operate and must set aside sufficient policy reserves to meet policy obligations as they become due, they differ in the type of business organization, the amount and type of representation, the quality of service, the types of policies offered, the specific clauses and riders in their policies, and the pricing of their policies.

You should attempt to find out as much as possible about several competing life-insurance companies. There are over eighteen hundred life-insurance companies in the United States, many of them newly formed companies doing business on a regional basis. They may be mutual companies or stock companies. The ratio of assets to insurance in force is a good indication of the financial strength of a company.

There are only 154 mutual companies, but these are generally the older and larger companies. They control over two-thirds of the assets of all U.S. life-insurance companies and account for slightly over half the life insurance in force. These companies usually issue participating policies. In theory, all policyholders are partners in the insurance venture. In practice, policyholders are generally not liable for any losses that the mutual company may incur. They receive a dividend only if the mutual company has a profitable operation.

The balance of companies, approximately nine-tenths of all insurance companies, are stock companies. Almost all new companies fall into this category. The policyholder usually must pay a set premium for the risk involved. He does not participate as a mutual owner, so his premium rates are lower, but he receives no dividends, which will equal out costs after about five years.

Representation Agents for insurance companies may be employees or independent contractors; each company sets its own policy about this important question. We discuss how to choose an agent in the next section of this chapter.

You may receive a direct-mail solicitation or read an advertisement in which a life-insurance company in a distant state offers what appears to be good protection at reasonable rates. You should be careful; these insurance companies may not be authorized to sell through agents in your state. This could create claims and service problems. It would be wiser to deal through local agents or at least with an insurance company based in your state. You can check the legality of any insurance company in your state by contacting the state insurance bureau or corporations department.

Quality of service The service rendered by an insurance company is most likely only as good as that of its representatives. Check with friends and neighbors to find out whether the company pays claims promptly, without undue red tape. Check to see if the company provides understandable brochures describing the benefits and coverage for your particular policy. Has the state insurance commissioner received many complaints?

Types of policies, clauses, and riders Does the company offer the type of policy that best suits your needs? If it does not, shop elsewhere for life insurance. Companies tend to sell you what they have, rather than what you need.

Pricing of policies The net cost of a policy is useful only if you compare two or more policies that are the same, or at least substantially similar. Buying a policy based on price alone is foolish unless it contains the benefits that best suit your needs. As noted previously, the net cost after dividends in participating policies should be similar to the premium charges of nonparticipating policies. About all you can do is to compare net cost of two or three competing policies.

You may wish to visit your local library and check the following references, which provide information about policy provisions and/or premium costs: *Best's Life Reports, The Spectator Insurance Year Book, Flitcraft,* and *Little Gem Life Chart.* Consumer magazines occasionally publish comparison charts of insurance premium costs. Once you decide which type of policy you desire, you might check the *Guide to Periodical Literature* for possible cost-comparison reports in consumer periodicals.

Recently Congress has begun investigations into sales practices and pricing in the life-insurance industry, scrutinizing large and small companies alike to find out why insurance costs may vary as much as 300 percent from one company to another. Investigators are also studying what amount of premium charge goes for savings and for protection. The result of this probe may be a federal truth-in-insurance law similar to the truth-in-lending law.

Furthermore, the Pennsylvania Insurance Department, in Harrisburg, Pennsylvania, has published a brochure comparing the costs of straight-life insurance offered by companies doing business in that state. The brochure, *A Shopper's Guide to Life Insurance,* can be ordered by mail.

The Life-Insurance Agent

In purchasing life insurance, you will deal with an agent. Keep in mind that you will probably deal with this person for a number of years as your insurance needs change. He or she should be someone that you can trust and be comfortable with. You can get acquainted with these insurance representatives when comparison shopping for life insurance. During the sales interview ask questions and get their recommendations. How well they explain the costs and benefits of their companies' policies will probably be a good criterion for choosing an agent. Remember, the agent represents the life insurance company, not you.

Agents may be salaried employees of an insurance company, or they may be self-employed and represent one or more insurance companies on a straight commission basis. All life-insurance agents receive a commission for their sales efforts, which usually amounts to 50 percent or more of the first year's premium payment and a small percentage paid as a residual each year the policyholder renews his insurance.

Because life insurance is such a complex subject, it is to your advantage to choose an agent who is knowledgeable. Find an agent who has completed some training beyond that offered by the life-insurance companies. An agent new to the business may be sincere, but does he really have the experience to serve you properly? If he has the initials *C.L.U.* after his name, he has been designated a Chartered Life Underwriter by the American College of Life Underwriters. This means that he has completed a college-level series of courses and has successfully passed a comprehensive examination.

In the final analysis you must choose the savings and insurance goals for you and your family. An agent, no matter how sincere, will have a tendency to sell you a policy offered by his company, whether or not it suits your particular needs. A self-employed agent may be more open-minded, but he too will have a natural tendency to sell you insurance rather than to provide for your needs. You decide.

Vocabulary and Concepts

Beneficiary	Group insurance
Cash value	Insurance
Coinsurance	Limited-payment life policy
Convertible-term policy	Mortality tables
Decreasing-term policy	Participating policies
	Risk
Dividends	Self-insurance
Endowment policy	Settlement options
Face value	Straight-life policy
Family plans	Term insurance

Questions for Discussion

1. How do people view life insurance? Discuss the more divergent views. Give a definition.
2. Why do people purchase life insurance?
3. When and for how long should a person carry life insurance?
4. What is meant by the term *insurance poor*? What is the underlying consideration in the cost of life insurance?
5. "The best reasons are the biggest economic risks." Explain.
6. Explain the features of the four basic types of life insurance.
7. Explain the difference among the three "family" insurance plans available.
8. The use of multiple policies and the concept of net costs can provide for flexibility in insurance planning. Explain.
9. Which types of clauses in a life-insurance policy are generally beneficial to the insured or his heirs? Which are not?
10. Why is it necessary to consider the difference between an independent insurance agent and an employee agent?

Projects

1. Compare the features and rates of straight-life and term insurance policies of a large and a small life-insurance company.
2. Calculate the value of your life. How much money would be required by your beneficiaries to *replace* your earnings or service value? If you have not begun your career, anticipate your future earnings or service value.
3. Determine what it will cost to purchase a straight-life and a term policy at your age rate. How much will it cost per year if you wait five years? Calculate the savings (if any) over a twenty-year time space. Use figures 6–3 and 6–4.
4. Buy term and invest the rest. Price a $30,000-face-value straight-life policy and a similar term policy. Invest the balance of your term premium in a savings account or a mutual fund for a period of twenty years. What are the results as compared with placing all your premium payments in straight-life insurance?
5. Compare the various settlement options available in the policies that you have

previously investigated. Which will provide the greatest security for your beneficiaries? Which will provide the greatest possible return?

Case Problem

At the present time, Art Able has a group term life-insurance policy of $20,000 provided by his company. Neither Art nor Barbara feel this is sufficient to provide for Barbara and their daughter. Why?

Advise them regarding how much more insurance should be purchased and for what period of time. Explain which type of policy will best provide protection for the family and yet accumulate a fund for their daughter to attend college. What alternatives and compromises are available to the Ables? Clarify and support any assumptions that you make. Assume that any premium payments must come from their budget as depicted in table 1–3. Calculate all costs and savings in your proposal. Present the Ables with your analysis of their insurance needs. Art is 26, Barabara is 23, and their daughter is 2 years old.

7 health insurance

Everyone needs some type of health-care service. It is questions of availability, cost, personal preference, and actual emergency that determine how much medical and health service to seek and when to seek it. Health care can take the form of a sensible personal program involving a good diet, plenty of exercise, and occasional visits to the doctor. It can also involve taking various medicines and drugs of doubtful value, or it can be an after-the-fact payment for emergency medical treatment. Whatever amount of health care you choose or have to procure for you and your family, it will cost money.

Because health is such a precious and expensive commodity, it must be included in your budget. The problem becomes one of how much and where money should be allocated for health expenses. To solve this dilemma properly you must answer certain questions: Can you budget for accident or illness? Do you prefer to pay a certain amount each month for medical security? Do you have a sufficient emergency fund to pay for most short-term illnesses? Could you and your family withstand the costs of a long-term illness? Could you and your family survive the loss of income for one or more months? Is the health of your family members unpredictable and therefore a risk that requires insurance? Should you purchase some sort of health insurance? Can you afford to purchase health insurance? Should the government provide for all medical services?

You will have ready-made answers for these questions, but what you really need is an economically sound plan to cover the high costs of everyday and emergency health care. You may budget for the routine health expenditures and the minor unexpected expenditures, but you will need some help to protect you and your family from the major expenses caused by extended illness and disability.

Frequency of medical care Health care is something that can be budgeted on an annual basis if your family is average. The average person visits a doctor 4.5 times and a dentist 1.6 times a year, according to the results of the latest national health survey conducted by the federal government. This information implies that an average family of four will visit the doctor 18 times during a year, or that some member of your family is going to the doctor every three weeks and to the dentist every two months.

Why Medical Expenses Are High

The high cost of medical service and the inability to predict when it will be needed are perhaps the most important reasons to consider the purchase of health insurance.

Medical costs, already high, are continuing to rise at a faster rate than that of other consumer expenditures.

Doctors, dentists, and other medical technicians have raised their fees for a number of reasons, only one of which is the high cost of their training. Their costs are higher especially if they are in private practice. Consumers forget that office, salary, equipment, and operational expenses must be met by the income produced by the doctor. To a degree the doctor has four alternatives, available at a time of rising costs: he may increase his fees, accept more appointments by increasing his workday, squeeze more patients into the present workday, or absorb the increased costs of running his business. Needless to say, doctors are reluctant to take the fourth alternative.

Consumers contribute to the rising costs of medical services because they demand more and better service. General practitioners have become preliminary analysts who often refer patients to specialists. There is an unfortunate rise in the number of malpractice suits, which in turn causes the doctor to check and double-check his diagnoses. Annual premiums for malpractice insurance in California run from $5,000 to $40,000, depending upon the medical specialty. Many doctors now seek advice from other doctors and require added tests, all of which add to your costs. Doctors are also quick to point out that many patients fail to keep appointments, thereby causing a loss of revenue that must be compensated for in some manner.

Hospital and equipment costs have risen at a faster rate than any other individual medical expense. New medical techniques developed as a result of using better facilities and equipment have lowered the average stay in the hospital to eight days, which helps offset these higher costs.

Individually prescribed drugs may also contribute to the higher costs of medical care. There are at least three reasons why drug costs are high: (1) Branded nonprescribed consumer remedies vary greatly in cost and advertised claims, causing great confusion; (2) individual prescriptions must often be compounded by pharmacists, which is usually expensive; and (3) the writing of more common prescriptions with brand names rather than generic names is usually more expensive.

TRENDS IN HEALTH CARE

A great number of changes are taking place in medical practice and in health insurance to meet the needs of the American public. Many of the changes result from an attempt to keep medical costs as low as possible for the average person and yet offer a complete health package.

Group Medical Practice

It has become almost standard in many areas of the country to form a group medical practice. The gathering of equipment and staff in one facility is an obvious saving. Consultation and treatment can become more specialized by utilizing the professional skills of a group of physicians. Some general practitioners and specialists become partners in clinics and similar medical facilities. More are becoming associates in nonprofit corporations. Most partnerships have been operated on a fee-for-service basis, but some are beginning to provide prepaid medical care. The nonprofit type of medical organization has generally been formed to provide prepaid medical care on a group basis. Individuals can also secure this prepaid medical care if the facilities are not too crowded by group members.

Prepayment for Health Care

A basic insurance principle is to shift some of the economic risk of a happening from the client to the insurer for a premium. The happening in this case is accident or illness. The prepayment concept takes some of the uncertainty out of your budget. This concept has now evolved into the next step: preventative medicine as practiced by a clinic or medical organization. Health-maintenance organizations, or HMOs, provide a complete health-care service by offering multiphasic physical examinations, general medical service with early detection and treatment of illnesses, and complete emergency services, all for a reasonable fee usually paid on a quarterly basis.

Broader Health Insurance

Prepaid health-care plans and commercial insurance-company indemnity plans now provide better benefits by covering a wider variety of health-care services, generally increasing the dollar amount that will be paid and lengthening the term for paying benefits. Our inflationary economy and consumer demand for greater protection against the high cost of medical care have had much to do with the trend toward providing broader and more comprehensive health insurance than was available in the past. Many labor unions and other employee groups receive health insurance as a fringe benefit. Wider coverage under a union contract often means a choice of several different health-insurance programs or extra benefits added to an existing contract. These plans often go beyond the basic coverages for hospital and surgical expenses by offering major medical insurance and general medical coverage to form a comprehensive insurance package that covers most remaining medical expenses. Many expenses formerly excluded in earlier health-insurance plans are now available at very little extra cost. These include such specialized treatments as dental care, care for mental illness, prescription drugs, pregnancy, optometry, and nursing-home care.

The dollar amounts for particular medical procedures have been increased to reflect the inflationary effects of rising costs. Insurance companies attempt to control their benefit-payment schedules by keying them to the average fees charged by physicians in a given area. They often use a *relative value schedule,* which evaluates each medical procedure in terms of its worth and complexity as compared to other medical procedures. If a particular doctor's fee or hospital charge appears to be too high, the insurance company may have it reviewed by a peer group to see if it is justified before paying the claim.

Health-insurance companies have increased the number of covered hospital days to insure longer-term illnesses. This provides better coverage against a true risk, that of exhausting your savings, which you would have to use if your hospital stay was of a long duration. Since the average stay in hospitals has declined, this change has allocated more protection to the unfortunate person whose illness exceeds the average. Disability (loss of income) insurance benefits have been lengthened for the same reasons.

Government Health Programs

The United States lags behind all other major nations in terms of a national health-care program. A person risks his health and his economic well-being when he has an accident or illness in the United States. Medical costs differ throughout the country; a person may or may not have health insurance; he may or may not have adequate coverage if he has insurance; he may or may not have the money to pay the medical bills; he may or may not be eligible to receive government monetary or medical aid; and he may or may not get medical treatment when needed. Nonprofit and commercial health-insurance companies partially fill the health-care needs of many people, but they do not and cannot provide complete medical coverage to their own insured policyholders, much less provide for those who are ineligible or who cannot afford their premiums.

Many people who are ineligible for private insurance policies are covered through Medicare if they meet the Social Security Administration requirements. Fortunately, persons with few assets and little income may be eligible for state and local medical care, assuming they meet certain legal requirements. It is the middle-income person who is really caught in a bind. There are few government medical services available to him.

A number of legislators have considered plans for a national health service that would be patterned after the Canadian, British, or Swedish plan. The medical profession as a whole is opposed to such a plan, calling it "socialized medicine." Although the term sounds sinister, we should remember that Medicare and Medicaid are already in operation and are the first steps toward adequate medical care on a nationwide basis. A national plan will probably be funded and administered through the Social Security system in association with commercial health insurers.

The trends in health care point to more group practices and to greater use of "preventive medicine." The spiraling costs associated with health care contribute to this trend. Government health care for all citizens may be the ultimate result of these trends. In the meantime a consumer should probably purchase health insurance if he is to protect himself adequately. The balance of the chapter explores the different types of health insurance available and the organizations offering various forms of health and accident insurance.

TYPES OF HEALTH INSURANCE

Health insurance may be broadly or narrowly defined. We will use a broad definition to include any form of insurance that is called *medical, health,* or *sickness and accident* insurance. Health insurance may be classified (1) by the nature of the medical expense covered, (2) by whether it is a service plan or an indemnity plan, or (3) by the type of organization offering the insurance. All three classifications have some economic importance to the consumer.

The type of medical-expense coverage in a policy is most important. The typical basic health-insurance plan provides for hospital expenses, surgical expenses, and specified general medical expenses. Major medical expenses are usually covered by a basic health plan through a package plan known as *comprehensive medical insurance.* In addition to basic health-insurance coverage, you may purchase dental insurance and disability-income insurance. These coverages are available on a group basis or an individual basis. Specialized policies are available through commercial insurance companies for persons desiring only a partial basic health-insurance plan. We will now look at the types of expenses covered.

Basic Health-Insurance Plan

This type of health insurance seems to be the most popular with the American public.

It fills the greatest need for coverage of an economic risk.

Hospital expense insurance This specialized coverage was the first of the "pure" medical insurances. Because there is a greater unknown expense factor in hospital costs than in other medical expenses, it is more of a risk. For example, a person can be confined for hospital treatment for long periods of time at rapidly increasing costs, while other medical expenses such as the doctor's fee may remain relatively stable.

Hospital-expense insurance covers daily room and board in a semiprivate, three-bed, or four-bed room, depending upon the benefits of the particular policy. Also covered is the cost of such items as anesthesia, operating rooms, emergency rooms, and recovery rooms. Most policies have added coverage to include such items as in-hospital drugs, X rays, laboratory fees, and ambulance service. Benefit periods for the maximum number of hospital days covered per illness or per year run from 30 days to 365 days. The daily dollar amount in a policy may not be sufficient to pay for all the costs that are "covered" under your policy.

Surgical-expense insurance Doctor's fees for surgical procedures may run quite high. Surgical-expense insurance acts as a prepayment for these fees. A schedule of fees is often published with the policy. The schedule covers each surgical or cutting procedure on a relative-value basis. A fee is set for certain basic operations, and the other operations are based on their relative complexity to the basic surgery procedures. The amounts scheduled for each cutting procedure may be the same or lower than the average rate for the surgical procedure. The cost of the policy usually has a direct relationship to the schedule of fees payable under the policy. Table 7–1 is an example of a schedule in an indemnity policy.

Table 7–1 Typical surgical allowance schedule

Abdomen	Allowance
Appendectomy	$385
Gall bladder removed	$610
Complete gastrectomy	$1,050
Removal of hernia by single incision	$385
Bowel resection, partial	$875
Bowel resection, total	$1,050

Source: Health Insurance Institute, New York.

Some policies operate on a service basis whereby the fee charged by the doctor is fully paid by the insurance company if it falls within reasonable ranges. Excessive fees are denied if the surgeon is unable to substantiate his claim for a higher-than-usual fee in a particular geographic area. Sometimes fee disagreements between the insurers and the doctor are arbitrated by an impartial panel of physicians.

Regular medical-care insurance Physicals, examinations, office visits, consultations, immunizations, and other routine doctor visits can usually be budgeted. Any policy covering these items cannot really be considered insurance but is a form of prepaying the inevitable. Any policy that insures this type of medical coverage must by its very nature cover expected costs. This type of coverage in a comprehensive policy is more expensive than other medical-expense insurance for the dollar value received. The inevitability of claims against this type of coverage based upon an average number of doctor visits requires high premiums.

Regular medical-expense insurance is usually available in group insurance plans or when combined with other medical expense insurance to form a basic package. Quite often limits apply to the type of doctor visits covered and the number of visits annually, or the policy may have a deductible feature.

Major Medical Expense Insurance

Major medical expense insurance is designed to cover prolonged illnesses and expensive accidents. It takes over after the benefits from hospitals and surgical expense policies leave off or where they do not apply. Sometimes major medical is known as catastrophe insurance because an unusually prolonged or expensive medical problem becomes a financial catastrophe. Major medical expense insurance, however, does not cover all possible expenses. Limitation on coverage is always spelled out in the policy.

To provide for catastrophe coverage the maximum benefits payable are usually rather high, ranging from $25,000 to $1,000,000. To keep the premium rates reasonable a *deductible* provision and a *coinsurance* requirement are featured in most major medical insurance policies.

The *deductible* clause establishes the dollar amount that the policyholder must pay before the major medical benefits are paid. The deductible sums vary with different policies. A deductible of $100 may apply to any policy that has the basic health-insurance coverage, and a $500 deductible may apply to major medical coverage that is not part of a basic plan. The greater the deductible, the lower the premium rates because the deductible effectively eliminates small claims.

Table 7–2 How comprehensive medical insurance works

	Total Charges	Covered by Base Plan*	Covered by Major Medical
Hospital room and board: 50 days at $82 per day	$4,100	$2,250	$1,850
Other hospital charges: Operating theater, X rays, blood tests, medicines, etc.	5,000	800	4,200
Registered nurses: $40 per day for 20 days	800	—	800
Physicians' fees	1,500	1,000	500
Totals:	$11,400	$4,050	$7,350
Less deductible of $100			–100
Balance subject to coinsurance			$7,250
Less coinsurance at 20%			–1,450
Amount paid by major medical			$5,800

SUMMARY	
Paid by base plan*	$4,050
Paid by major medical	5,800
Paid by patient	1,550
Total:	$11,400

* Hospital room and board and general medical expense. (Base room and board coverage = $45 per day.)

Source: Health Insurance Institute, New York.

Table 7–3 How major medical insurance works

Medical Expenses		
Physician's fee		$750
Specialists' fees		1,200
Private nurses		
10 days at $40 per day		400
45 days at $20 per day		900
Cardiographs, X rays, and laboratory examinations		800
Medicines		300
	Total	$4,350
Less deductible of $500		500
Balance subject to coinsurance		$3,850
Less coinsurance at 20%		770
Amount paid by major medical		$3,080
SUMMARY		
Paid by patient	$1,270	
Paid by major medical	3,080	
Total	$4,350	

Source: Health Insurance Institute, New York.

A *coinsurance* requirement becomes operative whenever major medical benefits are determined. The insurance company usually pays 80 percent of major medical benefits on covered expenses, and the policyholder pays the balance of 20 percent. The purpose of this plan is to keep medical costs under some control by requiring the policyholder to become a coinsurer. Many plans have a favorable "stop loss" provision that cancels further payments by the insured after he contributes a specific sum, such as $1,000. The insurance company then pays 100 percent of all further bills.

Tables 7–2 and 7–3 show how major medical insurance is integrated with basic medical coverage and how it can be used independently. Note that only the first table involves hospitalization.

Dental Insurance

This type of insurance has grown rapidly. It is usually available only to groups, through prepaid dental-service organizations chartered by the states in which they operate. Insurance companies do sell some individual coverage.

Dental insurance usually pays between 70 percent and 100 percent of the "usual, customary, and reasonable" fees in a given geographical area. Participating dentists are required to submit their schedule of fees for review by the dental-service organization. There is usually a calendar-year limitation on the dollar amount of dentistry allowed. Various plans offer limitations ranging from $500 to $1,000.

Dental insurance is really a prepaid service. It may be called an insurance, but the economic risk can effectively be delayed by not visiting a dentist. For this reason, dental insurance plans are designed to encourage preventive rather than corrective dentistry.

Table 7–4 is a schedule of covered dental services for the California Dental Service. This plan has an established table of allowances, which is used to determine payments to dentists. Patients pay any charges above the allowable fee. To create an incentive for regular dental care, the plan pays 70 percent of the fee the first year, 80 percent the second year, 90 percent the third year, and 100 percent thereafter. The insured must visit a dentist at least once a year and have all prescribed treatment rendered. Should he fail to do this, the percentage that CDS pays will revert to 70 percent. Prosthodontic services (bridges and dentures) are paid at a 50 percent rate at all times. Orthodontia is not covered. Some policies provide 50 percent coverage, with a $500 limitation.

Disability-Income Insurance

Other names for disability-income insurance are loss-of-income insurance or salary-continuance insurance. Similar to life insurance, its purpose is to provide an in-

Table 7–4 Typical dental insurance benefits

Out-of-state Services

Services rendered by an out-of-state dentist will be paid on the basis of the dentist's usual fee not to exceed the California customary range. However, non-CDS members within California are paid according to an established table of allowances.

Covered Dental Services
Basic Services (CDS pays 70%, 80%, 90%, 100%)

Diagnostic	—Procedures to determine required dental treatment.
Preventive	—Prophylaxis (teeth cleaning) once every six months; fluoride treatment; space maintainers.
Oral surgery	—Extractions, including preoperative and postoperative care.
General anesthesia	—When given for a covered oral surgery procedure performed by a dentist.
Restorative	—Simple fillings, and crown and gold fillings when simple fillings are not sufficient.
Endodontic	—Treatment of the tooth pulp.
Periodontic	—Treatment of gums and bones supporting teeth.

Prosthodontic Services (CDS pays 50% at all times)*

Procedures for construction of bridges, partial, or complete dentures. Prosthodontic appliances will be provided only once in any five-year period.
Payment for partial or full dentures is limited to 50 percent of the customary charge for a standard prosthodontic appliance regardless of special circumstances.

Dental Accident Benefits

Provides diagnosis and dental treatment rendered within 180 days following the date of an accident. There is a separate $1,000 maximum for covered services rendered as a result of an accident.

* An optional prosthodontic benefit is available at an extra cost. This would increase the copayment level for prosthodontic services to a constant 70%. Rates for this option are available upon request.

Source: California Dental Service, San Francisco.

come when the family breadwinner is unable to do so. The insured receives benefits whenever he is unable to work because of sickness or accident. If you are off the job and have no pay because of illness, lack of income just compounds the economic catastrophe. Disabled persons and their families often suffer greater economic hardships than the family of a deceased worker, because the disabled person continues to be an economic burden. His overhead continues after his income ceases.

Disability coverage Disability may be defined in a narrow or a broad sense in your policy. The broader the coverage or definition, the greater the premium. Under a narrow definition of disability, income loss payments will be made only if the insured cannot do any gainful work. Under a broad definition, income loss payments would be made if you are unable to perform any or all functions of your particular occupation. The broader interpretation provides for partial disability.

Benefits Insured salary-continuation plans normally pay you between 50 percent and 66-$\frac{2}{3}$ percent of your regular wages for a specified period of time. This dollar limitation is necessary to be certain that people would not take undue advantage of the plan. Full-pay benefits would create a tendency to be absent from work more often.

Most purchasers of disability-income insurance benefit from the low rates of group plans. Individual policies tend to be much more expensive. The actual cost is dependent upon the length of waiting period before it is effective, the weekly amount of benefits, the maximum benefit period, specified limitations, and the age and occupation of the insured. The length of the waiting period is most important, because the longer the period before benefits are paid, the lower the premium. Look at the waiting period as a form of time deductible. If you have sick-leave benefits from your employer, savings, or other disability payments, you can afford to wait until those benefits run out.

Since most disabilities are of short duration, it is better for you to have higher dollar coverage for a shorter period of time than to receive smaller benefit payments over an extended period. Most contracts pay you for two years if you are unable to perform your previous job—the broad interpretation—and then stop if you can perform other gainful employment. Liberal policies usually continue payments until age sixty-five if the disability is caused by sickness. Accidental injury may provide lifetime benefits. Short-term policies are those whose term is less than three years.

Special clauses A number of clauses relate specifically to disability insurance. These we will discuss now. Clauses that are common to most types of health insurance will be covered later in the chapter.

A *presumptive disability clause* defines the conditions under which the insured is deemed disabled. For example, total and permanent disability is presumed in many policies after unrecoverable loss of use of any two limbs or the loss of hearing, speech, or sight, even though some gainful employment may be carried out. Most hazards that lead to disability are covered. Common exceptions are noted in these clauses, such as war, military service, and pregnancy.

Proration clauses set the conditions for premium or benefit changes in your disability insurance. A change to a more hazardous occupation will increase premium rates. These clauses also contain provisions to prorate for misstatement of age and nonpayment of duplicate benefits covered by Social Security and workmen's compensation.

Miscellaneous Medical Insurance

Supplementary hospital insurance Many insurance companies offer supplementary hospital insurance. You use the money in any manner you see fit. It can be used to pay medical expenses, or it can help defray living expenses. The only requirement is that the insured be hospitalized in order to receive the benefits, which range from $10 to $50 per day. The various plans available have limitations that fix when payments begin and end. Premium rates would be affected by the limitations. This insurance constitutes disability-income insurance only if you are confined to a hospital.

A refinement of supplementary hospitalization insurance is the hospital and recuperation insurance plan, which pays a specific cash benefit while the patient is in the hospital and a lesser amount during a recuperation period. The recuperation period may be the same or a different length from the hospital period.

Accident insurance Accident insurance may be sold separately or as a rider on a life-insurance policy. It normally pays a lump-sum in case of death or dismemberment caused by any type of accident. It may also provide for monthly income benefits. The benefits vary from policy to policy but are characterized by a lump-sum payment that can be used for any purpose. Most policies contain a schedule of benefits paid whenever the policyholder becomes disabled by the loss of one or more vital limbs or organs. Some policies pay double indemnity—double payment of benefits—for particular types of accidents.

Automobile medical insurance This insurance is sold with your automobile casualty insurance. In case of an auto accident, it covers the medical expenses of you and anyone riding in your car to the limits of the policy. It also covers you as a pedestrian. Some policies provide primary coverage, your full cost regardless of other medical coverage, while some pay only medical expenses not covered by other medical insurance.

You may not need this insurance if you have a good basic health-insurance plan for you and your family. Guests in your car would be covered under your bodily injury liability insurance if you were legally liable for the accident. If the other party were liable, your guests would sue him.

Government health and accident insurance Federal, state, and local governments finance health insurance and health plans. Your age, income, assets, family status, and Social Security status determine your eligibility. The more noteworthy government plans will be presented later in the chapter, when we discuss government as an insuring agency.

FEATURES OF HEALTH-INSURANCE POLICIES

Common threads run through the fabric of most health-insurance policies. A prospective policyholder should look for certain features that are common to most policies in order to compare the benefits and limitations of a policy. By asking yourself certain questions in addition to noting these features, you should be able to select a policy that suits your needs and gives you value for your insurance dollar.

Deductible Amount

Hospital, surgical, and major medical policies often contain a deductible feature. By having the insured pay a certain portion of his medical expenses before the insurance pays, the insurance companies eliminate the administration and out-of-pocket expenses of small claims and probably reduce the number of marginal claims for health services.

The amount of the deductible varies with the type of insurance and with the level of protection offered. A single insurance company may offer two or three levels of protection for hospital, surgical, and major medical insurance. A company may offer no-deductible, $100-deductible, and $250-deductible policies, charging a higher premium for the no-deductible policy, which has the greatest insurance coverage.

Hospital and surgical policy premiums on the above deductibles might run $75, $60, and $40 per quarter, respectively. In such a situation you would have to weigh your potential need for hospital and surgical services. It would cost you $140 extra per year to protect yourself from paying the deductible. You would need a hospital claim every year to make the no-deductible policy worthwhile. The insurance company knows this will not happen very often.

Check the deductible clause closely to find out whether the deduction is applicable to each illness or injury claim, to all bills for the calendar year, or to hospital expense, surgical expense, and major medical expense separately. Find out how the deductible feature operates in your policy.

Double Benefits

A number of health-insurance policies have clauses denying cash medical benefits for the same coverage from more than one source. You should ascertain that a second health-insurance policy is actually needed and that it provides supplemental coverage. It would be unwise to double your basic coverage because policy provisions usually call for *coordination of benefits,* thereby negating the advantage of having two policies. The insurance companies will share the expenses, not pay you twice.

The many people who receive free basic health coverage through their employment need only supplemental hospitalization or accident insurance as a form of major medical. A supplemental policy can have a rather high deductible to take advantage of lower premium rates. Your basic health insurance may actually cover most of the deductible amount in any supplemental policy, since the supplemental (second) insuring company's policy usually states that it will not pay the first $250 (or stated amount of dollars) on a claim. Where you get the deductible amount is of no concern to the insurance company.

Coinsurance

Major medical policies usually contain this clause, but it may also be found in the other types of health insurance. The theory is that medical costs will be kept reasonable whenever the insured must pay a percentage of the bills. Coinsurance simply means that you and the insurance company become coinsurers, i.e., you assume the risk of medical expenses according to the policy percentage statement. Insurance companies usually pay 75 percent to 80 percent, and the policyholder pays the balance. Coinsurance limits the risk to the insurance company by the percentage that the insured assumes, subject to the stop-loss clause as mentioned previously.

Loss of Coverage

Loss of coverage can occur through nonrenewability, cancellation policies of the company, and preexisting conditions or illnesses. You should be sure that your policy contains a guarantee of automatic renewability. Most policies contain this feature. The premium rates may increase as you grow older or as your family increases, but no special qualifications should be necessary to renew your insurance policy. The original application questionnaire normally provides the insurance company with information to set up exclusions for existing or chronic illnesses.

Most policies do not require a formal renewal; you simply pay your premium when it is due. Protection remains in force until you reach sixty-five or until you are eligible for Medicare, whichever is earlier. Your policy, once in effect, is not normally cancellable because of your physical condition or because of utilization of benefits. However, make sure that it is noncancellable. A group policy normally provides continuous coverage as long as you are a member of the group. Check to see if your group policy is convertible to an individual policy without further qualifications if you should resign from the group.

Limitations and Exclusions

Every policy contains a maximum limiting the amount of benefits that the insurance company will pay. The maximum may be in dollar amounts or time limits, such as one hundred days of hospitalization. The maximum is similar to the face-value feature of a life-insurance policy. In placing a maximum on a policy, the insurance company effectively limits its risk against a stated premium payment. Your premium payments usually increase as the maximum benefits increase.

Most types of health insurance limit coverage of certain illnesses. Benefits sometimes do not begin at the inception of an illness or the beginning of hospitalization. Pregnancy expenses are usually not claimable until a policy has been in force for approximately ten months. Maternity benefits are often rather small or nonexistent on the theory that such a happening is either planned or that the expenses can be budgeted over a period of time. Medical treatment resulting from war or suicide attempts is often excluded, as is reimbursement for any medical treatment received in a government hospital. You must exercise extreme care to insure that any health-insurance policy you purchase provides the type of insurance benefits you desire, when you desire them.

Questioning the Policy Features

The purchase of health insurance involves deciding what coverage you want, compared to what is available and what you can afford. Consider the following points when comparing health-insurance policies:

1. How many days hospitalization are allowed?
2. Are the daily benefits realistic in comparison to actual charges in your area?
3. What related expenses are covered by your hospitalization policy?
4. Are surgical schedules realistic in comparison to actual charges in your area?
5. Is there a deductible, and does it apply for each illness or accident, or does it apply to an annual amount?
6. Does major medical insurance provide sufficient coverage to make up the deficiencies of the hospitalization and surgical expense policies?
7. What percentage of medical bills does the major medical policy pay?
8. Are there waiting periods before benefits begin for certain medical occurrences?
9. Do disability-income benefits provide a reasonable amount for a reasonable length of time?
10. What is whole and partial disability?
11. Are double benefits allowed? If so, how?

HEALTH-INSURANCE ORGANIZATIONS

There are about two thousand medical-insurance agencies in the United States. These include profit and nonprofit, private and government organizations such as Blue Cross–Blue Shield organizations, insurance companies, medical and dental society–sponsored plans, independent health-insurance plans, and federal, state, and local government health-insurance plans. A brief description of each major plan is offered below to help you decide which type of organization is most appealing to you.

Blue Cross–Blue Shield Organizations

These organizations are nonprofit and operate in cooperation with the hospitals and doctors in a given area. Blue Cross was originally designed to provide hospital-expense insurance, while Blue Shield was designed to pay surgical expenses. At present there are eighty Blue Cross plans and seventy-four Blue Shield plans in the United States. These plans operate either independently as competitors or in cooperation as one organization administered by the local Blue Cross plan. A nationwide communications network allows subscribers to be serviced anywhere in the country.

The "Blues" provide service benefits for hospital, surgical, and general medical protection rather than fixed dollar benefits (indemnity benefits). The exact benefits and premium rates will differ by locale, since each plan is locally operated. Benefits and the corresponding rates are reviewed regularly to provide semiprivate to four-bed-ward hospital rooms for subscribers and yet keep premium costs within reason. There are both individual and group plans. The former have somewhat more limited benefits and higher premium rates than the group plans.

Commercial Insurance Companies

Commercial insurance companies provide more health insurance than does any other type of private organization. These companies provide the widest range of coverage available, from hospital and surgical coverage to disability income and miscellaneous medical insurances, from group coverage to individual policies. Their plans tend to be the *scheduled-indemnity* type, where the insured receives specific cash benefits for medical services as specifically described in the policy. These companies do not contract with hospitals and physicians for service, nor do they attempt to control the quality of medical services rendered to their policyholders.

Most companies provide a choice of benefits and limitations based upon different premium rates. Typically the choice is between a high-benefit and a low-benefit policy. Premium rates tend to be competitive with Blue Cross–Blue Shield and independent plans. Commercial insurance benefits tend to be somewhat lower per premium dollar than those offered by the nonprofit service medical insurance organizations. Table 7–5 compares representative commercial insurance-company benefits and premiums for three typical households. These examples use a combination of individual insurance and group coverage to get the most for the premium dollar and provide wanted coverage.

Plans Sponsored by Medical and Dental Societies

Some state and local medical and dental societies have created plans in conjunction with, or in place of, Blue Cross–Blue Shield plans. They form and administer nonprofit corporations that offer prepaid medical services. Physicians and dentists have the option of participating. Since these plans are operated by their societies, and because they have a voice in the selling of benefits and premiums, most physicians and dentists tend to provide their services for the suggested fees. If their fees are greater than what the plan allows, the patient pays the difference. Two examples of the practitioner-sponsored plans are the California Dentists Service and the Wisconsin Physicians Service.

Independent Health-Insurance Plans

Many nonprofit group practices are not affiliated with insurance companies, Blue Cross–Blue Shield organizations, or local or state society-sponsored plans. Some are organized by labor unions, business enterprises, physicians, and interested people. They represent a rapidly expanding concept in medical care and health insurance. These

Table 7–5 Typical commercial medical-insurance programs based upon size of household

Single Person	Approximate Annual Cost
GROUP COVERAGE	
1. Comprehensive major medical plan: $50 deductible; 20% coinsurance; $15,000 maximum benefits	$70.00
INDIVIDUAL INSURANCE	
2. Disability income protection: Monthly indemnity of $300 for five years for accident and sickness; 30-day waiting period	110.00
Total:	$180.00

Husband and Wife	Approximate Annual Cost
GROUP COVERAGE	
1. Major medical expense insurance: $10,000 maximum benefit with $500 deductible and 20% coinsurance	$130.00
2. Disability income protection: Weekly indemnity of $100 for five years for accident and two years for sickness with waiting periods of one day and eight days, respectively; up to $1,000 for accidental death and dismemberment	75.00
INDIVIDUAL INSURANCE	
3. Hospital and surgical expense insurance: Each accident or illness up to one year, at $50 per day for room and board, with maximum allowances of $500 for extra charges and surgical benefits up to $400; additional maternity allowance, also in-hospital physician's expense $7 renewable	335.00
Total:	$540.00

Family of Five	Approximate Annual Cost
GROUP COVERAGE	
1. Hospital and surgical-in-hospital medical-expense insurance: Full semiprivate or intensive care for 120 days, with 100% for miscellaneous hospital services; surgical schedule $500; in-hospital medical $600; maternity same as any other disability, plus a $300 obstetrical fee for normal delivery Major medical expense insurance: $50,000 maximum benefit with $100 deductible and 20% coinsurance for each disability in benefit year	$220.00
INDIVIDUAL INSURANCE	
2. Disability income protection: Monthly indemnity of $600 to age 65 for sickness and lifetime for accident; 30-day waiting period, noncancellable	250.00
Total:	$470.00

Source: Health Insurance Institute, New York.

practices operate as health-maintenance organizations to prevent illness by providing medical services on a prepaid basis. Generally they provide their own salaried or partnership physicians, salaried paramedical technicians, and even hospitals. Costs are controlled by encouraging their subscribers to have regular medical checkups and to see their physicians as often as necessary. Subscribers are expected to use the plans' staff and facilities. They will not be reimbursed for using nonaffiliated services unless they are away from the geographic area of their particular plan. Group-practice health-insurance plans range from small organizations involving one or two physicians in a small town to large corporate complexes in metropolitan areas. Three widely known plans are the Health Insurance Plan of Greater New York (HIP), the Community Health Association of Detroit, and the Kaiser Foundation Health Plan of California, Colorado, Hawaii, Ohio, and Oregon. Figure 7–1 illustrates the services provided by the Kaiser Foundation Health Plan for individual members in Northern

Services are provided only by Doctors and Hospitals associated with the Plan.
The Service Area is the geographical area within a radius of 30 miles of any Kaiser/Permanente medical facility, within the following Counties: Alameda, Amador, Contra Costa, El Dorado, Marin, Napa, Placer, Sacramento, San Francisco, San Mateo, Santa Clara, Solano, Sonoma, Sutter, Yolo and Yuba.

PRESCRIBED MEDICAL AND HOSPITAL SERVICES		**"A" Coverage *For Subscriber and Dependents***
In the Doctor's Office Diagnosis and Treatment • Specialists' Care • Continued Care for Chronic Conditions • No Limit on Number of Visits • Physical Checkups • Pediatric Checkups for Children • Eye Examinations for Glasses	Doctor's Office Visits — Paramedical Services	$2 Charge per Visit
	Laboratory Tests, X-ray, X-ray Therapy	$2 Charge for Each Test, X-ray or Treatment
	Costs and Dressings	No Charge
	Physical Therapy	$2 Charge for Each Treatment Procedure
	Injections, Allergy Tests	Provided at Reasonable Rates
Prescribed Care In the Hospital There is No Limit to the Number of Covered Hospital Days	Physicians' and Surgeons' Services, Including Operations	No Charge
	Room and Board • General Nursing • Use of Operating Room	
	Intensive Care • Cardiac Care	
	Drugs and Medicines • Injections • Special Duty Nursing	
	Dressings • Casts • Blood Transfusions, if Blood is Replaced	
	Laboratory Tests • X-ray • X-ray Therapy	$2 Charge for Each Test, X-ray or Treatment
	Physical Therapy	$2 Charge for Each Treatment Procedure
Prescribed Care In a Skilled Nursing Facility	100 Days Coverage Per Benefit Period[1] Including: Room and Board • General Nursing • Physicians' Services • Drugs • Medicines • Injections • Supplies • Appliances and Equipment Provided by the Skilled Nursing Facility	No Charge
Ambulance Service	Provided Within the Service Area if Authorized or Approved	No Charge
Maternity Care Specified Charges Cover All Hospital and Medical Services.	Full Care Starting Early in Pregnancy • All Doctor and Hospital Services for Mother and Child During Confinement • Caesarean Section[2]	$95.00 Charge if Confinement Due After 10 Months Membership; Non-member Charges if Confinement Due Before 10 Months Membership.
	Interrupted Pregnancy	After 10 Months Membership a Maximum Charge of $64.00; Non-member Charges Before 10 Months.

[1] A "benefit period" begins when you enter a hospital or skilled nursing facility. It ends when you have *not* been a patient in either a hospital or a skilled nursing facility for 60 consecutive days. The term "benefit period" is used to define a period of time, not a condition of ill health. You can have several diseases or injuries in the course of a single benefit period. This period of time is not related to the calendar year.

[2] Non-member charges apply for maternity care if mother has had a Caesarean Section prior to the time she joined the Plan.

Figure 7–1 Typical Coverage Available in an Independent Service Plan. *(Kaiser Foundation Health Plan, Inc., Northern California Region, Oakland, California)*

California. A group-membership contract would have even greater policy benefits and/or lower premiums. The latest monthly membership fees for the individual plan service offered in figure 7–1 are:

Subscriber alone	$22.36
Subscriber and one dependent	44.22
Subscriber and two or more dependents	63.05

Federal Government Health Services

The Federal Social Security Act and subsequent amendments provide for health insurance or direct medical care for the elderly and the needy. The federal government provides for health insurance through Medicare. It provides direct care through funds dispensed to state and local agencies, which actually offer the service and the facilities. The federal funding program is known as Medicaid and is administered by the Department of Health, Education and Welfare. In addition, the federal government provides direct-care facilities through the Veterans Administration, the military services, and, for special diseases, the Public Health Service hospitals.

Medicare

This program is especially designed for those sixty-five and older, but it has been expanded to provide insurance for any disabled person who is receiving Social Security benefits. It comprises two parts, hospital insurance and medical insurance, both of which are automatically available to a person who is qualified for Social Security. Elderly persons not covered by Social Security may voluntarily enroll for Medicare and pay an extra premium.

Part A of Medicare is the hospital insurance, which helps pay for medical care to hospital in-patients. It does not pay doctor bills. The basic coverage is: (1) up to 90 "hospital days" in each benefit period; (2) up to 100 days of "extended care" (nursing or convalescent home) in each benefit period; (3) up to 100 "home health visits" in each benefit period. A benefit period starts whenever a person has not been an in-patient for a period of 60 days. In addition a patient has a "lifetime reserve" of 60 additional hospital days.

Part A requires a $104 deductible payment by the insured for each benefit period used. Almost all hospital charges are covered: a semiprivate room and board, regular nursing, operating rooms, drugs, and laboratory and X ray services. There is no premium charge for Part A coverage.

Part B of Medicare helps pay doctors' bills and some other services not covered by hospital insurance. The voluntary medical-insurance coverage costs the subscriber $6.70 per month. Persons covered by Social Security are automatically billed for medical insurance, but they may disenroll by contacting the Social Security Administration.

A deductible of $60 per year against the cost of reasonable medical services is required before Part B benefits become effective. The $60 is a cumulative deductible on total medical services for a year, not for each individual service. There are certain noncovered services, such as routine physical examinations, routine foot care, eye examinations and glasses, hearing aids, and most dental care.

State and Local Health Services

State and local health services vary greatly. Their common denominator is federal aid administered by HEW. Local services often receive state tax aid in addition to their own taxation revenue. Most counties and urban areas provide health services rather than health insurance for their client-patients. Health services usually include some or all of the following: (1) communicable disease control, (2) public nursing services, (3) public health nutrition services, (4) child and maternal health consultations, (5) medical care for the indigent and the elderly, (6) sanitation inspection, (7) vital statistics, (8) public health education, (9) school and industrial health services, and (10) general hospitals for people with chronic illnesses or without funds.

Workmen's compensation Another example of health and accident insurance offered by states is the workmen's compensation funds. You are covered while on the job for injuries and job-related sicknesses. Each state has a somewhat different law regarding who is covered and what benefits are offered. Almost all claims are due to accidents. Generally the employer pays into a state fund, or to a private insurance company approved by the state, to provide insurance for injuries resulting from work or working conditions.

Workmen's compensation benefits usually comprise three major categories: (1) medical treatment, (2) temporary disability payments, and (3) permanent disability payments. To receive benefits the injured employee files a claim through his employer. The medical treatment is under the control of the employer or his insurance carrier, but if the employee is dissatisfied with the medical treatment he may request a change of physicians, or if the injury is serious enough he may have a consulting physician of his choice. Temporary disability payments are made to help the injured worker meet his daily living expenses. Payments, based upon the worker's wages, may start immediately upon injury or may be subject to a waiting period. Table 7–6 illustrates the weekly disability payments under the California Workmen's Compensation Law. Whenever an injury results in permanent loss of earning power, causes impairment of the normal use of a bodily appendage, or creates a competitive handicap in the labor market, a worker becomes entitled to permanent disability payments. The degree of disability is usually rated as a "percent of permanent disability," thereby providing the injured worker something less than the maximum disability payment. Arbitration boards and the courts may be used to resolve disputes about the amount of disability allowed.

State short-term disability laws Many states have provisions for off-the-job disability coverage. These may be state-required plans or state-approved voluntary private plans. Weekly income benefits are paid to employees who cannot work because of sickness or injury not incurred because of employment. The actual benefit amount is based on one's wages. States apply different computation formulas but usually limit benefits to approximately 50 percent of wages. California also provides hospital benefits of $12 per day for twenty days in addition to any wage benefit paid. Benefits are not affected by personal-disability or hospital-insurance policies. In fact, you should coordinate other insurance with state disability-income insurance. Typical state insurance coverage provides benefits for a six-month period. You should purchase your own supplementary insurance to begin after state benefits are exhausted.

SELECTING YOUR HEALTH INSURANCE

According to a recent HEW report, approximately 78 percent of the U.S. popula-

Table 7–6 Workmen's compensation disability payment schedule: Weekly disability payments for injuries sustained on and after April 1, 1974

	Weekly Compensation			Weekly Compensation	
Weekly Wages	*Temporary Disability*	*Permanent Disability*	Monthly Wages	*Temporary Disability*	*Permanent Disability*
$30.00	$35.00	$20.00	$129.97	$35.00	$20.00
40.00	35.00	26.67	175.00	35.00	26.92
50.00	35.00	33.33	200.00	35.00	30.77
52.50	35.00	35.00	227.47	35.00	35.00
60.00	40.00	40.00	250.00	38.46	38.46
70.00	46.67	46.67	300.00	46.15	46.15
78.75	52.50	52.50	341.25	52.50	52.50
80.00	53.34	53.33	350.00	53.85	53.85
90.00	60.00	60.00	375.00	57.69	57.69
100.00	66.67	66.67	400.00	61.54	61.54
105.00	70.00	70.00	454.97	70.00	70.00
110.00	73.33	maximum	500.00	76.92	maximum
115.00	76.67		520.00	80.00	
120.00	80.00		540.00	83.08	
125.00	83.33		560.00	86.15	
130.00	86.67		580.00	89.23	
135.00	90.00		600.00	92.31	
140.00	93.33		620.00	95.38	
145.00	96.67		640.00	98.46	
150.00	100.00		660.00	101.54	
155.00	103.33		680.00	104.62	
160.00	106.67		700.00	107.69	
165.00	110.00		720.00	110.77	
170.00	113.33		740.00	113.85	
175.00	116.67		760.00	116.92	
178.50			773.47		
and over	119.00		and over	119.00	

Note: The rate of weekly compensation in most cases is based upon the employee's earnings at time of injury, but it may vary depending upon the facts in each case. If the date of your injury was before April 1, 1974, your compensation rate for either temporary or permanent disability will be different from the chart shown above. This is the most recent revision and is dated accordingly. In addition to money payments, tips, meals, room, and other advantages furnished by the employer are to be included in calculating earnings for compensation purposes. Contributions made by your employer to savings, wage continuation or replacement or stock plans, or other employee benefit programs, to a union or trust fund are excluded.

Source: State of California Department of Industrial Relations.

tion under sixty-five years of age have hospitalization insurance, while 75 percent have surgical insurance. Chances are that you, by receiving free health insurance as a fringe benefit of your employment, by your purchase of health insurance because of a definite need, or by a combination of these possibilities, will be a part of this majority.

It is a good idea to review your health-insurance policy every few years, because changes in your family's life-style might affect the amount and type of coverage you desire. Keep in mind the following points while reviewing your policy:

1. If your employment has changed, your policy might be cancelled.
2. A change of residence may limit the value of your policy if you are required to use specific medical facilities.
3. Changes in your family situation—marriage, divorce, birth, and death—may affect your policy coverage and rates.
4. Changes in your income and actual health needs may occur.

In any case you should follow certain steps in determining your health-insurance needs: (1) determine what medical insurance you already have or are entitled to; (2) determine what health insurance you and your family actually need; (3) determine what health insurance you can actually afford; (4) consider the risks of a self-insurance or coinsurance program; and (5) choose a good insurance organization that offers appropriate coverage.

What Do You Already Have?

With health insurance, as with any insurance program, you should consider what you already have to alleviate some of the risk. As mentioned earlier, the two economic risks in health care are high medical costs and the possible loss of income.

Medical insurance The public health laws of the federal and state governments may provide for medical care in the case of specialized illnesses. Unfortunately you cannot plan to have a specialized illness. Workmen's compensation insurance allows you to receive medical treatment through your employer, but you cannot plan to have a work-related illness or injury. Automobile medical insurance may cover limited medical expenses in an auto accident, but it too is a specialized coverage. The economic risk of high medical expense is still with you unless you have group or individual medical expense insurance.

Loss-of-income insurance You probably have some sick-leave benefits available at your place of employment. This may take care of your short-term loss-of-income needs but would generally not cover periods beyond six months. Your long-term need for income in the case of permanent disability would be covered by workmen's compensation if the disability is work-related or by state disability insurance or Social Security if it is not work-related. You will have problems, however, because of the rather low monthly benefits allowed under Social Security. A worse problem arises if your job is not covered by Social Security. The economic risk of loss of income is always with you unless you purchase a group or individual disability-income plan.

Group health insurance Many employers provide a basic health-insurance plan or one or more of the various medical-expense and disability-income insurances through fringe-benefit packages. By signing up large groups of people, the insurance company provides coverage at what amounts to wholesale rates. Coverage is usually made available to family members also. Sales and administrative costs are lessened by having the personnel department of the sponsor handle the clerical and claims work.

Sometimes employers contract with more than one health-insurance agency to give employees a choice of plans. This often takes the form of a choice between a health-maintenance organization and an indemnity carrier. For example, you may be given a choice between Kaiser Foundation Health Plan and New York Life Insurance Company.

One ominous feature of group health-insurance policies is that the insured may lose his coverage when he leaves the group. This may occur even if the policyholder was paying the premiums himself. Today most insurance carriers allow policyholders to convert to an individual policy at a higher premium rate and reduced benefits. Usually coverage will continue uninterrupted and without need for a renewal physical examination. It is usually better to get interim medical-insurance coverage until you are eligible for a new group plan.

Double benefits It is usually uneconomic to purchase duplicate coverage, because most indemnity carriers will insure only their prorated portion of the maximum medical expense as coinsurers if there is more than one insurance policy. If both husband and wife can obtain group insurance, it would be cheaper to purchase one policy covering the family than to have two separate policies. If the group insurance is paid by the respective employers, accept them both and use both policies by making coordinated claims to get 100 percent coverage for a particular illness or accident.

If a policyholder is injured by someone else who is held liable for his injury, the insurance company may sue the wrongdoer to recover the company's payments to the insured. This procedure stems from a subrogation clause in the insurance policy. If a policyholder sues the wrongdoer for damages and wins the case, he may have to reimburse the insurance company to the extent of any medical payments. All in all, it is rather hard to make a profit from double benefits of health-insurance policies.

What Do You Need?

After you determine what you have in the way of health insurance, figure out what you and your family really need. You may already have too much insurance. If you are paying for this surplus coverage, you should review and consolidate your coverage into the most acceptable policy, saving the excess premiums.

If you have too little coverage, you must determine what the medical-expense requirements are for you and your family. Then you must decide how much health-insurance coverage you desire and need. All too often a purchaser either does not get catastrophe coverage or else he gets basic coverage with a number of unessential features. You will need major medical insurance to protect you and your family against the greatest economic risks.

What Can You Afford?

Health insurance, like all other insurance, requires regular periodic payments. This simply means that you must make a place in your budget for the insurance premium or medical service prepayment. You are not attempting to budget something that *might* happen, but something that *will* happen, namely the regular periodic prepayment for medical care. Can you afford this payment as well as those for your auto loan, installment and charge accounts, mortgage or rent payment, and food? Unfortunately, you cannot afford *not* to have some health insurance because if you incur high medical bills, it is very likely that some of your more materialistic obligations will be left unmet.

If the breadwinner becomes disabled, his income will stop, and prior obligations as well as the new medical bills will now not be paid. Personal property being purchased on the installment plan may be repossessed. Creditors may make claims against paid-for assets, and the final result may be bankruptcy. A National Finance Association analysis of personal bankruptcies indicates that the chief reason given for filing bankruptcy was excess medical expenses added to crushing personal-installment debt. Obviously there was little if any health insurance or personal savings available to those who filed bankruptcy.

If you can afford only a small amount of health insurance, you should choose major medical. Set the deductible limits as high as possible to give you higher maximums. Disability-income insurance is also a must, because you must have income if you are disabled for any length of time. Workmen's Compensation may help, but 90 percent of disability claims are made because of off-the-job sickness. State disability and Social Security are good only for partial coverage. Both of these policies prevent the catastrophic expenses of a serious illness from bankrupting you.

Self-Insurance or Coinsurance?

Unless you have a considerable emergency fund and assets that you could or would sell in case of a major illness, it would be wise to consider a comprehensive health-insurance plan or, at the very least, a coinsurance program that will provide the best protection for your particular family situation. Total self-insurance, as noted above, may lead to bankruptcy.

Health insurance may cost you from 1 to 3 percent or more of your annual income. Selective coverage may very well be the answer. Should you purchase for your family's basic requirements and chance the rest? Will major medical and disability-income insurances be enough? Will a basic health-insurance plan be enough? How much medical/economic security do you need? Does your family have a history of illnesses, accidents? What is the *probability* of medical expenses compared to the *financial consequences* of high medical expenses?

If you receive free medical insurance through your employer, you may wish to purchase extra supplemental coverage to provide peace of mind—no coinsurance for you!

Choose an Insurance Carrier that Meets Your Needs

Your choice of a health insurer will probably determine the type of health care that you receive. Actually, the type of health care you need should determine your choice of health insurance.

Indemnity benefits Claims procedures and the type of health care provided distinguish an indemnity carrier from a service carrier. Commercial insurance companies usually offer indemnity policies that limit the dollar amount of benefits. This system eliminates the tendency to utilize unneeded medical services. Rates presumably would be lower, and you would have a complete choice of doctors and hospitals. You might choose a physician on the basis that his fees are no greater than your insurance indemnity. Otherwise, you would become a coinsurer of your medical expenses. Disability-income insurance, by its very nature, offers indemnity benefits.

Service benefits Policies paying service benefits cover hospital and physicians' charges either in full or up to a percentage of the usual and reasonable fees for a particular area. Premium rates are generally higher for service benefits than for indemnity benefits but your coverage better reflects the medical costs of your area. Blue Cross–Blue Shield pioneered the service concept whereby participating hospitals and physicians provide their health care at established rates. You and your family would have a wide choice of hospitals and independent physicians. You would be a coinsurer only to the extent that your hospital or physician's charges exceed the usual rates for the area and only for that part of the bill over the covered percentage.

Health-maintenance organizations also offer service benefits. Premium rates are generally slightly higher, but the medical care is most complete. The subscriber and his family pay up to $2 per doctor visit, no matter how routine or complicated the medical procedure may be.

Ask your physician Physicians and their receptionists deal with medical-insurance claims regularly. They can advise you which companies pay the benefits they claim to pay. You should also ask which companies pay the greatest portion of the doctor's fees. A frank discussion of fees will often result in more reasonable charges. Hospital billing offices can do the same for hospital expense insurance. If you prefer a particular hospital, ask which insurance carrier provides the best coverage for the services rendered by that particular hospital.

Mail-order health insurance Policies sold by mail and by Sunday-newspaper advertisement are usually depicted as supplements to other health-insurance policies. You can use them as a form of disability income or to pay the deductible and coinsurance amounts required by your basic policy. The advertisements tend to exaggerate benefits and minimize the policy limitations. Advertising copy tends to run to the emotional: "The siren wails, the ambulance pulls up and suddenly you're in the hospital. $33.33-a-day benefits (up to $1,000.00 per month) paid when you are hospitalized for any covered illness or injury."

The State Insurance Commissioner of Pennsylvania says, "Everything is wrong with these policies. People who have other coverage don't need it, and people who buy it as their only health insurance are not being adequately protected." According to a study, the average claim paid by some of the large mail-order firms was only $179. This is considerably less than the advertised figures! Most mail-order companies pay out about fifty-three cents of every premium dollar for benefits. The balance goes toward advertising, administration, and profit.

Special care must be taken to read and understand the clauses and innuendos of a mail-order policy. There is a considerable possibility of misrepresentation and fraud. For one thing, make sure the insurance company is licensed to do business in your state—check with your state's insurance department. Look for such items as the waiting period before benefits begin. Now figure the odds and see if the policy is still a good deal. You will not need a physical examination, but you will be required to complete a medical-history questionnaire. From this information the insurance company determines what preexisting health conditions are to be excluded from your coverage for a given period, usually two years. If you leave any blank spaces on the questionnaire, the company may refuse a claim because of a preexisting condition! The preexistent-condition clause is usually broadly interpreted in favor of the mail-order insurance company.

Do not be tempted by low premium rates. This is probably an indication that the company has a very low claim-acceptance rate. How else can it maintain low premium rates on a risk that should happen fairly regularly? Be aware of the advertisement with an "introductory" rate. This simply means that you have applied for health insurance at a premium rate that must increase after the first premium payment. It is good bait.

Not all mail-order insurance is inherently bad. Accident and hospitalization supplement insurance is offered directly by mail-order companies and through department stores and gasoline companies. The benefits may be reasonably good, or some of these retailers would not be sponsoring them. However, it is still much more prudent to deal face-to-face with the representatives of any insurance company than it is to attempt to purchase insurance and make claims by mail.

Vocabulary and Concepts

Coordination of benefits	Major medical
Deductible	Medicare
Disability income	National health plan
Group medical practice	Relative value schedule
Health-maintenance organization	Service plan
Indemnity plan	Socialized medicine
	Workmen's compensation

Questions for Discussion

1. Why are medical expenses so high? What can you do to curb your medical expenses?
2. What are the basic differences among health, life, and disability insurances?
3. Describe the workings of a supplementary hospital insurance plan. What type of insurance policy do these plans represent?
4. What medical expenses are usually covered in a basic health-insurance plan?
5. Describe how major medical insurance operates.
6. Explain the differences between a health-insurance indemnity plan and a service plan.
7. What coverages are usually available in a typical dental insurance plan?
8. How does workmen's compensation insurance differ from state disability insurance?
9. What are the disability-income features of the Social Security system?
10. What features should you compare when analyzing competitive health insurances?

Projects

1. Contact your congressional representatives to find their views on a national health plan. Research the position of the American Medical Association and other interested groups.
2. Compare the basic health-plan premium rates and benefits of a health-maintenance organization, Blue Cross–Blue Shield, and a commercial health-insurance policy in your area.
3. Compare the group-plan premium rates and benefits available at either your parents' or your own place of employment.
4. Determine the amount of disability-income insurance that would be appropriate for you. Shop two insurance companies for premium quotes. Do their features compare?

Case Problem

Art and Barbara Able have a basic health plan through Art's employer at a cost of

$120 annually. It is a commercial indemnity plan that pays $50 per day hospitalization for 365 days, $550 maximum surgical benefits, and $250 miscellaneous hospital services. The family's medical costs have averaged about $700 a year including the health-insurance premium. What advice would you offer the Ables? Elaborate.

8 property and casualty insurance

Great financial loss can accrue to a family if its possessions are stolen or damaged. Even greater loss can occur if you, your family, or your possessions damage or cause loss to another person, his family, or his property. It is for these reasons that almost all families pass some of the financial risk to an insurance company. It is very reassuring to many families that a premium payment can absorb at least some of the ever-present threat of economic disaster and its unknown payouts.

This chapter will describe how to protect assets in the sequence of the insurances purchased by most consumers. While we will concentrate on insurances available for automobiles, homes, personal possessions, and the liability that may attach to these items and their owners, there are many specialized insurance policies available for the right person, place, situation, and price. Since property, casualty, and liability insurance is usually marketed as either automobile or property insurance, we will follow this approach.

A person must have an insurable interest in an insurable risk to transfer his risks to an insurance company. A person must have some ownership or liability interest in the property or person to be insured. The insurance company must then be able to calculate the odds, and the insured must compare his priorities and desires with the amount of risk and the cost of insurance. Such diverse items as good vacation weather, pianists' hands, objets d'art, and unique inventions have been insured because of the criteria listed above.

WHY AUTOMOBILE INSURANCE?

There are many important reasons for purchasing some type of auto insurance. We will discuss the merits of each type of auto insurance later in the chapter, but it is a good idea to consider why auto insurance should be purchased. Among the reasons are the risk of sheer numbers of motor vehicles on the highway, the environment and physical surroundings of the auto, the requirements of law, and the need to protect your assets from loss.

Risk

The chances of being involved in an auto accident are perhaps greater than those of any other single hazard. In 1973, according to the National Safety Council and the Insurance Information Institute, there were 25.6 million reportable auto accidents that involved the death of 55,800 persons and injury to 5 million others. The cost of auto accidents amounted to $16.9 billion during the same year. During this time there were approximately 92 million registered autos on the nation's highways and streets. These figures do not include the many "fender benders" that could escalate into serious accidents by an error of judgment or slight change in timing. Table 8–1 shows that the number of auto accidents has increased each year until 1974. The sheer numbers involved indicate that the possibilities of an auto accident are always present. There are more multicar families and more persons reaching driving age.

Environment

The environment in which the auto is operated also increases the exposure to accident. Automobile and road designs, the relatively indiscriminate driver qualifications, and possible mechanical malfunctions form a mix that experts say contributes to our accident rate. Ralph Nader, the consumer advocate, often criticizes both the auto industry and government for car and road designs. The National Safety Council has often criticized various federal, state, and local governments for lax driver-safety regulations and enforcement of safety laws.

Because of esthetic and marketing requirements auto designs have not been as fully functional and safe as they should be. Protruding ornamentation, "bumpless" bumpers, and a terrible mix of large and small cars on the road have created safety problems. Road design, or sometimes the lack of it, contributes its share of accidents by having too few or too many intersections or by having them banked at the wrong angles. Often the lack of funds perpetuates road hazards caused by poor design.

The easiest change that might improve the driving environment is that of driver qualification. There are many persons, both young and old, who should not be driving

Table 8–1 Motor vehicle deaths and injuries, 1947–1974

Year	Deaths†	Injuries‡	Year	Accidents*	Deaths‡	Injuries‡
1947	32,697	1,365,000	1959		37,910	2,870,000
1948	32,259	1,471,000	1960		38,137	3,078,000
1949	31,701	1,564,000	1961		38,091	3,057,000
1950	34,763	1,799,000	1962		40,804	3,345,000
1951	36,996	1,962,000	1963		43,564	3,460,000
1952	37,794	2,090,000	1964		47,700	3,840,000
1953	37,955	2,140,000	1965		49,163	3,982,000
1954	35,586	1,960,000	1966	15,896,000	53,041	4,192,000
1955	38,426	2,158,000	1967	16,978,000	52,924	4,353,000
1956	39,628	2,368,000	1968	18,631,000	54,862	4,356,000
1957	38,702	2,525,000	1969	22,025,000	55,791	5,010,000
1958	36,981	2,825,000	1970	22,116,000	54,800	4,983,000
			1971	22,650,000	54,700	4,994,000
			1972	24,850,000	56,600	5,190,000
			1973	25,649,000	55,800	5,192,000
			1974	23,744,000	46,200	4,634,000

Sources: * Insurance Information Institute.
† National Safety Council.
‡ Prior to 1965, the Travelers Insurance Companies; 1965 to 1974, Insurance Information Institute.

cars. Driving is not a right, but a privilege licensed by the state upon provable competency. The passing of a simple written examination and the passing of a behind-the-wheel exercise do not necessarily mean that a motorist is a good driver. More stringent license suspension laws should be enacted as well as a mandatory driving test each time a person's license is renewed. Perhaps the state could develop a weighted scoring system that could be tied in with auto liability-insurance premium rates.

Finally, mechanical malfunctions are a part of the motoring environment. It might be your car or a nearby motorist's that is unsafe. In either case the malfunction could contribute to a serious accident. We need required preventative maintenance to reduce the incidence of mechanical failure. Government's problem becomes one of enforcement. Spot roadside inspections and required inspection at license-plate renewal times would help reduce the risk of accidents.

Financial Responsibility

By law you are required to furnish proof of your financial responsibility if you are involved in an accident. All states have some form of financial responsibility laws. If the accident is not the equal fault of the involved motorists, one will normally be found liable for money damages to the other. The judgment may easily go beyond the financial resources of the person causing the accident. If this happens, the offending motorist may have to pay the damages from his future wages. To prevent this situation, a motorist must provide proof that he is capable of indemnifying an injured party up to the limits prescribed by law. Since most motorists do not have sufficient assets to cover the legal indemnity, they purchase auto liability insurance to meet the requirements of the financial responsibility law. Table 8–2 lists the current financial responsibility requirements by state.

Often the minimum state requirements prove insufficient to cover a court judgment won by an injured party. We will discuss this in detail later in the chapter. Failure to meet the requirements of the law usually results in the loss of your driver's license and/or your auto license plates in addition to possible civil suits.

Asset Protection

In the final analysis, the most important reason to purchase auto insurance is to protect your current and future assets. You have probably worked hard to acquire your property, especially your expensive auto. It is subject to many forms of damage and loss. If driven negligently, it can injure another person or damage his property, thereby creating a liability for the owner. If you are adjudged liable, your assets will be used to settle the claim if you do not have liability insurance. You must remember that your auto is only one of your assets. Your house, furniture, investments, savings, and future earnings may be available to settle liability judgments. Few people can afford to let their assets be exposed to such liability risks.

TYPES OF AUTOMOBILE INSURANCE

It is important to be fully aware of the different types of auto insurance. Each provides coverage for a different risk. Auto insurance has a slight overlap in coverage. The risk coverage may already be duplicated wholly or in part by other insurance carried by you and your family. There are five basic

Table 8–2 Automobile financial responsibility laws in the United States and Canada

State	*Liability Limits**	*State*	*Liability Limits**
United States		Pennsylvania	10/20/5
Alabama	10/20/5	Rhode Island	10/20/5
Alaska	15/30/5	South Carolina	10/20/5
Arizona	15/30/10	South Dakota	15/30/10
Arkansas	10/20/5	Tennessee	10/20/5
California	15/30/5	Texas	10/20/5
Colorado	15/30/5	Utah	15/30/10
Connecticut	20/40/5	Vermont	10/20/5
Delaware	10/20/5	Virginia	20/40/5
District of Columbia	10/20/5	Washington	15/30/5
Florida	25/25/5	West Virginia	10/20/5
Georgia	10/20/5	Wisconsin	15/30/5
Hawaii	10/20/5	Wyoming	10/20/5
Idaho	10/20/5		
Illinois	10/20/5		
Indiana	15/30/10	**Canada**	
Iowa	10/20/5	Alberta	$35,000 inclusive†
Kansas	15/30/5		
Kentucky	10/20/5	British Columbia	$50,000 inclusive
Louisiana	5/10/1		
Maine	20/40/10	Manitoba	$50,000 inclusive
Maryland	20/40/5		
Massachusetts	5/10/5	New Brunswick	$35,000 inclusive
Michigan	20/40/10		
Minnesota	10/20/5	Newfoundland	$35,000 inclusive
Mississippi	10/20/5		
Missouri	10/20/2	Nova Scotia	$35,000 inclusive
Montana	10/20/5		
Nebraska	15/30/10	Ontario	$50,000 inclusive
Nevada	15/30/5		
New Hampshire	20/40/5	Prince Edward Island	$35,000 inclusive
New Jersey	15/30/5		
New Mexico	10/20/5	Quebec	$35,000 inclusive
New York	10/20/5		
North Carolina	15/30/5	Saskatchewan	$35,000 inclusive
North Dakota	10/20/5		
Ohio	12.5/25/7.5	Northwest Territories	$35,000 inclusive
Oklahoma	5/10/5		
Oregon	10/20/5	Yukon	$50,000 inclusive

* The first two figures refer to bodily injury liability limits and the third figure to property damage liability. For example, 10/20/5 means coverage up to $20,000 for all persons injured in an accident, subject to a limit of $10,000 for one individual; and $5,000 coverage for property damage.

† The "inclusive" limit means there is $35,000 of liability insurance available to settle either bodily injury or property damage claims—or both—up to that amount.

Amounts current to January 1, 1975.

Source: American Insurance Association.

auto coverages offered by most insurance carriers. These are:

1. Public liability
   a. Bodily injury
   b. Property damage
2. Comprehensive damage
3. Collision damage
4. Medical payments
5. Uninsured motorists

Some insurance companies also offer policies that have special coverage for autos such as:

1. Towing and road service
2. Death, dismemberment, or disability
3. Additional transportation expense

Public Liability

Auto liability insurance is sold as a package deal; you must purchase both bodily-injury and property-damage coverages. This is wise, because a person causing an accident does not plan to injure or kill a person, damage property, or do both. Liability coverage pays for the injuries and damages you cause to the other person. It does not pay for your injuries or damages. Both bodily injury (BI) and property damage (PD) are part of all state financial-responsibility laws.

Bodily-injury liability This coverage protects you if you are legally liable for the death or bodily injury of a third party caused by your negligence through the ownership, maintenance, or use of an insured owned or nonowned vehicle. Bodily-injury claims are composed of medical bills, lost income, and "pain and suffering" experienced by the injured third party. You, members of your household, and persons who use your car occasionally with your permission are covered to the limits of the policy for both BI and PD. You and members of your family are also covered when driving someone else's car with their permission.

Property-damage liability This coverage protects you from liability for damage to the property of others caused while operating an insured vehicle. Property of others includes their auto and any accompanying personal property and real property including contents.

Liability insurance pays claims of others to the amount of the policy limit. Property-damage claims are composed of direct damage to the other person's car, house, or any other property plus any consequential loss of use of the property. It also provides for unlimited legal-defense expenses if you are sued. It pays court costs, attorney fees, investigator fees, witness expenses and fees, and in many cases any other expenses, such as loss of earnings, that are incurred at the request of your insurance company.

The insurance company will settle claims and pay court judgments to the maximum policy limit. Any excess claim or award above the policy limit must be satisfied by the insured. You should carry sufficient liability insurance to cover most potential awards. Furthermore, your liability insurance must be able to satisfy your state's financial-responsibility law.

Your auto insurance policy will specifically indicate the company's liability limits. If "10/20/5" is noted on your policy, it means that $10,000 is the policy limit for bodily-injury liability claims for any one person and that $20,000 is the bodily-injury liability for any one accident involving bodily injury to more than one person. The "5" stands for a $5,000 property-damage liability limit. This is traditional *split-limit* coverage issued by auto-insurance companies.

The big disadvantage of split limits (other than the confusion about how much coverage one has) is that one person can sue and be awarded more than the policy maximum for one person. For example, if one person is awarded $20,000 against a typical 10/20/5 policy, the insured driver would have only $10,000 coverage and must pay the difference out of his pocket.

You can readily see that the minimums required to meet financial-responsibility laws of most states are very inadequate protection. You should insure yourself commensurate with the risk. Your legal liability for bodily injury or death and property damage can easily amount to $100,000 or more! Juries constantly award large amounts to families because of the loss of a breadwinner. If you should cause a multi-car accident or crash into a residence, property-damage claims can be quite high. A more practical approach is to purchase *single-limit liability* insurance in a large amount. For example, if you purchase a $300,000 single-limit policy instead of a more traditional $100,000/$300,000/$25,000 policy, your insurance will pay the first $300,000 of either bodily injury and/or property damage claims, whether or not one or more persons are suing. The company pays the losses until the $300,000 limit is exhausted. Under the traditional approach a single person could win a $150,000 judgment and the insured would be covered for only $100,000.

Finally, auto liability insurance satisfies the moral obligation to protect the other party if you are legally liable for his injury or damage. It is also a prudent obligation on your part to protect you and your family from the risk of having to relinquish current and possibly future assets to satisfy this legal liability.

Comprehensive Damage

Comprehensive is all risk coverage on your automobile. It is very broad in that all losses are covered unless specifically excluded. The main exclusion is collision damage, which will be described next.

Comprehensive coverage is often called fire and theft coverage, because these losses are featured. Certain types of losses that are technically collisions are arbitrarily defined as *not* being collisions and are therefore covered by comprehensive.

Losses caused by landslide, windstorm, earthquake, falling trees, animals, vandalism, glass breakage, and flood are covered. Auto parts permanently attached to the car are covered for theft unless specifically excluded from the policy. Stereo tape decks are usually excluded. Check your policy for specific exclusions. Some companies do not insure the contents of a car (personal property) for theft unless the entire car is stolen. Others require proof of breaking and entering before paying theft claims of property in the car. Some policies require that cars be locked before they will pay on a theft. Generally, the car itself is covered by theft even if unlocked. Other companies will not insure cars that are not permanently garaged. Finally, many companies have instituted a $50 deductible on comprehensive insurance to eliminate the many small nuisance claims.

Collision Damage

Collision insurance covers loss to your car due to collision with any object (unless defined as a comprehensive loss) or due to upset (i.e., rolling over). Your car will be restored to its former condition under collision coverage if the cost of repair does not exceed the actual cash value of the car. Actual cash value is the replacement cost less depreciation. If it is damaged beyond repair, you will receive the current actual cash value. Your policy will not state a repair limit, because potential repair costs on your particular car are considered in the calculation of the policy premium. If repair costs are estimated to be greater than the auto's value, the auto will be considered "totaled." An auto's actual cash value is usually based upon the current "blue book" value.

Collision coverage protects your car and your property. It covers collision with another car or any stationary object, and damage to your car caused by another moving vehicle, including hit-and-run damage. Damage to luggage and wearing apparel as contents in the car is usually covered up to a maximum of $200. Not all insurance companies provide this extended coverage. Collision does not provide any insurance protection to the other person's car or property; that is the function of liability insurance.

Collision insurance is expensive because of the high cost of auto repair and because of the abuses sometimes caused by overestimating damage so that a policyholder can pocket a little extra money. To cut premium costs, all policies make available a deductible, usually in $50, $100, and $250 amounts. In case of a collision, you pay the deductible amount. Some insurance companies waive the deductible payment if you collide with another car insured by their company. Others provide a "disappearing deductible": you do not pay any part of the deductible if the cost of repairs goes over a certain amount. It is wise to purchase a $100 or $250 deductible, because the premium is much less than that for a $50 deductible.

Medical Payments

The insured and each person riding in his car are covered to the limits of the policy for reasonable medical expenses incurred within one year from the date of the accident. The expenses must be a direct result of the accident. You and your family will also receive medical benefits if you are injured by a motor vehicle while walking or while riding a bicycle, providing the vehicle is not owned by a family member.

This coverage is primarily for the insured and guests riding in his car. It does not cover the medical expenses of the other party in an accident. Bodily-injury liability coverage is used for the other party if you are legally liable for his injuries. If you have separate health-insurance coverage, the auto medical-expense insurance may be duplicate coverage for you and your family. However, the "guest" laws of many states do not allow guests in your car to collect public liability coverage; therefore, you may need auto medical-expense insurance if you carry many guests. You should check with your insurance agent about this possibility. In such cases it is wise to carry auto medical-expense insurance.

Uninsured Motorists

Over 10 percent of the nation's motorists are not insured, either because of the high cost of liability insurance or because of the dismal financial responsibility enforcement procedures of most states. You can protect yourself from the risk of not being able to collect from a legally liable but financially incapable motorist by purchasing uninsured motorists insurance. Many states require that auto-insurance policyholders expressly waive this insurance; otherwise it is automatically included in the policy package.

This insurance covers only *bodily injury* sustained by you, your family, or guests riding with you when caused by a hit-and-run driver, by an uninsured motorist, or by a financially irresponsible motorist who is legally liable. You and your family are also covered if injured while walking or while riding bicycles. Damage to your car or other property is generally not covered. You are expected to purchase collision insurance to protect your car. Your homeowner's policy will protect your personal property. Some insurance companies will not sell uninsured motorists coverage unless you also purchase collision insurance.

Any person covered by your uninsured motorists policy who has a legitimate claim may collect damages up to the limits of the policy. Medical payments made to guests in your automobile reduce the uninsured motorists coverage available to you and your family if you must make a claim. The uninsured motorists insurance coverage is normally the minimum set by your state's financial responsibility law. For example, in Michigan you would be covered 20/40: up to $20,000 for any one person and up to a maximum of $40,000 for all insured persons sustaining injuries in the accident.

Theoretically you sue your own insurance company when injured by a hit-and-run driver or an uninsured or financially incapacitated motorist, because there is no incentive to sue the other party. Claims procedures or court decisions determine the award as if you had actually sued the liable party. The award generally goes beyond medical expenses to include damages for "pain and suffering." You buy the other party's liability insurance to protect yourself! Table 8–3 illustrates who benefits from the auto insurance coverages. Study the table to be sure that you are aware of who is being protected and who gets paid under each coverage.

Towing and Road Service

A number of insurance companies offer towing and road-service coverage. Many auto clubs such as the American Automobile Association and the National Automobile Club started by offering this "insurance" as a service to motorists. It is actually a prepaid service charge.

While the AAA requires you to use authorized service agencies, most insurance companies allow you to choose any road-service agency and apply for reimbursement. Your car is covered for towing to the nearest garage or for labor costs performed at the place your car becomes disabled. Often there is a $25 limit on this service.

Table 8–3 Beneficiary of auto insurance by type of coverage

Type of Coverage	Payments to Beneficiary				
	Insured and Family	*Other Persons*	*Insured's Car*	*Other's Car*	*Other's Property*
Bodily injury liability		×			
Property damage liability				×	×
Collision			×		
Comprehensive			×		
Medical payments*	×	×			
Uninsured motorists*	×	×			

* See text for limitations or expansion of coverage to beneficiaries.

Death, Dismemberment, and Disability

Few auto-insurance companies provide this coverage, which pays benefits for death or injury sustained in an auto accident. The policy states the benefit limits, which usually run between $5,000 and $20,000. This insurance is similar to the disability or loss-of-income plans offered by the health-insurance industry. The health-insurance policy covers death, dismemberment, and disability from any cause, while an auto policy pays benefits only for death and injury from an auto accident.

Additional Transportation Expense

Additional transportation expense coverage is available in a number of states. It pays between $20 and $100 a day while your car is being repaired for collision damage. The amount paid is a flat-benefit payment regardless of whether an expense is actually generated when you have your car in the repair shop for collision damage. The coverage is marketed as an extra benefit to help pay for such things as meals, car rental, motel, and incidentals that would arise because of a collision. The insured must also carry collision coverage to be eligible for additional transportation expense insurance.

HOW AUTO-INSURANCE RATES ARE DETERMINED

As an automobile owner, you are obviously concerned with the cost of auto insurance. Have you ever wondered how the insurance companies determine the premium rates? The companies are in general agreement that certain items have an effect on claims. These items form classifications that many companies use to set base rates.

The actual auto-insurance premium paid by an owner will be affected by the addition of surcharges or the subtraction of discounts. The items generally used to determine rates for auto insurance are sex, age, marital status, mileage driven, territory, driving record, and type of car. We will look at each of these.

Sex, Age, and Marital Status

Males pay more for auto insurance than females, at least until about age twenty-five or thirty. The reasons for this may be subject to some debate, but one has only to look at the auto accident statistics to prove that men are more likely to have accidents. Men drive more, and that is a good reason to increase the premium rate: greater exposure means greater risk to the insurance company.

"Age has its rewards." This saying may not be true in many instances, but it certainly applies to car insurance. The classification system offers a lower rate to drivers over age twenty-five or thirty. Presumably women become safe drivers at an earlier age than men.

Marriage is supposed to have a quieting effect on the marriage partners; it does in car insurance. Traveling with a group of peers and attempting to impress the opposite sex with driving prowess drop dramatically after marriage, and the exposure to various driving risks also decreases. Married women normally are charged the base rate. Married men must be over twenty-five years old to be eligible for the base rate. The married male under twenty five does pay less than the single male of the same age.

Mileage Driven

The mileage a car is driven, and by whom, affects the premium. Autos driven less than 5,000 or 10,000 miles per year usually get the lowest possible classification. Autos driven more than 3 to 10 miles one-way while commuting to work are usually in a higher rate classification. The less mileage, the less exposure to risk. The longer the commute, the greater the risk, and the more likely it will be on heavily traveled routes during the commute hours. National Safety Council statistics indicate that proportionately more accidents occur during the evening commute hours than at any other time.

Whenever an unmarried male under age twenty-five to thirty is the owner or principal driver, the car will be rated in the highest class. The operator in this case is a greater risk than an unmarried male who is not the principal driver. For example, if the car must be shared with parents, the unmarried male does not have unlimited use and is therefore not exposed to accidents as often as a sole owner or principal driver.

Territory

Risk occurs not only on the basis of who drives a car and how much it is driven, but also on the basis of where it is driven. Obviously an insurance company cannot follow you around to see where you are driving, but it can base its rates on where the car is parked or garaged.

The entire country is segmented into territories. Your auto registration address is used for insurance purposes. Rates are highest in metropolitan areas. The insurance companies, under regulation of the various state insurance departments, establish rural, suburban, and urban territories in each state.

To demonstrate how rates differ by territory, let us consider the liability insurance for a male under twenty-five who is principal operator of his car. For minimum 15/30/5 coverage he would pay $473 in San Francisco, $446 in Los Angeles, $319 in Oakland, and $261 in Redding, California. The rates were determined by the statistical chances of an accident. There are more cars per square mile in San Francisco than the other cities. Many commuter and tourist cars pour into San Francisco daily. The city is really one big intersection, complete with traffic jams and accidents.

Driving Record

You may have been driving for years and never have had an accident. A single accident can boost your insurance bill by up to 70 percent. Each auto-insurance company has its version of the accident-record rating plan, sometimes known as a good-driver rating plan. The purpose of this plan is to shift the cost of auto insurance to those drivers who cause accidents, rather than raising the cost of auto insurance for everybody.

The insurance companies' public-relations departments claim that such plans reduce the cost of auto insurance to good (accident-free) drivers. This is borne out by the method of charging for the insurance premium. After an accident, the company will add a surcharge either to your liability premium or to your entire auto package. The plan gets rather complex because it often depends upon the number of accidents you have already had, whether the accidents were chargeable to you, and the dollar amount that the company has paid against your policy.

Most companies use a point system to determine the surcharge. The surcharge may remain in effect from three to five years at

Table 8–4 A typical point system for chargeable automobile accidents and violations

Accident or Violation	Number of Points
Driving while intoxicated	5
Failure to stop in an accident	5
Manslaughter	5
Driving with suspended license	5
Accident involving minor personal injury liability	3
Moving motor vehicle violation	2
Accident involving more than $100 property damage liability	2
Equipment violation	1

Parking violations, property-damage accidents paid by the insured, and accidents for which the driver was not liable are not counted for points.

full charge, or it may be reduced each year until you are back to your normal rate. Table 8–4 shows a typical point system that weights accidents and moving violations according to the intensity of the violation or accident. Table 8–5 indicates what the point buildup will do to the insurance of a typical driver. Motorists may find it cheaper to pay for their own or the other person's damage than to submit a claim. However, if they have a moving violation, it may not make a difference—they have gained a point.

Table 8–5 Relationship of points to typical automobile insurance premiums

Point Accumulation	Reduction or Increase of Driver Classification Premium
0	20% reduction
1	10% reduction
2	no change
3	20% increase
4	40% increase
5	70% increase
6 or more	100% increase

Individual states and insurance companies will differ on the percentages, number of points, accumulation time, and length of time that a driver retains his "points."

Type of Car

The type of car you have has an obvious effect on your collision and comprehensive coverage. The more costly it is to repair, the more the insurance premium is going to be. In addition to what effect an accident may have on your car, companies have begun to see that the type of car you drive has a direct relationship to the liability claims that they must pay.

If you have a small car, theoretically you will do less damage to the other car. You might even drive defensively. However, if you have a big or powerful car you will probably do more damage. With a "muscle" car, you are much more likely to take chances because you have the power. Isn't that why you bought it in the first place? Most insurance companies have a list of what they consider "muscle" cars. Generally, it is any car that will accelerate from 0 to 60 miles per hour in less than eight seconds or that has a horsepower-to-weight ratio of less than 1 to 10. Sometimes all it takes is "four on the floor" to make your car into a premium-eating muscle car.

The actual surcharge is from 25 percent to 50 percent of your normal classification premium. Some insurance companies place the surcharge on the entire auto-insurance package, while others place it only on liability and sometimes on collision coverage.

HOW MUCH SHOULD YOU PAY FOR AUTO INSURANCE?

You should pay as little as possible for your auto-insurance needs. Attempt to keep your costs down as much as possible by basing your insurance on your needs and driving habits. If more than one person drives a car, insurance companies rate the car on the highest-rated person driving it. You have very little control over the factors that determine what premium rates you pay. You do not determine your sex or age; you usually do not get married or move to a given locale to save on auto insurance. That leaves only your driving record and type of car. These two items offer you a chance to get a discount from normal premium rates. However, since you probably already own a car and have compiled a good or bad driving record, your only option may be in the types of auto-insurance coverage you buy.

Coverage Needed

Carefully consider the types of coverage and the dollar amount of coverage when purchasing auto insurance; you may cut the cost somewhat. If you eliminate any coverages, you simply become self-insured; you bear the risk of the accident. Chances are that you will not become any more accident-prone because you have dropped part of your coverage. Actually you may drive more carefully, because you are now bearing the risk.

Liability Financial responsibility laws, your sense of responsibility, and the need for protection against personal-injury and property-damage suits make liability insurance a must. Unfortunately, not everyone agrees. Disregarding the legal and moral standards involved, it is not worth ruining your future by having to pay damages for an auto accident that is your fault. All it takes is one mishap or misjudgment, and you may be liable. You should carry sufficient liability insurance to cover your present worth and future average earnings. Limits of $100,000/$300,000/$50,000 are not unwarranted. This would provide you with protection against high economic risks. Increased liability limits do not cost much more than the minimum requirements. (See table 8–6.)

Collision damage Sometimes the cost of the premium for this coverage is more than the car is worth. You can readily determine the value of your car, compare it with the collision premium, and then attempt to determine your chances of having an accident that damages your auto.

Most banks and other lending institutions require that you carry comprehensive and collision to protect the lender if the car is damaged. They fear that a person would not continue his car payments if it were badly damaged and if he did not have the insurance money for repairs.

Assuming that you purchase an auto on the installment plan, you will have collision coverage for approximately three years. Then what? How long should you continue to carry collision insurance? Only as long as the car is worth the premium cost to you. For example, assume you have an auto worth $1,000. If you purchase $100 deductible, it may cost you $100 per year. If you have an accident costing $250, your out-of-pocket expense will have been $200, $100 in premiums and $100 in deductible. If you do not have an accident, it will cost you $100 in premiums. Apparently it is still economically feasible to purchase collision. But what are your chances of an accident in which you must pay your own damages? An average driver is involved in some sort of auto accident approximately every five years. If there is an even chance that the fault will be yours, then you would be likely to be liable for an accident once in ten years. Now the insurance does not look like too good a buy.

What each motorist and prospective collision-insurance purchaser must determine is whether the insurance is worth it to him. If you are a defensive driver, your chances of causing an auto accident are decreased.

Consider whether you would be willing to drive a dented automobile in order to forget about insurance premiums and repair bills. As a rule of thumb, a $1,000 "blue book" car value may be considered the break-even point for collision insurance. Below this value the premium cost cannot, in all probability, be recovered over one or more years. And remember that each succeeding year lowers the value of your auto.

Comprehensive damage Some insurance companies will not sell collision insurance unless comprehensive is purchased with it. Comprehensive normally costs about one-third to one-fourth as much as collision insurance. As stated earlier, theft and most damage other than collision is covered by comprehensive. Your need for comprehensive will be based on your car's value and the likelihood that anything might happen to it.

It is harder to apply a rule of thumb to comprehensive insurance, because the premium is lower, and the risk is much less. Consider such questions as where you park your car and whether it is susceptible to theft or vandalism. Is it in demand by either car thiefs or joyriders?

Medical expense If you have a good health-insurance plan you do not need medical-expense insurance for you or your family. Medical-expense insurance costs about 15 to 20 percent as much as liability insurance, depending upon the dollar amount of coverage you desire. If you pay $200 per year for liability, is it worth the $30 to $40 for your guests' medical expenses? Do you have many guests? Will you ever be responsible or legally liable in an accident? Are you a careful driver? What are the chances of an accident? Can your guests collect under your liability coverage? Consider all these questions before purchasing auto medical insurance.

Uninsured motorists This insurance costs about 10 percent as much as liability insurance. Most companies charge a flat rate for uninsured motorists insurance (UMI). They usually sell this insurance only to people who purchase collision insurance, because UMI covers only bodily injury to you and your passengers if the other person is legally liable for the accident and is unable to pay.

Since this insurance is inexpensive, you ought to buy it if you want as much protection as possible. If you want to consider self-insurance, find out the percentage of uninsured motorists in your state, figure your chances of an accident, admit to your driving habits, and then decide.

Towing and road service The older your car, the more likely you are to need this type of coverage. It usually costs a flat fee of $12 to $24 per year. Anyone who is not a mechanic should have this coverage. One use more than pays for the cost. Many things tend to go wrong with older cars, but even new cars run out of gas and break down.

Death, dismemberment, and disability Your best buy in this type of coverage is all-hazard disability insurance from your life-insurance company, usually in the form of a disability rider on your whole-life or term policy.

Additional transportation expense Most people can make alternate arrangements to secure a ride if their car is in the garage; they should be able to do the same if their car is in an accident. The car may be out of service for a greater period, but the cost of this insurance (up to $50 per year) makes it worth the trouble to find an alternative. Travel protection would be useful if one is on vacation, but is the cost commensurate with the risk and the exposure? You decide.

Premium Costs

Table 8–6 compiles premium quotations from various auto-insurance companies at various levels of coverage. You can readily see that higher levels of coverage are available at little increase in premiums. How much you should pay for auto insurance is based upon many factors. You should compare insurance companies and their rates by doing some comparison shopping. Before you can do this, however, you must be aware

Table 8–6 Automobile-insurance premium quotations comparing various levels of coverage*

	Limits		Premiums for 6 Months
	Each Person	*Each Occurrence*	
BODILY INJURY LIABILITY (Not available without P/D)	$15,000	$30,000	$32.60
	25,000	50,000	37.20
	50,000	100,000	42.40
	100,000	300,000	48.10
PROPERTY DAMAGE LIABILITY		$5,000	$24.70
		10,000	26.00
		25,000	26.70
		50,000	28.00
MEDICAL PAYMENTS		$500	$5.20
		1,000	6.50
		2,000	7.80
		5,000	10.40
	Deductibles		
COMPREHENSIVE	Full coverage		$22.10
	$50 deductible		12.40
COLLISION (Not available without comprehensive)	$50 deductible		$55.10
	$100 deductible		47.10
	$250 deductible		28.20
TOWING	$25 per claim		$18.00
UNINSURED MOTORIST	Bodily Injury		
	Each Person	Each Accident	
	$15,000	$30,000	$4.00
DEATH INDEMNITY	$10,000	Rate per person	$2.00
TOTAL DISABILITY	$50 per week		$3.00

* Six-month premium rates in effect January 1, 1975, for a 1974 Fiat 124 sports roadster, Reno, Nevada.

of certain features in automobile insurance that can either raise or lower your costs: policy fees, discounts, deductibles, special packages, and group insurance.

Policy fees These added fees are often known as acquisition fees. There is a $5 to $10 fee whenever a direct-writing insurance company issues new coverage for you. Any renewal without a change in coverage normally does not require a policy fee.

Discounts As premium costs rise throughout the nation, more and more drivers are cutting their coverage to save money. Many of these motorists feel they are good drivers and do not wish to pay the high insurance rates generated by poor drivers. Insurance companies have recognized this fact by lowering the premium rates to these *preferred risks.* A discount of up to 25 percent may be made available to drivers with accident-free records. Sometimes the discount is available only to certain occupations, or conversely certain occupations may be excluded.

Nondrinkers and nonsmokers often receive discounts because statistics prove that these people have fewer accidents, for rather obvious reasons. The same applies to young drivers who may be entitled to either a good-student discount or a driver-training discount. To get the good-student rate a person must normally maintain a B average, while the driver-training discount is available to a person completing a certified course of instruction.

The small-car or compact-car discount may be a published lower rate or a true percentage discount from the standard rate. As more small cars appear on the road, it is likely that this particular discount will disappear. The second-car discount should remain very much in evidence as more families acquire second and third cars. You must carry your auto insurance with the same company to get this benefit, which usually amounts to 10 percent off on the lower-rated auto. Since the second car seldom gets as much mileage as your first car, the insurance company benefits more from the risk reduction than you do from the premium reduction of 10 percent.

Deductibles Deductible coverage is available with collision and comprehensive insurance. You have a chance to become a coinsurer with the auto-insurance company under an arrangement where you pay the first part of the repair bill and the insurance company pays the balance.

Deductible coverage is often available in $50, $100, and $250 amounts on collision and $50 on comprehensive. Premium costs are normally halved when changing from nondeductible to $100 deductible on collision. It is a good buy. Deductible eliminates many small claims, which cuts paper work, and allows the insurance company off the hook for the first $100 of claims.

Special packages If you buy complete coverage, you may purportedly get a package deal at a price less than the aggregate costs of the individual auto insurance. The reduction supposedly amounts to about 10 percent. The special package, offered by direct-writing companies, is actually composed of separate coverage offered in conjunction with whatever public-liability coverage is being aggressively marketed at a particular time. For example, a company may offer a 30/60/10 policy with full coverage at rates slightly below the aggregate of each coverage separately listed.

Group insurance A relatively new concept in automobile insurance is the group plan sponsored by an employer. It is not the same as health or life insurance, where everyone pays the same rate and where the sponsor may pay all or a portion of the protection. It is actually an arrangement in which an insurance company contracts with a company to allow it to sell the company's employees auto insurance at a savings to both the insurer and the insured. Each employee is rated separately on his driving record, age, sex, and so on. The insurance company then discounts its rates on the average of 15 percent to the employee. The savings to the insurance company is in sales commissions and volume of new business.

Over three thousand group auto-insurance plans are now in force. Unions and employers alike consider them as a fringe benefit. Companies, however, are worried that unions may attempt to get the employers to pay a portion of the insurance as part of a pay package negotiated under collective bargaining.

Assigned Risks

You may not have a choice in choosing or shopping for auto insurance. Companies do not wish to accept clients who may cost them more in claims than the company receives in premium payments. An applicant may be rejected on the basis of his driving record or because of his age and status. Because it is imperative that a poor-risk driver be allowed to purchase liability insurance, many states require insurance companies to accept some poor risks. Generally any person who has been denied auto insurance may apply to his state's assigned-risk plan and be insured.

Each insurance company in an assigned-risk plan is required to accept its share of poor risks by rotation selection. Usually the insurance company offers only the lowest liability limits available at the highest premium rates allowable. Comprehensive and collision are not normally offered.

SHOPPING FOR AUTO INSURANCE

Auto insurance has almost as many different varieties as life insurance. You will have to determine what protection and company features are important to you. You must shop for coverage, price, claims procedure, and agent representation. By comparing different companies and different agents, you effectively consider coverage, price, and claims.

What to Look For in Auto-Insurance Companies

Auto-insurance companies, like other insurance companies, do not charge the same premiums for equivalent coverage. Their fees and allowable discounts are usually different. By not shopping for price you may pay up to 100 percent more for a policy. But do not immediately assume that a low price is good. It may mean lowered coverage or fewer claims allowed. You must find a number of low-priced companies and then check them out.

Rating interpretation You can make a good comparison when you can determine the meaning of the rating assigned to you and your car. All companies use ratings, but they apply them in different manners. To get this information you will invariably have to speak with an agent—you will receive very little cooperation by mail. You need to find out your rating code, its individual cost, and its relationship to other rates by the same company.

One company, for example, may set a commuter rate for travel between home and work as any mileage beyond three miles one way. Another company may base its commuter rate as any distance beyond ten miles one way. Companies may treat the sex, marital status, and age classifications differently.

Financial strength All insurance companies come under some regulation in their home states, and most come under some regulation in the states where they do business. Companies with representation by agents are required to register to do business. Most states now require mail-order insurers to be registered also.

Registration in itself is not proof of financial strength, but states normally require that the company meet certain minimum financial reserves to be registered. Whenever you are dealing with a relatively unknown company it would be wise to check with the state insurance department or the Better Business Bureau. You must assure yourself of the company's ability to meet claims.

Representation and service You really do not know how good your protection is until you file a claim—unless you have made a thorough scrutiny, then it is too late. One method of judging a company is its representation in your area. Good representation usually means that it has enough policies in an area to warrant the added costs of having employees or independent agents. Good service, in terms of sales, claim handling, and policy explanations, is the usual by-product of adequate representation.

A lack of representation means that you have the equivalent of mail-order insurance. This is not necessarily bad, because costs can be reduced by use of the mails, but you do not have personalized service. Companies that sell and service insurance by mail save on commissions and salaries. Hopefully they pass a portion of this on to you. If your mail-order company pays all its legally liable claims with reasonable promptness, there is no reason why you should not transact your business by mail. The big drawback may be slow and reluctant communication.

What to Look For in Auto-Insurance Agents

Auto insurance is sold by mail, by a company employee—an exclusive agent—or by an independent agent. If you have a choice, what sort of agent should you choose?

The larger insurance companies generally separate sales from claims for efficiency. Claims employees may have a tendency to protect their employer, but this cannot be certain. Smaller companies use direct mail or local independent agents who are responsible for both sales and claims.

Independent agents To a degree, an independent insurance agent is your broker or fiduciary. You contact him for professional assistance in procuring auto insurance. He can often explain the various coverages and find the best insurance values for your dollar. As an independent contractor, he can place your business with a number of companies. An exclusive agent can place business only with the company he represents, which might not always be to your benefit. Generally, the exclusive agents represent the larger, direct-writing auto insurers such as Allstate, American Automobile Association, Farmers, and State Farm insurance companies.

An independent agent is probably most valuable if you must file a claim. He will help file your claim to your best advantage if he desires your business. Since he can place insurance with a number of companies, he theoretically is not under the manipulation of a particular company. He does not have a claims settlement budget that he must account for.

An independent agent will often be a Certified Property and Casualty Underwriter—a CPCU. This designation is similar to a CLU in the life-insurance field. It indicates that the agent has taken and passed a number of courses in property and casualty insurance.

Dealer agents The large auto-finance companies, some of whom are subsidiaries of manufacturers, have their own insurance companies. This allows an auto dealer to arrange financing and insurance through one organization. The dealer acts as an agent for the financing and the insurance and receives a commission in the form of a rebate for this business. Because of this he may attempt a hard-sell approach.

You do not have to buy auto insurance from him, even though the bank or finance company demands collision and comprehensive insurance. You must get it somewhere, but to get it automatically from him eliminates any comparison shopping that you might otherwise attempt. In fact, a common practice is to sell you *vendor's single interest* (VSI) insurance that has a decreasing value which provides coverage only for the seller/lender while the automobile is being financed. The premium quoted may be deceivingly low because of this tactic. Be sure that you purchase dual interest coverage that does not decrease as your auto payments are made.

THE WHEN, WHERE, AND HOW OF CLAIMS

The procedures in filing claims are important. Failure to observe instructions or follow common sense may result in the denial of your claim. You should know what to do in case of accident, where and how to file a claim, and how to keep from having your policy cancelled. Your insurance agent should help you with all of these questions.

Claims Against the Other Party

If you think the other party is at fault, you file directly with his or her insurance company. Our legal and insurance systems are based on the principal of liability or fault. Insurance companies will settle a claim only if their insured policyholder is responsible or can be proved legally liable.

You must file a claim within one year of an accident to claim damages. This legal limitation is designed to give you an adequate time to determine your rights, your injuries, money damages, and who is responsible. Failure to file within one year of an accident bars any legal claim on your part. To have it any other way would be to hold all participants in an accident in legal jeopardy for an indeterminate period of time.

You will be visited by the other company's claims adjuster. He will be either an employee or an independent adjuster under contract to the insurance company. In either case, his job is to determine the merits of your claim and settle it for the least amount possible.

He will estimate the dollar amount that you will settle for, based on your injuries and damages. He will do so by asking various questions about your income, assets, medical history, and the accident. Do not say anything that will prejudice your claim. If you do not wish to answer him, advise him of this. The adjuster might then report to his insurance company that you are aware of your rights and knowledgeable about settlement procedures.

The adjuster figures your out-of-pocket costs by adding medical expenses, lost income, and other expenses. To this is added a pain and suffering multiplier, which determines the maximum allowable settlement within the policy limits of the other party's insurance.

After conferring with his insurance company, the adjuster is allowed this limit, which he may not exceed. He will then offer you a check for settlement in full of any liability claim that you may have against his company for the accident. When you accept the check, you relinquish the right of further claims. Do not be hasty in accepting the amount, even if it appears reasonable, if you have been physically injured. Injuries do not always make themselves immediately apparent. You may file an amended claim or suit unless you waive your right to do so by an early settlement. In cases of property damage, the adjuster simply determines the cost of repair, sets a limit, and then has you get two or more estimates of your choice. Sometimes he may have you take your auto to an insurance-company-recommended repair facility rather than give you a choice.

Whenever the other person's insurance company is reluctant to settle, the threat of a suit often speeds things up if you have a legitimate case. Litigated claims generally cost an insurance company more to settle; therefore, it has a tendency to settle out of court. There is an old adage in the liability and casualty insurance industry—settle quickly, or the claim will grow.

Claims Against Your Insurance Company

You can make claims against your insurance company to recover on collision, comprehensive, medical, uninsured motorists, towing and road service, additional transportation expense, and disability insurance. Other people can make claims against your company for personal injury and property damage for which you are legally responsible. Claims against an insurance company cannot exceed the policy limits.

When you file a claim against your insurance company, you go through most of the procedures that were mentioned above. The only major difference is that as a party to a contract with your insurance company you may be substantially limited in claims by the clauses, exceptions, and riders included in the policy contract. If you do not file a claim within the period of time stipulated in the policy, it may not be honored. Other parties who have claims against your policy do not know of and are not necessarily bound by these limiting clauses in your policy. The statute of limitations for injury and damage claims applies in all instances. You can also sue your insurance company if it does not settle with you within the terms of the contractual agreement.

Subrogation When the other party appears at fault, your insurance company will pay for the medical expenses and damages you sustained and then sue the other party's insurance carrier for repayment. This procedure, called *subrogation,* allows the substitution of your insurance company as plaintiff to sue on your claims for injury and damage.

Cancellation of Policy

If you or another party file a liability claim against your insurance company, this will cause a monetary loss to the company if the claim is honored. Consequently, you might be obliged to pay higher premiums at renewal time. Moreover, your policy might be cancelled if the terms of the policy and the laws of your state permit such action.

Check for a cancellation clause, a noncancellation clause, or a renewal guarantee. Buy a policy that provides you some protection against cancellation. Once you are cancelled, this information is passed along to a central insurance exchange. Few companies will then insure you, except at very high rates, and then only under an assigned-risk agreement.

The Allstate Insurance Company offers a reasonable renewal guarantee. After your auto-insurance policy has been in force for sixty days, the company guarantees in writing that your policy will be renewable for the next five years. The insurance cannot be cancelled because of accidents. You may still face an increase in premiums if you have an accident, but if you can keep from having an accident for the first sixty days, the company will keep you as a policyholder.

Double Coverage

Dual claims made against two separate policies seldom if ever prove profitable to the insured. There is usually a clause prohibiting payment of claims from more than one policy. Usually the wording is such that if more than one policy exists, payment will be coordinated between the policies. Two policies become rather expensive because you must pay two premiums for one potential claim payoff.

This is a standard clause in all property insurance, because it is possible that unscrupulous customers would tend to damage their own property if they could really profit by doing so. The double-coverage clause and claims settlements based upon the depreciation value of your auto largely eliminate the possibility of profit.

TRENDS IN AUTO INSURANCE

Regulation and Responsibility

The insurance industry is one of the most regulated industries in the country, but there are still abuses by unresponsive companies that charge too much and/or pay off too little. Perhaps government should regulate the amount of the premium dollar that is returned in claims settlements. Perhaps government or a concerned consumer group should publish a state-by-state list of typical rates charged by each company and compare the findings to the average claims payment.

Perhaps there is already enough regulation and not enough enforcement by government. Perhaps all the present system needs is more honest responsibility on the part of the insurance companies, the insured customers, the lawyers, other claimants, auto-repair shops, and the auto manufacturers.

No-Fault Insurance

The most controversial concept in auto insurance is no-fault insurance. At present you protect yourself by relying on the uncertainty of tort-liability lawsuits or by purchasing all sorts of insurance. A number of states, such as Massachusetts and Michigan, have passed legislation providing for a no-fault insurance system. Table 8–7 lists the state-by-state no-fault laws as of January 1, 1975. Note the diversity of benefits and restrictions.

No-fault insurance is a complete compensation system for bodily injury. Your insurance company pays your medical expenses, lost income, and other economic losses, subject to policy limits, regardless of who caused the accident. Pedestrians and guests in your car are also covered. There is no gamble about whether someone's insurance will pay for your medical bills.

No-fault eliminates much of the delay in claims settlement by reducing investigation and fault determination. Costs are lessened by eliminating much of the litigation. The limited form of no-fault insurance in-

Table 8–7 State-by-state no-fault laws

State	Effective Date	No-Fault Benefit Level	Restriction on Right to Sue
Arkansas	7/1/74	BODILY INJURY ONLY—$2,000 Medical and $7,280 loss of income with 7-day waiting period	None
Colorado	4/1/74	BODILY INJURY ONLY—$25,000 Medical, $25,000 Rehabilitation	Yes. Suits permitted only if: 1. Death. 2. Serious injuries. 3. Medical expenses exceed $500. 4. Intentional injury. 5. Product defect.
Connecticut	1/1/73	BODILY INJURY ONLY—$5,000 aggregate for various benefits.	Yes. Suits permitted only if: 1. Death. 2. Serious injuries. 3. Medical expenses exceed $400. 4. Expenses in excess of no-fault benefits.
Delaware	1/1/72	BODILY INJURY—$10,000 per person. $20,000 aggregate for various benefits. PROPERTY DAMAGE—Provided under UM	None, but permits subrogation against negligent party.
Florida	1/1/72	BODILY INJURY ONLY—$5,000 aggregate for various benefits	Yes. Suits barred unless injury results in death or if medical expenses exceed $1,000.
Georgia	3/1/75	BODILY INJURY ONLY—$5,000 aggregate for various benefits.	Yes. Suits permitted only if: 1. Death. 2. Serious injury. 3. Temporary disability exceeds 10 days. 4. Medical expenses exceed $500.
Hawaii	9/1/74	BODILY INJURY ONLY—$15,000 aggregate for various benefits.	Yes. Suits permitted only if: 1. Death. 2. Serious injury. 3. Medical expenses exceed $1,500.
Kansas	1/1/74	BODILY INJURY ONLY—$2,000 Medical. $2,000 Rehabilitation. $7,800 Loss of Income.	Yes. Suits permitted only if: 1. Death. 2. Serious injury. 3. Medical expenses exceed $500.
Kentucky	7/1/75	BODILY INJURY ONLY—$10,000 aggregate for various benefits.	Yes. Suits permitted only if: 1. Death. 2. Serious injury. 3. Medical expenses exceed $1,000.
Maryland	1/1/73	BODILY INJURY ONLY—$2,500 aggregate for various benefits.	None
Massachusetts	1/1/71	BODILY INJURY—$2,000 aggregate for various benefits. PROPERTY DAMAGE—Provides for three physical damage options under Property Protection insurance.	Yes. Suits permitted only if: 1. Death. 2. Serious injury. 3. Medical expenses exceed $500.
Michigan	10/1/75	BODILY INJURY—Unlimited Medical and $36,000 loss of income. PROPERTY DAMAGE—$1 million for nonvehicular PD and auto PD only when vehicle parked.	Yes. Suits permitted only if: 1. Death. 2. Serious injury. 3. Economic loss exceeding benefits provided by law.

Table 8–7 (continued)

State	Effective Date	No-Fault Benefit Level	Restriction on Right to Sue
Minnesota	1/1/75	BODILY INJURY ONLY—$20,000 Medical. $10,000 other economic loss. $1,250 Death benefits.	Yes. Suits permitted only if: 1. Death. 2. Serious injury. 3. Disability of more than 60 days. 4. Medical expenses exceed $2,000.
Nevada	2/1/74	BODILY INJURY ONLY—$10,000 aggregate for various benefits.	Yes. Suits permitted only if: 1. Death. 2. Serious injuries. 3. Injuries where medical expenses exceed $750. 4. Expenses for any benefit exceed the individual benefit limit.
New Jersey	1/1/73	BODILY INJURY ONLY—Unlimited medical and hospital expenses. $5,200 loss of income.	Yes. Suits permitted only if: 1. Death. 2. Serious injuries. 3. Medical expenses for actual treatment only exceed $200.
New York	2/1/74	BODILY INJURY ONLY—$50,000 aggregate for various benefits.	Yes. Suits permitted only if: 1. Death. 2. Serious injuries. 3. Medical expenses exceed $500.
North Dakota	1/1/76	BODILY INJURY ONLY—$15,000 aggregate for various benefits.	Yes. Suits permitted only if: 1. Death. 2. Serious injury. 3. Medical expenses exceed $1,000 or 60 days disability.
Oregon	1/1/72	BODILY INJURY ONLY—$5,000 Medical. $9,000 loss of income with a 14-day waiting period.	None
Pennsylvania	7/19/75	BODILY INJURY ONLY—Unlimited medical and rehabilitation expenses. Limits in funeral, wage loss, loss of service and survivor benefits.	Yes. Suits permitted only if: 1. Death. 2. Serious injury. 3. Medical expenses exceed $750 or 60 days liability. 4. Uninsured motorist.
South Carolina	10/1/74	BODILY INJURY ONLY—$1,000 aggregate for medical expenses, disability and economic loss.	None
South Dakota	1/1/72	BODILY INJURY ONLY—$2,000 Medical. $3,120 loss of income with a 14-day waiting period.	None
Texas	8/27/73	BODILY INJURY ONLY—$2,500 aggregate for various benefits.	None
Utah	1/1/74	BODILY INJURY ONLY—$2,000 Medical. $7,800 loss of income with a 3-day waiting period.	Yes. Suits permitted only if: 1. Death. 2. Serious injury. 3. Medical expenses exceed $500.
Virginia	1/1/72	BODILY INJURY ONLY—$2,000 Medical. $5,200 loss of income.	None

Source: American Insurance Association.

augurated by Massachusetts covers bodily-injury claims up to $2,000 in medical and hospital expenses and wage losses. On bodily-injury claims over $500, the driver retains the right to sue the other party and his insurance company. Even with this limited form of no-fault, premiums for bodily injury insurance were reduced by 15 percent in Massachusetts. Under the tort-liability system, a rate increase of 22 percent would have been necessary according to insurance industry sources.

What Would You Like?

The proposed legislation for a "pure" no-fault insurance plan contemplates three significant changes in our present system: (1) it will eliminate fault finding and dealings with the other party's insurance company; (2) it will lower premium costs, and (3) it will lessen "pain and suffering" damages and the right to sue for them, paying only direct economic losses. The Trial Lawyers Association has vigorously opposed the third change.

What do you think is the best solution? Many state legislatures are compromising between the present and proposed systems. Some states, such as Massachusetts and New York, are requiring compulsory auto-liability insurance. The federal government is in the process of formulating a national health plan. If it is properly coordinated with auto insurance, there would no longer be a need for auto medical-payment coverage. Contact your state and federal representatives and find out their views. Let them know yours. Consumers stand to gain from letting their views be known prior to being short-changed in the marketplace. Use your voting power where it might do some good.

PROPERTY INSURANCE

Your largest investment is probably your tangible property: your house, car, clothes, and physical possessions. Since you have probably worked hard for these things, you will want to protect them from unexpected happenings. One way to do this is by purchasing property insurance.

What Can You Insure?

You can usually insure yourself against economic loss of any property belonging to you. Property is categorized as real property or personal property. Real property is land, buildings, and anything that is attached to land. Personal property is any property that is not specifically real property, namely all other belongings.

Insurance companies will not insure land, because it is relatively indestructible. Anything attached to the land, such as a house, shed, trees, or shrubs, could be insured. Your personal property, on or off your premises, and someone else's property on your premises, may be insured. (In this case you have an insurable interest because you might be sued for its loss or destruction.)

What Can You Insure Against?

You can insure against *direct damage* to your property or to the *consequential loss of use* of your property. You ought to insure against both types of losses. The first type of loss is more prevalent in personal insurance lines, while the second is often used in business. There are times when the temporary loss of use of your home or auto requires you to rent a replacement at an expense to you. Additional living-expense insurance protects you against the first risk.

You can insure against any hazard that can cause you economic loss. Some of the more obvious hazards are easily identified: (1) fire and related calamities; (2) theft and related incidents; (3) weather and other acts of nature; (4) man-made equipment malfunction; (5) civil disorder and vandalism; and (6) legal liabilities resulting from damage to other people or their property when caused by you, your family, or any of your possessions.

All of these hazards and many more are insured against through fire, theft, and liability coverages. Autos are insured separately. Each hazard may be insured through a separate policy or several may be covered through a package policy or policy rider such as a *Homeowner's Policy* or a *Tenant's Policy*. Businesses also may purchase separate or package policies.

To understand what hazards you can insure against and some insurance limitations, we will look at the major coverages available. Whether you insure for direct damage or consequential loss or both, the choice of coverage may be narrowly or widely determined. This choice is between *named peril* or *all risk*. Named-peril policies enumerate the actual insurance coverage. If it is not named, you are not covered. In an all-risk policy the exclusions are enumerated. You are covered unless there is a specific exclusion not to insure against a particular hazard.

NAMED-PERIL COVERAGES

Fire and Lightning

The standard fire-insurance agreement insures against all direct loss to buildings and personal property by fire, lightning, and by removal from the premises of any articles endangered by these perils. The fire contract for residential property is written on a dwelling and contents form. Indemnity is provided for losses from hostile fires and not from friendly fires. Fire is defined as oxidation that produces a visible flame or glow. A hostile fire is one that is uncontrolled, while a friendly fire is one that is contained in a receptacle. Once a fire passes outside its receptacle it becomes hostile. Recovery generally cannot be made on articles thrown into a friendly fire, damage to the receptacle, or to scorching or smoke damage caused by a friendly fire. Once the fire escapes its confines, the insurance company is liable.

Lightning is the discharge of atmospheric electricity. The resulting damage is covered, whether a fire starts or not. Because it is difficult to determine lightning damage as compared to normal wear on electrical appliances, a $50 deductible is normally applied.

The standard agreement excepts certain causes of loss, for which the insurance company will assume no liability. These are loss by fire or other perils, directly or indirectly caused by:

1. Enemy attack, war, or civil insurrection
2. Neglect of the insured to use reasonable means to preserve the property when endangered by a peril
3. Losses caused by theft
4. Losses caused by explosion or riot unless fire ensues
5. Losses caused by the willful act of the insured

Extended-Coverage Endorsement

The extended-coverage endorsement, when attached to the fire-insurance policy, extends the policy to include the perils of windstorm, hail, explosion, riot, riot attending a strike, civil commotion, aircraft, vehicles, and smoke. The insured must accept all or none, since no deletions are permitted.

Windstorm and hail The extended-coverage endorsement applicable to windstorm and hail specifically excludes loss caused by frost or cold weather and ice (other than hail), snowstorm, waves, tidal wave, and high water or overflow, whether driven by wind or not.

A mandatory \$50 or \$100 deductible is applicable to windstorm and hail losses. The deductible does not apply to personal property located in a building; it does, however, apply separately to each building and separately to personal property in the open.

Explosion The coverage in the extended-coverage endorsement provides protection against all direct loss or damage by explosion, but it specifically excludes explosions originating within steam boilers, pipes, or machinery owned or controlled by the insured or located on the premises.

Riot and civil commotion The inclusion of these perils (riot, riot attending a strike, and civil commotion) supersedes the specific exclusion of such perils in the Standard Fire Contract. All physical damage caused by these perils is covered, although the definition of what constitutes a riot or civil commotion varies.

Aircraft and vehicles Direct loss attributable to aircraft or falling objects and vehicles also is covered by the extended-coverage endorsement. The term *vehicles* applies to vehicles running on land or tracks and excludes airplanes. Damage caused by vehicles owned or operated by the insured does not apply.

Smoke The smoke clause is intended to cover smoke damage caused by the sudden, unusual, and faulty operation of an on-premises heating or cooking unit, when such a unit is connected to a chimney by a smokepipe or vent. Smoke damage coming from fireplaces is usually excluded as coming from a friendly fire.

Vandalism and Malicious Mischief Endorsement

This coverage may be added to the Standard Fire Policy if the extended-coverage endorsement is also attached. Damage must be caused by willful and malicious physical injury to or destruction of the described property. Loss from pilferage, theft, burglary, or larceny is excluded, except for damage to the building caused by burglars. The endorsement also includes a vacancy clause, which permits vacancy up to thirty days.

Additional Extended-Coverage Endorsement

This comprehensive coverage applies to loss from extra perils or expanded earlier-named perils. These include: (1) water damage from plumbing, heating, or air-conditioning systems, (2) rupturing or bursting of steam or hot-water systems, (3) vandalism and malicious mischief, (4) vehicles owned or operated by the insured or by a tenant, (5) fall of trees, (6) objects falling from the weight of ice, snow, or sleet, (7) freezing of plumbing, heating, and the like, (8) collapse of buildings, and (9) glass breakage. This is not "all-risk" coverage. The basic liability to the insurance company is still "named perils."

Earthquake, Landslide, and Flood Insurance

Insurance against these specifically named perils is *individually* available by endorsement or by separate policy in selected areas of the country. These insurances are usually offered by commercial insurance companies in cooperation with the U.S. Department of Housing and Urban Development. The coverage for each is narrowly defined in most instances.

Dwelling Contents—Broad Form

This form incorporates all of the usual features of the regular dwelling and contents form and adds the perils of the extended coverage and additional extended-coverage endorsements as well as other extensions. For example, the broad form may include replacement-cost coverage where no deduction for depreciation is taken from the amount needed to replace the damaged property. Coverage often includes smoke damage caused by fireplaces and heating or cooking units not connected to a chimney. It is still on a named-peril basis.

Theft Insurance

Basic theft insurance covers burglary, robbery, and larceny. It usually does not cover damage caused by persons entering your property to commit theft, nor does it cover "mysterious disappearance." One is likely to incur more serious loss through breaking and entering than from actual theft. This coverage and coverage of losses from mysterious disappearance, where entry and theft cannot be specifically proved, is available by broad-form theft insurance or by special-form personal floaters. The property of guests is also covered by broad or special forms. Valuable items are covered only for a limited amount shown in your policy. Special schedules of valuable property may be covered by added premium payments.

Liability Insurance

Liability insurance protects your assets from claims arising from bodily injury and damage to the property of another person. Coverage varies among companies, but *comprehensive personal liability insurance* generally protects you from claims of others, except those arising from auto accidents, large-boat and aircraft accidents, libel, and slander. For all practical purposes you are insuring your present property (net worth) and future earnings from loss by lawsuit.

You can be sued for any wrongful act or omission that damages another party. Modern life continually exposes you to this possibility. The act or omission may be intentional, unintentional, or negligent (carelessness). The insurance company undertakes to settle a claim against you, your family, or your property. This may be done in or out of court. If the insurance company does not settle out of court, it will prepare a court defense on your behalf.

ALL-RISK COVERAGES

Dwellings—Special Form

This form covers only real property (buildings), not personal property. It departs from the traditional named-perils principle of insuring property. Coverage consists of "all risks of physical loss except as excluded." Exclusions include war, deterioration, insects, and termites, and any property unusually susceptible to damage. All-risk coverage by special form is the broadest insurance coverage available for dwellings. The exact wording of the form will differ from company to company and between rating territories.

Personal-Property Floaters

Floater policies are designed to provide all-risk protection for nonbusiness *personal property* of the insured and members of his household, wherever it may be located. The protection follows the property. The all-risk feature usually excludes loss by war, deterioration, and so on. Three types of personal floaters are available:

Personal-article floaters These provide all-risk protection on specified classes of valuable personal items on a scheduled basis. This means that the items must be listed and valued with the insurance company. New items must be added to the schedule and any extra premiums paid.

Personal-property floaters These floaters cover all risks on *all* personal property. Items of high and low value are included. High-valued items must be scheduled.

Personal-effects floaters This form of floater attaches to either of the aforementioned floaters to cover the personal property worn or carried by travelers. There is one blanket amount of insurance covering all personal property that a tourist normally carries. Money, securities, tickets, and the like are excluded, as are vehicles. Coverage does not normally apply while the property is located on the insured's premises or if stolen from an unlocked automobile.

APPROACHES TO SELECTING COVERAGE

A consumer may select coverage on a separate-policy basis or a package-policy basis. The separate-policy approach would require a contract for fire on buildings and their contents, with endorsements for extended and additional coverage. The consumer would have to purchase fire and theft for personal property. Separate policies would also be needed for personal liability, glass breakage, earthquake, landslide, and flood. All but the last three coverages can generally be purchased in a package policy. The best-known package policy is the homeowner's policy.

Homeowner's Policy

Homeowners and tenants need a multi-peril insurance to protect themselves from the many hazards of modern life. Homeowner's policies provide the coverage most desired in one package at a savings over individually purchased policies. This package is not directly available for rental units.

The extent of perils covered differs with the type of coverage purchased. The homeowner's policy is available in a series of coverages labeled H–1 to H–5. You choose which coverage you prefer based upon need and premium cost. Figure 8–1 illustrates the typical coverage available.

H–1, Standard Form Policy This policy covers your house and contents for such perils as fire, windstorm, explosion, vandalism, and smoke under the fire coverage. Theft coverage includes burglary, robbery, larceny, damage caused by burglars, and theft of contents from a locked car. Liability coverage includes bodily injury and property damage to others caused by you, your family, and your property. Medical expenses for other people injured by you are usually included. The policy lists the specific perils for which you are insured.

H–2, Broad-Form Policy This covers a wider range of perils than H–1. It includes

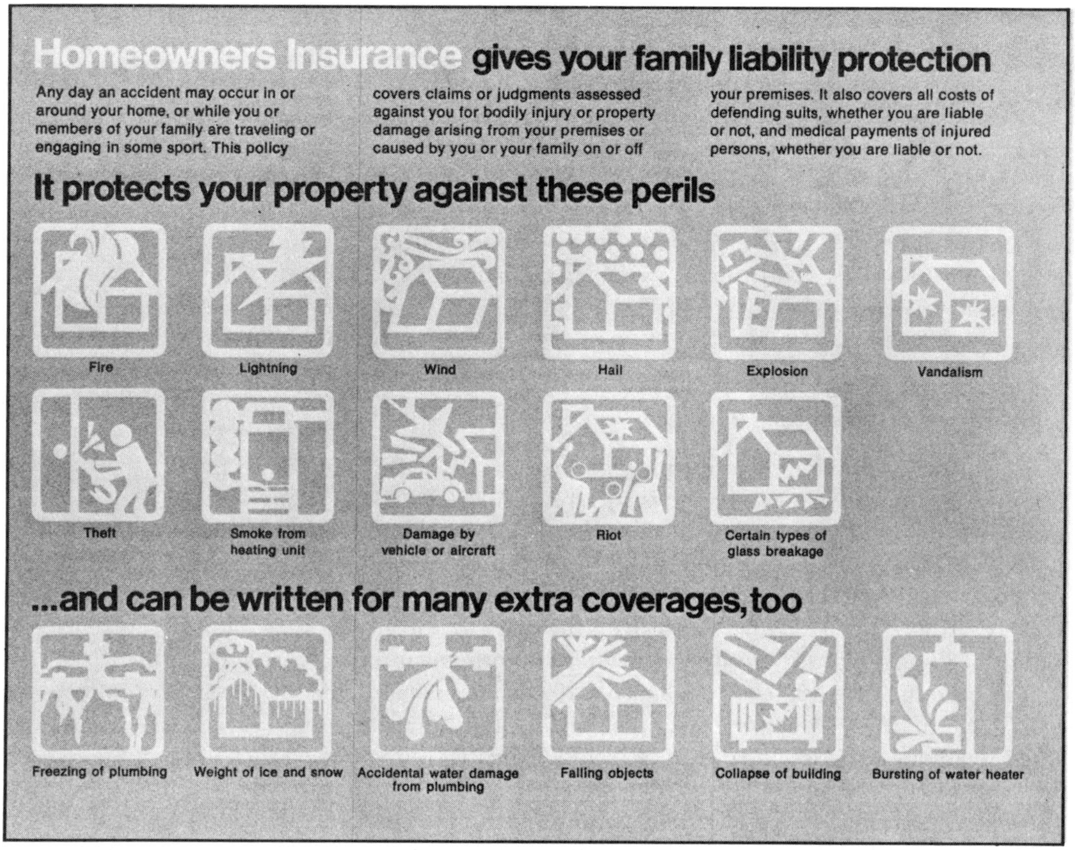

Figure 8–1 Homeowner's Package Policy. *(Farmers Insurance Group, Los Angeles)*

full smoke damage, glass breakage, freezing, water overflow, falling objects, and damage caused by another's auto. The specified coverage is broader and more costly than H–1.

H–3, Special-Form Policy This is an all-risk coverage on the building and a limited-risk coverage on personal property. This policy lists the exclusions rather than the coverage. It covers the named perils in H–1 and H–2 plus all physical loss to the building. This is the most popular homeowner's coverage.

H–4, Contents Broad-Form Policy Contents only are covered under this policy. It is specifically formulated for tenants and renters. These people have the same exposure to perils as a homeowner as far as contents are concerned. This policy covers contents to the extent of H–2, without the added expense of covering a dwelling.

H–5, Comprehensive-Form Policy This is an all-risk coverage on both the dwelling and the contents. It lists the specific exclusions to real and personal property. It includes scheduled coverage for your more valuable personal property, such as furs, jewelry, and paintings. It is the most expensive of the homeowner's policies.

A typical homeowner's policy will most likely consist of the following coverages: Dwelling–special form; Appurtenant private structures–special form; Personal property–on the premises; Personal property–away from your premises; Additional living expenses; and Personal liability–bodily injury and property damage.

Supplementary Umbrella Policies

These policies provide greater protection when used as a supplement to the insured's liability policy and major medical policy. There are two types of umbrella liability policies for individuals: excess-liability insurance and "drop-down" liability insurance. *Excess-liability insurance policies* in the amount of $1,000,000 to $5,000,000 pay excess liability damages on your behalf whenever your primary insurance is insufficient to pay a judgment rendered against you. For example, if your policy has a $300,000 public-liability limit and you have a $700,000 judgment against you, the umbrella policy pays the $400,000 excess. Your auto, boat, and homeowner's personal-liability policies provide your primary insurance. *Drop-down umbrella policies* "drop down" and provide primary coverage whenever your primary liability policy does *not* cover a particular liability loss. Libel and slander are normally covered in this manner. You have broader coverage and certainty of protection against high jury awards if you are found legally liable for damages.

A *personal umbrella major medical rider* provides up to $25,000 protection for each covered member of your family. There is a $10,000 deductible, which is usually covered by the major medical expense insurance of your family health plan. Eighty percent of the covered medical expenses in excess of the deductible will be paid by the umbrella until the limit of $25,000 has been reached.

If you do not find insurance for your particular needs, ask your casualty-insurance agent. For a price you can get any property or situation insured, providing the basic principles of insurance apply to your situation. Lloyds of London is an insurance syndicate that often underwrites unusual perils. Your agent can arrange the details.

INSURANCE CLAUSES THAT AFFECT YOU

Once you have a fairly good idea of what coverage you want, you must decide how much you need. At this point the clauses in your insurance policy help define the actual coverage you have, which in turn affects the premium that you must pay. The amount of protection you need should be related to the amount of exposure you have to a given risk. Let's look at some policy clauses to watch for and their underlying concepts before we figure the cost of insurance.

Coinsurance

The purpose of coinsurance is to force the insured to carry full face-value protection on his property. Under the coinsurance clause, the insured has any loss paid only in proportion to the amount of insurance that the company requires him to take to be fully insured. He is free to buy as little or as much insurance as he deems necessary, but loss payoff is prorated in proportion to what he actually carries. To be fully insured most companies require you to have a policy covering at least 80 percent of the actual value of the building. This amount is called the coinsurance percentage. Specifically, whenever you carry less insurance than required, the loss payoff will be less than the face amount of your policy. It will be proportional to the amount you should have carried. The insurance company formula for a coinsurance clause looks like this:

$$\frac{\text{Face value of policy}}{\text{Coinsurance percentage amount}} \times \text{Loss} = \text{Amount of payment}$$

A typical example of a policy involving the coinsurance clause follows: You have a home with a value of $50,000. To be fully insured you would have to carry $40,000 (80 percent of $50,000) face-value coverage. Any loss from the perils listed in your policy would be covered up to a maximum of $40,000 (less depreciation), as you are fully covered. Any face-value coverage of less than $40,000 would make you a coinsurer. You would be reimbursed on a prorated basis in an amount less than your actual loss. Let's see how coverage of less than full face value works.

Let us assume that you wish to save premium money by insuring your home for $30,000. You are actually carrying only three-fourths of the insurance required to be fully covered. In case of loss you would be reimbursed for only three-fourths of the loss because you insured yourself for only three-fourths of the required face-value coverage, as specified in the coinsurance clause. If you have a $10,000 fire, the computation would look like this:

$$\frac{\$30{,}000}{\$40{,}000} \times \$10{,}000 = \$7{,}500$$

You would be reimbursed for $7,500, less depreciation. You would need to provide the balance of $2,500 or more to replace your $10,000 loss.

Deductible Coverage

As in automobile and medical insurance, you can get a reduction in premium on homeowner's and glass-breakage insurance. Normally $100 deductible is available for a premium reduction of about $25. The assumption, of course, is that small insurance claims will be eliminated.

Duplicate Insurance

The purpose of duplicate insurance is to protect oneself from economic loss, not to make a profit. Insurance companies will make certain that you do not profit by having more than one policy covering a loss. Any one company will pay off only to the extent of its proportionate share of the total loss, not to exceed the policy limits. Because of this clause you cannot receive more than the actual loss from all the policies collectively. Some homeowner's forms use the duplicate-coverage clause as a pretext to void coverage completely if there is any other insurance present. Being overinsured is not economically sound.

Inflation-Guard Clause

Real property should be insured for replacement cost since it tends to appreciate. A good portion of the appreciation is caused by inflated prices of labor and materials needed to rebuild or replace your damaged property. In a period of three to five years you could become seriously underinsured to the point of becoming a coinsurer. See the definition of replacement cost in subsequent paragraphs.

The inflation-guard clause raises the coverage limit each year by a set amount or by a price-index percentage. This *automatic increase* in face value protects you to the full replacement cost. An additional premium is payable by separate billing or by an increase in premium at the policy renewal date.

Occupancy Clause

Your policy may be void if you leave your house unoccupied for sixty consecutive days. Some tenants' policies (especially those for theft coverage) become voidable if the premises are unoccupied for ten consecutive days. This clause is usually in standard-form policies, but not in broad-form or special-form policies. Check your policy carefully.

Reduced-Protection Clause

At one time fire policies reduced the amount of coverage (policy face value) by the amount of any claim. The lower coverage or balance was all that remained in force until the expiration of the insurance contract. For example, if you had a policy with a face value of $30,000 and had a fire loss of $18,000, your protection would be reduced to $12,000 for the balance of the term.

The premiums on reduced-protection insurance are lower than on the more popular nonreducing policies. The purchase of this insurance is usually not in the best interests of the policyholder. In fact this clause has been eliminated in most states. Catastrophies operate independently of one another. You can easily have two loss occurrences during the term of the policy that could separately exceed the original face value. If you *need* a certain amount of insurance protection, that is what you should purchase.

Replacement-Cost Clause

Insurance policies never pay more than the face value (coverage) of the policy; after all, that is what you paid for. However, the amount of the indemnity actually paid will be less if the value of the damaged property is less. This is known as *actual cash value* (ACV). ACV is the original cost less depreciation. It is not replacement cost.

For a higher premium as part of dwelling–special form, you may have buildings insured at replacement cost. Here again you must carry 80 percent or more of the value of the building to qualify for replacement-cost coverage. You and your agent must forecast what the cost per square foot will be to replace your dwelling during the period your insurance policy is in force. An inflation-guard clause provides for an automatic increase in the face value of a policy.

PREMIUM COSTS

The cost to purchase a homeowner's policy will differ greatly by area, type of house, face value of the policy, and type of coverage. For example, the number of fires or thefts in a given area affects the premiums of all residents in that area. Your proximity to a fire department and fire hydrants, and the efficiency rating of the fire department, also affect premiums. The construction material in the house, type of roof, and number of stories are also considered. If you have fire extinguishers in your home, some insurance companies allow a premium reduction.

As noted earlier, the face value and extent of coverage affect the premium you pay. Standard coverage on a $30,000 home should cost somewhere in the neighborhood of $150 per year. Broad and special coverage will be higher in cost. It is highly unlikely that two companies will quote the same rate. This is why shopping for insurance is a must.

You can reduce your premium costs by following these suggestions:

1. Compare two or more companies for rates.
2. Pay premiums in one lump-sum for the longest possible period: pay one-year premiums rather than half-year or monthly premiums.
3. Purchase multi-peril package policies rather than single-peril individual policies.
4. Purchase deductible coverage whenever possible.

SELECTING THE INSURANCE COMPANY

In selecting an insurance company, you should compare claims procedures, policy cancellations, and agent representation.

Claims Procedure

Insurance is only as good as your ability to collect. You can call upon your agent to assist you with a property-insurance claim. You should also check with any acquaintance who has had a property loss to see if he is satisfied with his insurance company's claims procedure.

You will probably be required to provide an inventory of personal property to prove your loss. Almost invariably you will not be able to remember what you owned, much less its original cost and date of purchase. To be properly prepared, make a list of all personal property and update it regularly. The list should be kept off the premises, at work or in a safe-deposit box. Photographs will further provide proof of loss, but keep these separate from the property.

Policy Cancellation

There will be a cancellation clause in your policy allowing you or the company to cancel. The company will have to give you five to ten days notice of cancellation. This allows you time to shop for new insurance. This is likely to occur only if you have filed too many claims with a company, or if the company has experienced a great upsurge of losses in your neighborhood.

If the company should cancel your policy, you will be given a prorated refund on your unused insurance premium. If you should cancel voluntarily, such as when you sell your house, you will receive a short-rated refund. This means that the company charges you for the insurance on a short-rate table, as if the shorter period is what you had originally contracted for. Shorter periods of insurance cost more per day, week, or month than longer terms.

Property and Casualty Agents

Property insurance is not often merchandised by mail. Chances are that you will deal through an independent insurance agent who will represent a company authorized to do business in your state. Your agent can advise you about the integrity of the companies he represents. He will have a tendency to recommend the companies that he is associated with.

While independent agents may deal with a few insurance companies on a steady basis, they can find just the right company to provide you with the right combination of premium, coverage, and service. By comparing two or more brokers' or agents' recommendations about particular companies, you will be able to make a more knowledgeable decision. Your agent should be a CPCU, as previously discussed in the section on automobile insurance.

Vocabulary and Concepts

Actual cash value	Coinsurance clause
Assigned risk	Collision damage

Comprehensive damage	Personal-property floater
Financial responsibility law	Replacement cost
Homeowner's policy	Subrogation
Liability insurance	Umbrella policy
No-fault insurance	Vendor's single interest

Questions for Discussion

1. Explain auto-liability insurance. Differentiate between single-limit and split-limit coverage.
2. Differentiate between auto comprehensive and collision insurance coverage.
3. What is uninsured motorists coverage?
4. What are the criteria for determining the premium rates for auto insurance? What can you do about this?
5. Explain how you can be either overinsured or underinsured in your auto policy.
6. What is the usual sequence in claims adjustment procedures whenever the other party is liable?
7. Explain the difference between named peril and all-risk property insurance coverage.
8. What are the five homeowner's policy forms? Explain each.
9. How would a claim pay off, if you were insured for $60,000 on a house valued at $80,000? What clause in your fire insurance policy covers this situation? What is the rationale for this clause?
10. Why is it important to have a replacement-cost or inflation-guard clause in your fire policy? What is the difference, if any?

Projects

1. Review your auto-insurance coverage. Ask for a detailed breakdown on your premium charge. Are you overinsured? Can you save on the premium?
2. Contact your state legislators to get their views on establishing or expanding the limits on a no-fault insurance system.
3. Find out how the point system, if any, operates to set auto-insurance premiums in your state. Find out how auto rates are set by your insurance company.
4. Inventory your personal property. Do you have sufficient insurance? What risks are present? What is the probability of loss in your locale?

Case Problem

Art and Barbara Able's balance sheet shown in table 1–2 indicates they own $13,400 in personal property and $40,000 in real property. After looking at the details, what face amounts of insurance in what types of policies would you suggest they purchase? Their friend Bart Baker also has $13,400 in personal property, of which $4,000 is a personal-size auto with the balance furnishings and effects in his apartment. Would you give him the same advice?

9

insuring your retirement

Retirement may be a means to an end, or it might be the real end. Money makes the difference between enjoying the leisure time at your disposal and struggling just to survive. The possible shortage of money, the potential for ill health, and an unknown time-factor all influence retirement.

THE RISKS OF RETIREMENT

At a young age it is hard to conceive of the very real peril of few assets, little income, and no way of replenishing your assets or increasing your income. A youth has a future in which to secure assets and income if he desires; it is not so when you are elderly. Many people would not retire at age sixty-five, but they are forced to by their employers. They have not amassed enough assets to live comfortably, because they did not plan ahead. They ran out of time.

There is a very definite possibility of outliving your assets after you retire if you have not planned ahead. Most retirees do not receive enough income from Social Security and other sources to keep their assets intact. If you must supplement your retirement income by drawing upon your savings or investment capital, the question becomes, how much should you take. If you withdraw too much, you will soon be penniless. If you withdraw too little, you must struggle. A further complication arises in the case of married couples: statistically, women live about five years longer than men, and wives are usually younger than husbands. Therefore, retirement planning must consider the likelihood of the woman outliving the man by five years or more.

The solution lies in providing yourself and your spouse with an adequate retirement fund. Our dispersed society and new life-styles have made it impractical, if not impossible, to have the retired person's family support him. Young families always seem to have enough troubles supporting themselves and raising their children without the added burden of supporting the elderly.

Social Security and welfare do not provide the solution to this economic risk. Social Security does provide a base income that you must supplement in order to have a decent standard of living. The Bureau of Labor Statistics figures there is at least a $150 difference between what the average couple receives in Social Security benefits and an average monthly budget needed to maintain a moderate standard of living. Welfare for the elderly does not make up this difference.

The lack of money or the possibility of outliving it is central to the risk of retirement. Careful consideration of the following questions will allow a couple to plan in a more orderly manner.

1. What sources of income will we have?
2. What assets will we have?
3. Where will we live?
4. What are our leisure-time goals?

SOURCES OF RETIREMENT INCOME

Most income during retirement comes from Social Security, partial employment, and savings or investment interest. Social Security requires little planning, but to supplement it with income from savings and investments demands careful thinking. Partial employment as a solution to reduced retirement income defeats the purpose of retirement and may not be economically feasible. Social Security benefits are reduced by fifty cents for each dollar earned over $2,760 annually by persons between age sixty-two and seventy-two. Once you reach age seventy-two, you can make any amount in outside employment or self-employment and still draw your full Social Security benefits.

In addition to Social Security, a person must plan ahead and look to other sources of income to balance his retirement budget. Other sources would be savings, company pension plans, annuities and retirement-insurance plans, real estate, rental income, and ownership of a business. We will expand on these sources of retirement income throughout this chapter and in the later chapters devoted to these specific subjects.

RETIREMENT ASSETS

Assets may be liquid (easily convertible to cash) or they may be fixed (nonliquid). What you own at time of retirement can increase, decrease, or have no effect on your actual income. Assets can appreciate (increase in value) or depreciate (decrease in value). They can also be sold, and the proceeds can be placed in a savings account or in an investment to produce current income.

The closer you are to retirement, the easier it is to estimate the assets you will have at retirement. In chapter 2 we learned that the value of your assets over your liabilities was called your net worth. The greater your net worth, the better your economic position. If you are many years from retirement, you may not be able to estimate your retirement net worth accurately, but you can formulate a plan to reach a certain goal.

The idea is to have your assets working for you by providing an income, by increasing in value, or both. If the asset does not accomplish either of these, it would be better to sell it. At retirement the most important economic need is current income, not asset growth, so you should place your assets with emphasis on income rather than growth or appreciation. It might be wise to sell your home and any other real estate or securities that are not providing current income and place the money in a savings account or an immediate annuity. Carefully figure cash flow, appreciation, and inflation factors before selling your home. Alternate accommodations may prove to be too expensive!

RETIREMENT RESIDENCE

What will housing cost? This question ties into the concepts of income and net worth, since the cost of housing is perhaps the greatest single expense of the retired person. Retired people who own their homes spend approximately one-fourth of their income on taxes, maintenance, and utilities, while those who rent spend approximately one-third of their income on rent and utilities. The difference may be more than made up if the house is sold and the proceeds are placed in a savings account. Again, remember that there are many factors to consider. In such a case, a fixed asset (your home) that causes expense will have been replaced by a liquid asset (savings) that produces interest income and is easily available if needed. Your net worth should remain about the same, because you have simply exchanged one type of asset for another.

You may wish to purchase a home in a retirement community or a condominium or cooperative apartment in an urban area to maintain a sense of ownership and gain some asset appreciation. Whether you rent or purchase, you probably desire to be with people who are of the same age and share some of your interests and problems. You may even wish to share housing expenses with someone. If you decide to move when you retire, two very important rules must be followed, or it will prove to be a very expensive and unwise move: (1) know the area where you are moving, and (2) do not sell your residence until after age sixty-five.

Know the area Retirement dreams may turn into nightmares if you are not familiar with the area in which you wish to retire. Many people exchange a nice home and friends for a small cottage or apartment in an area that is highly advertised as a retirement paradise. It would be better for you to try an extended vacation in your "dream" area as an experiment before completely moving with nothing more concrete than great expectations.

Sell your residence after age sixty-five Older people get a special tax break when they sell their residence. One spouse must be over sixty-five. You may elect to avoid income tax on the gain from the first $20,000 of the sales price of the residence. You must own the property and have lived in it at least five of the last eight years preceding the sale. You are entitled to this election only once in your lifetime.

LIFE-STYLE AND RETIREMENT GOALS

Planning for retirement requires that you assess your style of living very carefully. You must first determine the number of people who will still be dependent upon you after you retire. Many times a sixty-five-year-old person must still partly or wholly support parents who would be in their late eighties or older. If you have children late in life, you may have school-age dependents to support when you retire.

Next you must determine the standard of living you wish to maintain. What are your retirement goals? Part of this determination would include analyzing the cost of living in whatever geographical area you wish to retire. The Bureau of Labor Statistics annually reports this data for a two-person household in retirement. Your budget must be projected to cover basic living expenses and the extra leisure-time expenses associated with retirement.

Your leisure-time retirement activities will be the difference between a dull retirement and an enjoyable time. These activities will most likely add to your basic retirement expenses. Travel to foreign lands or to visit relatives on the other side of the country can be extremely expensive. Hobbies and country-club activities can also be expensive and must definitely be planned for in your budget. You must determine your retirement goals well before retirement—the earlier the better! You may be forced to change your life-style and your retirement plans drastically because of lack of money and lack of foresight.

Three specific plans have been devised to provide income during retirement. These are Social Security, individual and corporate pension plans, and annuities. We will examine each of these in turn.

Many fortunate persons have both OASDI (Social Security) and private-plan retirement insurance.

SOCIAL SECURITY

Until the Social Security Act of 1935, most people depended upon relatives and charity once they were forced to retire. The more fortunate planned ahead with insurance and annuities, or they were lucky enough to have a company pension that actually paid off.

Today over 90 percent of all workers are covered by Social Security. It is a mandatory retirement plan administered by the federal government and funded by contributions from the employee, the employer, and the self-employed. The contributions are made to provide economic protection against certain risks just as in any other insurance.

Your paycheck stub has a record of deductions for OASDI—Old Age, Survivors, and Disability Insurance. This public insurance program covers much more than just retirement benefits for the elderly. It is constantly being changed by Congress to improve the social well-being of all people who are covered. It is really an insurance designed to provide social security.

Types of Benefits Available

There are four major benefits available under the Social Security program. These are Retirement, Disability, Survivor, and Medicare. As each benefit is described below, consider how it fits into your overall insurance, investment, and retirement plans. Also remember that the benefits available at the present time are subject to change. Chances are that any change will liberalize benefits, as has been the case in the past.

Retirement The retirement benefit is the most widely known Social Security benefit. It is the benefit most widely received by persons covered by the act. It consists of monthly cash payments made to retired workers, their spouses, and dependent children, if any.

Retired workers may receive cash benefits beginning at age sixty-two. If the worker desires his full benefit he must wait until age sixty-five, the normal retirement age. Earlier retirement means a lower monthly benefit payment. The total benefits received during the retirement period are calculated to be about the same whether a worker retires at age sixty-two or sixty-five. Early retirement at lower but longer-lasting monthly benefits is an option available to the worker.

Wives of retired workers also receive monthly cash benefits. A wife may choose to receive retirement benefits under her own earnings record or that of her husband, whichever is greater. As a worker, a wife may also retire at age sixty-two with reduced monthly benefits, or she may wait and receive her full benefit at age sixty-five. However, in many cases a wife's wages as a worker may be too low to provide more than the minimum benefit, or else she may not have worked for a long enough period to qualify for her own retirement benefits. In these cases she may receive larger benefits as the wife of a retired worker.

The basic retirement benefit of a wife of a retired worker is 50 percent of her husband's full benefit. She must be sixty-five years old to receive this amount. At age sixty-two she could receive benefits approximating 38 percent of her husband's full benefit. Wives can make decisions independently of their husbands about when to retire. A wife with dependent children receives 50 percent of her husband's full benefit regardless of her age. Dependent children are unmarried children under eighteen, or between eighteen and twenty-two if they are full-time students. Unmarried disabled children eighteen and over who were disabled before age eighteen are also considered dependents for retirement-benefit purposes.

Dependent children of retired workers are also entitled to cash payments in their own name. They receive 50 percent of the retired worker's full benefit. A maximum family payment based upon the worker's past earnings applies to all beneficiaries, including the retired worker. Often the family maximum is less than the total of the individual cash payments allowable to family members. In such cases a working wife may possibly secure greater benefits by retiring under her own Social Security account, while dependent children may be attached to whichever account (husband or working wife) provides the greatest total money benefit for the family. Refer to table 9–1 to determine how cash payments may possibly be arranged to provide greater benefits to retired families with dependent children.

Disability Workers under age sixty-five who are unable to work because of a severe physical or mental condition may receive monthly cash payments. The disability must be expected to last at least twelve months or to result in death. The disability need not be job connected.

The amount of monthly disability payments is based upon past earnings and is generally calculated on the basis of the retirement benefit that the disabled worker would get if he were sixty-five years old. Payments may begin with the seventh full month of disability. Spouses and dependent children are usually eligible for payments in much the same manner as under the retirement benefit. Table 9–1 lists monthly cash payments under some of the various situations involving retirement, disability, and survivorship.

Survivor Survivors of a worker insured under Social Security may also receive monthly cash benefits. The amount of the monthly benefit is based upon the ages of the surviving children and what the deceased worker would have received had he retired at age sixty-five with his present earnings record.

The survivor's benefit is a form of term life insurance that provides monthly income to families with dependent children. Dependent children are unmarried children under eighteen (or twenty-two if full-time students) and unmarried dependent children of any age who were severely disabled before age twenty-two. The surviving wife also receives benefits if she is caring for the deceased worker's dependent children. There is a "widow's gap" in which the surviving wife receives no benefits at all once the deceased worker's children are no longer dependent. Her benefits resume as retirement income at age sixty (fifty if she is disabled).

A lump-sum payment benefit to survivors is paid at a worker's death. The amount is $255 or three times his monthly retirement benefit at age sixty-five, whichever is less.

Medicare Health-insurance protection under Medicare is available to nearly all persons age sixty-five and over, whether or not they were covered by Social Security. There are two main parts to Medicare: hospital insurance, which is automatic for those

Table 9–1 Examples of monthly cash payments under Social Security coverage

Benefits can be paid to	Average Yearly Earnings Since 1950									
	$923 or less	*$3,000*	*$3,500*	*$4,000*	*$4,500*	*$5,000*	*$6,000*	*$7,000*	*$8,000*	*$9,000*
You, the worker:										
Retired at 65	84.50	174.80	189.50	205.80	222.40	238.60	269.70	302.20	335.30	354.50
Under 65 and disabled	84.50	174.80	189.50	205.80	222.40	238.60	269.70	302.20	335.30	354.50
Retired at 62	67.60	139.90	151.60	164.70	178.00	190.90	215.80	241.80	268.30	283.60
Your wife:										
At 65	42.30	87 40	94 80	102.90	111.20	119.30	134.90	151.10	167.70	177.30
At 62, with no child	31.80	65.60	71.10	77.20	83.40	89.50	101.20	113.40	125.80	133.00
Under 65 and one child in her care	42.40	92.60	118.00	146.00	173.60	201.80	225.20	236.40	251.60	266.00
Your widow:										
At 65 (if you never received reduced retirement benefits)	84.50	174.80	189.50	205.80	222.40	238.60	269.70	302.20	335.30	354.50
At 60 (if sole survivor)	74.90	125.00	135.50	147.20	159.10	170.60	192.90	216.10	239.80	253.50
At 50 and disabled (if sole survivor)	56.80	87.50	94.80	103.00	111.30	119.40	135.00	151.20	167.80	177.30
Widowed mother and one child in her care	126.80	262.20	284.40	308.80	333.60	358.00	404.60	453.40	503.00	531.80
Maximum family payment	126.80	267.30	307.40	351.80	396.00	440.40	494.80	538.60	586.80	620.40

Source: United States Department of Health, Education and Welfare, Social Security Administration.

covered by Social Security, and medical insurance, which is voluntary and requires a small premium payment. Medicare benefits were discussed in greater detail in chapter 7.

Table 9–2 Years of credit to be fully insured under Social Security

Work Credit for Retirement Benefits	
If You Reach 62 in	*Years Needed*
1975	6
1977	6½
1979	7
1981	7½
1983	8
1987	9
1991 or later	10

Work Credit for Survivors Checks		
Born After 1929, Die at	*Born Before 1930 Die Before Age 62*	*Years You Need*
28 or younger		1½
30		2
32		2½
34		3
36		3½
38		4
40		4½
42		5
44	1973	5½
46	1975	6
48	1977	6½
50	1979	7
52	1981	7½
54	1983	8
56	1985	8½
58	1987	9
60	1989	9½
62 or older	1991 or later	10

Source: United States Department of Health, Education and Welfare, Social Security Administration.

Eligibility for Benefits

To be eligible for retirement, disability, and survivor's benefits under the Social Security system a person must either be a worker or the dependent of a worker who has contributed to the plan. All covered earnings throughout your working career are considered when your eligibility and the amount of your monthly cash benefit are determined.

You obtain credit for work if you earn $50 in covered wages during any three-month calendar quarter. You can get Social Security credit up to four quarters in any year. A person earning maximum wages subject to Social Security tax in any year will get four quarters of coverage even if he did not earn $50 in one or more calendar quarters. A self-employed person must have a net profit of $400 during a calendar year to earn four quarters of coverage.

The number of years of earned Social Security credit determines whether you are fully insured or currently insured. Credit is earned in quarters, which need not be consecutive. Table 9–2 indicates the amount of credit needed to be fully insured. Table 9–3 describes the benefits available to persons either fully or currently insured.

Fully insured To receive retirement benefits a covered worker and his dependents must be fully insured. No one is fully insured who has credit for less than 1½ years of work and no one needs more than 10 years of work (40 quarters) to be fully insured. The fully insured status means that certain benefits will be paid; it does not determine the amount payable. The amount will depend on your average earnings. Many people have become fully insured under Social Security and have then changed to jobs not covered by Social Security or vice versa. These people often receive benefits

Table 9–3 Insurance status and types of coverage under Social Security

Retirement	
Monthly payment to:	If you are:
You as a retired worker and your wife and child*	Fully insured
Your dependent husband 62 or over	Fully insured
Survivors	
Monthly payment to your:	If at death you are:
Widow 60* or over or disabled widow 50–59	Fully insured
Widow* (regardless of age) if caring for your child who is under 18 or disabled and is entitled to benefits	Either fully or currently insured
Dependent child	Either fully or currently insured
Dependent widower 62 or over and disabled dependent widower 50–61	Fully insured
Dependent parent at 62	Fully insured
Lump-sum death payment	Either fully or currently insured
Disability	
Monthly payments to:	If you are:
You and your dependents if you are disabled	Fully insured and if you meet certain work requirements

* Under certain conditions, payments can also be made to your divorced wife or surviving divorced wife.
Source: United States Department of Health, Education and Welfare, Social Security Administration.

from two retirement plans even though one or both may pay the minimum benefit.

Currently insured You will be currently insured if you have credit for 6 quarters or 1½ years of work within the three years before you die or become entitled to retirement benefits. The idea is to provide survivors' benefits to those who have not had time to become fully insured, minimum retirement benefits to those recently eligible for Social Security coverage, and disability benefits to those who have made contributions during at least half of their current working life of 1½ to 10 years. Specific details on disability insurance requirements are available through your nearest Social Security office. Table 9–3 relates benefit requirements to insurance status.

Estimating Retirement Benefit Payments

The amount of your monthly benefits under Social Security is based on your average earnings. The higher your average earnings, the larger the benefit payments. The exact amount of your benefit cannot be calculated until you retire, die, or become disabled, because all earnings up to the time of an application may be considered in figuring your benefit. The Social Security Administration will figure your exact benefit upon application. Table 9–1 can give you an approximation.

Changes in Retirement Benefits

Increased benefits Automatic increases in retirement benefits are generated whenever the *Consumer Price Index* rises by 3 percent or more from one year to the next, with the second quarter of each year being the measuring period. Congress has the option to act on the amount of increase. If it does not, the Secretary of Health, Education and Welfare is mandated to increase the benefits by the percentage of increase in the CPI by the following July 1.

Higher benefits may also result if you work after you retire. The Social Security Administration automatically refigures your benefits after the additional earnings are credited to your record.

Decreased benefits Too much earned income after retirement may also result in a temporary decrease in monthly benefits. If you are under seventy-two, the general rule is that $1 in benefits to you and your family will be withheld for each $2 you earn above $2,760 a year. This earnings limitation also increases by 3 percent or more per year, depending upon the percentage of increase in the CPI. The rule does not apply to people over seventy-two and to the monthly benefit of anyone earning less than $140 in any given month.

Financing the Social Security Program

Federal retirement, survivor, and disability benefits and hospital-insurance benefits are paid for by contributions based on earnings covered under Social Security.

If you are employed, you and your employer share the responsibility of paying contributions. If you are self-employed, you pay contributions for retirement, survivor, and disability insurance at a slightly lower rate than the combined rate for an employee and his employer. As long as you have earnings that are covered by the Social Security law, you continue to pay contributions regardless of your age—even if you are already receiving Social Security benefits.

How contributions are paid If you are employed, your contribution is deducted from your wages each payday. Your employer sends it, with an equal amount as his share of the contribution, to the Internal Revenue Service.

If you are self-employed and your net earnings are $400 or more in a year, you must report your earnings and pay your self-employment contribution each year when you file your individual federal income tax return. This is true even if you owe no federal income tax. Tables 9–4 and

Table 9–4 Maximum earnings subject to OASDI tax

Year	Amount
1937–50	$3,000
1951–54	3,600
1955–58	4,200
1959–65	4,800
1966–67	6,600
1968–71	7,800
1972	9,000
1973	10,800
1974	13,200
1975	14,100
1976 and after	subject to change

Source: United States Department of Health, Education and Welfare, Social Security Administration.

Table 9–5 Contribution rate to Social Security by type of contributor

Year	Employer and Employee (Each)	Self-employed
1971–72	5.2	7.5
1973–77	5.85	7.9
1978	6.05	8.10
1981	6.30	8.35
1986	6.45	8.50

Source: United States Department of Health, Education and Welfare, Social Security Administration.

9–5 illustrate the contribution rates of employers, employees, and the self-employed.

Other Government Retirement Programs

The federal government administers a number of retirement programs in addition to the Social Security program. Among them are the United States Civil Service Retirement System, the United States Military Retirement System, the Railroad Retirement System, and the Foreign Service Retirement System. These systems generally provide benefits equal to or greater than Social Security.

State and local governments offer retirement plans for their employees that are similar to Social Security. In addition, state and local government employees may now be covered by Social Security, their local pension plan, or both systems.

PENSION PLANS

Many medium-sized and large business organizations have established retirement pension plans for their employees. About one-third of the total employees in the United States are participating in an employer-sponsored or union-sponsored retirement plan. The vast majority of these plans are administered by the management of the employing company. These pension plans can provide appreciable amounts of retirement income and tax advantages to those who are eligible. Companies consider pension plans not only as an expense of doing business, but as an investment in good employer-employee relations and possible improved production or efficiency.

Private pension plans are not required by law. They are often created by labor-management negotiations. However, to provide some guaranteed protection to pension recipients, Congress has passed the Employee Retirement Income Security Act.

Employee Retirement Income Security Act

The Employee Retirement Income Security Act affects two different types of employee benefit plans—pension plans, which provide retirement benefits, and welfare plans, which provide other kinds of benefits, such as health, accident, etc. The welfare plans are the group-insurance plans discussed in chapter 7.

Two basic provisions apply to both welfare and pension plans. First, the act requires that all plans be *funded*. Funded plans require that the employer pay his contribution into a trust administered by a bank, trust company, or insurance company. These funds may be used only to provide benefits and to pay the necessary costs of the plans. No other use of the money may be made by either the employer or the fiduciary trust. The funds are invested or deposited according to the pension-plan provisions initially approved by the Internal Revenue Service.

The act calls for extensive reporting and disclosure of information about pension and welfare plans, their operations, and their financial condition to the Secretary of Labor and to those covered by the plans and their beneficiaries.

Provisions that apply solely to pension plans are:

Eligibility to participate In general, the law requires that a person eligible to participate in a pension plan must be twenty-five years old and have worked for the employer for one year. The act permits a plan to exclude from participation a person who starts a job five years before the normal retirement age under the plan.

All employees who work 1,000 hours per year are eligible to participate. Seasonal and part-time workers may be excluded from the act unless the customary work year is less than 1,000 hours. However, the plan must accrue benefits for less than full-time service on at least a pro rata basis.

Vesting The guaranteed right to receive your employer's contribution to the company's pension plan is known as vesting. Once vesting is achieved by an employee under the formula chosen by the plan, that individual has a right to receive a pension at retirement age, wherever he or she may be working at the time. The amount of the pension will generally depend on the amount of benefits earned by the employee during his or her service under the plan.

There are three alternative formulas for achieving vested pension rights under the new law:

1. Graded Plan—The employee must be at least 25 percent vested in his accrued benefit account after 5 years of covered service, with 5 percent additional vesting for each of the next 5 years, and 10 percent for the next 5 years. The employee would be 100 percent vested after 15 years.
2. Ten Year Plan—Each employee must be 100 percent vested after 10 years of service. No accrual formula is required as in the first plan.
3. Rule of 45 Plan—An employee with 5 or more years of service must be at least 50 percent vested when the sum of his age and years of covered service totals 45. Regardless of age there must be a 50 percent vested interest if the employee has 10 years of service. Once the 50 percent vestment has been attained, each succeeding year of covered service must provide 10 percent additional vestment until the employee has full vested interest in his employer's contributions.

All *employee contributions* are fully vested at all times.

The actual dollar amount of retirement benefits is still based upon the aggregate of both his and his employer's contributions. Generally, the earlier the retirement, the less the contributions, and the lower the benefits. Also, pensions are similar to annuities in that benefit schedules provide a lower periodic pay-out at younger ages because the accumulative pay-out period will be lengthened by earlier retirement.

Once an employee becomes eligible to participate in a pension plan, all of his years of service are to be taken into account for purposes of determining his place on the vesting schedule and the dollar amount of retirement benefits. Service before age 22, and any years in which the employee did not make mandatory contributions or opted not to participate in the plan, do not count. Breaks in the years of service generally will not affect vesting and benefits if the employee does not withdraw from his pension plan.

Pension-Plan Benefits

Pension-plan benefits are of obvious importance to an employee. Because pension plans are a very important fringe benefit, prospective employees should compare various retirement features whenever they have a choice of employers. An important time to begin planning for this type of retirement plan is now—even for you, the student!

Amount of retirement pension The actual amount received by an individual will be based upon a uniform formula applicable to all employees, whether the plan has been contributory or noncontributory. Plans may or may not be integrated (coordinated) with Social Security benefits. Under no circumstances, however, may plans decrease benefits because of an increase in Social Security benefits.

Among the various retirement formulas available are:

1. A flat amount for all employees.
2. A percentage of annual earnings.
3. A flat amount based on the number of years employed (longevity).
4. A percentage of annual earnings times the number of years employed.

The last formula is the one most widely used.

Pension-plan fundings are either "noncontributory," where only the employer makes the contributions to the fund, or "contributory," where joint compulsory contributions are made by the employer and the employee to provide for the basic pension. Retirement benefits are often larger in pension plans that allow extra voluntary contributions by employees. These contributions will then act as a form of additional retirement savings.

Survivor benefits Under the act, all pension plans must provide for a joint and survivor's annuity if the retirement benefit is in annuity form. A joint and survivor annuity must provide for continuing benefits of at least 50 percent of the stated payments to the survivor after the death of a spouse. This plan is automatically available to any employee participant who has been married for a one-year period ending on the annuity starting date.

Disability benefits Many plans allow pension rights to accumulate even if a worker is totally disabled. In such cases, contributions by the employer and employee (if any) are based either upon his disability pay or upon his normal pay.

RETIREMENT PLANS FOR THE SELF-EMPLOYED

A self-employed person now has retirement-plan advantages equal to or better than most wage-earners. Prior to the passage of the Keogh Act (HR 10) in 1962, the self-employed had to rely upon their own savings and investments for retirement purposes. They had to contribute about 1¼ times the rate of employees toward Social Security and they did not benefit from employer pension plans because they had no employers.

The Keogh Act and its 1974 revision do not change the Social Security contribution, but these provisions do offer persons receiving self-employment income the right to put up to 15 percent of such income into a tax-sheltered retirement program. This compensates for the lack of an employer pension plan. Keogh plans are available to any self-employed person or owner(s) of an unincorporated business. You do not need to be a professional person to take advantage of this combination retirement plan and tax break. Even income from hobbies and other part-time business qualifies; you may also be a wage-earner and still qualify. Many people are unaware of Keogh plans and fail to take advantage of this generous tax break.

A Tax Advantage

The amount you put aside for your retirement is deducted from your taxable income for the year, as if you never received it. The deduction is 15 percent of your self-employed earned income and it may not exceed a maximum deduction of $7,500. For example, the deduction can reduce the federal income tax on a $25,000 income by $1,240 a year. A married taxpayer filing jointly would pay $6,020 tax on $25,000 income, while he pays only $4,780 tax on $21,250 after the retirement adjustment. The $3,750 gross income adjustment for the self-employed retirement contribution in this example is partly paid for by the government. While you put $3,750 in a retirement fund, the out-of-pocket "extra" contribution is approximately $2,510, because otherwise $1,240 would be paid to the federal government in taxes. The government's portion of the contribution depends upon your tax bracket. The 15 percent deduction can apply to an income of any size; the greater your income and tax bracket, the greater your savings up to the limits of $50,000 of income and $7,500 of deduction. Further savings can be obtained on state income taxes if your state allows such a self-employment deduction.

In addition to deducting a portion of self-earned income off the top, you gain further tax-saving results by not being taxed on any income or capital gain generated by your retirement fund until you begin to withdraw it. For instance, any interest you earn in banks and other savings institutions must be included in your taxable income; "tax-sheltered" income or interest in an Internal Revenue Service (IRS)-approved retirement fund is not included. Your tax savings are significant. Also, the growth rate of an untaxed fund will be substantially higher than the growth rate of one subject to taxes. This is true because you have a much larger untaxed base upon which to compound interest or possible capital gains. The only "catch" is that tax on any "tax-sheltered" money earned is deferred only until you retire. At that time you will be taxed on it; however, your income will be substantially lower, and you will be in a lower tax bracket.

There are some restrictions on Keogh plans. You cannot withdraw funds from your program until age 59½ unless you agree to pay a tax penalty and not reenter a Keogh plan for a period of five years. There is an exception if you terminate a plan because of death or disability. Also, if you have full-time employees with three or more years of service, you must contribute the same amount for them as you do for yourself.

Finally, the plan of investment or savings must be approved by the IRS. Many large banks, insurance companies, and mutual funds have master plans that have already been approved by the Internal Revenue Service, making your enrollment in a plan a relatively simple matter. You have five main choices of investing your retirement funds under the Keogh Act:

1. You may purchase U.S. government retirement bonds.
2. You may purchase annuities from a life-insurance company.
3. You may purchase shares in an IRS-approved mutual fund.
4. You may deposit funds in an IRS-approved savings account at a bank, savings and loan association, or credit union.
5. You may open a bank trust account to act as custodian for your personal investment efforts.

INDIVIDUAL RETIREMENT ACCOUNTS

The Employee Retirement Income Security Act also has a provision to allow employees *without* a company pension plan to establish individual retirement accounts. The individual plan is patterned after the Keogh plans. Employees can contribute to an IRS-approved trust account and be allowed an income-tax deduction from gross income much the same as the self-employed. The maximum tax deduction is restricted to $1,500 or 15 percent of the employee's compensation, whichever is lower. The individual may make the payments into his account, or it may be done by his company or union through payroll deduction or other device. Mutual funds and savings institutions are now promoting this type of account.

Pension Transfers

Vesting and the individual retirement account provide the portability of pension plans that has been so lacking in the past. Now, pension plans generally remain in effect, if an employee does not withdraw his contributions. Also, if the new employer agrees, funds can be transferred tax-free to the new plan within sixty days of the old plan's distribution to the employee.

The transfers are called *tax-free rollovers.* They are also allowed between individual retirement accounts, but only once every three years. This situation would occur whenever an employee desired to change his retirement investment or savings account from one type of medium to another approved type.

ANNUITIES

An annuity is an insurance contract to protect the policyholder (annuitant) from the economic risk of outliving his income. Annuities provide for the payment of an income for the remaining lifetime of the annuitant. Life insurance protects the policyholder (actually his beneficiaries) from the economic risk involved in dying too soon to provide a sufficient continuing income for his family. Annuities and life insurance are really opposite forms of insurance based upon the economic consequences of the uncertainty of time of death.

Both annuities and life-insurance policies are sold by life-insurance companies to individuals and to groups, using the principle of spreading the risk over a large number of people. To set the price of life insurance, the company uses mortality tables to determine the likelihood of death; to set the price of an annuity, the company uses annuity tables to determine how long you are likely to live. Both tables differentiate by sex and age. The insurance company gambles that in any group of annuitants, enough members will die before their principal contribution is exhausted to pay for the others who will continue to live well beyond the principal repayment period of their individual contributions. Individually these people could not spend their savings without the fear that they would outlive their savings unless they spent them extremely frugally. This is the main reason to buy an annuity. You have a very safe investment, except for the hazard of inflation. No one, not even you, the annuitant, can touch the principal.

Purchasing an Annuity

You may purchase an annuity with a single lump-sum payment, or you may make payments on the installment plan. Annuities are usually sold in units of a $10,000 purchase price to provide a sufficient periodic payment to the annuitant to make the purchase worthwhile. One can purchase individual and group policies for larger or smaller amounts. Your annuity may start paying income immediately, or it may provide for periodic payments to begin at some future date. Your present age, financial status, and need for retirement income help determine when the repayment to you should begin and how often the periodic payments will be made.

Immediate annuity This type of annuity provides for payment to begin immediately, generally one period after the lump-sum purchase. The periodic payments may be monthly, quarterly, semiannually, or annually, as you desire. Annuitants usually receive periodic payments on a monthly basis.

Immediate annuities are purchased by people who are just retiring and wish to have a steady guaranteed income for the rest of their lives. Often the lump-sum used for the purchase of an immediate annuity comes from savings, from the sale of investments and real estate, and from the cash value of a life-insurance policy.

Deferred annuity Under a deferred annuity contract payments are deferred to a future date. This type of annuity may be purchased by a lump-sum. However, it is more likely to be purchased on the installment plan. Deferred-annuity purchasers are generally younger people who desire a guaranteed retirement plan in their later years. They do not wish to chance the possibility of not having saved a sufficient amount of money by retirement time to purchase an immediate annuity.

Most retirement plans that provide for the accumulation of funds to the date of retirement and then begin periodic payments are commonly called deferred annuities. Actually these are savings or insurance plans that automatically purchase an immediate annuity with the funds accumulated whenever the purchaser retires.

TYPES OF ANNUITIES

Annuities should be purchased to insure maximum income to you during retirement. You usually purchase an annuity to rid yourself of the worry of outliving your principal, but you pay for this lack of worry by receiving somewhat lower periodic payments than you would receive if you handled your own retirement money through savings or investment accounts. When you are managing your own money, you would have a tendency to "pay" yourself larger periodic sums from your principal. The specific type of annuity based on the terms guaranteed by the insurance company determines the amount of the periodic payment. Of course, the amount of money invested, and your sex and age at the time the periodic payments are to begin, also determine the amount of the periodic payment. We will look at each major type of annuity. Try to determine the reasons for the different amounts of periodic payments for each annuity type as shown in table 9–6 later in this chapter.

Straight-Life Annuity

The straight-life annuity is a pure annuity. It pays an income for life to the annuitant. When he dies, no further payments are made by the insurance company. The annuitant cannot bequeath his rights of payment. Nothing will be paid to his estate or to his beneficiaries. For this "all or nothing" approach, the annuitant receives the greatest periodic income for his annuity dollar.

If the annuitant lives longer than the length of time it takes the insurance company to repay his original purchase price and reasonable interest, he has received a bargain, and the insurance company has lost on his particular policy. If he should die shortly after purchasing the annuity, the insurance company will gain on his particular policy. The insurance company will gain more often than it loses. These "odds" are built into the annuity tables and premium rates to provide income for the rest of the annuitants in the company's portfolio and to provide a profit. Actually the deceased has not lost anything; he received exactly what he contracted for, income for a lifetime!

Relatives and heirs are often unhappy with straight-life annuities if it appears that the annuitant did not get his money's worth. This objection is overcome to a degree by the availability of a variety of annuities that guarantee minimum-dollar or time-period repayments regardless of when the annuitant dies.

A Life Annuity with Installments Certain

An installment-certain annuity guarantees the annuitant an income for as long as he lives. If he should die prior to receiving a certain number of installments, the balance of payments to meet the guarantee is paid to a beneficiary named by the annuitant. The usual guarantee is ten years. Some plans allow the balance to be paid to beneficiaries in one lump-sum at a discounted value.

The guarantee of a certain number of payments whether or not the annuitant lives solves the problem of at least partial repayment value for your purchase money. However, in return for this guarantee, the annuitant accepts lower periodic income payments. The longer the guarantee, the lower the periodic payments, which are usually on a monthly payment schedule.

Refund Annuity

If an annuitant wants to make sure that he or his beneficiaries get at least the dollar amount that he originally invested, he should purchase a refund annuity. The annuitant will receive a monthly income for life, and the dollar balance of his original investment will be guaranteed to be paid to his beneficiaries if he should suffer an early death. The actual "refund" may be made on the installment basis (an installment-refund annuity) or it may be made in a lump-sum (a cash-refund annuity).

The term *refund* does not mean that an annuitant can change his mind and get his money back on the annuity transaction. Once you purchase an annuity from an insurance company, you have an unbreakable contractual agreement. The only way your purchase money will be returned is through monthly periodic payments for life (all annuities), through guaranteed payments for a certain period of time (installment-certain annuity), or through guaranteed payments to the amount of the purchase price (refund annuity).

Joint Life and Survivorship Annuity

Most annuity contracts cover the life of one person. You can, however, insure two or more lives through the use of a joint survivorship plan. Usually a straight-life annuity is employed to pay a monthly income until the death of the last survivor of two or more annuitants.

The usual joint-survivorship annuity is an immediate annuity purchased by a husband and wife at the time of their retirement in order to avoid concern about income being terminated for the survivor if a single annuitant dies. The *installment-certain* and *refund* annuities do not provide protection indefinitely for the spouse. They terminate after a certain number of payments (ten years) or after a certain dollar amount has been paid. What is needed is an income to protect two people for both lifetimes, not just temporary protection for a certain time or temporary protection until the purchase price of the annuity is exhausted.

Joint and survivorship annuities are often

written to provide a reduced monthly income to the survivor on the theory that one person can live more cheaply than two persons. Usually the periodic payment is reduced by one-third to one-half. The smaller the amount of the continuing payments to the survivor, the less the original cost to the annuitants.

Women are usually the survivors, because they live longer and are often younger than their husbands. These facts tend to lessen the original amount of the monthly periodic payment to the joint annuitants and the continuing monthly amount to the survivor. This is an actuarial necessity for the insurance company because of the great possibility of a lengthy pay-out period from the moment the annuity begins until the wife finally dies.

Consider the case of a man of sixty-five having a wife ten years younger. The wife will statistically live five years longer than her husband, giving her a fifteen-year survivorship period (widowhood). To this, add an assumed ten-year retirement period for the husband and you have a twenty-five-year annuity period during which the insurance company is obligated to make monthly payments. Either the purchase price of the annuity will have to be high, or the periodic payments will be rather low.

Variable Annuity

Inflation has been a major deterrent to the purchase of the aforementioned annuities. Your purchase of an immediate or deferred annuity guarantees you a fixed-dollar periodic payment whenever you wish to retire. The real income-value of your contractual periodic repayment may soon be eroded, because the dollar loses purchasing power as inflation continues. In an inflationary economy, or in any period of rising prices, persons living on a fixed income face a deteriorating standard of living. Annuitants could be in worse financial shape than retirees who control their own capital, because annuitants cannot draw upon their principal to compensate for higher prices. Remember, the idea behind an annuity is to create an income from a principal amount that cannot be touched or outlived.

What is the solution? It may be a variable annuity designed to provide variable periodic payments. The monthly amount is determined by the value of an accumulated fund of common stocks. While the monthly income is guaranteed, the amount is not. In the long run, the cost of living has shown a steady rise. This is historically matched by an increase in the value of common stocks. Whenever stock prices and dividends increase, so does your annuity income. Unfortunately, this situation did not occur during the inflationary period 1973–74, giving many people second thoughts about variable annuities and pension plans.

Most variable annuities are deferred annuities; they are purchased on the installment plan to provide for better dollar-cost averaging. They are usually purchased through group-employment pension plans. They are now beginning to be offered to the individual annuitant who wishes to overcome the deficiencies of the fixed-income annuity. Some installment annuity plans provide for a combination of fixed-income and variable-income payments by investing portions of the purchase price in a combination of fixed and variable investments. These are called *balanced* annuities and usually require that one-half of the purchase price be placed in each type of investment medium.

A variable-annuity plan operates in a two-step manner when purchased in installments. First, you pay-in a stipulated amount each month, and this amount is credited to you in "accumulation units." The number of units accumulated is determined by dividing the unit price by the amount of your installment purchase. The unit price is the average value per share of the common stock in the particular investment fund established by the insurance company for its variable-annuity program. The number of units you accumulate each period will differ slightly based upon the unit value. For example, in one month you might get five accumulation units for a $50 installment payment: each unit cost $10. The second month you might get 4.5 units for the same $50 installment: each unit cost $11.11. In a third month, 6 units might be received: each unit cost $8.33 that particular month. The total number of units accumulated will increase with each additional monthly purchase.

The second step consists of exchanging your total accumulation of units for "annuity units" at the time you retire, when you wish to receive a monthly income. The actual number of annuity units you are entitled to receive will be based upon the insurance company's actuarial tables. You purchase annuity units with your accumulation units. The number of annuity units received is guaranteed for the remainder of your life. The dollar value of each unit will depend upon the value of the insurance company's variable-annuity investment portfolio. The dollar value of each annuity unit is computed each month by dividing the fund value by the number of annuity units in the fund. For example, you may be entitled to fifty annuity units per month. If the value of each unit in the portfolio is $6.00, you would receive $300 a month. If the value of the stock is $6.40 per share, you would receive $320 per month. If the value decreases to $5.00 per share, your monthly income would decrease to $250 a month.

You, of course, hope that the value of the investment portfolio increases to raise your income. If the value increases because of good investment management on the part of the insurance company, you have a real improvement in purchasing power. If the value of your annuity units increases only because of a general increase in prices throughout the economy, you have provided yourself a hedge against inflation and have not suffered a decline in purchasing power. Finally, if your units have decreased in value, you must live on less income. Carefully consider this last possibility, because insurance and investment companies do not provide a guaranteed minimum payment in a variable plan. You may receive a better yield from a long-term savings deposit than from a depressed variable annuity. Each generation can expect to live longer in retirement, which will mean longer exposure to the ravages of inflation without a guarantee that stocks underlying a variable annuity will rise along with the Consumer Price Index.

THE COST OF ANNUITIES

The price or cost of an annuity is based upon the income you will receive from it. You may examine the cost from two points of view: (1) the cost or purchase price needed to produce a certain income, or (2) the amount of income that can be received for a given purchase price that you can afford. Generally you apply the cost concept when purchasing an immediate annuity and the income concept when purchasing a deferred annuity. A higher cost in an annuity purchase may be associated with paying a greater dollar amount when buying an annuity, or it may be associated with receiving less money in each periodic income payment. How you view the cost of an annuity is up to you, the annuitant.

For ease of explanation we will examine cost from the first point of view. The following factors determine the cost of an annuity: (1) the amount of income desired; (2) the age of the annuitant at the time payment to him is to begin; (3) the type of annuity plan selected; and (4) the sex of the annuitant. Keep in mind that annuity policies are almost the exact opposite of life-insurance policies.

First, the greater the income desired, the greater the cost of the annuity. The insurance company needs a greater premium sum to invest to provide you with a greater income. If you purchase a deferred annuity, it will cost less out-of-pocket than an immediate annuity because of compounding the interest on the accumulated installments and because the insurance company has use of your money for a much greater period of time.

Second, the younger the annuitant, the greater the cost, because insurance companies must make periodic payments over a longer period of time. Annuity tables are used to calculate the cost based upon your age. Mortality tables are used to determine your life expectancy at any age you desire to begin receiving annuity payments. Health is not a factor because it is averaged based on your age. Insurance companies would just as soon have you be a rather unhealthy annuitant.

Third, the greater the guarantee to provide an estate for your beneficiaries, the greater the cost. Table 9–6 illustrates this concept. The greatest periodic income for your dollar is a straight-life annuity, while the lowest periodic income for your dollar would be a joint life and survivorship annuity. You must determine whether it is more important to have current income for yourself, to leave an estate for your beneficiaries, or to provide for a survivorship annuity.

Table 9–6 Typical periodic payments on $10,000 for various types of annuities for men and women at age 65

Annuity Type	Monthly Payment to: *Men*	*Women*
Straight life	84.68	74.07
Installment certain for 10 years	78.03	71.30
Cash refund	75.94	69.50
Joint and survivor (both spouses age 65)	65.04	
Joint and survivor (wife age 62)	62.94	

Source: Aetna Life Insurance Company, Hartford, Connecticut.

Fourth, women must pay more for annuities than men of the same age because women live longer. Generally whenever a woman purchases an immediate annuity, insurance companies apply the rates applicable to a man five years younger.

Another cost that must be considered involves both deferred and immediate variable annuities. Insurance-company variable-annuity investment funds are very similar to mutual funds. Whenever you purchase units there will be a sales charge (load) of about 8.5 percent every time you make an installment purchase. An immediate annuity will have a smaller sales-charge percentage because the investment amount is in a lump sum.

SHOULD YOU BUY AN ANNUITY?

Do you want a secure lifetime income without the worry of outliving your principal? This is a personal decision for the would-be annuitant. You would be free from investment-management worries. If you are a male at age sixty-five you would receive an annual income of approximately 9 percent of your immediate straight-life annuity purchase. This may be better than you could do on your own, but there would be no estate to bequeath to your beneficiaries. A second question now arises: do you want to leave an estate?

You do not need to purchase an annuity if you have a greater retirement income than your anticipated needs. Be sure to include Social Security and pension income in your planning. If your income is not sufficient, some combination of annuities and variable media investments such as mutual funds with systematic withdrawal plans can provide a good retirement income that might overcome the greatest drawback of an annuity, that of a single fixed income subject to inflationary pressures.

COMPREHENSIVE RETIREMENT PLANS

You should view Social Security as a foundation upon which to build your retirement. In itself, Social Security is insufficient to live on, but with a sound savings and investment program as a complement, you will be able to live comfortably as a retiree. We have already discussed savings, and we will cover investments in subsequent chapters.

There is a good possibility that you will be employed by a concern that offers a pension plan. Investigate and understand its provisions. By adding the fixed incomes generated by a pension plan and Social Security, you will have enough money to retire. Hopefully you will have your home paid for, which will help provide more comfortable living. At the least, your home can be converted to cash for use with your other savings and investments to produce either a greater fixed income or a supplementary variable income. Finally, you can purchase an annuity to provide a secure income for the rest of your life. All it takes is good planning and good follow-through.

Vocabulary and Concepts

Deferred annuity	Keogh Act
FICA/OASDI	Pension fund
Fixed annuity	Quarters of coverage
Immediate annuity	Tax-free rollover
Individual retirement account	Variable annuity
	Vesting

Questions for Discussion

1. Enumerate the various retirement assets available to persons who plan ahead.
2. What are the types of benefits available under Social Security?
3. How does a person become eligible for Social Security benefits? Differentiate between being fully and currently insured.
4. Under what circumstances can Social Security retirement benefits be increased or decreased?
5. Why is it advantageous to sell your residence after reaching age sixty-five?
6. Explain how annuities differ from life-insurance policies. How are they similar?
7. Explain how the Keogh Act (HR 10) acts as a tax shelter for the self-employed.
8. What is an Individual Retirement Account?
9. Why is vesting important to a pensioner? How does employee participation affect vesting?
10. What are the advantages and disadvantages of a variable annuity?

Projects

1. Find out all you can about the retirement system where you or your parents work. How does it compare to saving on your own? What benefits are you or your survivors entitled to at the present time?
2. Write to the Social Security Administration to determine the present status of your account.
3. Review the many points of view about financing the Social Security system. What steps must be taken to make it actuarily sound?
4. Investigate the withdrawal systems available from a bank or savings and loan association compared to an annuity.

Case Problem

Bartholomew Baker, aged thirty, desires to retire at age sixty-five. He is an unmarried, self-employed travel agent with an annual income of $27,000. How much can he save yearly in a Keogh retirement account? How much will he accumulate at 7 percent interest per annum? Use periodic compound interest tables to calculate. What sort of retirement income can he expect in addition to his retirement savings and interest? What life expectancy will he have? What advice can you offer? Would you offer the same advice to his friends Art and Barbara Able? Why or why not?

10

estate planning

Estate planning is the ultimate objective of personal money management. Personal money management takes place through accumulating, using, and transferring ownership of property. In a way, this broad definition means that the entire text has been devoted to estate planning. You follow certain money management patterns in the accumulation of an estate for your personal and family enjoyment. In your later years, you give thought about how to pass along your estate with a minimum of effort and taxation. Unfortunately, in most cases estate planning is an afterthought to transfer your property in contemplation of death. Effective estate planning would be much easier if you had included it from the beginning as one more aspect of your personal money management program. Most likely, you will want to bequeath as large an estate as possible to your heirs to provide for their welfare and enjoyment. Whatever is left from your living estate will be transferred to them by chance or by plan. The choice is yours.

DISPOSING OF YOUR ESTATE

Planning for the disposition of your estate is just as important as building your estate. By proper planning your business and investments can remain intact throughout your retirement period and through your death. Estate expenses and death taxes can be minimized by careful planning to allow you to leave a maximum amount to your heirs. In fact, part of your estate can be transferred while you are alive and still receiving substantial income. This procedure would enable you to reduce your current income-tax payments.

Estate planning involves consultation with a competent attorney to advise you and to draw up the assorted legal documents necessary to distribute your estate in an intelligent and balanced manner. You might also need the services of a financial counselor and a bank trust officer. Your comprehensive estate plan should consider wills, gifts, trusts, probate expenses, and taxes, which we will discuss in this chapter. Your plan should also account for retirement and survivor's benefits realized from life-insurance annuities, pension plans, and Social Security, all of which we have previously discussed.

WILLS

Title to all property, both real and personal, must pass to another upon your death. You cannot take it with you. You can, however, control its disposition. You say, "Why bother?" You may feel that you do not have enough property to worry about, or that everything will go to your wife anyway because it is all in both names. Perhaps you really do not care what happens after you are gone. It is more likely that you just have not gotten around to making a will. What can happen if you do not "get around to it"?

Property Disposition Without a Will

If you should die without leaving a will, you are said to die *intestate*. State law determines the distribution of your property. State laws vary but follow certain guidelines. Generally, all personal property is distributed according to the laws of the state where the deceased maintained residence. Real property is transferred under the laws of the state where the property is located. The state laws are called *rules of intestate succession* or *laws of descent*. Thus, by not making a will, a person decides to distribute his property according to state law. Therefore, you should know the rules of intestate succession in your state. In the event that there is no will and no heirs recognized by the state, your property (estate) reverts to the state by the process of escheat.

Intestate succession State laws generally provide for some property distribution to the surviving spouse in case the deceased was married. The percentage differs from state to state. In the community property states of Arizona, California, Idaho, Louisiana, Nevada, New Mexico, Texas, and Washington, the rule is that each spouse may dispose of his half of the community property by will. If he does not, it passes entirely to the spouse. In non–community property states various laws have been passed that provide for some sort of joint title to marital property. In the absence of a joint title provision, half of the deceased's estate normally goes to the spouse, with the balance to parents. When children are present, the spouse's portion often drops to one-third in non–community property states.

General guidelines for intestate succession for unmarried persons are:

1. Without children, property passes to parents equally or to surviving parent.
2. In absence of parents, property passes to brothers and sisters equally. Children of deceased brothers and sisters (nephews and nieces) take the share of the deceased *equally by right of representation.*
3. Further succession reaches out by lineal degree to *closest next of kin* such as grandparents, aunts, uncles, cousins, etc.
4. If there are no blood relatives, the property escheats to the state.

General guidelines for intestate succession for married persons are:

1. Without children one-half of deceased's property passes to spouse and one-half to parents.
2. With children, one-third to one-half to spouse, with balance divided among children or issue of a deceased child by right of representation.

As mentioned previously, the property and intestate succession laws surrounding married persons differ from state to state. Because the laws vary and are rather complicated, it definitely is a wise idea to transfer property by will rather than by the whim of state law. For example, table 10–1 shows the distribution effect of intestacy on a married person in three different states.

The value of a will A will can provide for a more rapid transfer of funds. It is not

Table 10–1 Intestate distribution of separate estate of married person in selected states

With Children		Without Children
California		
One Child $\frac{1}{2}$ to spouse, $\frac{1}{2}$ to child	Two or More Children $\frac{1}{3}$ to spouse, $\frac{2}{3}$ to children	All to spouse
Ohio		
One Child $\frac{1}{2}$ to spouse, $\frac{1}{2}$ to child	Two or More Children $\frac{1}{3}$ to spouse, $\frac{2}{3}$ to children	$\frac{3}{4}$ to spouse, $\frac{1}{4}$ to parents
Connecticut		
One Child $\frac{1}{3}$ to spouse, $\frac{2}{3}$ to child	Two or More Children $\frac{1}{3}$ to spouse, $\frac{2}{3}$ to children	$5,000 plus $\frac{1}{2}$ of balance to spouse, rest to parent(s); no parents: all to spouse

the best means of providing a fast transfer, but it has certainty. Your minor children may get most of your estate if you die intestate, leaving your widow without any funds to support them. Even with an emergency fund, she would eventually need to secure a court order to use the children's legacy for their support. This procedure would take time and would reduce the amount of money in the estate because of the expense involved. She would also have to account to the court regularly as the guardian of the children's estate.

Without a will an administrator will be appointed to dispose of your estate; there can be no charitable donations or tax-saving devices. You should be able to see the advantages of a will. Seldom does state law provide an acceptable substitute.

Administration of estate With or without a will, your estate will go through *probate proceedings* to make sure that taxes and creditors are paid and that title to property passes to your heirs properly. An administrator will be appointed by the probate court to administer and effect transfer of the deceased's estate whenever there is no executor named. Usually a close relative such as a spouse will be appointed. However, in the absence or incapacity of a close relative, a public administrator is appointed. The administrator must post a bond to protect the heirs and the creditors. He will take custody of all the assets of the deceased, pay creditor claims after court approval, defend or file law suits for the estate, and distribute the assets of the estate. He will be required to account to the court for his actions. He receives a fee for these duties.

If you had named an executor to administer your estate through your will, he would probably use up less of the estate than a court-appointed administrator. Relatives will often administer an estate for little or no charge. An executor would consider your wishes if he were required to sell property to raise funds to pay estate claims. An administrator would not necessarily be as considerate about what should be sold. A court-appointed administrator will perform his duties in an objective manner, but this may not be in accordance with your personal sentiments. As already mentioned, if you die intestate there can be no charitable donations or tax-saving devices.

Property Disposition With a Will

A will is a legal declaration that directs the disposition of a person's property after his death. The maker of a will is called a testator. Disposition of real property by will is called a *devise*; personal property, a *bequest* or a specific legacy; and money a *general legacy*. Anyone of legal capacity can make a will. This means that the testator must be of legal age and have the mental ability (sound mind) to understand that he is making a will to dispose of his property after his death. You must use precise language in your will, or your intentions may be misinterpreted, since the terms you use will be carried out as literally as possible. It is a good idea to employ an experienced attorney to make your intentions as precise as possible.

The primary reason for making a will is to control the disposition of your property. You can accomplish this control by making a will that designates:

1. An executor to carry out the directives in the will
2. Safeguards in the distribution of the property
3. The distributees or heirs of the property
4. The amount each heir should receive
5. The timing of the property transfer

Choosing the executor An executor or executrix should be chosen according to his or her ability and willingness to execute (carry out) the directives of your last will and testament. An executor performs the same duties as an administrator, hopefully in a more personally pleasing manner. He must take custody of all the decedent's assets, provide the probate court with an inventory of the assets, and publish a notice for creditors to file claims against the estate. He must also maintain real and personal property of the deceased in a prudent manner, operate or liquidate any business, and sell assets when necessary to pay court-approved taxes and other claims, expenses, and legacies. An executor is expected to defend lawsuits and bring lawsuits in the interest of the estate. Finally, he accounts to the probate court for all estate administration expenses and makes a final distribution of assets to the beneficiaries.

Choosing a guardian To safeguard your property further and provide for your dependents, you should also name a guardian for your minor children. This is especially important in case of a common disaster in which both spouses die. Jurisdictions may place minors in the care of foster parents or relatives whom you would not wish to have care for them. It is well worth making arrangements beforehand rather than relying on the judgment of the court.

Limitations on property disposition Generally, a person may dispose of his property in any manner he wishes. However, there are a few limitations. One spouse may not disinherit the other except under particular adverse conditions. Often the surviving spouse will receive the larger of the willed amount or the portion of the estate granted under the laws of intestate succession. Further protection for a widow takes the form of *dower*. This is a legal right to *use* one-third of a deceased husband's estate for so long as she lives. Community property states protect each spouse by providing that one-half of all property acquired after marriage belongs to each of them.

The testator may exclude or disinherit any person he chooses from receiving any portion of his estate. If the testator gives his entire estate to someone else, all persons who would inherit in the absence of a will are automatically excluded. No mention has to be made of those who are disinherited, nor does a nominal sum ($1) have to be left to the disinherited. However, children are given special protection. All children *must* be mentioned or acknowledged in a parent's will. This does not mean that they must be given anything. A clause for afterborn children is generally required in most states. Failure to mention living or afterborn children will result in their receiving whatever property they would receive under the laws of descent.

Any provision that is held to be against *public policy* is normally invalid. Requests or legacies requiring an heir to change his or her marital status are generally held to be against public policy. Provisions to control distribution of property in perpetuity are also held to be against public policy. The rule against perpetuities requires that the beneficiaries receive vested interest (control) within twenty-one years after the death of a designated person living at the time the interest is created. This is sometimes called the "lives-in-being plus twenty-one years rule." When interest is created by will, the date of interest creation is the date of the death of the testator. When interest is created by trust, the time that the trust interest vests in a beneficiary will be stated in the trust. The date can be relatively far into the future as long as it does not exceed the life-span of a person living at the time the trust is created plus another twenty-one years. The wording of the trust obviously will not indicate a specific trust termination date, since it cannot actually be determined at the time the will or trust is created. In either case, it will be somewhat short of perpetuity.

Types of Wills

There are three recognized types of wills differentiated by their method of preparation. They are the witnessed will, the holographic will, and the nuncupative will.

Witnessed will Sometimes known as a formal will, it is usually prepared by an attorney in typewritten form and signed by the testator in the presence of the required number of witnesses. Some states require two witnesses, and some require three. It is best to use three witnesses if possible because the devise of real property is based upon the state laws of its location (situs). Witnesses need not read the will nor have knowledge of its contents; however, they must sign in the presence of the testator and of each other. You should choose witnesses who are younger than you and who may be easily located if the validity of your will is questioned. They should also be of legal age and sound mind. Beneficiaries should not be witnesses because of possible undue influence.

Holographic will This will is one entirely written, dated, and signed, in the handwriting of the testator. It does not require any witnesses because a person's own handwriting must in fact be genuine. Not all states recognize this type of will because of the difficulty of proving the validity of the handwriting. A holographic will is often challenged.

Nuncupative will An orally made will before two or more witnesses is called a nuncupative will. It is allowed in about three-fourths of the states and then only to transfer personal property. Restrictions are placed on this type of will because it is generally made under emotional stress. Most states allow military personnel to make an oral will whenever they have been injured and are in peril of death. This will continues in force after the military man returns to civilian life. Military wills are also limited to the transfer of personal property.

The Will Format

There is no particular format required to formalize a will. Any words that convey the intention of the testator are sufficient. However, since the probate court will order the terms of a will to be carried out exactly, the wording should express the precise intent of the maker. It is probably better to be too wordy than leave the intent less clear. A lawyer should be able to tighten the wording with precise legal terminology. Your signature should be at the end of the will to prevent fraudulent additions.

A will has five distinct sections that express the testator's wishes and describe how the wishes are to be carried out. Figure 10–1 is an example of a simplified will. Note each distinctive part:

1. *The opening recitation*—The introduction section tells who you are, lists your address, and revokes all previous wills. It may also direct that funeral costs and just

> I, John Doe of 123 West 4th Street, Redwood City, California, do hereby make, publish, and declare this to be my last will and testament, and I do hereby revoke all former wills and codicils made by me at any time.
>
> First: I appoint as executrix of my will my wife; I request that she be permitted to serve without sureties on her bond and that, without application to or order of courts, she have full power and authority to sell, transfer, grant, convey, exchange, lease, mortgage, pledge, or otherwise encumber or dispose of, any or all of the real and personal property of my estate. I desire that my just debts, including the expenses of my last illness and funeral, be paid as soon as may be practicable after my death.
>
> Second: I devise and bequeath all of my property, real and personal, of every kind whatever and wheresoever situated, and whether now owned or hereafter acquired, to my wife Patricia for her own use and benefit forever.
>
> In Witness Whereof, I have hereunto subscribed my name this 4th day of July, 1976.
>
> John Doe
>
> On July 4th, 1976, John Doe, in our presence, subscribed the foregoing instrument and declared it to be his last will and testament, and requested us to witness it, whereupon we, still in his presence and in the presence of each other, have signed our names below. And we declare that at the time of the execution of this instrument said testator, according to our best knowledge and belief, was of sound mind and memory and under no constraint.
>
> Arthur Able   Ben Baker   Cal Charles
>
> Dated at Redwood City, California, this 4th day of July 1976.

Figure 10–1 The Essential Clauses of a Simple Will.

debts be paid. It may give instructions regarding burial if a separate letter of instructions has not been written.

2. *The administrative clause*—This section names the executor who will see that the provisions of the will are executed. It outlines his powers and what duties he is expected to perform. Coexecutors, trustees, and guardian for minor children would also be named. Sometimes funeral instructions and debt payments are mentioned in this section.
3. *The dispositive clause*—Who gets what and when they get it are described in the dispositive clause. Bequests, devises, and legacies are found in this section. A subsection called a *residuary clause* is often used to dispose of all property not otherwise specifically bequeathed.
4. *The testimonium clause*—This clause is your approval of the prior clauses and ends the will. You testify before witnesses that the prior clauses are correct. You testify by signing your signature.
5. *The attestative clause*—This statement signed by the witnesses attests to the fact that the testator was of sound mind and independent action.

Common-disaster clause Estate planners strongly recommend that a common-disaster clause be inserted in the will of a married person. This clause reinforces your intention to provide for your secondary beneficiaries. Simply stated, it provides that your estate go to your next of kin or whoever you wish designated as secondary beneficiaries. It is especially important in second marriages. The clause should state time limits for a transfer of an estate in the case of common disaster. Generally, the time limit should not exceed one month because longer periods would create too many other problems. A typical common disaster clause would read: "Any person who shall have died at the same time as I or as a result of injuries sustained within thirty days in a common disaster with me shall be deemed to have predeceased me."

Joint wills A single testamentary instrument that contains the wills of two or more persons either in common or in severalty is called a joint will. Responsible estate planners do not recommend its use because of future potential litigation or possible changes by one of the cotestators. Usually joint wills are executed by spouses who leave their property to each other. Both spouses should have separate wills since each person is a separate legal entity with some separate property. Each may have different blood relatives to whom each might wish to transfer property.

Keeping wills current No matter how well conceived and written, every will should be reviewed periodically. A will can go stale and become practically worthless. Changing circumstances can alter your will if it no longer reflects your intent.

Wills may be modified or revoked at any time during the life of the testator. The testator may amend a will or execute a completely new will. As a general rule, alterations should not be made to an existing will because different states vary the effect of alteration depending upon the nature and the extent of the alteration. The safest way to make changes is to have a new will drawn up. However, you may use a *codicil,* a separate writing that modifies a will. Except for the modified part, the original will remains in force. To insure validity, a codicil must be executed with all the formalities of the original will including the attestation of witnesses. It should be attached to the original will.

An outdated will may be revoked by destruction, alteration, or by execution of a later will. The safest way to revoke any will is to destroy it in the presence of witnesses.

Safeguarding Your Will

After going to the trouble and expense of preparing a will, you should keep your will in a safe place that is accessible to your executor after your death and available to you during life. If a will cannot be found, it is generally assumed to have been destroyed by the testator unless proof to the contrary can be presented to the probate court. You may leave your will with the attorney who drew the will. This procedure is highly recommended. You may also leave it with the executor or leave it in a jointly owned safe-deposit box. Many experts frown on this last suggestion because the deceased's safe-deposit box is sealed until probate court and tax officials inventory the contents.

Settling Your Affairs

Making a will is only one part of putting your affairs in order. It is the key element, but it cannot accomplish everything that you might wish to do. You may also wish to provide supplementary instructions about your finances or burial arrangements.

Even if a person does not make a will, he should prepare a *letter of last instructions.* It does not have any legal effect, but it will provide some direction for a survivor attempting to settle your affairs. You do not need to use legal jargon nor list the instructions in particular order. A useful letter should contain the following information:

1. Whom to notify in case of death.
2. List of relatives, their relationship, and addresses.
3. Location of the original copy of the will.
4. Funeral and burial preparations or preferences, if any.
5. List and location of important papers, such as birth certificate, Social Security card, marriage and divorce certificates, military service documents.
6. List of fraternal organizations and membership numbers of any that provide death benefits.
7. Pension plan information.
8. List and location of all insurance policies. A separate life-insurance list is helpful.
9. Location of safe-deposit boxes and their keys.
10. List of all savings accounts with location of passbooks and certificates.
11. List of all checking accounts and location of any cash not deposited.
12. List and location of any investment securities.
13. List of real estate property and location of the title documents.
14. List and location of important personal property and location of title papers. Automobiles, jewelry, and heirlooms are typical items.
15. Location of prior-year income-tax returns and supporting documents.
16. List of any substantial gifts given within the last three years for income-tax purposes.
17. List of creditors and debts outstanding.
18. Names and addresses of persons who can supply additional information as needed, such as your accountant, attorney, business associates, employer, insurance broker, and investment counselor.

PROBATE

The term *probate* brings thoughts of something rather sinister to some people. The probate concept is what the state does to make certain that creditors and legal heirs are rightfully protected. It is the *time* and *expense* associated with probate that can be sinister. Probate is the special court procedure concerned with the transfer of property from a decedent to a survivor. Only certain property—the probate estate—is subject to review by a probate court. Generally it consists of all property passed by will or, in the absence of a will, that property passed by the laws of descent or rules of intestate succession.

Probate procedure consists of determining whether a will is valid. If it is deemed to be, probate consists of the process of carrying out the instructions of the will to settle the estate of the deceased. The first step is to admit a will to probate. This is done by presentation to the court by the executor or executrix. After accepting a will to probate, the court will supervise the actions of the executor, who carries out his obligations as previously described. In the absence of an executor the court will appoint a qualified administrator to carry out the probate procedure.

Probate Delays

An extended period of time may pass between the death of a person and the final disposition of his property. For instance, after public notice, creditors have six months to file claims, during which time the executor verifies their validity. Once all claims have been paid, the executor files a *final account* and a petition for distribution. If the court finds that the final account is in order and that all estate taxes are paid, the court makes a decree of distribution. The decree will allow the remaining property in the estate to be transferred to the beneficiaries. Apportionment is made if the estate has shrunk to a lesser amount than specified in a will. If there is no will, the court will decree distribution in accordance with the rules of intestate succession. Probate is concluded when the executor files the receipts he obtained from the beneficiaries. The court then discharges the executor or administrator from further duties.

During this period, which must last at least six months, a widow and surviving minor children may petition for an allowance to support them until the estate is settled. This procedure in itself takes time and may cause serious inconvenience to the family. Furthermore, if there is any litigation or challenge to the will, it obviously will take much longer to complete the probate process. Remember, it takes time to secure a hearing if the court calendar is crowded.

Probate Costs

Critics argue that probate is a costly procedure because it is rather complicated and almost always requires the services of a lawyer and a professional executor. According to the Beneficial Life Insurance Company, total costs of probate generally run about 8.6 percent of the gross value of a $50,000 estate. The percentage decreases somewhat as the value of the estate increases. The recipients of these probate fees are lawyers, executors, appraisers, and the probate court, in descending dollar order. State law often stipulates the scale for these fees. Commission fees, in case property must be sold, and estate taxes must be added to the basic probate costs to figure the total expense of transferring your postmortem estate.

Avoiding Probate

Since probate is subject to excessive time and expense, it is desirable to have *some* property pass outside of your probate estate. Generally, it is impossible to have *all* property avoid probate. However, the more assets that pass outside probate, the sooner your beneficiaries will receive the property. And the less gross value in the probate estate, the less the probate fees.

Basically there are four ways to reduce your probate estate to keep the costs down: (1) life insurance, (2) gifts, (3) joint ownership, and (4) trusts. You must own or control property in order for it to pass through probate. The above devices divest you of some interests, allowing them to pass outside of probate. These devices do not necessarily reduce estate or gift taxes. We will discuss taxes later in the chapter. Sometimes it is not wise to avoid probate because the cost of avoidance may be greater than the probate fees.

Life Insurance

Life insurance passes outside of probate if a beneficiary is directly named in the policy. However, if the beneficiary named is your estate for distribution by will or by the rules of intestate succession, it becomes part of the probate estate and subject to the fees. Generally it is wise to name a new beneficiary upon the deletion of a prior beneficiary to keep from having your life insurance pass through probate. Life-insurance proceeds are also considered part of your gross estate for estate tax purposes.

Gifts

Obviously the simplest and least expensive way to reduce probate fees is to give away all your property, thereby leaving nothing for probate. This does not eliminate possible federal gift taxes or estate taxes. You may also create a problem by giving away too much; you might have to live off the recipients of your gifts! The practical solution is to give away only a portion of your estate or arrange for some form of living trust.

Joint Ownership

The main advantage of joint ownership of property lies in the personal usefulness inherent in jointly owned property, the possible ownership of more expensive property in this manner, and the possible methods of transfer in case of death. The disadvantages tend to be the inflexibility created by requiring approval of the joint owners before transferring title in some cases and possible liability of all owners in other cases. Bank accounts, stocks, automobiles, and real estate are often jointly owned. These *may* pass to the surviving owner automatically, not as part of a will. This property can therefore pass outside of probate, *if* it is the *right type* of joint ownership. There are four types of joint ownership: (1) joint tenancy, (2) tenancy by the entirety, (3) community property, and (4) tenancy in common. You should discuss the advantages and availability of each form of ownership in your state with your attorney when you arrange your will or when you purchase real property.

Joint tenancy This is the standard method used to bypass probate. Each tenant in a joint tenancy owns all of the property and has the right of survivorship. This means that when one joint tenant dies, the other still owns all the property. Since title is already vested in the survivor, there is nothing to pass. Joint tenancy property cannot be transferred by will because of the survivorship feature.

Tenancy by the entirety This provides the same survivorship advantages as joint tenancy. The difference is that it is available only to husband and wife. Tenants by the entirety may not sell such property without the other spouse's consent. Not all states recognize this form of joint ownership. Community property states do not. In some states, all property conveyed to married couples that would create a joint tenancy creates the tenancy by the entirety.

Community property This form of joint ownership is only available for spouses in community property states. The laws of these states hold that all property acquired jointly after marriage is community property and belongs to both spouses. Each spouse may dispose of his (her) half by will. In the absence of a will, the deceased's half of the community property goes to the surviving spouse. Separate property follows the laws of descent of the particular state.

Tenancy in common Property of this sort *does* pass through probate. It is joint ownership in the form of an undivided interest in property in which the owners' interest passes through their estate in case of death. All jointly owned property is considered tenancy in common if it does not meet the requirements of joint tenancy, tenancy by the entirety, or community property. For instance, in case of partnerships, ownership is generally tenancy in common, and the deceased's interest in the terminated partnership passes to his heirs.

Trusts

A popular way of avoiding probate costs, some estate taxes, and possible dissipation of an estate is to create a trust. It is the legal transfer of title to property by one person (called the trustor or grantor) to another person (called the trustee) to be held and administered by the trustee for the benefit of designated beneficiaries. You simply turn your property over to a person or institution to keep and manage it for your beneficiaries. There are many legal ramifications involved in trusts. It becomes an expensive way to lower probate costs if this is the only intent because of the need for formal trust documents, which involve the services of an attorney. There would also be the continuing services of a paid trustee. Typical commercial trust management fees average $4 per $1,000 principal on the first $100,000 and about 6 percent of the income produced on the first $25,000. Fee rates decline on larger trust funds. Trusts are used primarily to retain some control over property and reduce various taxes.

A trustor may be his own trustee or beneficiary, depending on the type of trust. Persons who are to receive the income from the management of the trust are known as *beneficiaries* or *life tenants*. Persons who are to receive the principal when the trust terminates are known as *remaindermen*. Because of the restrictions on perpetuities in most states, private trusts generally cannot exist for more than twenty-one years beyond the death of the last survivor named in the trust agreement. Charitable trusts are not subject to this time limitation.

There are two major types of trusts that have a bearing on estate planning. These are a *living* or *inter vivos trust*, which becomes effective during the lifetime of the trustor, and the *testamentary trust*, which is part of a trustor's will and becomes effective upon his death.

Living trusts Trusts may be established to manage the financial affairs of a trustor because he may be too busy or not feel competent. However, the primary reason is to lower probate costs and minimize income and estate taxes. A living trust can be effectively coordinated with a testamentary trust. A living trust will remain in effect upon the trustor's death. It will avoid the fees and delays of probate. Through the *power of appointment* a trustor can grant his beneficiary the power to determine the eventual distribution of the trust principal after the trustor's death. Figure 10–2 is a diagram example of how a living trust operates to provide retirement income from a mutual fund investment. Living trusts generally become effective as soon as they are established. They can be a revocable, irrevocable, or reversionary trust.

A *revocable trust* is a type that can be cancelled by the trustor at any time. The trustor retains control over the assets indirectly because of the ultimate right to

A Retirement Trust

John Wright has created a living trust which provides the enjoyment of a regular monthly payment to himself and then his wife through the use of a withdrawal plan. Then this trust will provide the benefits shown in the diagram for their three sons.

THE JOHN WRIGHT TRUST

Provisions for John Wright:

1. Mr. Wright receives a monthly check from income and principal.
2. Mr. Wright retains the right to amend his trust and withdraw principal.
3. The trustee may use principal for Mr. Wright's support in case of his illness or incapacity.

OTHER TRUSTS

Mr. Wright may make the property or other trusts payable to the John Wright Trust.

WILL

Mr. Wright's will provides that his assets will be distributed to The John Wright Trust.

NO PROBATE

PROBATE

MRS. JOHN WRIGHT
(Beneficiary)

1. Mrs. Wright will receive a monthly check from income and principal.
2. Mrs. Wright will retain the right to amend and withdraw principal.
3. The trustee may use principal for Mrs. Wright's support in case of her illness or incapacity.

NO PROBATE

TRUST DIVIDES IN EQUAL SHARES FOR CHILDREN

John, Jr. **Paul Henry** **Michael**
(Remainder Beneficiaries)

1. Each child receives his share of income quarterly.
2. The trustee may pay to each son any part or all of his share of the principal for support and education in its discretion prior to the son's reaching age 35.
3. Each child may withdraw principal at age 35.

Figure 10–2 A Trust Operating Plan. *(The Massachusetts Company, Inc., Boston)* cancel the trust. The revocable trust is used to pass property outside of probate, not to save on taxes.

An *irrevocable trust* is a trust agreement that cannot be cancelled once it has been put into effect. The trustor loses control of the trust assets. This feature reduces his income-tax liability during his lifetime because the trust assets and the income from the assets are no longer the legal property of the grantor. Gift taxes will still have to be paid, but these are somewhat lower than comparable income and estate taxes.

A *reversionary trust*, often called a short-term trust, is one that must be irrevocable for a period of ten years if it is a private trust and two years if it is a charitable trust. The beneficiary must be other than the grantor. Such a trust is a gift of income, with the principal reverting to the grantor who would be the remainderman when the trust terminates. A reversionary trust is primarily used to reduce income taxes paid by the trustor during his lifetime.

Testamentary trusts The formation of a testamentary trust is provided by will. It does not become effective until the death of the testator. Often the executor of a will is the trustee in this type of trust. However, this provision is not mandatory. Again, individuals or commercial banks and trust organizations can be trustees. The main advantage of a testamentary trust is that the trustor does not relinquish control of his estate during his lifetime. He can change his will and the trust at any time. A postmortem trust is designed to preserve the principal in a trust fund for the financial benefit of the recipients. It passes through probate as part of the gross probate estate. One exception to this rule is a life-insurance trust, where the proceeds payable to beneficiaries may be protected by trust arrangements. This trust is by separate agreement with the life-insurance company and would not be mentioned in the will and therefore passes outside of probate.

There is no immediate financial advantage to testamentary trusts because probate costs and estate taxes must be paid. However, a trust established for a minor does not need to be supervised by the probate court because it theoretically is in effect before probate proceedings. This should save accounting and guardianship expenses. Furthermore, since the state tax is levied upon the transfer of the assets from the trustor to the trust, no further estate taxes would be payable until the trust is dissolved. At that time any principal balance would go to the remaindermen. A trust could remain in effect until the death of a trustor's grandchildren. During the period the trust is in existence, it would pay income taxes as would the beneficiaries.

ESTATE TAXES

Federal and state governments may tax a person's right to pass title to his property at death and also tax the right to receive such property. In the former instance, the tax is called an *estate tax*; in the latter it is called an *inheritance tax*. The federal government levies a tax on the deceased's estate but does not have an inheritance tax.

State Death Taxes

State governments vary in their methods of taxing the transfer of property upon death. Some levy the tax on the estate, some on the amount that each beneficiary receives. Nevada is the only state without death taxes. Some states levy both types of taxes. Generally states tax at a lower rate than the federal government, even though the states tend to require taxes on much smaller es-

Table 10–2 Federal estate tax table

Amount of Taxable Estate	Tax on Amount in (A)	Amount of Taxable Estate in Excess of (A) But Not in Excess of (C) Is Taxed at Rate Shown in (D)	
(A)	(B)	(C)	(D)
$0	$0	$5,000	3%
5,000	150	10,000	7%
10,000	500	20,000	11%
20,000	1,600	30,000	14%
30,000	3,000	40,000	18%
40,000	4,800	50,000	22%
50,000	7,000	60,000	25%
60,000	9,500	100,000	28%
100,000	20,700	250,000	30%
250,000	65,700	500,000	32%
500,000	145,700	750,000	35%
750,000	233,200	1,000,000	37%
1,000,000	325,700	1,250,000	39%
1,250,000	423,200	1,500,000	42%
1,500,000	528,200	2,000,000	45%
2,000,000	753,200	2,500,000	49%
2,500,000	998,200	3,000,000	53%
3,000,000	1,263,200	3,500,000	56%
3,500,000	1,543,200	4,000,000	59%
4,000,000	1,838,200	5,000,000	63%
5,000,000	2,468,200	6,000,000	67%
6,000,000	3,138,200	7,000,000	70%
7,000,000	3,838,200	8,000,000	73%
8,000,000	4,568,200	10,000,000	76%
10,000,000	6,088,200	. . .	77%

Column (A) shows the amount of the taxable estate; that is, the total gross estate less all deductions and an exemption of $60,000.
Column (B) shows the estate tax on the corresponding taxable estate in Column (A).
Column (D) shows the rate applicable to any amount in excess of the taxable estate shown in Column (A) but not in excess of the taxable estate shown in Column (C).
The tax computed by use of this table is the estate tax liability without allowance for any credit for gift tax, for death taxes paid to the States, for foreign death taxes, and for taxes on transfers from prior decedents; it is therefore the maximum Federal estate tax payable by any estate.

Source: Prentice-Hall, Inc., *Federal Tax Course 1975.*

tates. State estate tax rates tend to run about 3 percent of the net estate and increase with the size of the estate. State inheritance tax rates are approximately the same, with higher rates applicable to beneficiaries who are not the spouse or direct lineal relatives.

State death tax payments may be required in more than one state if the deceased's property is located in more than one state. A competent estate planner is needed to calculate the potential tax liabilities in such instances. We will investigate only the federal estate tax because of the variety of state laws and rates. It usually is not worth the effort to avoid the state taxes because they begin on a much smaller taxable estate. The federal taxing concepts illustrate how death taxes operate.

Federal Estate Tax

The federal estate tax is levied on the gross value of the estate of the deceased. The gross value includes *all* personal and real property *belonging* to the decedent at time of death.

Net taxable estate Outstanding debts, funeral expenses, and expenses of administering the estate are deducted from the gross estate. The resulting amount is called the adjusted gross estate. If the deceased was married, a marital deduction is allowed. Finally, all recognized charitable gifts and a $60,000 specific exemption may be deducted from the adjusted gross estate to arrive at the net taxable estate. The estate tax return is filed by the executor on IRS Form 706 (United States Estate Tax Return) within nine months of the date of death, if the deceased's gross estate exceeds $60,000.

Marital deduction The government allows you to transfer one-half of your adjusted gross estate to your surviving spouse free of federal estate tax, providing your spouse has full powers of disposition of the property either during lifetime or at death. Basically this means that whatever property is transferred to the surviving spouse would otherwise be taxable to the survivor's estate. The deceased spouse's property can be passed by will or by the laws of descent. In effect, the marital deduction provides for dividing the deceased's property with his spouse where there are no community property laws. In community property states a surviving spouse already owns one-half of all property that is not the separate property of the deceased spouse. The marital deduction in these states applies only to one-half of the testator's *separate* property.

Computing the Federal Estate Tax

You compute the federal estate tax by applying the rates illustrated in table 10–2 to the net taxable estate. We will compare an example of a married person and an unmarried person. Both have recently died leaving an estate as listed below. The estate expenses were the same as for both. The only difference was Mr. Able leaves his entire estate to his wife, while Mr. Baker leaves his estate to a son by prior marriage:

	Mr. Able		*Mr. Baker*	
Gross Estate:				
Personal and real property	$150,000		$150,000	
Gifts in contemplation of death (causa mortis)	50,000		50,000	
Life insurance	50,000	$250,000	50,000	$250,000
Deductions:				
Funeral expenses	5,000		5,000	
Estate administration	8,000		8,000	
Outstanding debts	7,000	20,000	7,000	20,000
Adjusted gross estate		$230,000		$230,000
Marital deduction	$115,000		-0-	
Recognized charities	15,000		$ 15,000	
Exemption	60,000	190,000	60,000	75,000
Net taxable estate		$ 40,000		$155,000
Gross Federal Estate Tax		$ 4,800		$ 37,200

GIFT TAXES

One way to reduce high federal and state death taxes is to give away your property over an extended period of time. If you can plan your giving properly, there may be very little estate left to tax. A gift, however, must be given at least three years before death to be considered a gift; otherwise it will be included in your estate for tax purposes. You will receive a tax credit on your estate tax for all or part of the gift taxes paid if the IRS does require estate tax payment on a gift made "causa mortis." As you will see, the government encourages giving as the most effective way of minimizing estate taxes. First, there are certain exclusions and exemptions, the deductions that will reduce the taxable gift considerably. Second, the federal gift tax rates are only three-fourths of the estate tax rates. We will look at the federal gift tax because only a few states have gift taxes.

Federal Gift Tax

A gift is a gratuitous transfer of property during a taxpayer's lifetime. A gift can be any real or personal property in which the donor passes title and a current interest to the donee without retaining control. Current market value at the time of the gift is used to determine value for tax purposes. Gifts of securities are valued at the original purchase price of the donor plus the gift tax cost if there is a capital gain to the donee; they are valued at market price if there is a loss. In the latter instance, it would be better to sell the securities, take a loss for tax purposes, and give the money away. Gifts to the United States and any of its political subdivisions and to recognized charitable, religious, and educational institutions are exempt from gift taxes no matter how large the gifts may be. A general rule of thumb is that any charitable deduction allowed for income-tax purposes is a nontaxable gift. There are no carryover gift tax considerations. The gift tax is paid by the donor. He must file IRS Form 709 (U.S. Quarterly Gift Tax Return) on a quarterly basis and submit payment (if any) at that time.

Gift Tax Reductions

There are three noteworthy reductions available before the gift tax is applied. These are the annual exclusion, a lifetime exemption, and the marital deduction. Beneficial rates can also result from married couples splitting their gifts.

Annual exclusion Each person has a $3,000 annual exclusion for each donee to account for all the small gifts that people usually do not record. A married couple would have a $6,000 exclusion. The exclusion is allowable *each year* for gifts to *each separate donee.* Under the concept a married couple could give $6,000 to each of six grandchildren for a total of $36,000 without payment of gift taxes. This individual exclusion cannot be increased by simultaneous cross-gift. For example, Mr. Able and Mr. Baker would *not* have been able to double their individual exclusions by arranging for each of them to make simultaneous gifts of $3,000 each to their own son and the other's son, thereby arranging an inter-vivos gift of $6,000 to save taxes on the amount over the $3,000 individual exclusion.

Lifetime exemption In addition to the annual individual exclusion, there is an overall specific exemption of $30,000 available to offset all taxable gifts that a person may make in a lifetime. This exemption is *per donor.* It may be spread over a number of recipients. You may use the total lifetime exemption in one year or spread it over several years. In effect, a married couple can give an inter-vivos gift of $66,000 during any one year without incurring a gift tax liability if they have not previously used their lifetime exemptions.

Marital deduction A marital deduction by one-half of the value of a gift between husband and wife is allowed in much the same manner as in estate taxes. In community property states it would affect only separate property. This deduction is taken before and in addition to the annual individual exclusion. Therefore, one spouse could give the other $6,000 without paying gift taxes, i.e., $3,000 (½ of gift) and $3,000 annual exclusion.

Joint gifts to third parties A husband and wife can split a joint gift to a third party in order to be separately taxed at lower rates. Table 10–3 illustrates the federal gift tax rates. Separate Form 709s must be filed by each spouse. Each uses his (her) own exclusion and exemption (if applicable). As mentioned earlier, a married couple can jointly give $66,000 to one donee in one year without gift tax, if they have not previously used their lifetime exemption. Let us assume

Table 10–3 Federal gift tax table

Amount of Taxable Gifts	Tax on Amount in (A)	Amount of Taxable Gifts in Excess of (A) But Not in Excess of (C) Is Taxed at Rate Shown in (D)	
(A)	(B)	(C)	(D)
$0	$0	$5,000	2¼%
5,000	112.50	10,000	5¼%
10,000	375	20,000	8¼%
20,000	1,200	30,000	10½%
30,000	2,250	40,000	13½%
40,000	3,600	50,000	16½%
50,000	5,250	60,000	18¾%
60,000	7,125	100,000	21%
100,000	15,525	250,000	22½%
250,000	49,275	500,000	24%
500,000	109,275	750,000	26¼%
750,000	174,900	1,000,000	27¾%
1,000,000	244,275	1,250,000	29¼%
1,250,000	317,400	1,500,000	31½%
1,500,000	396,150	2,000,000	33¾%
2,000,000	564,900	2,500,000	36¾%
2,500,000	748,650	3,000,000	39¾%
3,000,000	947,400	3,500,000	42%
3,500,000	1,157,400	4,000,000	44¼%
4,000,000	1,378,650	5,000,000	47¼%
5,000,000	1,851,150	6,000,000	50¼%
6,000,000	2,353,650	7,000,000	52½%
7,000,000	2,878,650	8,000,000	54¾%
8,000,000	3,426,150	10,000,000	57%
01,000,000	4,566,150	. . .	57¾%

Source: Prentice-Hall, Inc., *Federal Tax Course 1975.*

that they give a $106,000 gift to a relative. After joint reductions, there would be $40,000 taxable on the whole gift. The gift tax table indicates that the tax would amount to $3,600. Now, if the gift was split to show two $53,000 gifts and each spouse filed a separate return, the taxable gift would be $20,000 each. The gift tax table indicates that only $1,200 would be owed on each return—a substantial saving over a joint gift tax return.

Computing the Gift Tax

Since the gift tax is a device to tax persons who would otherwise avoid estate taxes by divesting themselves of their assets over a period of years, the gift tax is based on the total accumulation of gifts over the years. Fortunately, you have the individual exclusion each year to help reduce the tax bite. The cumulative effect becomes rather expensive in large estates, but it is still lower than estate taxes. Current gifts are taxed at rates that include the cumulative effect of gifts made in prior years and prior quarters of the current year. For example, let us assume that Mr. Charles and Mr. Davis each made taxable gifts of $100,000. Mr. Davis had previously given taxable gifts in the amount of $50,000, while Mr. Charles had not. The gift tax on the current $100,000 gift would be calculated for each donor as follows:

Mr. Charles:	Tax on $100,000	$15,525
	Current gift tax liability	15,525
Mr. Davis:	Tax on $150,000	$26,775
	Less tax on $50,000 previously paid	5,250
	Current gift tax liability	$21,525

To give you insight into the tax effects of gift giving, we will go back to Mr. Able's and Mr. Baker's estate plans. If both had arranged planned gifts to their beneficiaries over a period of years, the tax results would be somewhat different. We will assume that $100,000 of their property is given over a ten-year period as irrevocable inter-vivos gifts of $10,000 annually. Also, the cash value of the life insurance policy when given to the named beneficiary would have been $15,000 with all rights vested in the beneficiary. The tax results of this particular strategy would be:

		Mr. Able		*Mr. Baker*
Gift totals		$115,000		$115,000
Deductions:				
lifetime exemption	$30,000		$30,000	
ten-year exclusions	30,000		30,000	
marital deduction	57,500	117,500	-0-	60,000
	$ -0-			$ 55,000
Federal gift tax	$ -0-			$ 6,188

By giving the actual life insurance policy to your beneficiary without retaining *any* interest in it, there will be a further savings of $35,000 ($50,000 face value – $15,000 current cash value). The former beneficiary and new owner of the policy would have to make all premium payments in order for the IRS to agree that the insured has no interest in the policy. The balance of the estates, $100,000 each, would be subject to payment of estate taxes as follows:

		Mr. Able		*Mr. Baker*
Balance of estate		$100,000		$100,000
Less expenses		20,000		20,000
Adjusted gross estate		$ 80,000		$ 80,000
Marital deduction	$40,000		-0-	
Recognized charities	15,000		15,000	
Exemption	60,000	115,000	60,000	75,000
Net taxable estate		-0-		5,000
Gross Federal Estate Tax		-0-		$ 150
Total tax for periodic gift and estate transfer		-0-		$ 6,388
Amount saved by gift giving		$ 4,800		$ 30,812

Neither of the estate plans computed the probate costs. However, it is obvious that a $200,000 estate would entail more fees than a $100,000 estate. One insurance company estimates the approximate expenses of probate for these estates at $15,000 and $8,000 respectively.

Uniform Gift to Minors Act

All states have adopted the Uniform Gift to Minors Act to some degree. It permits adults to make gifts of securities or money to minors and manage the ownership for the benefit of the child without court approval of the custodian's stock market transactions. There are no formal legal documents. Money is paid into an account with a broker or bank in the name of the minor and under the custody of the donor. Securities are registered as follows: "(Custodian's name), as a custodian for (minor's name), a minor."

It is primarily used by parents for their children. Stocks, bonds, cash, and mutual fund securities may be given under the act. A major income tax benefit accrues to the donor. Any income from property given to a minor under the Act is taxed to the minor and not to the donor, unless the income is used for the support of the minor. If it is used for support, the income will be taxable to the parent. Otherwise, the income-tax benefits allow the donor-parent to shift his high tax-bracket income to a donee's lower tax bracket (if he has any tax at all). Furthermore, in terms of capital gains, there is none for the donor because there was no sale. The donee's capital gain is based on the donor's adjusted cost plus any gift tax, while the donee's loss would be based on fair market value at time of gift.

MINIMIZING ESTATE SHRINKAGE

Estate planning is a continual process. It should start early in your personal money management career. Life insurance will probably be your first estate endeavor. It should not end at that point. Make a will early in life. Draw a balance sheet to ascertain where you are financially and where you want to go. Above all, realize the value of your property and how easily it can shrink. Probate costs and estate taxes can reduce your estate by 25 percent.

Review your will and your financial status regularly. Remember that the purpose of estate planning is to transfer the maximum amount of your property at a minimum cost to you and your beneficiaries. This can only be accomplished by planning your estate with the help of family members and a competent attorney. Assistance should be sought from accountants, bankers, brokers, insurance agents, and trust officers as needed.

Basically, you can reduce estate costs by passing property outside of probate and paying gift taxes rather than estate taxes. Timing is of the utmost importance. Your age and financial status and that of your beneficiaries should be considered in the process of reducing total death taxes.

Periodic gifts and joint tenancy are *probably* the least expensive method of transferring title between relatives if they are capable of managing their financial affairs. Trusts can be used to transfer appreciating property and to provide management safeguards for the principal. Trusts can be rather expensive if the principal is under $250,000. Trust costs can run above 1 percent of the principal value which could reduce income to the beneficiaries. Fortunately, costs are partially offset by being tax deductible. Also, if the trust is successfully managed, the principal may be increased to an even greater extent than when under your control.

Finally, an estate planning program must provide liquid funds to pay gift and estate taxes, especially the latter. You and your family may not wish to dispose of collectibles, securities, heirlooms, or residences. There may be no ready market or the timing may be inopportune. Guard against a forced sale by giving property away rather than money whenever possible. However, be sure to maintain sufficient liquidity to cover taxes and sufficient assets to provide for your needs until death.

Remember that the economy will change, estate laws will change, your financial and family status will change, and your beneficiaries' needs will change. A periodic review of your will and total estate plan should allow you to retain liquidity and provide for you and your family.

Vocabulary and Concepts

Administrator	Marital deduction
Community property	Perpetuities
Estate	Probate
Executor	Remaindermen
Holographic will	Reversionary trust
Inter vivos trust	Separate property
Intestate succession	Tenancy in common
Joint tenancy	Testamentary trust

Questions for Discussion

1. What are the general rules of intestate succession?
2. Explain the three types of wills.
3. Why should you have a will? What should be in it? How should you safeguard it?
4. What techniques may be employed to avoid or reduce probate costs?
5. Explain the two major types of trusts and how they are formed.
6. What is the difference between an inheritance tax and an estate tax?
7. How is the federal gift tax computed?
8. Enumerate and explain the four major types of joint ownership.
9. Explain the Uniform Gift to Minors Act.

10. Generally how does one go about minimizing estate shrinkage? Expand on the various techniques available.

Projects

1. Prepare your own will and letter of last instructions.
2. Find out the costs and time delays involved in probate proceedings in your area. Ask your local bank about restraining orders on joint accounts in case of death.
3. Determine the death and/or estate tax rates in your area. Calculate the state and federal taxes on your anticipated estate. Determine if it would be less expensive to set up a trust of some type.

Case Problem

Bart Baker, who is unmarried, desires to transfer his estate of approximately $200,000 upon his death to his heirs at the lowest possible cost. How can this be accomplished? At what approximate cost?

three

Once you have mastered the financial problems of everyday living through planning and budgeting, you are ready to implement your investment plans. As mentioned in parts one and two, your understanding of consumerism, credit, savings, and insurance concepts is very important in any financial plan. You should allow for a reasonable standard of living in your budget before you begin to invest seriously. You should have savings over and above an emergency fund and sufficient insurance for your family's protection in order to invest in a prudent manner.

People generally invest to increase their incomes, safeguard their assets from inflationary losses, and provide for growth of their assets. Savings, real estate, securities, business ownership, and tax planning each accomplish these tasks in varying degrees. We have already looked at savings. We will look at tax planning and ownership of homes and real estate as the first steps toward building an investment portfolio. These are activities most likely to be engaged in by most people. We will then analyze security investments and business ownership. No attempt will be made to endorse any investment medium over another. You should be aware of the concepts, opportunities, types, costs, and risks of all investments and then choose according to your needs.

invest for the present and the future

CONCEPTS AND OPPORTUNITIES

Whenever you invest you become an owner of an asset, which may be either personal property or real property. You exchange one asset (money) for another (an investment). All segments of the economy benefit from your investment. You and your fellow consumers, business, and government have gained to varying degrees when you invest. You hope to make a profit on your money. Businesses will use your funds for operations, expansion, and profit. Government also uses your funds for operations whenever you lend it money by saving or investing in government securities. Your fellow consumer benefits from the jobs, services, and products made available through investment. Investment, especially in business, means you become a part owner, not only in the specific business, but in the free enterprise system.

OBJECTIVES

Before choosing a particular investment, you need to determine your specific investment goals. The four basic investment objectives you should consider are: (1) safety, (2) liquidity, (3) current income, and (4) growth. Unfortunately, you cannot meet all these objectives in any one investment. Therefore, you should diversify your investments. Besides, you may wish to change your investment objectives at various stages in your life cycle.

Safety

No one wants to lose his investment. Your choice of investment will reflect the amount of risk you are willing to take. Conservative investments such as savings, government securities, and some corporate bonds are relatively safe, but they do not provide a very high yield. As a generality, the greater the safety, the lower the yield, but the more stable it is.

Liquidity

The ability to exchange your investment for cash on short notice is called liquidity. You may desire a short-term investment because you will need the money in the near future. Government and corporate securities and some savings certificates provide almost immediate conversion to cash. Loans, business ownership, real estate, and long-term savings certificates are examples of investments that may not be easy to sell or convert to immediate cash.

Current Income

There are times when a person desires or needs a regular income to supplement or supplant his or her wages. Usually an investment that regularly pays a fixed income, such as interest-bearing securities and loans or corporate preferred dividends, does not increase in value to any great extent. Also, the greater the regularity, the greater the safety, and the less the risk, the lower the rate of return on your investment.

Growth

Price appreciation (growth) is the glamorous part of investing. You often hear of persons investing in some property or a company that increases in value. You also hear of persons who have invested in something that loses much of its value. Gain results from selling at a price higher than you paid. Loss results from selling at a price lower than you paid. The amount of the capital gain (or loss) often depends upon the risks and the time involved. Many investors would be happy to gain enough to cover the effects of inflation. Hopefully you will be more successful. Investments that provide for possible growth (capital gains) include common stock, real estate, commodities, and collectibles such as antiques and paintings.

TYPES OF INVESTMENTS

The average investor has a bewildering choice of saving and investment possibilities. He usually opts for a savings passbook or certificate of deposit and home ownership, because he is not familiar with many investment opportunities, or he has heard nothing but ill-founded rumors about particular investments. The more adventuresome person sometimes invests in common stock or mutual funds or even starts his own business.

Some of the lesser-known investments that we will discuss in part three include mortgage lending, corporate bonds and commercial paper, government bonds and notes, commodities, and collectibles. These are in addition to the major investment media of real estate, corporate stocks, and mutual funds.

COSTS OF INVESTMENT

Part of analyzing an investment opportunity consists of determining the costs of buying, selling, and servicing the investment. For example, there are loan fees and closing costs in the purchase of a home, followed by the sales commission when you sell your home. Banks and brokerage houses charge a fee for the service of buying and selling securities for you.

Management fees are charged for the management of real estate and investment portfolios. Trust accounts have administration fees.

All these fees are in addition to the actual purchase cost of the investment. Transaction fees often differ between individual banks and broker-dealers. The fees will definitely differ with the kind of investment. These transaction fees pay for the information and research services of the investment broker, in addition to paying for the salesman's commission. It will pay you to become aware of competitive charges for investment transactions in your area.

Risks of Investment

All investments have some degree of risk. The amount of risk allows us to differentiate among gambling, speculating, and investing, all of which involve a degree of risk. The degree of uncertainty as to potential loss determines the amount of risk.

Gambling is dependent on pure chance. There is no honest way to reduce the uncertainty of the anticipated event. True gambling, Nevada style, is gamesmanship, an artificially created risk for "fun and profit." Business and investment risk-taking may be considered gambling only if no thought whatsoever goes into the investment. Some time ago, a researcher using a computer and a random-selection process showed that in at least one series of "investments" you could best the average rate of return experienced by a number of leading investment institutions. That was gambling; the possibility of selecting other profitable investments at random is indeed remote.

Speculating is the business person's gamble. Speculation is the deliberate assumption of risks in transactions that offer the home of a good profit if they prove successful. The profit may be in the form of a large income or yield, but is more likely to be in the form of a capital gain. The speculator is usually an asset trader who seeks price appreciation in a relatively short time. He may also take longer-term risks such as developing new products and new industries. Speculating is high-risk investment.

Investment is a commitment to use money under conditions relatively free from risk. A true investor attempts to find long-term money commitments that will provide (1) a reasonable rate of return, (2) safety for his principal, and (3) modest capital appreciation. A true investor looks to the long-term conservative approach to money management, not to the quick profit.

There is a direct relationship between the degree of risk and the potential return on an investment. No one, investor, speculator, or gambler, wants to assume a risk unless it is worthwhile in terms of anticipated gain. As the degree of risk (the chance of loss) goes up, so does the potential rate of return, or there would be no takers. All risk takers (investors) can choose which type of risk they care to undertake by which type of investment they choose.

Investors attempt to identify the types of risks found in business investments. These risks can be reduced to four distinct types, which are present in varying degrees in all investments. These risks are commonly called (1) business, (2) interest-rate, (3) market, and (4) price-level risks.

Business Risk

This is often called the earning-power-of-business risk. The financial capacity of an organization may change to the point that its earning power is impaired, or even nonexistent in the case of business failure. The risk may be caused by competition, change in demand, management problems, high costs, or any other factor that could cause an organization to reduce its power to generate earnings. Both local government and businesses offer securities that suffer from the earning-power-of-business risk.

Interest-Rate Risk

This risk is also known as the money-rate risk. An investor in any fixed-rate, fixed-term investment must make a financial commitment and then await the consequences. The risk is that after the commitment, the interest rates in the money market may go up but may leave the investor already committed at the lower rate. He cannot take advantage of the higher rates currently available because of contractual maturity dates. This predicament is really a form of lost opportunity.

Generally, the shorter the fixed term, the less the interest-rate risk, because the investor soon has another opportunity to invest. Longer-term fixed-rate investments are offered at higher rates of interest to offset the effects of the interest-rate risk and to entice investment. These generalities are especially true in an inflationary economy.

Common stock and real estate may also provide a yield on investment. Even though these assets may be purchased with the objective of capital gains, they do provide the equivalent of an interest rate in the form of dividends and rental profits. If you could receive a better return on your investment elsewhere, you suffer from the interest-rate risk. If interest rates decline after the investor makes his commitment, he has successfully overcome the interest-rate risk. Both the investor and the investment issuer/seller are exposed to the same risk.

Market Risk

The risk arises from the uncertainty of the future price or value of an investment. Even though earning power of an asset may not change, demand for an asset may increase or decrease, causing the price to increase or decrease. The intrinsic value and earning power of an investment asset helps to determine its market price. In the final analysis, however, it is investor expectations about the future value that create current demand for the asset and determine its current market price.

Investors who buy low and sell high have successfully met the market risk. Those who do the opposite have taken the market risk and have lost. Both the investors and the investment issuer/seller are exposed to the risk. An investor purchases with the intent of making a long-term commitment, while a speculator expects a short-term upward change in price. Both conceivably evaluated the risk. A gambler would have taken the chance without investigation.

Price-Level Risk

The price-level risk is also known as the purchasing-power risk. The buying power of the U.S. dollar decreases annually as worldwide inflation continues. All investments and all savings suffer from this hazard. Your investment may provide income or capital gain, but in either case you will receive your return in dollars that will purchase fewer goods and services. As mentioned earlier, an investor may have an investment objective of safety of principal, that of keeping it intact. To accomplish this, one must have a return at least as great as the rate of inflation.

RISK REDUCTION

The risks in any investment can be reduced considerably. You must gather facts about business trends and the economy as a whole. Specific industries and selected firms within the industry must be analyzed in terms of your investment objectives, the appropriateness of the investment, the opportunity presented, the costs of investment, the current rates of return, and future expectations.

Know the alternatives available, procure knowledgeable advice, and have an understanding of investment concepts. In this manner you can hopefully reduce your investment risks. The next few chapters should be very useful to you.

11

income tax

"Taxes are what we pay for a civilized society." This observation is as true today as when it was so eloquently stated by Justice Oliver Wendell Holmes, Jr., of the Supreme Court. Today we expect a lot in the way of "civilized" social services. We pay for these services with higher taxes on the federal, state, and local levels. This chapter will examine in detail the federal income tax, because this is the one tax that you can individually defer or reduce to some degree. Each year Congress makes changes in the tax laws, but the concepts within this chapter should remain fairly constant.

PRINCIPLES OF TAXATION

Before we discuss the federal income tax in detail, we must make some general remarks about all types of taxes. No one wants to pay taxes if he or she can help it. If offered the opportunity, you would probably suggest that "the other guy" pay more. Our federal, state, and local legislators give considerable thought to taxation because of this. Some people would even say that legislators spend too much time thinking about ways to raise taxes and too little time trying to reduce government spending.

Certain principles must be analyzed whenever taxation is being considered. Unfortunately, these principles are subject to differing interpretations by lawmakers, special-interest groups, and the average citizen. Some of these principles are diametrically opposed to each other.

1. Taxes are necessary to support government operations. The controversy arises over what operations the government should be engaged in and who should be taxed for them.
2. Taxes must be mandatory and equally applied. Even a well-meaning concept such as this creates controversy. Equitable taxation has different meanings. The source of income, the tax rate, to whom it is applied, and for whose benefit all have a bearing on equitable taxation.
3. Taxes must be easy to administer. The ease and cost of collecting the tax must be considered. If the effort and expense of collecting are too great, a government bureaucracy is created that may not pay for itself because of low net revenues. If a tax becomes unenforceable, citizens will often avoid payment and develop a worse attitude toward voluntary compliance.
4. Taxes must be politically expedient. Taxes are often hidden in the price of goods and services because legislators do not wish to be noted for raising consumer taxes. Taxes may be levied on producers and middlemen who pass them on as part of the pur-

chase price. Some taxes are promoted by pressure groups to be placed on items such as tobacco, alcohol, and other nonfavored products.

5. Taxes should be paid by those who benefit from the service provided by the tax revenue. Roads and bridges may be mostly financed by their users through gas taxes and tolls, but all citizens benefit from them to a degree. The benefits derived from a court system, national defense, and local government cannot be allocated to specific citizens. Education provides benefits to the entire country while personally benefiting the local recipients.
6. Taxes must be based on the ability to pay. This concept is more easily understood and accepted than the other principles of taxation. What constitutes ability? Is it income, or is it accumulated capital? Should a person pay a property tax on real estate or personal property because he has accumulated this property? Hasn't he already paid a tax on the income used to purchase the property?
7. Taxes must be easy to understand. The first five principles eliminate any chance that taxes will be easy to understand. Each of these principles is considered by legislators when they try to predict the impact a tax change will have on the economy. Of all the taxes levied, income taxes are the most complicated.

Why We Have Taxes

The taxes we pay provide the funds for the services rendered by all levels of government. Government is a nonprofit activity that receives its income from taxes and borrowing and dispenses its income to citizens through its public services. As individuals we can do little to provide for needed services, but as a group formed by the common bond of government we are able to accomplish a lot in the name of public good.

The cost of government at all three levels has been rising sharply over the years because of population increases, our affluent society, inflation, and the demand for more and better government services. A change in the attitude of taxpayers, citizens, and legislators is needed to slow the continuous upward spiral of demand for services, which triggers a need for more taxes, if indeed this attitude can be changed or should be changed.

Sources of Taxes

Because of the need for new sources of revenue to finance government expenditures, legislators and administrators grasp at almost any source of taxation. Traditionally each level of government has its own prime source of revenue. Some of these may change in the near future because of constitutional challenges, federal revenue sharing, or a more enlightened tax philosophy.

Federal government Over half of federal revenue comes from income taxes, of which individual taxes comprise 41 percent and corporate taxes 14 percent. About 23 percent comes from Social Security taxes, which are returned to the citizens in Social Security and unemployment benefits. Seven percent of the federal income is received from excise taxes, and 5 percent comes from miscellaneous taxes. The balance of income, 10 percent, is borrowed through the debt media of government bonds and U.S. Treasury notes.

State government Each state has its own system of raising funds. The tax burden on citizens of each state differs with the taxing power of the state government, its spending philosophy, and the amount of urbanization and industry.

The major sources of tax revenue for

states tend to be sales taxes, income taxes, and licenses. Sales taxes still are the greatest source of revenue for the aggregate of the fifty states, although the U.S. Department of Commerce points out that income taxes have replaced the sales tax as number one revenue producer in twelve states.

Local government The nation's local taxing districts are composed of counties, cities, towns, and special-purpose taxing districts. These political entities need funds to provide the many local services needed in a civilized society. Property tax, sales tax, and licenses tend to be the biggest producers of revenue. School systems, police and fire protection, parks, recreation, and health services tend to be the chief users of local tax funds.

Classification of Taxes

The principles of taxation become theoretical when government is faced with finding sufficient revenue to pay for its many activities. Legislators will tax almost anything and anyone if the objections are not too loud. As mentioned earlier, the average taxpayer believes in equality of taxation as long as the other person is taxed for whatever benefits he receives. This idea essentially amounts to a user's tax. Objectively it may be fair and equitable; then again, it may not. To get a better perspective on taxes, we will classify them as direct or indirect and progressive or regressive.

Direct vs. indirect taxes A direct tax is paid by the person upon whom it is levied. He cannot shift its cost to someone else. An indirect tax is paid as part of the cost of a product or service.

The individual income tax is the best example of a direct tax. Government holds the individual responsible for this tax by direct withholding from his income. Sales and property taxes are also paid directly out of the taxpayer's pocket. You can "feel" the cost of government when you pay direct taxes.

Excise taxes are included in the sales price and may therefore be considered indirect. Taxes paid by corporations, partnerships, and sole proprietorships (actually all taxes on business) are indirectly paid by consumers when they purchase that particular business's goods and services. The common idea of having business pay higher and higher taxes tends to backfire in the final analysis, since consumers buy that business's products and services at higher and higher prices.

Progressive vs. regressive taxes The principle of ability to pay determines whether a tax is progressive or regressive. If the tax rate increases on a percentage basis as one's ability to pay increases, the tax is a *progressive* tax. The income tax accomplishes this even though there is disagreement about the rates that should be applied to the various income levels. Figure 11–1 shows the federal income tax rates for 1975. Are these rates equitable and progressive? If the income tax were applied at the same rate for all, it would be considered *proportional.* Those with higher incomes would pay more money because of more income, but they would pay the same rate as those with lower incomes.

A *regressive* tax is levied on all applicable taxpayers at the same rate, regardless of their income. Regressive taxes are not based upon ability to pay and hence are termed regressive because they take a greater percentage of the wages of lower-income families than of higher-income families. Sales taxes, property taxes, and gasoline taxes are considered regressive, as are any taxes not directly based on ability to pay.

1975 Tax Rate Schedules

If you do not use one of the Tax Tables, figure your tax on the amount on Form 1040, line 47, by using the appropriate Tax Rate Schedule on this page. Enter tax on Form 1040, line 16a.

SCHEDULE X—Single Taxpayers Not Qualifying for Rates in Schedule Y or Z

Use this schedule if you checked the box on Form 1040, line 1—

If the amount on Form 1040, line 47, is: / Enter on Form 1040, line 16a:

Not over $500 ... 14% of the amount on line 47.

Over—	But not over—		of the amount over—
$500	$1,000	$70+15%	$500
$1,000	$1,500	$145+16%	$1,000
$1,500	$2,000	$225+17%	$1,500
$2,000	$4,000	$310+19%	$2,000
$4,000	$6,000	$690+21%	$4,000
$6,000	$8,000	$1,110+24%	$6,000
$8,000	$10,000	$1,590+25%	$8,000
$10,000	$12,000	$2,090+27%	$10,000
$12,000	$14,000	$2,630+29%	$12,000
$14,000	$16,000	$3,210+31%	$14,000
$16,000	$18,000	$3,830+34%	$16,000
$18,000	$20,000	$4,510+36%	$18,000
$20,000	$22,000	$5,230+38%	$20,000
$22,000	$26,000	$5,990+40%	$22,000
$26,000	$32,000	$7,590+45%	$26,000
$32,000	$38,000	$10,290+50%	$32,000
$38,000	$44,000	$13,290+55%	$38,000
$44,000	$50,000	$16,590+60%	$44,000
$50,000	$60,000	$20,190+62%	$50,000
$60,000	$70,000	$26,390+64%	$60,000
$70,000	$80,000	$32,790+66%	$70,000
$80,000	$90,000	$39,390+68%	$80,000
$90,000	$100,000	$46,190+69%	$90,000
$100,000	....	$53,090+70%	$100,000

SCHEDULE Y—Married Taxpayers and Qualifying Widows and Widowers

If you are a married person living apart from your spouse, see page 5 of the instructions to see if you can be considered to be "unmarried" for purposes of using Schedule X or Z.

Use this schedule if you checked the box on Form 1040, line 2 or 5—

Married Taxpayers Filing Joint Returns and Qualifying Widows and Widowers (See page 5)

If the amount on Form 1040, line 47, is: / Enter on Form 1040, line 16a:

Not over $1,000 ... 14% of the amount on line 47.

Over—	But not over—		of the amount over—
$1,000	$2,000	$140+15%	$1,000
$2,000	$3,000	$290+16%	$2,000
$3,000	$4,000	$450+17%	$3,000
$4,000	$8,000	$620+19%	$4,000
$8,000	$12,000	$1,380+22%	$8,000
$12,000	$16,000	$2,260+25%	$12,000
$16,000	$20,000	$3,260+28%	$16,000
$20,000	$24,000	$4,380+32%	$20,000
$24,000	$28,000	$5,660+36%	$24,000
$28,000	$32,000	$7,100+39%	$28,000
$32,000	$36,000	$8,660+42%	$32,000
$36,000	$40,000	$10,340+45%	$36,000
$40,000	$44,000	$12,140+48%	$40,000
$44,000	$52,000	$14,060+50%	$44,000
$52,000	$64,000	$18,060+53%	$52,000
$64,000	$76,000	$24,420+55%	$64,000
$76,000	$88,000	$31,020+58%	$76,000
$88,000	$100,000	$37,980+60%	$88,000
$100,000	$120,000	$45,180+62%	$100,000
$120,000	$140,000	$57,580+64%	$120,000
$140,000	$160,000	$70,380+66%	$140,000
$160,000	$180,000	$83,580+68%	$160,000
$180,000	$200,000	$97,180+69%	$180,000
$200,000	....	$110,980+70%	$200,000

Use this schedule if you checked the box on Form 1040, line 3—

Married Taxpayers Filing Separate Returns

If the amount on Form 1040, line 47, is: / Enter on Form 1040, line 16a:

Not over $500 ... 14% of the amount on line 47.

Over—	But not over—		of the amount over—
$500	$1,000	$70+15%	$500
$1,000	$1,500	$145+16%	$1,000
$1,500	$2,000	$225+17%	$1,500
$2,000	$4,000	$310+19%	$2,000
$4,000	$6,000	$690+22%	$4,000
$6,000	$8,000	$1,130+25%	$6,000
$8,000	$10,000	$1,630+28%	$8,000
$10,000	$12,000	$2,190+32%	$10,000
$12,000	$14,000	$2,830+36%	$12,000
$14,000	$16,000	$3,550+39%	$14,000
$16,000	$18,000	$4,330+42%	$16,000
$18,000	$20,000	$5,170+45%	$18,000
$20,000	$22,000	$6,070+48%	$20,000
$22,000	$26,000	$7,030+50%	$22,000
$26,000	$32,000	$9,030+53%	$26,000
$32,000	$38,000	$12,210+55%	$32,000
$38,000	$44,000	$15,510+58%	$38,000
$44,000	$50,000	$18,990+60%	$44,000
$50,000	$60,000	$22,590+62%	$50,000
$60,000	$70,000	$28,790+64%	$60,000
$70,000	$80,000	$35,190+66%	$70,000
$80,000	$90,000	$41,790+68%	$80,000
$90,000	$100,000	$48,590+69%	$90,000
$100,000	....	$55,490+70%	$100,000

SCHEDULE Z—Unmarried (or legally separated) Taxpayers Who Qualify as Heads of Household (See page 5)

Use this schedule if you checked the box on Form 1040, line 4—

If the amount on Form 1040, line 47, is: / Enter on Form 1040, line 16a:

Not over $1,000 ... 14% of the amount on line 47.

Over—	But not over—		of the amount over—
$1,000	$2,000	$140+16%	$1,000
$2,000	$4,000	$300+18%	$2,000
$4,000	$6,000	$660+19%	$4,000
$6,000	$8,000	$1,040+22%	$6,000
$8,000	$10,000	$1,480+23%	$8,000
$10,000	$12,000	$1,940+25%	$10,000
$12,000	$14,000	$2,440+27%	$12,000
$14,000	$16,000	$2,980+28%	$14,000
$16,000	$18,000	$3,540+31%	$16,000
$18,000	$20,000	$4,160+32%	$18,000
$20,000	$22,000	$4,800+35%	$20,000
$22,000	$24,000	$5,500+36%	$22,000
$24,000	$26,000	$6,220+38%	$24,000
$26,000	$28,000	$6,980+41%	$26,000
$28,000	$32,000	$7,800+42%	$28,000
$32,000	$36,000	$9,480+45%	$32,000
$36,000	$38,000	$11,280+48%	$36,000
$38,000	$40,000	$12,240+51%	$38,000
$40,000	$44,000	$13,260+52%	$40,000
$44,000	$50,000	$15,340+55%	$44,000
$50,000	$52,000	$18,640+56%	$50,000
$52,000	$64,000	$19,760+58%	$52,000
$64,000	$70,000	$26,720+59%	$64,000
$70,000	$76,000	$30,260+61%	$70,000
$76,000	$80,000	$33,920+62%	$76,000
$80,000	$88,000	$36,400+63%	$80,000
$88,000	$100,000	$41,440+64%	$88,000
$100,000	$120,000	$49,120+66%	$100,000
$120,000	$140,000	$62,320+67%	$120,000
$140,000	$160,000	$75,720+68%	$140,000
$160,000	$180,000	$89,320+69%	$160,000
$180,000	....	$103,120+70%	$180,000

Figure 11–1 1975 Tax Rate Schedules. *(Internal Revenue Service)*

Sales taxes are a tax on consumption. For example, in some states you pay a 5 percent state sales tax on the purchase of most goods other than food. No consideration is given to your income. If you earn $5,000 per year you will definitely spend all your earnings. You may spend 50 percent of your income —$2,500—on taxable items. At 5 percent you would be taxed $125 on your $5,000 income. Now let us assume that you earn $10,000 per year and still spend $2,500 on taxable items. This amounts to 25 percent of your income. The actual tax is the same as in the prior example, $125. If you earned the lower income, you would pay sales tax equal to $2\frac{1}{2}$ percent of your total income; if you earned the higher income, you would pay a sales tax equivalent to $1\frac{1}{4}$ percent of your income.

A similar example would involve the purchase of gasoline, tobacco, or alcohol. If the same amount of these items were purchased by a low-income person and a high-income person, the low-income person would pay a proportionately higher percentage of his income for the tax on these items.

Property taxes may also be considered regressive because they do not take ability to pay into account. There may be some relationship between income and the value of one's property, but it is not consistent. Actually, you are penalized for holding property or improving it. You may have little or no income with which to pay your tax. In fact, you could be forced to sell your property to pay the taxes on it.

Your Fair Share

No one wants to pay more than his or her fair share. Your fair share of income tax is the tax that you are legally liable to pay after honestly reporting all income, adjustments, deductions, and exemptions. Proper financial planning and a good understanding of tax law can reduce your taxes to a minimum. This procedure is known as *tax avoidance* and is encouraged by the government to keep you from paying more than your fair share. Unfortunately, tax rulings and computations are very complex. You must learn to reduce your tax burden legally or secure competent help in preparing your return.

You must *never evade taxes.* This is illegal. Willful failure to report income or subtracting unallowable deductions, exemptions, and adjustments is considered tax evasion. Severe penalties may result from such activities. Be sure of the distinction between legal tax avoidance and illegal tax evasion.

Businesses and wealthy individuals hire lawyers and tax accountants to help them take advantage of every favorable loop-hole in the tax laws. You can use this same advantage on a much smaller scale if you are aware of your legal tax-avoidance procedures. The so-called tax-free millionaires pay little or no federal income tax because they usually invest in tax-sheltered ventures. They plan their financial activities to save on taxes. The special treatments and suggestions near the end of the chapter are some of the more important tax considerations that influence the financially sophisticated. They should also influence you.

FACTORS IN PREPARING YOUR FEDERAL INCOME TAX RETURN

All taxes are important because they are an expense; they subtract from your income. While the federal income tax is the most

File a return if you are:	And your gross income is at least:
Single (legally separated, divorced, or married living apart from spouse with dependent child) and are under 65	$2,350
Single (legally separated, divorced, or married living apart from spouse with dependent child) and are 65 or older	3,100
A person who can be claimed as a dependent on your parent's return, and have taxable dividends, interest, or other unearned income	750
A qualifying widow(er) with dependent child and are under 65	2,650
A qualifying widow(er) with dependent child and are 65 or older	3,400
Married filing jointly, living together at the end of 1975 (or at date of death of spouse), and both are under 65	3,400
Married filing jointly, living together at the end of 1975 (or at date of death of spouse), and one is 65 or older	$4,150
Married filing jointly, living together at the end of 1975 (or at date of death of spouse), and both are 65 or older	4,900
Married filing separate return or married but not living together at end of 1975	750
A person with income from sources within U.S. possessions	750
Self employed and your net earnings from self-employment were at least $400.	

Figure 11–2 Who Must File a Return? *(Internal Revenue Service)*

equitable tax, it is also the most complicated and usually the most expensive. Therefore the balance of this chapter will be devoted to explaining it. We cannot turn you into an expert. Only considerable practice can do that, and then only to the degree necessary to do your taxes with reasonable skill and understanding.

Who Must File a Return?

The amount of *gross income* you received during the year determines whether you must file a return. Figure 11–2 illustrates the basic filing requirements. It would be wise to check the latest IRS tax-form booklet for any change in gross-income requirements. Gross income includes all income in the form of money, property, or services that are not specifically exempt by law. In practice, however, if you have earned any wages from which income tax has been withheld, you must file a return. The government does not automatically refund the withheld income tax if your gross income is below the stated figures; you must file a return to claim the refund.

When and Where to File a Return

Most taxpayers use the calendar year ending December 31. Then you have 3½ months to compute and file your federal income tax return for the just-ended calendar year. You must file on or before April 15, although if April 15 falls on a Saturday, Sunday, or legal holiday, you have until midnight of the next business day. The IRS tax-form booklet will specify the latest date that you can file a timely return.

Your return is timely if it is postmarked before midnight of the date it is due. If you cannot make that deadline because you waited until the last minute, you will be subject to a penalty. Advance planning should eliminate this problem. If you realize that you will be unable to make the timely deadline, you may file for an automatic two-month extension. This is accomplished by filing Form 4868 and attaching a check for the estimated amount of tax due for the year, which may already be taken care of by the tax withheld from your pay.

Where to file You file your return with the IRS service center for your region.

This information will be listed in the tax-form booklet. After you have filed for the first time the IRS will mail you the information booklet with the tax forms that you will normally need.

Payment of Tax

Our income-tax system operates on a pay-as-you-go basis. Your tax is paid either by withholding a portion of your wages or by sending quarterly payments of your estimated annual income to the IRS if you do not receive wages. Both procedures are really estimates of the actual tax, which must be calculated and filed by April 15 of the following year. The withholding of tax from your wages and the filing of a Declaration of Estimated Tax will not relieve you from filing your regular return.

Tax withholding An employer must withhold income tax from each employee's pay in each pay period. Gross pay and the number of allowances claimed determine the amount of tax withheld.

Every new employee should fill out and file with his employer an Employee's Withholding Allowance Certificate, Form W–4, to claim the number of allowances to which he is entitled. An employee may claim fewer exemptions than he actually has, but he may not claim more. Some taxpayers use withholding as a form of forced savings that they cannot touch except at tax-filing time.

Form W–4E, Exemption from Withholding, is used by employees who had no tax liability in the preceding year and expect to have none in the current year. An employee who files this form will be exempt from tax withholding on wages paid to him during the year. Form W–4E is particularly useful to students, so they will not have to file a return solely to claim a refund. Filing of Form W–4E has no effect on a taxpayer's liability for payment of Social Security (FICA) tax, which will still be withheld from your wages.

At the end of the year your employer will give you three copies of Form W–2, Wage and Tax Statement. This statement is to be given to you on or before January 31. It shows total wages paid and the amount of income tax and Social Security tax (FICA) withheld during the year. You should file one copy with your federal tax return, and a second copy with your state return to substantiate the credit for taxes already paid. The other copy should be kept with your copy of the return. If you work for more than one employer during the year, you will have more than one W–2 to submit with your return.

Declaration of Estimated Tax Business owners, professional people, investors, and others not receiving income from wages must file a Declaration of Estimated Tax for Individuals, Form 1040–ES. Persons who have income over and above that subject to withholding may also be required to file Form 1040–ES.

Your estimate will be based on the preceding year's return and anticipated added income not subject to withholding for the upcoming year. The declaration must be filed not later than April 15 if your total estimated tax is $100 or more.

The declaration comes with attached vouchers that are sent in with payments due April 15, June 15, September 15, and January 15. A percent penalty is incurred if you underestimate any payment by more than 20 percent. You may change your estimate from quarter to quarter if you discover that your income is different than anticipated. The penalty is imposed on the difference between 80 percent of the amount that you should have paid and the amount you actually did pay.

Keeping Records

Record keeping is an important part of your tax planning and preparation. Do not trust your memory. Keep all receipts, bills, and cancelled checks accumulated throughout the year. These are especially important for itemized deductions and any type of investment or business enterprise. Furthermore, these documents may be needed to substantiate your return if you are audited by the IRS.

Your supporting records for income-tax purposes should be kept for a minimum of three years, the basic statute of limitations. However, the IRS may go back as far as six years to question a tax return. There is no time limitation in case the IRS suspects fraud in a return.

For practical purposes keep your returns and supporting documents for six years. Keep the actual return, Form 1040 and other schedules, for an indefinite period. You may wish to use income averaging, determine your place of residence, or refer to some other item. Sometimes new legislation is passed that gives the taxpayer new benefits based upon past years' transactions. The old returns do not take up much space and are well worth retaining.

When disposing of supporting documents at the end of the sixth year, do so with caution. You may need some of the information when selling an asset to determine the correct capital gain. Keep any document that pertains to the acquisition costs including all sorts of fees above the actual purchase price. Documents that indicate the cost of improvements to property should also be saved because these, in effect, are part of the cost of the property.

Cash vs. accrual Most individuals are wage earners and operate on a cash basis for record-keeping purposes and therefore file their tax return on a cash basis. This means that all items of taxable income actually or constructively received and all deductible-expense items actually paid during the year are shown on your income tax. "Constructively received" includes income that has been credited to your account, dividends that have been reinvested, and uncashed checks and similar items that have been constructively received.

Under the accrual basis it is not the actual receipt of income but the right to receive it that governs the amount you report. Income is accounted for when it is earned and expenses are deducted when they are incurred.

Once you have chosen your accounting method, you ordinarily may not change it without permission from the IRS. If you are a business person, you may use different methods of accounting for different businesses.

FINDING YOUR TAXABLE INCOME

Your taxable income is the amount upon which you calculate your federal income tax. To get your taxable income, follow the sequence of instructions on Form 1040. It looks very confusing, but if you take each line on the form in proper sequence, it will prove to be easier than it looks. The basic formula for determining taxable income is as follows:

Add:	Income (from all taxable sources)
Subtract:	− Adjustments to income
Equals:	= Adjusted gross income
Subtract:	− Deductions (standard or itemized)
Subtract:	− Exemptions
Equals:	= Taxable income

This formula is essentially the same for both Form 1040 and Short Form 1040A. Figures 11–3, 11–4, 11–5, and 11–6 illustrate the front and back sides of Form 1040 and Form 1040A. The short form is for simple income tax returns not involving adjustments or itemized deductions. You must choose which form is more beneficial to you. The IRS instructions will help you decide. The IRS will make changes in the forms whenever necessary, but the forms should follow the basic tax formula regardless of any change.

Who May Use Short Form 1040A

You may use Short Form 1040A if all your income was from wages, salaries, tips, other employee compensations, dividends, and interest. There is no limitation on the total amount of income.

You may not itemize your deductions using the short form, so you must decide whether itemizing will lower your tax. A general rule of thumb to help you decide is discussed later in the section on itemized deductions.

Who Must File Form 1040

You should file Form 1040 if your itemized deductions make it worthwhile. You *must* file Form 1040 under certain circumstances. The most important reasons are:

1. You had income other than wages, salaries, tips, dividends, or interest.
2. You received more than $400 in dividends or interest payments.
3. You received $20 or more in tips in any one month, and you did not fully report these tips to your employer.
4. Your Form W–2 shows uncollected employee tax (Social Security tax) on tips.
5. You claim any of the following:
   a. a retirement income credit,
   b. an investment credit,
   c. a foreign tax credit,
   d. a credit for federal tax on special fuels,
   e. a credit from a regulated investment company.
6. You choose the benefits of income averaging.
7. You could be claimed as a dependent on on your parents' return, and you had dividend or interest income, and your combined dividend and interest income was $750 or more.
8. Your spouse files a separate return and itemizes deductions.
9. You received capital-gain dividends or nontaxable distributions (return of capital).
10. You claim an adjustment to income for any of the following:
    a. a sick-pay exclusion,
    b. a moving-expense deduction because you changed jobs or were transferred,
    c. a business expense as an ouside salesperson or for travel for your job,
    d. a payment to a Keogh retirement plan,
    e. a payment to an individual retirement account,
    f. forfeited interest penalty.
11. You have a financial account in a foreign country.

Perhaps the best way to learn the intricacies of income tax is to do a return. We will use the sequence of Form 1040 to expand upon the basic formula for determining your taxable income. The short form may be the easy way out, but the long form will better acquaint you with how to save on taxes.

Form **1040** US Department of the Treasury—Internal Revenue Service
Individual Income Tax Return 1975

For the year January 1–December 31, 1975, or other taxable year beginning ...., 1975, ending ...., 19...

Please print or type

Name (If joint return, give first names and initials of both) | Last name | Your social security number | For Privacy Act Notification, see page 2 of Instructions.

Present home address (Number and street, including apartment number, or rural route) | Spouse's social security no. | For IRS use only

City, town or post office, State and ZIP code | Occupation: Yours ▶ Spouse's ▶

Requested by Census Bureau for Revenue Sharing ▶ A In what city, town, village, etc., do you live? | B Do you live within the legal limits of the city, town, etc.? ☐ Yes ☐ No ☐ Don't know | C In what county and State do you live? County State | D In what township do you live? (See page 4.)

Filing Status

1 ☐ Single *(check only ONE box)*
2 ☐ Married filing joint return (even if only one had income)
3 ☐ Married filing separately. If spouse is also filing give spouse's social security number in designated space above and enter full name here ▶
4 ☐ Unmarried Head of Household (See page 5 of Instructions) ▶
5 ☐ Qualifying widow(er) with dependent child (Year spouse died ▶ 19). See page 5 of Instructions.

Exemptions

6a Regular ☐ Yourself ☐ Spouse Enter number of boxes checked ▶
b First names of your dependent children who lived with you .... Enter number ▶
c Number of other dependents (from line 27) ▶
d Total (add lines 6a, b, and c) ▶
e Age 65 or over ☐ Yourself ☐ Spouse
Blind ☐ Yourself ☐ Spouse Enter number of boxes checked ▶
7 Total (add lines 6d and e) ▶

8 **Presidential Election Campaign Fund** ▶ Do you wish to designate $1 of your taxes for this fund? Yes No
If joint return, does your spouse wish to designate $1? Yes No
Note: If you check the "Yes" box(es) it will not increase your tax or reduce your refund.

Please attach Copy B of Forms W-2 here

Income

9	Wages, salaries, tips, and other employee compensation (Attach Forms W-2. If unavailable, see page 3 of Instructions.)	9
10a	Dividends (See pages 7 and 14 of Instructions) $........, 10b Less exclusion $........, Balance ▶ *(If gross dividends and other distributions are over $400, list in Part I of Schedule B.)*	10c
11	Interest income. [If $400 or less, enter total without listing in Schedule B; If over $400, enter total and list in Part II of Schedule B]	11
12	Income other than wages, dividends, and interest (from line 36)	12
13	Total (add lines 9, 10c, 11, and 12)	13
14	Adjustments to income (such as "sick pay," moving expenses, etc. from line 42)	14
15	Subtract line 14 from line 13 (Adjusted Gross Income) (If less than $8,000, see page 8 of Instructions on "Earned Income Credit.")	15

- **If you do not itemize deductions and line 15 is under $15,000, find tax in Tables and enter on line 16a.**
- **If you itemize deductions or line 15 is $15,000 or more, go to line 43 to figure tax.**
- **CAUTION.** If you have unearned income and can be claimed as a dependent on your parent's return, check here ▶ ☐ and see page 7 of Instructions.

Tax, Payments and Credits

16a	Tax, check if from: ☐ Tax Tables ☐ Tax Rate Schedule X, Y, or Z ☐ Schedule D ☐ Schedule G OR ☐ Form 4726	16a
b	Credit for personal exemptions (multiply line 6d by $30)	b
c	Balance (subtract line 16b from line 16a)	c
17	Credits (from line 54)	17
18	Balance (subtract line 17 from line 16c)	18
19	Other taxes (from line 63)	19
20	Total (add lines 18 and 19)	20
21a	Total Federal income tax withheld (attach Forms W-2 or W-2P to front)	21a
b	1975 estimated tax payments (include amount allowed as credit from 1974 return)	b
c	Earned income credit	c
d	Amount paid with Form 4868	d
e	Other payments (from line 67)	e
22	Total (add lines 21a through e)	22

Pay amount on line 23 in full with this return. Write social security number on check or money order and make payable to Internal Revenue Service.

Please attach Check or Money Order here

Balance Due or Refund

23	If line 20 is larger than line 22, enter **BALANCE DUE IRS** ▶ (Check here ▶ ☐, if Form 2210, Form 2210F, or statement is attached. See page 8 of Instructions.)	23
24	If line 22 is larger than line 20, enter amount **OVERPAID** ▶	24
25	Amount of line 24 to be **REFUNDED TO YOU** ▶	25
26	Amount of line 24 to be credited on 1976 estimated tax. ▶ 26	

If all of overpayment (line 24) is to be refunded (line 25), make no entry on line 26.

Sign here

Under penalties of perjury, I declare that I have examined this return, including accompanying schedules and statements, and to the best of my knowledge and belief it is true, correct, and complete. Declaration of preparer (other than taxpayer) is based on all information of which preparer has any knowledge.

▶ Your signature Date | ▶ Preparer's signature (other than taxpayer) Date

▶ Spouse's signature (if filing jointly, BOTH must sign even if only one had income) | Address (and ZIP Code)

Figure 11–3 Form 1040: Individual Income Tax Return (Front). *(Internal Revenue Service)*

Other Dependents

(a) NAME	(b) Relationship	(c) Months lived in your home. If born or died during year, write B or D.	(d) Did dependent have income of $750 or more?	(e) Amount YOU furnished for dependent's support. If 100% write ALL.	(f) Amount furnished by OTHERS including dependent.
				$	$

27 Total number of dependents listed in column (a). Enter here and on line 6c . . . ▶

Part I Income other than Wages, Dividends, and Interest

28 Business income or (loss) (attach Schedule C)	28	
29a Net gain or (loss) from sale or exchange of capital assets (attach Schedule D)	29a	
29b 50% of capital gain distributions (not reported on Schedule D—see page 9 of Instructions)	29b	
30 Net gain or (loss) from Supplemental Schedule of Gains and Losses (attach Form 4797)	30	
31a Pensions, annuities, rents, royalties, partnerships, estates or trusts, etc. (attach Schedule E)	31a	
31b Fully taxable pensions and annuities (not reported on Schedule E—see page 9 of Instructions)	31b	
32 Farm income or (loss) (attach Schedule F)	32	
33 State income tax refunds (does not apply if refund is for year in which you took the standard deduction—others see page 9 of Instructions)	33	
34 Alimony received	34	
35 Other (state nature and source—See page 9 of Instructions) ▶	35	
36 **Total** (add lines 28 through 35). **Enter here and on line 12** ▶	36	

Part II Adjustments to Income

37 "Sick pay." (attach Form 2440 or other required statement)	37	
38 Moving expense (attach Form 3903)	38	
39 Employee business expense (attach Form 2106 or statement)	39	
40a Payments to a Keogh (H.R. 10) retirement plan	40a	
40b Payments to an individual retirement arrangement from attached Form 5329, Part III	40b	
41 Forfeited interest penalty for premature withdrawal—see page 10 of Instructions	41	
42 **Total** (add lines 37 through 41). **Enter here and on line 14** ▶	42	

Part III Tax Computation (Do not use this part if you use the Tax Tables to find your tax.)

43 Adjusted gross income (from line 15)	43	
44 (a) If you itemize deductions, check here ▶ ☐ and enter total from Schedule A, line 41 and attach Schedule A (b) If you do not itemize deductions and line 15 is $15,000 or more, check here ▶ ☐ and: If box on line 2 or 5 is checked, enter 16% of line 15 but not more than $2,600; if box on line 1 or 4 is checked, enter $2,300; if box on line 3 is checked, enter $1,300	44	
45 Subtract line 44 from line 43	45	
46 Multiply total number of exemptions claimed on line 7, by $750	46	
47 **Taxable income.** Subtract line 46 from line 45	47	

(Figure your tax on the amount on line 47 by using Tax Rate Schedule X, Y, or Z, or if applicable, the alternative tax from Schedule D, income averaging from Schedule G, or maximum tax from Form 4726.) Enter tax on line 16a.

Part IV Credits

48 Retirement income credit (attach Schedule R)	48	
49 Investment credit (attach Form 3468)	49	
50 Foreign tax credit (attach Form 1116)	50	
51 Contributions to candidates for public office credit—see page 10 of Instructions	51	
52 Work Incentive (WIN) credit (attach Form 4874)	52	
53 Purchase of new principal residence credit (attach Form 5405)	53	
54 Total (add lines 48 through 53). **Enter here and on line 17** ▶	54	

Part V Other Taxes

55 Tax from recomputing prior-year investment credit (attach Form 4255)	55	
56 Tax from recomputing prior-year Work Incentive (WIN) credit (attach Schedule)	56	
57 Minimum tax. Check here ▶ ☐, if Form 4625 is attached	57	
58 Tax on premature distributions from attached Form 5329, Part V	58	
59 Self-employment tax (attach Schedule SE)	59	
60 Social security tax on tip income not reported to employer (attach Form 4137)	60	
61 Uncollected employee social security tax on tips (from Forms W–2)	61	
62 Excess contribution tax from attached Form 5329, Part IV	62	
63 **Total** (add lines 55 through 62). **Enter here and on line 19** ▶	63	

Part VI Other Payments

64 Excess FICA, RRTA, or FICA/RRTA tax withheld (two or more employers—see page 10 of Instructions)	64	
65 Credit for Federal tax on special fuels, nonhighway gasoline and lubricating oil (attach Form 4136)	65	
66 Credit from a Regulated Investment Company (attach Form 2439)	66	
67 **Total** (add lines 64 through 66). **Enter here and on line 21e** ▶	67	

Figure 11–4 Form 1040: Individual Income Tax Return (Back). *(Internal Revenue Service)*

Short Form 1040A **U.S. Individual Income Tax Return** Department of the Treasury Internal Revenue Service **1975**

Please print or type

Name (If joint return, give first names and initials of both) | Last name | Your social security number | **For Privacy Act Notification, see page 2 of Instructions.**

Present home address (Number and street, including apartment number, or rural route) | Spouse's social security no. | For IRS use only

City, town or post office, State and ZIP code | Occupation: Yours ▶ Spouse's ▶

Requested by Census Bureau for Revenue Sharing ▶ A In what city, town, village, etc., do you live? | B Do you live within the legal limits of the city, town, etc.? ☐ Yes ☐ No ☐ Don't know | C In what county and State do you live? County | State | D In what township do you live? (See page 5.)

Filing Status

1 ☐ Single (*check only ONE box*)

2 ☐ Married filing joint return (even if only one had income)

3 ☐ Married filing separately. If spouse is also filing give spouse's social security number in designated space above and enter full name here ▶

4 ☐ Unmarried Head of Household (See page 4 of Instructions) ▶

5 ☐ Qualifying widow(er) with dependent child (Year spouse died ▶ 19). See page 4 of Instructions.

Exemptions

6a Regular ☐ Yourself ☐ Spouse — Enter number of boxes checked ▶

b First names of your dependent children who lived with you — Enter number ▶

c Number of other dependents (from line 22) . ▶

d Total (add lines 6a, b, and c) . . . . ▶

e Age 65 or over . ☐ Yourself ☐ Spouse — Enter number of boxes checked ▶

Blind . . . . ☐ Yourself ☐ Spouse

7 Total (add lines 6d and e) . . . . ▶

Attach Copy B of Forms W-2 and Check or Money Order here

8 Presidential Election Campaign Fund . . ▶ Do you wish to designate $1 of your taxes for this fund? . . Yes | No — If joint return, does your spouse wish to designate $1? . . Yes | No — **Note:** If you check the "Yes" box(es) it will not increase your tax or reduce your refund.

9 Wages, salaries, tips, and other employee compensation (Attach Forms W-2. If unavailable, see page 6 of Instructions) . . . 9

10a Dividends (if over $400, see Instructions at top of page 3) $.......... 10b Less exclusion $.......... **Balance** ▶ 10c

11 Interest income (if over $400, see Instructions at top of page 3) 11

12 Total (add lines 9, 10c, and 11) **(Adjusted Gross Income)** (If less than $8,000, see page 18 of Instructions on "Earned Income Credit.") . . 12

- **If you want IRS to figure your tax, see page 6 of Instructions.**
- **If line 12 is under $15,000, find tax in Tax Tables (on pages 8–18) and enter on line 13a, on the back.**
- **If line 12 is $15,000 or more, figure your tax using the Tax Computation Worksheet on page 18 of Instructions.**

Figure 11–5 Short Form 1040A: Individual Income Tax Return (Front). *(Internal Revenue Service)*

FORM 1040 SEQUENCE

Start by reading the instruction booklet that comes with the tax forms. Complete all applicable lines on the form. The IRS reports a very high percentage of all returns omit some important information. Omissions often delay a refund that you may have coming. Just follow the numbers on the form. Refer to figures 11–3 and 11–4 for an illustration of Form 1040 as we proceed through the sequence.

Identifying the Return

Your correct name (and spouse's name if a joint return), address, Social Security number(s), and occupation(s) are needed to insure that the proper individual(s) get credit for the return. Use the special gummed label if the information on it is correct; this will speed up the processing of your return. The Social Security number of whichever spouse is named first should be carried forward to any supporting schedule or form. This consistency is for ease of identification, especially if your return becomes separated from its supporting documents.

The correct address and county of residence information is used by the federal government to provide revenue-sharing funds to counties and municipalities.

Filing Status

You can have only one possible filing status—check one box only. The actual tax

Form 1040A (1975) Page 2

13a Tax, check if from: ☐ Tax Tables (pages 8–18) OR ☐ Tax Computation Worksheet (page 18)	13a	
b Credit for personal exemptions (multiply line 6d by $30)	b	
14a Balance (subtract line 13b from line 13a). If less than zero, enter zero.	14a	
b Credit for contributions to candidates for public office (see page 7 of Instructions)	b	
15 Income tax (subtract line 14b from line 14a). If less than zero, enter zero.	15	
16a Total Federal income tax withheld (attach Forms W–2 to front)	16a	
b Excess FICA, RRTA, or FICA/RRTA tax withheld (two or more employers—see page 7 of Instructions)	b	
c 1975 estimated tax payments (include amount allowed as credit from 1974 return)	c	
d Earned income credit	d	
17 Total (add lines 16a, b, c, and d)	17	
18 If line 15 is larger than line 17, enter **BALANCE DUE IRS** ▶	18	
19 If line 17 is larger than line 15, enter amount **OVERPAID** ▶	19	
20 Amount of line 19 to be **REFUNDED TO YOU** ▶	20	
21 Amount of line 19 to be credited on 1976 estimated tax ▶	21	

Pay amount on line 18 in full with this return. Write social security number on check or money order and make payable to Internal Revenue Service.

If all of overpayment (line 19) is to be refunded (line 20), make no entry on line 21.

Other Dependents

(a) NAME	(b) Relationship	(c) Months lived in your home. If born or died during year, write B or D.	(d) Did dependent have income of $750 or more?	(e) Amount YOU furnished for dependent's support. If 100% write ALL.	(f) Amount furnished by OTHERS including dependent.
				$	$

22 Total number of dependents listed in column (a). Enter here and on line 6c ▶

Under penalties of perjury, I declare that I have examined this return, including accompanying schedules and statements, and to the best of my knowledge and belief it is true, correct and complete. Declaration of preparer (other than taxpayer) is based on all information of which preparer has any knowledge.

Sign here ▶ Your signature — Date ▶ Preparer's signature (other than taxpayer) — Date

▶ Spouse's signature (if filing jointly, BOTH must sign even if only one had income) — Address (and ZIP Code)

Figure 11–6 Short Form 1040A: Individual Income Tax Return (Back). *(Internal Revenue Service)*

rate differs according to your filing status. Figure 11–1 should demonstrate that federal income tax progresses at different rates for different marital and household statuses. There is approximately a 5 percent to 10 percent progressive increase in the tax rate for single taxpayers over married taxpayers filing a joint return.

Single If you were single, divorced, legally separated, or a "married person living apart from your spouse" on December 31, consider yourself single for the whole year.

Married If you were married on December 31, consider yourself married for the whole year. If your spouse died during the year, consider yourself married for the whole year.

Joint return In a joint return you include all income, adjustments, deductions, and exemptions of both husband and wife, even if one has no income. This procedure allows for a theoretical income splitting on federal income tax to equalize the taxable income for taxpayers residing in non–community property states. In community property states the earnings of a married couple belong equally to the husband and to the wife without regard to which spouse earned them.

Separate return If you file a separate return, you report only your separate income, adjustments, deductions, and exemptions. If one spouse separately itemizes, the other must also—both must figure their tax the same way. Unless both husband and wife have substantial incomes, filing a joint return will usually lower the amount of income tax to be paid. Always compute the tax liability both ways whenever both spouses have roughly equal incomes.

Unmarried head of household To use this status you must be single or legally separated on December 31 and meet either of the following tests:

1. You paid more than half the cost of keeping up a home for a parent whom you can claim as a dependent.
2. You paid more than one-half the cost of keeping up your home, which was occupied all year by:
   a. Your unmarried child, grandchild, foster child, or stepchild. This person does not have to be your dependent.
   b. Any other relative you can claim as a dependent.

The head-of-household tax rate is one-half the difference between the single and joint-return rates.

Widow(er) with dependent child You may use the joint return tax rates under this filing status if:

1. Your spouse died in the two years preceding this tax year.
2. You have not remarried.
3. You have a child or stepchild you can claim as a dependent.
4. Your home was the main home of the child.

If you qualify, you should use this rate rather than the head-of-household rate because it offers the greater tax saving.

Exemptions

Check the appropriate number of boxes for you (and your spouse, if filing a joint return). An exemption of $750 from your adjusted income is allowed for each exemption that you can legitimately claim. The taxpayer and his spouse are allowed extra exemptions if they are blind or over age sixty-five on December 31. Age and blindness exemptions are not available to other dependent exemptions.

One exemption is allowed for each dependent who meets certain tests:

1. *Relationship* See IRS booklet for detail.
2. *Support* Received over half his support from you.
3. *Income* Received less than $750 income for year (unless child is under nineteen, or full-time student).
4. *Citizen or resident* Of U.S., or resident of Canada, Mexico, Republic of Panama, or Canal Zone.
5. *Married dependent* Did not file a joint return with spouse.

Presidential Election Campaign Fund

You have the right to earmark $1 ($2 on joint returns) of your taxes for a *general* fund to help meet the campaign expenses for legitimate candidates in the next presidential election. This is an *allocation* of your tax. It does not increase your tax or decrease your refund. It simply allows you to advise the IRS to put one of your tax dollars into this fund.

This check-off procedure is an attempt to give the American public the chance to finance part of the presidential campaign costs without regard to party politics. The fund is to be distributed on the basis of political party voter registration.

Income

All income must be reported in the year it was received (under the usual cash basis) unless it is specifically exempt by law. Payment to you may be in cash or the fair value of property or services. For example, a paycheck dated December 31 must be included in this year's income, while one dated January 1 or later would be next year's income even though both checks represented payment for the same period of work. Payments-in-kind such as reduced rent or furniture for your fix-up talents would be considered income. Table 11–1 indicates the taxability of the usual sources of income.

Employee compensation All wages, salaries, bonuses, commissions, fees, and tips are reported on the appropriate line of Form 1040. This income will usually be supported by Form W–2 issued by your employer. If you have more income to report, such as tips or fair value of property, a memo should be attached to your return explaining the circumstances.

Dividends Any payments you receive as corporate dividends are generally taxable if they represent company earnings and profits. You will usually be notified by the company if a dividend is fully taxable, nontaxable, or excludable by Form 1099 (similar in function to Form W–2).

Taxpayers often confuse "dividends" from insurance companies with corporate dividends. The former are a return or reduction of your premium payment.

Table 11–1 Taxability of income for reporting purposes

Taxable Items	Nontaxable Items
Alimony	Accident insurance proceeds
Annuities (non-contributed portion)	Annuities (return of contributions)
Bad debts previously deducted	Bequests
Bonuses	Disability and death payments
Business profits	Federal income tax rebate or refund
Capital gains	Fellowships (under some circumstances)
Cash dividends (corporate)	Gifts
Commissions	Grants (under some circumstances)
Fees	Inheritances
Gambling winnings	Insurance company dividends
Interest (except municipal bonds)	Interest on municipal securities
Pensions (non-contributed portion)	Life-insurance proceeds
Prizes and lotteries	Military allowances
Rents	Pensions (return of contributions)
Royalties	Personal injury awards
Salaries	Scholarships (under some circumstances)
State tax refund (if itemized)	Sick pay
Strike benefits	Social Security benefits
Tips	Unemployment benefits
Trust and estate income	Veteran's benefits
Tuition paid by employer	Workmen's compensation
Wages	

"Dividends" paid by savings and loan associations, mutual savings banks, and credit unions are really interest and should be reported as such.

You are allowed to exclude $100 of dividends received from qualified domestic corporations. On joint returns $200 can be excluded provided each spouse was a joint owner of the underlying stock or received $100 of dividends on stock owned separately. Neither can use any part of the $100 exclusion not used by the other. For example, if a husband had $300 in dividends, and his wife had $20, only $120 can be excluded.

Interest income You must report all interest you actually or constructively received during the year regardless of the amount. Interest credited to your account even though not yet entered in your passbook would be available for your withdrawal and must therefore be included as interest income for the year.

Income Other than Wages, Dividends, and Interest

Most people get their income from wages, dividends from a few shares of stock, and interest on savings. If this is the extent of your income, you probably can use the short form and disregard the other forms of income listed on Form 1040. This would be a mistake! As mentioned earlier, you will have a much better concept of income, how it is taxed, and how it is retained if you follow Form 1040 and its schedules.

Schedules to Support Form 1040

The more important types of income additions and subtractions are explained to the IRS by attaching supporting schedules. The following is the list of schedules for the tax year 1975.

"A"	Itemized Deductions
"B"	Dividend and Interest Income (for aggregate amounts over $400)
"C"	Profit or (Loss) from Business or Profession
"D"	Capital Gains and Losses
"E"	Supplemental Income Schedule (used to report income from rents, royalties, pensions, annuities, partnerships, trusts, estates, etc.)
"ES"	Declaration of Estimated Tax for Individuals
"F"	Farm Income and Expense
"G"	Income Averaging
"R"	Retirement Income Credit Computation
"SE"	Self-Employment Social Security Tax

We will not cover all types of extra income in detail, nor will we analyze all schedules in detail. Often the reverse side of a schedule gets too detailed and technical for our needs.

Business Profit or Loss—Schedule C

To compute profit or loss from a business or profession complete a Schedule C and attach it to your return. Schedule C is used for sole proprietorships. Partnerships and corporations file a different set of forms. The format is similar to a profit and loss statement for a business. You first determine total income and then deduct business costs. These would include such things as cost of merchandise, salaries, taxes, rent, repair, depreciation, and supplies. Include only income and expenses related to your business. If you use your home and car for both personal and business use, include only the business portion. A partial list of expenses is printed on the schedule, with blank space left for expenses peculiar to a particular business.

Capital Gains and Losses—Schedule D

Schedule D is used for reporting details of gain or loss from the sale or exchange of capital assets. Capital assets are any property you own and use for personal, pleasure, or investment purposes. These would include stocks and bonds held in your personal account, your residence, real estate holdings for investment, household furnishings, and your automobile(s).

Gain or loss determination Whenever you sell or exchange a capital asset, you will gain, break even, or lose on the transaction. The government generally taxes all your gains from personal or investment property and allows an offset against income for your capital losses on investment property—never on personal property.

Gain is the excess of the amount you realize in the sale or exchange over the adjusted basis of the property. *Loss* is the excess of the adjusted basis of the property over the amount you realize in the sale or exchange. The *adjusted* basis is your original cost (including all fees and commissions) adjusted for such things as casualty losses, improvements, and depreciation.

Here is an example of calculating taxable gains on investment property. Imagine that you purchase a duplex for $50,000, add $3,000 of improvements for an adjusted basis of $53,000, and then sell the property for $63,000, paying a commission of $3,780. The $3,780 selling fee would be added to the adjusted basis. The selling price less $56,780 would leave a gain of $6,220 to be reported.

Taxable gains from capital assets of a personal nature would include any gain from any asset, but for all practical purposes they are limited to the appreciation of your residence or vacation home and valuable jewelry. Almost all other property such as automobiles and furniture depreciates (loses value) as you use it. The IRS laws do not allow you to report losses on personally used property because it was ostensibly purchased for pleasure and not with expectations of making a profit. You must, however, report any *gain*, because it is a form of income.

Time of asset ownership The length of time you hold an asset determines the tax treatment it will receive when sold or exchanged. Gain or loss on property held six months or less is considered *short term* and is reported in Part I of Schedule D. Gain or loss on property held more than six months is considered *long term* and is reported in Part II of Schedule D. We will discuss capital gains and losses more thoroughly later in the chapter.

Supplemental Income—Schedule E

This schedule is used to report income from pensions and annuities (Part I), rents and royalties (Part II), and partnerships and trusts, etc. (Part III).

Pensions and annuities If your pension or annuity was fully paid by someone else, such as your employer, it is fully taxable. All income from such pensions and annuities is reported directly on Form 1040, line 3b. Part I of Schedule E is used to calculate the portion of pension and annuity income that is taxable when you have made some contribution toward your retirement. Veterans' pensions and Social Security are not to be reported.

The actual calculations to determine what portion of your income from a pension or annuity plan is taxable are rather involved. We will not go into detail; however, each partly taxable pension or annuity needs a separate Part I.

Rents and royalties The production of income through the rental of property or the royalties from the results of your personal endeavor must be shown in Part II of Schedule E. Current itemized expenses may be deducted from rental income. Depreciation may be deducted from both rental and royalty income during the lifetime of the property. The depreciation concept will be discussed more fully later in the chapter under the heading of special tax treatments.

Partnerships, trusts, etc. Part III of Schedule E is used to show the net income or loss from partnership, estates or trusts, and small-business corporations. The taxpayer receives notification of his reportable income or loss by special schedule from the source organization.

Farm Income or Loss—Schedule F

A special schedule is used to report income or loss from a farm or agricultural operation. Special tax rules apply to farm income and expenses. For example, the costs of installing certain irrigation systems may be treated as current expenses rather than as capital expenditure that requires depreciation.

Miscellaneous Income

Space is allowed on Form 1040 in Part I, Income other than Wages, Dividends, and Interest, to report miscellaneous types of income that cannot be appropriately reported elsewhere on Form 1040. We have already discussed the schedules that require complicated mathematical computations for specialized income production. Special lines allow you to report state income-tax refunds and alimony received. A line labeled "Other" is used to report miscellaneous items of income not reported elsewhere, such as bad debt recoveries that were deducted in a prior year, gambling winnings, prizes, and tuition paid by your employer.

Adjustments to Income

At this point you will have added all forms of income together. Some schedules (C, D, E, and F) may show a loss, which is netted with income to provide your total gross income. Now you may be able to make certain adjustments to gross income to arrive at your adjusted gross income. Adjusted gross income is used to determine your allowable standard deductions. If you itemize deductions, it is used to determine limitations on medical, charitable, and sales-tax deductions. You subtract adjustments from gross income, as if you had not received this amount of income.

Each tax year, you should review the possibility of subtracting certain adjustments from your gross income to lessen your tax burden. You may adjust for forfeited interest, sick pay, moving expenses, employee business expense, and payments to IRS-approved retirement plans. These adjustments are subtracted from total income to arrive at the *adjusted gross income.*

Forfeited interest penalty You are allowed to deduct the amount of forfeited interest that you lose as a penalty for early withdrawal from a certificate of deposit. The savings institution will notify you of the penalty amount.

Sick pay To qualify for the sick-pay adjustment you must meet the requirements set by the IRS. First, you must be covered by an employer-paid wage continuation plan. Second, you must be sick or injured sufficiently to remain off work for a certain period. The sickness or injury does not have to be connected with your work.

The procedure for figuring your sick-pay percentage and waiting period is rather complicated. The instructions on the back of Form 2440, Sick-Pay Exclusion, lead you through, line by line and step by step.

Moving expense Any employee or self-employed person may subtract reasonable moving expenses from his gross income. This is accomplished by attaching Form 3903, Moving Expense Adjustment, to your income tax return. This adjustment is allowed because the move must be in connection with securing a job at a new principal place of work. You do not have to itemize your deductions to get the benefit of this adjustment.

Two major requirements must be met to claim moving expense: (1) A change in job locations must *add* at least fifty miles to the commute distance from your old residence. (2) You must be employed full-time at your new job location during at least thirty-nine weeks of the twelve-month period following the move.

The types of expenses allowed are described on Form 3903. These include unlimited reasonable expenses related to transportation of household goods and personal effects; and travel, meals, and lodging expenses to move from your former residence to your new residence. Travel, meals, and lodging expenses incurred before the move to search for a new residence after obtaining employment, and *temporary* expenses for meals and lodging at the new location during any period of thirty consecutive days, may be allowed up to a maximum of $1,000. Expenses incident to the sale, exchange, or lease settlement of the old residence and expenses incident to the purchase or lease acquiring of the new residence are also allowed.

The moving expense is then subtracted from gross income unless you received reimbursement for the move. Any reimbursement will reduce your expense deduction. If the reimbursement amounts to more than the total moving expense, any excess must be reported as additional income.

Employee business expenses Certain employee travel expenses are deducted from gross income as an adjustment to income. These expenses do not require that you itemize on a Schedule A. Form 2106, Employee Business Expenses, is used to substantiate the adjustment.

Business travel expenses away from your "tax home" are deductible in full. These would include such items as transportation expenses (air, railroad, bus fares), meal and lodging expenses, and automobile expenses. In your home area, only transportation and automobile expenses are deductible. Food and lodging would be considered personal living expenses and are therefore not deductible. All of these expenses must be provable and must be reduced by any employer reimbursement. You must, of course, report any excess reimbursement as income.

Retirement contributions The final adjustment allowable is the contribution made to an IRS-approved retirement plan. The amount is limited to 15 percent of earned income or $7,500 for the self-employed person, whichever is lower, and 15 percent or $1,500 for the individual whose wage, salary, or compensation is not covered under an employer-financed retirement plan. The advantages of the Keogh Act and the Individual Retirement Act were discussed in chapter 9.

1975 Tax Tables

For individual taxpayers with incomes under $15,000 who do not itemize deductions

Table 1—Returns claiming ONE exemption (and not itemizing deductions)

If adjusted gross income is— At least	If adjusted gross income is— But less than	And you are— Single, not head of household	And you are— Head of household	And you are— Married filing separate return claiming— Low income allowance	And you are— Married filing separate return claiming— %Standard deduction
		Your tax is—			
0	900	0	0	0	0
900	925	0	0	0	2
925	950	0	0	0	5
950	975	0	0	0	8
975	1,000	0	0	0	11
1,000	1,025	0	0	0	14
1,025	1,050	0	0	0	17
1,050	1,075	0	0	0	20
1,075	1,100	0	0	0	23
1,100	1,125	0	0	0	26
1,125	1,150	0	0	0	29
1,150	1,175	0	0	0	32
1,175	1,200	0	0	0	35
1,200	1,225	0	0	0	38
1,225	1,250	0	0	0	41
1,250	1,275	0	0	0	43
1,275	1,300	0	0	0	46
1,300	1,325	0	0	0	49
1,325	1,350	0	0	0	52
1,350	1,375	0	0	0	55
1,375	1,400	0	0	0	58
1,400	1,425	0	0	0	61
1,425	1,450	0	0	0	64
1,450	1,475	0	0	0	67
1,475	1,500	0	0	0	70
1,500	1,525	0	0	0	73
1,525	1,550	0	0	0	76
1,550	1,575	0	0	0	79
1,575	1,600	0	0	0	83
1,600	1,625	0	0	0	86
1,625	1,650	0	0	0	89
1,650	1,675	0	0	0	92
1,675	1,700	0	0	0	95
1,700	1,725	0	0	2	98
1,725	1,750	0	0	5	101
1,750	1,775	0	0	9	105
1,775	1,800	0	0	12	108
1,800	1,825	0	0	16	111
1,825	1,850	0	0	19	114
1,850	1,875	0	0	23	117
1,875	1,900	0	0	26	120
1,900	1,925	0	0	30	123
1,925	1,950	0	0	33	127
1,950	1,975	0	0	37	130
1,975	2,000	0	0	40	133
2,000	2,025	0	0	44	136
2,025	2,050	0	0	47	139
2,050	2,075	0	0	51	142
2,075	2,100	0	0	54	146
2,100	2,125	0	0	58	149
2,125	2,150	0	0	61	152
2,150	2,175	0	0	65	156
2,175	2,200	0	0	68	159
2,200	2,225	0	0	72	162
2,225	2,250	0	0	76	166
2,250	2,275	0	0	79	169
2,275	2,300	0	0	83	172
2,300	2,325	0	0	87	176
2,325	2,350	0	0	91	179
2,350	2,375	2	2	94	183
2,375	2,400	5	5	98	186
2,400	2,425	9	9	102	189
2,425	2,450	12	12	106	193
2,450	2,475	16	16	109	196
2,475	2,500	19	19	113	199
2,500	2,525	23	23	117	203
2,525	2,550	26	26	121	206
2,550	2,575	30	30	124	209
2,575	2,600	33	33	128	213
2,600	2,625	37	37	132	216
2,625	2,650	40	40	136	219
2,650	2,675	44	44	139	223
2,675	2,700	47	47	143	226
2,700	2,725	51	51	147	230
2,725	2,750	54	54	151	233
2,750	2,775	58	58	155	237
2,775	2,800	61	61	159	241
2,800	2,825	65	65	163	244
2,825	2,850	68	68	167	248
2,850	2,875	72	72	171	251
2,875	2,900	76	75	175	255
2,900	2,925	79	79	179	258
2,925	2,950	83	82	183	262
2,950	2,975	87	86	187	266
2,975	3,000	91	89	191	269
3,000	3,050	96	95	197	274
3,050	3,100	104	102	205	282
3,100	3,150	111	109	213	289
3,150	3,200	119	116	221	296
3,200	3,250	126	123	229	303
3,250	3,300	134	130	238	310
3,300	3,350	141	137	246	318
3,350	3,400	149	144	255	326
3,400	3,450	157	152	263	334
3,450	3,500	165	160	272	342
3,500	3,550	173	168	280	350
3,550	3,600	181	176	289	358
3,600	3,650	189	184	297	366
3,650	3,700	197	192	306	374
3,700	3,750	205	200	315	382
3,750	3,800	213	208	324	390
3,800	3,850	221	216	334	398
3,850	3,900	229	224	343	406
3,900	3,950	238	232	353	414
3,950	4,000	246	240	362	422
4,000	4,050	255	248	372	430
4,050	4,100	263	256	381	438
4,100	4,150	272	264	391	446
4,150	4,200	280	272	400	454
4,200	4,250	289	280	410	462
4,250	4,300	297	288	419	470
4,300	4,350	306	296	429	478
4,350	4,400	315	305	438	486
4,400	4,450	324	314	448	494
4,450	4,500	334	323	457	502
4,500	4,550	343	332	467	510
4,550	4,600	353	341	476	518
4,600	4,650	362	350	486	526
4,650	4,700	372	359	495	534
4,700	4,750	381	368	505	542
4,750	4,800	391	377	514	550
4,800	4,850	400	386	524	558
4,850	4,900	410	395	533	566
4,900	4,950	419	404	543	574
4,950	5,000	429	413	552	582
5,000	5,050	438	422	562	589
5,050	5,100	448	431	571	597
5,100	5,150	457	440	581	605
5,150	5,200	467	449	590	613
5,200	5,250	476	458	600	621
5,250	5,300	486	467	609	629
5,300	5,350	495	476	619	637
5,350	5,400	505	485	628	645
5,400	5,450	514	494	638	653
5,450	5,500	524	503	647	661
5,500	5,550	533	512	657	669
5,550	5,600	543	521	666	677
5,600	5,650	552	530	676	685
5,650	5,700	562	539	685	694
5,700	5,750	571	548	696	703
5,750	5,800	581	557	707	712
5,800	5,850	590	566	718	721
5,850	5,900	600	575	729	731
5,900	5,950	609	584	740	740
5,950	6,000	619	593	751	749
6,000	6,050	628	602	762	758
6,050	6,100	638	611	773	768
6,100	6,150	647	620	784	777
6,150	6,200	657	629	795	786
6,200	6,250	666	638	806	795
6,250	6,300	676	647	817	805
6,300	6,350	685	656	828	814
6,350	6,400	695	665	839	823
6,400	6,450	706	674	850	832
6,450	6,500	716	684	861	842
6,500	6,550	727	693	872	851
6,550	6,600	737	703	883	860
6,600	6,650	748	712	894	869
6,650	6,700	758	722	905	879
6,700	6,750	769	731	916	888
6,750	6,800	779	741	927	897
6,800	6,850	790	750	938	906
6,850	6,900	800	760	949	916
6,900	6,950	811	769	960	925
6,950	7,000	821	779	971	934
7,000	7,050	832	788	982	943
7,050	7,100	842	798	993	952
7,100	7,150	853	807	1,004	962
7,150	7,200	863	817	1,015	971
7,200	7,250	874	826	1,026	980
7,250	7,300	884	836	1,037	989
7,300	7,350	895	845	1,048	999
7,350	7,400	905	855	1,059	1,008
7,400	7,450	916	864	1,070	1,017
7,450	7,500	926	874	1,081	1,026
7,500	7,550	937	883	1,092	1,036
7,550	7,600	947	893	1,103	1,045
7,600	7,650	958	902	1,114	1,054
7,650	7,700	968	912	1,125	1,063
7,700	7,750	979	921	1,136	1,073
7,750	7,800	989	931	1,149	1,082
7,800	7,850	1,000	940	1,161	1,091
7,850	7,900	1,010	950	1,174	1,100
7,900	7,950	1,021	959	1,186	1,110
7,950	8,000	1,031	969	1,199	1,119
8,000	8,050	1,042	978	1,211	1,128
8,050	8,100	1,052	988	1,224	1,138
8,100	8,150	1,063	997	1,236	1,149
8,150	8,200	1,073	1,007	1,249	1,161
8,200	8,250	1,084	1,016	1,261	1,174
8,250	8,300	1,094	1,026	1,274	1,186
8,300	8,350	1,105	1,035	1,286	1,199
8,350	8,400	1,116	1,046	1,299	1,211
8,400	8,450	1,128	1,057	1,311	1,224
8,450	8,500	1,140	1,068	1,324	1,236
8,500	8,550	1,152	1,079	1,336	1,249
8,550	8,600	1,164	1,090	1,349	1,261
8,600	8,650	1,176	1,101	1,361	1,274
8,650	8,700	1,188	1,112	1,374	1,286
8,700	8,750	1,200	1,123	1,386	1,299
8,750	8,800	1,212	1,134	1,399	1,311
8,800	8,850	1,224	1,145	1,411	1,324
8,850	8,900	1,236	1,156	1,424	1,336
8,900	8,950	1,248	1,167	1,436	1,349
8,950	9,000	1,260	1,178	1,449	1,361
9,000	9,050	1,272	1,189	1,461	1,374
9,050	9,100	1,284	1,200	1,474	1,386
9,100	9,150	1,296	1,211	1,486	1,399
9,150	9,200	1,308	1,222	1,499	1,411
9,200	9,250	1,320	1,233	1,511	1,424
9,250	9,300	1,332	1,244	1,524	1,436
9,300	9,350	1,344	1,255	1,536	1,449
9,350	9,400	1,356	1,266	1,549	1,461
9,400	9,450	1,368	1,277	1,561	1,474
9,450	9,500	1,380	1,288	1,574	1,486
9,500	9,550	1,392	1,299	1,586	1,499
9,550	9,600	1,404	1,310	1,599	1,511
9,600	9,650	1,416	1,321	1,611	1,524
9,650	9,700	1,428	1,332	1,624	1,536
9,700	9,750	1,440	1,343	1,637	1,549
9,750	9,800	1,452	1,354	1,651	1,561
9,800	9,850	1,464	1,365	1,665	1,574
9,850	9,900	1,476	1,376	1,679	1,586
9,900	9,950	1,488	1,387	1,693	1,599
9,950	10,000	1,500	1,398	1,707	1,611
10,000	10,050	1,511	1,408	1,721	1,624
10,050	10,100	1,521	1,417	1,735	1,637
10,100	10,150	1,531	1,426	1,749	1,651
10,150	10,200	1,541	1,435	1,763	1,665

Continued on next page

Figure 11–7 1975 Tax Table for One Exemption. *(Internal Revenue Service)*

Tax Tables

The amount of your adjusted gross income and whether you wish to itemize your deductions on Schedule A determine whether you should use the tax tables (figure 11–7) or the tax rate schedules (figure 11–1). The tax tables may not be used when the adjusted gross income is in excess of $15,000 or by someone with *unearned* income who is claimed as a dependent. An example would be an unmarried full-time student who has dividend or interest income to report on his own separate return while being claimed on his parents' return.

Figure 11–7 illustrates the first of a series of twelve tax tables that automatically determine your tax liability for the year. There is a separate table for the number of exemptions you claim, from one to twelve. The standard deduction and number of exemptions are taken into account in figuring the taxes shown in these tables.

ITEMIZED DEDUCTIONS

You must decide whether to take the standard deduction or to itemize your actual deductions for charitable contributions, medical expenses, interest, taxes, etc. Because the standard deduction varies at different income levels, it will generally be helpful to follow these guidelines provided by the IRS. If you are:

Married filing jointly or a qualifying widow(er) with dependent child, you should itemize on Form 1040 if your income on line 12 of Short Form 1040A is: less than $11,875 and your itemized deductions total more than $1,900; between $11,875 and $16,250 and your itemized deductions total more than 16 percent of line 12; or over $16,250 and your itemized deductions total more than $2,600.

Married filing separately, divide the dollar amounts specified for joint returns in half and be sure to use only the total of your own deductions.

Single or unmarried head of household, itemize on Form 1040 if your income on line 12 of Short Form 1040A is: less than $10,000 and your itemized deductions total more than $1,600; between $10,000 and $14,375 and your itemized deductions total more than 16 percent of line 12; or over $14,375 and your itemized deductions total more than $2,300.

Using the standard deduction means you cannot use any of the itemized deductions discussed on the following pages.

If you itemize, you use Schedule A, Itemized Deductions. This schedule is represented in figure 11–8. The schedule shows the main categories under which deductions are allowed. The schedule does not show each possible deduction. It is up to you to be aware of what expenses you can legally deduct. Allowable deductions are sometimes a matter of interpretation. If you feel you have a legitimate claim, take it. You must, however, be able to substantiate the expense through cancelled checks, receipts, log books, diaries, and account books.

We will list the major types of deductions that you may take, but we should first point something out. The dollar amount that is itemized is not all a tax saving. The total of all deductions is subtracted from your taxable income, giving you a smaller amount upon which to figure your taxes. You save only a portion of the expenses deducted. This portion is the same percent as the tax rate that you end up paying. For example, if you have made a contribution to a recognized charity in the amount of $200, you would realize a tax savings of $50 if you were in the 25 percent tax rate bracket ($200 × 25%). The $200 is still an

Schedules A&B—Itemized Deductions AND Dividend and Interest Income

(Form 1040)
Department of the Treasury
Internal Revenue Service

▶ Attach to Form 1040. ▶ See Instructions for Schedules A and B (Form 1040).

1975

Name(s) as shown on Form 1040 | Your social security number

Schedule A—Itemized Deductions (Schedule B on back)

Medical and Dental Expenses (not compensated by insurance or otherwise) (See page 11 of Instructions.)

1 **One half (but not more than $150) of insurance premiums for medical care. (Be sure to include in line 10 below)** . . .
2 Medicine and drugs . . . .
3 Enter 1% of line 15, Form 1040 . . .
4 Subtract line 3 from line 2. Enter difference (if less than zero, enter zero) . .
5 Enter balance of insurance premiums for medical care not entered on line 1 . .
6 Enter other medical and dental expenses:
a Doctors, dentists, nurses, etc. . . .
b Hospitals . . . .
c Other (itemize—include hearing aids, dentures, eyeglasses, transportation, etc.) ▶
7 Total (add lines 4 through 6c) . . .
8 Enter 3% of line 15, Form 1040 . . .
9 Subtract line 8 from line 7 (if less than zero, enter zero) . . . .
10 **Total (add lines 1 and 9).** Enter here and on line 35 . . . . ▶

Taxes (See page 11 of Instructions.)

11 State and local income . . . . . .
12 Real estate . . . .
13 State and local gasoline (see gas tax tables)
14 General sales (see sales tax tables) . .
15 Personal property . . . .
16 Other (itemize) ▶
17 **Total (add lines 11 through 16).** Enter here and on line 36 . . . . ▶

Interest Expense (See page 12 of Instructions.)

18 Home mortgage . . . .
19 Other (itemize) ▶
20 **Total (add lines 18 and 19).** Enter here and on line 37 . . . . ▶

Contributions (See page 12 of Instructions for examples.)

21 a Cash contributions for which you have receipts, cancelled checks or other written evidence . . . .
b Other cash contributions. List donees and amounts. ▶
22 Other than cash (see page 12 of instructions for required statement) . . . .
23 Carryover from prior years . . . . .
24 **Total contributions (add lines 21a through 23).** Enter here and on line 38 . . . ▶

Casualty or Theft Loss(es) (See page 13 of Instructions.)
Note: *If you had* **more than one loss,** *omit lines 25 through 28 and see page 13 of Instructions for guidance.*

25 Loss before insurance reimbursement .
26 Insurance reimbursement . . . . .
27 Subtract line 26 from line 25. Enter difference (if less than zero, enter zero) .
28 Enter $100 or amount on line 27, whichever is smaller . . . .
29 **Casualty or theft loss (subtract line 28 from line 27).** Enter here and on line 39 ▶

Miscellaneous Deductions (See page 13 of Instructions.)

30 Alimony paid . . . .
31 Union dues . . . .
32 Expenses for child and dependent care services (attach Form 2441) . . . .
33 Other (itemize) ▶
34 **Total (add lines 30 through 33).** Enter here and on line 40 . . . . . . ▶

Summary of Itemized Deductions **A**

35 Total medical and dental—line 10 . .
36 Total taxes—line 17 . . . .
37 Total interest—line 20 . . . . . .
38 Total contributions—line 24 . . . .
39 Casualty or theft loss(es)—line 29 . .
40 Total miscellaneous—line 34 . . . .
41 **Total deductions (add lines 35 through 40).** Enter here and on Form 1040, line 44 . . . . ▶

Figure 11–8 Schedule A: Itemized Deductions. *(Internal Revenue Service)* out-of-pocket expense for something. If you had not made the contribution, you would owe the government an extra $50, but you would still have $150 of the original $200.

Medical and Dental Expenses

Medical and dental expenses are deductible but are subject to certain limitations. They are deductible only to the extent that they exceed 3 percent of your adjusted gross income. The government contends that the 3 percent represents personal living expenses and only the amount above that represents an unusual, and deductible expense.

We will not attempt to list every conceivable medical and dental expense. The following paragraphs will attempt to cover the more important deductions and nondeductions.

You can deduct one-half (up to $150) of the amount you pay for medical care insurance, even if you have no other medical expenses. This amount is not subject to the 3 percent limitation. If you have auto medical insurance, it may be considered medical care insurance. Life insurance and disability-income insurance are not deductible.

Only that portion exceeding 1 percent of your adjusted gross income is allowed for medicine and drugs, but you must include that portion in the 3 percent overall limitation. Toiletries, toothpaste, and nonprescribed vitamins are not deductible.

Payments to hospitals, doctors, dentists, specialists, and medical-dental technicians are normally deductible. Expenses of artificial limbs, crutches, guide dogs, glasses, and the like are deductible. Nursing expense is deductible, but domestic help is generally not.

You may deduct ambulance service and other travel costs necessary to get medical care. This would include taxi, rail or air fares whenever necessary. Trips for the general improvement of your health are not deductible. Also deductible are auto expenses incurred in securing medical care. Auto expenses may be based on the actual operating costs of gas, oil, and parking fees, or you may deduct seven cents for each mile you use your car for medical care, plus parking fees.

The total medical expenses of you and your dependents for the year must be reduced by any reimbursements from insurance or other sources.

Taxes

Certain taxes imposed upon you and paid by you during the year may be deducted. Generally, most state and local taxes are deductible, while most federal taxes are not.

State and local income taxes that have been withheld or paid are deductible. Any refund of these deductions must subsequently be included as income on your next federal income tax return.

Real estate taxes, including foreign taxes, are deductible. This tax deduction by homeowners often marks the difference between itemizing and taking the standard deduction of 16 percent.

State and local (not federal) gasoline taxes are deductible. You may use receipts to prove the actual taxes or approximate the taxes paid by use of the gas tax tables for each state that are published in your annual tax-form booklet. If you have a four-cylinder or smaller car, you are allowed only one-half of the tax deduction shown in the gas tax tables.

General state and local sales taxes are deductible on the basis of the actual amount paid or by approximation through the use of the optional state sales tax tables also included in your tax-form booklet. You can add extra sales tax from a boat, airplane, mobile home, automobile, or building materials to the tax-table amount. Invariably the tax-table procedure will be easier to figure and will generally lead to a greater deduction. Personal property taxes are deductible to the extent that they are based on the value of the taxed item and are not purely a standard license fee. An example is an auto license fee and tax. The base amount charged to all motorists would be considered a license fee; any amount above that would be a tax.

Interest Expense

The biggest deduction is usually the mortgage interest on your home. Home ownership is encouraged by government through the real estate tax and interest deductions allowable. Mortgage loan points when you buy a home, and mortgage prepayment penalties when you sell or refinance your home, are also deductible, while seller's loan fees and points are not.

All revolving charge-account finance charges, installment-plan interest, and term-loan interest are deductible. Credit-investigation fees and interest on loans used to purchase tax-exempt securities are not. Interest must actually be paid in order to deduct it unless you use the accrual method of accounting.

Contributions

You can deduct gifts to organizations operated for religious, charitable, educational, scientific, or literary purposes, or to prevent cruelty to children or animals. Such organizations would include churches, Scout groups, the Red Cross, United Fund, and similar organizations. You can also deduct contributions to fraternal organizations if the gifts are used for the above purposes, to government agencies that will use the gift for public purposes, and to nonprofit organizations designated by the IRS. You cannot deduct gifts to relatives, friends, foreign organizations, social clubs, labor unions, chambers of commerce, or similar organizations. Political contributions may be deducted under the miscellaneous heading.

The gift may consist of cash or property. You may not deduct for the value of your time or services. You may, however, total your out-of pocket expenses such as postage, uniforms, etc., while working as a volunteer. Such items as gas, oil, and tolls may be itemized, or you may take seven cents a mile.

Casualty or Theft Losses

A loss caused by theft or a sudden, unexpected, unusual identifiable happening called a casualty is deductible wholly or in part. Damage from fires, storms, car accidents, and similar happenings may be deducted to the extent that the loss exceeds $100. Each casualty has a separate $100 deduction from loss. Business casualty losses have no such limitations. Any reimbursement from insurance would have to be subtracted from the amount of the loss.

Expenses for Child and Dependent Care

Married persons and heads of households who incur employment-related expenses for the care of dependents may claim these under miscellaneous deductions on Schedule A. Children must be under the age of fifteen; other dependents or spouses must be physically or mentally incapable of taking care of themselves. Married persons claiming this exemption must be gainfully employed on a full-time basis or seeking gainful full-time employment.

The actual dependent-care expenses for employed persons must be for (1) household services, such as the wage of a cook or domestic maid, or (2) personal care for the dependent, such as the wage paid to a baby-sitter, governess, or nurse, or cost of a nursery school. Payments to dependents or relatives are not deductible.

Limitations apply to this deduction. Form 2441, Expenses for Household and Dependent Care Services, may be used to determine the actual deduction. Expenses are figured on a monthly basis, which helps complicate the preparation of this form.

Other Miscellaneous Deductions

A taxpayer may deduct alimony, certain job-related expenses, expenses necessary to produce income or protect income-producing property, political contributions, and gambling losses to the extent of the amount won.

Alimony You may deduct alimony or separate-maintenance payments to your ex-wife (ex-husband). It is very important to determine the tax consequences of all post-marital payments, because not all such payments are deductible or reportable as income by the former spouse. Child support is not alimony but may entitle the payer to a dependency exemption. Lump-sum cash or property settlements are not deductible, nor are installment property settlements disguised as alimony. Loan repayments, payments paid before the agreement, and any payments not required are not deductible.

Employee expenses Even though you are not self-employed, you may have certain job-related expenses. Employment-agency fees, union dues, uniforms not adaptable to general use, travel expenses, tools and supplies, and employer-required physical examinations are generally deductible. Some education expenses are deductible, as well as dues to professional societies and subscriptions to professional journals.

Income-producing expenses Almost all expenses used in producing income are deductible. Such items as legal fees and the cost of publications, investment counsel, clerical help, office rent or office-in-home, and safe-deposit box rentals necessary to produce income are deductible. Whenever an expense is part personal and part business, only the business portion may be deducted.

Political contributions The contribution must be made to a political party, a candidate for local, state, or national office, or to a committee supporting such candidates. Contributions for political causes, no matter how "good," are not deductible.

You may claim up to $100 ($200 on a joint return) as an itemized deduction. Those people who do not itemize may claim one-half of their contribution, not to exceed $25 single or $50 married filing jointly, as a special credit on page two of Form 1040. You choose the better of the two choices.

How Much Should You Deduct?

The deductions that have just been discussed comprise the more readily apparent ones. Special situations may justify deductions that would seem to be unacceptable to the IRS. Often a memo attached to an unusual claim to substantiate the claim will keep you from being audited.

The more you deviate from the average, the more likely it is that your return will be audited. The following figures represent the averages for 1973, the latest year available. If you are audited, you must be able to substantiate your deductions, average or not.

Adjusted Gross Income	Contributions	Interest	Taxes	Medical
$10,000–15,000	$347	$1,090	$1,025	$455
20,000–25,000	350	1,538	1,764	394
30,000–50,000	964	2,221	2,965	558
50,000–100,000	2,121	3,919	5,142	639

TAX COMPUTATION

Once you have determined your itemized deductions, you subtract this amount or the standard deduction, whichever is more beneficial, from your adjusted gross income. You then multiply the number of exemptions you have claimed by $750. Subtract this result from your adjusted gross income to arrive at your taxable income. Space for this procedure is available on the back side of Form 1040 (figure 11–4). You calculate the amount of tax using the federal income tax rate schedule (figure 11–1). From this figure you may subtract certain credits, other taxes, and other payments to the federal government. Form 1040 will give you an indication of what types of credits may be allowed. The details are too complex to discuss in a single chapter.

Your tax return is completed once you indicate whether a balance is due the IRS, whether an overpayment has been made, and whether you desire a refund. You must then sign the return, which in effect means that you declare the return to be "true, correct, and complete."

IRS Will Figure Your Tax

The Internal Revenue Service advises that it will figure your tax if your adjusted gross income is $20,000 or less, and if the income was only from wages, salary, tips, dividends, interest, pensions, and annuities. You must, however, take the standard deduction.

All you have to do is complete the Form 1040 heading, filing status, exemptions information, and all the lines pertaining to your sources of income. You then indicate any credits, other taxes, and the amount of taxes withheld from your pay on the appropriate lines and sign the return. The IRS will figure the tax and either bill you for the balance or send you a refund check.

The IRS has not released any figures on what percent of taxpayers exercise this option. It would appear that once he had gathered this information, anyone with a pencil and a piece of paper could figure his own tax. The only apparent advantage is that if you owe the IRS and do not have funds available, if you follow the above procedure you will get a short reprieve from paying the balance due the IRS.

SPECIAL TAX TREATMENTS

As we have mentioned before, the more you know about taxes, the better off you will be financially. Even if you know how to fill out the tax forms as previously described, you should be aware of the theory of taxation, at least as it relates to special tax treatments. Do you know that capital investments, when sold at a gain, are taxed at rates that are half the rate for wages and earned income? Some of these investment assets may be depreciated, which allows an expense against current income, theoretically to replace the asset. Do you know that you can average your income over a five-year period to decrease your tax rate if you have an unusually high income in any one year, or that you can invest in "tax shelters" that defer income while they appreciate?

Capital Gains

Investment funds create plant, equipment, and employment opportunity to keep the economy going and the government stable. The government therefore encourages long-term investment by allowing long-term gains to be taxed on only 50 percent of the amount of the gain. Capital-gains income from asset appreciation is given preferential tax treatment when compared to income earned from wages, businesses, professions, and rent which is taxed on 100 percent of the actual amount. Part of the reason stems from the speculative nature of investment and the need for an incentive to encourage the placement of capital.

Capital gains and losses may be categorized by time the asset was held, whether there was a gain or a loss, and the taxable amount of income to be reported in your return. Short-term assets are those owned for six months or less. Long-term assets are those owned for more than six months.

Short-term capital gain —
    100 percent included as income.
Short-term capital loss —
    100 percent allowable as deduction from income.
Long-term capital gain —
    50 percent deduction from income to be reported.
Long-term capital loss —
    50 percent deduction from income to be reported.

This breakdown means that short-term gains and losses are treated as ordinary income and loss at the full 100 percent reported amount. Long-term capital gains and losses are given special treatment: only 50 percent of the gain or loss is eventually reported.

You may make further tax savings from capital gains because the amount of capital gain may not be the "profit" that you think you have made. The gain or loss is the difference between the gross sales price and the "cost or other basis as adjusted." The key is "other basis as adjusted." Often real estate property costs must be adjusted because of changes caused by depreciation, alteration, or improvements. The basis for securities is normally the purchase price (cost), including any taxes and commissions.

A further reason to invest for special tax treatment lies in the concept of a capital loss. A loss incurred as a result of the sale of an investment is subtracted from either capital gains or ordinary income, thereby reducing your taxes. We will discuss the timing aspects of this later. In any case, you can afford the risk of investment if a loss results in paying fewer taxes. You might consider this capital-loss deduction as a form of government subsidy. Capital losses are limited to $1,000 in any one year. However, you may carry over any excess loss to subsequent years until the entire loss is completely absorbed.

Sale of residence Your residence is a capital asset subject to capital gains. However, tax laws do not allow you to take a loss on it. If you expect a loss, it might be better to convert your home to rental property before selling it. This allows you to take a legitimate tax loss on the sale of an income-producing property. Also, you can take depreciation during its use as income property. Depreciation is not allowed on your personal residence or any personal-use property.

Special rules apply to the sale of your principal residence. It may be a house, condominium, cooperative apartment, mobile home, or houseboat. You can defer the capital gain (not pay taxes on the gain) if the following conditions are met:

1. You must purchase and use as your principal residence a new home within 12 months before or after the sale.
2. If you build a new home, construction must begin within the period of 12 months before to 12 months after the sale and it must be occupied not later than 18 months after.
3. The cost of the new home must equal or exceed that of the old home.

You can regularly sell your present residence for a net gain and defer the capital-gains tax by always purchasing a more expensive residence. The deferred gain is subtracted from the cost of your new residence. When you sell the second house the new net gain will include prior gains on which the tax was deferred. This procedure can continue through the sale of several homes until eventually you must pay a capital-gains tax.

Actually the capital gains can be further lessened if you do not sell your last home until you are over age sixty-five. Remember that persons over sixty-five can exclude the first $20,000 gain on the sale of their residence. Also, you are more likely to be in a lower tax bracket as a sixty-five-year-old retiree.

Depreciation

Business property with a useful life of more than one year may not be deducted as an expense when purchased. These asset purchases are considered capital expenditures, and the cost is spread over the life of the asset. The IRS has set useful-life guidelines to assist in determining depreciation. Depreciation is a loss in value of a property. Depreciation is an allowable business expense that may be caused by wear and tear, obsolesence, or other factors, and it may be used to recover the cost of the property during its useful life. Then a new purchase would most likely be made, and the process would start over.

To be able to depreciate your property it must have a limited life and be used in your trade or business or held for the production of income. The property may be new or used. Depreciation must be taken in the year that it is allowed. Failure to take it will result in its loss as an expense. You may not claim depreciation on your home, furnishings, auto, or other items used only for personal or pleasure purposes. Items that are used for both business and personal reasons may be depreciated to the extent that they are used for business (prorated).

Three methods are allowed when computing depreciation. The method chosen must be consistently applied. The three methods are: (1) straight-line, (2) declining-balance, and (3) sum-of-the-years-digits.

Straight-line depreciation is determined by dividing the adjusted basis of the property, less salvage value, by the remaining useful life of the property. It is the easiest to understand and the most popular method. For example, a truck may be purchased for $4,000 with a planned salvage value of $400 after a useful life of three years.

$4,000 cost
— 400 salvage value
$3,600 ÷ 3 = $1,200 allowable depreciation each year

The amount of the depreciation must be prorated if the truck was not owned during an entire year.

Declining-balance depreciation is determined by subtracting the current depreciation from the cost or the remaining adjusted basis before computing the next year's depreciation. The same depreciation rate applies to the reduced balance each year. The rate used may be 200 percent, 150 percent, or 125 percent of the rate you would use under the straight-line method. Rate limitations are based on the type and age of the property to be depreciated. The declining-balance method increases the expense taken during the first years of the property's life. It probably reflects a more accurate figure for the remaining market value of the property. The concept of motor vehicle depreciation is a good example of declining-balance depreciation.

The *sum-of-the-years-digits* method applies a different fraction to the property basis each year. The denominator remains constant; it is the sum of the numbers representing the useful life of the property. If we use the truck example again, the denominator would be 6 ($1 + 2 + 3 = 6$). To find the depreciation amount, you multiply the cost by the fraction for that year.

$4,000 cost
– 400 salvage value
$3,600 × 3/6 = $1,800 allowable depreciation the first year
$3,600 × 2/6 = $1,200 (second year)
$3,600 × 1/6 = $ 600 (third year)

Table 11–2 compares the three methods of depreciation. A businessman can control his "paper" expense and affect his taxes by choosing a faster depreciation method. An *additional first-year depreciation* expense may be allowed on personal business property having a useful life of six years or more. This additional 20 percent is deducted before computing the regular depreciation for the life of the asset.

Table 11–2 Depreciation methods compared

	Amount of Annual Depreciation		
	Straight-line	*Declining Balance* 200%	*Sum-of-the years-digits*
Cost	$4,000	$4,000	$4,000
Salvage value	400	(*)	400
Adjusted basis	$3,600	$4,000	$3,600
Year 1	1,200	2,400†	1,800
Year 2	1,200	1,067	1,200
Year 3	1,200	133‡	600
Total depreciation	$3,600	$3,600	$3,600

* Salvage value is not deducted in determining declining-balance depreciation.
† Declining-balance depreciation may not exceed 200%, 150%, or 125% of the straight-line amount.
‡ Property must not be depreciated below reasonable salvage value.

Income Averaging

Income averaging permits taxpayers with fluctuating income or an unusually high income in a particular year to be taxed at lower rates averaged over the preceding four-year base period. Almost all types of income are eligible for averaging. You can take advantage of capital-gains income and still use the income-averaging techniques.

The procedure involved is rather complicated. Schedule G of Form 1040 can be followed to compute the tax. The eligibility rules may require explanation from the IRS or a tax practitioner. Basically, you must have a current income that exceeds 30 percent of the total of the last four years by at least $3,000.

Credits Against Taxes

Even when you have computed your taxes, you may still be able to save money through credits against taxes. A current list of such credits is printed on Form 1040. Here are several representative credits:

Retirement-income credit If you are retired, you may be allowed up to 15 percent of your income as a credit.

Investment credit If you are a business person and you purchase and use depreciable property you may be allowed up to 10 percent of the purchase price as a credit.

Contributions to candidates for public office If you do not itemize, one-half of your contribution, up to $25 single or $50 married filing jointly, may be claimed.

Federal tax on special fuel Farmers and nonhighway users of gasoline and oil may receive credit. Motorboat owners may take advantage of this credit.

Earned income credit A refundable credit may be granted if your earned income is less than $8,000.

Excess FICA tax withheld If you worked for two or more employers and had excess FICA tax withheld, you may claim the excess as a refundable credit.

All of these credits have various eligibility rules and limitations. They may change from year to year as economic and political expediencies become law. You should seek advice if you seem eligible for their benefits.

PLAN TO SAVE ON TAXES

Your every action should not be predicated on what its tax consequence will be, but you should give some thought to taxes on a year-round basis. By proper planning and awareness you can receive some of the advantages offered by special tax treatments.

Plan Ahead

Timing is a very important aspect of taxes. Such decisions as when to retire, when to sell your house, when to take a capital gain or capital loss, and even when to deduct an expense become important. When to take capital gains and losses is part of the current-year decisions. You may shift the timing on expenses or income or on both items. This will hopefully have the effect of reducing your taxes.

Marginal Tax Rates

The shifting of income and expense may put you in a different tax bracket. Higher tax rates are charged against higher incomes; our progressive-income-tax system produces this result. You must decide if earning additional income is worth the trouble, because the additional income may mean a higher tax rate. Despite statements to the contrary, you will always end up with more money than you started with, even at these higher tax rates. The rate attributable to the last income earned is known as the marginal rate. The highest marginal tax rate at the present time is 70 percent. Theoretically, 70 percent of each dollar of taxable income earned over $100,000 for single taxpayers would go to the federal government. Actually, taxpayers seldom reach this marginal rate because of special tax treatments and tax shelters.

Shifting Expenses

The standard deduction is limited to a maximum of 16 percent or $2,600. You could very well be in a position where any tax-deductible expenses incurred at the end of the year would be "wasted" if they would not cause you to exceed the standard deduction. Often medical and dental services or the payment of them can be deferred until the new year. Such major services as orthodontia can be scheduled and paid for during a one-year period, to receive the best possible tax break. Sales taxes and interest can be deferred by not purchasing an automobile or other major item until the new year. You can also defer the purchase of tools and equipment needed for your job until the first of the next year. Also, if you anticipate an increase in taxable income next year, it may be advantageous to defer deductible expenses until the next year in order to remain in the same tax bracket during that year.

Through advance planning you can also transfer your expenditures to the current year if you are certain that you have sufficient itemized deductions to use them to full advantage. If you have already surpassed the 3 percent deductible for medical and dental expenses, schedule these services during the current year. Perhaps you can make your contributions early, pay your taxes early, or purchase tools or uniforms for work. However, any time you move deductible expenses forward to the current year, you will have that much less to deduct next year.

Shifting Income

One way of shifting income for tax purposes is to invest in "tax shelters," which are various investments that defer income to sometime in the future, provide for current losses to offset your current ordinary income, and/or grow in value to realize a capital gain in the future.

Other ways to shift income include not billing clients for services until the new year or billing them early for current-year payment. Salary payments to you on a bonus or multi-year contract may be spread over a longer time to reduce the tax burden. If you are selling property, accept installment payments to spread income. Finally, you can time the sale of investments to take advantage of short-term losses and long-term gains if at all possible. You can at least place the gain or loss in the year of your choice.

Tax Decisions for Investment

One possible solution to high tax rates is to purchase tax-free municipal bonds whose interest income is not taxable. If an investor is in the 50 percent tax-rate bracket, he would have to earn a 12 percent return on a taxable investment to net the same income as a 6 percent tax-free municipal bond.

The sale of an investment asset invariably means a capital gain or loss. Multiple sales or trades may be offsetting to result in a net gain or a net loss. You may reduce your taxable income (gains) by selling a security at a loss this year rather than waiting until next year and taking the loss. Gains and losses cannot be completely isolated, but they can be categorized and timed for taxation purposes:

1. Take capital gains long-term instead of short-term for a lower tax rate.
2. Take capital losses short-term instead of long-term because loss allowance is more favorable.
3. Offset long-term losses against short-term gains whenever possible.
4. Offset short-term losses against short-term gains whenever possible.

There are many other possibilities available, but they would tend to create confusion at this point. Consult your stock broker and tax accountant to see if you have capital gains or losses that may be beneficially shifted between two years.

Income Splitting

Income splitting causes income to be shifted from one individual to another. This is usually done when a person in a high income-tax bracket shares his income with a person in a lower tax bracket. The most common method occurs when spouses file a joint tax return. Theoretically, each spouse then shares an equal amount of income, lowering the bracket for the couple. This is the automatic effect of the laws in community-property states. Residents in the other states get the same benefit by filing a joint tax return.

Another form of income splitting can occur if you transfer interest-bearing paper or instruments to another person so that you no longer receive the income or control the investment. Trust funds for children or other relatives are a good example of this concept.

PREPARING YOUR TAX RETURN

We have discussed the use of adjustments, deductions, and special tax treatments as methods of reducing taxes. It was suggested that you plan ahead to effect savings in the tax year of your choice. However, tax preparation does not end with the planning and computation of taxes. You must file a correct timely return which means you must prepare your return with care before the due date. Failure to do so will cost you a penalty or at the very least result in a delayed refund check.

Checklist for Preparation of Forms

The IRS keeps records of the most common errors and omissions on taxpayers' returns. If you double-check these points, you will be less likely to have the processing of your return delayed or to be singled out for audit.

1. Use preprinted address labels.
2. Be sure to use your correct Social Security number.
3. Place entries on proper lines.
4. Prepare return legibly.
5. Check your arithmetic.
6. Sign the return. Photocopies must bear *original* signatures.
7. Assemble return in following order in proper sequence: Form 1040, lettered schedules, numbered forms, your own memos, and supporting documents.
8. Staple remittances, W–2s, and all attachments firmly.

Amended Returns

If you discover that you have either underpaid or overpaid your income tax, you may file an amended return. Form 1040X

(Amended U.S. Individual Income Tax Return) is designed to complement your original return. It shows the original amounts reported, the net changes, and the amended totals.

Penalties

Penalties may be assessed if you fail to file your return, fail to file it on time, erroneously fail to pay a sufficient amount of tax, or deliberately defraud the government. The penalty for failure to file a return is 5 percent added to the tax due for each month or fraction of a month in which the tax is not paid. The maximum penalty is 25 percent of the total tax due.

The penalty for failure to pay any tax when due is 7 percent of the amount due annually. The maximum late-payment penalty is 25 percent of the amount due. The penalty rate is based on the prime interest rate and is subject to annual change.

Seeking Help

If you learn to prepare your tax return before it gets complicated, you will not have to regularly seek the services of professional tax preparers. You can prepare your tax return with the aid of the instruction booklets provided by the IRS. Furthermore, you can always telephone or visit the IRS for more detailed technical information. Finally, you may secure IRS Publication 17, *Your Federal Income Tax*, or any of the commercial books on the market, such as J. K. Lasser's *Your Income Tax*.

Tax-preparation services Check the yellow pages under the heading Tax Return Preparation, and you will find listings for attorneys, certified public accountants, and tax practitioners. These people are generally professionals, but you get what you pay for. Fees start at $5, and most services quote definite fees for each form completed. Additional charges are usually made for long interviews made necessary if the taxpayer does not have his tax information properly organized. Fees for complete returns may cost hundreds of dollars, but they invariably pay for themselves through the legal reduction of taxes.

Tax practitioners are not regulated to any great extent. Attorneys, CPAs, and enrolled agents have had training and have passed certain tests; however, anyone who wishes may offer his services as a tax preparer. You should determine what you want in the way of service, a form-completion expert or a tax counselor. Ask whether the preparer will stand behind the return. The preparer should be responsible for the mathematical accuracy and tax-procedure accuracy of any return he signs. He should also agree to pay for any penalties or interest charges caused by his errors. You are responsible for the correctness of the information embodied in the return and must pay any tax that the IRS determines is still due.

The Tax Audit

Taxpayers usually worry about appearing before the IRS to explain their tax reasoning and document their tax claims. You should not worry if your reasoning and documentation are honest and correct. Tax claims are often a matter of interpretation. When in doubt, take the reasonable deduction, but be able to document it.

All tax returns are processed by IRS computers for arithmetic, tax calculation, deduction averages, and all-around reasonableness. The processing in itself is an audit, but the IRS carries out detailed auditing on a random basis and also on a select basis for certain occupations and income levels.

According to authoritative estimates you stand a one in fifty chance of a detailed audit. The IRS claims that the chances are greater than this.

Audit procedure Audits of individual returns generally require you to visit the nearest IRS district office to explain and document a particular deduction or exemption.

If you prove your claims to the satisfaction of the IRS auditor, your case is closed. If not, you will be asked to pay the income tax on whatever is disallowed. Interest at 7 percent will be added to the tax. You will be asked to sign a statement agreeing to the IRS-amended return. It is best to consider the amended results for a few days before agreeing to the IRS calculations. You do not have to sign immediately; the IRS agent may have made a mistake or misinterpretation in his zeal to perform his duty, which is to collect taxes! Generally, if the amount of additional tax calculated is less than $25, your case will be closed.

If, during an office audit, you believe an agent to be wrong, it is perfectly legitimate to ask for the agent's supervisor. This will often result in a compromise satisfactory to all concerned. However, if you feel that you are right in your claims, and if the IRS still disagrees, you may follow formal appeal procedures. This may involve a series of conferences and court litigations. Figure 11–9 illustrates the steps involved in an appeal. Of course, you can terminate your appeal at any point in the process if you reach a satisfactory compromise.

STATE AND LOCAL TAXES

For many years the greatest source of revenue for states has been the sales tax, but almost all states now have an income tax, which has become an increasingly important source of revenue. Unfortunately, each state has developed its own forms, making a broad review impossible except in generalities.

Most states follow the general format of the federal income-tax return Form 1040 and the supplementary letter schedules. Few states have developed the highly specialized numbered forms, so you simply file a copy of the federal numbered form. Probably the best way to cope with a state income tax is to find how it differs from your federal tax. Often the difference will be in types of taxable income, types of deductions (federal income tax and education deductions are often allowed), veterans' exemptions, amount of standard deduction, and a lower tax rate.

A PARTING COMMENT ABOUT TAXES

Our country came into being because of oppressive taxes levied without the consent of the citizens. Times may have changed, and the need for federal taxes may be much greater today, but the government should still seek the general consent of the citizenry on tax policy. You have the right and the duty to elect representatives to foster tax reform. At present, our complex tax laws seem to imply that "there is no taxation without misrepresentation."

The many problems of tax reform engender an annual debate in Congress. What should be done? How should income tax be collected, and at what rate? Congress passes the laws, and the IRS carries them out. The IRS attempts to make the return as simple as possible, considering all the variable possibilities of income, allowances, deductions, and credits. Unfortunately, there is no way

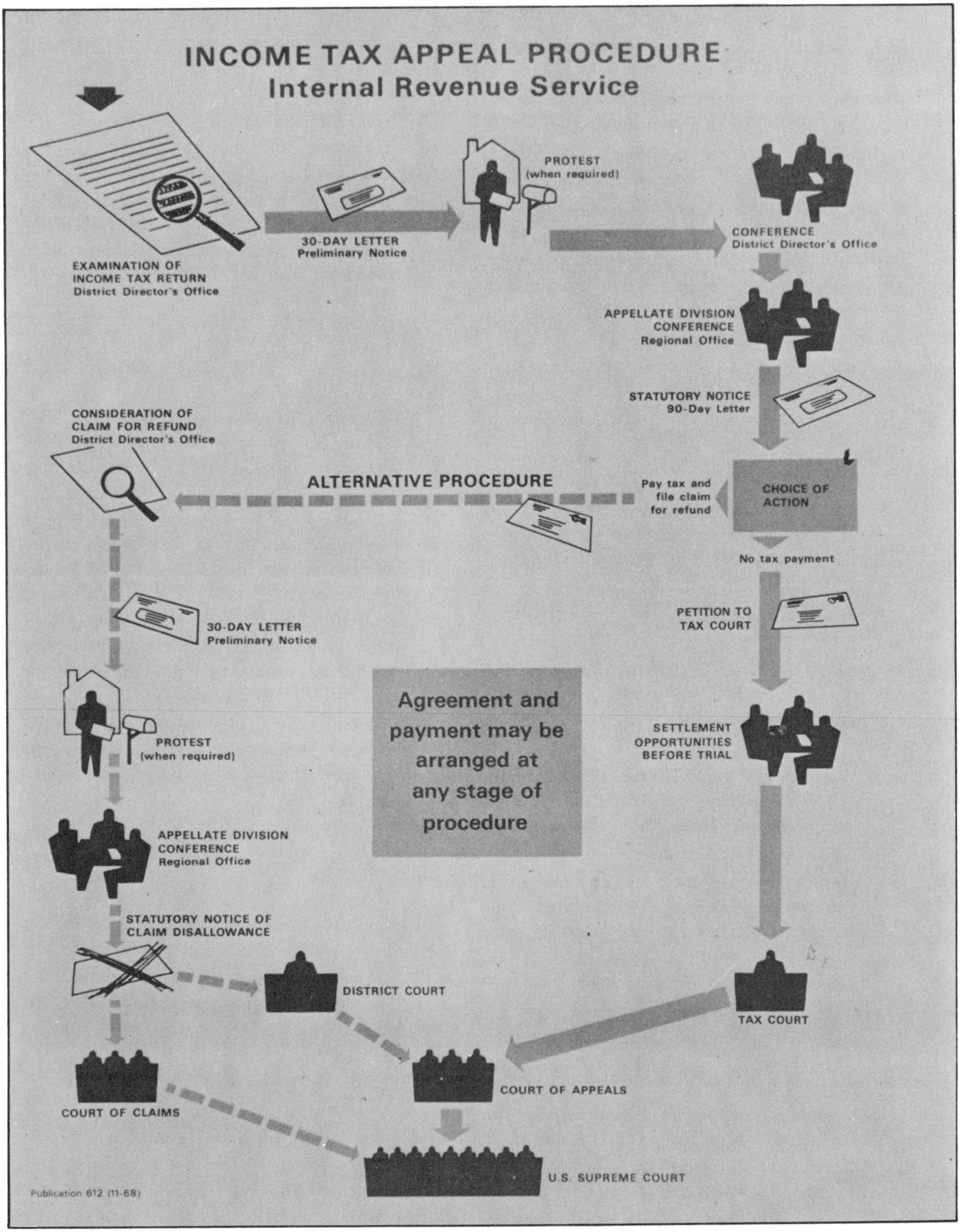

Figure 11–9 Income Tax Appeal Procedure. *(Internal Revenue Service)*

that the forms can be really easy to understand in light of the present complex laws. A realistic answer must lie in larger standard deductions, fewer exceptions, and fewer special tax treatments. This simplistic solution would hopefully provide a more equitable and understandable tax structure, one so clear that you would not have to pay someone else to determine what taxes you must pay the government.

Vocabulary and Concepts

Adjusted gross income	Exemptions
Amended returns	Filing status
Capital gains and losses	Income averaging
Depreciation	Itemized deductions
Estimated tax	Taxable income
	Tax rate schedule
	Tax table

Questions for Discussion

1. Classify the many different taxes on the basis of direct vs. indirect and progressive vs. regressive. How fair are these taxes?
2. Who must file a return?
3. Enumerate various types of income other than wages, dividends, and interest. What tax schedules must be completed for those listed?
4. What are capital gains? How do they work? Is this method fair?
5. Enumerate the adjustments to income. Why are these important? Why are these adjustments allowed?
6. Explain how income shifting and income splitting can decrease your income taxes.
7. When should a taxpayer file the short tax return, Form 1040A?
8. Enumerate the major classifications of itemized deductions.
9. What are the three methods of depreciation allowed by the IRS? Why is depreciation important?
10. Under what conditions will a taxpayer have to submit quarterly payments of his estimated taxes? Under what conditions will a wage earner not have income taxes withheld from his paycheck?

Projects

1. Compile a list of all the types of taxes that you are subject to in your area. Discover the taxing districts and the amounts they assess.
2. Contact your local, state, and federal representatives. Get their viewpoint on tax reform and the need for increased or decreased taxes.
3. Find out what types of tax credits and reductions are available to you on your federal and state income tax and your residential property tax.
4. Compare your state's income-tax return with the federal Form 1040. Where is it different? Does it have to be different?

Case Problem

Bart Baker purchased a six-room house on July 1, 1975, for $40,000. His monthly payment is $400 per month, which includes $100 for taxes, $50 toward principal, $230 for interest, and $20 for insurance. He rents one-third of his home to a friend for $200 per month. Bart is using straight-line depreciation and estimates his home will have a salvage value of $10,000 at the end of thirty years. What would his taxable rental income be for the year 1975? We will not count other expenses. Contributions toward the principal cannot be expensed.

12

home and real estate investment

The purchase of a home is likely to be your largest single investment. Home-ownership is an "American Dream" that nearly everyone hopes to share. But are you really prepared to buy a home, or are you just conforming to expectations? Purchasing a home is a serious matter. You must give careful thought to your life-style and your financial situation.

LIFE-STYLE

You may not fit the general classifications of the life cycle because of personal or family preferences. For instance, you may have a variety of interests and hobbies that require more room; you may be a member of a large, close-knit family; or you may just enjoy spaciousness and feel that your home is your castle. Your life-style tends to dictate your housing needs. Do you spend a lot of time at home? Are you willing to give up other important things to have the house or apartment of your dreams?

FINANCIAL SITUATION

If major nonhousing expenses appropriate a large portion of your budget, you may have to keep your housing expenditure to a minimum. For instance, your family may have large medical bills, college and school tuition, business expenses, or repayment of past debts that limit all other expenditures for an extended period of time. Good budgeting practice dictates that you do not box yourself into a financial corner by making fixed commitments that you cannot handle.

No matter where you are in the life cycle or what life-style you pursue, the basic housing question is how much you can afford to pay for housing. Current income and future earning power should be considered. Housing should always be scaled to income. You must exercise extreme care when planning your budget *before* upgrading your housing.

TO RENT OR TO OWN?

Perhaps the most challenging decision that a family must make is deciding whether to rent or buy. For some people it is clear-cut; how would it be for you? We are a home-owner-oriented society despite the high initial purchase price and the high continuing maintenance costs. Since this situation is not likely to change in our inflationary society, a wrong decision can be very costly indeed. There is no guarantee that you can retrieve your investment if you are unhappy with home-ownership.

Advantages of Renting

1. *Mobility* You may move on relatively short notice. Your job may require this.
2. *Less maintenance* If you do not like to use your leisure time for house and yard upkeep, you can enjoy your free time. Smaller quarters usually mean less housework.
3. *Predetermined costs* Your rent covers major repairs and replacement. It also covers taxes, decorating, insurance, and other associated costs.
4. *Financial flexibility* You can change your housing expenses as your income changes. You are not "boxed in." If you should lose your job, you would not lose your investment through foreclosure.
5. *Community living* If you like people, you will have a much greater chance to become acquainted. Compact quarters mean you will be close to your neighbors.
6. *Investment alternatives* Your investment need not be fixed. Savings, mutual funds, stocks and bonds, commodities, and other business ventures including income property may be purchased with funds that would otherwise be earmarked for a home down payment and upkeep.

Advantages of Buying

1. *Roots in the community* You will have a sense of belonging. You will have stability and standing in the community.
2. *Pride of ownership* Upkeep of your own "castle" is more enjoyable. Psychologically, you may actually enjoy garden and house care and even become a "do-it-yourself" fan.
3. *Better location* Single-family residences are usually in better locations than apartments. Access to schools and open space contributes to the welfare of your children.
4. *Extra living space and privacy* You can accumulate and store your possessions much more easily. Family members are not on top of each other. You can be independent and relatively free to live in whatever life-style you wish.
5. *Forced savings investment* You have ownership of real property to show for your monthly payments. You build an equity rather than a pile of rent receipts.
6. *Less costly than renting* The quality and quantity of living space being equal, costs will be lower to buy. You can also control them to a greater extent. You receive income-tax benefits in addition to purchasing an equity.

You can probably come up with a larger, slightly different list of advantages for each housing-cost alternative. The advantages of buying tend to be the disadvantages of renting and vice-versa. Which set of advantages best suits your family?

Cost Comparisons

Many times the final decision rests on the total monthly costs associated with renting or buying. You can compound the mistake of not being suited for a particular house or for home-ownership in general by not thoroughly checking into all aspects of the monthly costs involved in renting or buying.

Table 12–1 provides an analysis of the out-of-pocket monthly costs for a family of four, including two elementary school children. They live in a comfortable two-bedroom unfurnished apartment and desire more space. They have saved enough money to provide for a $6,500 down payment and closing costs on a $35,000 three-bedroom home in the suburbs. The mortgage amounts to $28,500 at 9 percent for twenty-five years. The individual expenses will vary in different parts of the country and with different life-styles.

It appears that the monthly out-of-pocket

Table 12–1 Monthly cost comparison for three-bedroom home, three-bedroom apartment, and two-bedroom apartment

Monthly Cost Items	Own Home	3-bedroom apartment	2-bedroom apartment
Mortgage or rent	$239	$300	$250
Real estate taxes	80	—	—
Insurance (owner/tenant)	10	5	5
Maintenance	30	—	—
Heating and cooling	20	15	10
Electricity	15	13	11
Water	10	—	—
Garbage	5	—	—
Telephone	15	10	10
Added comute expense	30	—	—
Out-of-pocket expenses	$454	$343	$286

The amounts assume that larger space means greater costs. Apartments are located closer to work. No consideration is given to cost or need for second automobile. See text for further analysis.

cost of owning a home is greater than that of renting an apartment. The increased costs are associated with more space and commuting. Close analysis is needed at this point because of the many variables. It is hard to be objective if you are sold on the psychological advantages of home-ownership.

Analysis of the table indicates an apparent difference of $168 between the present two-bedroom apartment and the three-bedroom home. There is a $57 difference between the two-bedroom and three-bedroom apartments. Therefore, roughly $50 extra per month provides more adequate space, and another $100 provides still more space and ownership equity.

If we carry the analysis a little further, we would have to consider other noncash financial projections such as depreciation, current appreciation and/or inflation, and return on investment of the down payment and principal payments. Changes in value will be considered next, while return on investment will be discussed later in the chapter, when we look at income property as an alternative investment.

You need a roof over your head, and if the house is a good investment, you are in most instances way ahead of renting. The big exception is if you plan to remain in one place only for a relatively short time. A rough rule of thumb to determine the break-even point of when to rent or buy is two years. Appreciation and inflation will most likely cause the value of your house to rise enough during this period to return your purchase price and cover the costs of the sale. The longer you stay, the more equity and appreciation you build. Rent receipts offer nothing as an investment.

For example, if you assume a 5 percent appreciation factor on your $35,000 home, the increase of approximately $1,750 per year will almost cover the costs of selling your home. Approximately $2,500 will be absorbed by sales and mortgage fees with the balance of $1,000 allocated to the added costs of living in the home during the two-year period. Other rates of appreciation or depreciation will change these approximations.

Finally, you must consider the federal income-tax savings that accrue to those who itemize. If you are in the 25 percent tax bracket, property tax and mortgage interest deductions of $3,525 in the first year would amount to an $881 annual tax saving which substantially lowers the home-ownership costs as presented in the table.

We can safely summarize by stating that there is generally an economic advantage to home-ownership over renting through property appreciation, forced savings, and income-tax deductions.

HOW MUCH CAN YOU AFFORD TO SPEND FOR HOUSING?

Now that you have determined that buying a home is more economical than renting over the long term, how much can you afford to pay? Once you decide, you can look at the alternatives available in your price range. You may want to take the opposite approach, in which you determine your needs and wants first and then narrow your selection to match your ability to pay. Actually prospective homeowners base their buying decision on their ability to pay and their desires concurrently. Lenders tend to look at your ability to pay in terms of original cost and continuing monthly payments.

Initial Purchase Price

The selling price of a home will differ by size, location, and construction features. You therefore modify your desires to match the general selling prices in your location. Metropolitan areas command higher sales prices simply because of the law of supply and demand. With less land available and more people wanting homes, prices rise.

Inflationary trends in the United States are pushing the initial price of homes completely out of range for many prospective purchasers. The average purchase price for a home is approximately $35,000 and a much higher rate prevails in metropolitan areas. Scare stories abound of homes being resold for $5,000 more within a year of purchase. This may mean that you should compromise your desires and needs and perhaps purchase a minimum acceptable home rather than saving for something closer to your dream house. This inflationary approach has the advantage of giving you the benefit of any increase in local real estate values. Otherwise you may continue to save and find that the price goes up faster than your ability to save.

In any case, your choice of housing must be limited to what you can comfortably pay for. The "dream house" may become a nightmare if you cannot maintain and improve your home to your satisfaction and yet have funds available for the many other things that make for a comfortable life. Therefore, you must not be saddled with a monthly mortgage payment that you cannot afford.

There are two ways to accomplish this: one is to buy less house; the other is to make a larger down payment. The immediate funds that you have available and your monthly income determine what you can initially afford. Also you must consider such move-in expenses as the closing costs, actual moving and storage expenses, and any improvements and decorations needed to make your home livable. Additional furniture and appliances are often needed.

A detailed approach to initial housing expenses should follow this format:

Down payment	$ ________
Closing costs (including prorated taxes and insurance)	________
Immediate repairs and modernization (if any)	________
Immediate purchase of furniture, appliances, and household items	________
Moving cost	________
Total	$ ________

Down Payments

The average down payment runs between 10 percent and 20 percent depending upon the mortgage lender and his requirements. The larger the down payment, the less mortgage money that has to be borrowed. The down-payment money available effectively limits the amount of house you can buy. If you are required to put down 20 percent on a $35,000 house, you must come up with $7,000, a considerable effort for the average young couple. One general rule for obtaining a mortgage is not to borrow more than 2½ times your annual gross income.

If you have extra funds to make a larger down payment, you are confronted with the dilemma of deciding whether to reduce your monthly payments or to reduce the total interest amount paid over the life of the mortgage.

Monthly Mortgage Payments

A second general rule for obtaining a mortgage is that the monthly payment should not exceed one week's gross income. The balance of your income is needed for other expenses in your budget.

A relatively conservative way to measure your ability to pay is to examine your budget closely in order to determine what is available. Add up all nonhousing expenses, including savings; the balance should be available for housing. Hopefully you have not underestimated expenses in your desire to show extra funds available for housing. Your housing expenses should include monthly mortgage payments (principal, interest, insurance, and taxes), repair and maintenance, and heat and utilities.

HOUSING ALTERNATIVES AVAILABLE

Once you decide to own a home, you will find a wide choice of housing locations and housing types available. You may choose among new homes (tract, custom, and manufactured), used homes, condominiums, cooperatives, and mobile homes.

Your choice of housing should reflect your finances and your life-style. Your home's location, appearance, size, design, and type must be suitable to your needs, or you may wish that you had never committed yourself and your money to it.

Location

The neighborhood in which you live is at least as important as the house itself. All too often, home buyers pick the home of their dreams only to find the surroundings unpleasant or inconvenient. Use the checklist below to evaluate whether you would like to live in a particular neighborhood:

Physical Attractiveness

Do zoning laws protect the residential character of the neighborhood?
Are street and lot patterns arranged for appearance, convenience, and safety?
Are the site plans and designs of houses in the neighborhood compatible?
Is the neighborhood landscaping pleasing to the eye?
Are most homes in the same general price range?

Congenialty

Will the educational and social background and the income of your neighbors be similar to yours?
Will there be neighbors in your age group?
Will there be children in the same age group as your children?

Accessibility

Will you be within walking or easy riding distance of:
- schools?
- parks and playgrounds?
- a church of your denomination?
- convenience stores?
- athletic and entertainment facilities that your family enjoys?

Is there fast, frequent, and convenient bus or train transportation to:
- your place of employment?
- larger business and shopping areas?
- entertainment and cultural attractions?

Community Services

Are streets paved and well maintained?
Is there a proper sewage and storm drainage system?
Are water, electricity, gas, telephone service, and other utilities provided at reasonable costs?
Is there mail delivery, garbage pickup, and police and fire protection?
Is the community tax level within your budget and consistent with the services provided?
Will your budget be able to meet the expenses of special assessments or new bond issues if any are planned?

If the answer is yes to most of the above questions, you may then want to look for housing in that particular location.

Specific Housing Needs

You will probably never find the one house that meets all your family's needs. However, certain basic requirements are common to all families, and some are different for each family's life-style. A suitable checklist of questions like the following makes selection easier:

Lot Size and Orientation

Is the lot large enough to insure adequate privacy if adjacent construction is started?
Is the lot graded so that rainwater drains away from the house in all directions?
Is the house oriented so that the living room is not exposed to the hot afternoon sun?
Is the view from the house pleasant and likely to remain unchanged?

Space

Is there enough total space for your family?
Can your whole family be seated in the living room without crowding?
Are there enough bedrooms for you, your children, and children to come?
Are bathroom facilities sufficient for periods of peak use by your family?
Is there closet space for each member of the family and adequate utility space?
Is there space for children to play indoors?
Can the whole family eat together in the kitchen?
Can additions be built on the house at reasonable cost?

Design

Do you think the design of the house will prove attractive to you over a period of years?
Is it appropriate to whatever furnishings and household goods you have or will want?
Does the design take advantage of sunlight and natural ventilation?
Are bedrooms separated from living areas for privacy and silence?
Is the traffic pattern throughout the house convenient to everyday living?
Does it have a step-saving kitchen?

Is there some separation between the front or guest entrance and the main living area?
Does the design avoid styling which may rapidly go out of fashion, reducing market value?

Construction

Is there adequate protection against termites, including complete separation of wood construction from the ground?
Is the foundation free of large cracks and signs of seepage?
Will the drainage and storm sewer system prevent basement flooding?
Are insulation and weather stripping adequate?
Is there a vapor barrier in the walls to help prevent paint from peeling or blistering?
Does the trim fit neatly around doors and windows?
Is the roof free of leaks?
Is the heating system adequate and efficient?
Is the hot water system adequate for your needs?
Is the house adequately wired for the variety of electrical appliances to be used?

A New or Used Home?

Your choice of a new or used home should be based upon more than just your liking new things. Any home you buy will be new to you. Once you add your furnishings you will soon forget that your home was previously owned by someone else. Let's look at some of the advantages and disadvantages of new and used homes before deciding.

New homes Most new homes are placed on raw land rather than replacing an older home, which means that they are likely to be located in the suburbs. Is this an important factor? Everything in it will be brand new, including the latest time-saving and energy-saving appliances. Is this important? Usually the actual housing space is small but extremely functional, to get the most out of each construction dollar. The quality of construction will vary greatly among builders, and you should investigate thoroughly before buying.

Consideration must be given to what is missing in a new home. Carpets, drapes, fencing, and landscaping costs must be added to the base price for comparison. The added costs in time, money, and possible gasoline shortages are also distinct disadvantages if the new house is not located near your place of employment.

Used homes Location and stability of a neighborhood are the greatest plus factors for purchasing a used home. The character of a neighborhood is well established; you know what you are getting. The extras that must be added to new homes are usually part of the used home: drapes, carpets, landscaping, finished attics, basements, or family rooms. These extras are usually reflected in the price of the used home. Another good reason to choose a used home is the wide variety of architectural styles available. You should find something to your liking. The used home will probably be more spacious and have better-quality materials used in its construction.

There are problems with used homes, though. You may be buying someone else's headaches. The older home may need extensive repair or improvements. Heating, cooling, plumbing, and electrical systems may be inadequate for today's needs. The general cost of maintenance may be higher than in a new home. Finally, you will probably not get a "buy" unless some work does have to be done, because the previous owner will most likely wish to make a profit on his pioneering effort, the law of supply and demand, and inflation.

Tract, Custom, and Manufactured Homes

These terms bring emotional images to many people. They are really just terms used to describe how or where a house has been built. You should not automatically eliminate any of these designations from your choices, as you may well miss out on a good purchase.

Tract home A tract home can be objectively described as one of a similar group of homes built in a certain location. This method of home construction tends to bring economy of scale and keeps the price within reach of the average consumer. It does not necessarily connote cheap construction. There are expensive and inexpensive tracts, depending upon location, size, materials, and number of models available.

A suburban tract generally becomes differentiated with landscaping, additions, improvements, and the aging process. Often people are unaware that older portions of town were or are tracts—they just do not fit the popular concept of a tract because time brings differentiation. City row houses, duplexes, apartment blocks, and town houses may be just as "tracty" as a suburban ranch house development. The high cost of land and its reasonably efficient use dictate less land per family than what most of us would like.

Custom-built home One of these may be in your future. These are homes that are built singly to individual design. Custom-built homes generally do not look like all the surrounding homes; however there is often not much difference in a given area. After zoning considerations, custom homes are built to a customer's needs and finances. You may hunt for an individualized used home to your liking or you may "build" to your taste.

How custom is custom? The price may come to no more than a good tract home if you thoroughly investigate some of the cost-saving possibilities. For example, you can purchase ready-made plans from an architect or builder. Chances are you will find a plan that matches what you want where you want it. You can act as your own general contractor to award and supervise the various subcontractors needed to complete your home. You can specify various grades of materials and equipment for your home. You can have a builder construct your home using his plans and your lot.

Manufactured home Choosing a manufactured house is very similar to choosing a custom house if it meets your needs and the various zoning and labor union regulations in your area. These are homes that are prefabricated in a manufacturing plant and shipped in large pieces to a site for erection. At one time they were called prefabs. The name was changed due to a rather poor reputation for quality. This does not have to be the case if you choose your dealer with care. Premanufactured homes are generally less expensive than homes completely erected on the building site. Cost savings comes from labor-saving techniques and the use of less skilled labor in the manufacturing plant.

Cooperatives and Condominiums

Co-ops and condominiums are relatively new housing alternatives. Both may offer the same physical layout and extra amenities. They may be detached, semidetached, townhouses, or multi-family apartment-like structures. They usually feature swimming pools, tennis courts, clubhouses, or some public areas for use by all tenants.

The advantage of this type of housing is that the tenant-owner gets the benefits of maintenance-free home-ownership, income-tax deductions, and equity appreciation. Since they usually occupy less land and are built on a large project basis, they are usually priced lower than a comparable single-family dwelling.

The main disadvantage lies in the management agreement required by these communal housing alternatives. There is a monthly assessment to pay for the administration and maintenance of common areas, taxes, insurance, and the like. Unfortunately, you may underestimate this monthly expense. You may find yourself in a minority position on various management problems that can occur in the administration of a housing complex. If at all possible, check out your prospective neighbors and fellow owners before committing yourself to the purchase of these units. The difference between a co-op and a condominium lies in the form of ownership. In both cases you can sell your ownership subject to certain covenant restrictions.

Cooperative apartment Membership in a cooperative is like ownership in a corporation. You purchase ownership in the cooperative equal to the percentage of living space you occupy. If your apartment comprises 4 percent of the entire living space, you become a shareholder-owner of this amount of the cooperative including the common areas. You receive a proprietary lease on your apartment for life.

Condominiums Under condominium ownership, you purchase your unit outright. The price includes a proportionate share in all the common areas. You receive a certificate of title, which you pass along to the next owner when you sell. Condominiums have proven to be very popular because one can own a particular unit.

Mobile Homes

You should also consider purchasing a mobile home, a very popular form of housing. Their popularity is twofold: the relatively low complete package price, and their increasingly greater size. You can purchase a mobile home now that has carpeting, heating, and air conditioning. Costs range from approximately $10,000 to $30,000 depending upon the size, layout, and appliances selected. Mobile homes are not very mobile in most cases. They tend to range between 10 and 20 feet wide and are over 54 feet long.

The main disadvantage of a mobile home is the location of the mobile home park. While it is not always the case, local planning commissions tend to relegate them to less desirable areas near freeways and commercial-industrial zones. Monthly space-rental costs together with the installment purchase are generally lower than those of any other form of housing. Therefore, if you do not mind a less desirable location and a feeling of impermanence, you will get more housing for your dollar with a mobile home than with any other housing form.

THE HOUSING SPECIALIST

When you begin to think seriously of purchasing a home, the time comes to enlist the aid of a specialist. Realtors, appraisers, attorneys, lenders, and insurance agents all provide various helpful services. Without question you should see a realtor if you have never purchased a home previously. He can handle the whole transaction. The other specialists are concerned only with portions of a transaction.

The Realtor

A realtor, also known as a real estate broker, maintains an office complete with salespersons who are licensed to sell real estate. The broker acts as a go-between for the seller and the buyer. Actually, he is an agent for the seller and is required to secure the highest possible price for him. For all practical purposes, however, he represents himself; he provides the expertise and balancing needed in real estate negotiations and earns a fee. Both buyers and sellers benefit from his services even though his commission fee is paid by the seller. The seller often attempts to pay the fee by raising the selling price. Six percent of the sale price is the usual commission rate paid to the selling broker, who then splits the fee with his salesperson and the listing broker.

Buyers benefit from a realtor's service because he has extensive knowledge of what is on the market. A buyer can tell a broker exactly what he wants and at what price. This will save the buyer a great deal of time and effort, since most realty offices have a multiple-listing service, which entitles them to sell houses on behalf of any seller who has signed for the service.

The seller's big benefit from using a realtor is in exposure to prospects. The realtor is the focal point of buyer interest because he has the knowledge of what is available, so buyers naturally visit one. The broker can have the salesperson show the house and handle the complete transaction, including negotiation, counter-offer, financing, and escrow arranging. A "lock-box" security device allows the house to be shown by any multiple-listing salesperson in the absence of the occupant.

Sellers often attempt to sell a house without the aid of a realtor. This takes considerable patience and some skill. A seller will probably become a prisoner of his house while waiting for telephone calls and possible prospect visits. The advantage to the seller lies in "saving" the commission. Unfortunately, the buyer is also aware of this saving and would like to share in the windfall. You, as a buyer, should investigate the purchase of a home from a private party if you find a house that matches your housing needs and price requirements. A little negotiation may reduce the selling price, because the seller may not have had many interested prospects.

The Attorney

Experts say you should engage the services of an attorney in a real estate transaction to insure that your interests are protected in the contract. Both buyers and sellers may not get what they expect unless the purchase agreement states specifically what real and personal property is included in the transaction. Occupancy, financing arrangements, zoning changes, and repair requirements that are part of the transaction should also be in writing. This is extremely good advice and worth the attorney's fee of $100 to $500 if you do not have the services of a realtor or if you wish to feel extra secure. A trustworthy realtor will help you through the legal entanglements, but you are still liable for your contractual agreements.

The Appraiser

After you have definitely decided upon a particular home, you should arrange an independent appraisal of the property. The seller and the broker tend to become overenthusiastic about the merits and value of the house. At a cost of about fifty dollars, an appraiser will check the construction soundness and the plumbing, heating, and electrical systems. He will check for termites and advise you of any building code violations. He should provide you with an estimate of any repairs necessary. This will provide you with negotiating information and perhaps save you from a mistake. Most lenders require a termite inspection before they will loan mortgage money on a property. Since a termite inspection will cost a buyer about thirty-five dollars, just a few dollars more will provide you with a more detailed and informative report.

Other Specialists

Mortgage-money lenders should be shopped to get the best possible interest rates. Title-insurance companies and escrow companies should likewise be shopped. We will look into the activities of these specialists as we progress through our home purchase transaction.

HOME MORTGAGE FINANCING

Prospective home buyers worry about the purchase price of the home that they want. This is only right because through negotiation a buyer can often save several thousand dollars over the asking price. Then they turn around and accept the first home mortgage interest rate that is offered. At 9 percent interest the home buyer will double the cost of his mortgage in twenty years and triple it in thirty-five years. Since the average person actually pays more in interest charges than he pays for the house, you should at least give equal attention to the costs of financing your home. We will examine the variables of mortgage financing in detail.

What Is a Mortgage?

Most home loans are secured by a mortgage on the real estate being purchased. The mortgage is a security device used by a lender to provide him with a remedy in case the debtor should fail to perform (pay) according to contract. The real estate mortgage conveys an interest in the real property to the mortgagee (lender). To get a loan the mortgagor (borrower) conveys an interest in the property by deed of trust to the mortgagee. The interest in the property is in the amount of the loan balance. The deed is recorded as a matter of public record so that as an "owner," the lender can proceed against the debtor to claim the property through foreclosure if the borrower defaults. The mortgage is evidence of the secured debt so that the lender does not have to bring a suit to prove the debt. State laws govern whether a formal suit must be brought in foreclosure proceedings.

A real estate mortgage loan is granted by the mortgagee upon the conveyance by the mortgagor of a deed of trust. In practice the real estate sale and financing transaction is sorted out during escrow. The lender puts the mortgage loan money into the escrow account to pay off the old loan and/or the seller, while the buyer (mortgagor) conveys a partial interest to the mortgagee by his deed.

A deed of trust may be a first or second conveyance, with the senior debt having the first and greatest right to remedy a default.

Real Estate Loan Sources

A number of sources are available from which to borrow your mortgage money:

1. Commercial banks
2. Savings and loan associations
3. Mutual savings banks
4. Mortgage companies
5. Insurance companies
6. Individual lenders

If you see a realtor, he will have contacts with mortgage lenders and know the availability of money and the current interest rate. You, too, should investigate the mortgage money picture because a mortgagor can often shop around and secure better terms by negotiating and comparing. The granting of a mortgage loan requires a formal application, an extensive credit investigation, and signing of documents. You can telephone various sources to get preliminary quotes on their best available rates before starting the formal procedures.

Types of Mortgage Loans

Three widely used types of real estate loans are available to the borrower: conventional loans, F.H.A. loans, and V.A. loans. Additionally, individual states often guarantee or actually lend mortgage money to selected citizens. An example of this is the Cal-Vet program in California.

Conventional loans Any real estate loan that is not insured or guaranteed by the government may be considered a conventional loan. The lender sets his rates, terms, and requirements based on good lending practices and the competitive money market. As a generality, the lender will require a 20 percent or greater down payment and a shorter loan period such as twenty-five years to lessen the risk of borrower default. These precautions mean that a borrower must be in extremely good financial position. If this is the case, you may receive an extremely favorable interest rate.

F.H.A. loans The Federal Housing Administration (F.H.A.) was established by Congress in 1934 to promote home ownership by the average citizen by permitting low down payments. The borrower actually negotiates with his mortgage lenders and pays a ½ percent insurance premium that is passed on by the lender to the F.H.A. The F.H.A., in turn, insures the lender against any loss on his loan commitment. This insurance means that a lender will accept a lower down payment, a longer term, a greater credit risk, and even a slightly lower rate of interest.

Current F.H.A. loan formulas call for 3 percent down payment on the first $15,000, 10 percent on the next $10,000, and 20 percent on the amount over $25,000. The current maximum loan insured by the F.H.A. is $30,000. The interest rate allowable under the F.H.A. changes with money market conditions. Currently it is 9 percent plus ½ percent insurance.

V.A. loans The Veterans Administration has been helping veterans purchase homes since the end of World War II. A veteran must qualify by serving in the military for at least 180 days. A GI applicant has a time limit in which to take advantage of the loan guarantees provided by the Veterans Administration.

The V.A. guarantees a portion of the mortgage loan offered by approved lenders. There is no extra insurance premium charged the borrower as in F.H.A. loans. Low down payments are also featured by V.A. loans. No down payment is required on the first $15,000, 10 percent down on the next $10,000, and 15 percent down over $25,000. The maximum interest rate allowed currently is 9 percent.

Alternative Financing

There are alternatives to the three types of real estate financing just mentioned. You can assume an existing loan, give a second mortgage, or refinance your existing mortgage.

Assuming a loan Sometimes you can

buy a house without securing a new real estate loan. This saves some closing costs and higher interest payments. You simply take over the existing loan of the seller. You pay the seller the difference between the selling price and what he owes on the house (his equity). You as the new owner take full responsibility for the balance of the mortgage payments. Often the buyer does not have quite enough to cover the seller's entire equity. This is where a second mortgage may be accepted by the seller to make up the difference.

The agreement to assume a mortgage is usually subject to the approval of the first mortgage holder. The buyer must meet the standard credit requirements of the lender, but this is normally no trouble if you offer a substantial down payment. Under a conventional assumption agreement the seller of the property is released from any payment liability by the lender (mortgagee). However, if the old interest rate is much lower than the current rate available on conventional loans, the mortgagee may not wish to continue the loan. For example, you may wish to assume a 5 percent loan when new loans are being made at 9 percent. When this happens conventional loans must be renegotiated. F.H.A. and V.A. loans, however, can still be assumed by a separate contract between the seller and the buyer. Under a separate agreement assumption the seller remains liable for any default by the new buyer. In today's inflationary real estate market the risk of default and subsequent loss is not very great.

Second mortgages A second mortgage is a lien on real property that has a lower priority than the first mortgage. The second mortgagee's claim is honored only after the first mortgage holder is protected. In practice, if the second mortgagee needs to foreclose, he will make normal payments to the first mortgagee. This can be very costly.

When purchasing a house you may use a second mortgage on a conventional loan if the first mortgage lender is agreeable (F.H.A. and V.A. regulations prohibit the use of second mortgages at purchase time). This procedure is advantageous to the buyer who cannot meet the down-payment requirements. Unfortunately, the necessary second monthly payments are relatively large and may create a monthly budget problem. Second-mortgage interest rates are higher, and the terms are shorter than those of the first mortgage. Currently, second mortgages run 10 percent or more.

Often homeowners borrow on the equity (ownership build-up) in their home. They negotiate a "homeowner's" loan from a finance company, using their equity as security. Occasionally home improvements are financed in this manner, but homeowner's loans are almost invariably debt consolidation loans needed by the debtor to bail himself out of the burden of many budget-ruining debts. Usually a second mortgage of this type is a prelude to losing your home and possibly going into bankruptcy.

Refinancing your mortgage Another method of borrowing on your equity is to refinance your home by renegotiating your mortgage with your current lender or his competitor. You negotiate the loan as if you were purchasing your home for the first time. This procedure allows you to keep your present home yet get some of the equity out of it without selling it. You may then use the money for whatever purpose you desire. Hopefully it will be for improvements or another real estate investment. The disadvantages of refinancing lie in wasting the money you receive from your equity plus the probable extending of the term of the loan or the increasing of the interest rate payable on the new loan.

Refinancing with today's high interest rates will require you to make large monthly payments and pay an extremely large total amount of interest over the years if you hold your mortgage until maturity. You must therefore be aware of the going interest rates on real estate loans. If they should drop by 1 percent or more, it might be beneficial to refinance your first mortgage loan to secure lower monthly payments and/or a lower total interest if you reduce the term of the loan. Prepayment penalties (if any) would have to be considered when determining whether a refinancing procedure would be beneficial.

REAL ESTATE LOAN COSTS

There are many variable factors that determine the cost of your real estate loan. Many of these factors are interconnected. A decision on one factor affects another, as the interest formula ($P \times R \times T = I$) indicates. Most of these factors can be negotiated with the lender or personally selected from alternatives. As stated earlier, you may also shop various lenders to compare these factors.

Interest Rate

All other things being equal, the interest rate that you pay for your real estate mortgage is the most obvious indicator of financing costs. The higher the interest rate, the higher the monthly payment and the higher the total interest paid. Table 12–2 illustrates this principle. It is quite easy to figure the cost of different mortgage amounts at different rates of interest using the table. For example if you borrow $25,000 at 8½ percent, the total interest paid during a twenty-five-year mortgage is $35,300 ($60,300 – $25,000). If borrowed at 9½ percent, the total interest would amount to $40,400 ($65,400 – $25,000). It pays to shop for the lowest interest rate. Interest rates have been climbing steadily since World War II with the exception of a slight drop in the early 1960s. Just a few years ago real estate mortgages were available at 7 percent; now they are going at approximately 9½ percent interest.

Table 12–2 Effect of varying interest rates on a twenty-five-year, $25,000 mortgage

Interest Rate	Monthly P/I Payment	Total Payments to Maturity
7½%	$185	$55,500
8%	193	57,900
8½%	201	60,300
9%	210	63,000
9½%	218	65,400
10%	227	68,100

Monthly principal and interest payments are rounded to nearest dollar. Monthly payments do not include impound fees for taxes and insurance.

Variable interest rates A concept that is being given serious nationwide consideration is a variable interest rate tied to the money market. The interest rate would be on a sliding scale and change as needed at least once a year. Several methods of implementing the concept have been considered. One would be to increase or decrease the monthly mortgage payments; another would be to extend or contract the term of the mortgage while leaving the payment unchanged. The main advantage of a variable interest rate is that lenders would not be as reluctant to lend long-term mortgage money when interest rates are continually rising. Until better protection is offered to the borrower, you will probably be better off with a fixed interest rate mortgage. You should be able to refinance to a lower rate if the interest rates on mortgages take a significant drop, but would not have to pay a higher rate if interest rates were to rise.

The Mortgage Amount

The more that you borrow, the more cash you will have available for other uses. The amount that you borrow is closely associated with your down payment, which we will discuss next. The dollar amount that you can borrow is negotiable because the lender will interpret your total income and your ability to make the monthly payments. Your debt structure, available assets, employment longevity, and types and amount of income are weighted somewhat differently by different lenders. The broadest range of interpretations occurs in the area of what is consistent income. The salaries of both spouses are counted if the income is consistent.

Down Payment

The amount of the down payment can be negotiated with the lender. You should realize that the greater the down payment, the less you will have to borrow. The more you borrow, the more you eventually pay back with interest. Table 12–3 points up the economic benefits of borrowing less money.

A lower down payment may be justified under the following circumstances: (1) if you can save on a home purchase price before inflation raises the price; (2) if you use your excess funds to purchase all the accouterments necessary to make your new home more comfortable and customized to your family's life-style and taste; and/or (3) if you use your excess funds for investment at a yield greater than you are paying on your mortgage. These circumstances, especially the third one, represent the opportunity costs of making a larger down payment.

Generally lenders increase the interest rate charged whenever a borrower desires a low down payment on a conventional loan. As previously mentioned, minimum down payments, minimum terms, and interest rates are prescribed by law for F.H.A. and V.A. loans.

The Length of the Loan

The term of the loan affects the total interest paid during the life of the loan.

Table 12–3 Effects of varying down payments on 9 percent mortgage for a twenty-five-year term

Down %	Payment Dollars	Amount Borrowed	Monthly P/I Payment	Total Payments to Maturity
5%	$1,500	$28,500	$239	$71,700
10%	3,000	27,000	227	68,100
20%	6,000	24,000	201	60,300
25%	7,500	22,500	189	56,700
30%	9,000	21,000	176	52,800
50%	15,000	15,000	126	37,800

A home purchase price of $30,000 is used in the above table. Monthly principal and interest payments are rounded to nearest dollar. Monthly payments do not include impound fees for taxes and insurance.

Table 12–4 Effect of various mortgage lengths on a 9 percent mortgage of $25,000

Term in Years	Monthly P/I Payment	Total Payments to Maturity
10	$317	$38,040
15	254	45,720
20	225	54,000
25	210	63,000
30	201	72,360

Interest is based on the amount of time that the rate is applied to the principal. The longer the time, the more interest is paid. A shorter term will result in larger monthly payments but significantly lower overall interest charges. Table 12–4 illustrates the effect of various mortgage lengths on a $25,000, 9 percent mortgage loan.

Lenders often charge a higher rate of interest on a longer-term loan. The rationale is the risk involved because of the continuing exposure to default. Longer-term loans do have the benefit of lower monthly payments because the repayment of principal is spread over more months. If longer terms and lower monthly payments are a factor in comfortably paying for your house, they should definitely be considered. A further potential benefit for a longer term is the repayment in future dollars that are likely to be inflated and worth less than the current dollars being borrowed on the real estate mortgage. This is also a reason why lenders increase the rate on longer-term loans.

Loan Fees and Points

When shopping for real estate mortgage money, you will soon find what the current rate of interest happens to be. If the F.H.A. or V.A. rate is appreciably below the conventional loan rate, lenders will not grant the government-insured loans. This reluctance can be overcome through the charging of "points," a one-time loan fee for the privilege of getting the loan. A point is 1 percent of the principal. The number of points charged will vary depending upon the spread between F.H.A. and V.A. rates and the yield provided by a conventional mortgage. F.H.A. regulations prohibit a buyer from paying more than one point. The seller must pay any extra points to secure the loan for the buyer. Needless to say, the seller passes this extra cost along to the buyer by raising the sale price of the house. Points or loan fees are sometimes required on conventional loans before the lender will grant the loan. The amount of points and loan fees (if any) reflects the availability of real estate mortgage money. The tighter the supply of available funds, the higher the interest rate and the higher the extra loan fees or points.

Prepayment Clauses

Be sure you have the right to pay off your mortgage prior to the maturity date. If you do not have such a clause, you must pay off the mortgage as agreed by contract. This means that you may end up paying up to three times the amount of mortgage borrowed. This was illustrated earlier in this chapter. Because interest rates have historically been on an uptrend, most lenders allow you prepayment privileges but attach a penalty for doing so. Even though you expect to keep your home and mortgage for the contractual term of twenty to thirty years, you will probably change your mind. Fewer than 25 percent of home mortgages go to the complete term, usually because the mortgagor moves and sells the house, thereby triggering an early payoff of the mortgage.

The penalty ranges for prepayment usually amount to 1 or 2 percent of the outstanding balance or from 90 to 180 days interest. On a $30,000 mortgage balance at 9 percent this would have a dollar range of $300 to $600 or $650 to $1,300, depending upon the penalty method. As you can see, the penalty can add up to a rather substantial amount. You have theoretically "breached" the contract, and the penalty presumably soothes the lender.

F.H.A. and V.A. mortgages require prepayment privileges without penalty. Lenders do not particularly like this arrangement and either tend to discourage these loans or charge points before they will grant the loan. Sometimes conventional loans allow partial prepayment without penalty. For example, extra principal payments not to amount to more than 20 percent of the original mortgage may be allowed without penalty in any calendar year. This way you could accelerate your mortgage payments and pay off your loan in five years without penalty. Finally, some lenders waive the penalty if you refinance a loan through them or borrow from them on a new property.

Impound Accounts

The regular monthly payment made to the lender includes more than just the payment of principal and interest. It usually includes a charge for property taxes, special assessments, and fire/homeowner's insurance. The total annual sum needed to pay these items is estimated in advance by the lender. One-twelfth of the estimated charges is collected as part of your regular monthly payment and deposited in a special account. As they become due, the annual charges are paid out of this fund, known as an impound account. Figure 12–1 illustrates a loan statement with a transaction breakdown.

This procedure seems to be a convenience to the home buyer/mortgagor. It helps him budget his housing expenses. Unfortunately, the impound account does not pay interest. You should be able to deposit the same impounded amounts in an interest-bearing savings account or have the mortgagee pay interest for the use of your money. Theoretically, the money is not used by the lender because it is in a trust account. Legislation is now being passed in some states requiring that interest be paid on these accounts.

Closing Costs—Escrow Fees

The mortgage factors previously mentioned would be negotiated with the mortgage lender. The buyer and the seller must also negotiate with each other as to who will pay what parts of the closing costs and what the final purchase price of the home will be.

Closing occurs as the last major step of a real estate purchase when the buyer, seller, mortgage lender, and their legal representatives come together to complete the transaction. No matter how long it takes to complete the individual details, in law all these things happen at once. The usual escrow is the deposit of the deed to the property by the seller or his mortgage company and the deposit of money by the buyer and/or his mortgage company with an impartial third party known as an escrow agent. This agent acts as an impartial middleman for both buyer and seller. Once all agreed-upon conditions of the real estate contract have been met, the escrow agent

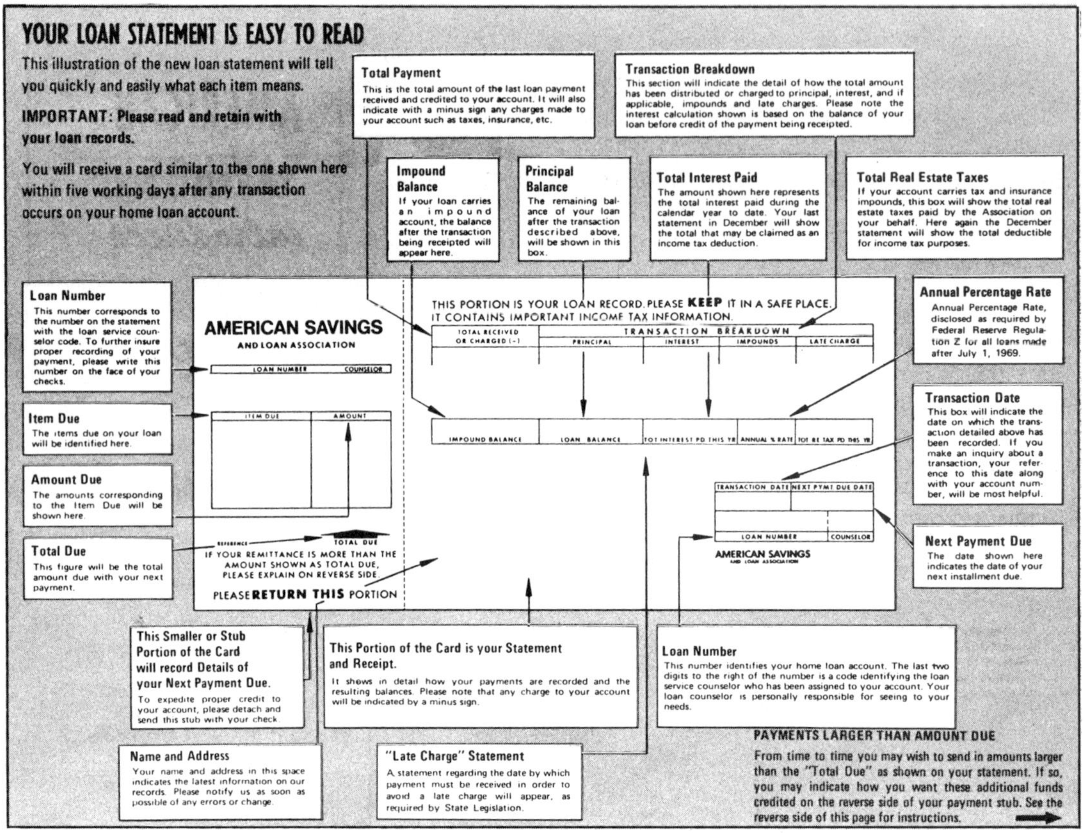

Figure 12–1 Real Estate Loan Statement and Payment Card. *(American Savings & Loan Association)*

hands over the deed to the buyer and the money to the seller. An escrow agent may be a bank, lawyer, specialized escrow company, or title-insurance company.

The escrow procedure (or last settlement) prorates taxes and interest impounds, fire-insurance premiums, and any temporary rental between the buyer and seller. The deed, mortgage, and other legal papers are notarized and recorded. Payments are made for termite inspection, property repair required by the purchase agreement, commission to selling realtor, prepayment penalties, mortgage to the old lender, and loan fees to the new lender. Figure 12–2 shows the type of form used for apportionment.

Title insurance Figure 12–3 shows a typical title-insurance policy that enumerates the conditions of insurance. Title insurance protects the buyer and his mortgage lender from a recorded claim against title to the property. Lenders require title insurance as a condition of making a real estate mortgage loan. A buyer should carefully read the policy of title insurance to determine whether the policy covers the full property

STEWART TITLE

STATEMENT OF ESCROW NO.:
TO:

CLOSING DATE:
OFFICE:

PROPERTY:	CHARGES	CREDITS
CONSIDERATION OR SALES PRICE	$	$
Paid outside of Escrow		
Deposits		
Deposits		
Deposits		
By First Trust Deed		
By Second Trust Deed		
By Assignment of Trust Deed		
PRO-RATIONS MADE AS OF		
Taxes for ½ year $ paid to		
Personal Property Taxes		
Taxes paid		
$ Ins. expiring Premium $		
New Insurance Premium		
Interest on $ @ % paid to		
Rent @ $ per paid to		
Commission paid to		
Policy of Title Insurance		
U.S. Internal Revenue Stamps		
Recording Deed		
Recording Trust Deed		
Recording		
Conveyancing $ Notary $		
Processing Charge		
Termite Inspection $ Termite Work $		
Principal of Encumbrance paid to		
Interest @ from to		
Prepayment Charges		
Forwarding Fee		
Reconveyance Fee		
Loan Trust Fund		
Principal of Encumbrance paid to		
Interest @ from to		
Reconveyance Fee		
Loan Discount Fee $ Loan Fee $		
Credit Report $ Tax Service $		
Tax Reserve $ Fire Ins. Reserve $		
Appraisal Fee		
Interest @ $ paid to		
BALANCE DUE YOU FOR WHICH OUR CHECK IS ENCLOSED		
TOTALS		

Figure 12–2 Escrow Statement. *(Stewart Title Guaranty Company, Houston)*

POLICY OF TITLE INSURANCE ISSUED BY

STEWART TITLE
GUARANTY COMPANY

SUBJECT TO SCHEDULE B AND THE CONDITIONS AND STIPULATIONS HEREOF, STEWART TITLE GUARANTY COMPANY, a Texas corporation, herein called the Company, insures the insured, as of Date of Policy shown in Schedule A, against loss or damage, not exceeding the amount of insurance stated in Schedule A, and costs, attorneys' fees and expenses which the Company may become obligated to pay hereunder, sustained or incurred by said insured by reason of:

1. Title to the estate or interest described in Schedule A being vested other than as stated therein;
2. Any defect in or lien or encumbrance on such title;
3. Unmarketability of such title; or
4. Any lack of the ordinary right of an abutting owner for access to at least one physically open street or highway if the land, in fact, abuts upon one or more such streets or highways;

and in addition, as to an insured lender only:

5. Invalidity of the lien of the insured mortgage upon said estate or interest except to the extent that such invalidity, or claim thereof, arises out of the transaction evidenced by the insured mortgage and is based upon
   a. usury, or
   b. any consumer credit protection or truth in lending law;
6. Priority of any lien or encumbrance over the lien of the insured mortgage, said mortgage being shown in Schedule B in the order of its priority; or
7. Invalidity of any assignment of the insured mortgage, provided such assignment is shown in Schedule B.

COPY

Signed under seal for the Company, but this Policy is to be valid only when it bears an authorized countersignature.

Sanctity of Contract

STEWART TITLE
GUARANTY COMPANY

Countersigned:

STEWART TITLE GUARANTY CO. INCORPORATED 1908 TEXAS

Chairman

President

Authorized Countersignature

Page 1 of
Policy Serial No. CNJP

Figure 12–3 Specimen Policy of Title Insurance. *(Stewart Title Guaranty Company, Houston)* value or just the amount of the mortgage. The latter is the usual case.

The escrow or handling fees for the real estate sales transaction are usually standard and not subject to much negotiation with the escrow agent. However, you may attempt to reduce the cost of title insurance. The one-time premium runs about $200 for a $30,000 home. If the house has been previously sold within the last few years, there is less public-record searching for liens and encumbrances to be done by the title company. If the property is already insured by the same company, they are not taking much additional risk and may well accept a lower premium. The buyer has his choice of title companies; he can use this as a lever to reduce his closing costs. He can always choose a different title company if the company refuses to negotiate the costs involved.

Home Purchase Price

You should attempt to negotiate with the seller for a lower purchase price without considering the mortgage negotiations, which are separate. Prices of similar houses, the seller's desire for a quick sale, and any defects in the house may affect the price. The final price may also be affected by escrow fees.

Standard procedure, legal and customary, historically divides the escrow fee transactions between the buyer and seller according to local formula. The participants do not have to abide by this formula because they can agree privately to a different arrangement. This alternative will normally take the form of an increase or decrease in the sales price of the home to compensate the payer of the fees required in the escrow transaction. For example, the seller may increase the sale price of the house if he is required to pay most of the escrow costs. Likewise, the buyer may secure a lower purchase price if he is required to pay most of the closing costs because of local procedure.

REAL ESTATE AS AN INVESTMENT

If your life-style is not compatible with home-ownership, you can still receive many benefits by purchasing a condominium or by investing in real estate for income or appreciation. Homeowners also can purchase other real estate as their investment medium.

There is a rather firm belief that you cannot make an investment mistake in real estate because inflationary and population pressures tend to increase the value (or price) of existing and new construction; leverage and easy credit allow access to more expensive properties and greater profits; and real estate management is easily understood and foolproof. While these advantages are generalities ascribed to real estate by realtors and other promoters, they are not necessarily true for a particular person or a particular piece of property. As with any other investment, you must thoroughly investigate the possibilities and evaluate the specifics of a particular property. You will invest in a particular real property for one or more of these main reasons:

1. Income
2. Price appreciation
3. Tax advantages

After looking at different real estate investments, we will analyze a specific property for profit potential.

Types of Investment

In addition to home-ownership, which is the most prevalent form of real estate investment, there are many other opportunities available to persons who seek the relative security inherent in real estate. Among the investment possibilities are residential property, commercial property, unimproved or raw land, farms, real estate syndicates, real estate investment trusts, real estate companies, and mortgage lending.

Residential property Any real property that people live in and pay rent for may be considered an investment. Homes, condominiums, duplexes, apartments, and vacation cabins meet this definition. The investment possibility is determined primarily by current and future income, property appreciation, or a combination of both. Size, neighborhood, and local vacancy factor determine rental income and, to a degree, property appreciation. Multi-unit structures and higher-priced, single-unit residences generally provide a greater return on investment through both income and price appreciation.

Commercial property Business and industrial property is considered commercial income property. Zoning becomes important to the investor if he wishes to choose a particular type of renter or lessee. Generally, commercial property returns higher rents than residential property and is more likely to provide stable, long-term leases from financially solvent tenants.

Land For the average investor, raw, unimproved land without buildings tends to be a more speculative investment than residential or commercial property. He must anticipate where housing demand and development will occur. Often it is hard to rent such land for income unless some commercial use can be found for it. Usually land investors end up with a monthly outgo for mortgage payments and taxes, and no income. They hope for growth and a generous capital gain, which require population increases and urbanization. In recent years, land developers have been pushing resort properties, many of which have failed. These properties may make good vacation homes, but are seldom good investments.

Farms Both income and growth are possible from a farm investment. The property can be leased for a flat sum or it can be share-cropped for a portion of the farming profits. Price appreciation may occur because the value may increase due to urbanization, inflation, and agricultural trends. The average investor is least likely to have a knowledge of farm values, so close investigation and good counsel are needed.

Real estate syndicates Limited partnerships provide the relatively small investor with the chance to own a portion of a large real estate complex. These syndicates offer the advantages of accelerated depreciation when investing in multi-unit residential property, which in turn provides a tax-free cash flow. As long as the basic property is paying for itself, this is a good deal. Unfortunately, this type of investment offers little diversification and no liquidity whatsoever. It is at the mercy of the syndicate's managerial judgment. Again, thorough investigation and good advice are needed.

Real estate investment trusts These trusts pool the money of the small investor. They are similar to a closed-end investment company; they might be considered real estate mutual funds. REITs can invest only in real property and in mortgages. They tend to spread the risk over a number of different properties and mortgages, including construction loans.

Real estate investment trusts are often

subsidiaries of major banks and insurance companies and may be listed on major stock exchanges. In addition to the advantages of diversification and professional management, they have the added advantage of the same liquidity that you would find in a mutual fund. Special tax considerations accrue to the REIT if it follows certain IRS rules, such as distributing 90 percent of its income to shareholders, limiting its capital gains to 30 percent of its gross income, and not directly managing any property. Your stockbroker can give you more details and recommend various REITs. Recently many of these organizations have been caught in the squeeze of high construction costs and high interest rates.

Real estate companies These are corporations in which an investor can buy common stock. No special tax break is available to them, nor must they follow the IRS rules for REITs. They can retain their earnings if they so desire and speculate by purchasing and selling real estate for capital gains profit. There is no limit on capital gains earnings. Corporations that specialize in investment of real estate are really an alternative form of securities investment. There is no direct real estate tax benefit, only the chance to receive income from corporate dividends or capital gains or losses from the sale of the stock in the real estate company.

Mortgage lending First or second mortgage lending is a peripheral method of real estate investment. The idea is not to create ownership of property but to provide a fixed-rate interest investment (a loan) secured by real estate. Upon default of a loan and after following prescribed legal procedures, the investor may foreclose on a loan and secure title to mortgaged property.

High interest rates characterize second mortgages, as mentioned earlier. As a lender/investor you can expect to receive interest approximating 10 percent. You can procure your own second mortgage business by dealing directly with people in need of financing. Often a notice in the classified newspaper advertisements will solicit many inquiries, as will personal contacts with realtors.

Another method, especially in your first endeavor, is to use the services of a commercial second mortgage loan broker. These organizations are often home loan companies. They offer loans from $500 to $25,000, requiring the borrower's real property for collateral. They usually lend the money in their name and then sell the loan certificate to private investors. You generally get 10 percent interest less a service fee.

Real Estate Investment Evaluation

Proper evaluation of an investment property includes many considerations. Since the objective is to make a profit from operating income, price appreciation, or both, the property must be appraised as accurately as possible to determine what the property is worth to you. The three most common appraisal methods are: (1) income value, (2) fair market value, and (3) replacement value. There are various modifications to these methods, but they do point out the different approaches to the same problem. An investor may appraise the same property, using each method as a double or triple check.

Income value A property that earns a reasonable income on your equity is probably a sound investment. You can estimate annual income and expenses rather accurately. These figures can also be projected over a five- to ten-year period. If the property is already used for income, you may have actual figures to work with; otherwise you can compare income and expense figures from comparable property.

Actual income value is determined by the rate of return on your investment. Net figures are used. You divide the annual net earnings by the amount of your net investment. For example, if the property nets $2,000 per year and you have to invest $40,000, you would be getting a return of 5 percent annually. This procedure does not provide the investor with an accurate idea of the value of the property unless you compare the income value with other investments. Five percent makes a rather poor comparison with savings.

We have not taken leverage, financing, taxes, operating costs, growth, or property management into consideration. All of these have a bearing on your rate of return. These items will have to be investigated as soon as we look at the other methods of real estate appraisal.

Fair market value The easiest method of real estate appraisal is fair market value. It simply means that property is valued at a price consistent with similar properties in an area.

Replacement value Lenders and insurers use replacement appraisal because of their prospective interests in possibly repossessing or replacing a building. It is primarily used for residential units. Building costs in each locality are determined on a square-foot basis. The size and type of building are used to weigh the cost per square foot. The weighted square-foot unit is then multiplied by the number of square feet in the building to determine the basic replacement cost. This amount is increased or decreased by above-average or below-average features in the home, such as kitchens, bathrooms, family rooms, fireplaces, basements, garages, and similar items. Finally, the current market value of the lot is added to the replacement cost of the dwelling to give a true appraisal of the property.

Investment Objective

Obviously you should not pay more for a property than it is worth. All you can really do is secure an accurate estimate of what the property is worth and proceed with your analysis. However, first you must determine what your investment objectives are in terms of growth (price appreciation), income, and tax advantages. The evaluation methods used tend to reflect your objectives. The property you select should definitely reflect your specific real estate objectives.

Growth There is every reason to believe that real estate prices will continue to rise. Inflation and population pressures will help continue the upward spiral. Only those properties that are of intrinsically poor quality or are located in a declining neighborhood will not rise along with prices in general. Even in these cases, if you can buy at an extremely low price, you may still have price appreciation. This is why property appraisal is so important.

Inflation usually causes rents to increase, which in turn causes greater price-level pressure on all dwellings. Renters hunt for a residence that they can purchase, and investors hunt for property that will provide a good rental return on their investment.

Property values are affected by changes in zoning, traffic patterns, and neighborhood population patterns. This can be detrimental. Property can also decline in value. Older properties tend to reflect the aggregate changes more clearly than newer properties. On a national average, single-family dwellings under twenty-five years old often sell for 100 to 150 times their monthly rental value, while homes over twenty-five years old bring only 75 to 125 times their monthly rental value. These prices generally reflect maintenance expectations and housing fashions in addition to the aggregate changes mentioned earlier.

You should also consider that real estate is a rather nonliquid investment. It is relatively hard to turn to cash quickly. Only if you have plenty of time can you afford to wait for your cash price.

Income A real estate investment earns income through rent. The net income after expenses should be sufficiently high to justify the purchase or continued holding of the property for income. Other alternative investments including savings will prove more attractive to the investor if a high rate of rental return is not available.

Income property is especially subject to the *financial risk* of having its earning power decline because of any of a number of reasons:

1. You may not be able to rent the property.
2. You may not receive the amount of rent anticipated.
3. Your expenses may be higher than expected.

These specific risk problems are intertwined not only with specific localities, but also with the problems of management.

All real estate investment requires some management, but income property requires considerably more supervision than most types of investment. You may manage your own income property or have a realtor or other professional manage your property for either a flat fee or a percentage of gross rents. Some of the management problems that must be overcome include such items as:

1. Determining the amount of rent
2. Selecting tenants
3. Collecting rents
4. Controlling expenses
5. Physically maintaining the property

The first-time rental buyer should thoroughly investigate these problem areas and get a "feel" for income property management by talking to someone who has tried such an investment. Many investors are not psychologically equipped to handle a real estate investment properly.

Tax advantages Whether your investment objective is income or price appreciation, you will receive some tax advantages from real estate investment. Persons in higher income-tax brackets often invest in real estate that takes a "paper" loss through depreciation in order to reduce their personal income tax on their ordinary income. The basic tax advantages in real estate investment are capital gains and depreciation allowance.

Capital gains are derived from price appreciation resulting from selling your property for more than you paid for it. Actually the capital gain is the difference between the selling price and the tax basis of your property. The tax basis will be different from the original purchase price because actual or allowed depreciation must be subtracted from the original cost, while improvement costs would be added.

As you have already learned, the tax advantage of a capital gain is that if the property has been held for more than six months, any gain will be taxed on only one-half of the dollar amount of the gain. The rest of your income, including rents, is fully taxable. As mentioned in chapter 11, this tax advantage promotes investment. Look at this example. If you purchase income property for $30,000 and sell it for $45,000 five years later, the transaction would appear thus:

Add net selling price:		
Selling price	$45,000	
Less cost of sale	2,700	$42,300
Less tax basis:		
Purchase price	30,000	
Less depreciation	5,000	25,000
Long-term capital gain:		$17,300

You would show only $8,650 as taxable income, a 50 percent savings in taxes. If you are in the 30 percent tax bracket the extra capital gain income is taxed at $2,595 ($8,650 × .30). In comparison, ordinary income in the same amount would be taxed at $5,190, or twice the amount.

A further advantage when selling real estate at a profit is the *installment sale concept*. Under IRS rules the capital gain becomes taxable only as the proceeds are collected. This procedure defers the tax and avoids an unusually high income-tax bracket in the year of sale. It allows the capital gain income to be averaged over the years it is actually received.

The *depreciation allowance* represents a major tax advantage, because it allows the investor to recapture a portion of a business property cost or the potential replacement cost on an annual basis. Depreciation is an expense of doing business because buildings and machines do become less valuable as they wear out with use. Land does not depreciate; only the improvements (buildings, etc.) on it depreciate.

Depreciation may be apportioned equally over the life of the business asset, or it may be allowed in greater amounts during the first few years of ownership. Equal apportionment is called the straight-line method of depreciation. Accelerated methods of depreciation are called the declining balance method and the sum-of-the-digits method. Further explanation of these methods appeared in chapter 11. The depreciation in the capital gain example was arrived at as follows:

Property cost	$30,000	
Less land value	5,000	
Adjusted price of property		$25,000
Estimated life of asset	25 years	
Annual depreciation ($25,000 ÷ 25 yrs.)	$1,000	
Depreciation taken during period of ownership (5 yrs.)	$5,000	

Since you were in the 30 percent tax bracket, you save $300 on taxes annually by taking a $1,000 depreciation expense deduction from the operating income of your investment property. This is an ordinary income deduction resulting in a savings of $1,500 in taxes over five years. By *not* taking the depreciation, you would save only $750 in taxes at the time of sale. The extra $5,000 in capital gains is taxed on only $2,500 with less tax savings as a result.

Financing Your Investment

Earlier in the chapter we discussed financing your home. The financing of business and rental property involves the same considerations. You must find a lender and negotiate with him. The mortgage interest rate, amount of the mortgage, the down payment, the term of the loan, loan fees and points, prepayment rights, and impound accounts are all worth the negotiating and shopping effort. Conventional loans are used to finance most business property.

One of the biggest problems in real estate investment is that large sums of money are needed to purchase property. Common stock and savings investments, on the other hand, can be made with much less capital. However, mortgage financing can be arranged to amortize the principal balance after a down payment is made. The borrowed amount is someone else's money used to generate income for you; this procedure is known as using leverage.

The leverage concept The ratio of other funds to yours is the leverage ratio. The greater the ratio, the greater will be your return, provided you can earn more than the interest cost for the borrowed money. This is not always easy to do. The income generated by a highly mortgaged, expensive piece of property may not be enough to make the mortgage payments. Since mortgage payments are fixed, you may lose your property because you cannot afford to pay the difference out of your own funds indefinitely. Leverage can be risky if the ratio is too high.

When you have a rental property with *stable income,* you can be reasonably safe with a high leverage ratio. A simplified example of leverage is provided by your purchase of a $30,000 single-family residence for income purposes. If you receive $300 per month rental, the annual gross income would be $3,600. After taxes of $700, you would net $2,900, assuming no other expenses. On your investment of $30,000 you would realize a rate of return of 9.67 percent ($2,900 ÷ 30,000). If you had negotiated an 80 percent mortgage at 8 percent, you would be borrowing $24,000 with a down payment of $6,000. This is a 4:1 leverage ratio. Your annual interest payments would be $1,920, which must be deducted from your gross income along with taxes. Your net on your investment of $6,000 is $980 ($3,600 – $1,920 – $700). This amounts to a return of 16.33 percent ($980 ÷ 6,000) on your actual cash outlay.

In effect, you have been able to earn a higher rate of return on a smaller investment. You can use your remaining $24,000 for other investments. Theoretically, you could buy four more $30,000 properties using the same leverage. Each would then return $980 net income annually. Multiply this by five houses and your total net return is $4,900 on a $30,000 investment using leverage as compared to $2,900 for one house without leverage. Again, the rates of return are 16.3 percent and 9.7 percent respectively. These are approximate figures with assumptions. Unfortunately, you cannot expect to find similar investments so neatly packaged. We have not yet considered depreciation, closing costs, loan fees, and operating expenses, nor have we weighed the possibility of price appreciation and rental increases.

Rental Property Financial Analysis

Much of the profit motive surrounding real estate involves the financial operations of the rental enterprise. Cash flow, leverage, depreciation, out-of-pocket expenses, and rental income all play an important part in the financial analysis of real property. We will look at the annual financial operation of the $30,000, single-family rental unit. Original closing costs and loan fees are included. The land is valued at $5,000, the building at $25,000. A $24,000 mortgage at

8 percent is on the property, which has an anticipated gross rental income of $300 per month. No vacancy loss is anticipated.

Estimated annual income statement The financial operations of a business enterprise over a period of time, normally a year, are reported in an accounting document called the income statement. It deserves critical analysis before investing for income. We will estimate the first-year financial operation of the rental unit as follows:

Gross income (12 × $300 monthly rental)		$3,600
Less expenses:		
Utilities (12 × $30)	$ 360	
Taxes	700	
Insurance	75	
Maintenance/repair (1% of building)	250	
Depreciation ($25,000 ÷ 25 yrs)	1000	
Total expenses		2,385
Net income from property		$1,215
Less interest on $24,000 mortgage at 8%		1,920
Net loss on $6,000 owner equity		($ 705)

At this point the analysis shows a loss because you have $685 direct operating expenses that we did not count in our prior example. We only considered taxes at $700. We also did not deduct $1,000 for depreciation.

Cash flow Cash flow is the actual money flowing into and out of a business. Cash flow analysis will indicate the amount of money that is actually available to the investor through the operation of the business. It will indicate whether the business generates enough funds to be self-sufficient or whether the investor must plan on adding out-of-pocket capital to the business in order to remain solvent.

In our example, out-of-pocket (cash) expenses still would amount to $1,385. Cash flow includes the actual mortgage payments of $2,248.32, the annual amount fully amortizing a loan of $24,000 at 8 percent for 25 years. An amortization schedule would be needed to break down the annual mortgage into separate principal and interest payment amounts. Our example will continue to show $1,920 as the annual interest with the balance of $328.32 as payment toward the principal.

Income	*Outgo*	
$3,600 rents	$1,385	cash expenses
	2,248	mortgage payment
$3,600	$3,633	
Operating cash loss:	($33)	

Note that the operating statement loss ($705) differs from the cash flow loss ($33). For income statements and for tax purposes you do not show the total mortgage payment because a portion of the payment represents a contribution to principal—your installment purchase. It is neither income nor operational expense. The owner's principal contribution becomes important only when you wish to know the extent of your investment in an asset for purposes of sale, refinancing, or calculating a rate of return.

In our example, you are losing money at the moment. The $33 loss is an out-of-pocket loss. The $705 "paper loss" would be subtracted from your other source of income for tax purposes. If you are in the 30 percent tax bracket, you would pay $212 less income tax because of your "paper loss." You would have an investment that is likely to appreciate in value to provide a capital gain. It will become self-sustaining, given a stable demand for rentals, no major repairs, a continued shortage of single-family dwellings, and inflation at an annual rate of 5 percent or more.

Rental property appreciation We have considered the possibility of price appreciation over the years. Let us apply a conservative forecast for growth. In the capital gains illustration we had the property appreciate at the simple annual rate of 10 percent. We will now conservatively figure price appreciation at 7.5 percent compounded annually (5 percent inflation and 2.5 percent demand):

Cost	$30,000	
Appreciation at 7.5% for 5 years	13,069	
Market value		$43,069
Gross sale price		43,000
Less 6% sales commission	2,580	
Other sale costs	420	3,000
Net sale price		40,000
Less cost		30,000
Net gain		$10,000

To figure your *rate of return* on your five-year investment you would divide your net gain by your investment:

Down payment	$6,000	
Principal payments	1,250	(approximate)
Cash input requirements	165	($33 × 5 years)
Five-year total investment	$7,415	

$\$10,000 \div 7,415 = 134.86\%$ total
$135\% \div 5$ years $= 27\%$ annual yield

Your *cash flow* on the sale will be the net sale price ($40,000), less mortgage balance ($22,750), less marginal income tax ($2,700). This will be approximately $14,550.

To figure your *marginal income tax* on your capital gain you would have to recapture your depreciation since the property has appreciated:

Add:	Net sale price		$40,000
Less:	Purchase price	$30,000	
	Less depreciation	5,000	25,000
	Long-term capital gain		$15,000
Net cash profit before taxes			$17,250
Taxable gain (50% of $15,000) = $7,500			
Amount of tax payable for person in 36% tax bracket*			2,700
Net cash profit after taxes			$14,550

Summarizing Your Real Estate Investment

Rental property has the possibility of producing income or at least providing a self-sustaining cash flow in most cases. Rents should go up faster than expenses because mortgage payments, your biggest expense, remain relatively stable. As rents increase and inflation and demand for property continue, your property will rise in value. This actually increases the rate of return on your investment because you have purchased the property using fixed mortgage financing. You hopefully garner big gains from a small original investment. Finally, in addition to income and growth possibilities, real estate provides considerable tax advantages.

Real estate cannot be considered a "surefire" investment. Income may not materialize, or expenses may be too great to provide a positive cash flow. If you carry too big a mortgage for the income potential, you may be forced to sell if you cannot provide out-of-pocket cash to cover unexpected expenses

* Taxable gain of $7,500 will probably move you from 30 percent to 36 percent tax bracket.

caused by some misfortune. Finally, your real estate investment may not increase in value. Also, you may take a loss when trying to sell it quickly; real estate is not as liquid as securities or savings.

Vocabulary and Concepts

Appreciation	Installment sale
Cash flow	Leverage
Closing costs	Mortgage
Condominium	Points
Cooperative apartments	Prepayment penalty
Depreciation	Real estate investment trust
Down payment	Refinancing
Escrow	Title insurance
Impound account	

Questions for Discussion

1. Compare all the advantages and disadvantages of renting vs. buying. When is it economically feasible to purchase?
2. How do you go about assuming an existing mortgage loan?
3. What is the difference among F.H.A., V.A., and conventional mortgage loans?
4. What is a variable mortgage loan?
5. Name the various items that are worth negotiating when arranging for the purchase and financing of a home.
6. What are the usual sources of real estate mortgage money?
7. What are the possible financial consequences of speculating in unimproved land purchases? Explain in detail.
8. What is meant by cash flow in a rental property? How is it determined?
9. Explain how a rate of return can be projected in the purchase of income property.
10. Discuss how to get $10,000 equity out of a $50,000 home with a $30,000 first deed of trust. Which would be less costly, a second mortgage or refinancing the present mortgage?

Projects

1. Price the various types of housing available in your locale. What other considerations must you make besides price?
2. Contact two competing lenders from each type of mortgage lender. Compare these mortgage rates in your area.
3. Answer an advertisement for the purchase of a duplex. Determine the cash flow and tax situation by applying financial analysis procedures.
4. There is more involved in a home purchase than the down payment and closing costs. Visit an open house or model home. Estimate the fix-up and furniture expenses necessary to make the property "livable."

Case Problem

Art and Barbara Able are considering the purchase of a new residence one mile from Art's office. They can sell their present home for $55,000 with selling expenses of $4,000. It has a mortgage of $18,000. The new three-bedroom condominium is selling for $75,000. They can get a $60,000 mortgage at 9 percent for 30 years or a $50,000 mortgage at 8 percent for 25 years. The monthly payments including impound accounts will be $600 at 9 percent and $500 at 8 percent. Closing costs and some new furnishings will come to $5,000. Can the Ables afford the new residence? Do they have enough cash? How will their budget be affected? What do you recommend and why?

13

the stock market

Our free-enterprise system allows businesses and consumers an enormous choice of what goods and services to produce and to use. The choices are usually made in an economic context, one based on profits and benefits in relation to value. Furthermore, our system promotes private ownership of property and the means of productivity. This is called capitalism. Money, called capital, is needed to purchase equipment and property and to own and operate businesses. Businesses need capital and actively seek it from many sources. Individuals, on the other hand, often have money available to invest in savings and other profitable endeavors. The stock market performs a very valuable economic service by bringing business and the investor together. The stock market provides access to capital for businesses and access to investment for investors.

CAPITAL NEEDS

Corporations have more assets than any other type of business organization, and they are the biggest users of capital. They attempt to gather capital funds in large quantities at the lowest possible cost. Basically they have two methods to generate their needed capital: they may use equity funding or debt funding.

Equity Funding

Funds invested by shareholders are called equity. These funds form the bulk of capital needed to organize, operate, and expand a corporation. Individual shareholder equity in a corporation is based on the number of shares issued. For example, if a company has 100,000 shares outstanding and you own 10,000 shares, you own 10 percent of the company. Whenever a corporation desires extra funds that would not create a creditor claim against its assets, it seeks funds from present shareholders first and then offers ownership shares to outside investors.

Equity funds may also be raised by the device of *retained earnings.* This occurs whenever the after-tax earnings are not distributed to the stockholders in the form of dividends but are retained by the corporation for working capital purposes. Retained earnings are profits that are plowed back into the corporation in the form of cash or other assets. This increases the asset value of the company, which theoretically increases the value of each share of stock outstanding. Retained earnings might be considered a form of pay-as-you-go financing.

Debt Funding

Sometimes the present shareholders do not wish to increase the amount of shares outstanding, which could possibly dilute their current ownership percentage and profit-sharing potential. Sometimes only a relatively small amount of capital is needed. Sometimes current or prospective investors cannot be enticed to contribute more capital by purchase of a new issue of stock because of money market or stock market conditions. Whenever any such situation occurs, it is usually more desirable for the corporation to borrow the funds that it needs. The borrowed funds may be long-term bonds or shorter-term notes. In either case, borrowed funds create a claim against earnings that must be satisfied before residual profits can be paid to shareholders. Debt financing does not create a permanent claim, since the principal will eventually be repaid by the maturity date. The corporate earnings beyond the fixed interest repayment amount accrue to the current shareholders and do not have to be shared with any new shareholders.

INVESTMENT NEEDS

Private individuals, businesses, financial organizations, and private and government institutions often have funds that are not immediately needed for living or operational purposes. These funds must be put to work to earn a return for their owner. Not to do so would create waste and inefficiency and make the owner suffer an inflation loss. Savings deposits, loans, and ownership investment constitute the usual placement of these funds. Savings institutions absorb the savings deposits and then recirculate the funds throughout the economy by lending. Many more loans and ownership investments are bought and sold in the securities market. Bonds represent loan (debt) investment, while stocks represent ownership investment. Distribution of these securities is handled in the primary and secondary investment markets.

PRIMARY MARKETS

Corporations occasionally sell new securities directly to the public. Because of the logistics involved, direct sales are confined to present stockholders and a few large institutional buyers. Usually the marketing of new securities for corporations and government is conducted by investment banks. New-issue transactions constitute the primary market, the first issuance of securities to raise money for a corporation or government entity. A new issue must be accompanied by a *prospectus,* a booklet that describes the company, its officers, its assets, the number of shares of stock authorized and outstanding, the rights of stockholders, the intended use of the proceeds, and the price per share of the new issue. The prospectus is required by the Securities and Exchange Commission.

Underwriting the Offer

Investment bankers raise capital for companies by underwriting the security offer. This procedure occurs when the underwriter purchases the entire issue for resale or guarantees to purchase the balance of any issue that cannot be readily sold to the public. Since the securities offering to raise capital may range from $100,000 to $100,000,000, no one investment banker can successfully handle the responsibility. An underwriting syndicate is then formed to share the risks and profits of the offering.

Rights and Warrants

Rights and warrants basically provide the same investment function; they are options to purchase shares of stock. *Rights* are usually issued to existing shareholders to allow them to purchase additional shares of stock whenever a new issue is offered. Company bylaws often give existing shareholders the *preemptive right* to maintain their proportionate ownership in the company. The company must offer the new shares to the present shareholders first. A certificate is sent to the shareholder of record indicating the number of shares, the cost, and the date that the right terminates. The shareholder may then exercise his rights and purchase his allotment of the new shares, or he may sell the rights to other investors, who may then do the same thing. *Warrants* are options to purchase stock at a set price during a stated period of time. Warrants differ from rights in that they are usually given with the original sale of bonds or preferred stock to sweeten the deal, or with a corporate merger to secure approval. Warrants remain in effect for a longer period of time than rights, because rights are used to help subscribe new issues of common stock and must be exercised quickly (usually within thirty days). Both rights and warrants have value.

Valuing Your Option

You may exercise your option by purchasing the stock, or you may sell your option, or you may do nothing and lose the value of the right or warrant when it expires. Theoretically, the value of a right or warrant can be determined by mathematical formula; practically, the value can be determined by checking the market price. Rights and warrants are usually sold on the same stock exchange as the underlying common stock.

The market value of a common stock "rights-on" (with rights) includes the value of the rights. The stock loses value when the stock goes "rights-off" or "ex-rights." The theoretical value of the right is the difference between the market value of the present stock traded on an exchange and the offering price of the new issue. Stocks with and without warrants are valued in the same manner. Warrants, however, are normally separate from the underlying stock and offer the owner the option to subscribe to one share of common stock for each warrant. Warrants will be listed separately in the stock quotation.

SECONDARY MARKETS

The subsequent buying and selling of securities by owners of securities is called the secondary or continuing market. It is comprised of organized stock exchanges, brokerage houses, and securities dealers that provide wholesale and retail trading centers. When people talk about the stock market, it is really the secondary market that they are discussing. The overwhelming majority of stocks and bonds that are for sale are previously owned. Once stocks and bonds have been originally sold by the issuing corporation, it receives no further cash from subsequent sales. The owner of the shares receives the sale price. There is an analogy in the automobile sales market—when the auto is first sold, the manufacturer makes a sales profit; when it is later resold or traded, the car owner or dealer receives the sales price.

Liquidity

The secondary market apparatus offers the investor the chance to meet at least two investment objectives: liquidity and either growth or income, perhaps both. The whole concept of the secondary market is to provide a trading forum for the investor. Any investor who wishes to buy, sell, or trade may do so quickly. Usually your transaction will be consummated within one hour of contacting your broker. There is always a ready market for securities. This liquidity adds to the value of your investment. You know that it can be converted to cash quickly if your price is right.

Theoretically, you can buy and sell stock yourself for whatever price someone is willing to sell or pay for it. Unfortunately, it would be rather hard to find someone who wanted to sell or buy the particular stock you have in mind. This inability to find a trading partner brought rise to the secondary securities market. Brokers and organized exchanges make up the key elements of the securities market. The actual market places, both wholesale and retail, exchange and broker-dealer, exist to provide a market trading post and serve the needs of the investor. Brokers charge a commission for their services, which are basically to provide liquidity for the investor by providing a trading partner and handling the details of the transfer. By looking at the niche occupied by brokers and stock exchanges, we will get an overall idea of how the securities market works.

Brokers

A stockbroker is licensed to buy and sell securities for himself, his brokerage house, and for clients. He is well versed in the concepts and methodology of the securities markets because of a thorough training program at the brokerage house he represents. Stockbrokers are also known as account executives and registered representatives. These more professional titles reflect the range of services and types of securities transacted by the broker. They buy and sell listed and unlisted common stocks, preferred stocks, corporate bonds, government securities, mutual funds, and commodity futures.

Brokerage Firms and Securities Dealers

The term *brokerage* means being in a business as agent, middleman, or a representative of another for a commission. A dealer buys and sells for his own account and risk. Brokerage firms should really be called broker-dealers. The brokerage house usually represents its clients in the securities market place, which consists of organized or unorganized exchanges, but may represent itself after first servicing the client. Brokerage firms deal with each other directly and join national and regional organized stock exchanges to carry out the orders of their clients. Often known as securities dealers, brokerage firms are listed in the Yellow Pages under the heading of Stock and Bond Brokers.

THE OVER-THE-COUNTER MARKET

Whenever brokers deal directly with each other they are said to be in the over-the-counter market (OTC). Actually any security transaction not made on an organized exchange takes place over the counter. Any buyer or seller, not just dealers, may participate in OTC transactions. Institutions, corporations, estates, trusts, unions, individuals, and all types of organizations with investment funds or securities participate regularly. All private placement transactions may be considered OTC even if they consist of listed securities, meaning that any stock, bond, or negotiable government security may be handled OTC. New issues are always transacted in the over-the-counter market.

Until 1971, the OTC market was mainly a loose-knit network of securities dealers who contacted each other to buy and sell the securities of the forty thousand corporations not listed on any exchange. Dealers would telephone or telegraph around to buy or sell specific securities for their clients. This procedure is still carried out with the many less actively traded stocks. The National Association of Securities Dealers (NASD) has now developed an automated quotation system (NASDAQ) that provides instant computer communication to its member firms on over three thousand OTC stocks.

Making a Market

Dealers specialize in making a market in a few of the actively traded OTC stocks. They carry these stocks in inventory and sell them to investors on a negotiated basis. Any dealer making a market in an OTC stock must be willing to trade in the stock actively. He will buy it at a quoted *bid price* and sell it at a quoted *asked price*. The spread between the bid and asked price is part of the dealer's profit. Dealers also receive brokerage commissions on all securities transactions.

THE ORGANIZED STOCK EXCHANGES

Organized exchanges came into being because of the inconvenience of trying to find a trading partner for a particular stock. Organized exchanges may be considered as wholesale trading locations, while dealers' branches may be considered the retail outlets. Only securities formally listed with the exchange may be traded on the floor of an exchange and then only by members of the exchange. Members may be partners or officers in brokerage and investment firms, or they may be wealthy individual investors. Members must buy a seat (membership) on the exchange. Presently seats on the New York Stock Exchange are selling for about $200,000.

There are a number of stock exchanges throughout the country. By far the largest is the New York Stock Exchange (NYSE), followed by the American Stock Exchange (Amex), also located in New York City. Smaller exchanges are located in Chicago, San Francisco, Los Angeles, Toronto, Boston, Detroit, Honolulu, and other metropolitan centers. These smaller exchanges trade a combination of securities ranging from regional companies to national corporations that are already traded on the NYSE and Amex. The Pacific Coast Exchange, which has trading floors in San Francisco and Los Angeles, offers a chance to trade listed securities for two hours after the big exchanges are closed because of the East Coast–West Coast time difference. Currently, the NYSE and Amex are open 10:00 A.M. to 4:00 P.M. EDT. Sometimes large blocks of listed stocks move on regional exchanges so as not to affect dramatically the price on the NYSE or Amex.

The New York Stock Exchange

The NYSE traces its history back to 1792. The oldest and largest stock exchange in the country does a sales volume in excess of $140 billion. There are approximately 1,300 corporations listed on the exchange with a total of 1,700 common and preferred stocks traded. Another 1,200 bonds are traded on the New York Bond Exchange, which is a part of the NYSE.

The most widely held and best-known corporations have their securities listed on the NYSE. To be eligible for listing on the exchange, a company must agree to make public an annual report about its corporate and financial affairs and must meet the following criteria:

1. Earnings before taxes of $2.5 million
2. Tangible net assets of $16 million
3. One million publicly held shares
4. Two thousand shareholders owning at least 100 shares

In addition to the above requirements, a company pays an initial listing fee of $25,000 and must be approved by the NYSE board of governors, who look at a company in terms of its reputation, stability, market quality, and degree of nationwide interest in its stock. An annual review is made to insure that listed companies maintain their eligibility. An annual listing fee of $10,000 is charged.

The American Stock Exchange

As the second largest stock exchange, the Amex has a volume greater than all of the regionals combined, yet it does only a third of the volume of the NYSE. It specializes in smaller companies and those that are either new or less established than those on the NYSE. The requirements for listing on the Amex are less restrictive than those for the NYSE. Most companies that desire a national listing and are unable to qualify for the NYSE list on the Amex. These companies often have a great growth potential, and investors who wish to speculate or seek growth do so on the Amex.

MAJOR SECURITIES

Now that we have discussed how investment in securities benefits both the investment and the investor and have looked at the various institutions that accomplish this in the primary and secondary investment markets, we should look at the investments themselves. What are a common stock, a preferred stock, and a corporate bond? How can they be compared for income, capital gain potential, ownership, voting rights, and claims in case the company is liquidated?

Common Stock

All business corporations must have some common stock because this security represents the residual ownership in the corporation. Common stock has the basic voting control of a corporation and is entitled to all assets and earnings after debts are paid. Common stock is said to have the risks and successes of the enterprise. It receives the income from operations and the growth in value caused by price appreciation. As an investor, you would probably like safety, liquidity, income, and price appreciation in any stock investment that you make. You will have to determine your priorities within these objectives. Then, by understanding the classification and characteristics of various securities, you will be better prepared to make a decision based upon your objectives. At this point you can be reasonably sure that all common stock, like most securities, is a relatively liquid investment, but does it have safety, income, and growth characteristics?

Classification of Common Stock

Common stock is often classified in terms of its reaction in the market place rather than its investment objectives. It is given such names as blue-chip, speculative, glamour, defensive, and cyclical stock, in addition to the familiar terms of income or growth stocks.

Blue-chip stocks These are stocks of well-established companies and they offer minimal risks of investment. These stocks have consistent earnings records and long-term growth potential. They usually have a high price-earnings ratio because they are of good quality. Eastman Kodak, Sears, DuPont, and Standard Oil of New Jersey are typical of this category.

Speculative stocks If blue-chip stocks are not very risky, then speculative stocks are. They comprise securities of companies which are small, new, or whose chances of success are not established. While speculation is relative, you take a greater risk in stock that has not been tried or that has not proved very successful in the past. Stocks of mining companies, development companies, and newly emerging industries are usually found in this category.

Glamour stocks These are common stocks that are currently the upward movers in the market. They do fluctuate, but the primary trend is upward because of the industry they are in. Aerospace, electronics, energy, motor homes, and recreational equipment companies have been expanding and earning large profits. They were the latest group of successful speculative growth stocks.

Defensive stocks Defensive stocks are those whose price generally resists a primary decline in the stock market. They tend to be stocks that pay a high income or whose profits are only slightly affected by a recession. The rationale is that if they continue to pay a high yield, their price cannot drop too much because this would lower the price-earnings ratio, thereby making them appear more attractive. This would discourage selling, which depresses the price. They are countercyclical stocks that are bought as a hedge against a declining market. Banks and insurance companies tend to be defensive stocks.

Cyclical stocks The business cycle fluctuations tend to guide the movement of cyclical stocks. These stocks are primarily those of companies whose earnings reflect the economy, so their price rises or falls correspondingly. Generally, all stocks are affected by recession and expansion of the economy, but cyclicals are nearly congruent with the economy. Automotive, construction, machinery, and steel stocks are usually considered cyclical.

Income stocks Any stock that consistently pays a high percentage of its earnings to its owners in the form of dividends is considered an income stock. They differ from cyclical stocks in terms of consistency.

Income stocks usually have limited growth potential, but many are blue-chip investments. These are the securities of companies that offer staple products and services such as banking, beverages, food, and utilities.

Growth stocks The stocks of companies that have had a record of continued earnings over the last three to five years are generally considered growth stocks if they retain most of their earnings in the company for future growth. They usually pay very little in dividends. The market value of these stocks tends to rise steadily because of the plowback of earnings and the expectations of the investor. The price-earnings ratio tends to be high for the same reason. These stocks are traded with the expectation of capital gain rather than income. Glamour stocks are growth stocks that have caught the current attention of the investing public, but not all growth stocks may be considered glamour stocks.

Characteristics of Common Stock

All securities have certain common characteristics. For example, all common stock has certain corporate income, voting, and liquidation rights.

Corporate income Common stock has the ownership rights to all of a company's earnings after expenses and claims are satisfied. A stockholder's claim to income is essentially the same as any partnership or sole proprietorship with the exception that the shareholder must abide by the earnings distribution plan approved by the board of directors. Corporate profits are distributed by means of dividends. However, corporate directors are under no liability to declare and pay dividends. Company earnings may be retained for company use. Your rights of ownership, income, and loss are proportionate to your ownership share in the company.

Corporate ownership and control Since a common stockholder is the residual owner of the company, he should have a say in the management of the company. You, as owner, exercise your say by voting for the directors of the corporation on the basis of one vote for each share owned. Presumably the directors carry out the wishes of the majority of the shareowners. If you are unsatisfied with the decisions of one or more of the directors, you can theoretically vote them out of office at the annual meeting. You will need the concurrence of 50 percent of the shares voted. This is usually hard to achieve unless current management is doing an extremely poor job. Small shareholders have little say in corporate affairs because their ownership share is insignificant and unorganized. The time and expense involved usually does not justify your participation. However, you may vote by *proxy.* This is a legal procedure that allows a person to select someone to vote for him. Proxy votes are usually solicited by management to reelect the board of directors to continue the present policies and to get shareholder approval of major corporate programs. Disenchanted shareholders may challenge present management by soliciting your proxy to vote for a change of directors and a change in corporate policy. This challenging procedure results in a *proxy fight,* a struggle by opposing shareholders for management control of a company. Often this is done when outsiders buy in with the hope of improving the profitability of a company or when shareholders wish to change dividend policies.

Some corporations have a nonvoting class of stock. None of these securities are listed on the NYSE, and few are listed on the other exchanges. Nonvoting stock is issued with the intent of retaining control by the original shareholders while receiving the benefits of new equity capital.

Common shareholders are also entitled to maintain their pro rata ownership share in the company by common law. Unless the corporate charter bylaws expressly forbid it, this is a preemptive right and is unique to common stock.

Evidence of ownership is vested in a negotiable instrument known as a stock certificate. There is a trend toward developing a computer record of ownership; instead of receiving the actual stock certificate, a shareholder would receive a statement indicating the number of shares held.

A common stock certificate often has a par value indicated on its face. Par is the arbitrary value assigned by the issuing corporation. Most companies now issue no-par stock or low-par stock because par in common stock has no face-value significance.

Claims if business is dissolved Common stockholders have the residual ownership in the corporation in proportion to the number of shares that are outstanding. As a pro rata owner, you are entitled to your share of any remaining assets if the company is liquidated. As a matter of practicality, there is seldom much in the way of assets available after all creditor claims have been paid. Successful companies do not liquidate. Any distribution of assets upon liquidation is called a liquidating dividend. All possible assets are sold for cash (liquidated), and the money is disbursed to creditors and owners, in that order.

Preferred Stock

Preferred stock has an ownership interest in a corporation, but differs significantly from common stock and bonds. The ownership and claims status of preferred stock falls about halfway between a common stock and a corporate bond. Preferred is similar to common stock because preferred holders receive dividends and have "first owner" preference as to dividends and liquidating assets. It is similar to bonds because its shares usually receive a stated yield as listed on the certificate. It is a hybrid security.

Very little preferred stock has been issued by corporations in recent years because it is an expensive way to raise capital. Preferred dividends, and for that matter any dividend, must be paid from after-tax profit. Instead, most companies are selling bonds, which become a legal liability of the company and are an expense payable *before* taxes. Given the same dollar expense for bond payments and preferred dividends payments, the common stockholders will receive a greater residual of profits by using bond financing. The following example explains the concept:

	Financing by	
	Preferred	*Bond*
Operating income	$1,000	$1,000
less bond interest	0	−200
Taxable income	1,000	800
less income tax at 50% rate	500	400
After-tax profits	500	400
less preferred dividends	200	0
Common stockholder residual	$300	$400

Characteristics of Preferred Stock

Preferred stock may be traded over the counter or on the exchange where it is listed. In addition to income, corporate control, and liquidating characteristics, it has some rather unique features that make it more or less valuable than the same company's common stock. More than one class of preferred stock may be issued. They would be called first preferred, second preferred, and so on. Preference would be according to seniority. Different dividend rates could accompany each issue.

Corporate income Whenever the board of directors declares a dividend, it must do so for the company's preferred shareholders before declaring any dividend for common shareholders. Of course, all expenses including dividends must first be met. Sometimes preferred dividends are paid even though a company has not had a profitable year. Directors may use internally held funds to pay any type of dividend if they feel it would be beneficial to the company. If dividends are not paid when due, they are normally lost forever.

The exact dividend amount per share is stated as a percentage of the par value of a preferred stock. Therefore, par value in preferred stock bears a direct relationship to the earning power of the share. Market value will probably remain at about par if the yield remains competitive with current interest rates and if the stock is a straight preferred with regularly paid dividends. *Cumulative preferred* is the name given a preferred stock that has a continuing cumulative claim on corporate dividends, if and when they are paid. Common shareholders may not receive dividends until any arrearage in cumulative preferred is brought up to date. The cumulative status helps a company sell out an original offer. While cumulative status does not guarantee payment, it presumably increases the possibility of some payment. It should not affect the market value of the stock once the shares are issued unless the company fails to pay a dividend. Then it may not lose its value quite as rapidly. If the nonpayment continues for any length of time, the cumulative status is of doubtful value.

A preferred stock's value will have some relationship to its common stock market value if it has *participating* status. This means that the preferred has a right to participate in residual dividends with the common shareholders on an equal basis once the original preferred dividends are paid and the common shareholders receive an equal amount. This is the best of two investment worlds, first preference as to dividend and then a sharing of extra profits. Participating status will enhance the value of any preferred. Invariably, participating preferred will sell at a higher market price than the common stock or the par value of the preferred. An unusual situation occurs when a preferred stock is both cumulative and participating. A company that offers such a package is probably financially weak.

Corporate ownership and control Usually preferred shareholders have no voting rights and little interest in exercising them if they did have the vote. As a standard rule, corporate charters allow preferred holders voting rights only if their dividends are significantly in arrears, normally two years. In some instances, voting is allowed on any corporate measure that affects the status or value of the preferred stock.

Further proof that preferred is a hybrid security is the fact that while it is called an equity, it is *callable* at the option of the corporation. Some or all of the preferred stock may be retired according to charter provisions whenever the company deems it desirable. The call feature is a device favorable to the company. It allows the company to retire high-yield obligations for the benefit of the common shareholders.

The call feature effectively limits the market value of a preferred stock because it will seldom rise much above the call price and any premiums. The call price and any premium payable upon call are usually stated in the corporate charter. The call price is usually par value plus 5 to 15 percent premium.

Convertibility If preferred stock is convertible to common stock at the option of the holder, it becomes more desirable. Most convertible stock is also callable so that a corporation can either retire the issue or force its conversion. The stock may be converted at any time or during a specified period. Preferred stock is usually converted when the market price of the underlying common stock rises above the specified conversion price. The value of convertible preferred rises and falls with the value of common stock. More detailed discussion of the value of convertibility follows in our treatment of bonds.

Claims if business is dissolved Preferred stock is a safer, more secure investment than common stock. Preferred shareholders are entitled to receive the par value of their shares if the company is liquidated. However, any debts, including bonds, must be paid before preferred holders are satisfied. At least there is some possibility of enough residual assets to protect the preferred holder.

Corporate Bonds

Bonds are used by both corporations and governments to raise long-term funds. We will discuss government securities in more detail in chapter 16. Corporate bonds represent debt funding rather than the equity funding of stock. The corporation borrows the money rather than increasing ownership equity by issuing more shares. A bond is a negotiable debt instrument of the issuing corporation, signifying that it is part of a mass borrowing arrangement. Evidence of ownership is a bond certificate. The certificate features include the denomination, interest rate, maturity date, and any special conditions attached to the bond. Individual bonds are sold in denominations of $1,000 and up, with $1,000 being the most common denomination.

Bonds are normally registered with the corporation's trustee, meaning that the trustee has your name and address; your name must be inscribed on the bond. Some *bearer* bonds that do not require a registered owner are available. These bonds are negotiable by delivery, without endorsement, while registered bonds require your signature to pass title.

Each bond certificate in a single offering will have the same features. Interest is normally paid semiannually either by coupon or by mail. For example, if the interest is 8 percent per annum, the coupon would be redeemed at $40 twice a year. Usually the *interest coupons* are attached to the bond. Bondholders clip the due-dated coupon from the bond and submit it to the trustee by mail or redeem it through their local bank.

Characteristics of Corporate Bonds

Bonds are issued for a period of twenty or more years. They are negotiable promissory notes that promise to repay the money borrowed at a specified maturity date while paying a semi-annual interest charge. If the maturity date is July 1, 1994, that is when the holder will receive the face value of the bond. You would receive $80 each year until maturity for a $1,000 bond paying 8 percent. A twenty-year bond would return $1,600 interest over the period of indebtedness, and the principal would be repaid at maturity.

Corporate income Bondholders are creditors and as such have a claim on corporate income before preferred and common shareholders. The interest is a fixed charge that must be paid or else the corporation is in default. Even if a company does not make a profit, it is legally liable for bond interest payments.

Investors purchase bonds for interest income and security. There is relatively little price appreciation on bonds. If they are held to maturity, they will be redeemed by the issuing corporation at par value, the denomination indicated on the certificate.

Occasionally a special limited-liability bond is issued. These are called *income bonds*. In such cases, interest is paid only if the company earns enough to pay part or all of the interest. Payments are not fixed, but based upon income. Usually income bonds are former debenture or mortgage bonds reissued to save a corporation from going bankrupt.

Corporate ownership and control Bondholders have no voting rights or direct control over the operations and profit distribution of corporations. Often there is a debt-limiting covenant that limits the corporation from incurring further long-term debt except under certain conditions. For example, the covenant may require that any further long-term debt not exceed two-thirds of the dollar value of the capital assets to be purchased by the future indebtedness.

Bonds may be *callable* at the option of the corporation. This provision is similar to that of preferred stocks. Sometimes a call may be exercised only during a specified period of time. A call is inserted in a bond contract whenever possible because it allows the company to refinance elsewhere should interest rates decline or if earnings are such that the company can pay off its indebtedness early. A premium is usually payable whenever a call is exercised.

Another feature that may be attractive to investors, especially in lower-rated bonds, is the provision for a *sinking fund.* This arrangement requires systematic contributions to a fund in order to redeem the bonds at or before maturity date. If redeemed before maturity date, the sinking fund acts as the fund accumulator to call the bond. *Serial bonds* accomplish redemption by issuing a number of bonds in sequence with progressive maturity dates. This system allows both the investor and the corporation to plan ahead for repayment of the bond. There is no surprise call for redemption on a serial bond.

Convertibility This is a feature of bonds and preferred stock that benefits the investor by allowing him to convert holdings to the residual ownership status of common stock according to the provisions set forth in the bond or preferred stock. You would do this whenever the market price of the common stock rose to the point where you would profit by the exchange. Convertibility allows an investor to receive relatively high and secure income until such a time that he can make a satisfactory gain through the exchange. The issuing corporation finds that convertible securities are easier to sell, often at lower interest rates.

The actual conversion agreement will state that each bond or preferred stock is convertible into a certain number of shares of common stock or that it is convertible into common stock at a certain value per share. For example, a $1,000 bond may be converted into 40 shares of common stock, or the $1,000 bond may be converted into shares of common stock at $25 per share. Both procedures provide the same result.

If you wish to purchase a convertible bond or preferred stock with intentions of making a capital gain on the exchange, you must determine what chance the common stock has of rising to a price where the convertibility feature is worth exercising. If the chances are remote it would be better to purchase a security that is nonconvertible but pays a higher interest rate.

Claims if business is dissolved Since bonds are debts of the issuing corporation, bondholders' claims will be recognized before those of preferred or common shareholders. Usually bondholders will not wait until a corporation is to be liquidated before asserting their claims unless they are unaware of the true financial status of the company. Many bankrupt corporations attempt reorganization, restructuring their debt by issuing income bonds.

Bonds may be secured or unsecured. Unsecured bonds are general obligations of the company. They are called *debentures.* Secured bonds add to the safety of the investment but often yield slightly less interest. Your decision to purchase a bond should be based on whether you think a corporation will service its debt. Obviously there should be some hesitance on your part to buy any bond, secured or unsecured, in a company that faces default possibilities. Assuming that there is no way of telling the future, and there is no specter of default, you are generally better off to have a secured bond. There are a number of different types of secured bonds: mortgage bonds, collateral trust bonds, and equipment trust bonds.

INVESTMENT INFORMATION SOURCES

Once you have a basic understanding of the securities market and recognize the different types of securities, it would only seem natural that you would be ready to invest. You really need a lot more information before you are ready. To buy at this point would be a gamble because you need to know what is a good investment and how it can be evaluated. Frankly, you need to know what is happening in the dynamic world of investment. The more knowledge you have and the more different sources of information you have available, the better equipped you will be to make your decision.

Newspapers

All major metropolitan newspapers and many suburban newspapers carry business and financial news. You can often get an insight into the economy, an industry, or a specific company by looking over the business pages. Newspapers usually provide the daily prices of stocks listed on the NYSE. Sometimes they offer the stock quotations of the other exchanges and commodity markets plus occasional over-the-counter coverage. Many newspapers provide their readers with the general trend of market prices by printing market indexes. Comments by the financial editor about the prior day's market happenings can be combined with price quotes, indexes, and news of the day to provide you with lots of valuable current information.

The Wall Street Journal A dedicated investor should read the *Wall Street Journal* regularly. Many banks and other businesses provide their executives and customers with this newspaper. It is available in all public libraries. The *Wall Street Journal* is published by the Dow Jones Company weekdays in a number of regional editions that provide up-to-the-minute financial and business news on a national scale. The regional edition concept is used to facilitate distribution and to provide for regional advertising. It is not only the largest and most influential investment-oriented newspaper, but it also has the second largest daily circulation of any U.S. newspaper, with over 1,250,000 subscribers.

The paper publishes industry and individual company information and proposals in addition to general economic news. It also contains editorials; index averages; comparative business activity graphs; and over the-counter, security, and commodity exchange price quotations. Page one offers specialized columns called "What's News" that capsulize the latest developments in national and international finance. Specialized reports are also columnized on page one each day, under the headline of "The Outlook" (trends), "Labor Letter," "Tax Report," "Business Bulletin," and "Washington Wire."

How to Read Financial Information

You can get a capsule summary of financial news by reading the editorial comments of financial columnists. However, to get specific information, you must know how to read the indexes and stock and bond quotations.

Indexes The format for the reporting of the various exchanges, indexes, and market indicators is very similar in all papers. Figures 13–1 and 13–2 illustrate examples from a Sunday newspaper summary and the daily *Wall Street Journal.* Averages when placed in graphic form provide a visual trend line of the market place. Both graphs indicate a down trend. Figure 13–1 covers a one-year period, while figure 13–2 covers a much shorter period but tends to provide more specific information. Averages are weighted index numbers, not actual dollars. The summary list of "Most Active Stocks" (figure 13–1) is significant to speculators and investors because the activity often reflects accumulative positive or negative business transactions of these companies.

Dow Jones Averages The "Dow" is the oldest and most closely watched stock price measurement index. The industrial average is the one usually printed in daily papers and quoted on radio and television. It is not a dollar average, but an index of values for a select group of stocks. Figure 13–3 indicates the current composition of stocks in the four averages computed by Dow Jones, (1) thirty industrial stocks, (2) twenty transportation stocks, (3) fifteen utility stocks, and (4) a composite of the sixty-five aforementioned stocks.

Market Highlights

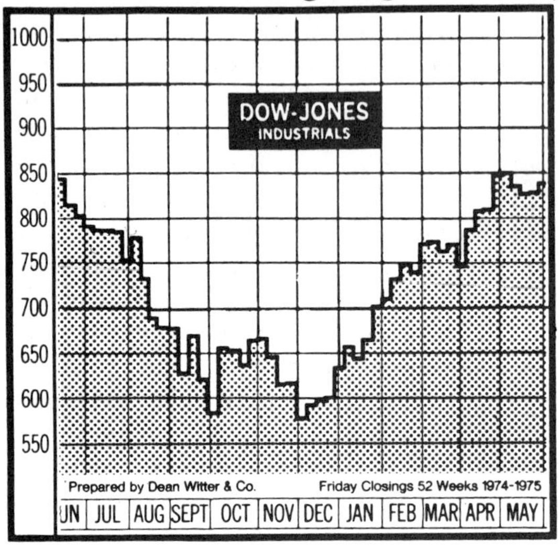

Dow Jones Averages

For the week ended June 6: stocks (intra-day highs and lows)

	Open	High	Low	Close	Net Change
30 Industrials	839.25	855.44	829.94	839.64	+ 7.35
20 Transportations	168.84	171.95	167.08	170.52	+ 2.67
15 Utilities	80.07	83.78	79.63	82.82	+ 3.00
65 Stocks	256.20	261.37	254.69	258.15	+ 3.74
40 Bonds	67.85	67.91	67.78	67.91	+ 0.09

Standard & Poor's

	High	Low	Close	Net Change
425 Industrials	104.49	103.87	103.87	+ 1.22
15 Railroads	39.11	38.79	39.11	+ 0.37
60 Utilities	43.12	41.56	43.12	+ 2.26
500 Stocks	92.89	92.48	92.48	+ 1.33

Most Active Stocks

Sales	Stock	Close	Change	Sales	Stock	Close	Change
2,102,500	Searle G D	19⅜	− 4⅞	641,900	Williams Co.	35¾	+ 2¾
1,123,900	Occid Pet	18¾	− ⅞	615,200	Am El Power	19½	+ 1⅜
1,107,200	Coastal St Gas	10½	+ 1⅜	605,300	Polaroid	31¾	− ⅜
924,300	Southern Co	12⅝	+ 1¾	593,500	West Elect	18⅞	+ 1
917,500	Gulf Oil	21½	+ 1⅛	588,400	Control Data	22⅝	+ 1⅛
794,700	Teleprompter	8⅜	− ½	583,500	La Land Exp	29⅜	+ 3⅞
731,100	Texaco	25⅞	unch	583,000	Gen Motors	44½	+ ½
693,500	Am Tel & Tel	49⅛	− ⅛	580,600	Clorox Co	11	+ ¾
675,100	Sony Corp	11⅝	+ 1	564,000	Amax Inc	54⅛	+ 8¼
653,900	Std Oil Calif	31⅞	+ 2⅛	560,600	Levitz Furnit	4⅞	+ ⅛

Figure 13–1 Market Highlights and Indexes. *(San Francisco* Examiner *and* Chronicle, *June 8, 1975)*

The averages were developed before electronic computers became available to calculate a larger list of stocks. The Dow Jones Company defends the continued use of this rather limited selection of stocks on the basis that they are a representative sample that follows (leads?) the primary trend of the stock market. Since the indexes are only trend-measuring devices, Dow Jones is probably right. Besides, the DJ Averages are an important part of the lore of the market. At the beginning of 1973, the DJ

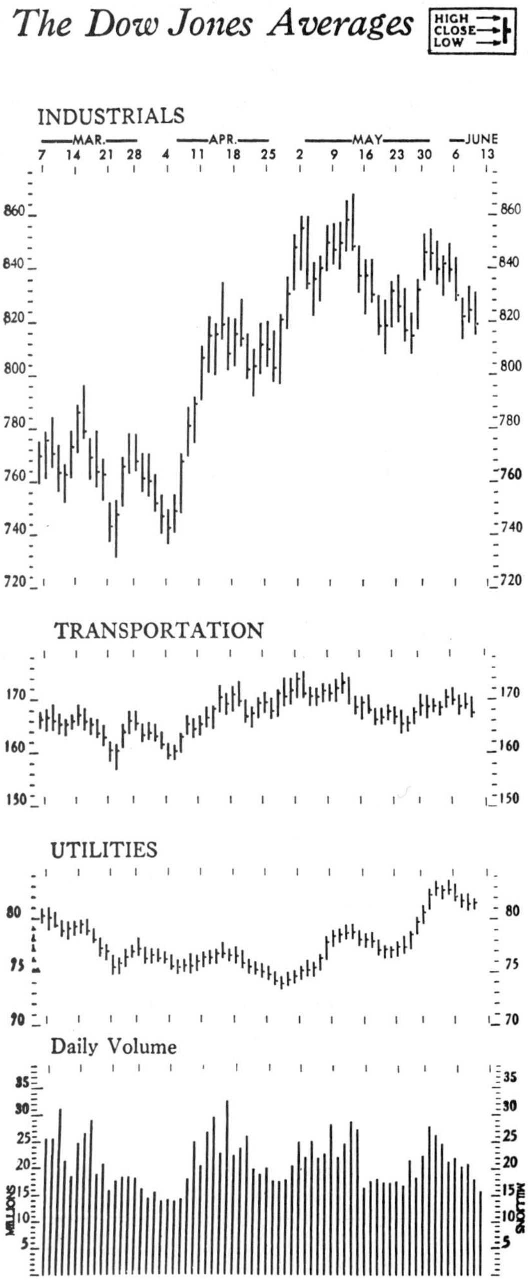

Figure 13–2 The Dow Jones Averages. *(Reprinted with permission of The Wall Street Journal, © Dow Jones & Company, Inc. 1975. All Rights Reserved.)*

WEEKLY LISTING OF 65 STOCKS

Thirty stocks used in Dow Jones Industrial Average are:

Allied Chemical	Esmark Inc	Owens-Illinois
Aluminum Co	Exxon	Procter & Gamb
Amer Brands	General Electric	Sears Roebuck
Amer Can	General Foods	Std Oil of Calif
Amer Tel & Tel	General Motors	Texaco
Anaconda	Goodyear	Union Carbide
Bethlehem Steel	Inter Harvester	United Technologies
Chrysler	Inter Nickel	US Steel
Du Pont	Inter Paper	Westinghouse El
Eastman Kodak	Johns-Manville	Woolworth

Twenty Transportation Stocks used are:

American Air	Norfolk & West'n	Seaboard Coast
Burlington North	Northwest Air	Southern Pacific
Canadian Pacific	Pan Am World Air	Southern Railway
Chessie System	Penn Central	Transway Int'l
Consolfd Freight	St.Louis-SanFran	Trans World Air
Eastern Air Lines	Santa Fe Indust	UAL Inc
McLean Trucking		Union Pac Corp

Fifteen Utility Stocks used are:

Am Elec Power	Consol Nat Gas	Panhandle EPL
Cleveland E Ill	Detroit Edison	Peoples Gas
Colum-Gas Sys	Houston Lt & Pw	Phila Elec
Comwlth Edison	Niag Mohawk P	Pub Serv E&G
Consol Edison	Pacific Gas & El	Sou Cal Edison

Figure 13–3 Stock Composition of the Dow Jones Averages.

industrials reached 1051.7, the all-time high. The average then dropped because of inflation, tight money, and the oil crisis of fall 1973. By late 1974 the average hovered around 600. The DJ industrial average appears to reflect the sentiment of the investor, as noted in figure 13–4.

Other indexes The Standard and Poor Corporation average computes an index comprised of 425 industrials, 50 utilities, 25 railroads, and a composite of all 500 stocks. Because it covers a greater and more diverse cross section of the stock market, the *Standard and Poor's averages* are regarded as a better measurement of the stock market. The *New York Stock Exchange Index* and the *American Stock Exchange Index* record the average price and net change of all common stocks listed on their respective exchanges. Since both indexes record all stock price movements, they are the most precise measurements of market trends. The National Association of Securities Dealers provides an index for

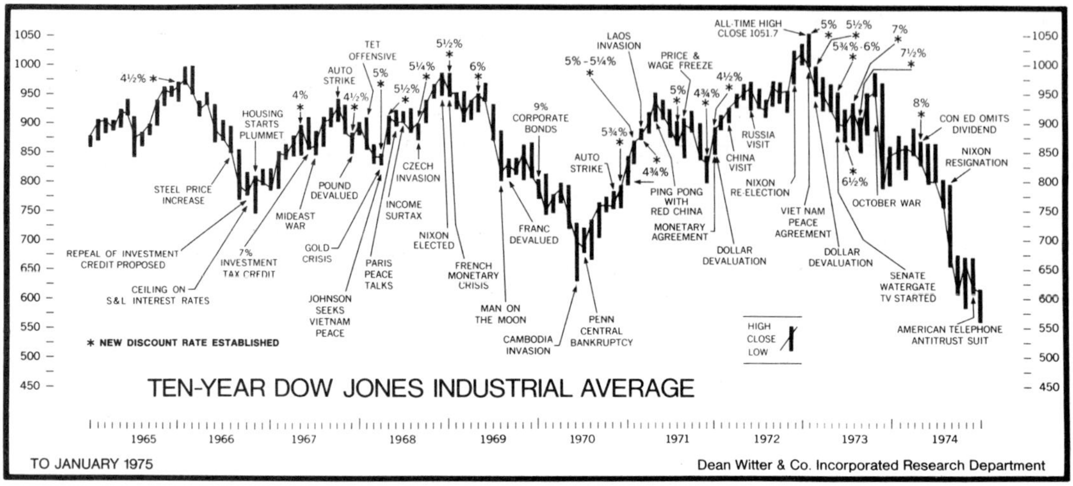

Figure 13–4 Ten-Year Dow Jones Industrial Average. *(Dean Witter & Co., Incorporated, San Francisco)*

active OTC stocks. These newer indexes are computerized to provide for their full market compilation.

Stock price quotations You can learn a number of important things about a stock by looking at the latest stock price quotation in your daily paper or the *Wall Street Journal.* Figure 13–5 is an extraction of the NYSE quotations of June 13, 1975. The Amex quotation follows the same format. Over-the-counter price quotations contain somewhat less information. We will take three well-known stocks from figure 13–5 to see what the quotations indicate:

The first two columns give the high and low sales price range per share for the calendar year 1975. During the first few months of a year, the prior year's ranges are included to offer a longer time span. Quotations and actual stock sales are made in $\frac{1}{8}$ of a dollar, which is $12\frac{1}{2}$ cents or 1 bit. The range for American Telephone and Telegraph during calendar year 1975 is from a high of $52.00 to a low of $44.75. The next column lists the name of the stock. All listings are common stock unless followed by the designator "pf" for preferred. The "Div." column records the current annual

1975 High	1975 Low	Stock	Div.	P/E Ratio	Sales 100s	High	Low	Close	Net Chg.
52	$44\frac{3}{4}$	AmT&T	3.40	9	878	49	$48\frac{3}{4}$	$48\frac{3}{4}$	$-\frac{1}{8}$
$227\frac{3}{8}$	$157\frac{1}{4}$	IBM	6	17	894	$208\frac{3}{4}$	206	$206\frac{1}{8}$	$-2\frac{3}{8}$
$60\frac{1}{2}$	$26\frac{3}{4}$	McDonald's		29	216	$52\frac{1}{4}$	$50\frac{1}{2}$	52	$+1\frac{1}{4}$

New York Stock Exchange Transactions

Friday, June 13, 1975

Friday's Volume
16,300,000 Shares; 230,100 Warrants

Volume since Jan. 1:	1975	1974	1973
Total shares	2,430,674,190	1,570,800,065	1,770,560,235
Total warrants ..	60,379,900	13,292,000	21,438,100

ACTIVE STOCKS

	Open	High	Low	Close	Chg.	Volume
Texaco Inc	25⅝	26⅛	25⅝	26	+ ⅜	280,800
Occiden Pet	18¼	18⅜	17¾	18⅛	− ¾	268,000
Wllms Cos	32⅞	32⅞	31	31¼	−1⅝	248,000
Searle GD	18¾	19⅜	18½	19⅜	+ ¾	215,800
Gen Motors	42⅞	43⅝	42½	43⅝	+ ¼	151,700
Pittston Co	70	70⅜	67¾	69⅜	−2⅛	141,800
Gulf Oil	22⅛	22½	21¾	22½	+ ½	139,300
WnAir Lin	7½	7¾	7⅜	7¾	+ ½	117,700
Howrd John	11½	12⅜	11⅜	12⅛	+ ½	110,900
Whittakr	3¾	4	3⅝	4	+ ¼	110,400

Average closing price of most active stocks: 25.41.

— A–A–A —

1975 High	1975 Low	Stock Div.	P.E. Ratio	Sales 100s	High	Low	Close	Net Chg.
75⅝	46½	AbbLab 1.44	17	87	72¾	71½	72¼	...
45¾	33¼	ACF In 2.60	9	16	43⅛	42¾	43	+ ⅛
10⅜	7	AcmeClv .50	5	3	9¼	9	9¼	+ ¼
4⅛	1¾	AdmDg .04e	9	1	3⅞	3⅞	3⅞	+ ⅛
10½	7¾	AdmEx .77e	...	26	10⅛	9¾	9⅞	......
3⅝	2⅛	Adms Millis	..	4	2⅞	2⅞	2⅞	......
9⅜	3¼	Addressog	76	309	7⅝	7¼	7⅝	......
10	7¼	AdvInv .28e	...	54	9	8⅞	9	......
28⅜	20	AetnaLf 1.08	12	541	27⅝	26⅝	27	......
42	31	AetnaLf pf 2	...	16	43	42	43	+ 1¾
7	4¾	Aguirre Co	7	1	5⅝	5⅝	5⅝	......
12	6⅞	Ahmans .20	7	35	10¾	10⅝	10⅝	− ¼
3¾	1⅝	Aileen Inc	8	8	3¼	3⅛	3¼	......
78⅜	44¾	AirPrd .20b	18	70	71⅝	70⅜	71⅝	+ ⅝
21¼	10½	AircoInc .90	5	46	18⅜	17⅞	18⅛	......
2⅝	1	AJ Industris	...	107	2½	2⅜	2½	......
17¼	10½	Akzona 1.20	14	61	15⅛	14¾	15⅛	......
13	7⅞	Ala Gas 1.18	7	7	12¾	12⅜	12¾	+ ⅝
17⅜	9	Alaska Intrs	11	23	15½	15	15¼	+ ⅛
19⅝	13⅞	AlbanyIn .60	6	4	17	16¾	17	+ ¼
7⅜	4⅝	AlbertoC .36	17	8	6⅜	6⅜	6⅜	.....
18¾	12¼	Albertsn .60	9	44	17¾	17½	17¾	+ ⅝
24⅜	18⅞	AlcanAlu .80	6	332	22⅝	22¼	22⅜	− ¼
12⅝	7½	AlcoStd .48	5	35	12⅛	11⅞	12⅛	+ ⅛
29	15¼	AlconLb .24	26	19	26¼	26	26¼	.....
5⅞	2½	Alexdrs .16e	10	8	5⅜	5¼	5¼	.....
6⅜	3	Alison Mtg	16	29	3⅞	3¾	3¾	− ⅛
11⅜	6⅞	AllegCp .45e	10	50	10¼	9¾	10⅛	+ ¼
26⅞	20⅜	AllgLud 1.80	3	36	24¼	23½	24¼	+ ¾
36⅞	31⅝	AllgLud pf 3	...	3	34¼	34	34¼	+ ¼
18½	12⅞	AllgPw 1.52	9	31	17⅛	16⅞	17	+ ⅛
8½	4⅛	AllenGrp .40	9	2	7¾	7¾	7¾	+ ⅛
42	27	AlldCh 1.80	7	198	37⅜	36⅝	37⅛	+ ⅛
15⅜	8⅝	AlldMnt .54	8	27	14	13¼	13¼	− ¾
15⅜	12½	AlldProd 1	5	9	13⅝	13½	13½	− ⅛
34½	15⅞	AlldStr 1.50	7	44	33⅛	32⅞	33⅛	− ⅛
4	2⅛	Alld Supmkt	...	21	2⅝	2½	2⅝	+ ⅛
11¾	6⅝	AllisChal .26	6	43	10½	10⅜	10½	......
10⅞	7⅜	Alpha Pl .72	5	1	10⅝	10⅝	10⅝	......
50¼	27⅛	Alcoa 1.34	9	488	42¾	41¼	42¼	+ ⅝
56¼	28¾	Amax 1.75	9	973	53½	52⅛	53	− ⅝
46⅞	26¾	AmalgSug 3	2	21	34¼	33¾	34¼	+ 1
135½	77	Amax pf5.25	...	2	129	128	129	− ¾
5⅛	3	Amcord .26	7	2	4¾	4⅝	4¾	+ ⅛
18¾	13¼	Amerce 1.20	5	8	17⅛	17⅛	17⅛	.....
22⅜	15⅛	A Hess .30b	4	194	20⅛	19⅞	19⅞	+ ⅛
55½	42	A Hes pf3.50	...	33	51½	51	51½	+ ½

1975 High	1975 Low	Stock Div.	P.E. Ratio	Sales 100s	High	Low	Close	Net Chg.
10¼	7⅛	BuddCo .60	10	8	8¾	8⅝	8⅝	.....
5	4½	BudCa pf.60	...	2	5	5	5	.....
4¼	2¾	Budget Ind	...	4	3⅞	3¾	3¾	.....
9⅜	6¾	BulovaW .20	5	22	7¼	7	7¼	+ ⅛
22⅛	18½	BunkHil 1.92	...	2	20½	20⅜	20½	+ ⅛
7½	3¼	BunkrRa .40	51	39	6⅝	6⅜	6⅝	.....
28¼	14⅞	BurlInd 1.20	12	115	26¼	25⅞	25⅞	.....
42⅞	33	BurlNor 1.70	8	68	37¾	37⅛	37⅜	− ⅝
7⅝	6⅝	BurlNo pf.55	...	2	7	7	7	.....
31⅝	11¾	Burndy .78	10	10	30⅝	30⅝	30⅝	+ ¼
110	61⅛	Burrghs .60	27	250	100¾	98½	100	+ 1

— C–C–C —

1975 High	1975 Low	Stock Div.	P.E. Ratio	Sales 100s	High	Low	Close	Net Chg.
5½	2⅝	CabCab For	..	14	4⅛	4	4	− ⅛
2[illegible]	15¾	Cabot Cp .92	110	26	17⅞	17½	17⅝	+ ⅜
3⅝	1⅝	Cadence Ind	...	7	3⅛	3	3⅛	.....
6¼	2⅜	Caesars Wrl	8	16	5⅛	4⅞	4⅞	− ¼
4⅜	2⅛	Cal Finanl	...	7	3⅝	3½	3⅝	.....
15¾	13⅝	CalP Ut 1.52	7	6	15½	15¼	15¼	.....
13⅝	7½	Callahn .15r	11	43	13⅛	12½	12¾	− ⅜
3⅜	1⅝	Camrn Brn	...	5	2¼	2⅛	2¼	+ ¼
36¾	26¼	CamRL .60a	19	64	31⅞	31¼	31⅜	− ⅝
33⅞	27⅜	CamSp 1.24	12	131	32	31⅝	31⅞	+ ⅛
17⅛	13¾	CdnPac .86e	6	92	14¾	14⅝	14⅝	− ⅛
42⅝	22	CapCit Com	14	51	40¼	39⅝	40¼	− ¼
28½	21⅝	Cap Hold .34	16	201	28⅝	28	28¼	− ⅛
3¾	1¾	Capit Mtg	...	6	2¼	2⅛	2⅛	− ⅛
47¾	28¼	Carbor 1.70	6	20	45	44½	45	+ ¼
3	2	Carling OKe	...	14	2¾	2½	2¾	+ ⅜
14⅜	10¼	Carlisle .88	4	10	12	12	12	.....
66	53⅝	CaroC&Oh 5	...	z50	57¼	57¼	57¼	− ¼
6¼	4⅝	CaroFrg .20	67	1	5⅜	5⅜	5⅜	+ ⅛
17	11	CaroPw 1.60	7	356	17⅝	17	17½	+ ½
25½	24½	CarP pf2.67	..	9	25	24¾	24¾	− ¼
24¾	15⅞	CarTec 1.60	4	24	20⅞	20⅜	20⅞	+ ¼
13½	6⅞	CarrCp .52	41	41	10¾	10½	10¾	+ ⅛
30	28	Carr pf2.25	...	z50	29⅝	29⅝	29⅝	− ⅜
12⅛	10⅜	CarrGn .90e	...	3	11⅜	11¼	11¼	− ⅜
24⅛	13¼	Cart Hwl .80	12	39	21	20½	20½	.....
41¼	24¾	CartHw pf 2	...	12	35½	34½	35¼	− ½
10½	6⅛	CartWall .40	10	19	8⅞	8⅝	8⅞	.....
9⅛	6½	CascNGs .92	68	4	8⅛	8⅛	8⅛	.....
16⅜	13¼	CastlCk .80b	5	57	15½	15⅛	15⅛	+ ⅛
69½	48	CaterTr 1.80	14	383	63	61¾	63	+ 1½
51⅛	28⅞	CBS 1.46	13	85	50	49⅜	49⅝	− ¼
2⅜	⅞	CCI Corp	...	29	2	1⅞	1⅞	− ⅛
16	13¾	Ceco Cp 1.15	5	10	15⅞	15⅝	15⅞	+ ¼
36	25⅞	Celanse 2.80	7	92	34⅝	34⅛	34⅛	− ¼
50¾	41	Celn pfA4.50	...	2	50¾	50½	50¾	.....
7⅝	3½	CencoInc .20	...	94	7	6½	6⅞	+ ⅜
10½	5	Centex .12	23	84	8¾	8½	8⅝	− ⅛
17½	12½	CenHud 1.72	7	1	17	17	17	− ⅛
16¼	11¼	CenIllLt 1.60	8	43	16¼	16	16¼	.....
29½	25¼	CnILt pf2.87	..	z1350	26¾	26⅝	26¾	+ ⅛
13½	9⅜	CenIlPS 1.20	9	144	12⅞	12¾	12¾	.....
19⅛	14⅛	CenLaE 1.28	8	7	18⅞	18⅝	18⅞	+ ¼
13⅝	10⅞	CeMPw 1.34	9	22	12¾	12⅝	12¾	− ⅛
17	13⅜	CenSoW 1.16	9	644	16¼	16	16⅛	+ ⅛
15½	10	CenSoya .60	10	45	14	13⅞	13⅞	− ¼
20½	16½	CenTel 1.12	9	31	20⅛	19¾	20⅛	+ ⅜
22¼	6½	Centrn Data	12	60	19	18¼	19	+ ⅜
16½	11⅜	Cerro 1.20	8	19	15⅜	15⅜	15⅜	.....
12¾	6¾	Cert-teed .60	...	14	11	10⅞	11	+ ⅛
17½	11⅞	CessnaAir 1	6	30	16¼	15¾	16	+ ⅛

1975 High	1975 Low	Stock Div.	P.E. Ratio	Sales 100s	High	Low	Close	Net Chg.
11⅛	3¾	HouFab .20e	13	96	9⅞	9½	9⅞	+ ½
18½	11⅞	HouseFin 1	7	436	16¾	16¼	16⅝	+ ⅛
32¾	25½	HouF pf2.50	...	29	30¾	30¾	30¾	.....
26⅜	20⅜	HousLP 1.56	9	83	24	23¾	23¾	− ⅛
14½	4½	HowJohn .24	13	1109	12⅜	11⅜	12⅛	+ ½
14⅞	10⅜	Howmet 1	6	13	13⅞	13⅝	13¾	.....
15⅜	9⅝	Hubbrd 1.60	9	31	15¼	14⅝	14¾	− ¼
19¼	13⅜	HudsA 1.60	5	1	18	18	18	+ ⅛
94⅜	61¾	Hughs TJ .50	19	82	91¼	90	91¼	+ 1⅝
12⅝	4⅛	Humana	8	64	10⅝	10⅛	10⅛	− ¼
17¾	11¼	HuntCh .24	20	161	17¼	17	17	− ⅛
15¾	6⅝	HuttnEF .52	7	12	12½	12⅜	12½	+ ⅛
19⅝	14½	Huyck .40	14	2	17¼	17⅛	17¼	+ ⅜
7⅜	4½	Hydromt .24	4	9	6¼	6⅛	6¼	.....

— I–I–I —

1975 High	1975 Low	Stock Div.	P.E. Ratio	Sales 100s	High	Low	Close	Net Chg.
15⅛	10¾	ICInds 1.30	5	70	13¾	13⅝	13¾	+ ⅛
73	62	ICInds pf 6	...	3	67½	67½	67½	+ ¼
35¾	27¾	ICInd pf3.50	...	17	34	33½	34	+ ⅜
4⅞	1⅝	ICN Pharm	...	170	4½	4⅛	4½	+ ⅛
29	23⅝	IdahoP 1.96	8	25	27⅛	26¾	27⅛	.....
18¾	11¼	IdealBasic 1	7	38	16⅞	16¼	16¼	− ⅝
6⅝	2⅝	IdeaToy .10t	6	146	6½	6⅛	6⅜	+ ¼
17¼	4⅛	IDS Rl 3.23e	...	31	5¼	4¾	4¾	− ½
25½	17½	IllPowr 2.20	9	168	24	23¼	23⅝	− ⅛
24½	22	IlPow pf2.13	...	z30	23½	23½	23½	− 1
27¾	17	IllToolW .50	15	1	27	27	27	+ ¼
11⅜	7½	ImplCpA .20	6	96	10¾	10⅝	10⅝	− ⅛
39⅜	28⅛	INA Cp 2.10	11	117	38	37⅝	38	+ ½
18¾	14⅞	INA Inv 1.59	...	29	17¾	17⅛	17¾	+ ½
5⅛	2¾	Income Cap	...	5	4⅞	4⅞	4⅞	− ⅛
20¼	13	IndplPL 1.82	9	49	18½	18½	18½	.....
15⅜	10	IndlNat 1.20	19	2	14⅜	14¼	14⅜	+ ⅜
8	5½	Inexco Oil	...	250	7¼	7	7¼	+ ¼
84⅜	61⅛	IngerR 2.48	13	297	80⅛	79	79½	− 1
51½	38	IngR pf2.35	...	182	49⅞	49	49	− 1⅜
35½	21¾	InlCon 1.40a	5	2	32¼	32¼	32¼	− ¼
44¼	32¼	InldStl 2.40a	5	49	38¼	37¾	38¼	+ ¼
8⅛	5⅛	Inmont .40	5	89	7¾	7½	7⅝	+ ⅛
8½	5⅞	Insilco .70	5	32	7⅞	7¾	7⅞	+ ⅛
13	10½	Insil pfA1.25	.	10	12½	12½	12½	...
40½72	½	InspirCop 2	15	5	30¾	30½	30¾	+ ¼
7½	4⅛	Integon .28	7	2	6¾	6¾	6¾	+ ⅛
35⅞	18¾	Interco 1.46	8	18	34¾	34⅜	34⅝	− ⅛
2⅜	1⅜	Intrcntl Div	6	118	2½	2⅛	2⅜	+ ¼
35	27	Interlake 2a	3	26	32	31½	32	+ ¾
227⅜	157¼	IBM 6	17	894	208¾	206	206⅛	− 2⅜
35⅛	23⅝	IntFlav .30b	37	127	31⅛	30¾	31	+ ¼
30½	19¾	IntHarv 1.70	5	175	28¼	27⅞	27⅞	− ⅛
11⅝	6⅛	IntHold .68e	...	6	11⅝	11½	11⅝	+ ⅛
48½	30⅞	IntMinCh 2	4	407	38⅜	37½	37½	− ⅝
11⅞	6½	Int Mining	11	44	9¾	9¼	9⅜	− ⅛
26	17¾	IntMulti 1.36	6	1	23½	23½	23½	+ ⅛
29⅛	21⅜	InNick 1.40a	7	101	27	26¼	27	+ ¾
54¾	34⅝	IntPaper 2	8	218	46⅛	45½	46⅛	+ ½
6½	3½	IntRect .12e	7	7	5⅞	5¾	5⅞	.....
24¾	14⅝	IntTT 1.52	6	486	23⅝	22⅞	23½	+ ⅝
47½	32¾	IntTT pfH4	...	2	47½	47½	47½	+ 1
49⅝	34¼	ITT pfI4.50	...	1	48⅝	48⅝	48⅝	.....
44¾	31⅞	IntTT pfJ4	...	71	44	43	44	+ 1
44½	32½	IntTT pfK4	...	33	43½	42½	43½	+ ¾

1975 High	1975 Low	Stock Div.	P.E. Ratio	Sales 100s	High	Low	Close	Net Chg.
30	19⅜	LaLand 1.12	10	176	28¼	27⅜	28⅛	+ ¼
16½	8⅜	LaPacif .20	9	141	14½	14¼	14⅜	.....
22	17¼	LouisGs 1.84	10	16	21¾	21½	21¾	.....
13¼	8⅞	Lowenst .40	..	x31	11	10⅝	11	+ ⅛
19¾	9	LTV Corp	2	216	13¾	13⅜	13⅝	.....
73¾	48	LTVCp pf 5	..	27	48½	47¾	47¾	− ⅞
56⅝	35¼	Lubrizol 1	20	60	52⅛	51⅝	52⅛	+ ¼
15⅛	8	LuckStr .64b	11	53	13½	13¼	13½	.....
11⅞	8⅛	Ludlow .72	9	9	8⅜	8¼	8⅜	− ⅛
30	22½	LukenSt 1.60	5	62	26¼	25	25	− ⅞
18⅞	13½	LykeYng 1e	1	30	14½	14⅜	14⅜	.....
36¼	26⅝	Lykes pf2.50	..	19	28⅜	28	28¼	.....
5⅜	3½	LynCSys .20	8	9	4¼	4⅛	4¼	+ ⅛

— M–M–M —

1975 High	1975 Low	Stock Div.	P.E. Ratio	Sales 100s	High	Low	Close	Net Chg.
8⅝	6¼	MacAF .60b	9	43	8⅛	7⅞	8⅛	+ ¼
4½	1¼	MacDonal	4	24	3⅞	3¾	3¾	.....
5	2⅝	Macke .30	8	1	4⅜	4⅜	4⅜	.....
6¾	3⅜	Macmill .25	6	65	5⅝	5¼	5⅝	+ ¼
23⅛	12⅜	Macy 1.10	8	26	20⅛	19¾	20⅛	.....
49½	43	Macy pf 4.25	...	z30	45	45	45	− 1¼
9⅜	7⅛	MadisFd .60	...	33	9¼	9⅛	9¼	+ ⅛
6¼	3¼	MadSq Gar	...	18	5¾	5⅝	5⅝	− ⅛
6¼	3¼	MagicCf .32	...	115	6¼	6	6⅛	− ⅛
8¾	3⅞	Magnavox	...	17	8⅝	8⅝	8⅝	.....
20	11½	Mallory 1	12	16	19⅝	19	19⅝	+ ¼
25¼	16½	MalHyd .44b	14	3	24½	24	24½	+ ¼
5½	2	Manhat Ind	...	22	5⅛	5	5⅛	.....
12½	9	Manpwr .88	5	32	11⅞	11⅜	11⅞	+ ⅜
37¼	25¼	MfrHan 1.72	8	130	34¼	33⅝	34¼	+ ⅝
44⅜	27¼	MAPCO .70	17	60	41⅝	40⅝	41⅝	+ 1⅛
12	5⅜	Marathn Mf	5	27	10⅞	10¾	10⅞	+ ¼
44⅞	29⅞	MaraO 1.80a	8	64	42⅜	41⅜	42⅜	+ ⅞
29	13⅞	Marcor 1	8	347	25¼	24½	24¾	− ¼
57	28½	Marcr pf A2	.	26	49¾	48¾	49¼	− ⅜
15⅛	8⅛	Maremt .40	13	65	13⅞	13¾	13¾	+ ⅛
18⅞	14¼	MarMid 1.80	6	277	17¼	16⅞	17⅛	+ ⅛
27½	16¾	MarionL .48	14	19	21¼	21⅛	21¼	...
37	13⅞	Marley .60	12	54	30⅝	30¼	30½	− ½
11⅛	6⅞	Marqtt .50e	6	24	10	9¾	9⅞	...
17	6½	Marriot .37t	18	247	12⅞	12¼	12⅝	− ⅜
60¾	41	MrshMc 1.60	22	97	60	59½	59¾	+ ⅛
26⅜	15⅝	MarshF 1.24	11	181	22⅛	21½	21½	− ½
17¾	13⅛	MartMa 1.30	5	24	16	15¾	15⅞	− ⅛
20½	5¾	MartPr .50e	10	75	19¼	18¾	19¼	+ ⅛
16⅜	11⅝	MrldCup .54	7	18	13⅞	13½	13⅞	+ ⅜
51¼	30	MascoCp .32	22	252	49½	49⅛	49½	+ ¼
26¾	16½	Masonite .54	38	84	23⅝	23½	23⅝	− ⅛
17⅞	13⅝	MassyFer 1	4	43	15¾	15¼	15½	− ¼
11⅜	7¾	MasMt 1.24e	8	17	10⅜	10⅛	10⅛	− ⅛
16¼	11¾	MasCp 1.59e	...	15	14¾	14⅝	14⅝	...
12⅞	10⅛	Mas Inc 1.02	...	82	12	11⅝	11⅝	− ⅛
19¼	12	Matsu E .31e	11	5	18	18	18	....
44⅜	22⅛	MayDSt 1.60	14	154	43¼	42⅜	43	+ ⅝
27½	20	MayD pf1.80	..	5	27¼	27	27¼	+ 1¼
21⅝	14⅞	MayerOs .92	7	4	21⅜	21	21⅜	+ ⅜
5⅜	3⅜	MaysJW .28	8	1	4	4	4	.
31½	19⅜	Maytg 1.30a	19	26	29	28⅝	28⅞	− ⅛
10½	5¾	MBPXL .20e	10	9	9¾	9⅜	9⅜	− ¼
64½	27¾	MCA Inc 1	8	x58	59½	58¼	59⅜	+ ½
12½	7¾	McCord .96	5	6	11¼	11⅛	11¼	.....
4½	2⅛	McCrory Cp	..	3	3⅛	3⅛	3⅛	.....
97	59¾	McDer 1.60	11	224	95	93	95	+ 1¾
60½	26¾	McDonalds	29	216	52¼	50½	52	+ 1¼
18	8⅛	McDonD .40	6	103	17⅛	16½	16⅝	− ⅜
18¾	11½	McGEd 1.20	14	88	18¼	17⅞	18	+ ⅛
13⅝	6	McGrwH .56	10	103	11⅜	11	11⅜	+ ⅜
2⅜	1¼	McGrg Don	..	32	2	1⅞	2	+ ¼
51	29⅛	McIntyre	9	z50	45½	45½	45½	− ½
26½	10⅝	McKeeCo 1a	9	78	27⅝	25½	27½	+ 1⅞
29¾	16	McLean .72	8	9	28⅞	28⅜	28⅜	− ¾
17½	13¼	McLout 1.60	5	10	15⅞	15⅝	15⅞	+ ⅛
10	7½	McNeil .80	6	3	9½	9½	9½	.....
17½	13⅛	MeadCp 1.20	4	33	15⅝	15⅜	15⅜	− ⅛

Figure 13–5 New York Stock Exchange Stock Price Quotations. *(Reprinted with permission of The Wall Street Journal, © Dow Jones & Company, Inc. 1975. All Rights Reserved.)*

dividend amount as calculated by the latest quarterly or semiannual dividend paid by the company. This means that the amount listed may be inaccurate if the dividend paid has changed during the last three quarters. This annual rate is calculated only to provide a common measurement. In the example, the IBM stock shows an annual dividend of $6. This may reflect $1.50 paid in each of the last four quarters, or $1.50 paid in the last quarter with either more or less than that amount paid in earlier quarters. Footnotes often classify the dividend status of a stock.

The next item is the price-earnings ratio, computed by dividing the earnings per share into the closing price. In our example, the P/E ratio indicates IBM is selling at seventeen times the most recently reported twelve-month earnings. You can estimate the company's annual earnings by dividing the P/E ratio into the closing price. IBM must have earned about $12.13 per share and paid a dividend of $6 per share. You can assume that the balance of earnings was retained for expansion or operational use in the company.

"Sales 100s" indicates the trading activity in the listed stock. There were 87,800 shares of AmT&T traded during the day. The high, low, and close columns are the price at which the stock sold for the day. Of the three stocks, IBM had the widest price fluctuation for the day. "Net Change" indicates the dollar amount of change, plus or minus, from the previous day's close. IBM was down $2.375. McDonald's was up by $1.25 per share.

Further arithmetic calculations on your part will give you some idea of the volatility of a stock by determining the percentage of the range between high and low for the day and for the year represented. You can also determine the percentage of change as compared to the closing price. On any one day's stock prices, you can tell today's price trend by the plus or minus change, but you cannot tell whether this is a continuing situation without consulting prior editions or other information sources. Also, the prices of these three stocks in themselves do not say which is the best buy. We will discuss evaluation procedure in the next chapter.

Bond quotations Corporate bond quotations are sometimes found in daily newspapers. You are sure to find the NYSE and Amex bond transactions listed in the *Wall Street Journal.* Figure 13–6 illustrates the price quotations for bonds. Note that a corporation often floats more than one issue of bonds. American Telephone & Telegraph Company is an obvious example of multiple issues. Utilities often need large amounts of capital to carry on construction. They float bond issues whenever they have a need for debt financing. The various interest rates and maturity dates on ATT bonds reflect the money market at the time of issue. We will compare some well-known companies as an explanation of the bond price quotation format:

Bonds			Cur. Yld.	Vol.	High	Low	Close	Net Chg.
AAirl	11s	88	11.0	16	100	100	100	—
AAirl	$4\frac{1}{4}$s	92	cv	61	$43\frac{1}{8}$	43	$43\frac{1}{8}$	$-\frac{5}{8}$
ATT	$2\frac{3}{4}$s	80	3.4	99	81	$80\frac{1}{2}$	$80\frac{1}{2}$	$-\frac{3}{8}$
ATT	$2\frac{5}{8}$s	86	4.3	74	61	$59\frac{3}{4}$	$59\frac{3}{4}$	$-\frac{1}{4}$

New York Exchange Bonds

Tuesday, June 10, 1975

Total Volume, $24,680,000

SALES SINCE JANUARY 1

1975	1974	1973
$2,519,097,000	$1,691,596,100	$2,029,197,800

	Domestic Tues	Domestic Mon	All Issues Tues	All Issues Mon
Issues traded	826	818	839	829
Advances	376	391	383	392
Declines	218	215	219	221
Unchanged	232	212	237	216
New highs, 1975	71	56	74	56
New lows, 1975	5	4	5	8

Dow Jones Bond Averages

−1973− High	−1973− Low	−1974− High	−1974− Low	−1975− High	−1975− Low		TUESDAY −1975−	TUESDAY −1974−	TUESDAY −1973−
75.34	71.33	73.50	64.13	69.74	66.16	40 Bonds	68.27 + .23	68.84 − .11	74.25 + .03
55.27	52.37	54.58	45.60	50.35	47.30	10 Hi Rails	49.00 + .15	49.77 − .15	54.75 + .04
69.73	65.05	68.36	61.28	63.52	61.31	10 2nd Rails	61.66 + .14	65.13 − .04	67.28 ....
92.00	88.85	91.70	78.52	88.05	81.03	10 Utilities	85.42 + .01	84.46 − .09	91.01 + .01
85.90	77.55	80.82	70.81	78.27	74.51	10 Industrial	77.02 + .65	75.98 − .17	83.98 + .07
54.61	49.97	54.26	44.07	47.83	42.75	Inco Rails	42.75 − .76	47.38 − .03	51.52 + .10

CORPORATION BONDS

Volume, $24,490,000

Bonds	Cur Yld	Vol	High	Low	Close	Net Chg
AddM 9⅜95	13.	15	72	72	72	.....
AirRe 3⅞87	cv	19	75	75	75	.....
AlaB 10½99	10.	50	101	101	101	.....
AlaP 9¾s04	10.	3	94	94	94	.....
AlaP 9s2000	10.	10	89½	89	89	− ½
AlaP 8⅞s03	10.	11	87	87	87	+ ½
AlaP 8½s01	10.	8	80⅜	80⅜	80⅜	.....
AlaP 8¼s03	10.	12	81½	81½	81½	+1½
AlaP 7⅞s02	10.	15	77½	77½	77½	+ ½
Alison 8¾79	14.	3	59	59	59	+ ½
AllnG 11½94	cv	3	88⅝	88⅝	88⅝	+3⅝
AldCh 5.2s91	7.2	10	71½	71½	71½	− ¼
AlldSt 4½92	cv	4	80¼	80¼	80¼	− ¼
AldSu 5¾87	cv	18	41¼	41	41¼	+ ¼
Alc 9.45s2000	9.1	14	103	103	103	.....
Alcoa 9s95	9.0	8	100	100	100	.....
Alcoa 6s92	7.5	29	79¼	78	79¼	+2¼
AluCa 9½95	9.7	10	97	97	97	− ⅞
AMAX 8½84	8.5	5	99¼	99¼	99¼	.....
AMAX 8s86	8.8	13	91	90	90	− ¼
AAirFil 6s90	cv	20	93	92⅞	93	+1½
AAirln 11s88	11.	16	100	100	100	.....
AAirl 4¼s92	cv	61	43⅛	43	43⅛	− ⅝
ABrnd 9⅝79	9.1	35	105¾	105	105⅜	.....
ABrnd 8⅛85	8.1	52	99⅞	99½	99⅞	.....
ACeM 6¾91	cv	9	34	34	34	.....
ADist 4⅜s86	8.1	1	53⅝	53⅝	53⅝	.....
AExC 7.8s92	10.	15	74¼	72	74¼	.....
AForP 5s30	10.	85	46½	46⅜	46½	.....
AFoP 4.8s87	8.3	22	59	57½	57½	−1½
AGnIn 6½94	6.1	5	106	106	106	−1
AHosp 5¾99	cv	5	127⅞	127⅞	127⅞	−2⅝
AInvt 9½s76	9.6	35	99¼	99	99	.....
AInvt 8¾s89	11.	5	76	76	76	+1
AMed 9½98	13.	20	68	67⅞	68	.....
AMedcp 5s97	cv	13	45½	44¾	45½	+ ¾
AmMot 6s88	cv	2	61¾	61¾	61¾	−1¾
ASug 5.3s93	7.7	2	68	68	68	.....
ATT 8.80s05	8.6	737	101⅞	101⅛	101⅞	+ ⅞
ATT 8¾2000	8.5	505	102⅜	101½	102⅜	+1
ATT 8.7s02	8.6	228	101	100½	100⅞	+ ¼
ATT 8⅝s07	8.6	309	100	99½	100	+ ⅝
ATT 7¾s82	7.7	202	100	99¾	100	+ ⅛
ATT 7.75s77	7.5	35	102⅞	102½	102½	.....
ATT 7⅛s03	8.2	13	86¾	86	86¾	+1
ATT 7s01	8.1	103	86	85	86	+ ½
ATT 6½s79	6.6	30	97⅛	97	97⅛	+ ¼
ATT 4⅜s85	5.7	31	76	75⅝	75⅞	+1⅝
ATT 4⅜s85r	..	10	75	75	75	.....
ATT 3⅞s90	6.0	19	63½	63	63½	+ ½
ATT 2⅞s87	4.7	58	61	60⅞	61	+ ⅛
ATT 2¾s75	2.7	2	98 9-16	98 9-16	98 9-16	+1-16
ATT 2¾s80	3.4	99	81	80½	80½	− ⅜
ATT 2⅝s86	4.3	74	61	59¾	59¾	− ¼
Ampx 5½94	cv	45	45	45	45	.....
Anhr 9.20s05	8.8	1	103¾	103¾	103¾	− ¼
ApcoO 5s88	cv	1	59	59	59	− ⅜
APL 5¾s88	cv	15	93	92½	92½	− ½
AppP 11⅛83	10.	208	101⅜	101	101⅜	+ ⅜
AppP 8⅝s76	8.5	10	100⅝	100⅝	100⅝	.....
Arco 8.70s81	8.4	50	103	102¼	103	.....
Arco 8s82	7.9	43	100½	100⅜	100½	+ ¼
Aristr 9½89	12.	10	79	77	79	−1
ArizP 9½s82	9.3	60	101⅜	100¾	101⅜	+ ⅝
AriP 7.45s02	9.9	4	75	75	75	.....
ArmSt 8¼75	8.2	30	101⅜	100 5-16	100 5-16	−7-16
ArS 4.35s84	5.6	26	77	77	77	− ¼
Armr 5s84	7.7	7	64⅞	64⅞	64⅞	.....
Armr 4½83	cv	1	90¼	90¼	90¼	+ ⅛
ArCk 8.45s84	8.2	5	101⅞	101⅞	101⅞	.....
ArmstC 8s96	9.0	15	88⅛	88⅛	88⅛	−1⅞
Asarc 8.8s83	8.7	134	100¾	100⅜	100¾	+ ½
AshlO 4¾93	cv	5	64½	64½	64½	.....
AsCp 8½77	8.4	2	101	101	101	+ ¾
AsInv 4½76	4.6	11	96½	96½	96½	.....
AsInv 4⅜84	7.6	3	57¼	57¼	57¼	−2¾
AsInv 5⅛79r	..	10	82½	82½	82½	.....
Atchsn 4s95	7.4	10	54	54	54	− ⅞
Atchn 4s95st	7.5	8	54⅛	52⅞	53	.....
ARf 7.7s2000	8.8	5	87⅛	87⅛	87⅛	+ ⅛
AtlRich 7s76	7.0	13	100	99⅞	99⅞	.....
ATO 4⅜s87	cv	17	52	49	49	−1
AvcoC 7½93	14.	7	52½	52	52	− ½
AvcoC 5½93	cv	32	42⅛	42	42⅛	− ⅜
AvcoF 8⅞77	8.8	105	100	100	100	.....
BalG 10⅛83	9.6	10	105⅜	105⅜	105⅜	+ ⅜
BalGE 8¾75	8.7	5	100	100	100	+5-32
BalGE 3s89	5.6	40	53	53	53	.....
B&O 4¼s95	9.0	12	47	47	47	.....
B&O 4s80	5.3	3	75⅜	75⅜	75⅜	− ⅝
BangP 8¼94	cv	3	56	56	56	−1½
BkNY 6¼94	cv	5	87⅞	87⅞	87⅞	− ⅛
Banka 8⅞05	9.0	46	98½	97⅞	98½	+1
Banka 7⅞03	9.0	13	86⅝	86⅝	86⅝	.....
BectD 5s89	cv	3	77	77	77	.....
BecD 4⅛s88	cv	10	92⅛	92⅛	92⅛	− ⅞
BeecA 4¾93	cv	5	59⅞	59⅞	59⅞	.....
Belco 4¾s88	cv	14	60½	60½	60½	+ ¼
BellPa 9⅝14	9.1	23	105	105	105	.....
BellPa 8⅝06	8.6	11	99¾	99¾	99¾	.....
BellPa 7⅛12	8.7	10	81⅜	81⅜	81⅜	+ ⅜
BellPa 7s80	7.2	5	97	97	97	+1
Bendx 9¼81	9.0	17	103	102½	102½	+ ¼
Bendx 6⅝92	8.4	10	78	77	78	−1
BenCp 9⅜78	9.1	13	102½	102	102	− ½
BenCp 8½76	8.3	37	102	101¼	102	+ ⅜
BenCp 6¾77	6.9	1	97	97	97	−1¼
BetSt 8.45 05	8.6	60	98	97½	98	+ ¾
BlkD 8.45s85	8.3	45	101⅛	101⅛	101⅛	+ ⅞
BobbB 5¼81	cv	14	50	48	50	+1

Bonds	Cur Yld	Vol	High	Low	Close	Net Chg
Dow 8⅞2000	8.7	25	101½	100	101½	+ ½
Dow 7.75s99	8.7	5	89	89	89	.....
Dow 4.35s88	6.1	3	70½	70½	70½	+5⅜
DPF 5½87	cv	1	54	54	54	− ½
Dressr 4⅛77	4.4	10	93⅛	93⅛	93⅛	+1¼
duPt 8.45s04	8.4	5	100	100	100	− ⅞
duPont 8s81	7.8	46	102½	102¼	102½	+ ¼
DukeP 13s79	11.	20	109¾	109½	109½	.....
DukeP 9¾04	10.	4	96⅞	96⅝	96⅞	+ ¼
DukeP 9½05	10.	10	94⅞	94⅞	94⅞	+1⅜
DukeP 7¾03	9.6	5	80	80	80	+1
DukeP 7⅜01	9.5	3	76⅞	76⅞	76⅞	+2⅞
DupIn 5½94	cv	5	31⅛	31	31	.....
DuqL 8¼76	8.0	26	102	101⅛	102	− ½
E Sys 4½s92	cv	5	57	57	57	+ ½
EasAir 5s92	cv	25	39⅞	39⅝	39⅞	+ ¼
EaAir 4¾93	cv	34	39⅞	39¾	39¾	− ¼
EGG 3½s87	cv	4	60	60	60	+ ½
ElPa 8½95A	cv	46	97¼	96⅝	96¾	− ½
Englh 5¼97	cv	15	84½	84	84	− ½
vjEriR 5s20f	..	10	5⅞	5⅞	5⅞	+1⅞
vjEri 3⅛90f	..	25	13½	13½	13½	.....
Esmk 8.4s82	8.4	3	99⅛	99⅛	99⅛	.....
Evans 6¼94	11.	26	53½	52¾	53⅜	+ ⅝
Exxon 6½98	7.8	25	83	82½	83	+ ¾
Exxon 6s97	7.6	64	78⅞	77½	78⅞	+1⅜
ExxnP 9s04	8.6	25	103⅞	103	103⅞	.....
Fairch 4⅜92	8.9	29	49	48½	48⅞	− ⅝
Feddr 8⅞94	13.	7	64¼	64¼	64¼	.....
Feddrs 5s96	cv	20	39½	39½	39½	.....
FedN 4⅜96	cv	71	92	91¼	91⅜	− ⅛
FedSt 7⅛02	8.1	5	87¾	87¾	87¾	+2¾
FsNOr 7⅞78	8.0	5	97⅜	97⅜	97⅜	+ ⅜
FsNBos 8s82	8.0	10	100	99¾	99¾	− ¾
FNBo 7.6s81	7.7	13	98¾	98½	98¾	+ ¼
FtSec 10½99	10.	35	101½	101¼	101¼	− ⅛
FsWis 8½96	11.	10	76⅞	76⅞	76⅞	.....
FWiN 6.8s80	7.9	7	86⅛	85⅞	86⅛	+ ¼
FlPLt 10¾81	10.	57	106	104½	105	.....
FlaPL 9⅛84	8.9	176	107⅜	101¼	101½	+ ¼
FlaPL 8⅞82	8.7	55	101	101	101	+ ½
FlaPL 8⅛75	8.1	25	99⅝	99⅝	99⅝	− ⅛
FMC 9½2000	9.5	10	99¼	99¼	99¼	.....
FMC 4¼92	cv	15	61	61	61	.....
FoodF 4s79	5.4	2	73¼	73¼	73¼	− ¼
Ford 9¼94	8.9	62	104¼	103⅜	103⅜	− ⅛
Ford 7.40s80	7.4	10	98¾	98¾	98¾	.....
Ford 7¼77	7.2	25	100½	100⅜	100⅜	.....
FrdC 10½94	9.7	9	107⅜	107⅜	107⅜	+2⅜
FrdC 8⅞90A	9.1	20	97	97	97	.....
FrdC 8⅞90N	9.3	25	95	94½	94½	−1½
FrdC 8½91	9.5	17	88⅞	88⅞	88⅞	− ⅛
FrdC 8⅜76	8.2	16	101¾	101⅝	101⅝	− ⅛
FrdC 7¼79	7.4	10	97	97	97	.....
FrdC 4⅞98	cv	15	64⅞	64½	64½	− ¾
FrdC 4½96	cv	20	60½	60½	60½	− ½
FoMcK 6s94	cv	3	70¼	70¼	70¼	+ ¼
Frueh 5½94	cv	26	60	60	60	+ ½
FruF 9.15s83	9.0	20	100⅝	100⅝	100⅝	+ ⅛
Fuqua 9½98	13.	27	69½	69	69	− ¼
GAC 5⅞s94	cv	16	29	29	29	+ ½
GAC C 12s75	12.	20	93½	93½	93½	−5¾
GAC C 11s77	15.	66	72	69⅛	72	+2½
GnATr 5¾99	cv	19	73	72	72	−1
GnEl 7½96	8.0	2	93	93	93	+1
GnEl 6¼79	6.5	3	95	95	95	− ½
GnEl 3½76	3.5	78	97¾	96⅝	97¾	+ ½
GElC 8.6s85	8.5	4	101	101	101	+ ⅛
GElCr 8½76	8.3	20	102⅜	102¼	102⅜	+ ⅜
GElCr 7⅛78	7.2	25	98½	98	98½	− ½
GElCr 7s80	7.2	14	96	96	96	+ ½
GnInstr 5s92	cv	20	56	55¾	56	− ¼
GMills 8s99	8.6	5	93	93	93	+3
GMA 8⅞99	8.9	93	99⅝	99¼	99⅝	+ ⅛
GMA 8¾77	8.4	1	103¾	103¾	103¾	+ ⅜
GMA 8s93	8.4	5	95	95	95	+3⅛
GMA 7.85s98	8.7	17	90	89⅞	90	.....
GMA 7¾94	8.7	18	88¾	88¾	88¾	.....
GMA 7⅛90	8.2	25	86⅛	85½	86⅛	+1
GMA 7⅛92	8.4	5	84¼	84¼	84¼	− ¾
GMA 6¼88	7.7	40	81⅝	81⅛	81⅛	+ ⅛
GMA 5s77	5.2	63	95⅞	95⅛	95⅞	+ ⅞

Bonds	Cur Yld	Vol	High	Low	Close	Net Chg
Medus 5¾88	cv	5	73	73	73	.....
Mellon 10s89	9.9	253	100⅝	100⅜	100½	+ ¼
Melln 7.8s82	7.9	2	98¾	97⅝	97⅝	+ ⅛
MGM 5s93	cv	4	77	77	77	−2½
MGIC 8⅜88	10.	6	79	79	79	.....
MGIC 5s93	cv	19	54	53½	53½	−1
MichB 7¾11	8.6	50	89⅝	88	89⅝	+1⅝
MichB 7s12	8.8	9	79	79	79	+1⅛
MichB 6¼78	6.5	15	96	96	96	.....
MicW 10⅝95	10.	41	104¾	104¼	104¾	+ ½
Micr 10s2000	12.	8	83	82¾	83	+ ¼
MidMt 8s80	17.	16	45	44¾	45	.....
MSPS 4s91	9.6	1	41⅝	41⅝	41⅝	+ ½
MMM 8.20s	7.9	18	103½	103	103	+ ½
MKT 5½33f	..	2	7¼	7¼	7¼	+ ¼
MoPac 5s45f	..	86	40¾	40¾	40¾	+ ¼
MPac 4¾30f	..	6	39	39	39	.....
M Pac 4¼05	9.4	32	45	44½	45	+ ½
MoAl 8.45 05	8.5	19	98¾	98¾	98¾	+3¼
Mob O 7⅜01	8.2	10	89	89	89	+1½
Moh D 5½94	cv	51	25½	25	25¼	+ ¾
vjMoM 4s91f	..	3	60¼	60¼	60¼	+5⅛
Monog 10s99	12.	6	80⅛	80	80⅛	+1½
Mons 9⅛s00	8.7	15	103¾	101½	103¾	+2⅝
Mnt W 4⅞90	7.3	10	66⅛	66⅛	66⅛	+ ½
Mnt W 7⅜88	8.8	2	83	83	83	+2
Mnt W 6½87	8.7	5	74	74	74	+ ¾
Morgn 4¾98	cv	15	95⅞	95⅞	95⅞	− ⅜
vjMrE 3½00	..	1	14½	14½	14½	− ½
MtS Tl 9s10	8.8	33	101¾	101¼	101¾	+1
N Can 5s93	cv	11	65	65	65	+4
N Cash 6s95	cv	59	81	81	81	.....
N City 6½91	cv	8	46	45⅜	45⅜	+1⅜
N City 5½88	cv	25	44½	44½	44½	+ ¼
N Dist 4½92	cv	17	65¾	65½	65½	− ⅜
N FGs 8⅝75	8.6	5	100 1-32	100 1-32	100 1-32	−3-32
N Ind 5¾88	cv	3	55	55	55	+1
NRU 8.95s85	8.8	20	100¾	100¾	100¾	+ ¾
Nat Stl 8s95	8.7	4	91¼	91¼	91¼	.....
NStl 3⅞86r	..	5	63⅛	63⅛	63⅛	.....
Ntrl G 6⅞80	7.8	5	87½	87½	87½	+3½
NCR 9¾2000	9.4	35	103	102½	103	.....
NCR 9s85	8.7	200	102⅝	101	102⅝	+1⅝
N EnT 8⅝09	9.1	30	95¼	94¼	94¼	− ⅝
NEnT 8.2s04	8.9	10	91¾	90½	91¾	+2
NEngT 8s03	9.0	1	88½	88½	88½	+ ⅛
N EnT 7⅜07	9.0	10	81½	81½	81½	+ ⅛
NJBl 9.35s10	8.9	24	104	103½	104	.....
NYBS 10s81	9.9	62	101¼	100⅞	100⅞	− ¼
vjNYC 6s80f	..	15	10⅜	9¼	10⅜	+1
vjNYC 6s90f	..	4	53	53	53	.....
vjNYC 5s13f	..	7	8½	7¾	7¾	.....
vjNYC 4½13	..	5	5⅝	5⅝	5⅝	.....
vjNYH 4½sf	..	1	1⅞	1⅞	1⅞	− ⅜
NYE 10.6s82	9.9	5	106¼	106¼	106¼	+ ¼
NYEG 9⅜05	9.5	3	98	98	98	+1
NY Tl 9¼10	9.0	31	102½	102	102	.....
NY Tel 9s14	8.8	240	101¾	100½	101¾	+ ⅞
NY Tl 8⅞15	8.8	141	100	99½	100	+ ½
NY Tl 8.3s12	8.7	37	95	93½	95	+1¾
NY Tel 8s08	8.7	30	91½	91	91½	+ ½
NY Tel 8s83	7.9	19	101⅛	100¾	101⅛	+ ⅛
NY Tl 4⅛93	7.1	5	57⅝	57⅝	57⅝	+ ⅜
NiM 12.6s81	11.	5	108¾	108¾	108¾	+ ¼
NiM 10.2s05	10.	87	97½	97	97	.....
Ni MP 4⅞87	7.9	3	61	61	61	+1
Ni MP 2⅞80	4.1	10	70	70	70	−5
NLT 8.80s85	8.6	13	101⅞	101¾	101⅞	.....
NorfWe 4s96	7.4	3	53⅜	53⅜	53⅜	+ ⅜
Norlin 9s88	12.	5	74	74	74	.....
NAMg 5½79	8.4	23	65	63½	65	+1½
NoIllG 8½76	8.3	31	101¾	101¾	101¾	− ¾
NoNGs 9s85	8.8	10	102⅛	102⅛	102⅛	+1
No NGs 8s91	9.0	5	88¾	88¾	88¾	.....
No St P 4s88	6.4	3	62	62	62	+1
NwnMu 6s91	cv	1	66	66	66	−1¼
NortS 6s98	9.6	29	63	62½	62½	− ½
Oak In 4⅜87	cv	5	52½	52½	52½	.....
Occidt 7½96	cv	274	96½	94⅛	96	−1¼
Ogden 5s93	cv	17	60⅝	60	60	.....
OhBIT 7⅞13	8.7	10	90	90	90	−2
OhEd 10s81	9.3	76	107⅜	106¼	107⅜	+ ¼
OhP 12⅛81	11.	22	106¾	106¾	106¾	.....
OhP 10⅛82	9.9	29	101½	100¾	101½	+ ¾

Bonds	Cur Yld	Vol	High	Low	Close	Net* Chg
Sw BlT 7s78	6.9	10	100½	100½	100½	+ ½
Sw BT 6⅞11	8.3	141	82	79	82	+3
Sw BT 6½79	6.7	10	96	96	96	.....
Sprag 4¼92	cv	26	44	43½	44	+ ½
StO Cal 7s96	7.8	31	89⅜	89	89	+ ⅛
S OCal 5¾92	7.4	41	77⅝	77	77½	+ ½
StOIn 9.7s89	9.7	153	99⅞	99⅞	99⅞	.....
StOIn 9.2s04	8.7	2	104¾	104¾	104¾	.....
StO Ind 6s91	7.4	10	80½	80½	80½	+ ¼
StdOh 7.6s99	8.9	10	84½	84½	84½	+1½
St Pkg 5¼90	cv	1	41⅛	41⅛	41⅛	.....
St Pru 6½90	cv	3	62⅛	62⅛	62⅛	.....
StaMut 9s80	16.	28	54	54	54	− ¼
StaufC 4½91	cv	19	130	128	128	−2
Stevens 4s90	cv	3	68⅛	68⅛	68⅛	+ ⅛
Stkl 10¼2000	10.	5	101	101	101	.....
Suave 5s97	cv	6	37¾	37¾	37¾	.....
SunOil 7¾76	7.6	5	101½	101	101	− ¼
SunOil 4⅝90	6.6	20	70	70	70	+1
Sundstr 5s93	cv	7	60	60	60	+3
Sutro 6¾82	10.	13	62	61	62	+1
Sybrn 9⅛85	9.0	30	101	101	101	.....
Sybrn 4½87	cv	5	69½	69⅛	69⅛	− ⅜
Talctt 9¾76	10.	34	95	95	95	.....
TalcNtl 6s94	cv	26	35½	35	35⅛	− ⅜
Tandy 10s94	11.	15	87	86¾	87	+1¼
Tapp 5½s94	cv	1	50	50	50	.....
Teledy 10s04	12.	41	79½	78¾	79½	.....
Teledy 3½92	cv	15	46½	46¼	46½	.....
Telex 9s96	20.	29	45⅛	44	44½	− ⅝
TennCp 9s78	8.8	5	102¼	102¼	102¼	.....
TenCp 8⅜75	8.3	16	100¼	100¼	100¼	+3-16
TenCp 6¼92	cv	28	87¼	86¾	86¾	− ¼
TenInc 9⅞s	9.6	25	102	101⅞	101⅞	+ ⅝
TenInc 6s79	6.6	15	90¾	90¾	90¾	.....
TVA 9¼s95	8.6	10	107	107	107	− ¾
TVA 8.10s79	7.7	26	104½	104	104½	+ ½
TVA 8.05s99	8.3	20	97	96¾	96¾	− ¼
TV 7¾s98C	8.3	25	92⅞	92⅞	92⅞	+1⅞
TVA 7.4s97	8.3	45	89	88½	88½	− ½
TV 7.35s97B	8.3	28	89	87½	88	+ ⅛
TV 7.35s97C	8.3	10	88½	88½	88½	+ ½
TV 7.35s98A	8.2	95	89½	88	89½	+1⅞
TV 7.35s98B	8.3	28	88⅛	88	88⅛	+1⅛
TV 7.35 98Br	..	15	88¼	87½	87½	.....
TVA 7¼s76	7.2	20	100¾	100½	100¾	+ ½
TVA 7s97	8.1	50	85¾	85¾	85¾	+ ¼
TVA 7s97r	..	10	84¾	84¾	84¾	.....
Tesoro 5¼89	cv	126	105⅜	104	105	−2½
Texco 8⅞05	8.6	88	102	101⅝	102	+ ⅜
Texco 7¾01	8.4	50	92	92	92	+ ¾
Texco 5¾97	7.5	12	77	76½	76½	+ ½
TxGsT 8¾84	9.1	20	96	96	96	−2
Texfi 4¾96	cv	30	34	34	34	.....
Tol Ed 7½02	9.6	5	77¾	77¾	77¾	−2¼
TWA 11s86	11.	4	94	94	94	+1
TWA 10s85	11.	25	90	89	90	.....
TWA 6½78f	..	19	68⅞	67⅞	67⅞	−1
TWA 5s94	cv	177	35⅛	34¼	34½	− ⅛
TWA 4s92	cv	44	27½	27¼	27¼	− ¼
TranF 10s77	9.6	13	103¾	102⅝	103¾	+1¼
TranF 7⅞91	10.	1	74	74	74	.....
TriSM 7¾80	19.	113	40	39¼	40	.....
TriSoM 7s92	cv	11	33	33	33	+ ¼
TucsG 8⅛01	10.	2	79½	79½	79½	.....
UCarb 8½05	8.5	55	99	99	99	+ ½
U Car 5.3s97	7.2	54	73	72⅛	73	+1½
U OilC 8¼76	8.1	60	101⅞	101¾	101⅞	+ ⅝
UP Cp 8.6 83	8.3	5	103¼	103¼	103¼	+1
UP Cp 4¾99	cv	3	138½	138½	138½	−1½
UPR 7.20s76	7.1	10	100⅝	100⅝	100⅝	.....
UPRR 2½91	5.3	25	48	47	47	−1
Uniryl 5½96	cv	22	57½	57¼	57¼	− ½
UnAirL 5s91	cv	21	61	60½	60½	−1
UnAL 4¼92	cv	21	48½	48	48	− ½
UBrnd 9⅛98	16.	45	55⅛	55	55⅛	.....
UBrnd 6¾88	14.	5	48	48	48	.....
UBrnd 5½94	cv	52	37½	37	37½	+ ½
UGP 10⅛90	10.	2	94⅛	94⅛	94⅛	+ ⅜
UGsP 5¼77	5.5	10	94¾	94¾	94¾	+1¼
UGsP 5⅛78	5.6	11	90¼	90¼	90¼	+ ¼
UJer 7.95s79	8.4	5	94¼	94¼	94¼	.....
Un Mer 4s90	cv	3	47½	47½	47½	+ ½
UnNucl 5s88	cv	25	70	69⅝	70	.....
US Ho 5½95	cv	12	46½	46	46	− ⅛
US In 7¾97	12.	10	63½	63½	63½	.....
US L 7.65s77	7.9	3	96¾	96¾	96¾	+ ¾
US Stl 7¾01	8.6	5	90	90	90	.....
US Stl 4⅝96	7.2	85	63⅞	62½	63⅝	+1⅛
US Stl 4½86	6.0	16	74¾	74½	74¾	+ ⅛
UnTec 9s85	8.8	10	102	102	102	+ ¼
UnTec 5⅜91	cv	67	85	84	85	.....
UnTec 4½88	8.6	1	52⅛	52⅛	52⅛	.....
UnTec 4½92	cv	222	75½	73½	74½	−1
Upjhn 8⅛85	8.0	33	100⅝	100⅝	100⅝	.....
UtaP 10¼83	9.4	10	108½	108½	108½	+3½
UVInd 5¾93	cv	31	67	66½	66¾	− ¼
UVInd 5⅜95	10.	20	52⅛	51	51	−2
Ver P 9⅝98	10.	19	94	93¾	94	+1½
Va EP 3⅝86	cv	5	58½	58½	58½	+ ½
Va EP 3s78	3.5	5	85½	85½	85½	−3
VaRy 6s2008	10.	17	58	57	58	+1⅞
WalMt 6½95	cv	5	106½	106½	106½	−1
WallM 6½91	cv	11	69	68¾	68¾	.....
WarL 8.3s85	8.1	12	102⅜	102¼	102¼	+ ⅛
Wean 5½93	cv	5	52	52	52	.....
Wean 5½93n	cv	2	52¾	52¾	52¾	.....
WAirL 5¼93	cv	5	75½	75½	75½	.....
WUC 10¾97	13.	26	79⅛	79	79	.....
WUC 5¼97	cv	27	42	42	42	.....
WUT 8.10s98	12.	5	67	67	67	.....
WUT 7.90s97	12.	21	64½	64	64	−1

Figure 13–6 New York Stock Exchange Bond Price Quotations. *(Reprinted with permission of The Wall Street Journal, © Dow Jones & Company, Inc. 1975. All Rights Reserved.)*

The name of the company is listed under "Bonds," followed by the face value or nominal coupon interest rate of the bond and the maturity date. The first listing in the example taken from figure 13–6 is American Airlines' 11 percent bonds maturing in 1988. The current yield is also 11 percent because the bonds are selling at face value. Note that the $4\frac{1}{2}$s due in 1992 do not show a current yield because they are convertible issues (cv) whose real yield is tied to the underlying stock. Both ATT current yields are higher than the nominal interest rate because the bonds are selling at a discount (less than the par value).

"Vol." indicates sales volume in thousands of dollars at par value. This should also indicate the number of securities that changed hands in most cases. The high, low, close, and net change columns operate in the same manner as stock quotations. Bond quotations in newspapers drop the last digit of the sales price. Bonds selling at par ($1,000) would be listed at 100. Quotations over 100 indicate that a premium is being paid, while below 100 indicates a discount is received. In our example, your purchase of ATT $2\frac{3}{4}$s 80 at $80\frac{1}{2}$ means you would pay $805.00 for a $1,000 bond maturing in 1980. During the next $4\frac{1}{2}$ or so years before maturity, you would receive interest amounting to approximately $123.75 ($27.50 per yr. × $4\frac{1}{2}$ yrs.), plus the discount of $195.00 to be received by you when the bond is redeemed for $1,000 at maturity. The exact method of calculating yield on bonds will be discussed in chapter 14.

Periodicals

There are many general, business, and investment publications available on a semiweekly to monthly basis. Most of these are available in your local library. Consumer, family, women's, and men's magazines often contain feature articles about the investment world. If you are a novice, start by reading these. Then move up to *Time, Newsweek, U.S. News and World Report,* and *Business Week.* The serious investor would probably subscribe to one or more of the following: *Barron's, Financial World, Forbes, Fortune,* and *The Magazine of Wall Street.* These are the better-known periodicals. Browse through your local library; you will become immersed in a sea of investment information.

Financial Reporting and Advisory Services

There are a number of research, reporting, and advisory services available. The better-known companies that offer these services are *Fitch Investment Service, Moody's Investors Service, Standard and Poor's,* and the *Value Line.* These organizations publish information manuals and provide advisory services for substantial fees. You can obtain information on individual corporations and industry groupings from any of the services. They compile comparative statistics covering a period of years to provide trend analysis on the assets, earnings, dividends, financial ratios, and stock prices of all corporations listed on the NYSE and many more Amex and OTC companies.

Moody's Manuals, Standard and Poor's Standard Corporation Records, and the *Value Line Investment Survey* are large loose-leaf volumes that are updated almost daily. Their subscription cost is too great for the small investor, but you do have access to these publications through your broker's office or public and college libraries. Figure 13–7 is an explanatory example of one of 1,550 Value Line Reports from the *Value Line Investment Survey.*

Investment Counselors

For the truly personalized, all-inclusive approach to investing, a substantial investor should employ the services of an investment counseling firm. These individuals and organizations will tailor an investment program to the individual's investment objective and pocketbook. Usually a minimum of $100,000 in liquid assets is required to engage their services. Counseling fees range upward from 1 percent to about 5 percent of the portfolio value. Many management fees, which include performing the actual timing of transactions, may run to 10 percent, depending upon the size of the portfolio and the number of services included.

Brokerage Firms

The large nationwide brokerage firms offer lots of investment information for the asking. Various investment brochures and bulletins are published regularly by the larger brokerage firms. Usually they are free. Often you can be placed on a mailing list. Brokerage houses also maintain a supply of information booklets published by the NYSE. A very good one, obtainable free, is *The Language of Investing*, a glossary of investment terms. As you become a recognized customer, your investment funds will be solicited and investment suggestions will be made regularly by your account executive. If your account is small, you will not get much portfolio supervision because account executives will first service those clients who are earning them greater commissions.

Annual Corporate Reports

Another good source of information to the investor is the annual corporate report. These reports may be rather plain, fact-filled documents or slick, full-color magazines. All will have full accounting with comparative balance and income statements covering the last few years, plus a message from the company's president or chief executive officer. Information about the company's current operations and future plans embellishes most annual reports.

Extreme care must be taken to insure that the glowing accomplishments and plans in the text of the report match the actual facts of the accounting statements. Both the NYSE and the Securities and Exchange Commission are pushing for "full disclosure" in annual corporate reports. Companies seldom sort out their most important problems for report readers. Also the reports seldom indicate exactly where the company's earnings came from. This important information would probably reveal very marginal operations in many divisions of a company.

The annual report gives you a "feel" for the company. Most corporations will send you their annual report upon request. If you are a shareholder, you will automatically receive one so that you will be informed of what is happening at your company. Brokerage firms are usually well supplied with annual reports from major companies. They, too, will be happy to give you a copy.

REGULATION AND PROTECTION

People cannot always be protected from themselves. Even with all the information sources available, an investor can sustain a costly loss by an unwise decision. If your loss is caused by speculation, wrong expectations, misinterpretation of facts, or a general economic decline, you must be prepared to take your lumps. If losses happen regularly, you probably are not very knowledgeable or are relying on the wrong advice. In any case, you can generally expect to get an honest deal in the investment world if you are knowledgeable. Self-regulation by the industry and government regulation and protection have greatly reduced churning of accounts and misrepresentation of investment facts.

Self-Regulation

The investment industry has always had to police its ranks because of the nature of the business. The passing of fraudulent information, the churning of accounts, and self-serving investment transactions by investment industry representatives tend to be the activities that most need regulating. Fraudulent information has been given to get the client to purchase a particular security. Churning consists of advising a client to trade more often so that the salesperson can earn more commission. A self-serving purchase occurs when the sales representative buys for his personal account at the best price but does not do the same for his client.

Individual *broker-dealer* firms watch the performance of their salespeople very carefully. The companies have a good reputation to uphold, so they require their employees to maintain the highest degree of integrity. Most brokerage houses are members of the Better Business Bureaus in their local area. They actively suggest the use of such facilities whenever a consumer feels he has been cheated in some manner by anyone who purports to be a member of the investment community.

Industry regulation comes from two sources: the National Association of Security Dealers, who have a professional membership and a code of ethics, and the stock exchanges. Every exchange has rules governing floor trading and members' relations with clients. The exchanges require member

Here is a sample Value Line Report: →

- **A** Performance Rank
- **B** Safety Rank
- **C** Beta

These three reflect thousands of hours of research. They express Value Line's evaluation of practically everything you need to know to select a stock for purchase or sale or for holding according to Value Line's recommended strategy.

- **D** Price-Earnings Ratio
- **E** Dividend Yield
- **F** Recent Price
- **G** Indices of Price Stability and Growth Persistence
- **H** Annual Price Range
- **I** 12 Months Earnings Per Share Plotted Quarterly
- **J** Index of Insider Decisions
- **K** Historical Growth Trends
- **L** Annual Rates of Change
- **M** Current Position
- **N** Capital Structure
- **O** Quarterly Sales (Company Basis)
- **P** Earnings (Per Share) as Reported
- **Q** Quarterly Dividend Paid (Per Share)
- **R** Dividend Record
- **S** Stock Comment
- **T** Business Comment
- **U** Statistical Milestones (Company Basis)
- **V** Statistical Milestones (Per Share Basis)
- **W** Estimates of Sales, Earnings, Dividends, Etc.
- **X** Value Line
- **Y** Percentage of Outstanding Shares Traded Monthly
- **Z** "Cash Flow" Multiple used to Describe Historical Price-Earnings Relationship
- **ZZ** Estimated Range of Average Annual Prices, 1976-78

AMERICAN SMELTING NYSE-AR

RECENT PRICE 20 | DIV'D YIELD 6.0% (NORM 5.0%) | P/E RATIO 4.3 (NORM 11.5) | 1157

	1964	1965	1966	1967	1968	1969	1970	1971	1972	1973	
	[illegible]1.2	28.6	30.9	28.1	49.7	49.3	36.1	28.8	23.5	26.1	←High
	[illegible].7	18.0	19.1	21.3	24.3	27.0	21.2	16.4	17.5	17.3	←Low

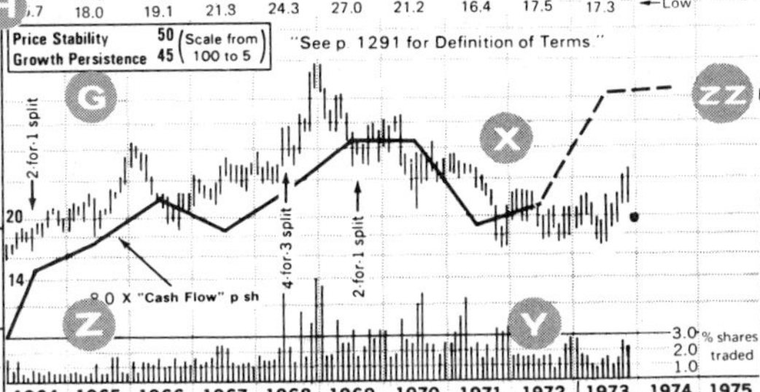

PERFORM'CE Next 12 Mos. **1** Highest

SAFETY **3** Average

(Scale: 1 Highest to 5 Lowest)

BETA 1.04 (NYSE Avg. = 1.00)

Nov. 16, 1973 Value Line

Shares Held by Investment Companies			
9/30/72	12/31/72	3/31/73	6/30/73
1,350,166	1,223,766	1,241,666	1,147,900
(15 funds)	(15 funds)	(13 funds)	(13 funds)

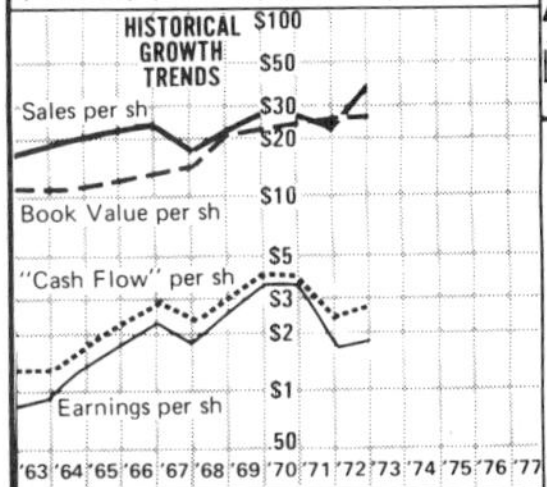

	1964	1965	1966	1967	1968	1969	1970	1971	1972	1973	1974	1975	© Arnold Bernhard & Co., Inc. 76-78 E
Sales per sh	20.50	21.10	22.46	17.58	21.78	26.65	26.84	24.53	30.54	*38.95*	*43.05*		*46.65*
"Cash Flow" per sh	1.87	2.20	2.76	2.30	2.96	3.96	3.89	2.39	2.74	*5.20*	*5.25*		*4.95*
Earnings p sh (yr-end)	1.41	1.80	2.38	1.94	2.52	3.44	3.32	1.72	1.84	*4.25*	*4.15*		*3.50*
(A) Egs p sh as reported	1.41	1.80	2.85	1.94	2.52	3.42	3.16	1.72	1.84	*4*[illegible]	*[illegible]4.15*		*3.50*
(B) Div'ds Decl'd per sh	0.79	1.05	1.24	1.13	1.32	1.90	1.90	1.73	1.20	1[illegible]	*[illegible]1.20*		*2.00*
Cap'l spending per sh	0.39	0.38	1.24	1.61	1.28	0.87	2.68	1.40	3.04	*3.25*	*4.00*		*2.50*
Book Value per sh	11.61	12.31	13.47	14.53	20.17	22.14	25.30	25.14	25.60	*28.65*	*31.55*		*37.30*
(C) Common Shs Outst'g	29.66	29.13	29.10	29.08	29.11	28.93	26.75	26.78	26.67	*26.70*	*26.70*		*26.80*
Avg Ann'l P/E Ratio	13.2	12.1	8.3	12.9	12.5	9.9	8.9	13.6	10.9	'73-'74 italic figures are VL estimates			*11.5*
Avg Ann'l Div'd Yield	4.2%	4.8%	5.2%	4.5%	4.2%	5.6%	6.8%	7.4%	6.0%				*5.0%*
Sales ($mill)	608.0	614.6	653.8	511.2	634.1	771.0	717.8	656.8	814.4	*1040*	*1150*		*1250*
Operating Margin	12.1%	13.3%	10.7%	8.2%	6.0%	7.8%	8.2%	4.3%	6.1%	*8.0%*	*10.0%*		*8.0%*
Depreciation ($mill)	13.5	11.5	11.0	10.6	12.9	15.2	15.2	17.9	23.9	*26.0*	*30.0*		*38.0*
Net Income ($mill)	41.9	52.5	69.2	56.3	73.2	99.4	88.8	46.0	49.1	*113.5*	*110*		*94.0*
Depreciation Rate	4.3%	4.4%	3.8%	3.2%	3.5%	3.9%	3.5%	3.7%	4.4%	*4.5%*	*4.5%*		*4.5%*
Income Tax Rate	39.1%	37.2%	30.2%	22.5%	14.6%	21.4%	22.4%	11.0%	16.8%	*25.0%*	*25.0%*		*25.0%*
Net Income Margin	6.9%	8.5%	10.6%	11.0%	11.6%	12.9%	12.4%	7.0%	6.0%	*10.9%*	*9.6%*		*7.5%*
Funded Debt ($mill)	40.9	40.0	36.4	35.2	33.5	24.0	23.7	38.1	51.0	*50.0*	*45.0*		*60.0*
Net Worth ($mill)	344.5	358.6	392.1	422.5	587.1	640.7	676.6	673.3	682.6	*765*	*842*		*1000*
Working Cap'l ($mill)	186.2	191.7	213.5	186.7	185.9	204.9	191.7	173.7	130.7	*150*	*150*		*225*
% Earned Total Cap'l	11.4%	13.6%	16.6%	12.7%	12.1%	15.1%	12.8%	6.7%	7.0%	*14.5%*	*12.5%*		*9.5%*
% Earned Net Worth	12.2%	14.6%	17.7%	13.3%	12.5%	15.5%	13.1%	6.8%	7.2%	*15.0%*	*13.0%*		*9.0%*
% All Div'ds to Net Inc	56%	59%	52%	58%	52%	56%	61%	101%	65%	*28%*	*29%*		*57%*

ANNUAL RATES of change (per sh)	Past 10 Yrs	Past 5 Yrs	Est '70-'72 to '76-'78
Sales	5.0%	6.0%	*10.0%*
"Cash Flow"	10.0%	4.5%	*8.0%*
Earnings	12.5%	2.5%	*7.5%*
Book Value	8.5%	13.5%	*14.5%*

CURRENT POSITION ($mill.)	1970	1971	12/31/72
Cash Assets	17.9	10.4	15.1
Receivables	64.4	73.3	82.9
Inventories	212.2	217.2	208.7
Other	19.7	24.6	25.8
Current Assets	314.2	325.5	332.5
Accts Payable	84.0	97.4	108.0
Debt Due	--	--	63.6
Other	38.5	54.4	30.2
Current Liab'ties	122.5	151.8	201.8

CAPITAL STRUCTURE as of 12/31/72

Debt $51.0 mill. **Interest** $2.4 mill.

Pfd Stock None **Pfd Div** None

Common Stock 26,665,777 shares

Cal-endar	QUARTERLY SALES ($ Millions) Mar. 31	June 30	Sept. 30	Dec. 31	Full Year
1970	180.4	203.6	173.5	160.3	717.[illegible]
1971	182.9	201.6	111.6	160.7	65[illegible]
1972	210.2	206.7	191.4	206.1	81[illegible]
1973	256.0	273.9	250.6	*259.5*	*1040*
1974	*283.5*	*301.5*	*278.5*	*286.5*	*1150*

Cal-endar	EARNINGS AS REPORTED (per sh) (A) Mar. 31	June 30	Sept. 30	Dec. 31	Full Year
1970	1.07	1.07	.60	.42	3.1[illegible]
1971	.46	.75	.11	.40	1.7[illegible]
1972	.47	.46	.36	.55	1.84
1973	.63	1.04	1.56	*1.02*	*4.25*
1974	*1.05*	*1.10*	*.90*	*1.10*	*4.15*

Cal-endar	QUARTERLY DIVIDENDS PAID (B) Mar. 31	June 30	Sept. 30	Dec. 31	Full Year
1969	.475	.475	.475	.475	1.90
1970	.475	.475	.475	.475	1.90
1971	.475	.475	.475	.30	1.73
1972	.30	.30	.30	.30	1.20
1973	.30	.30	.30	.30	1.20

BUSINESS: American Smelting & Refining Co. is the world's largest custom smelter of nonferrous metals. Metal interests are worldwide and include copper, lead, zinc, gold, and silver. Federated Metals Division processes a wide variety of nonferrous metal products. Sales breakdown: copper, 36%; silver, 16%; lead, 8%; zinc, 6%; gold, 3%; other products and services, 31%. Major subsidiaries: Mt. Isa Mines in Australia (52.7%-owned), Southern Peru Copper (51.5% owned), Asarco Mexicana, S.A. (49%-owned). Has 14,800 employees, 59,500 stockholders. Chrmn.: C.F. Barber. Pres.: R.L. Hennebach, Inc.: N.Y. Address: 120 Broadway, N.Y., N.Y. 10005.

A superior relative market performance may be expected in the coming year for Asarco shares. Since the beginning of 1969, the shares have not been a rewarding investment. Now, however, earnings gains in the past two years (particularly in 1973) combined with the increasing visibility of future earnings have attracted a following on Wall Street. Note also, that insider decisions have been on the buy side since the start of 1972. Investment companies, up until June 1973 anyway, were net sellers; however, we suspect that trend will reverse by the time year-end figures are available.

This is not a stock to lock up for the long pull. Although the Safety Grade is Average and the Beta Index of 1.04 suggests that the stock moves with the market, Asarco's earnings have been quite cyclical, more or less matching the ups and downs of metal prices, particularly that of copper. There is some feeling in the industry that the price of copper is likely to be less volatile in the years ahead. Planned capacity expansion and the cost structure within the industry are cited as evidence that copper will fluctuate less widely in the future and, consequently, peaks and valleys will become less pronounced in Asarco's earnings. As yet there has not been sufficient evidence of this to convince us. As a result, our 1976-78 projections of share results are actually lower than the earnings estimated for both 1973 and 1974.

The 1973 estimate includes 44¢ from a sale of securities. Because accountants have now decided to eliminate extraordinary items which are usually excluded and footnoted on our data sheets, the net gain of $11 million from the sale of 3.7% of M.I.M. stock has been included in reported results. Earlier in the year (before the accounting change) the company established loss reserves (of an extraordinary nature) of 37¢ a share that have been excluded from the 1973 estimate. Consequently, on a *reported* basis, this year's earnings are expected to exceed next year's, but on an *operating* basis the company is expected to earn about $3.80 a share this year and $4.15 a share next year. *R.J.D.*

(A) Based on avg. shs. outstanding. Excludes extraordinary gains: '64, 10¢; '70, 81¢. Loss: '73, 38¢. Includes pretax gain of $21 million from sale of securities in '73. (B) Next div'd meeting about Jan. 25. Goes ex about Jan. 31. Div'd payment dates: Feb. 28, May 31, Aug. 31, Nov. 30. Div'd reinvestment plan available. (C) In millions, adjusted for stock splits and div'ds.

Figure 13–7 Sample *Value Line* Report. (The Value Line. *New York: Arnold Bernhard & Co., Inc.*)

firms to be audited so that they maintain financial strength. The NYSE has had a special fund to which all members contribute for the payment of creditors whenever a member firm becomes bankrupt.

Government Regulation

Federal and state laws regulating the investment community for the protection of the consumer are constantly being revised to account for new investment situations and to promote a new era of consumerism. Federal laws are primarily concerned with investment activities involving interstate and foreign commerce. State laws govern investment activity wholly within the individual states. These state laws are often called blue-sky laws.

The Federal Securities Acts The Federal Securities Act of 1933 and the Securities Exchange Act of 1934 were passed in response to the "Great Stock Market Crash." These acts required that new securities be fully and clearly described in the offering literature and the sales presentation; that the Securities and Exchange Commission (SEC) be established; that all securities listed on the national securities exchanges be registered with the SEC; that manipulative practices to change prices artificially or create sales be prohibited; and that officers, directors, and principal stockholders (those owning over 10 percent of total shares) report any transaction by them involving shares of their company to the SEC by the tenth of the month following the transaction. Investment companies and credit requirements have also come under the federal regulation of the Securities and Exchange Commission.

The SEC regularly makes headlines in the financial chronicles by investigating suspected activities, but even with all this "protection" an investor can become a victim of illegal practices. Your best protection is to help yourself by being aware, by being careful, and by realizing that "you never get something for nothing." There is no insurance against your stupidity in the market place—*caveat emptor*!

Securities Investor Protection Corporation Another form of protection available to investors since 1971 is custodial account protection available through the Securities Investor Protection Corporation (SIPC). All registered brokers must contribute to this government-sponsored corporation, which insures investors who allow their brokers to keep their securities for safety and trading convenience. The SIPC offers insurance of $50,000, of which only $20,000 has to be repaid into a cash account. The loss coverage is limited to customer losses as a result of brokerage house bankruptcy. It is similar to the FDIC in this respect. It is depository insurance, not poor-investment insurance.

Vocabulary and Concepts

Averages	Liquidity
Call feature	Over-the-counter
Capital	Participation feature
Common stock	Preferred stock
Convertibility feature	Rights
Corporate bonds	Stock exchange
Debt funding	Underwriting
Equity funding	Warrant
Index	

Questions for Discussion

1. How are capital needs of American businesses met? Explain why different methods are used to raise funds.
2. What is the difference between the primary and secondary markets?

3. Explain how rights and warrants operate. What is their importance?
4. Describe the basic procedures behind a buy or sale stock transaction.
5. What is a common stock? Describe its characteristics.
6. What is a preferred stock? Describe its characteristics.
7. What is a corporate bond? Describe its characteristics.
8. What are the main features of the *Wall Street Journal*?
9. How is the investing public protected from unscrupulous securities dealers? Is there sufficient protection?
10. What information do the daily stock quotations usually supply? In what manner may this information be used?

Projects

1. Visit your city or college library to compile a list of periodicals available that provide current articles on the stock market. Which offer advice? Which report factual information?
2. Read the business pages of your local newspaper or the *Wall Street Journal*. Secure the latest annual corporate report of a well-recommended and an unrecommended company. Note the president's letter to the stockholders. Is there a difference in the outlook and terminology of the letter? Are annual reports useful and informative tools?
3. For a one-month period compare the price movement of four common stocks selected at random with the movement of the Dow Jones industrial averages. Compare four common stocks recommended for purchase by a broker or periodical. What conclusions can you reach concerning your random selection vs. recommended stock?

Case Problem

Art and Barbara Able and Bart Baker have discussed the possibilities of investing in securities. The Ables desire stocks or bonds that will supplement their income because they are gaining appreciation on their home. Bart disagrees with this idea. He suggests that they invest for growth. What do you suggest? Considering current market conditions, how would you invest $10,000? Support your advice.

14

buying and selling securities

An important part of buying and selling securities is deciding what to buy and when to buy. In the final analysis you must decide on both of these factors. If you have little or no information on a security or the market as a whole, you are not an informed buyer. You are gambling on someone else's decision about what and when to buy. Try doing some research on your own before getting professional advice on buying securities that interest you. Finally, make your decision and act on it. Later in the chapter we will find that investment decisions should be based on a combination of factors such as the economic situation, financial analysis, market price, and opportunity. Learn what and when to buy through a combination of self-instruction, advice, and experience.

DO-IT-YOURSELF RESEARCH

The adage that "experience is the best teacher" may be true in many endeavors, but it is not necessarily true in the investment field. Knowledge is a more useful first tool. All investors are exposed to some information from the numerous sources available, but you should want to find useful information and then read it at your own pace. Once you have gained a knowledge of the concepts and terminology of investment, you can discuss it more intelligently to obtain and understand advice.

Investment Clubs

These organizations provide an excellent way to gain understanding and experience with securities transactions at very little cost. Typical clubs consist of ten to twenty members who contribute $10 to $25 monthly into a pool to provide cash for actual stock purchases. The purpose is to learn by doing, to experience the research and decision-making process.

Each member may specialize in a particular industry and then make a report and recommendation on various companies within an industry. Companies may also be selected and analyzed on a random basis. In either case, everyone participates in security selections. Decisions are made by vote of the membership after thoroughly discussing the proposals. An investment club can provide very valuable experience in portfolio management. You can obtain information about starting a club from brokerage houses or from the National Association of Investment Clubs, 1515 E. Eleven Mile Road, Royal Oak, Michigan 48067.

Cash Reserves?

Before you actually begin an investment program, you must determine how much of your cash reserve you should keep for emergencies. It would be foolhardy to purchase securities with your extra funds only to have to cash them within a very short time. This may cause you to sell at a loss because you would be at the mercy of the market place. You should not place all your extra funds in securities. Obviously, you should not invest monies that have been saved for a specific purpose to be used at a specific time. For example, funds saved for a home could be greatly reduced if you are forced to sell securities at a specific time.

BUYING AND SELLING PROCEDURES

Perhaps it is not vital that an investor understand the mechanics of buying and selling securities, but as with just about everything else, the more you know, the better off you usually are. Our discussion on buying and selling will revolve around the secondary market, the stock market of the financial pages, where investors buy and sell stock through intermediaries.

Opening a Brokerage Account

As mentioned in the last chapter, you must deal with a broker in order to buy or sell a stock because of the nature of the market place. Without the use of brokerage houses and securities exchanges, very little trading would be accomplished because buyers and sellers would not be likely to find each other. Therefore, you must open an account with a broker in order to participate in the stock market to any degree. Opening an account requires that you fill out an application with relevant personal and financial data. It is similar to applying for credit. You can apply by mail or in person. Once an account is established, most transactions can be handled by telephone.

You will be assigned an *account executive* by the brokerage firm. This person is known to the public as a stockbroker. He will probably be a broker-salesman with considerable training in the investment field. You may select a particular account executive by recommendation. Your broker should work with you to assist you in reaching your investment goals.

Placing an Order

Let us assume that after thorough investigation of the market, you decide to purchase 100 shares of McDonald's common stock. You tell your broker the price at which you wish to buy. You may give him a *market order,* the best price obtainable when the order is executed, or a *limit order,* a specific price at which you are willing to buy. Your limit order to buy will be executed at a price lower than you specify if the market price is down. Orders to sell use the same terminology.

The actual sequence of events for giving your order to a local broker's office and its execution on the exchange occurs somewhat in this manner: Your broker will take your order over the telephone and obtain a "quote" from an electronic terminal linked to a computer center (Market Data System) that provides current prices on listed stocks. (Active OTC stock quotes are also available by electronic retrieval.) You then decide on the market or limit price at which you wish to purchase. We will assume you decide to buy at market. Your broker wires his firm's floor broker at the NYSE. This man maintains a communication center at the edge of the exchange floor in order to carry out transactions desired by his firm's customers.

The floor broker takes your order to one of the eighteen trading posts that handle buy and sell transactions. Each stock listed on the NYSE is assigned a specific location. At the trading post handling McDonald's, your floor broker contacts other floor brokers who are attempting to sell. Your broker asks, "How's McDonald's?" Another broker may say, "Bid 51, asked $51\frac{1}{4}$." Armed with this information, your floor broker can enter the auction process at the trading post. Brokers are required to protect the interests of their customers, so yours will not necessarily buy at $51\frac{1}{4}$. He will bid at 51, then $51\frac{1}{8}$, before meeting the asking price of $51\frac{1}{4}$. In the meantime, other brokers, selling the McDonald's stock on behalf of their clients, offer it at $51\frac{1}{4}$. If no takers, they will try $51\frac{1}{8}$, and finally 51. Chances are the brokers will compromise at $51\frac{1}{8}$. There is a true auction process operating at all times. If your broker does not accept an offering price, a competing broker may very likely purchase the shares for his client.

The transaction is completed as each broker notes the agreement and reports this information back to his respective communications center. The transaction is then reported back to your local broker, who will telephone you. In the meantime, an exchange employee will complete an optical scan card on the transaction so that the latest selling price can be entered in the Market Data System central computer. The latest transaction price is then displayed on the ticker system throughout the nation.

Shortly after you receive word from your broker, you will receive a billing from the brokerage house. You will have five business days to pay the amount due. In this case it will be $5,112.50 for the stock plus commission fees. We will discuss buy and sell costs later. Your copy of the transaction should be kept for income-tax purposes.

The specialist The auction process sounds very time consuming; actually it is not. In a market order transaction, there is usually quick agreement. In a limit order, however, the floor broker often leaves the order with a specialist.

A specialist "makes a market." He specializes in one or more stocks at a specific trading post. He is required to maintain a fair and orderly market in the stocks he handles. To "make a market," he will buy or sell for his own account whenever there is a temporary gap between supply and demand for his stock. He keeps the action going to help maintain liquidity in the market.

Whenever a floor broker cannot execute his client's order, he leaves the order with a specialist who will try to execute it whenever the price reaches the stipulated level. He acts as a broker's broker. The specialist keeps a "book" where all the pending buy and sell orders are kept and matched up as prices change. He is highly regulated and may not buy or sell for his own account until all clients have been accommodated. Critics of the stock market accuse the specialist of manipulating prices for the benefit of "insiders" by opening his book up or down to provide for a prearranged profit.

In addition to market orders and limit orders, there are other orders that you can place with your broker. These are good for both buying and selling situations.

GTC order A "good till cancelled" order is just that, an *open order* good until the broker executes the order or until the customer cancels the order.

Stop order A stop order is a hedging device. It is primarily used to sell at a price above or below the current market price. It is used to protect a "paper profit" or limit the loss on stock holdings. It is often called a stop-loss order. A sale stop order directs a broker to sell at market when a stock reaches a specific price. Buy stop orders are usually entered to protect unrealized profits or to limit losses in a short sale.

Short Sale

You can make a profit in a declining market by a short sale, a very speculative practice. You sell first and buy later, the reverse of a normal transaction. If you believe that the price of a certain stock will decline, you may borrow shares from your broker, sell them, and later purchase and return the same stock at a lower price (you hope). Your profit is the difference between the two prices, less commissions and interest. If you later pay more for the stock you borrowed and returned, the difference would be a loss.

The Securities and Exchange Commission, the stock exchanges, and brokerage houses limit the conditions under which a short sale may be made. A margin account must be used, and you will be required to deposit the current margin plus the proceeds from the sale of the borrowed stock. You cannot sell short on a "down tick"; a short sale must be made at a price higher than the last transaction involving a price change of a particular stock. This means that the ticker price must show a plus difference over the last transaction. There can be a number of no-change transactions occurring between the price changes required for a short sale.

Margin

Stocks can be purchased on credit, which is called margin in the investment field. The object of buying on credit is to increase your purchasing power through leverage. Rather than paying 100 percent cash for a stock purchase, you make a down payment equaling a required percentage of the purchase. The balance of the purchase price is borrowed from your broker, to whom you pay interest. Obviously, your dollars can purchase more shares of stock if you can borrow in a margin transaction. The extra shares then allow you greater gains in a market price increase or greater losses in a price decline. Margin usage is a speculative practice for the sophisticated trader who is willing to take the risk involved.

Persons who desire to use margin must meet certain requirements of the SEC, the exchanges, and the individual brokerage house. The Federal Reserve System sets the margin percentage that must initially be met in a stock transaction. Currently, a purchaser is required to put up 50 percent. Figure 14–1 illustrates the changing margin requirements over the years. If you purchase stock worth $1,000 today, you would have to post $500 and be able to borrow $500 from your broker.

The NYSE requires that $2,000 be left on deposit with your broker if you open a margin account. The NYSE also requires that a 30 percent equity margin be maintained on any margin account. However, individual brokerage houses may require larger deposits or greater maintenance margins. Brokers use these requirements to protect themselves in a declining market.

We will look at an example of how margin works using the purchase of 100 shares of McDonald's common stock. You purchased it at 51⅛ for a total cost of $5,112.50. Present initial margin requirements allow you to pay your broker 50 percent or $2,556.25 and borrow $2,556.25 from him. If margin credit is not available to you, you would be able to buy only 50 shares. If McDonald's returns to its former high for

Initial Margin Requirements

Percent of Total Value Required to Purchase Stock

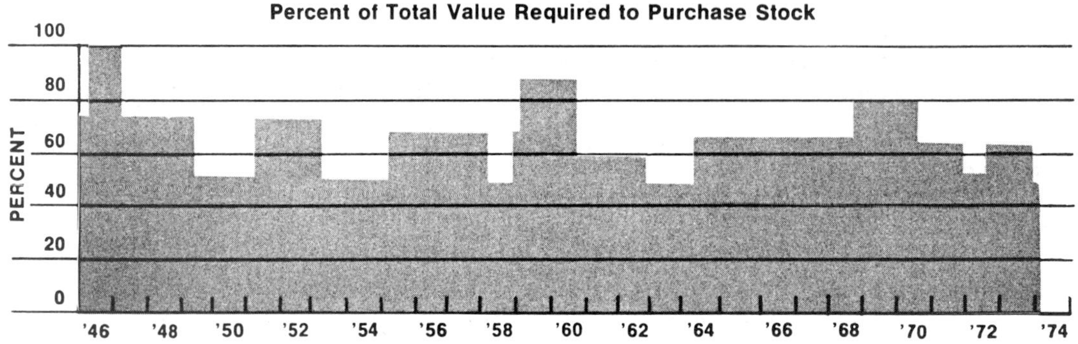

Effective	Rate	Effective	Rate	Effective	Rate
10/15/34	45%	1/17/51	75%	7/10/62	50%
2/1/36	55	2/20/53	50	11/6/63	70
11/1/37	40	1/4/55	60	6/8/68	80
2/5/45	50	4/23/55	70	5/6/70	65
7/5/45	75	1/16/58	50	12/6/71	55
1/21/46	100	8/5/58	70	11/24/72	65
2/1/47	75	10/16/58	90	1/3/74	50
3/30/49	50	7/28/60	70		

Figure 14–1 Initial Margin Percentage Requirements, 1934–1974.

the year (60½, as illustrated in chapter 13), a margin and a cash account would show different results:

50 percent MARGIN ACCOUNT		
Buy 100 shares at 51⅛		$5,112.50
cash outlay	$2,556.25	
borrowed	$2,556.25	
Sell 100 shares at 60½		6,050.00
difference		$937.50
CASH ACCOUNT		
Buy 50 shares at 51⅛		$2,556.25
cash outlay	$2,556.25	
borrowed	-0-	
Sell 50 shares at 60½		3,025.00
difference		$ 468.75

The profit difference between the margin and cash accounts is $468.75, less the cost of borrowing, which currently is about 12 percent per annum. If it took three months for the price of the McDonald's stock to reach your selling point, interest would amount to $76.69 ($2,556.25 × .03), leaving $392.06 ($468.75 – $76.69) as profit. If you had purchased 1,000 shares, the gross profit before commission and taxes would be ten times as much.

Margin is used for trading and speculation. It is not designed for long-term holdings because of the interest that must be paid while you are using borrowed funds. In fact, the price may go down, leaving you with a leveraged loss. For example, if McDonald's returns to the year's low of 26¾ at the end of our three-month period, the results would appear as follows:

50 percent MARGIN ACCOUNT		
Buy 100 shares at 51⅛		$5,112.50
cash outlay	$2,556.25	
borrowed	$2,556.25	
Sell 100 shares at 26¾		2,675.00
difference		$2,437.50
CASH ACCOUNT		
Buy 50 shares at 51⅛		$2,556.25
cash outlay	$2,556.25	
borrowed	-0-	
Sell 50 shares at 26¾		1,337.50
difference		$1,218.75

You have suffered a loss in both cases, but a greater loss was caused by the greater number of shares involved in the margin account. The extra $1,218.75 loss would be multiplied by 10 if you had purchased 1,000 shares. Incidentally, you still have the $76.69 interest to pay on the margin account, plus commissions and taxes due on both accounts.

Finally, if you try to ride out a decline on margined stock, you will be subject to a margin call if your equity gets too low. Assume your broker requires the greater of a 30 percent maintained margin on current market value or $2,000. To simplify our example, if you had purchased $5,000 in stock on 50 percent margin, you would have a $2,500 equity. The broker will also have loaned you $2,500. If the stock declines in value to $4,000, your equity drops to $1,500, which is well below the $2,000 minimum equity deposit even though it is above the 30 percent maintained margin requirement of $1,200. You will have five business days to bring your margin account up to requirements by adding $500, or the brokerage firm will sell enough of your securities to meet its requirements. In practice most people buy more than one stock on margin and are able to cover the call with equity from the net balance of all their stocks in the margin account. All margin accounts are in street names and kept in the possession of the broker to facilitate a sell-off. A street name is simply the broker's name.

In summary, buying on margin is a speculative practice. A margin account will increase your profit or your loss through leverage as compared to the same amount of money used in a cash account. You can be certain only that you will have to pay the interest charges on whatever amount you borrow.

INVESTMENT COSTS

When determining in which particular investment or savings medium to place your funds, you should consider the cost of making the investment. Often in the case of an income-producing investment, the yield is lowered too much by investment costs to make the investment competitive with savings certificates. This is especially true for relatively short investment periods. If you are investing for growth, you must expect sufficient price appreciation on your investment to surpass the interest that you would otherwise receive from savings certificates.

Investment costs are sometimes rather hard to determine in advance. Typical costs would include such items as commissions, taxes, service charges, load charges, finder's fees, price spreads, interest charges, and assorted closing costs. Most of these differ so widely that broad comparisons are not much help. Sometimes these charges are added to both the purchase price and the sale price, sometimes to just one end of a transaction. You simply must compare the alternative costs at investment time. We will deal only with charges associated with securities investments in this chapter.

Odd-Lot Transactions

Transactions to buy or sell on an organized exchange are executed in round lots, which are trading units of 100 shares of a particular stock or a multiple thereof. Commission rates are based on round-lot sales because brokerage firms' floor representatives usually handle transactions involving round lots. If you buy or sell less than 100 shares, your order is sent to an odd-lot dealer located at your stock's trading post. He will actually buy or sell the odd-lot shares. Consider him an odd-lot specialist who maintains an inventory in his specialty of stocks at all times. Whenever his inventory does not permit an odd-lot order to be filled, he purchases a round lot and breaks it.

Odd-lot differential Odd-lot prices are geared to the auction market. An odd-lot price is based on the first round-lot transaction price that occurs after receipt of the odd-lot order at the trading post of the stock involved. Once this market price is established, a differential is added to the round-lot price per share to cover the odd-lot dealer's commission. Currently this is $.125 per share on all stocks on the major exchanges. The differential is added for purchases and subtracted for sales.

In the McDonald's example involving a 50-share purchase without margin, the differential would be shown thus: Buy 50 shares at 51¼ for total of $2,562.50 instead of 51⅛ for $2,556.25. Sell 50 shares at 60⅜ for total of $3,018.75 instead of at 60½ for $3,025. The differential in either of these odd-lot transactions involving 50 shares amounted to $6.25. On the transaction confirmation card the price per share reflects the round-lot price plus or minus ⅛ ($.125). The point to remember is that odd-lot shares cost you ⅛ more per share when purchasing and return ⅛ less per share when selling, in addition to the normal brokerage commission.

Brokerage Commissions

Stocks and bonds bought and sold through an organized exchange will normally be charged a commission on both ends of the transaction. The seller and the buyer representatives charge a commission. At one time, the minimum commission rate was set by the exchange, but commissions are now negotiable, especially on volume transactions. Table 14–1 portrays typical brokerage fees. Commissions for over-the-counter transactions generally run higher than exchange transactions. They consist of the dollar spread between the asked and bid prices of the OTC stock plus a small additional fee.

On the purchase of 100 shares of McDonald's, the approximate commission would be figured as follows:

Buy 100 shares at 51⅛	$5,112.50
Commission	78.13
SEC fee	.11
Total cost	$5,190.74

The buying cost of $78.24 as a percentage of the purchase amounts to 1.53 percent.

Transaction Taxes

The SEC levies a federal registration fee on all transactions made on an organized exchange. It amounts to one cent per $500. No federal taxes as such are levied.

Table 14–1 Typical brokerage fees

Round-lot Orders	
Dollar Value of Order	*Minimum Commission*
Less than $100	$5.00
$100 but under $800	2.3% plus $7.45
$800 but under $2,500	1.5% plus $14.00
$2,500 and above	1.0% plus $27.00
Odd-lot Orders	
Odd-lot differential plus round-lot commission less $2.30	
Bonds per $1,000	
Minimum commission $2.50	
In practice, commissions charged are $2.50 to $7.50 each based upon the number of bonds in the trade.	
Maximum Transaction Charge	
Less than $5,000	$75.00
$5,000 and above	$78.50

Above fees were charged prior to May 1, 1975. Since then, all commissions are subject to negotiation. In practice, only transactions involving orders over $2,500 are negotiated.

A few states charge a securities transaction tax. Almost invariably you will be charged the New York State tax, which is applied to all transactions on the NYSE and Amex. The transfer tax is charged to the seller and approximates $.025 per share on a sliding scale.

INVESTMENT DECISION BASED ON GENERAL ECONOMIC CONSIDERATIONS

There are many considerations that should influence a securities selection. Some considerations are more general than others and apply to all investments. Once you have covered the generalities, you should move on to specific stock or bond selections. *General considerations tend to be qualitative.* They involve the nature or condition of the economy, the industry, and the company. The timing of a securities purchase or sale is often based on these considerations. We will consider timing when we talk about specific stock selection, even though it is appropriate at this point also. Some investment counselors call the qualitative approach a *fundamentalist* approach. If you know the fundamentals involving a security, you can weed out securities that do not appear to have potential and zero in on those that do. Your final analysis will be *quantitative,* whereby you rate and compare the specific security in terms of the many mathematical ratios and formulas available. Some investment counselors also call the quantitative approach a fundamentalist approach.

Economic Conditions

Both institutional and individual investors react to stock market conditions, which in turn reflect the economy or at least an important segment of it. A robust or weak economy, a lagging or increasing gross national product (GNP), employment figures, housing starts, consumer durable sales, interest rates, and the consumer price index all affect the stock market. These and other indicators allow you and professional analysts to judge whether market conditions are settled or unsettled and to tell in which direction the market is headed.

Bulls and bears The aggregate investor reaction to national and worldwide political and economic happenings constitutes stock market behavior. The anticipated and actual resignation of former President Nixon is a perfect example. Investor reaction is one of expectations:

great expectations if the news or indicators are good; pessimistic expectations if the news or indicators are bad. The roles played by investor expectations often create a primary market trend.

If enough people expect the market to rise, they will buy stock, forcing an upward pressure on stock prices. If this uptrend is prolonged and is a recognizable rise in the stock averages, it is called a *bull market.* The buyer is known to be "bullish." A *bear market* is just the opposite. If enough people expect the market to decline, their selling in anticipation of a stock market decline actually forces prices downward. These sellers are known as "bears." As you can see, stock market behavior to a great degree is a self-fulfilling activity.

There may be a reason to buy or sell a security because of the economy, but it is the "herd instinct" that creates and perpetuates the great extremes that occur in the stock market. The market seems to turn in the opposite direction (it tops out or bottoms out) whenever economic reasoning returns. Generally stock prices drop whenever they become overpriced and when investor expectations turn pessimistic about company earnings or further price appreciation. Conversely, a downward trend will slow and turn as the investor increasingly recognizes good buys based upon yield and price. At some point, buyer resistance fades as the "bargain hunter" starts buying.

Industry Analysis

Performance of industrial groupings is a qualitative measuring device. Generally companies within a grouping will perform somewhat the same relative to the stock market as a whole. Industries change in profitability because of the national and worldwide economic and technical environment. This is reflected in the market price of the stock of companies in that particular industrial grouping. Figure 14–2 illustrates an industry performance analysis. All the major reporting services and brokerage houses offer an industry analysis. They do not necessarily agree on the composition of an industry by activity or by company included.

It is easy to associate an industry with a business cycle or an economic or political happening. Investor expectations and reactions are even more important under these circumstances. A prime example is/was the energy crisis. Petroleum-reliant industries like public utilities, plastics, auto manufacturers, and highway business suffered severe profit and stock price declines, while the petroleum industry showed correspondingly higher profits and stock price increases. Raw-material shortages, war, and political instability cause numerous industry stock averages to fluctuate. Heavy machinery and consumer durables are very susceptible to the business cycle.

Company Analysis

An investor will eventually reduce his industry selections to a few choices, and he must then select a company or companies whose securities meet his investment objectives. Brokerage houses and reporting services offer an avalanche of advice. These services, the annual corporate reports, trade publications, and general business news can provide you with a lot of valuable information. You should look for management success and product market shares of the companies selected for your further analysis.

Management There should be a positive relationship between managerial talent and competitive success. This is not always the case. Some companies succeed

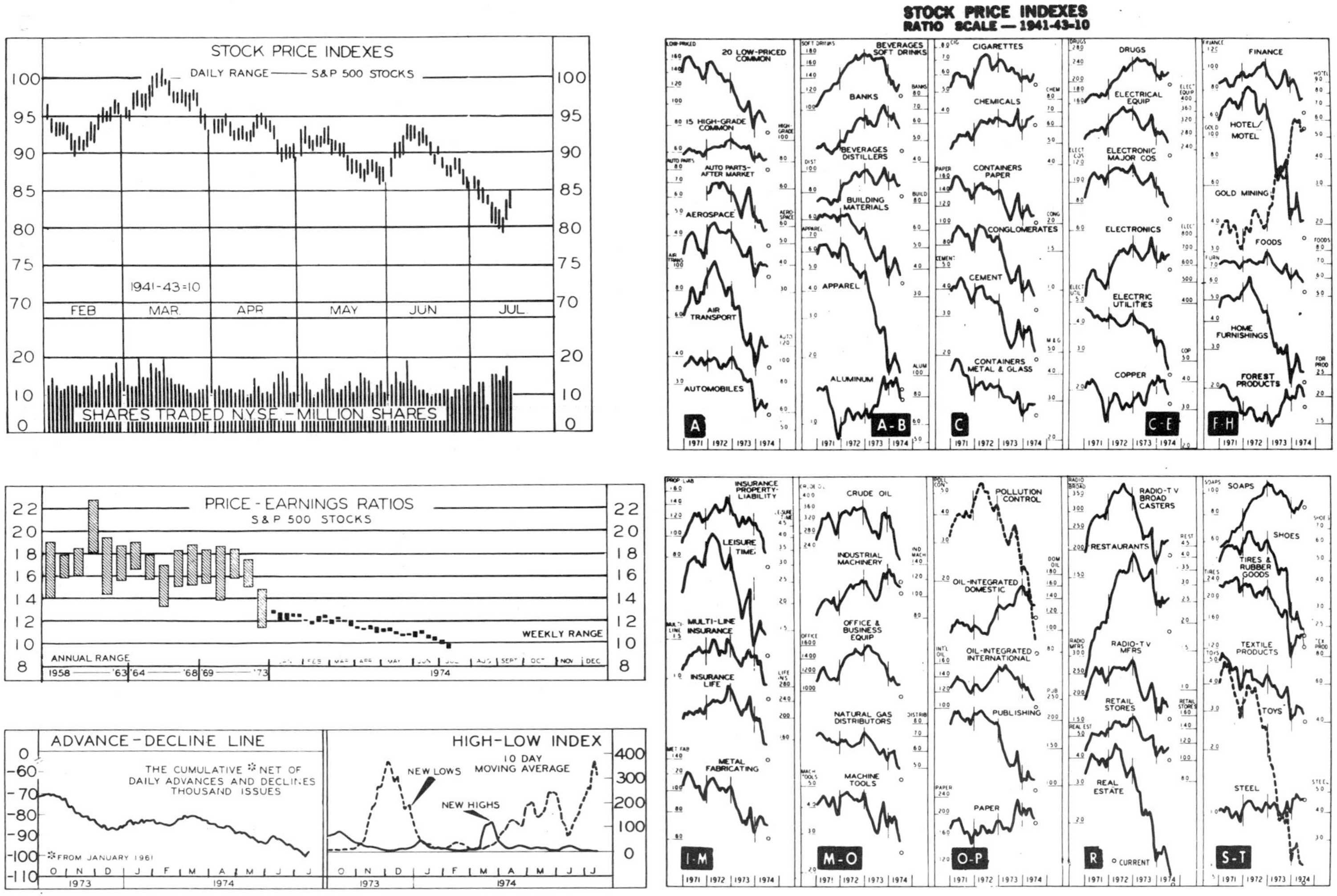

Figure 14–2 Industry Performance Indexes. *(Standard & Poor's Corporation, New York)*

despite their management and vice versa. Generally, however, you can judge a management team by its financial results and its relationship with clients, employees, and stockholders. No management is perfect; companies make mistakes in customer, employee, and shareholder relations. A knowledgeable investor will ferret out this information and analyze the effect on corporate profitability. For example, a company may have a bad customer image that, while not important now, may affect future sales. There may be labor strife at a company, or talented employees may leave for better working conditions elsewhere. Finally, there may be infighting between various shareholder groups that may eventually affect corporate policy.

Competition Whenever there is competition, management competency will surely surface. Management may be able to control intracompany situations but can seldom control the competition. Management must devise ways of securing a greater share of the product market, while competitors are attempting the same thing. You should ask your broker for historical data on market shares, or you could do some statistical research. Trade groups and individual companies are good sources. You will find the research fascinating if you have the time.

Competition does not necessarily have to be limited to the industry of the company you are investigating. Often a company's products are subject to *substitution*. When this happens, especially if the substitute is lower priced, profits may be subject to severe decline.

A final competitive consideration involves *monopoly* companies where, either by government franchise or patent protection, a company has little apparent competition. A large product market share caused by a unique product is a temporary monopoly position that may be subject to future competition. Sales of monopoly companies are basically protected. Monopolies offer you a good deal if all other qualitative and quantitative factors are satisfactory.

You should investigate a monopoly company just as thoroughly as any other because its costs may be high even though its sales may be "guaranteed." For example, utility companies are now paying extremely high prices for fuel, causing their profit margins to shrink. An analysis should be made regarding raw materials and labor costs. Actually you should also look at the "sales guarantee." Many dominant companies are hiding behind patents that may soon expire. Polaroid, IBM, and Xerox are examples of firms that may remain dominant in their fields or that may become just other competitors in a competitive industry.

A Diversified Portfolio

You probably realize that the risks of investment are very real. Any look at the stock pages tells you this. If your investment funds are narrowly invested in one or a very few corporations, you will gain or lose as these few investments fluctuate. You have all your eggs in one basket. It would be to your advantage to diversify your investment portfolio. Obviously, the smaller your funds for investment, the smaller your variety of securities. You can provide some protection against declines in one security by purchasing a second security in a different industry.

You start with a *portfolio* approach. This means you select your securities to provide for some balance while planning your investment objective. You may desire an aggressive or defensive portfolio, or something in between. You attempt to remain consistent by contemplating the effect that each securities transaction has on your objective. This approach will provide you with an orderly acquisition rather than a random selection of "good deals." It requires more portfolio management, but any worthwhile investment requires some management.

The more securities you acquire, the more you can diversify. You build your portfolio with this in mind. At no time should an investment program be without an objective. Market conditions will force you to manage your portfolio, cause you to review it regularly, and cause you to buy and sell securities. The irregularities of the business cycle suggest that a portfolio be diversified by containing common stock, preferred stock, government and corporate bonds, and cash reserves at various times.

Economic Factors Affecting Security Prices

Security selection involves more than general considerations. You must quantify your decision. But before doing so, there is a gray area in portfolio building that must also be considered. Security prices do react to economic happenings, and investors react to security prices.

A general knowledge of what economic factors affect what securities is an important tool for the competent investor. You can switch from one type of security to another and from one industry to another as the economy and stock market behavior dictate.

Common stock Price changes in common stock are directly related to good or bad economic news on an international, nationwide, industrywide, and individual company scale. How strong the reaction (price change) is depends on how close the company is to the action. As mentioned previously, it is really investor expectations that affect prices. For every buyer there is a seller who must have different expectations about price changes.

Common stock is bought for income, price appreciation, or a balance of both. Investors will purchase common stock for *income* when the dividend yield is sufficiently high and stable as to nearly equal the interest rate available in savings certificates or bonds. An investor is willing to accept a slightly lower yield because he has the added possibility of price appreciation. We will discuss the mathematics of yield later in the chapter. Common stocks will not normally be purchased for income when the price becomes too high for a good dividend yield. You may balance the advantages of a good yield against price appreciation and still buy an overpriced common stock if you feel the price will continue to rise and provide you with a capital gain. You have now switched to a *growth* objective. So long as prices are rising, most purchases of common stock are for price appreciation.

Preferred stock Investors popularly consider a preferred stock as a balance between a bond and a common stock. Perhaps it is, with its preferred claims on income and possible participation and convertibility features. Investors will bid the price down to where a good dividend yield is obtainable in a straight preferred stock because there is no other reason to purchase it. However, most investors like to emphasize the equity concept in preferred stock by purchasing only participating or convertible preferred stock. Prices of such a preferred stock will rise and fall with the fortunes of the underlying common stock.

Bonds Corporate bonds are purchased for income; they are not purchased for price appreciation. There is little "expectation" of growth. The debt claim against the corporation will never be more than the par value of $1,000 payable at maturity. During an economic expansion and a bull market, stock prices rise and high-grade bond prices decline. Strong demand for money pushes interest rates up, thereby lowering the market price of low-coupon-rate bonds. The closer the bond's coupon interest rate is to the current interest rate, the closer the market price will be to par ($1,000). Finally, the closer the date to maturity, the closer the market price will be to the bond redemption price of $1,000.

Bonds are debt securities that must pay semiannual interest claims and eventually be redeemed. The bond investor does accept a number of risks: (1) a business risk (will he receive his interest regularly and the entire obligation when due?), (2) an interest-rate risk (will there be better coupon rates available during the term of the bond?), and (3) a price-level risk (will inflation over the term of the bond lower the true interest and cause redemption in lower-purchasing-power dollars?).

A bondholder accepts a *business risk* because the corporation might not be able to meet its obligation. Probably he will minimize the risk by purchasing a high-grade bond as rated by one of the reporting services. Figure 14–3 illustrates the bond rating symbols. Rating opinions may vary among the services, so it is a good idea to compare ratings before buying. The top four ratings in bonds are generally considered satisfactory for investment-grade securities. There is relatively little business risk attached to them. Safety is a key element. The speculative element becomes significant by the fifth rating and predominates by the seventh rating. As a company's fortunes change, its credit-worthiness as represented by bond ratings will change. Ratings, in turn, affect the market price.

Fitch's	Moody's	Standard & Poor's
AAA	Aaa	AAA
AA	Aa	AA
A	A	A
BBB	Baa	BBB
BB	Ba	BB
B	B	B
CCC	Caa	CCC
CC	Ca	CC
C	C	C
DDD		DDD
DD		DD
D		D

Figure 14–3 Bond Rating Symbols.

All bonds feature an *interest-rate risk* simply because the changing demand for credit forces interest rates up and down. Theoretically all similarly rated bonds maturing at the same time will sell at the same market price. Higher or lower ratings will have higher or lower prices. The market price of a bond reflects the coupon (face value) interest-rate relationship to current-yield interest rates. You purchase a bond at par only when the coupon interest rate matches the current interest rate for new bond issues. Otherwise you pay more or less than $1,000 for a bond. You pay a *premium* (over $1,000) if the coupon rate is higher than the current interest rate for bonds. Your interest-rate risk is reduced through the purchase of a bond at a *discount* (below $1,000). For example, we will assume a current interest rate of 10 percent. If a bond pays a 5 percent coupon rate and is due to mature in 10 years, it would sell for $500. The concept operates in this manner: The discount enables the purchaser to get a yield equivalent to the current interest rate of 10 percent. The $500 discount or savings is prorated over the remaining ten years of the 5 percent bond. A discount of $50 plus $50 interest equals $100 per year on a $1,000 bond for ten years, giving a 10 percent yield to maturity. The further from maturity that a discounted (under $1,000) bond happens to be, the lower will be its market price in order for the buyer to recoup the continuing low interest rate. Bond tables indicate the market value of any nominal (coupon) rate based upon varying current yield and the number of years to maturity.

All investments suffer from *price-level risks.* Investors buy bonds with current dollars and receive interest and the eventual return of their principal in inflated dollars. While common stock has price appreciation to act as a possible hedge against inflation, a bondholder will get only his fixed $1,000 back at maturity date—probably less at any time before then. If the principal is to be used for a purchase of any consumable item the loss can be measured in terms of lost purchasing power. The same situation applies to any other investment liquidation. However, if the investor reinvests the principal in another security that pays the current rate of interest, he theoretically does not lose any purchasing power. This is why financial institutions and large investors continue to purchase bonds when interest rates would otherwise appear to be unacceptable. Many banks, other financial institutions, and trusts are limited by law to safe investments such as high-grade bonds.

Finally, the market prices of bonds are affected by some of their features, notably their *call* and *conversion* options. Since bond market prices reflect the yield to maturity, consideration must be given to a premature redemption, or conversion. These options would be reflected in the price.

Bonds with a *conversion* feature sell at a higher price than similarly rated bonds without this feature. The higher price tends to reflect the exact value of the gain to be made by converting to the common stock. Now we have a case where common-stock prices affect bond prices. If a bond can be converted to twenty shares of common, you would multiply twenty times the current market price of the common stock to find the bond value. This should be the bond market price.

INVESTMENT DECISION BASED ON FINANCIAL STATEMENT ANALYSIS

The various qualitative considerations that help determine what investments to make should be influenced by how well the company under scrutiny has done. These results are dollar measurements found in a company's financial statements. Market prices of the company's stocks are at least partially affected by the operating results portrayed in its financial statements. You must at least be able to read and understand a balance sheet, an income statement, and a retained earnings statement to find out how well the company is doing. Follow tables 14–2, 14–3, and 14–4 as we explain the major components of financial statements. Note that the prior year's figures are printed for comparison. The percentage of change from the preceding year is shown in the far right column. More sophisticated financial statements sometimes provide a five- to ten-year comparison. The financial statement formats illustrated in the figures are somewhat simplified. A company's actual operations and financial transactions may require considerably more detail. Accepted accounting practice allows some choice of terminology and format detail. The end result should be the same regardless of the detail.

Many of the following ratios are published by credit reporting companies like Dun & Bradstreet, Inc., whose subscribers generally use it prior to granting credit to a company. Investment reporting services publish and analyze ratios significant to investors. However, the only sure way to get to know a company is to read and interpret its financial statements yourself.

The Balance Sheet

The balance sheet represents the financial status of a company at one particular moment in time. You might consider it a photographic "still shot." It is called a balance sheet because it should balance out mathematically. Assets (what the company owns) balance with liabilities (what the company owes) and stockholders' equity (what is left for the owners of the company). Another way of looking at the "balance sheet equation" is assets less liabilities equals stockholders' equity. We will now look at the component parts of a balance sheet.

Assets Assets include all goods and property owned by the company as well as claims against others yet to be collected. They are usually subdivided into current assets and fixed assets. *Current assets* are those assets that can be turned to cash more readily than fixed assets. During the normal course of business they are expected to be turned to cash within a year. These assets include cash, investment securities, accounts receivable, and inventories. Inventory is usually valued on a conservative basis of *cost* or *market,* whichever is lower. This is done so as not to overstate the assets or earnings of a company whenever price increases occur. A consistent method of valuing inventory must be used. Footnotes in a statement will normally advise readers of the method used.

Fixed assets include land, buildings, and equipment, which by their nature are expected to be useful for a number of years. They represent assets not intended for sale. Except for land, all fixed assets will wear out in time. *Depreciation* is the accounting technique used to represent the deteriorating value of these assets. Cost minus accumulated depreciation is the recognized accounting practice. Depreciation techniques were discussed in chapter 11. Total assets represent one half of the balance sheet. It is everything that is owned or has value to the company.

Liabilities These are claims against assets, otherwise known as claims against the company or debts owed by the company. *Current liabilities* are all debts that fall due within the coming year, such as accounts payable, accrued liabilities, notes payable, and income and other taxes payable. *Long-term liabilities* constitute the debt that does not mature during the coming year. Portions of debt that become due are transferred to current liabilities. Sums that have already been paid are eliminated as liabilities. The company uses an asset (cash) to pay the debt.

Stockholders' equity These figures represent the balance of assets that have not been claimed (on paper) by creditors. This

Table 14–2
YOUR INVESTMENT, INC.
BALANCE SHEET
December 31, 1975 and 1974
(in millions of dollars)

	1975	1974	% of Change
ASSETS			
Current Assets			
Cash	$ 7.1	$ 6.7	6.0
Investment Securities	2.0	2.0	0
Accounts Receivable	14.0	11.2	25.0
Inventories	26.0	24.0	8.3
Total Current Assets	$ 49.1	$ 43.9	11.8
Fixed Assets			
Land	9.0	9.0	0
Buildings	60.3	55.9	7.9
Machinery	35.7	33.9	5.3
	105.0	98.8	
Less Accumulated Depreciation	32.1	29.0	10.7
Total Fixed Assets	72.9	69.8	4.4
Total Assets	122.0	113.7	7.3
LIABILITIES AND STOCKHOLDERS' EQUITY			
Current Liabilities			
Accounts Payable	6.1	5.0	22.0
Accrued Liabilities	4.6	4.1	12.2
Notes Payable	1.0	—	—
Income and Other Taxes Payable	9.6	8.4	14.3
Total Current Liabilities	21.3	17.5	21.7
Long-term Liabilities			
Notes Payable—5%	—	1.0	—
5% Debentures due January 1, 1985	25.0	25.0	0
Total Liabilities	46.3	43.5	6.4
Stockholders' Equity			
Common Stock, no par, 2,000,000 authorized and outstanding	25.0	25.0	0
Total Capital Stock	25.0	25.0	0
Retained Earnings	50.7	45.2	12.2
Total Stockholders' Equity	75.7	70.2	7.8
Total Liabilities and Stockholders' Equity	122.0	113.7	7.3

Table 14–3
YOUR INVESTMENT, INC.
STATEMENT OF RETAINED EARNINGS
for the years ending
December 31, 1975 and 1974
(in millions of dollars)

	1975	1974
Balance at beginning of year	45.2	40.6
Add		
Net income for year	12.0	11.1
Subtract		
Dividends paid common stock 2,000,000 shares at $3.25 per share	6.5	6.5
Balance at end of year	50.7	45.2

amount is what is left for the stockholders. It is sometimes called proprietary interest or owners' net worth. *Preferred stock* indicates the number of shares of this type outstanding and the amount payable per share. *Common stock* indicates the number of common shares outstanding and what the issuing value (amount received by the company) happened to be. *Retained earnings* are often called earned surplus. These are earnings not paid out in dividends but retained in the business for expansion and operations. There is no *earned surplus fund* as such. It has become part of the assets and expenses of the company over the years. It has become reinvested in the company and is part of stockholders' residual equity.

The Balance Sheet Figures Analyzed

You need an accounting background in order to understand the balance sheet fully. You can, however, draw certain interpretations from balance sheet relationships. Here are some of the most significant factors that can be gleaned from the balance sheet.

Net working capital This is the difference between total current assets and total current liabilities. It shows the ability of a company to meet its current debts and have some funds remaining. It is a true measure of liquidity. Your Investment, Inc., has $27.8 million ($49.1 – 21.3) net working capital available in 1975.

Current ratio This is the ratio of current assets to current liabilities. It shows how many times the company can meet its debts. It is found by dividing current assets by current liabilities. "Yours" meets it 2.3 times in 1975 and 2.5 times in 1974. A 2-to-1 ratio is standard.

Capitalization ratio The proportion of each type of funding in a company to the total capital is known as the capitalization ratio. Because bond and preferred-stock payments must be made before any common-stock dividends are paid, you will probably want to know what percentage of capital these funds represent. Long-term liabilities plus stockholders' equity represent the total capitalization of a company. The total capitalization for Your Investment, Inc., in 1975 was:

	$ in mil	%
Bonds	25.0	24.8
Common stock	25.0	24.8
Retained earnings	50.7	50.4
	$100.7	100.0%

The percentage figure is the ratio. The common-stock ratio should include retained earnings, because reinvested earnings belong to the common stockholders. This amounts to 75.2 percent of the total capital in the corporation.

Your Investment, Inc., has rather low *leverage*, since only 24.8 percent of the capital is coming from other than the common stockholders. This is a conservative position that will allow common stockholders to keep more of the profits rather than pay them out. High leverage is more a speculative position using someone else's money.

Book value per share This is found by adding the common-stock value contributed by shareholders to the retained earnings and dividing by the number of common shares outstanding. This is the common stockholders' equity per share. In 1975 Your Investment, Inc., had an equity of $25 million plus retained earnings of $50.7 million. The book value per share for common stock was $37.85 ($75.7 ÷ 2).

The Income Statement

The income statement represents the financial record of a company's operations for a given period of time, usually a year. You might consider the income statement a photographic "moving picture" as compared to the balance sheet's "still shot." The income statement is often known as an *earnings report* or *profit and loss statement.* It shows how much money a company makes or loses during a year by matching income against outgo. The "bottom line" is a net profit or a net loss for the year. This statement is of prime interest to an investor. We will look at its component parts.

Sales Sales represent the primary source of money received for goods sold or services rendered. They are sometimes termed *revenues* or *operating revenues. Net sales* refer to the amount received after deducting returned goods and price reduction allowances.

Table 14–4
YOUR INVESTMENT, INC.
INCOME STATEMENT
for the years ending
December 31, 1975 and 1974
(in millions of dollars)

	1975	1974	% of Change
SALES	$124.8	$111.7	11.7
Less:			
Cost of sales	78.4	70.2	11.7
Gross profit	$ 46.4	$ 41.5	11.8
Less:			
Selling and admin. expenses	16.7	15.0	11.3
Depreciation	3.1	2.5	24.0
Operating profit	$ 26.6	$ 24.0	10.8
Other income			
Interest earned	0.2	0.2	0
	$ 26.8	$ 24.2	10.7
Other deductions			
Interest charges	1.3	1.3	0
Earnings before income taxes	$ 25.5	$ 22.9	11.4
Provision for income taxes	13.5	11.8	14.4
Net profit	$ 12.0	$ 11.1	8.1

Cost of sales This is also termed *cost of goods sold* or *operating costs.* These figures reflect the productivity costs of manufacturing, servicing, or purchasing for resale. Wages and materials costs make up the bulk of the cost of sales.

Gross profit The difference between sales and cost of sales.

Selling and administrative expenses This group of expenses differs with the type of business. These expenses consist of advertising, travel costs, sales commissions, wages, office expenses, and any other expense incurred whether or not any production, service, or purchase for resale activity is carried out.

Depreciation This item has already been discussed in detail. It is not an actual cash outlay but an accrued expense that is taken annually as a claim against income, because at some future point the asset will have to be replaced.

Operating profit The operating profit reflects the company's ability to generate income from its usual operations. It excludes financing costs (interest expense), which in the case of highly leveraged companies, may have a significant impact on earnings before income taxes.

Other income and other deductions The *other income* category includes income from any nonoperational source, usually investments. Sometimes called *miscellaneous income,* it can and should reflect the one-time sale of capital assets, which if included in operating income would distort earnings. Nonrecurring expenses are generally listed under other deductions. These might be substantial bad-debt loss, inventory revaluation, special discounts, uninsured asset losses, and so on. Interest expense is listed as a separate item because of its significance as a before-tax expense of financing.

Earnings before income taxes The operating profit plus and minus other income and other deductions including interest.

Provision for income taxes This includes federal, state, and local income taxes. At present, the maximum federal rate for corporations is approximately 48 percent on profits over $50,000 and 20 to 22 percent below this amount.

Net profit This item is often called *net income* because it is the final result of all income less all deductions listed on an income statement. It is also called *net earnings.* It is the amount available to pay dividends on preferred and common stock and to reinvest in the business.

The Income Statement Figures Analyzed

The income statement can tell you a lot if you make a few detailed comparisons. Here are the most significant factors that can be gleaned from the statement:

Operating profit margin To find this ratio one divides the operating profit by sales. The result shows the operational success of the company without confusing the results with other income and deductions. In 1975 "Yours" had an operating profit margin of 21.3 percent ($26.6 ÷ $124.8). This means that for each dollar of sales there remained 21.3 cents as profit from operations.

Interest coverage ratio This ratio is used to determine how many times the interest charges are covered by earnings before taxes. Bonds and interest-bearing notes represent a claim against income. They are an operating expense of business. Common stockholders would be interested in this ratio only if there was some doubt about availability or residual earnings. Bondholders are very interested in this ratio because it represents their safety of income. Your Investment, Inc., covered the interest expense on its notes and bonds 20.6 times ($26.8 ÷ $1.3) in 1975.

Preferred dividend coverage The net profit is divided by preferred dividend payment to find how many times the preferred dividend is earned. Net profit is used because preferred dividends are paid after taxes. Your Investment, Inc., does not have any preferred stock outstanding.

Cross-Analyzing the Financial Statements

An investor often must apply ratios from figures to be found separately in the balance sheet, the income statement, and the statement of retained earnings.

Earnings per common share This item should be located at the end of all income statements because of the great concern investors place on it. Earnings per share or the prospective earnings per share influence stock market prices. This item is calculated by subtracting preferred dividends (if any) from net income and then dividing the available earnings by the number of common-stock shares outstanding. The earnings per common share of Your Investment, Inc., for 1975 would be calculated as follows:

Net income
$12,000,000 ÷ 2,000,000 shares = $6.00 per share

Common-stock dividends per share This item is actually found in the retained earnings statement. If it is not, simply divide the common-stock dividends amount by the number of shares of common stock outstanding as shown on the balance sheet. A $3.25 dividend was paid by Your Investment, Inc. ($6,500,000 ÷ 2 million shares).

Dividend payment This refers to the percentage of earnings per share on common stock actually paid in dividends per share. You have already calculated earnings per share and dividends per share for 1975. Therefore the dividend payment on percentage of earnings paid is 54.2 percent ($3.25 ÷ $6.00).

Sales to fixed assets ratio Sales are divided by fixed asset values before this year's depreciation. "Yours" has a 1.71-to-1 ratio for 1975. This ratio is important because it helps point up whether the funds spent for fixed assets are being used efficiently.

Sales to inventory Sales are divided by the year-end inventory. "Yours" has a ratio of 4.8-to-1 for 1975. This ratio is also called the *inventory turnover.* It acts as a guide to determine whether the company is investing too heavily in inventory. The true inventory turnover is determined by dividing sales by average inventory, which is not available in our statements. A high ratio generally means updated merchandise, while a low ratio often means stale merchandise.

Net income to net worth How much the company is earning on its owners' investment is a very significant ratio. You figure your net return on all of your other investments, so it is only natural to determine the company's ratio. Net profit is divided by total stockholders' equity including preferred stock, common stock, and retained earnings. Your Investment, Inc., shows a return of 15.9 percent ($12.0 ÷ $75.7) on owner's equity for 1975.

INVESTMENT DECISION BASED ON MARKET PRICE

When you finally get down to selecting an individual security, quantitative analysis becomes a must. Fortunately, the reporting services and brokerage houses have many of the important ratios already quantified. Their individual methods of presentation may differ, but their reports will probably involve an investment recommendation with a full statistical analysis. The facts are often presented in the form of texts, tables, and graphs to let you make your own judgment. Still, you must answer these questions about a common stock: (1) Is the price acceptable? (2) Is there a profit potential? and (3) What type(s) of profit are there and for what time period? We must now look to the price of the security for analytical data.

Corporate earnings are what make profits. Dividends will generally not be paid and stock market prices will generally not rise if there are no earnings or potential earnings. The more important investment measurements revolve around earnings per share and market price. None of these measurements are ends in themselves, but taken in context with other indicators, including all the qualitative and quantitative factors already discussed, they provide insight into stock buying, holding and selling.

Earnings per Share

We will mention this again because the buyer of common stock is often more concerned with the earnings per share than he is with the dividend. This measurement indicates the dollar amount that the corporation earned on each share of common stock after taxes during the latest reporting period. Total net profits (after preferred-stock dividends, if any) are divided by the number of common stock shares outstanding.

Price-Earnings Ratio

The P/E ratio tells how many times a stock price exceeds its earnings per share. It is sometimes called the P/E multiple. The stock market price is divided by its earnings per share. This ratio can be misleading if the price and earnings are not taken from the same time period. If you are purchasing a stock, you would use the latest market price and the latest earnings for the year. Many newspapers now offer P/E ratios with the stock price quotations.

A high or low P/E multiple can be interpreted in many ways, but it is generally understood that the "average" for an investment-quality stock is about 10 to 20 times earnings. A higher multiple can mean that there is investor expectation of increased profits in the future or that a stock is overpriced. A look at the qualitative measurements and statistical trends may suggest that earnings are about to increase. If the whole market is up because of investor euphoria, the stock may well be overpriced and overspeculative. A low P/E multiple generally suggests that a company is having difficulty earning a profit. No multiple at all means there was no profit. In either case, it is wise to look for the reasons behind reduced earnings.

There are very few bargains in the investment world, because prices decline if earnings or expectations of earnings are low. Prices increase if the earnings increase or are expected to increase. The P/E ratio is a measure of actual and potential stock value. As such P/E ratios are used by capital-gains investors who wish to evaluate the market price of a stock.

Investors interested in dividend income use P/E ratios to figure how long it will take a company to earn enough per share to return their initial investments. Earnings do not mean dividends, but investors hope that the company uses whatever earnings are retained in the company for the benefit of shareholders. Retained earnings should generate greater earnings, prompting greater dividend income.

Dividend Yield

Yield shows a percentage return on investment. Percentage provides a common method of comparing net returns on different types of investments involving different principal sums. Cash distribution of earnings is called *cash dividends* and need not be the full earnings of a company. The dividend can be declared and paid on a regular or erratic basis.

Dividend yield is calculated by dividing the cash dividend by the current market price. We will repeat our three stock quotations from chapter 13 in order to find out how profitable these stocks are in terms of dividend yield.

1975 High	1975 Low	Stock	Div.	P/E Ratio	Sales 100s	High	Low	Close	Net Chg.
52	$44\frac{3}{4}$	AmT&T	3.40	9	878	49	$48\frac{3}{4}$	$48\frac{3}{4}$	$-\frac{1}{8}$
$227\frac{3}{8}$	$157\frac{1}{4}$	IBM	6	17	894	$208\frac{3}{4}$	206	$206\frac{1}{8}$	$-2\frac{3}{8}$
$60\frac{1}{2}$	$26\frac{3}{4}$	McDonald's		29	216	$52\frac{1}{4}$	$50\frac{1}{2}$	52	$+1\frac{1}{4}$

AmT&T provided a dividend yield of 6.97 percent, IBM 2.91 percent, and McDonald's nothing, based on the closing purchase price. What does all this mean? It means you would get a money return equal to the above percentages if you invested in the stocks at these prices. Each stock's current yield should be considered in terms of alternative investment yields, the average of all common stock yields, and in terms of the concept of total return. The first two considerations are especially important to investors who desire income.

The total return concept has more appeal to investors who desire price appreciation. While common stocks do not have a maturity date, you can arbitrarily choose a time period (say five years) to gauge a potential price rise in a stock. For example, if qualitative and quantitative forecasts look good it would not be out of line to expect a price to double in the next five years. This is a 100 percent increase over current price. The average gain would be 20 percent per year. Add this unrealized 20 percent capital gain to the current dividend yield of 3 percent and you have a forecasted annual return of 23 percent on your investment. Unfortunately, an important variable makes this concept just another measurement device to add to all the others. Your calculation is only as good as your forecast. But is this not the case with all investments?

Stock dividends These represent the distribution of new stock certificates to shareholders of record in proportion to the number of shares they already hold. It might be called an illusory dividend because the value of a shareholder's total holdings does not change. The corporation offers stock dividends rather than cash dividends to conserve the company's earnings for other uses or because its earnings are insufficient to provide a satisfactory cash dividend. The only value in a stock dividend is the psychological affluence brought on by its receipt plus the potential of a market price rise based on a greater number of shares.

Financially, the end result is the same with or without the stock dividends. If you receive one share for each ten shares you hold, you are getting a 10 percent stock dividend. You now have eleven shares, but they are earning the same amount in total as the original ten shares because the number of shares outstanding has no effect on total earnings of the company. If a company earned $2,000,000 on 200,000 shares, each share of stock would have earned $10. After a 10 percent stock dividend, a company would still earn the $2,000,000 but on 220,000 shares or an earnings per share of $9.09. The market price of your stock would decline in the same ratio. For instance, if 200,000 shares were valued at $40 per share, they would represent aggregate worth of $8 million. The ownership value or net worth of the company is still the same, but we have more shares over which to spread this worth. ($8,000,000 ÷ 220,000 = $36.36 per share.) The market price could deviate because of other factors but should be near $36\frac{3}{8}$ per share.

Any cash dividends received later are part of an aggregate dollar distribution by the company. A company as a matter of course disburses as much of its earnings as possible. If it earns $1 million, it might disburse $500,000. At the original 200,000 shares, each would receive $2.50; while at 220,000 shares, each would receive $2.27. With 10 shares you receive $25.00; with 11 shares you would also receive $25.00.

Stock splits The division of the outstanding shares of a corporation into a larger number of shares is called a stock split. It is usually done on a two-for-one or three-for-one basis. A shareholder with 100 shares would now have 200 or 300 shares. His equity in the corporation would remain the same just as in the case of stock dividends. A stock split does not bring any new capital into the corporation.

The market price of the stock will react in proportion to the number of new shares issued. A stock priced at $100 will drop to $50 on a two-for-one split, and to $33.33 ($33\frac{3}{8}$) on a three-for-one split. The main reason for a stock split is to bring the market price down to a more popular trading range. Psychologically, investors seek out stocks in the $25 to $50 range more often than higher priced stocks. Perhaps it is because they can purchase in round lots if the price is low enough. Generally, if a stock is more active, all things being equal, a greater demand is created for it, pushing the stock price upwards. On our three-for-one split, the stock could easily rise to $34 because of demand.

INVESTMENT DECISION BASED ON OPPORTUNITY

Since most people invest because they see an opportunity to make a profit, one might ask just what an investment opportunity is. It is any market price situation that lends itself to profit either by growth or income. You will be more prone to take advantage of opportunities if you are an aggressive investor rather than a defensive investor. Your investment objectives help determine your courses of action. Again, think of the *total return* when buying, selling, or holding securities. Take all the dividends and interest you can get along with price appreciation. Since younger persons will generally invest for long-term growth, we will look to growth as our primary objective. However, long-term growth does not mean you must stay with one stock or group of stocks. If your objective is long-term growth, you should build your portfolio through careful *acquisition* and *sales* over the years. In this manner you expect to increase your total portfolio value by considerably more than you would from staying with your original purchases. To do this with any degree of success means you must time your purchases and sales with care.

Timing

Most of the trading opportunities in the stock market relate to knowing when to buy and sell. We already know the answer to that—buy when stock prices are lowest, and sell when stock prices are highest! Ok, but when do these happy events occur? The knowledgeable investor recognizes the *primary* and *secondary trends* of the stock market and buys or sells according to carefully thought-out plans. He does not trade on an emotional basis.

Primary trends These are long-term and broad-based rises and declines in the stock market. They are affected by the general economy, the outlook for business profits based on the general economy and government policy, speculation (expectation), and the availability of money for investment. These elements are interrelated and fundamentally qualitative.

Secondary trends These are short-lived rises and declines in the stock market, usually of a few weeks duration. Speculation is the cause of these "market tremors." Anticipating market changes, speculators and traders may purchase or sell a substantial volume of stock during a short period. On many occasions their actions will be wrong, triggering a corrective action on their part.

Day-to-day movements A look at your newspaper will confirm that day to day, and even minute to minute, there are changes in the market price of many stocks traded on the organized exchanges. Political, economic, and business news partly causes these changes by influencing individual investors who want to invest or divest themselves of a specific stock. These minor fluctuations are not the concern of the long-term investor, for whom it is not profitable to juggle stocks daily. They are not the concern of the small investor because he has no time to watch the market. Day-to-day trading is for the speculator with ample funds who can profit on small price changes.

The Dow Theory

Perhaps the best known of the many ideas for anticipating stock market movements is the Dow Theory. It is based on the assumption that it is profitable to take advantage of the primary trend and not to resist it. Since primary trends *usually* last one or more years and change upward or downward from their base by 25 percent or more, you can eventually recognize one and join the action.

The second part of the Dow Theory advises that an upward primary trend exists when each succeeding secondary cycle produces a market-price peak and subsequent trough that is higher than the preceding peak and trough. The reverse applies to a downward trend, when each subsequent trough and market-price peak is lower than the preceding one. The primary trend will be confirmed by similar activity on other stock market indexes as they too break through their previous high or low quotations.

What and When to Buy and Sell

A sophisticated investor who wants to do more than just buy for the long term can use as much information and advice as he can absorb. He should build his portfolio in such a manner that he can easily change his position from growth to income and back to growth again. You can do this, too. Do not become enamored with a particular stock because it has been successful. Times change.

A dynamic approach This approach will have you carefully analyze a number of stocks for all the qualitative and quantitative features previously discussed. Then purchase the one(s) that best suit your portfolio. Buy growth stocks during the early stages of a primary trend. You should time your purchase when prices are lowest, but this point is seldom identifiable until later. If you attempt to forecast market price levels before a trend has been identified, you are risking the very great possibility of loss as the market continues its decline. On the other hand, if you wait too long to confirm the bull market, stocks will be overpriced, and your chances of a capital gain will be diminished. When prices are rising in the later stages of an uptrend, it is emotionally hard to stay out of the market. However, it is the best possible decision you could make.

Convertible bonds and preferred stock should be purchased for income during the period when a bull market has peaked and is starting its downward trend as a bear. Obviously you should sell your high-priced common stocks to finance your income-oriented purchases. As soon as a primary downtrend is confirmed, get out of stocks because their capital gains have been wrung out. With some luck and the adoption of the *total return concept,* an investor can have income and capital gains from all of his securities by buying, selling, and holding them at the proper time.

A defensive approach A truly conservative and defensive approach to long-term capital gains investment is to sell your common stock upon recognition of a downtrend and place the funds in government securities or savings-institution time certificates. This approach eliminates any discount of capital loss that would occur by purchasing a bond near par only to lose part of its purchase price because of the interest-level risk and price-level risk.

An aggressive approach For this approach you analyze a number of stocks for all the qualitative and quantitative features. Then you rely on market analysis to anticipate the primary trend. You do not wait to confirm the primary trend. An aggressive investor attempts to make his stock purchases as close to the high as possible and his sales as close to the low as possible. You do not buck the trend, you beat the trend. You would also purchase bonds after selling your common stock in anticipation that the money market would follow historical patterns. You would eventually sell your bonds at high prices caused by low interest rates for new issues as the market nears its anticipated low. Then back to stocks! Obviously, this is a speculative approach that is expected to provide profits commensurate with the risks taken.

Timing Transactions for Taxes

Tax selling can be an aggressive or defensive action. Its purpose is to keep income taxes as low as possible, something that we all want to do. Sales at year-end affect that year's taxes. In an upward primary trend you must consider whether an early selling (at year-end for tax savings) will result in greater gains to you than holding the stock for further price appreciation. Your tax bracket for both years should also be considered.

INVESTMENT DECISION BASED ON FORMULA APPROACH

Some people try to solve their investment timing dilemma by reducing their buy, hold, and sell decisions to a formula. There are a number of different plans that attempt to eliminate the human element from decision making. To be human in this instance means to be emotionally involved with the stock, to make judgments based on intuition and wishes rather than the hard cold facts. We will look at a few of the better-known formulas.

Dollar-Cost Averaging

Sometimes known as dollar averaging, this is a systematic stock-purchase plan that involves investing the same number of dollars each period. Purchases are made each month or quarter and must be in the same stock or group of stocks in order to create an average. The buyer frees himself of decisions about how much and when to buy through regular purchases. He ends up investing steadily during periods of high market prices and low market prices. His *average cost* turns out to be lower than the *average price* of the stock.

Table 14–5 is an example of how dollar averaging works over a period of five years. We will invest $250 in each quarterly investment period. Note that the market price will not always allow you to purchase full shares because of the amount of money you have available. Therefore, you purchase to the last full share.

Table 14–5 Example of dollar-cost averaging

Period	Current Price per Share	Number of Shares Purchased	Purchase Price	Cumulative Cost of Shares	Cumulative Shares	Average Cost per Share
1.	$44	6	$264	$264	6	$44.00
2.	48	5	240	504	11	45.82
3.	50	5	250	754	16	47.13
4.	60	4	240	994	20	49.70
5.	63	4	252	1,246	24	51.92
6.	56	4	224	1,470	28	52.50
7.	52	5	260	1,730	33	52.42
8.	48	5	240	1,970	38	51.84
9.	41	6	246	2,216	44	50.36
10.	37	7	259	2,475	51	48.53
11.	30	8	240	2,715	59	46.02
12.	34	7	238	2,953	66	44.74
13.	39	6	234	3,187	72	44.26
14.	37	7	259	3,446	79	43.62
15.	35	7	245	3,691	86	42.92
16.	36	7	252	3,943	93	42.40
17.	40	6	240	4,183	99	42.25
18.	43	6	258	4,441	105	42.30
19.	47	5	235	4,676	110	42.51
20.	50	5	250	4,926	115	42.83

Dividends and commission charges have been ignored in the example. Note that at current market price at the end of the five years you would have 115 shares worth $50.00 each, for which you paid $42.83 each. In the example there were times when the average cost per share was greater than the market price. The current price in the tenth period was $37 per share. The average price over the ten periods was $49.90 ($499 ÷ 10, the sum of prices each period divided by the number of periods). Your dollar-cost average was $48.53. The dollar-cost average will be lower than the average price at which the stock was bought. The reason for this is that as the market price drops, you purchase more shares.

There is no guarantee of profit using this formula. In the final analysis, you must still sell your stock at a market price higher than your cost price, but if you do not need to sell there is no reason to do so unless the particular stock has no possibility of returning to higher market prices. Perhaps the hardest part of dollar-cost averaging is the necessity to maintain a systematic purchase plan in the face of a declining market. You need a stout heart because psychologically it appears that you are throwing good money after bad. Actually, you are lowering your dollar cost per share. Investors often attempt to beat the system by withholding funds during a decline or by purchasing more stock during an upswing or by changing the period between purchases. This destroys the whole automatic concept. Whatever result you get, it is not dollar averaging.

Monthly Investment Plans

The New York Stock Exchange provides the small investor with a means to invest his money systematically through any member broker. The Monthly Investment Plan (MIP) is a pure form of dollar-cost averaging, because a fixed dollar amount is invested each month for the accumulation of stock shares. Payments are set between $40 and $1,000 per period. You have the choice of monthly or quarterly schedules. Commissions and odd-lot charges are deducted from the payment, with the balance purchasing full shares and fractional shares.

Any stock listed on the NYSE can be purchased in this manner. Dividends are credited to your account on full and partial shares. Since it is noncontractual, you may stop at any time. The main drawback is the high commission rate on small purchases.

Employee stock plans Many organizations offer their employees the option to participate in the fortunes of the company through an employee stock plan. These are similar to the NYSE's Monthly Investment Plan. We urge you to take advantage of your company's offer if it is a sound company. If not, you had better find other employment!

The advantages are manifold: (1) Most plans are handled through payroll deduction—very systematic; (2) generally there is no commission charge; the company pays for it; (3) there is no odd-lot differential because it often comes from unissued stock, or the company buys in round lots; and (4) best of all, many companies actually match all or part of an employee's contribution—a very good bargain if the stock is sound.

Automatic Trend Following

Another major formula in wide use is automatic trend following. This technique varies with the individual investor but basically follows the Wall Street "herd instinct." You follow the trend of market prices by taking a buy or sell action whenever the market reverses direction. This type formula also takes the guesswork out of timing transactions, much the same as dollar-cost averaging. You do not forecast market trends; you wait for a trend to develop. The results of your action will be different from dollar-cost averaging because you are attempting to trade (speculate?) rather than invest in a company for the long term. Here is what you must do to apply an automatic trend-following system:

1. Base your purchases or sales on one of the published averages that indicate market trends. Any of the composite or industrial averages or specific industry averages will do if there is some relation to your securities.
2. Select a percentage figure to trigger your automatic response to the market average that you have chosen to follow. Many investors use a 10 percent turn-around figure as evidence of a new trend. A lower percentage may cause undue trading (churning) in your account. A higher percentage may cause you to respond too late to take advantage of the trend for profit.
3. An automatic buy signal will occur whenever your index average increases by this percent.
4. An automatic sell signal will occur whenever your index average decreases by this percent.

With such a trend-following plan you never buy at the lowest point or sell at the highest point of the index that you are following. The particular stock(s) that you buy or sell may "top out or bottom out" at times somewhat different than the index.

Ratio and fixed-sum plans Two such plans that follow trends automatically are the constant-ratio plan and the fixed-dollar-sum plan. In the *constant-ratio plan,* you keep a constant percentage of common-stock dollar value in your portfolio at all times; let's say 60 percent. Whenever common-stock prices rise, you shift the excess percentage to bonds. Whenever common-stock prices decline, you sell bonds and buy additional stock to maintain your constant ratio. To make the plan work you must (1) have a separate portfolio of stock, bonds, and cash, and (2) set a deviation point spread from the ratio at which you will take corrective action to rebalance your ratio. In the *fixed-dollar-sum* plan, you have a fixed number of dollars and then determine how much to keep in stocks. Whenever the dollar value rises in common stock, you remove the excess, and as prices fall, you buy extra shares. This plan is generally less successful than the constant-ratio plan because it does not limit the amount of extra funds that may go into stocks in a depressed market. Losses can reduce your portfolio to the point where all funds are in stocks in order to maintain the dollar amount. Conversely, you tend to get out of a rising market too soon.

Charting A refinement of automatic trend following involves the use of charts. A chartist plots daily or periodic price movements in select stocks or industry and composite averages. The charted trends presumably indicate certain patterns that may be interpreted. Some patterns are widely accepted as indicators. Past performance of select stocks or industries is constantly reviewed for the same patterns. Chartists then buy and sell based upon the assumption that what has happened in the past will happen again.

There is a lot of tedious work involved in charting. Fortunately a number of firms provide daily, weekly, or quarterly charts for your interpretation. Among them are Chartcraft, Inc., Securities Research Company, and Trendlines, Inc. Figures 14–4 and 14–5 reproduce a representative charting

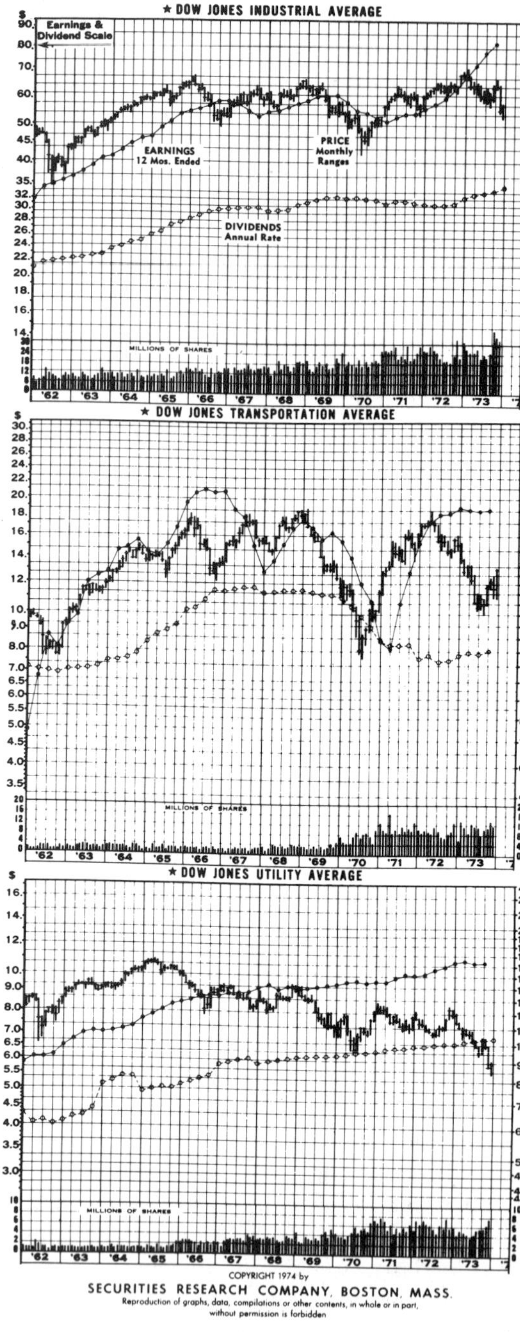

THE THREE AVERAGE DIAGRAMS IN ACTION

This Transparent Overlay Sheet provides a unique means for comparing the market profiles of individual stocks with their respective Dow-Jones Industrial, Rail, or Utility Average. This is accomplished by laying the corresponding "average" chart over the stock chart under study, with the initial price bars to the left coinciding. The comparison quickly indicates whether the stock has fluctuated more or less widely than its related average, whether the pattern of the market profile appears to be basically "growth", "cyclical", etc. as shown in the examples on page 1, whether the stock tends to anticipate or lag a general market movement, or may be undergoing a basic change in character.

USING THE RULERS

PERCENTAGE RULER

Advances and declines are measured by placing the zero line at the start of the advance or decline. The point reached on the scale shows directly the percentage gain or loss.

PRICE-EARNINGS RULER

The number of times annual earnings at which a stock sells is measured by placing the 15 line on the charted earnings. The point of the scale reached by the price shows directly the price-earnings ratio.

DIVIDEND COVERAGE

With the 10 line (of the P-E ruler) placed on the charted dividend line, the point reached by the earnings line shows 10 times dividend coverage. Thus, if the earnings are found at 23 on the ruler, divide that figure by 10 and the result is the dividend coverage – 2.3 times.

YIELD RULER

The dividend yield is measured by placing the 6.7% line on the charted dividend. The point of the scale reached by the price range shows the yield on the annual dividend rate.

USING THE GROWTH CHART

To approximate the extent of the market advance of individual issues over the full 12-year time span – as compared with annually compounded interest rates – use the growth chart below. Place the lower left corner of this chart at the start of the stock's price range 12-year's back and read on the right the rate at which the issue has appreciated. Increases in per share earnings and dividend rates may be similarly measured.

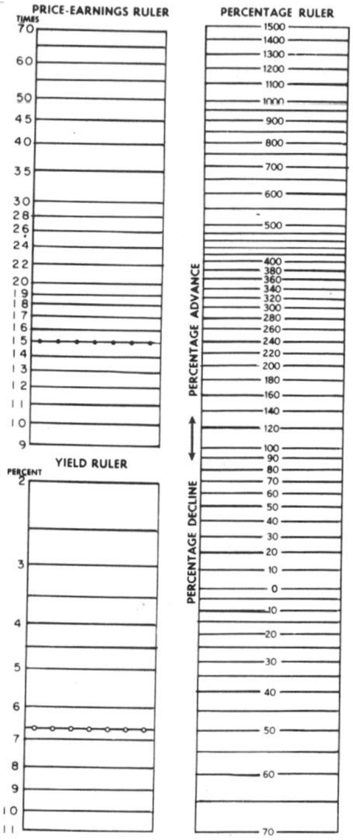

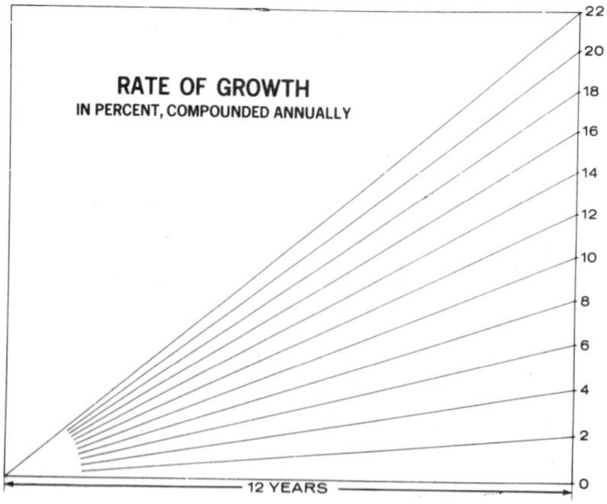

Figure 14-4 Market Diagram Comparators. *(Securities Research Company, Boston)*

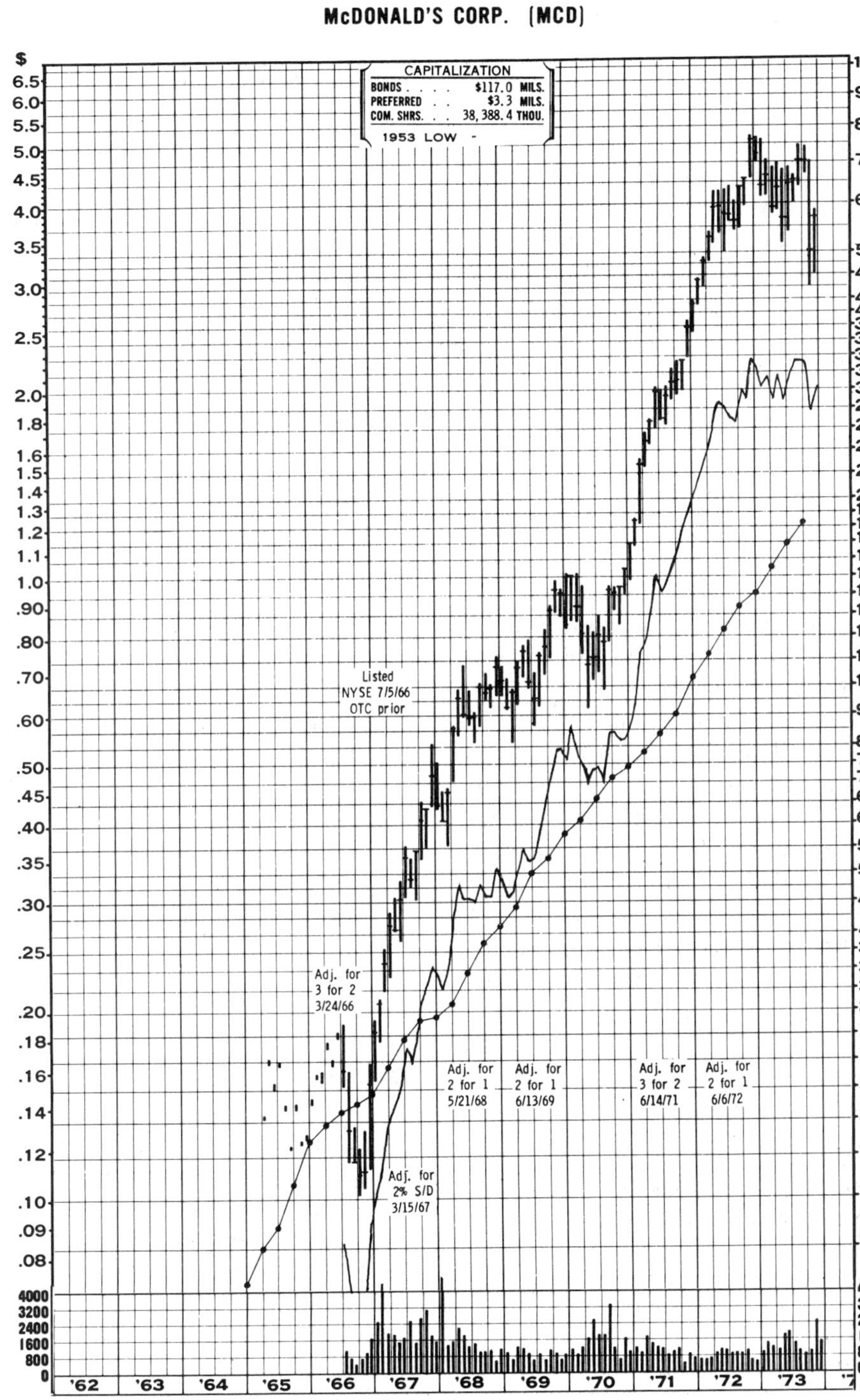

Figure 14–5 Trend Chart of a Selected Stock. *(Securities Research Company, Boston)*

system that provides trend analysis. They are part of the chartbook *3-Trend Cycli-Graphs* published by Securities Research Company. Figure 14–4 is an overlay that allows three of the Dow Jones averages to be superimposed upon specific stock charts as shown in figure 14–5.

IT'S STILL YOUR DECISION

In the final analysis, it is still your decision about what to buy and when to buy. All the advice in the world will not stop you from making expensive mistakes in the stock market. Listening to the advice and using all the analytical tools available should certainly cut your losses. If you follow good investment practices, your gains should outpace your losses. We are in an inflationary world where the primary trend is up over the long term. The choice of the fundamentalist approach using individual timing and selection or the choice of the formula approach to timing will be equally successful if you think rationally rather than emotionally. In any case, an investment decision must be based on a number of equally important factors that we have discussed.

Vocabulary and Concepts

Balance sheet	Odd lot
Dividends	Operating profit
Dollar-cost averaging	Portfolio
Dow Theory	Price-earnings ratio
GTC order	Retained earnings
Income statement	Round lot
Margin	Short sale
Monthly Investment Plan	Stock dividend
	Stock split
Net working capital	Stop order

Questions for Discussion

1. Explain in detail the procedure for buying securities on credit.
2. How can the trader protect himself from an unexpected decline in the price of a stock?
3. Explain why it is important to analyze both the industry and a company before investing. What should you look for?
4. How can common-stock profits be made in a declining market? Explain.
5. Under what economic conditions is it generally better to purchase bonds, rather than common stock? Why?
6. What important balance-sheet ratios should be analyzed? Why?
7. What important income statement figures should be analyzed? Why?
8. What important figures should be cross-analyzed on both financial statements? Why?
9. Explain the various "timing theories" for buy and sell securities transactions.
10. How would you describe dollar-cost averaging? Is this a speculative or investment technique?

Projects

1. Survey your local security brokers. Find out which ones encourage the small investor. Assume you purchase 100 shares of a recommended stock and corporate bonds of approximately the same value. Compare the investment costs at two brokerage houses and at a bank. Also compare costs between the securities.
2. Research a common stock that has been recommended by a broker, a newspaper

columnist, or your instructor. Make an investment decision based on general considerations, financial statement analysis, market price, opportunity, and a formula approach. Report it to the class.

3. Calculate the yield of a corporate bond that is selling at a premium and one that is selling at a discount. What conclusion do you reach about bond yields in general?

Case Problem

Bart Baker desires to invest $200 per month in the stock market. His investment objective is growth. Provide him with a list of alternative plans that he may use to make the investment. Indicate the approximate investment costs of each alternative you suggest. Based on your knowledge of Bart's finances, is he in a position to speculate?

15

investment companies

After looking into the various aspects of individually selected investments, you will probably come to the conclusion that you might need help with your investments. Investment companies will be glad to assist you. You may turn to these organizations whenever you do not have the time, energy, or perhaps the ability to make meaningful investment decisions. An investment company is a business organization that sells shares in itself to the investing public (both institutions and individual investors). It uses the proceeds to buy securities in other companies. Investment companies are popularly known as *mutual funds*, but this designation is not technically correct because not all investment companies are mutual funds.

Investment companies buy, sell, and hold the securities of other companies according to their analysis of the economy and the stock market. In the continuous process of accomplishing these investment chores, they provide you with their two main reasons for existence: *portfolio management* and *diversification.*

Investment companies seem to have a rather cyclical association with investors. Public confidence flows and ebbs with the marketplace performance of the funds. Their marketplace performance is quite closely tied to the performance of the stock market as a whole, because most funds are fairly well diversified. In the 1920s, public confidence was very high, but it fell because of the 1929 stock market crash, which caused a number of investment companies to fail. Confidence and public interest in mutual funds became very strong in the 1950s and 1960s during bull markets. In the early 1970s there was a net outflow of small-investor money from the mutual funds.

TYPES OF INVESTMENT COMPANIES

There are open-end and closed-end investment companies, differentiated by their organization structures. By far the most important, with over 90 percent of all investment company assets, are the open-end funds, which are the true *mutual funds.* Unless we mention specifically the closed-end funds, we will be referring to open-end mutual funds.

Open-end Investment Companies

Mutual funds are capitalized entirely by purchases of common-stock shares from the fund. A fund continually sells and redeems its shares as requested by the investor. It has the theoretical possibility of unlimited growth because as more persons purchase shares, their money becomes available for more security purchases by the fund. If the fund's manager succeeds in earning a good profit for his shareholders, "smart" investors will flock to purchase more shares, making the investment company still larger. However, all funds are really self-limiting because there are never enough good investments to keep the funds' performance at the top. As their performance declines, so does investor interest. Shareholders then redeem their shares. Sometimes mutual funds decrease in size until they liquidate. If enough shareholders redeem, the portfolio holdings of a mutual fund may need to be sold in order to satisfy the redemption demand. This lowers asset value, which may entice others to redeem, which in turn lowers the asset value, and so on.

Asset value Open-end companies offer to sell or buy their shares on the basis of current net asset value. Mutual funds calculate their per share value in this manner:

Add:	Market value of securities in fund's portfolio.
Add:	Cash on hand available for investing or redemption.
Subtract:	All liabilities (expenses payable).
Difference:	Net asset value of fund.
Divide:	Net asset value by number of shares issued.
Result:	Net asset value per share.

The share price in a mutual fund is computed daily after the stock market closes. It is the per share value of the fund's entire portfolio less any liabilities owed by the fund. Perhaps you can see why share values in mutual funds react in unison with the composite securities that they represent. Figure 15–1 illustrates the price per share as quoted by NASD and published in the *Wall Street Journal*.

Closed-end Investment Companies

Closed-end companies differ from the more popular mutual funds in three important ways: (1) they do not redeem their shares, (2) they will not issue new shares on demand, and (3) they may receive capital from sources other than common stock. In other words, closed-end investment companies are organized in much the same way as any other corporation and deal with their shareholders in the same manner as any other corporation.

Capitalization is relatively fixed. Debt capital may be raised to purchase additional securities if it is financially feasible. Once all the authorized stock has been sold, a new buyer of closed-end shares may obtain them only in the secondary market. Just like any other listed or unlisted stock, the stock price of a closed-end company reflects the laws of supply and demand. There is no fixed or constant relationship between the market prices of closed-end stocks and their underlying asset values. The market price per share is based on expectations of how well the portfolio of stocks owned by the closed-end company will perform. Shares may sell at higher or lower prices than their net asset values indicate. Premiums and discounts from net asset value per share in a particular closed-end company may fluctuate widely within a single year just as would any other stock.

Asset value Closed-end funds calculate their net asset value per share in the same manner as open-end funds. However, the closed-end shareholder is not as interested in the net asset value per share as is the open-end shareholder because he is not as directly affected by it. His buy or sell price is based on market price, while the mutual fund shareholder purchases and redeems his shares at net asset value per share.

Mutual Funds

Friday, June 13, 1975

Price ranges for investment companies, as quoted by the National Association of Securities Dealers. NAV stands for net asset value per share; the offering includes net asset value plus maximum sales charge, if any.

	NAV	Off. Prc.	NAV Chg.
Adm Gwth	3.58	3.92	...
Adm Incm	3.29	3.61+	.01
Adm Insur	6.89	7.55+	.03
Adviser Fd	3.39	3.70	...
Aetna Fnd	6.80	7.43+	.02
Aetna InSh	11.71	12.80+	.03
Afuture Fd	7.60	N.L.+	.09
AGE Fund	4.24	4.33+	.02
Allstate	9.63	10.35+	.06
Alpha Fnd	10.05	N.L.+	.07
Am Birthrt	10.26	11.27+	.02
Am Equity	4.36	4.78−	.01
American Express Funds:			
Capital	5.92	6.47+	.03
Income	7.72	8.44+	.03
Invest	6.81	7.44+	.02
Spec Fnd	5.96	6.51+	.04
Stock Fd	6.41	7.01+	.03
American Funds Group:			
Amcap F	4.61	5.04+	.03
Am Mutl	8.00	8.74+	.03
Bnd FdA	x14.00	15.30−	.33
Gth FdA	4.16	4.55+	.02
IncF Am	13.02	14.23+	.02
I C A	12.10	13.22+	.06
Nw Prsp	15.05	16.45+	.12
Wash Mt	11.26	12.31+	.05
Am Grwth	4.48	4.90−	.01
Am Ins Ind	4.47	4.89−	.03
Am Invest	4.76	N.L.+	.01
AmNat Gw	2.16	2.36	...
Anchor Group:			
Daily Inc	1.00	N.L.	...
Growth	6.45	7.07	...
Income	6.46	7.08+	.03
Reserv	10.31	11.30+	.01
Spectm	4.20	4.60+	.02
Fund Inv	6.33	6.94+	.02
Wa Natl	9.47	10.38+	.03
Audax Fnd	6.90	7.54+	.04
Axe-Houghton:			
Fund A	4.34	4.72	...
Fund B	6.63	7.21+	.02
Stock Fd	5.73	6.26+	.02
BLC Gwth	9.32	10.18+	.05
Babson Iv	9.82	N.L.+	.05
Bayrock	5.32	...+	.03
Bayrok Gr	4.51	...+	.02
Beacon Hll	8.19	N.L.+	.02
Beacon Inv	9.12	N.L.+	.01
Brksh Cap	6.53	7.14+	.03
Bondsk Cp	4.10	4.48+	.01
Bos Found	8.53	9.32+	.02
Brown Fnd	(z)	(z)	(z)
Burnham	(z)	(z)	(z)
Calvin Bullock Funds:			
Bullock	11.47	12.54+	.07
Canadn	8.91	9.74+	.01
Div Shrs	2.92	3.20+	.01
Ntwide	8.78	9.60+	.04
NY Vent	10.35	11.31+	.07
C G Fund	9.18	9.92+	.01
CG Inc Fd	7.86	8.50+	.03
Cap Presv	94.93	N.L.+	.02
Century Sh	10.09	11.03+	.05
Chalng Inv	8.92	9.75+	.04
Channing Funds:			
Amercn	1.10	1.20	...
Balanc	8.52	9.31+	.01
Bond Fd	7.97	8.71+	.02
Eqty Gth	6.48	7.08+	.04
Eqty Prg	2.61	2.85+	.02
Fnd Amr	6.09	6.66+	.02
Growth	4.09	4.47+	.02
Income	5.89	6.44+	.01
Prov Inc	3.33	3.64+	.01
Special	1.49	1.63+	.02
Venture	8.38	9.16+	.17
Charter Fd	10.23	11.32−	.03
Cust K 1	6.60	7.24+	.02
Cust K 2	5.06	5.51+	.03
Cust S 1	18.39	20.15+	.08
Cust S 2	8.70	9.53+	.03
Cust S 3	7.25	7.94+	.03
Cust S 4	3.12	3.42+	.02
Apollo	3.81	4.17+	.04
Polaris	3.12	3.41+	.03
Lndmk Gw	6.46	7.06+	.02
LD EdieCa	13.07	13.98+	.05
Lexington Group:			
Cp Ledrs	13.29	14.64−	.10
Growth	6.19	6.77+	.02
Income	10.30	11.26+	.01
Resrch	12.27	13.41+	.04
LifeIns Inv	6.04	6.60+	.01
Lincoln National Funds:			
Linc Cap	5.88	6.43+	.01
Selct Am	6.41	N.L.+	.02
Selct Op	9.10	N.L.+	.09
Selct Spl	13.07	N.L.+	.01
Loomis Sayles Funds:			
Cap Dev	10.17	N.L.+	.05
Mutual	12.59	N.L.+	.05
Lord Abbett:			
Affilatd	6.79	7.33+	.03
Am Bus	2.88	3.11+	.02
Bond deb	9.51	10.39+	.04
Lutheran Brotherhd Fds:			
Broth Fd	9.42	10.30+	.04
Broh Inc	8.50	9.29+	.03
Broth US	10.05	10.98	...
Mass Company:			
Freedm	6.66	7.30+	.02
Indep Fd	6.89	7.55+	.02
Mass Fd	9.72	10.65+	.02
Mass Financial Svcs:			
MIT	9.86	10.78+	.05
MIG	9.94	10.86+	.05
MID	12.29	13.43+	.05
MFD	11.39	12.45+	.05
MCD	12.01	13.13+	.09
Mates Invs	1.43	N.L.	...
Mather Fd	9.68	N.L.+	.07
Mid Amer	4.49	4.91	...
Money Mkt	1.00	N.L.	...
MONY Fd	9.20	10.05+	.05
MSB Fund	13.21	N.L.+	.07
Mutl BnFd	(z)	(z)	(z)
M I F Fd	7.29	7.88+	.05
M I F Gro	3.39	3.66+	.03
Mutual of Omaha Funds:			
Amer	11.60	11.78−	.01
Growth	4.20	4.57+	.01
Income	8.04	8.74+	.06
Mutl Shars	19.84	N.L.+	.04
Mutl Trust	1.75	N.L.	...
Natl Indust	9.00	N.L.+	.05
National Securities Funds:			
Balanc	7.63	8.34−	.01
Bond	4.10	4.48	...
Dividnd	3.22	3.52+	.02
Preferd	5.40	5.90+	.01
Income	4.39	4.80+	.01
Stock	6.53	7.14+	.06
Grwth	5.32	5.81+	.01
New Eng Life Fds:			
Equity	14.51	15.77+	.03
Grwth	8.54	9.28+	.06
Income	13.40	14.57	...
Side	13.30	14.46+	.08
N E A Mut	7.93	...+	.04
Neuwirth	7.78	N.L.+	.03
Newton Fd	11.05	12.07+	.08
New World	10.50	11.48+	.04
Nichlas Fd	12.82	N.L.+	.07
Noeast Inv	13.34	N.L.+	.02
Omega Fd	7.74	7.86−	.06
One Wll St	14.26	N.L.+	.02
Chase Group of Boston:			
Fnd Bost	6.58	7.19+	.04
Front Cp	4.03	4.40+	.01
ShTr Bos	6.38	6.97+	.03
Special	5.21	5.69+	.01
Chem Fnd	8.34	9.11+	.05
CNA Management Funds:			
Knick Fd	5.38	5.90+	.03
Knick Gr	5.71	6.25+	.08
Liberty	3.85	4.21+	.02
Manhtn	2.98	...+	.01
Schus Fd	6.41	7.01	...
Colonial Funds:			
Convert	x8.26	9.03−	.14
Equity	2.41	2.63+	.02
Fund	9.12	9.97+	.02
Growth	4.90	5.36+	.03
Income	x7.98	8.72−	.17
Ventur	2.16	2.36+	.01
Col Grwth	12.23	N.L.+	.06
Columb Fd	6.58	N.L.	...
Commonwealth Trust:			
A & B	.91	.98+	.01
C	1.33	1.44	...
Cmpass Gr	5.18	5.66+	.03
Comp Cap	4.00	4.38−	.01
Comp BdSt	7.81	8.49	...
Composit	7.68	8.35+	.02
Concord F	8.40	N.L.+	.04
Consol Inv	9.25	9.75	...
Constlatn	5.33	N.L.+	.02
Cont Mtlv	6.33	N.L.−	.02
Coutry Cap	11.42	12.35+	.06
Davidg Fd	6.29	N.L.	...
Delaware Group:			
Decatr	9.37	10.24+	.02
Delw Fd	8.99	9.83+	.02
Delta Td	4.05	4.43+	.01
DeVegh M	59.48	N.L.+	.09
Oppenheimer Funds:			
Aim Fnd	8.32	9.09+	.04
Opp Fnd	5.93	6.48+	.04
Income	7.25	7.92	...
Mony Br	9.62	...	...
Time Fd	5.43	5.93+	.06
OTC SecFd	9.82	10.67+	.01
Paramnt	6.52	7.13+	.07
Partners	7.58	N.L.+	.04
Paul Revr	5.35	5.85+	.03
Pegasus F	3.41	3.74+	.02
Penn Mutl	2.41	N.L.+	.04
Penn Squ	6.74	N.L.+	.03
Phila Fund	6.59	7.20	...
Phonx Cap	7.84	8.57+	.05
Pilgrim Group:			
Pil Frml	11.69	12.78+	.06
Mag Cap	2.92	N.L.+	.01
Mag Inc	7.81	8.54+	.02
Pilgr Fd	6.78	7.41−	.01
Pine St Fd	9.72	N.L.+	.05
Pine Trée	(z)	(z)	(z)
Pioneer Funds:			
Pionr Fd	11.26	12.31+	.03
Pionr II	9.98	10.91	...
Planned In	10.09	10.97	...
PLIGRO	10.12	11.06	...
PLITRN	6.23	6.81+	.03
Price Rowe:			
Growth	10.65	N.L.+	.04
Income	9.61	N.L.	...
New Era	11.00	N.L.+	.07
Nw Horz	7.25	N.L.+	.06
PRO Fund	5.97	N.L.+	.03
Provdr Gt	7.33	8.01+	.05
Pru SIP I	8.49	9.28+	.03
Putnam Funds:			
Convert	9.69	10.59+	.01
Equitie	8.88	9.70+	.08

Weekly Mutual Funds

Friday, June 13, 1975

	Bid	Asked
acorn Fund Inc	9.54	N.L.
AmExpGov Sec	24.32	24.75
Am Gen Growth	15.94	...
Capital ExchFd	28.44	...
Combined Shrs	(z)	(z)
Congress Str Fd	29.44	...
Constitution Fd	46.87	...
Daily IncomeFd	10.02	N.L.
DelchsterBd Fd	8.45	9.23
Deposit FndBos	20.85	...
Devnshire St Fd	11.42	...
Divesifcatn Fd	33.42	...
Drexel Inves Fd	(z)	(z)
Edie Spl InstFd	44.09	N.L.
Empire Fnd Inc	17.52	...
Exchang FdBos	38.11	...
Exeter Fund	33.97	...
Federal StFund	27.08	...
Fiduciary ExFd	21.13	...
44 WallStreetFd	(z)	(z)
Josten GrwthFd	10.67	...
Lincoln Nat Inc	7.90	8.63
MassFnclBd Fd	14.88	16.26
Nassau Fund	11.24	N.L.
Ocean TechnFd	(z)	(z)
Ohio Capital Fd	(z)	(z)
Safeco IncomeF	8.26	9.03
Scudder Dev Fd	41.29	42.13
2nd Congress St	33.47	...
2nd Fiduciary	27.88	...
Sentinel Trustes	10.90	11.85
Transam InvFd	8.33	9.05
VanceS Income	13.28	14.51

Dual Purpose Funds

Friday, June 13, 1975

Following is a weekly listing of the unaudited net asset values of dual-purpose, closed-end investment funds' capital shares as reported by the companies as of Friday's close. Also shown is the closing listed market price or the dealer-to-dealer asked price of each fund's capital shares, with the percentage of difference.

	Cap. Shs. Price	N.A. Val Cap. Shs.	% Diff.
Am DualVest	4 1/8	5.64	−26.9
Gemini	9 1/2	13.79	−31.1
Hemisphere	1 5/8	0.57	+185.1
Income and Cap	4 7/8	7.69	−36.1
Leverage	7 1/4	11.03	−34.3
Pegasus Inco&Cap	4 1/2	4.09	+10.0
Putnam Duo Fund	4 1/4	5.51	−22.9
Scudder Duo-Vest	5 1/2	8.05	−31.7
Scudder D-V Exch	14	25.39	−44.9

Lipper Analytical.

Figure 15–1 Mutual Fund Price Quotations. *(Reprinted with permission of The Wall Street Journal, © Dow Jones & Company, Inc., 1975. All Rights Reserved.)*

INVESTMENT COMPANY OBJECTIVES

Many investors believe a professional management team will invest their money with better results than they could obtain by direct investing. This may be true because professional management should be continually on top of market happenings while the individual investor does not have the time or resources to do so. If you should decide that professional management is for you, pick a fund that matches your investment objectives. You may choose from over five hundred different funds. Fortunately a number of reporting services classify funds by their investment objectives. You may also learn about a fund's objectives and policies in its offering prospectus.

Common-Stock Funds

A common-stock fund portfolio consists of at least 80 percent common stock. Investor preference over the years has been building rather steadily toward capital growth rather than current income. This preference has spurred more offerings of common-stock funds. For the majority of mutual fund buyers, the question is not whether they should invest for growth, but how much risk they should take to get potential growth.

Growth funds No set description can apply to all funds that seek capital appreciation. It is a matter of risk degree and how aggressive an investment policy the funds have. This is spelled out in the prospectus. A fund that seeks "maximum capital gain" will state that higher-than-average risks will be taken in an effort to achieve it. Acceptable risks would include: (1) investments made in some little-known companies, (2) rapid portfolio turnover, (3) use of short-sales positions, (4) use of borrowed money to provide leverage, and (5) very little yield from investment income. These are *capital gains* funds. They perform well in rising markets and suffer substantial losses when the market declines. Somewhat less aggressive are *growth funds* and *growth income funds*. They, too, are speculative, but they are slightly more diversified to cushion advances and declines in the market.

Specialized funds A few funds limit their holdings to a specialized field or industry. They normally hold bonds and preferred stocks. Most of these funds are not as specialized as the name implies, but they do offer the investor an opportunity to invest in a particular industry. Aerospace, airlines, electronics, mining and exploration, chemicals, and petroleum are the industries usually featured. Real estate investment trusts (REITs) could be classified as a form of specialized fund. Special funds may be open- or closed-end.

Balanced Funds

The objective of a balanced fund is to minimize investment risk as much as possible without unduly sacrificing long-term growth and current income potential. This objective is accomplished by maintaining a "portfolio balance" of bonds and common stock. Balanced funds also hold some government notes, preferred stock, and other securities. How balanced the fund really is can be determined by capital-gains performance and current yield.

Generally, balanced funds are less volatile than common-stock funds. Their managers also continually analyze their portfolio and change investment position as the stock market dictates.

Other Investment Objectives

While common-stock and balanced funds account for the vast majority of investment companies, there are a few other types of funds that deserve mention.

Income funds Income is extremely important to some investors. A number of mutual funds stress the largest possible current income. These funds may utilize common stock, preferred stock, or bonds in their portfolio. While they attempt to de-emphasize capital growth, a number of income funds behave more like balanced funds. A convertible fund behaves this way. A true current income position is available if you invest in *bond and preferred stock funds* or in tax-exempt *municipal bond funds.*

Hedge funds The dictionary defines hedge as "to sell out, as against previous purchases, so as to avoid loss, to bet on both sides." This amply describes the activity of a hedge fund. Profits are enhanced in a rising market through leverage and long positions, and losses are minimized in a declining market by extensive use of short sales. These funds are trading oriented. They have all the features of capital-gains funds plus the leverage possibility of borrowed money and short sales. If you invest in this type of fund, you can expect to obtain large gains in a rising market or incur sharp losses in a declining market if the hedge does not work.

Dual-purpose funds These funds are unique because one fund is used for two completely different investor objectives. They are often called *leverage* funds because of the two classes of shares and their method of dividing profits and losses. The classes in these closed-end funds are usually called *income shares* and *capital shares.* Income shares are entitled to the total net investment income of the portfolio, while capital shares gain the fund's entire asset appreciation. This simply means that each class uses the other's funds for its particular investment objective. With twice as many shares working for you, the leverage is 2-to-1 on an original issue purchase.

Dual-purpose funds are organized to operate as closed-end funds for a definite duration, usually fifteen years, after which time the income shares are callable. Capital shares would then operate as an open-end fund with the right of redemption.

The income shares in most funds are cumulative and are guaranteed a minimum dividend with the right to receive all income over the guarantee. Income shares may be traded over the counter at market price at any time before they are called. Since these shares resemble preferred stock, their market price tends to reflect current interest rates and the fund's dividend performance.

Capital shareholders receive no dividends. Capital gains realized by the fund are automatically reinvested in other stocks. The fund's net asset value increases whether the capital gain is realized by sale or unrealized by holding the portfolio investment. Capital shareholders obtain their capital gains (or losses) by selling their shares in the fund in the over-the-counter market. The dual-purpose nature of the fund means that the capital shareholders have everything to gain or lose. The market price of capital shares is listed in the *Wall Street Journal* every Monday.

INFORMATION AND PROTECTION FOR THE INVESTOR

You must keep yourself reasonably well informed about the market place and the particular mutual funds that interest you. Even if you are purchasing a fund in order to have professional management and diversification, you cannot shirk your responsibility. It is your money that is being invested. You can suffer considerable losses by relying entirely on someone else. You can also do the same by relying entirely on yourself.

Periodical Information

There are many sources of information about particular investment companies and the mutual fund industry as a whole. As in any investment, you should first be aware of the state of the economy and the stock market, and then get down to specifics. The most comprehensive information on investment companies is available in a number of annual guides published by Fundscope, Inc., Wiesenberger Services, Inc., Johnson's Charts, Inc., the Hirsch Organization, Inc., and Vicker's Associates. The respective titles are *Fundscope Mutual Fund Guide, Investment Companies, Johnson's Investment Company Charts, Mutual Funds Almanac,* and *Vickers Guide to Investment Company Portfolios.* Your broker or local library will have access to some or all of them. Each service provides supplements at various times during the year.

The *Wall Street Journal* publishes the daily net asset value of the open-end and weekly NAV of ask prices on closed-end funds. Of course, some closed-end funds are quoted in the regular stock quotations of the NYSE. *Barron's, Forbes,* and *Fortune* publish comparative ratings and analyses of the industry and selected funds at regular intervals. For the most current information on articles available, check the *Business Periodicals Index* and the *Readers' Guide to Periodical Literature.* Occasionally general-interest publications have rather informative articles.

Mutual Fund Salesmen

Since open-end funds are not sold on any exchange, the funds attempt to reach the investor in a more direct manner. Each fund's marketing department usually has a representative agreement with a number of dealer-broker organizations and also with a direct sales organization. In the first instance, brokerage-house account executives receive a commission for selling the fund shares as broker representatives. In the second instance, mutual fund salesmen make sales visits to your home or office as direct agents for the fund. A number of insurance companies have organized mutual funds that are sold by their insurance agents. In such cases the agent can offer you a fixed-income savings plan as part of a straight life or endowment life-insurance policy, or he can combine the life-insurance plan with the systematic purchase of mutual funds to provide a variable-income savings plan. In all person-to-person sales the commission, called a *load,* is added to the net asset value of the shares. We will discuss this later in the chapter.

The Mutual Fund Prospectus

Knowledgeable investors can secure a vast amount of important information from an investment company's prospectus. These are offered to the investing public as a factual disclosure of information, as required by the Securities and Exchange Commission. Figure 15–2 presents selected pages from the prospectus of United Funds, Inc. Most funds follow this general format.

The cover provides the name of the fund, its manager and sales organization, and other pertinent information. The United Funds prospectus differs from most other funds because it offers four different funds, each with its own objectives. This approach may be helpful to an investor who has a choice of investment objectives. It is helpful to Waddell & Reed, Inc., because it shows all their "wares" in one offering.

Waddell & Reed

One Crown Center
Kansas City, Missouri 64141
(816) 283-4000

April 30, 1975

PROSPECTUS

UNITED FUNDS, INC.

United Funds, Inc. (the Corporation) is an investment company managed by Waddell & Reed, Inc. (See page 7 for information about the Manager.) Its combined total net assets of $1,330,505,677 on December 31, 1974 represented the beneficial interests of over 367,595 shareholder accounts. The Corporation issues four classes of capital shares; each class represents ownership of a separate mutual fund.

The shares of each Fund afford a convenient way to obtain wide diversification and the continuing services of a professional management organization.

For important information concerning Waddell & Reed, Inc. and the financial difficulties of its parent corporation see page 21

THE FOUR FUNDS

United Accumulative Fund is designed primarily for investors who are interested in capital growth of their investments with current income a secondary consideration.

United Income Fund is designed primarily for those who are interested in the maintenance of current income subject to market conditions.

United Science Fund is designed to provide opportunities for long-term capital growth through investment in a portfolio emphasizing science securities.

United Bond Fund is designed for investors who are primarily interested in investing in a portfolio of fixed dollar type securities offering a reasonable return with more emphasis on preservation of capital invested.

The minimum initial order is $500, except in the states of California and Illinois and plans or trusts that qualify under Section 401 or 408 of the Internal Revenue Code, the minimum initial order is $100. Subsequent orders must be at least $25. A Payroll Deduction Plan is also available. See page 16.

The offering price of the shares of each Fund is its net asset value per share next determined plus a maximum sales charge of 9.59% of the amount invested (8.75% of the offering price) on purchases of less than $25,000 (reduced on certain larger purchases).

THESE SECURITIES HAVE NOT BEEN APPROVED OR DISAPPROVED BY THE SECURITIES AND EXCHANGE COMMISSION, NOR HAS THE COMMISSION PASSED UPON THE ACCURACY OR ADEQUACY OF THIS PROSPECTUS. ANY REPRESENTATION TO THE CONTRARY IS A CRIMINAL OFFENSE.

RETAIN THIS PROSPECTUS FOR FUTURE REFERENCE

Figure 15–2 Selected Pages from a Mutual Fund Prospectus. *(Waddell & Reed, Inc., Kansas City, Mo.)*

TABLE OF CONTENTS

Numerous investment companies continuously offer their shares to investors. Investment companies have different investment objectives and techniques and involve varying degrees of risk. Sales commissions which are paid to compensate persons who sell investment company shares vary as do management charges and expense ratios. For the last fiscal year, total operating expenses (including advisory fees) as a percent of average net assets for each Fund were: United Accumulative Fund, 0.49%; United Income Fund, 0.48%; United Science Fund, 0.49%; and United Bond Fund, 0.35%.

INTRODUCTION

United Funds, Inc. is an investment company incorporated in Maryland on February 21, 1974 as successor to a Delaware Corporation. An investment company is an arrangement by which a number of persons invest in a company that itself invests in securities. The Corporation is an open-end investment company because, upon demand of a shareholder, the Corporation has a legal duty to acquire the shares of any Fund of the Corporation held by the shareholder and pay him the net asset value of the shares. (See discussion of computations of redemptions and net asset value, pages 17 and 18.) This type of investment company is commonly called a *mutual fund.*

Mutual funds invest their assets in accordance with their investment objectives and policies. The Corporation's investment objectives and policies are stated starting on page 4.

Waddell & Reed, Inc. determines what securities each Fund shall purchase and sell and is paid an investment advisory fee pursuant to a contract. This fee on an annual basis is .5 of 1% of the Corporation's average net assets on the first $500 million of such assets and is reduced on larger amounts. A separate fee of .3125 of 1% of average net assets is charged for United Bond Fund. (See page 7 for a discussion of the investment adviser and the advisory agreement.) Waddell & Reed, Inc. pays all the other expenses of the Corporation except directors' fees, taxes, custodian, legal and auditing fees, and any extraordinary expenses. (For information concerning expense allocation under the terms of a proposed new management agreement, see page 7.)

The value of the Funds' shares fluctuates because the value of the securities in which each Fund invests fluctuates. When a Fund sells portfolio securities it may realize a gain or loss, depending on whether it sells them for more or less than their cost. Each Fund will earn dividends and interest income to the extent that it receives dividends and interest from its investments. (The tax consequences of these dividends and distributions to shareholders of the Corporation are discussed on page 16 under the caption Dividends, Distributions and Taxes.)

— 2 —

Figure 15–2 (continued)

UNITED FUNDS, INC.

PER-SHARE INCOME AND CAPITAL CHANGES

(For a Share Outstanding throughout each Year)

	INCOME AND EXPENSE				CAPITAL CHANGES						
Fiscal Year Ended Dec. 31	Income	Operating Expenses	Net Income	Dividends from Net Income	Net Asset Value at Beginning of Year	Net Realized & Unrealized Gains (Losses) on Investments	Distributions from Capital Gains and Other Capital Sources	Net Asset Value at End of Year	Ratio of Operating Expenses to Average Net Assets	Ratio of Net Income to Average Net Assets	Shares Outstanding at End of Year (000 omitted)
UNITED ACCUMULATIVE FUND (Adjusted to give retroactive effect to a two for one stock split February 16, 1968)											
1965	$ .27	$ .04	$ .23	$ .22	$ 8.28	$ .99	$ .13	$ 9.15	.46%	2.6%	135,105
1966	.25	.04	.21	.22	9.15	(.76)	.20	8.18	.41	2.4	150,932
1967	.23	.03	.20	.21	8.18	.85	.50	8.52	.38	2.3	163,218
1968	.16	.03	.13	.13	8.52	.48	.49	8.51	.37	1.5	171,585
1969	.19	.03	.16	.16	8.51	(1.11)	.25	7.15	.39	2.1	175,563
1970	.19	.02	.17	.18	7.15	(.38)	.01*	6.75	.38	2.7	169,054
1971	.17	.03	.14	.07	6.75	1.04	—	7.86	.39	1.9	147,833
1972	.16	.03	.13	.13	7.86	.85	.19	8.52	.42	1.6	128,201
1973	.16	.03	.13	.14	8.52	(1.69)	.20	6.62	.43	1.7	117,994
1974	.18	.03	.15	.14	6.62	(1.96)	.05	4.62	.49	2.8	111,977
UNITED INCOME FUND											
1965	$ .45	$ .07	$ .38	$ .37	$13.80	$ 1.31	$ .43	$14.69	.47%	2.6%	46,614
1966	.43	.06	.37	.37	14.69	(1.35)	.50	12.84	.41	2.7	49,282
1967	.39	.06	.33	.34	12.84	2.68	.58	14.93	.39	2.3	50,836
1968	.36	.06	.30	.30	14.93	1.95	.66	16.22	.37	2.0	52,551
1969	.44	.06	.38	.33	16.22	(1.91)	.68	13.68	.39	2.6	56,700
1970	.46	.05	.41	.43	13.68	(.22)	.58	12.86	.38	3.4	60,519
1971	.39	.05	.34	.42	12.86	1.61	.06	14.33	.40	2.5	60,757
1972	.40	.06	.34	.33	14.33	1.81	.53	15.62	.43	2.3	57,527
1973	.45	.06	.39	.39	15.62	(2.82)	.68	12.12	.43	2.8	57,911
1974	.48	.05	.43	.42	12.12	(3.19)	.62	8.32	.48	4.4	60,959
UNITED SCIENCE FUND											
1965	$ .16	$ .04	$ .12	$ .12	$ 7.47	$ 2.56	$ .30	$ 9.73	.49%	1.4%	30,504
1966	.15	.04	.11	.12	9.73	(1.02)	.43	8.27	.42	1.2	36,459
1967	.16	.04	.12	.12	8.27	2.45	.54	10.18	.39	1.3	42,373
1968	.14	.03	.11	.11	10.18	.22	.63	9.77	.37	1.1	48,226
1969	.18	.03	.15	.14	9.77	(1.18)	.55	8.05	.40	1.8	55,394
1970	.20	.03	.17	.21	8.05	(.87)	.05*	7.09	.39	2.6	58,212
1971	.20	.03	.17	.13	7.09	1.11	—	8.24	.39	2.1	53,762
1972	.17	.04	.13	.15	8.24	.23	.11	8.34	.43	1.6	47,716
1973	.16	.03	.13	.12	8.34	(1.85)	.16	6.34	.40	1.8	44,166
1974	.17	.03	.14	.10	6.34	(1.94)	—	4.44	.49	2.6	42,768
UNITED BOND FUND											
1965	$ .35	$ .03	$ .32	$ .30	$ 9.23	$ (.18)	$ —	$ 9.07	.35%	3.5%	118
1966	.41	.03	.38	.32	9.07	.31	—	9.44	.31	4.4	335
1967	.54	.03	.51	.43	9.44	.18	.30	9.40	.30	5.2	371
1968	.57	.03	.54	.51	9.40	(.23)	.30	8.90	.28	5.9	422
1969	.60	.02	.58	.57	8.90	(1.16)	—	7.75	.30	7.0	633
1970	.63	.02	.61	.59	7.75	.28	—	8.05	.27	8.1	710
1971	.62	.02	.60	.74	8.05	.45	—	8.36	.29	7.3	1,009
1972	.59	.03	.56	.60	8.36	.11	.10	8.33	.33	7.1	9,249
1973	.64	.03	.61	.60	8.33	(.59)	—	7.75	.33	7.6	14,505
1974	.62	.02	.60	.60	7.75	(1.26)	—	6.49	.35	8.7	17,837

* Distributions in 1970 of $.01 for United Accumulative Fund and $.05 for United Science Fund were from paid-in surplus.

—3—

Figure 15–2 (continued)

INVESTMENT OBJECTIVES AND POLICIES

The Corporation has certain investment objectives, policies and restrictions which may be changed only by vote of the outstanding shares.

Diversification and Concentration

The market risk inherent in any securities investment tends to be reduced because of wide diversification in the investments of each portfolio. No purchase may be made that would result in more than 25% of the total assets of United Accumulative Fund or United Income Fund being invested in any one industry, or more than 5% of the total assets of any Fund being invested in the securities of any one company, or that would result in any Fund owning more than 10% of the voting securities or 10% of the securities of any class of any one company. United Science Fund is concentrated in science securities. (See page 5.)

Investments

The greater part of the assets of United Accumulative, United Income and United Science Funds at December 31, 1974 was in common stocks. The present policy is to invest largely in common stocks. However, cash and senior securities such as bonds and preferred stocks may be held in these Funds in any proportions at any time. While investments are made in these Funds which may be expected to increase in value over the years, fluctuations in market values can result in decreases as well as increases from any given level. The assets of United Bond Fund are invested in bonds, notes, debentures or obligations of similar nature. Due to market risks inherent in any investment, there is, of course, no guarantee that the investment objectives will be achieved.

While securities are bought for investment purposes rather than for short-term trading profits, complete freedom is reserved to make changes in the several Funds' portfolios whenever the shareholders' interest will be better served thereby. The rates of portfolio turnover for each of the four Funds during the years ended December 31, 1974, 1973 and 1972 were as follows:

	1974	1973	1972
United Accumulative Fund	9.85%	46.13%	76.69%
United Income Fund	14.97	28.03	73.20
United Science Fund	22.77	39.16	117.15
United Bond Fund	76.05	30.92	25.09

Portfolio turnover is calculated by dividing (1) the lesser of purchases or sales of portfolio securities (excluding U. S. Government and short-term securities) for the year by (2) the monthly average of the market value of such securities during the year.

The lists of investments as of December 31, 1974 are included in the financial statements.

Other Investment Restrictions

Other investment restrictions provide that the Corporation may not: (1) borrow money; (2) invest in the securities of companies which have a record of less than three years' continuous operation; (3) pledge, mortgage or hypothecate any of its assets; (4) purchase securities issued by other investment companies except securities of closed-end investment companies in a regular transaction in the open market, or as a part of a plan of merger or consolidation, provided that as a result of such purchase not more than 10% of the total assets of the Corporation are invested in such securities; (5) buy securities on margin or sell short; (6) underwrite or participate in the underwriting of any securities; (7) purchase or sell real estate, commodities or commodity contracts; (8) deal with its own directors or officers acting as principal; (9) purchase restricted securities or securities (other than commercial paper) not having readily available market quotations; (10) purchase securi-

Figure 15–2 (continued)

ties of foreign governments if as a result of such purchases more than 5% of the total assets of the Corporation is invested in such securities; (11) purchase puts, calls, straddles or spreads; (12) invest for the purpose of exercising control or management of other companies; or (13) lend money or securities other than through the purchase of a portion of an issue of publicly distributed debt securities and other obligations customarily acquired by institutional investors or through lending portfolio securities collateralized in cash at 100% each business day. The Corporation intends to loan portfolio securities under the following conditions (which, except for the 100% collateral requirement, may be changed without a vote of shareholders): (a) loans will be made to broker-dealers and financial institutions; (b) the borrower must agree to increase the collateral on a daily basis if the securities increase in value but the borrower may require the return of the collateral if the securities decrease in value; (c) the loan will be made in accordance with the New York Stock Exchange rules, which presently require the borrower, after notice, to redeliver the securities within the normal settlement time of five business days; (d) the collateral will be invested only in short-term investments, (a portion of the yield on which may be paid to the borrower) which gives maximum liquidity so that the collateral may be paid back to the borrower when the securities are returned; (e) in the event the voting rights or rights of dissent pass to the borrower, and a material proposal affecting the securities borrowed is to be voted upon, the loan will be called in time for the Corporation to vote the proxies; and (f) the Corporation will limit the amount of lending of securities so that the aggregate amount received from borrowers of securities measured by dividends and interest on such securities will not cause the Corporation to lose its status as a regulated investment company and thereby subject it to the payment of Federal income taxes. It is anticipated that less than 10% of the Corporation's total assets will be lent at any one time.

SPECIFIC POLICIES

United Accumulative Fund

In operation since 1940, this Fund is primarily intended for investors who are interested in capital growth of their investments with current income as a secondary consideration in selection of portfolio securities. The major portfolio emphasis is on securities which provide opportunities for capital growth. Current income is a secondary consideration. Ordinarily the portfolio will be largely invested in common stocks or securities convertible into common stocks. When management believes that a more defensive economic position is desirable, the Fund may hold a relatively large portion of its assets in cash or in fixed income or defensive equity securities.

United Income Fund

In operation since 1940, this Fund is intended for those who are primarily interested in the maintenance of current income subject to market conditions. At times investment emphasis may be on the securities of companies which provide opportunities for capital growth and at other times emphasis may be on the securities of companies which are expected to show resistance to deflationary influences. Such securities will usually consist principally of common stocks and securities convertible into common stocks; preferred stocks and fixed income securities selected for their income possibilities may also be held. The portion of the portfolio held in such preferred stocks and fixed income securities or in cash may be substantial when management believes that a more defensive economic position is desirable.

United Science Fund

In operation since 1950, this Fund is intended for those who wish an investment designed to provide opportunities for long-term capital growth through investment in a portfolio emphasizing science securities. Science securities are securities of companies whose products, processes or services, in the opinion of management, are being or are expected to be significantly benefited

—5—

Figure 15–2 (continued)

UNITED ACCUMULATIVE FUND

INVESTMENT SECURITIES

December 31, 1974

	Shares	Cost	Market Value
COMMON STOCKS			
AIRLINES—0.77%			
Braniff International Corp.	100,000	$ 1,470,674	$ 500,000
Northwest Airlines, Inc.	190,000	7,044,449	2,280,000
Trans World Airlines, Inc.*	226,500	7,742,082	1,189,125
Total		*16,257,205*	*3,969,125*
BANKS—1.72%			
Citicorp	140,000	6,191,998	3,972,500
First International Bancshares, Inc.	67,000	3,238,991	2,345,000
Morgan (J.P.) & Co.	50,000	3,129,422	2,587,500
Total		*12,560,411*	*8,905,000*
BEVERAGES—0.88%			
Heublein, Inc.	150,000	8,924,552	3,018,750
Pabst Brewing Company	92,000	6,561,875	1,541,000
Total		*15,486,427*	*4,559,750*
BUILDING FINANCE—1.29%			
Federal National Mortgage Association	363,600	6,786,606	6,681,150
BUILDING & RELATED SERVICES—2.46%			
Champion International Corporation	330,000	6,469,179	3,465,000
Fedders Corporation	268,900	4,609,339	773,088
Fleetwood Enterprises, Inc.†	300,000	2,854,215	2,700,000
Jim Walter Corporation	225,000	6,626,274	5,175,000
U.S. Home Corporation	250,000	4,442,465	593,750
Total		*25,001,472*	*12,706,838*
CHEMICALS—3.92%			
Allied Chemical Corp.	100,000	3,541,091	2,837,500
Dow Chemical Company	110,000	6,771,218	6,050,000
Hercules Incorporated	100,000	3,971,669	2,400,000
Monsanto Company	105,000	6,701,939	4,278,750
Raychem Corporation*	27,500	2,835,000	4,716,250
Total		*23,820,917*	*20,282,500*
COSMETICS & TOILETRIES—2.70%			
Avon Products, Inc.	60,000	$ 4,599,678	$ 1,725,000
Gillette Company	152,900	6,610,381	3,879,838
Revlon, Inc.	175,000	12,419,179	8,334,375
Total		*23,629,238*	*13,939,213*
DIVERSIFIED—1.28%			
Fuqua Industries, Inc.*	200,000	3,127,900	650,000
International Telephone and Telegraph Corporation	260,000	8,405,224	3,835,000
Kidde (Walter) & Co.	233,200	8,486,792	2,157,100
Total		*20,019,916*	*6,642,100*
DRUGS—13.06%			
American Home Products	230,800	9,888,928	7,674,100
Bristol-Myers Company	187,700	11,736,561	9,385,000
Marion Laboratories, Incorporated	132,600	5,462,691	2,237,625
Merck & Co., Inc.	60,000	5,444,248	3,982,500
Pfizer Inc.	127,300	4,870,376	4,184,988
Richardson-Merrell Inc.	102,400	4,105,758	1,664,000
Schering-Plough Corporation	111,000	7,933,858	5,827,500
Searle (G.D.) & Co.	285,740	9,387,366	3,928,925
Squibb Corporation	200,000	8,668,367	5,750,000
Syntex Corporation	169,400	6,046,591	6,670,125
Upjohn Company	200,000	12,997,261	10,125,000
Warner-Lambert Company	235,300	8,384,568	6,117,800
Total		*94,926,573*	*67,547,563*
FOOD PRODUCTS & SERVICES—2.83%			
McDonald's Corporation*	260,000	16,190,125	7,637,500
Norton Simon Inc.	131,676	4,317,220	1,431,977
Ralston Purina Company	150,000	6,293,869	5,587,500
Total		*26,801,214*	*14,656,977*

See Notes to Schedules of Investments on page 38.

—25—

Figure 15–2 (continued)

United Funds, Inc.

STATEMENT OF ASSETS AND LIABILITIES December 31, 1974

	United Accumulative Fund	United Income Fund	United Science Fund	United Bond Fund
ASSETS				
Investment securities—at market value*—(Note 1)	$ 512,999,255	$ 504,491,204	$ 189,193,004	$ 111,479,985
Cash	560,518	529,023	315,500	240,172
Receivables:				
Investment securities sold	2,144,832	—	270,699	1,008,860
Fund shares sold	74,612	410,556	121,918	632,977
Dividends and interest	1,884,283	3,859,848	359,965	2,424,880
Other	21,937	21,977	8,186	6,307
Total assets	517,685,437	509,312,608	190,269,272	115,793,181
LIABILITIES				
Payables:				
Investment securities purchased	36,012	1,693,351	43,732	—
Fund shares redeemed	80,835	92,403	49,030	4,698
Other	221,801	217,452	81,248	34,259
Total liabilities	338,648	2,003,206	174,010	38,957
NET ASSETS	$ 517,346,789	$ 507,309,402	$ 190,095,262	$ 115,754,224
Capital shares outstanding ($1.00 par value)	*111,976,906*	*60,959,471*	*42,767,996*	*17,836,750*
Net Asset Value per Share				
(net assets ÷ capital shares outstanding)	***$4.62***	***$8.32***	***$4.44***	***$6.49***
Add: Selling commission (8¾% of offering price**)	***.44***	***.80***	***.43***	***.62***
Offering Price per Share (net asset value÷91¼%)	***$5.06***	***$9.12***	***$4.87***	***$7.11***

**On sales of $25,000 or more the offering price is reduced as set forth on page 12.

Capital shares authorized	*205,000,000*	*120,000,000*	*95,000,000*	*30,000,000*
Total paid-in capital	*$ 746,075,935*	*$ 655,526,163*	*$ 302,219,561*	*$ 140,843,905*
**Identified cost of securities*	*$ 720,944,736*	*$ 686,320,281*	*$ 268,816,450*	*$ 135,436,084*

See notes to financial statements.

Figure 15–2 (continued)

UNITED FUNDS, INC.

STATEMENT OF OPERATIONS For the year ended December 31, 1974

	United Accumulative Fund	United Income Fund	United Science Fund	United Bond Fund
Investment Income:				
Income				
Dividends from:				
Affiliates	$ 218,391	$ 498,000	$ —	$ —
Other investments	15,884,645	17,425,255	4,359,394	—
Interest	4,290,960	10,281,616	2,382,527	9,904,526
Other Income (Note 9)	386,473	302,332	212,575	6,380
Total income	20,780,469	28,507,203	6,954,496	9,910,906
Expenses (Note 4):				
Investment management fees	2,820,542	2,658,397	1,029,948	342,154
Legal and auditing expenses	102,486	96,901	38,320	17,776
Franchise taxes (Note 8)	45,438	41,529	16,574	6,973
Other	60,766	50,655	21,871	13,075
Total expenses	3,029,232	2,847,482	1,106,713	379,978
Net investment income	$ 17,751,237	$ 25,659,721	$ 5,847,783	$ 9,530,928
Ratio of operating and management expenses to total investment income	*14.85%*	*10.10%*	*16.42%*	*3.84%*
Realized and Unrealized Gain (Loss) on Investments (Note 7):				
Realized gain (loss) on sale of investments (excluding commercial paper and U.S. Government securities):				
Proceeds from sales	$ 151,567,839	$ 95,657,843	$ 51,285,939	$ 70,084,111
Cost (identified cost basis)	183,249,119	63,982,031	62,027,496	71,013,494
Net realized gain (loss)*	(31,681,280)	31,675,812	(10,741,557)	(929,383)
Realized loss on sale of U.S. Government securities:				
Proceeds from sales	—	—	—	4,769,776
Cost (identified cost basis)	—	—	—	4,942,631
Net realized loss	—	—	—	(172,855)
Net realized gain (loss) on sale of investments*	(31,681,280)	31,675,812	(10,741,557)	(1,102,238)
Unrealized appreciation (depreciation) of investments:				
Beginninig of year	(12,089,330)	42,083,454	(6,261,538)	(5,678,487)
End of year	(207,945,481)	(181,829,077)	(79,623,446)	(23,956,099)
Unrealized depreciation during year	(195,856,151)	(223,912,531)	(73,361,908)	(18,277,612)
Net realized and unrealized loss on investments	$(227,537,431)	$(192,236,719)	$(84,103,465)	$(19,379,850)
**Including realized gain on sale of affiliates*	*$ 37,835*	*$ —*	*$ —*	*$ —*
For the year just ended:				
Purchases of investment securities, excluding commercial paper and U.S. Government securities	*$ 58,168,834*	*$ 85,840,774*	*$ 46,837,786*	*$100,260,751*
Purchases of U.S. Government securities	—	—	—	*9,933,530*
At end of year:				
Accumulated realized gain (loss) on investments	*(31,200,156)*	*32,486,417*	*(35,760,820)*	*(1,331,238)*

See notes to financial statements.

— 40 —

Figure 15–2 (continued)

United Funds, Inc.

STATEMENT OF CHANGES IN NET ASSETS For the year ended December 31, 1974

	United Accumulative Fund	United Income Fund	United Science Fund	United Bond Fund
From Investment Activities:				
Net investment income	$ 17,751,237	$ 25,659,721	$ 5,847,783	$ 9,530,928
Dividends paid to shareholders (Note 6)	(16,236,886)	(25,125,192)	(4,354,782)	(9,462,570)
Increase in undistributed net investment income	1,514,351	534,529	1,493,001	68,358
Realized gain (loss) on sale of investments	(31,681,280)	31,675,812	(10,741,557)	(1,102,238)
Distributions paid to shareholders (Notes 5 & 6)	(5,864,801)	(36,044,371)	—	—
Net decrease	(37,546,081)	(4,368,559)	(10,741,557)	(1,102,238)
Unrealized depreciation during year	(195,856,151)	(223,912,531)	(73,361,908)	(18,277,612)
Decrease in net assets derived from investment activities	(231,887,881)	(227,746,561)	(82,610,464)	(19,311,492)
From Capital Share Transactions:				
Proceeds from sale of shares*	5,923,898	39,730,817	8,496,496	33,745,774
Proceeds from reinvestment of dividends and/or capital gains distributions*	20,365,676	34,511,791	3,844,822	3,784,584
Cost of shares redeemed*	(58,078,646)	(40,914,835)	(19,815,587)	(14,867,565)
Increase (decrease) in net assets derived from capital share transactions	(31,789,072)	33,327,773	(7,474,269)	22,662,793
Net increase (decrease) in net assets	(263,676,953)	(194,418,788)	(90,084,733)	3,351,301
Net Assets:				
Beginning of year	781,023,742	701,728,190	280,179,995	112,402,923
End of year:				
Capital	506,930,298	506,183,503	186,835,295	115,556,568
Undistributed net income	10,416,491	1,125,899	3,259,967	197,656
	$ 517,346,789	$ 507,309,402	$ 190,095,262	$ 115,754,224
***Number of shares:**				
Issued from sale of shares	*1,103,208*	*4,013,850*	*1,641,715*	*4,885,941*
Issued from reinvestment of dividends and/or capital gains distributions	*3,534,806*	*3,283,079*	*716,512*	*548,183*
Redeemed	*(10,655,480)*	*(4,248,195)*	*(3,756,491)*	*(2,102,729)*
Increase (decrease) in outstanding capital shares	*(6,017,466)*	*3,048,734*	*(1,398,264)*	*3,331,395*

See notes to financial statements.

Figure 15–2 (continued)

Pages 2, 4, and 5 of the prospectus describe the investment company, its *objectives*, and its *operating policies*. The table of contents describes the prospectus. Of special interest to an investor is the percentage of operating expenses to average net assets (page 2), rates of portfolio turnover (page 4), and the corporation's investment restrictions. Specific policies for each fund are spelled out on page 5.

Per-share income and *capital changes* illustrated on page 3 offer you a chance to compare performance over a number of years. We will look at this in greater detail later in the chapter. The data for all four funds allow you to compare whatever financial ratios are important to you.

Management and brokerage fees are discussed in the prospectus, as is required by the SEC. Investment companies often contract with management firms to provide research, investment management, and actual brokerage services for the fund. An explanation of charges and fees as listed in a prospectus can give you an insight into the "hidden costs" of your investment company.

Shareholder services such as open purchase accounts, optional withdrawal accounts, combining of investments, self-employed retirement plans, payroll-deduction plans, exchange rights, dividends, distributions, taxes, share redemption, and reinvestment privileges are described in the prospectus. We will discuss some of these topics later in the chapter.

The performance of any fund is only as good as the portfolio and the transaction timing of its managers. A prospectus will offer a complete list of all securities owned by it as of the date of its financial statements. Page 25 shows a partial portfolio listing of the United Accumulative Fund. Different securities are purchased for different investment objectives. You must ask yourself if the particular portfolio is what you would purchase if you had sufficient cash to build your own diversified portfolio. It is important to compare the portfolio composition of competing funds.

Financial statements such as balance sheets and income statements are also illustrated in the prospectus. The format and name of the financial statements are changed somewhat to match the operating characteristics of investment companies. Pages 39, 40, and 41 of the United Funds prospectus are typical of investment company financial statements. Of special interest are the *Realized and Unrealized Gain (Loss) on Sale of Investments*, the *Unrealized Appreciation (Depreciation) of Investments*, and the *Statement of Changes in Net Assets.* Note that as of December 31, 1974, all United funds had lost net asset value because of a decline in the market price of their investments. This is known as unrealized depreciation. Practically all stocks and all investment companies lost value during the year, so our illustration is typical. Buyers in a bear market often switch to conservative investments. Note that the United Bond Fund had an increase in capital because of an influx of investor money to purchase bonds.

Financial statements are issued quarterly to investors in mutual funds. This gives the shareholder the opportunity of appraising the performance of the fund.

Investment Company Regulation

Investment companies come under a variety of federal and state security laws designed to inform and protect the investing public. Federal laws are applicable only to those securities marketed in more than one state or sold through an organized exchange. State laws apply only to securities offered wholly within a state. States provide varying degrees of protection and enforcement.

Wherever state law is more restrictive, it supersedes the federal laws within the state. These laws and regulations merely provide that a minimum amount of information be made available to the investor. They are attempts to keep dishonest manipulators from fleecing the public. Therefore, even with the information available in the prospectus, you must still evaluate that information in the light of future profit potential. Regulating laws do not protect you against your own bad judgment or the sales enthusiasm of a mutual fund salesman.

Two general investment acts contain specific information regulating investment companies. The Securities Act of 1933 required that mutual funds offer a prospectus and regular financial statements to potential investors and required that interstate funds register themselves with the Securities and Exchange Commission. The Securities Exchange Act of 1934 established the minimum standards for dealings between a fund, its managers, and its brokers. These regulations were amended in 1962.

The Investment Company Act of 1940 voluntarily regulated the management operation of investment companies: (1) No more than 5 percent of a regulated company's assets can be invested in the securities of any one company, (2) financial leverage is not allowed in open-end companies, (3) only limited amounts of bonds and preferred stock may be issued by closed-end companies, and (4) nonofficers must be included on the board of directors of regulated investment companies. Funds choosing to be regulated by the Act are called *regulated investment companies.* Almost all mutual funds have voluntarily become regulated because of certain tax advantages that go hand in hand with regulation. Basically, they become tax-exempt *conduits* of investment income.

SPECIAL FEATURES OF MUTUAL FUNDS

A number of special voluntary features, called *shareholder services,* are offered to mutual fund investors. Most of these features are designed to make acquisition and redemption of shares as easy as possible for the potential investor.

Open-Purchase Plan

This arrangement is simply an open account; orders for shares are placed whenever the investor desires. Purchases are subject to initial and subsequent minimum dollar requirements. Payment may be made by cash or billing within seven days. Some companies sell in full-share amounts only and hold the dollar balance for your future investment, while others credit your account with a fractional share.

Accumulation Plans

These plans may be voluntary or contractual.

Voluntary plans You make an agreement with the mutual fund to invest a certain dollar amount each month or each quarter. The dollar amount under such a plan may be less than the minimums required under an open-purchase contract. The purpose of the voluntary plan is to get you into a systematic savings/investing plan. You pay the applicable load fee (if any), and you may vary the amount of the periodic accumulation. There is no penalty for failure to comply with the original agreement. Basically, an accumulation plan is similar to the Monthly Investment Plan of the New York Stock Exchange. If your periodic investments remain at the same dollar amount, you are doing dollar-cost averaging.

Contractual plans These require a formal contract. If you do not abide by the terms of the contract you suffer a penalty. The purpose of contractual plans is to have a forced investment program and to reduce the sales charge percentage if the contractual obligation is large enough. Generally you contract for a specific dollar investment goal over a specific period of time. Ten thousand dollars in ten years is a popular amount. Failure to maintain your scheduled payments penalizes you in terms of not only not reaching your goal, but the sales charge for the *whole* contract is deducted from the lesser amount you actually did invest. This is known as a *front-end load.* You would receive nothing for your investment if you terminate the plan before there is sufficient cash to pay the load.

Mutual fund salesmen have sold the contractual accumulation plans with enthusiasm because they are assured a large commission regardless of your ability to complete the contract. Some government and industry authorities are attempting to end contractual plans.

Payroll Deduction Plan

A number of mutual funds offer payroll deduction for the purchaser of fund shares. An employer must allow such a program or have a sufficient number of employees investing a minimum amount in a single plan to make the effort worthwhile. Ask your employer or fund sales representative about such a program.

Tax Sheltered Retirement Plan

Most mutual funds are approved as prototype tax sheltered retirement plans by the Internal Revenue Service. Investors using mutual funds for this purpose should pay attention to custody agreements and reinvestment requirements in order to receive income-tax deferment benefits. Keogh plans and Individual Retirement Accounts are usually available.

Exchange Rights

Multi-fund, open-end investment companies offer the opportunity to exchange shares of one fund for another. Under the *conversion privilege* you may be able to switch between growth and income funds or between diversified common stock and special industry or bond funds. There is usually a small charge for this privilege. Exchange rights provide the mutual fund investor with a chance to speculate or to change his portfolio position with respect to the primary trend of the market or to switch because his investment objectives may change.

Automatic Reinvestment Plan

All mutual funds generally provide for automatic reinvestment of dividends and capital-gains distribution at no additional sales charge. If you do not want your dividends and gains to be reinvested, you must usually inform the company. Automatic reinvestment is especially favorable in the case of growth funds because accumulation of capital is your objective. The effect is similar to that of compounding savings.

Tax Status

Corporate dividends and interest received by the mutual fund are paid to you as dividends after fund operating expenses have been deducted. Capital-gains distributions may be automatically reinvested or they may be distributed to you. They represent the capital gains that the fund has realized on the profitable sale of its portfolio securities. You will be taxed on them in the year in which they are declared. Investment companies act as conduits, passing their investment tax status through to their shareholders.

Dividends are always taxed as ordinary income. All capital-gains distributions are taxed as long-term capital gains. It does not matter how long the fund held the specific investment in its portfolio. This special capital-gains treatment is an advantage to mutual fund investors. However, in any years in which the fund has realized capital losses, there will be no capital-gains distribution and the loss cannot be reported for tax purposes.

When you sell your shares, any profit you make from the sale of your shares in an investment company is taxed as ordinary income if the shares were held for six months or less, and taxed as capital-gains income if they were held for more than six months. A capital loss can be reported when you actually sell your shares at a loss. Sometimes distributions of invested capital may be made by mutual funds during periods of capital loss. These distributions are returns of your investment capital and are not taxable. Investment companies normally advise shareholders of the tax status of shares held when they mail copies of Form 1099–DIV to their investors for income tax reporting purposes.

Withdrawal Plans

Most mutual funds provide for one or more automatic withdrawal plans. These plans are especially desirable for persons like the retired who wish to receive current income. Usually you must have at least $10,000 invested before a fund will set up a withdrawal account. You simply authorize the fund to send you a check for a specified amount each month or quarter until you change the authorization or until the money runs out.

HOW MUTUAL FUNDS OPERATE

At this point we have covered most of the salient features of mutual funds. Now we will see how they operate, what are the costs involved in the purchase and redemption of shares, and how investment company shares should be selected.

A typical investment company is an open-end mutual fund, that sells an unlimited number of shares upon demand and redeems the shares upon direct request. The purchase and redemption price would be based upon net asset value of the investment portfolio of the fund. The company would submit to being regulated under the Investment Company Act of 1940 in order to pass all dividends and distributed capital gains through to shareholders without a second corporation income tax. In order to be a regulated investment company, at least 90 percent of its shareholder distribution must be from dividends, interest, and securities profits.

The portfolio of a typical mutual fund will probably contain about one hundred diversified common stocks, with a slight emphasis on growth. No more than 5 percent of the fund's assets would be invested in any one company. Any amount invested in a single company would represent less than 10 percent of that particular company's voting stock. The portfolio might contain a few preferred stocks and bonds to lend some balance. Any uncommitted cash would be in a bank or would be used to purchase short-term Treasury notes. Fund managers attempt to keep all monies fully invested in some manner in order to earn income or gain capital appreciation.

A bank or trust company is usually the custodian of the mutual fund's securities, which are typically worth over $100 million. The same bank would act as transfer and disbursement agent. The bank issues quarterly dividend checks upon order from the fund's management. Capital gains would be disbursed once a year. Quarterly and annual reports to shareholders are made available by the fund to comply with federal regulations.

A mutual fund's board of directors consists of eight or more members, half of whom would be officers in the management company involved with the fund. The balance of members would come from various financial institutions and legal counsel. There is usually one educator on the board. Most likely the research and management functions of the fund would be contracted to a firm specializing in such activity. The marketing and sales activity would also be handled by a separate organization on a fee basis. Often management and sales are handled by the same organization.

INVESTMENT COSTS

An investor must weigh the cost of acquiring his investment in mutual funds just as he should for the purchase of any other savings, insurance, or investment medium. Mutual fund sales charges cost anywhere from nothing to about 9 percent. If you contemplate a long-term investment, a percentage of the cost can be spread over the number of years involved, thereby lowering the rate per year. However, the acquisition cost of a short-term investment cannot be amortized. The whole amount is added to the purchase price in the year of purchase. You will also pay for a continuing management in addition to any sales charge.

Sales Charges

Closed-end investment companies do not have sales charges per se. Their shares, like those of any corporate security, are purchased in the open market, and the normal stockbroker's commission applies to the purchase and later sale of the shares.

Open-end investment companies, known as mutual funds, operate as their own principals in securities transactions. They sell shares through agents to the investor and later redeem the shares from the investor upon his direct request. The sales charge, if any, applies only to the purchase transaction. Redemption of shares requires no additional charge. The sales charge is called a *load.* Approximately one-third of the load is the salesman's commission, one-third goes to the broker's office, and one-third covers expenses and the profit of the underwriting organization. Not all mutual funds require a sales charge. Those that do are called load funds; those that do not are called no-load funds.

Load funds The accessibility of load funds is what makes them popular to the investing public. Salesmen and brokerage houses acting as agents for a mutual fund have strong incentive to "sell" load funds for a commission that is at least twice the commission rate for a standard securities transaction. The salesman earns his commission entirely on the selling end of the transaction, a one-time event. Later the mutual fund redeems its shares directly from the investor without charge.

Figure 15–1 illustrates the mutual fund price quotations published in the *Wall Street Journal.* These quotations identify the load funds and their load charge amounts per share. The difference between the offered price and the net asset value (NAV) per share is the amount of the load per share. This typically amounts to 8.75 percent of the offering price and 9.59 percent of the amount invested after deducting the load. This means that an investor pays $87.50 in commission on each $1,000 of mutual funds he purchases. This would leave $912.50 invested in shares and working for the investor. The load of $87.50 becomes 9.59 percent of $912.50, the amount invested. The mathematics are similar to the way one discounts a bank loan.

You can figure the load charge percentage on any fund by subtracting the NAV from the offering price and dividing the answer by the offering price. This is a simple percentage problem. Using the *American Express Capital Fund* in figure 15–1 as an example, we find that the load per share is $.55 ($6.47 − $5.92); the load percent on the offering price ($.55 ÷ $6.47) is .0850 or 8.5 percent. Some funds do have a lower charge. Front-end loads do not affect the rate of commission if the contractual agreement to purchase shares is carried to completion. If the agreement is terminated short of the agreed time—two years instead of ten years, for example—an investor could end up paying a much higher rate because the front-end load is based on the total contract price.

Mutual funds do lower the commission rates on large purchase transactions. However, most investors do not have sufficient capital to make a large enough purchase to lower the commission rate. If you expect to purchase enough shares of a particular fund (or group of funds in a multi-fund group) to qualify for lower rates, you may sign a *letter of intent*. This statement may be part of the original purchase application or a subsequent letter within ninety days of purchase, guaranteeing to buy a specific dollar value of shares during a thirteen-month period following the original purchase. Purchases over $25,000 and under $50,000 generally have a commission rate of 6 percent of the offering price, a savings of 2.75 percent. Each purchase during the period is charged the "intended" lower commission rate. Sufficient shares (5 percent of the intended investment) will be held in escrow from the original purchase to insure completion of the intended purchase amount. If the investor fails to purchase the intended amount the fund will liquidate enough escrow-held shares to pay the higher sales commission rate on the number of shares actually purchased.

No-load funds You have to work a little harder to find and invest in a no-load fund because there are no salesmen or brokers offering their shares; you must deal directly with this type of fund. It may be worth the savings of 8.75 percent. Newspaper price quotations help you differentiate between a load and a no-load fund. As you will note in figure 15–1, approximately one hundred of the mutual funds listed have the same NAV and offering price. This means that they are no-load funds because they do not have a sales charge built into the offering price. They sell their shares at asset value. One hundred percent of your purchase price is invested for you and working for you.

No-load funds often advertise in the *Wall Street Journal* and in other financial publications. You may have to contact the companies directly because they do not actively seek new shareholders through sales agents. As mentioned earlier, a number of publications provide information on mutual funds, both load and no-load. You can also check reader's guides to periodicals for the latest articles on mutual funds and their performance records.

Management Fees

All investment companies have management fees, which are quite distinct from commission or load fees. Management fees are the operating income of the professional securities management organization. Management fees typically run .5 percent of the average daily net asset value of the fund being managed on the first $500,000,000. Fees are then scaled down slightly as the assets of a fund increase.

The .5 percent does not seem high, but it amounts to $2,500,000 per annum. This fee is not based on performance, but on the aggregate amount of investment monies in the fund. If we look at the management fee in terms of investment income, we get a completely different percentage figure. Page 40 of the United Funds prospectus shows that operating and management expenses amount to 14.85 percent of investment income for the Accumulative Fund. These expenses include legal and auditing charges, taxes, and other miscellaneous expenses. The actual management fee is 15.89 percent ($2,820,542 ÷ 17,751,237).

You can see why there has been some criticism of "high" management fees. The fees as a ratio to income tend to be higher during bear markets because few realized capital gains are available for income purposes. No-load funds are reputed to have slightly higher average management fees than load funds. The expense ratios of various funds are compared in a number of the previously mentioned investment company periodicals. Some mutual funds, especially those whose investment objective is specifically capital gains, have an additional *management incentive fee* based upon the performance of the fund.

MEASURING FUND PERFORMANCE

Investors must be as selective in purchasing mutual fund shares as they are in purchasing any other investment. This selectivity should be the result of studying the performance of the mutual fund in question over both the short term and the long term. Short-term performance may be determined by looking at the latest statements of total income, per-share income, and capital changes. Long-term performance is measured by the comparison of the financial results of the fund over a selected period, usually ten years. An investor should also measure in terms of the stated objectives of the company and in terms of management efficiency. One should make comparisons with other major fund competitors, investment company indexes, and the three major common-stock averages: Dow-Jones, Standard & Poor's, and the NYSE.

Total Return

A fund's performance should be measured by evaluating the three sources of possible gain: (1) realized capital gains, (2) dividends from net income, and (3) unrealized capital gain or loss (appreciation or depreciation of net assets). These evaluations will give you an accurate picture of a fund's performance. No one will dispute that dividends and capital gains actually received or reinvested should be figured as part of your return, but some investors do not believe that paper profits and losses should be considered as part of return on investment until they are actually received or realized. However, total return should include all sources of gain or loss, because the shares underlying the unrealized capital gains or loss are measurable and salable at any time. This is called the *liquidating value concept.* It is the potential return if the shares are liquidated.

The per-share income and capital change statistics illustrated on page 3 of the United Fund prospectus (figure 15–2) may be used to *calculate* and *compare* both short-term and long-term performance of a fund. Per-share statistics appear for the years 1965 through 1974. Careful study must be made of the tabular headings to determine what is being represented. The illustration in our example shows the per-share results of four different funds in the United group.

We will examine and calculate the total returns for 1972 and 1974, a "good" year and a "bad" year. We will start with *net income,* which may be distributed as dividends. Looking at the column *Ratio of net income to average net assets,* we find that the results are 1.6 percent and 2.8 percent for 1972 and 1974. These results are calculated by dividing the *net income* (not the dividend) by the year's beginning and ending *net asset value* (NAV). This result really does not tell you much because it is not the total return. By adding the *distributed capital gains* to *dividends* (not net income), you have the *actual return* per share. This would be calculated thus:

	1972	*1974*
Dividends	$ .13	$ .14
Distributed capital gains:	.19	.05
Actual returns per share:	$ .32	$ .19

To get the rate of actual return per share, it is necessary to divide the actual return by *your* purchase price. We will arbitrarily use the beginning-of-the-year NAV. Therefore, your 1972 return would be 4.07 percent ($.32 ÷ $7.86) of your investment, while 1974 would be 2.87 percent (.19 ÷ $6.62). Your rate of actual return in these instances would not have covered the load charge of 9.59 percent of the amount invested during the year.

To get the *rate of total return* we must add-in the unrealized gain or loss per share on the mutual fund's investments.

	1972	*1974*
Actual return per share	$ .32	$ .19
Unrealized gain or loss per share	.85	(1.96)
Amount of total return per share	$1.17	$ (1.77)

The rate of total return assumes that you sell (liquidate) your shares at the end of the year to realize your gain or loss against your original purchase price. The unrealized gain or loss per share would be the difference between your original purchase price and the year-end NAV with the realized gain added back to the NAV (otherwise you would be counting realized capital gains twice.)

In the above case we will use the NAV at the beginning of the year and the unrealized gain or loss per share as stated for the specific year. The 1972 total rate of return would be 14.89 percent ($1.17 ÷ $7.86) and in 1974 it would be −26.74 percent (−$1.77 ÷ $6.62). The 1972 results reflect a market price increase, while the 1974 results reflect a market price decrease.

A further refinement of the rate of total return or liquidating value concept can be made by using a five- or ten-year average in the above example. (1) To calculate a ten-year average dollar return, one adds the amounts received for each year and divides by ten. (2) Then one calculates the difference between the original purchase and the end-of-ten-year selling price and divides by ten. (3) Finally one divides these "realized" profits by the original purchase price to determine the average annual rate of total return over the period of the investment. The United Accumulative Fund example would show the following results for a 1965 purchase:

rates of return: (1) The timing of the sale of an investment will have an effect on the rate of return; (2) any comparison of performance must cover the same time period; (3) the same measurement calculations must be used and accurately reflect the *liquidating value rate of return*; and (4) history may not repeat itself; what has happened in the past may not happen again.

(1)

	Dividends	*Capital Gains Distribution*
1965	$ .22	$ .13
1966	.22	.20
1967	.21	.50
1968	.13	.49
1969	.16	.25
1970	.18	.01
1971	.07	—
1972	.13	.19
1973	.14	.20
1974	.14	.05
	$1.60	$2.02

$1.60 dividends
2.02 distributed gains
$3.62
$3.62 ÷ 10 = $.362
average dollar return per year per share

(2)
$ 8.28 purchase price per share 1965 beginning of year
— 4.62 selling price per share 1974 end of year
$ 3.66 (loss per share)
($3.66) ÷ 10 years = ($.366) per year depreciation of asset

(3)
$ .362 average dollar return per year
— .366 average asset depreciation per year
$ (.004) average total return per year
$ (.004) ÷ $8.28 = (.05) % average total return (loss) per year per share during the period 1965 to 1974.

The loss was caused by the *loss on the sale of the fund shares* at a particular time. If the shares had been sold at the end of 1972 for $8.52 each the result would have been a 5.02 percent total average return based on an eight-year average! These results point out four important observations about figuring

Effects of a Load Charge

The 9.59 percent load on the net asset value per share was not considered in the performance example. The load charge is not included in your investment, so it will not change the operating results. However, rate of return on your first two years of investment would be "lost" because of the load. Let us spread the 9.59 percent load over the eight and ten years, respectively. This amounts to approximately 1 percent per year. The amortized load results in a reduced average rate of return of 6.4 percent for the eight-year period ending in 1972 and (1.01) percent for the ten-year period ending in 1974.

Mutual funds do not like to publicize loads of 9.59 percent on net asset value; they would prefer to talk about an 8.75 percent sales charge discounted from the offering price, which includes the load. Using their calculations, if you invest $10,000, the load would be $875 (8.75%), leaving $9,125 actively invested in the shares of the fund. The load sum of $875 also represents 9.59 percent of your remaining investment of $9,125. The load, as a dollar amount or a percentage, must be recovered in order to compete with a no-load fund.

Fundscope has published data that finds no significant correlation between load and no-load fund performance records. *Mutual Funds Scoreboard,* a quarterly newsletter using the same data, maintains that the average no-load fund over periods of 5, 10, 15, and 20 years dating back to 1952 has consistently outperformed the average load funds. In any case, a load fund must recover the 9.59 percent load to compete effectively with a no-load fund. During a ten-year holding period a load fund would need to exceed a no-load fund by .96 percent each year; in a five-year period 1.92 percent extra each year would be needed to match the no-load performance. The longer the period of time that a fund is held, the better the chance you have of recouping the load charge because of the greater amortization period.

Accumulation Concept

Some mutual funds provide supporting sales literature to accompany their prospectus. These show how much a $10,000 investment would increase in asset value providing all dividends and realized capital gains are automatically reinvested. Figure 15–3 illustrates such an assumed investment. The reinvested shares create a form of compounding on the original $10,000 principal. Unfortunately, mutual funds provide variable rates of return subject to the whims of the market place. A return cannot be guaranteed. Your redemption timing would have an effect on the rate of return. Also, you must remember that history does not necessarily repeat itself, that accumulation may not occur to the same extent.

Index and Fund Comparison

Investors can make comparative measurements of mutual fund performances using line charts, bar charts, and tabularized material. The most popular form of index measurement is the line chart, which imposes income, net asset value, or total return on trend lines for comparison with industry averages or with major stock indexes. *Fundscope, Johnson's Charts,* and *Wiesenberger Services* all specialize in this area. They all offer one or more of the following mutual fund averages: (1) a growth fund average, (2) an income fund average, (3) a balanced fund average, and (4) a general mutual fund average.

Caution should be taken when making an absolute comparison with any market average. Performance statistics of averages presume an expense-free, pure-profit investment, while mutual funds or for that matter all securities investments are saddled with

Waddell & Reed

UNITED INCOME FUND

ILLUSTRATION OF AN ASSUMED INVESTMENT OF $10,000

With Capital Gains Distributions Accepted in Shares and Income Dividends Paid in Cash

The chart below covers the period from January 1, 1959, through December 31, 1973. This period was one of generally rising common stock prices. The results shown should not be considered as a representation of the dividend income or capital gain or loss which may be realized from an investment made in the Fund today.

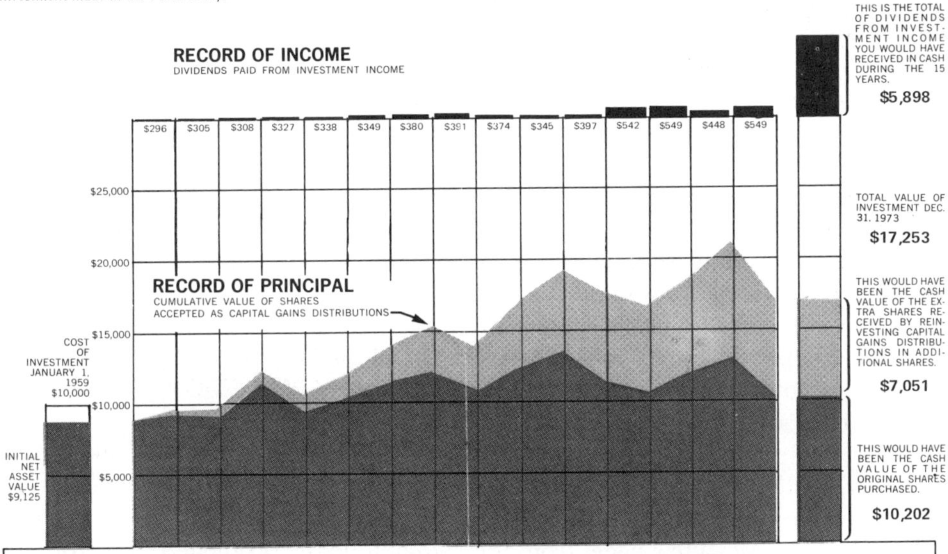

YEAR END DEC. 31	1959	1960	1961	1962	1963	1964	1965	1966	1967	1968	1969	1970	1971	1972	1973
VALUE OF 842 SHARES INITIALLY ACQUIRED THROUGH INVESTMENT OF $10,000	$9,361	$9,201	$11,288	$9,487	$10,438	$11,617	$12,366	$10,808	$12,567	$13,654	$1 ,532	$10,826	$12,063	$13,148	$10,202
VALUE OF SHARES ACCEPTED AS CAPITAL GAINS DISTRIBUTIONS (CUMULATIVE)	332	673	1,187	1,357	1,878	2,496	3,106	3,244	4,434	5,595	5,532	5,928	6,688	8,069	7,051
TOTAL VALUE	$9,693	$9,874	$12,475	$10,844	$12,316	$14,113	$15,472	$14,052	$17,001	$19,249	$17,064	$16,754	$18,751	$21,217	$17,253
SHARES (CUMULATIVE)	872	903	930	962	993	1,023	1,053	1,094	1,139	1,187	1,246	1,303	1,308	1,358	1,424

Initial net asset value is the amount received by the Fund after deducting from the cost of the investment the sales commission as described in the prospectus. No adjustment has been made for any income taxes payable by shareholders on capital gains distributions accepted in shares. The dollar amounts of capital gains distributions accepted in shares were: 1959–$330; 1960–$341; 1961–$362; 1962–$364; 1963–$377; 1964–$409; 1965–$441; 1966–$529; 1967–$638; 1968–$758; 1969–$815; 1970–$730; 1971–$78; 1972–$694; 1973–$924. Total–$7,790.

ASSUMING DIVIDENDS WERE REINVESTED AND CAPITAL GAINS DISTRIBUTIONS WERE ACCEPTED IN SHARES

Initial Investment January 1, 1959–842 shares $10,000
Cost of 565 shares purchased
with reinvested dividends 7,458
Total Amount Invested $17,458
Value of 2,143 shares, December 31, 1973 . . . . $25,972*
*Includes capital gains distribution of $9,925 reinvested into shares with an end value of $8,927.
*Includes dividend income of $7,458 reinvested into shares with an end value of $6,843.

ASSUMING RECEIPT OF CAPITAL GAINS DISTRIBUTIONS AND DIVIDENDS IN CASH

Capital Gains Distributions in Cash . . . . $ 5,950
Value of 842 Shares, December 31, 1973 . . . . $10,202
Investment Income Dividends in Cash . . . . $ 4,522

This illustration is authorized for use only when accompanied or preceded by the delivery of a currently effective prospectus setting forth details of United Funds, Inc., including the sales commission and other material information.

Figure 15–3 Illustration of an Assumed Investment of $10,000. *(Waddell & Reed, Inc., Kansas City, Mo.)*

brokerage charges, taxes, and operating expenses. A mutual fund by necessity must have some noninvested cash on hand because of the sale and redemption of its shares plus the cash from investments-in-process (both buying and selling). These "true-life" needs probably lower performance by 2 percent. However, there is no reason why you cannot make a relative comparison of the averages with a number of funds, because each fund would reflect the above expenses.

A popular tabularized performance measurement is the annual *Forbes* Fund Ratings published by the magazine each August 15. Funds are grouped by load and no-load stock funds, closed-end investment companies, foreign investment funds, load and no-load balanced funds, bond and preferred stock funds, exchange funds, dual-purpose funds, and a complete listing of new funds. Figure 15–4 reproduces a few pages from the 1975 ratings.

Fund Objective Comparison

The stated investment objectives and investment policies of a fund should be measured against actual performance. Did the fund manage its portfolio in a manner consistent with its objectives? Performance of any investment is measured in terms of income, growth, and total return. Too many mutual funds are sold on past performance, rather than in light of their stated objectives.

Comparison of Managerial Efficiency

A final comparison among funds can be made on the basis of management efficiency. Reaching the investment objectives noted above is only part of the comparison. Management might accomplish its intended performance goals, but in a costly manner. Cost control is a measurement of managerial efficiency. Cost control has the effect, if done properly, of increasing the margin of profit. Therefore, you should examine the expense ratios of comparable funds. Most experts consider an expense of .5 percent ($\frac{1}{2}$ of 1 percent) of a fund's assets as being within cost goals. This information is usually available in the publications of the leading reporting services and in the financial statements of each fund.

GUIDELINES FOR INVESTMENT COMPANY SELECTION

There is no "easy" way to take care of your investment needs. Investment companies are better equipped than the average investor to handle the problems of portfolio selection and transaction timing. They give you the advantages of diversification and professional management. They constantly monitor the securities market. And you have the relative ease of buying and redeeming your shares in open-end investment companies. Unfortunately, you pay for all these advantages through management fees and in many cases through sales charges. These fees and charges may be excessive. Your costs may be even higher than anticipated because the fund may not perform according to the assurances that you receive.

Once you decide that the cost differential is worth all the advantages attributable to investment companies, you must still make the most important choice—which fund among the many diverse types available meets your objectives and performance standards. Do not be sold; *take ample time* to study the facts, and decide for yourself. The market price of investment company stock should not fluctuate so rapidly that you cannot take the time to consider and evaluate each of the following:

1. Do the investment objectives of the fund match yours? They ought to, or you will be unsatisfied.
2. Is the company an open-end or closed-end fund? Open-end funds offer purchases in relatively small quantities and direct redemption based on net asset value. Accumulation, reinvestment, and withdrawal plans are available. Closed-end funds offer speculative trading possibilities because of stock market price fluctuations. They are often priced below net asset value. The brokerage commission is far less than the standard mutual fund load charge.
3. How much is the sales charge or brokerage fee? Open-end funds charge up to 9.5 percent on the purchase transaction only. Closed-end fund brokerage fees run approximately 3 percent on each end of the brokerage transaction. All things being equal, no-load mutual funds are less costly.
4. How long an investment period do you contemplate? Can you amortize the load charge over a long period? Watch out for contractual front-end loads.
5. What is the expense ratio of the fund? How does it compare with other funds? Your fund should be in the 0.5 to 1.0 percent range of expenses to assets.
6. Is it a balanced fund or a common-stock fund? A balanced assortment of securities has more price stability and is generally safer. However, a common-stock fund offers a more professional use of management fees. You should not need as much professional attention for bond investments. A bond and savings program separate from a common-stock fund would provide you more flexibility. You may not need to buy and sell all types of securities at the same time as would be the case with balanced fund shares.
7. Is it a large or a small fund? Large funds (over $100,000,000) offer greater diversification, research, and sale and redemption security. They became large because they were successful. Small funds are more flexible; they can make investment shifts without creating a market impact. A rather small fund (under $25,000,000), if recently successful, will probably receive an influx of new share money, which it may not be able to invest properly. If this happens, it will have a poor performance record in the following year.
8. Is it a new fund? Does it have new management? Can it weather economic adversity? Choose a fund with proven managerial ability under all market conditions. That a fund performs well in a bull market does not indicate that it will do so in a bear market, and vice versa. A change of managers should forecast a change in fund performance.
9. What is the fund's past performance? Past performance does not necessarily mean that the future will bring the same results, but this record is still the most important tool available to the investor.

Vocabulary and Concepts

Accumulation plan	Income fund
Automatic reinvestment plan	Load fund
Balanced fund	Net asset value
Closed-end fund	No-load fund
Dual-purpose fund	Open-end fund
Growth fund	Prospectus

Questions for Discussion

1. Explain the fundamental differences between an open-end and a closed-end investment company.
2. What is meant by the statement "mutual funds are self-limiting"? Do you agree?
3. What is the difference among balanced, income, and growth funds?

Performance Ratings: In UP Markets	Performance Ratings: In DOWN Markets		Dollar Results: Latest 12 Months	Dollar Results: 9-Year Average Annual Growth Rate	Dollar Results: Dividend Return	Total Assets 6/30/75 in Millions	Total Assets % Change 1975 vs. 1974	Maximum Sales Charge	Annual Expenses Per $100
—	—	Standard & Poor's 500 Stock Average	10.7%	0.1%	4.0%				
C	C	FORBES Stock Fund Average	13.8%	–0.5%	3.1%				
		Stock Funds (Load)							
		Admiralty Funds							
C	D	Growth Series	7.1%	–7.6%	5.0%	$12.9	6.6	†	N.A.
C	C	Insurance Series	–0.6	–0.9	6.8	2.2	–4.4	†	N.A.
D	D	Advisers Fund	–11.0	–6.9	2.0	1.4	–22.2	8.50%	$1.50
D	B	Affiliated Fund	25.4	1.2	3.9	1,540.6	21.0	7.25	0.46
B	F	All American Fund	–10.6	–10.6	none	N.A.	—	†	N.A.
• •A	•D	Allstate Enterprises Stock Fund (started 2/70)	14.0	—	1.1	196.9	16.6	7.00	0.82
• •A	• •D	AMCAP Fund (started 4/67)	31.3	—	2.6	62.5	33.0	8.50	0.77
• •C	•B	American Equity Fund (started 1/69)	17.4	—	1.7	3.1	34.8	8.75	2.01
		American Express Funds							
A	F	Capital	13.7	–0.5	2.4	120.8	8.4	8.50	0.96
• •C	•C	Special (started 4/69)	2.9	—	1.6	31.7	–1.3	8.50	1.14
C	D	Stock	11.6	–1.8	3.8	44.8	5.4	8.50	0.76
C	C	American Growth Fund	12.2	0.8	5.4	13.4	13.6	8.50	1.32
• •A	• •B	American Insurance & Industrial Fund	23.5	—	2.5	6.3	85.3	8.50	1.01
• •D	•B	American Leaders Fund (started 2/69)	12.6	—	4.3	22.3	2,130.0	1.50	1.44
D	A	American Mutual Fund	15.2	1.1	5.7	322.9	11.4	8.50	0.62
A	F	American National Growth Fund	26.0	1.6	3.8	15.7	49.5	8.50	0.90
B	F	Anchor Growth Fund	14.9	–3.8	2.5	249.2	8.4	8.75	0.65
• •A	•D	Audax Fund (started 11/69)	31.8	—	1.1	3.9	39.3	8.50	1.50
C	C	Axe-Houghton Stock Fund	13.6	3.7	3.8	102.8	69.9	8.50	1.18
• •C	•C	Berkshire Capital Fund (started 12/68)	15.2	—	5.7	4.7	95.8	8.50	1.50
• •B	•C	BLC Growth Fund (started 10/69)	13.9	—	2.0	8.0	23.1	8.50	1.00
• •C	•B	BLC Income Fund (started 10/69)	22.3	—	5.4	7.0	34.6	8.50	1.01
D	C	Bondstock Corp.	15.1	–2.5	4.4	20.9	16.1	8.50	0.84
• •C	• •D	Boston Mutual Fund* (started 1/69)	7.8	—	2.0	5.0	150.0	8.50	1.01
C	C	Broad Street Investing Corp.	11.7	1.6	4.2	335.8	8.6	8.50	0.44
B	D	The Brown Fund of Hawaii	30.1	0.3	1.3	4.5	21.6	3.00	1.50
C	C	Bullock Fund	19.4	0.9	3.9	139.3	18.6	8.50	0.66
D	A	Capamerica Fund	20.0	–0.2	0.5	2.5	19.1	8.75	1.53
C	F	Capital Shares	21.0	–5.5	1.4	29.1	25.4	8.75	1.47
• •C	• •D	The Cardinal Fund** (started 12/66)	24.5	—	3.0	12.3	392.0	8.50	1.58
B	D	Century Shares Trust	16.9	0.3	2.9	73.5	8.9	8.50	0.56
• •A	• •C	CG Fund (started 2/68)	22.9	—	2.3	128.4	42.5	7.50	0.77
• •D	• •A	CG Income Fund (started 11/68)	7.8	—	8.4	29.6	190.2	7.50	0.49
		Channing Funds							
D	C	American Fund	6.5	–3.1	3.5	20.2	11.0	8.50‡	1.03
B	F	Growth Fund	11.7	–3.7	2.3	180.7	12.7	8.50	0.90
A	F	Special Fund	14.4	–3.3	1.3	56.3	7.9	8.50‡	0.99
• •A	• •B	Charter Fund (started 7/67)	22.6	—	1.2	4.5	66.7	8.50	1.50
• •A	• •F	Chase Frontier Capital Fund of Boston (started 3/68)	11.9	—	1.5	20.9	1.5	8.50	1.32
A+	F	The Chase Fund of Boston	20.5	–0.3	2.0	49.1	9.1	8.50	0.92
• •A	•C	Chase Special Fund of Boston (started 7/69)	24.9	—	1.5	14.8	20.3	8.50	1.43
B	B	Chemical Fund	5.0	4.4	1.8	985.2	15.2	8.50	0.59
• •C	• •F	Colonial Equities (started 11/66)	6.3	—	1.2	43.6	2.8	8.50	1.00

• Fund rated for one period only; maximum allowable rating A. • • Fund rated for two periods only; maximum allowable rating A.
* Formerly Boston Mutual Equity Growth Fund. ** Formerly Knowledge Communication Fund. N.A. Not available.
† Fund no longer selling new shares; existing shares traded over-the-counter. ‡ Sold only to present shareholders.

EXPLANATION OF COLUMN HEADINGS

*The Performance Ratings are based on the following **UP** and **DOWN** markets: **UP,** 10/7/66—11/29/68; 5/26/70—1/11/73; 10/3/74—6/30/75. **DOWN,** 2/9/66—10/7/66; 11/29/68—5/26/70; 1/11/73—10/3/74. In determining both the performance ratings and the percentage figures in the Dollar Results section, all capital gains distributions have been reinvested, but income dividends have not. All results are based on investments at net asset value and do not allow for sales charges. In the Dollar Results section, the latest 12 months covers the period from June 30, 1974 to June 30, 1975; the 9-year average annual growth rate covers the period from February 9, 1966 to June 30, 1975. Dividend Return is based on June 30, 1975 net asset value and the income payout for the preceding 12-month period. Annual expenses include management fees and operating expenses as a percentage of average net assets.*

Figure 15–4 *Forbes* Fund Ratings, 1975. (Forbes *Magazine*)

Performance Ratings: In UP Markets	Performance Ratings: In DOWN Markets		Dollar Results: Latest 12 Months	Dollar Results: 9-Year Average Annual Growth Rate	Dollar Results: Dividend Return	Total Assets 6/30/75 in Millions	Total Assets % Change 1975 vs. 1974	Maximum Sales Charge	Annual Expenses Per $100
—	—	**Standard & Poor's 500 Stock Average**	10.7%	0.1%	4.0%				
C	C	**FORBES Stock Fund Average**	13.8%	−0.5%	3.1%				

Stock Funds (No-Load)

In UP Markets	In DOWN Markets	Fund	Latest 12 Months	9-Year Average Annual Growth Rate	Dividend Return	Total Assets 6/30/75 in Millions	% Change 1975 vs. 1974	Maximum Sales Charge	Annual Expenses Per $100
• • B	• F	Spectra Fund (started 7/69)	29.1%	—	0.8%	$ 2.0	25.0	none	N.A.
• • B	• F	Standard & Poor's/In'cap Dynamics Fund (started 5/69)	11.9	—	2.2	4.3	−2.3	†	$1.53
• • C	• • C	State Farm Growth Fund (started 3/68)	27.1	—	2.5	60.5	57.1	none	0.79
• • D	• • A	State Farm Income Fund (started 3/68)	16.8	—	5.3	9.2	50.8	none	0.80
C	F	Steadman American Industry Fund	11.0	−4.9%	2.8	22.4	7.2	none	3.01
C	D	Steadman Investment Fund	4.6	−2.1	5.2	25.9	2.4	none	1.48
A	D	Stein Roe & Farnham Capital Opportunities Fund	8.8	1.3	1.7	21.2	3.9	none	0.75
A	D	Stein Roe & Farnham Stock Fund	18.3	1.9	2.3	178.8	27.3	none	0.61
• • D	• C	Tudor Hedge Fund (started 6/69)	39.7	—	none	11.0	39.2	none	1.97
		Twentieth Century Investors							
A+	F	Growth Investors	34.1	−0.4	none	12.4	36.3	none	1.53
D	C	Income Investors	40.6	−0.3	1.7	1.3	30.0	none	1.52
C	F	Vanderbilt Growth Fund*	−1.4	−3.2	0.6	5.4	−26.0	†	3.58
B	F	Vanderbilt Income Fund**	−7.3	−6.8	0.5	3.4	−20.9	†	5.70
C	C	Variable Stock Fund	10.1	0.5	2.7	3.7	19.4	none	1.48
B	D	Viking Growth Fund	22.2	0.1	none	1.7	13.3	none	N.A.
• • A	• • F	Weingarten Equity Fund (started 3/67)	31.1	—	none	11.1	60.9	none	1.00
• • D	• • B	Clarence M. Whipple Fund (started 5/68)	0.6	—	3.6	0.6	−14.3	none	3.78

Closed-End Investment Companies

In UP Markets	In DOWN Markets	Company	Latest 12 Months	9-Year Average Annual Growth Rate	Dividend Return	Total Assets 6/30/75 in Millions	% Change 1975 vs. 1974	Where Traded	Annual Expenses Per $100
C	A	Adams Express	18.8%	2.5%	3.6%	$186.3	18.5	NYSE	$0.66
C	A+	ASA Limited	−3.7	1.7	2.3	318.1	−3.7	NYSE	0.43
• • D	• • A	Baker Fentress & Co.	6.2	—	2.4	142.4	3.9	O-T-C	0.61
D	B	Carriers & General Corp.	13.7	1.1	3.6	19.6	11.4	NYSE	1.00
B	F	Central Securities	19.6	−4.1	4.1	38.0	23.4	ASE	1.10
C	D	Consolidated Investment Trust	13.7	−0.3	3.3	60.4	5.4	O-T-C	0.28
• • D	• B	Diebold Venture Capital (started 4/68)	−9.7	—	none	10.8	−9.2	ASE	2.00
• • D	• F	Emerging Securities Fund (started 11/68)	16.9	—	none	2.8	27.3	O-T-C	1.91
B	C	General American Investors	9.3	2.5	1.7	104.5	10.2	NYSE	1.23
C	C	International Holdings	14.5	0.4	3.4	79.1	9.6	NYSE	1.21
B	A+	Japan Fund	8.6	19.7	0.9	126.0	25.5	NYSE	0.86
A	C	The Lehman Corp.	10.5	4.4	2.0	480.8	6.3	NYSE	0.50
B	C	Madison Fund	29.8	2.1	4.2	324.7	29.7	NYSE	0.71
D	B	National Aviation	11.6	−3.6	3.7	82.7	13.0	NYSE	1.00
B	C	Niagara Share Corp.	8.6	4.3	1.4	101.3	4.0	NYSE	0.81
• • B	• • D	OTF Equities*** (started 7/68)	31.8	—	none	1.1	22.2	O-T-C	4.40
B	A	Petroleum Corp. of America	34.4	6.6	3.6	100.2	31.3	NYSE	0.60
• • D	• • A	Source Capital (started 10/68)	15.2	—	5.5	166.5	−3.8	O-T-C	1.13
B	C	Standard Shares	38.6	5.0	1.4	86.8	38.7	ASE	0.77
B	C	Tri-Continental Corp.	7.4	1.5	3.7	595.8	6.3	NYSE	0.40
D	A	The United Corp.	10.7	−0.2	5.6	121.1	10.5	NYSE	0.79
C	C	U.S. & Foreign Securities	12.9	−0.4	2.9	109.6	10.0	NYSE	1.18
• • D	• • B	Value Line Development Capital Corp. (started 2/68)	−6.8	—	0.2	12.0	−7.0	ASE	1.47

Funds for Investing Abroad

In UP Markets	In DOWN Markets	Fund	Latest 12 Months	9-Year Average Annual Growth Rate	Dividend Return	Total Assets 6/30/75 in Millions	% Change 1975 vs. 1974	Maximum Sales Charge	Annual Expenses Per $100
D	A+	Canadian Fund	−2.6%	10.9%	3.7%	$28.3	−5.4	8.50%	$0.89
D	A+	International Investors	3.7	16.0	4.8	130.5	12.7	8.75	0.99
C	A	Scudder International Fund****	7.2	3.5	1.6	18.9	−5.5	none	1.48
C	A+	Templeton Growth Fund	13.5	13.5	1.7	18.5	6.9	8.75	0.99
C	A+	Transatlantic Fund	19.6	8.8	3.4	12.9	−3.0	†	1.10

• Fund rated for one period only; maximum allowable rating A. • • Fund rated for two periods only; maximum allowable rating A.
* Formerly The Pegasus Fund. ** Formerly Vanderbilt Mutual Fund. *** Formerly Ocean Technology Funds. N.A. Not available.
† Fund no longer selling new shares; existing shares traded over-the-counter. **** Formerly Scudder International Investments.

4. What type of funds would be considered aggressive if not speculative? What tools do the managers use to accomplish their objectives?
5. Why are there load and no-load funds? Which fund would be better for short-term investment? Why?
6. Describe the advantages and disadvantages of investing in mutual funds.
7. Explain the different ways in which mutual funds may be purchased over long periods of time.
8. What are exchange rights? Are they useful?
9. What is meant by the total return concept in mutual funds?
10. In what manner are investment companies and their investors taxed?

Projects

1. Find a mutual fund that tends to specialize in an industry in which you work or are interested. Compare the fund's daily price performance with the common stock price of one particular company in the industry.
2. Visit your local library or securities brokerage office to locate mutual fund research periodicals. Find the recommendation these periodicals offer for the specialized fund in project one.
3. Select a mutual fund on the recommendation of a brokerage house or fund salesman. Write for the prospectus of a no-load fund with the same objectives selected at random. Compare the performance currently and over the past few years.
4. Compare the sales charges and management fees for two load and two no-load funds selected at random.

Case Problem

Art and Barbara Able have finally decided that a growth mutual fund is their best investment. They have been told that if they had invested $10,000 on January 1, 1965, their shares would have been worth about $19,000 as of December 31, 1975, had they reinvested their distributions. Compare the rate of return per annum over this period for a typical load fund and a no-load fund. Do you have any precautionary suggestions for the Ables?

16

more investment opportunities

When people consider investment, they usually think first of the stock market and then of real estate. However, there are many more investment opportunities available. Some are extremely safe and liquid; others are extremely speculative, whether liquid or nonliquid. We will now explore the more accessible alternative investments such as government securities, both federal and municipal; speculative trading in the options market and in commodity futures; foreign investments; investment in collectibles such as art, memorabilia, antiques, jewelry, and the like; and investment in yourself through ownership and operation of a small business.

GOVERNMENT SECURITIES

Government securities are debt instruments issued by federal, state, and local authorities. Debt financing is the method used by government to raise funds in excess of its current income. This form of funding is widely known as *deficit financing*. Equity financing cannot be used to raise funds because there are no ownership shares in government. According to the Constitution, we are the government.

United States Government Securities

The major reasons for purchasing U.S. government securities are the quality and marketability or redeemability of the security. There is no question about repayment of U.S. government securities, which are backed by the "full faith and credit of the United States." Every government's debt obligations are rated for quality on the basis of its ability and willingness to pay. This affects an investor's response to an original issue by the government and the subsequent marketability in the secondary market. The U.S. government has never defaulted on any security when it matured. The same cannot be said about many other governments.

U.S. government securities set the standards for *safety of principal* in any investment. Short-term and long-term obligations of the federal government affect the commercial money market of the United States and vice versa. Federal government securities provide a *lower yield* than corporate securities because of their highest-quality rating. They are always included in the legal investment portfolio of banks, trust funds, and insurance companies. Many corporations and individuals also purchase federal government securities. Often these investors purchase government securities as a *residual investment medium,* to be bought only when higher-yield loans or investments are not obtainable at a particular time.

Treasury (direct) obligations comprise the largest portion of the national debt. Other fully guaranteed obligations are primarily those issued by the Federal Housing Administration (FHA) and the Government National Mortgage Association (called "Ginnie Mae"). Nonguaranteed obligations equal about 5 percent of the national debt but are not legally a part of it. These obligations yield slightly higher returns than can be had on direct or fully guaranteed obligations, even though it is highly unlikely that Congress would allow a federal agency to default. Securities that are nonguaranteed include those issued by such agencies as the Federal Land Bank, World Bank, U.S. Postal Service, Federal National Mortgage Association (called "Fannie Mae") and others. Each of these agencies assists in guaranteeing some form of economic development.

Marketability The Treasury issues two types of securities, marketable and nonmarketable. We have already discussed the nonmarketable (nonnegotiable) issues in chapter 4. Most nonmarketable government securities are Series E and H savings bonds that can be redeemed only by the Treasury. These are registered to the owner and cannot be transferred. They are designed for the small investor to hold to maturity. Redemption prior to maturity date results in a lower yield. Marketable securities are negotiable and can be transferred by endorsement or delivery.

Types of securities There are three major types of securities issued by the Treasury through the Federal Reserve Banks. These are Treasury bills, Treasury notes, and Treasury bonds, each with differing maturity terms. All three types offer denominations as low as $1,000, but they are subject to a minimum $10,000 purchase by the investor and usually carry the $10,000 denomination. Figure 16–1 illustrates the price quotations of various federal securities available in the secondary market.

Treasury bills are short-term direct obligations of three to six months duration. They are offered by the Federal Reserve Banks each week by auction to the highest bidder. Individuals may purchase bills by direct bid to the Federal Reserve Banks at no charge or through banks and brokers for a flat service fee. (Current service fees for some banks are $25 regardless of the dollar amount of bills purchased.) This fee would have a dramatic effect on the yields of a small investment. Bills do not carry a coupon interest rate but are sold at discount for redemption at face value at maturity.

Bills are a highly liquid investment subject to the fluctuation of the money market. They are fully negotiable and can be transferred to others any time prior to maturity. Individuals and financial institutions often hold them for a few days in order to keep cash working. They provide relatively low yields because of their short-term and absolute safety features.

Treasury notes are obligations of one to five years duration. These negotiable securities are regularly traded in the over-the-counter market. Institutions and individuals use them for intermediate term investments. The yield is generally about 1 to 1.5 percent greater than that of bills. Interest is paid by coupon redemption on a semiannual basis and is stated on the security. Notes are affected by interest-rate and purchasing-power investment risks.

Treasury bonds are issues with maturity periods of more than five years. These are irregularly offered in various denominations for varying periods of maturity. Most issues are available in registered or coupon bond form. The interest is paid semiannually at

Government, Agency and Miscellaneous Securities

Thursday, June 12, 1975

Over-the-Counter Quotations: Source on request.

Decimals in bid-and-asked and bid changes represent 32nds (101.1 means 101 1-32). a-Plus 1-64. b-Yield to call date. d-Minus 1-64.

U.S. TREASURY BONDS & NOTES

Rate	Mat.	Date		Bid	Asked	Bid Chg.	Yld.
5⅞s,	1975	Aug	n	100.2	100.4	.....	5.02
8⅜s,	1975	Sep	n	100.27	100.31	+ .1	4.90
7s,	1975	Nov	n	100.18	100.22	+ .1	5.27
7s,	1975	Dec	n	100.23	100.27	.....	5.39
5⅞s,	1976	Feb	n	100:2	100.6	+ .1	5.59
6¼s,	1976	Feb	n	100.7	100.15	.....	5.53
8s,	1976	Mar	n	101.21	101.25	+ .1	5.67
5¾s,	1976	May	n	99.28	100.0	.....	5.75
6½s,	1976	May	n	100.18	100.22	+ .2	5.72
6s,	1976	May	n	100.5	100.9	+ .2	5.69
8¾s,	1976	Jun	n	102.27	102.31	.....	5.77
6½s,	1976	Aug	n	100.18	100.22	.....	5.88
7½s,	1976	Aug	n	101.21	101.25	+ .1	5.90
5⅞s,	1976	Aug	n	99.28	100.0	+ .1	5.88
8¼s,	1976	Sep	n	102.25	102.29	+ .5	5.88
6½s,	1976	Oct	n	100.17	100.19	.....	6.04
6¼s,	1976	Nov	n	100.4	100.8	+ .1	6.06
7⅛s,	1976	Nov	n	101.11	101.15	+ .2	6.06
7¼s,	1976	Dec	n	101.14	101.18	+ .1	6.17
8s,	1977	Feb	n	102.15	102.19	+ .1	6.34
6s,	1977	Feb	n	99.13	99.17	+ .2	6.29
6½s,	1977	Mar	n	100.5	100.7	+ .2	6.37
7⅜s,	1977	Apr	n	101.21	101.25	+ .3	6.35
6⅞s,	1977	May	n	100.26	101.2	+ .1	6.28
9s,	1977	May	n	104.12	104.20	+ .1	6.40
6¾s,	1977	May	n	100.17	100.19	+ .3	6.43
7¾s,	1977	Aug	n	102.15	102.23	+ .1	6.39
7¾s,	1977	Nov	n	102.15	102.23	+ .1	6.52
6¼s,	1978	Feb	n	99.4	99.12	− .3	6.52
7⅛s,	1978	May	n	100.26	101.2	− .1	6.72
7⅝s,	1978	Aug	n	102.2	102.6	− .3	6.83
8¾s,	1978	Aug	n	105.4	105.12	+ .1	6.83
6s,	1978	Nov	n	97.11	97.19	− .1	6.81
7⅞s,	1979	May	n	102.24	103.0	− .2	6.99
6¼s,	1979	Aug	n	97.12	97.20	− .2	6.92
6⅝s,	1979	Nov	n	98.16	98.24	.....	6.97
7s,	1979	Nov	n	99.26	100.2	− .2	6.99
4s,	1980	Feb		87.28	88.28	+ .6	6.82
6⅞s,	1980	May	n	99.4	99.12	.....	7.02
9s,	1980	Aug	n	107.14	107.22	.....	7.19
3½s,	1980	Nov		84.4	85.4	− .4	6.83
7s,	1981	Feb	n	98.22	98.30	.....	7.23
7⅜s,	1981	Feb	n	100.6	100.14	− .2	7.28
7s,	1981	Aug		98.16	99.16	+ .2	7.10
7¾s,	1981	Nov	n	101.27	102.3	− .1	7.34
6⅜s,	1982	Feb		94.2	95.2	− .26	7.32
8s,	1982	May	n	102.31	103.3	+ .2	7.42
3¼s,	1978-83	Jun		80.12	81.12	− .4	6.24
6⅜s,	1984	Aug		94.16	95.16	.....	7.05
3¼s,	1985	May		80.8	81.8	− .2	5.76
4¼s,	1975-85	May		81.30	82.30	− .12	6.63
6⅛s,	1986	Nov		91.14	92.14	+ .6	7.11
3½s,	1990	Feb		80.8	81.8	− .4	5.37
8¼s,	1990	May		103.2	103.10	− .10	7.87
4¼s,	1987-92	Aug		80.28	81.28	− .14	5.94
4s,	1988-93	Feb		80.12	81.12	− .6	5.69
6¾s,	1993	Feb		90.30	91.30	− .2	7.59
7½s,	1988-93	Aug		97.12	98.12	.....	7.67
4⅛s,	1989-94	May		80.16	81.16	− .4	5.74
3s,	1995	Feb		80.20	81.20	+ .4	4.41
7s,	1993-98	May		91.0	92.0	.....	7.75
3½s,	1998	Nov		80.8	81.8	− .8	4.85
8½s,	1994-99	May		104.4	105.4	− .14	8.02
7⅞s,	1995-00	Feb		99.16	100.16	.....	7.92
8¼s,	2000-05	May		102.20	102.31	+ .4	8.06

n — Treasury Notes.

U.S. Treas. Bills

Mat	Bid Discount	Ask Discount	Mat	Bid Discount	Ask Discount
6-17	5.14	4.46	10- 2	5.08	4.90
6-19	5.21	4.55	10- 9	5.12	4.96
6-26	5.07	4.65	10-16	5.15	4.99
6-30	5.13	4.59	10-21	5.17	4.97
7- 1	4.97	4.61	10-23	5.17	5.01
7- 3	4.99	4.63	10-30	5.20	5.04
7-10	5.04	4.68	11- 6	5.20	5.04
7-17	5.02	4.62	11-13	5.23	5.09
7-24	5.00	4.76	11-18	5.23	5.07
7-29	5.01	4.77	11-20	5.24	5.08
7-31	5.01	4.81	11-28	5.23	5.11
8- 7	5.00	4.80	12- 4	5.28	5.12
8-14	4.98	4.82	12-11	5.19	5.09
8-21	5.00	4.80	12-16	5.24	5.06
8-26	4.99	4.82	1-13	5.36	5.20
8-28	4.98	4.86	1-31	5.36	5.28
9- 4	4.95	4.81	2-10	5.44	5.28
9-11	4.89	4.81	3- 9	5.47	5.31
9-18	4.97	4.81	4- 6	5.47	5.33
9-23	5.03	4.85	5- 4	5.49	5.33
9-25	5.04	4.86	6- 1	5.40	5.32

Fed. Home Loan Bk.

Rate	Mat	Bid	Asked	Yld
7.15	8-75	100.8	100.12	5.06
7⅞	8-75	100.13	100.17	4.96
7.95	8-75	100.13	100.17	5.03
6½	11-75	100.8	100.16	5.32
7.05	11-75	100.16	100.24	5.29
9.10	11-75	101.12	101.20	5.30
7⅜	2-76	100.24	101.4	5.68
8.70	2-76	101.24	102.4	5.50
8¾	2-76	101.24	102.4	5.55
9.20	2-76	102.0	102.12	5.63
7.20	5-76	100.24	101.8	5.81
7.45	5-76	101.0	101.16	5.78

FNMA Issues

Rate	Mat	Bid	Asked	Yld
6.80	9-75	100.8	100.12	5.08
7½	9-75	100.13	100.17	5.10
5.70	12-75	99.28	100.4	5.43
8¼	12-75	101.4	101.12	5.32
5.65	3-76	99.24	100.4	5.46
7⅛	3-76	100.24	101.4	5.52
5.85	6-76	99.20	100.4	5.72
6.70	6-76	100.12	100.28	5.77
10	6-76	103.16	104.0	5.76
5.85	9-76	99.8	99.24	6.05
6⅛	9-76	99.20	100.4	6.01
7½	9-76	101.8	101.24	5.99
6¼	12-76	99.16	100.0	6.25
7.45	12-76	101.4	101.20	6.28
8.45	12-76	102.16	103.0	6.30
4½	2-77	96.4	96.28	6.52
6.30	3-77	99.8	99.24	6.45
7.05	3-77	100.16	101.0	6.42
6⅜	6-77	100.4	100.20	6.04
6½	6-77	99.12	99.28	6.57
7.20	6-77	100.20	101.4	6.58
6⅞	9-77	99.28	100.12	6.68
7.85	9-77	101.28	102.12	6.68
7¼	12-77	100.24	101.8	6.70
7.55	12-77	101.12	101.28	6.72
8.45	3-78	103.12	103.28	6.86
6.70	3-78	99.12	99.28	6.75
7.15	6-78	100.8	100.24	6.87
7.45	6-78	101.6	101.14	6.91
7.15	9-78	100.4	100.20	6.93
6¾	12-78	99.0	99.16	6.91
8.95	12-78	105.16	106.0	6.98
7¼	3-79	100.0	100.16	7.09
7.85	6-79	101.16	102.0	7.26
9.80	6-79	107.16	108.16	7.30
6.40	9-79	96.28	97.12	7.13
7.80	9-79	101.12	101.28	7.27
6.55	12-79	96.24	97.8	7.28
7¾	12-79	101.13	101.17	7.34

Figure 16–1 Government Security Price and Yield Quotations. *(Reprinted with permission of The Wall Street Journal, © Dow Jones & Company, Inc., 1975. All Rights Reserved.)*

the rate stated on the security. Yields are slightly lower than the Treasury notes. Bonds are very definitely affected by interest-rate and purchasing-power investment risks.

State and Local Securities

States, counties, cities, school districts, and other units of local government also need capital to build and maintain various local projects such as roads, transit systems, hospitals, airports, and schools. Bond issues constitute their major form of debt financing. The nature of the promise to pay and the source of funds used to repay the debt vary considerably among the nearly one hundred thousand different political jurisdictions in the United States. For the sake of convenience all state and local bonds are collectively known as *municipals*. These obligations are long-term in nature, usually with a maturity period of twenty years or longer. They suffer the interest-rate and purchasing-power investment risks as do all long-term fixed-rate obligations. Their greatest appeal is their tax-exempt status.

Marketability Municipal bonds vary greatly in their marketability. Bonds of prominent political subdivisions are traded throughout the country. Regional dealers in close proximity to the issuer's area handle local obligations. New issues are generally sold at competitive bidding to banking syndicates or investment underwriting firms. These organizations buy the bonds outright for resale to the public.

Individuals and commercial banks are the main purchasers of municipal bonds. They provide for over 75 percent of all purchases. Municipals are traded over the counter in the secondary market. The securities of nationally known bond issuers are much more liquid than local issues because they enjoy a broader market. Investors became somewhat wary of municipals in late 1975 because of the debt problems of New York City.

Bond types There are three major types of state and local bonds. These are (1) general obligation bonds, (2) revenue bonds, and (3) assessment bonds.

General obligation bonds are also known as full faith and credit bonds. They are backed by the full taxing power of the government unit issuing them. The tax base for state issues is generally sales and income taxes, while the assessed value of real estate is used for local issues. In general, fully taxed supported obligations command the highest prices for the sellers and the lowest yields for the buyers.

The investment quality of general obligation bonds is based upon the legality of the obligation and the ability and willingness of the political subdivision to repay the debt with interest.

Revenue bonds are debt obligations of business activities conducted by state and local governments. The debt service is paid solely out of revenues from the project. Examples of such activities include such publicly owned businesses as water departments, toll roads and bridges, and airports. The borrowing government agency establishes rates high enough to pay off the debt from the patronage of the particular project. Voters often approve the issue of revenue bonds because they are based on the benefits-received principal of a *use tax*. They like the idea that local debt and tax rates on real property are not increased by revenue bonds.

Investment quality of revenue bonds is determined by whether the revenues from the project will be sufficient to service the debt. An additional investment risk (the business risk) is present on municipal revenue bonds because of the possibility that insufficient revenue will be generated by the project.

Assessment bonds are not very important as an investment opportunity. They are used to finance improvements in a given area. A special property tax assessment is levied against all property in the benefit area to pay for the bonds. Willingness to pay any municipal bond often seems to be closely associated with the ability to pay without inconvenience. This is especially true of assessment bonds.

Rating and Purchase of Government Securities

You should still take care when evaluating and purchasing government securities. Since federal government securities and most municipals are considered to be almost risk free, you might decide to purchase without questions. However, you should first check Moody's *Bond Survey*, Standard & Poor's *Bond Outlook*, or the Bond Buyer *Prices and Yields* for rating information. Quotations and current news items of bond offerings are usually listed in the *Wall Street Journal*. Major brokerage houses and bank securities departments often publish daily quotation sheets listing federal securities.

Price and Yield

Government securities are calculated in $\frac{1}{32}$ of a dollar as shown in the price quotations of figure 16–1. Bonds quoted in dollar prices are actually priced in "points." A point in bond terminology is 1 percent of the face value. On a $1,000 bond a point would be $10; on a $10,000 bond, it would be $100. For reading and space purposes the last zero is dropped from the quote.

Government securities, like corporate bonds, may sell above or below face value. Over 100 results in a premium; below 100 results in a discount. Because of the interest-rate investment risk and the upward pressures of inflation and money demand, most governments sell at a discount in the secondary market. The market price constantly adjusts to money market conditions to provide a competitive current yield.

Yields Yields to maturity on government securities may be calculated in the same manner as corporate bonds. *Current yield* is the percent relation of the annual interest received to the current asking price of the bond. It is simple arithmetic if you have a $1,000 bond with a 5 percent coupon rate due in twenty years. The current yield would be 5 percent through to maturity, *if* you pay $1,000 for it.

Bond yield calculations are complicated because it is necessary to determine present values of future payments to find exact yields. Fortunately, current yields are published with price quotes. You can also determine particular bond yields from *bond tables* as shown in figure 16–2. To find the net yield to maturity, find the table with the correct coupon (nominal) interest rate, find the column that corresponds to the number of years and months to maturity, go down the column until you find your market price for the bond, and then read the net yield as listed in the first column on the left. This is easier than calculating it!

Perhaps you should settle for the concept that there is an inverse relationship between bond prices and yields. The higher the bond price, the lower the yield. The higher the yield, the lower the bond price. Finally, remember that all bonds sell at prices that reflect the current loan value of money. Even though they may have different coupon rates, bonds of similar quality can be compared on the basis of yield. You will pay a similar price for similar value.

Tax Status

Income from federal securities is taxable on federal income-tax returns and on most state returns. It is the tax-exempt status of municipals that makes them appealing to wealthy individuals and to corporations. Interest income on municipals is nontaxable on federal returns. A single person with a taxable income of $20,000 would be in the 38 percent tax bracket; he would have to earn a yield of 9.68 percent in order to match a 6 percent tax-exempt bond yield.

Many people criticize tax-exempt municipals as a subsidy for the wealthy. However, without this exemption there would be a hindrance in fund raising by state and local governments because it would be

YEARS AND MONTHS — COUPON **5**

YIELD	19-5	19-6	19-7	19-8	19-9	19-10	19-11	20-0
3.00	129.27	129.36	129.45	129.55	129.64	129.73	129.82	129.92
3.05	128.41	128.50	128.59	128.68	128.77	128.85	128.94	129.04
3.10	127.56	127.65	127.73	127.82	127.90	127.99	128.07	128.16
3.15	126.72	126.80	126.88	126.96	127.05	127 13	127.21	127.30
3.20	125.88	125.96	126.04	126.12	126.20	126.28	126.36	126.44
3.25	125.05	125.13	125.20	125.28	125.36	125.43	125.51	125.59
3.30	124.23	124.30	124.38	124.45	124.52	124.59	124.67	124.75
3.35	123.41	123.49	123.55	123.62	123.69	123.76	123.84	123.91
3.40	122.60	122.67	122.74	122.81	122.87	122.94	123.01	123.08
3.45	121.80	121.87	121.93	122.00	122.06	122.13	122.19	122.26
3.50	121.00	121.07	121.13	121.19	121.25	121.32	121.38	121.45
3.55	120.22	120.28	120.34	120.40	120.45	120.51	120.58	120.64
3.60	119.43	119.50	119.55	119.61	119.66	119.72	119.78	119.84
3.65	118.66	118.72	118.77	118.82	118.88	118.93	118.99	119.04
3.70	117.89	117.95	117.99	118.05	118.10	118.15	118.20	118.26
3.75	117.13	117.18	117.23	117.28	117.32	117.37	117.43	117.48
3.80	116.37	116.42	116.47	116.51	116.56	116.61	116.65	116.70
3.85	115.62	115.67	115.71	115.75	115.80	115.84	115.89	115.94
3.90	114.88	114.92	114.96	115.00	115.05	115.09	115.13	115.18
3.95	114.14	114.18	114.22	114.26	114.30	114.34	114.38	114.42
4.00	113.41	113.45	113.49	113.52	113.56	113.60	113.64	113.78
4.05	112.68	112.72	112.76	112.79	112.82	112.86	112.90	112.94
4.10	111.97	112.00	112.03	112.06	112.10	112.13	112.17	112.20
4.15	111.25	111.29	111.32	111.34	111.38	111.41	111.44	111.47
4.20	110.55	110.58	110.60	110.63	110.66	110.69	110.72	110.75
4.25	109.84	109.88	109.90	109.92	109.95	109.98	110.01	110.04
4.30	109.15	109.18	109.20	109.22	109.25	109.27	109.30	109.33
4.35	108.46	108.49	108.51	108.53	108.55	108.57	108.60	108.62
4.40	107.78	107.80	107.82	107.84	107.86	107.88	107.90	107.93
4.45	107.10	107.12	107.14	107.15	107.17	107.19	107.21	107.23
4.50	106.42	106.45	106.46	106.47	106.49	106.51	106.53	106.55
4.55	105.76	105.78	105.79	105.80	105.82	105.83	105.85	105.87
4.60	105.10	105.11	105.12	105.13	105.15	105.16	105.18	105.19
4.65	104.44	104.46	104.46	104.47	104.48	104.50	104.51	104.57
4.70	103.79	103.80	103.81	103.82	103.83	103.84	103.85	103.86
4.75	103.14	103.16	103.16	103.17	103.17	103.18	103.19	103.20
4.80	102.50	102.51	102.52	102.52	102.53	102.53	102.54	102.55
4.85	101.87	101.88	101.88	101 88	101.88	101.89	101.90	101.91
4.90	101.24	101.25	101.25	101.25	101.25	101.25	101.26	101.27
4.95	100.61	100.62	100.62	100.62	100.62	100.62	100.62	100.63
5.00	100.00	100.00	100.00	99.99	99.99	99.99	100.00	100.00
5.05	99.38	99.38	99.38	99.37	99.37	99.37	99.37	99.38
5.10	98.77	98.77	98.77	98.76	98.76	98.75	98.75	98.76
5.15	98.17	98.17	98.16	98.15	98.15	98.14	98.14	98.14
5.20	97.57	97.57	97.56	97.55	97.54	97.54	97.53	97.53
5.25	96.97	96.97	96.96	96.95	96.94	96.93	96.93	96.93
5.30	96.39	96.38	96.37	96.36	96.35	96.34	96.33	96.33
5.40	95.22	95.21	95.20	95.18	95.17	95.16	95.15	95.14
5.50	94.07	94.06	94.05	94.03	94.01	94.00	93.99	93.98
5.60	92.95	92.94	92.91	92.89	92.88	92.86	92.85	92.84
5.70	91.84	91.82	91.80	91.78	91.76	91.74	91.72	91.71
5.75	91.29	91.27	91.25	91.23	91.21	91.19	91.17	91.15
6.00	88.62	88.60	88.56	88.54	88.51	88.49	88.46	88.44
6.50	83.58	83.55	83.51	83.47	83.44	83.40	83.37	83.34
7.00	78.93	78.90	78.85	78.80	78.76	78.72	78.68	78.64

Figure 16–2 Sample Bond Table.

necessary for municipals to offer a higher interest rate to compete with other borrowers. The average taxpayer would end up paying extra taxes to cover the cost of higher debt service by local government.

SPECULATIVE INVESTMENT

A number of other investment opportunities are available for the person who is willing to take a greater risk for a greater gain. Most of these opportunities involve trading on specialized exchanges or in foreign investment of some sort. These are not recommended for the small investor who cannot afford to risk his capital in speculative positions.

OPTION MARKETS

An option is a speculative contract that allows a trader to buy or sell 100 shares of a specific stock at a specific price during a specific period of time, regardless of the market price during that period.

Puts and Calls

Option contracts are often referred to as puts and calls. A *put* is an option contract giving a holder the right to sell the stock, while a *call* is an option giving a buyer the right to purchase the stock.

Puts and calls have been traded over the counter for a number of years by speculators who dealt through put and call dealers. Many options are still transacted in this manner, as evidenced by the brokerage firm advertisement in the *Wall Street Journal* in figure 16–3. The premium or price of the actual option, while negotiable, is related to the market value and volatility of the underlying stock and the length of the option period. The bigger any of these factors are, the higher the premium for the put or call option.

In figure 16–3 the *call* option for Westinghouse Electric Company means that a buyer is willing to purchase an option to buy at $12.75 per share, while holders will accept a call option at $13.50 per share. The expiration date of the option is November 4 of the current year. The premium will cost the buyer $125. The option allows the buyer to purchase the Westinghouse shares at a negotiated option price (we will use $13) at any time prior to the expiration date. If the price increases by $1.25 per share, the call option holder will break even on the round-lot option of 100 shares. If the price rises to 16 he can be expected to exercise his option and then resell the shares like this:

Buy

$ 125.00	cost of option
1,300.00	purchase 100 shares
$1,425.00	total cost

Sell

$1,600.00	sale of shares
–1,425.00	cost
$ 175.00	net profit

If he had purchased the 100 shares instead of the option, he would have netted $300, less commission. With the option, he protected himself against the possibility of market decline (the most he could lose would be $125) and also provided a form of leverage for the purchase of the shares with an actual cash outlay of only $125.

In the advertisement, the Reynolds Metals *put* means that a holder is offering

PUTS & CALLS

Plus tax—Subject to prior sale or price change

PUTS					
9⅜	ALASKAN INTERSTATE	9⅞	OCT	21	$187.50
12¼	AMERICAN STANDARD	13.30	NOV	25	175.00
13⅞	BOISE CASCADE	14½	JAN	29	237.50
6½	ELSBURG GOLD ADR	6¼	FEB	3	150.00
19½	GIANT YELLOWKNIFE	15⅝	JAN	28	125.00
75½	HEWLETT PACKARD	74	OCT	21	725.00
14¾	HARMONY GOLD ADR	14⅝	FEB	3	287.50
60¾	MONSANTO CO.	62	FEB	4	650.00
27½	MC LOUTH STEEL	27¾	NOV	1	225.00
18	REYNOLDS METALS	19	7-23-75		337.50
CALLS					
95⅝	ASA LTD.	86	JAN	27	$2075.00
3⅜	AMPEX	31½	NOV	18	50.00
7¾	AMERICAN AIRLINES	7⅞	NOV	4	100.00
12¼	AMERICAN STANDARD	14½	DEC	3	50.00
4⅜	AVCO CORP	5½	DEC	17	75.00
5⅛	BODIN APPAREL	5½	NOV	4	75.00
5	BRACKEN GOLD ADR	4⅝	DEC	24	187.50
3½	DATA PRODUCTS	4	NOV	18	50.00
21⅝	DOORNFONTEIN ADR	21⅝	FEB	10	550.00
6½	ELSBURG GOLD ADR	6½	FEB	10	225.00
14¾	EASTDRIEFONTEIN ADR	14¾	FEB	10	412.50
5¼	EVANS ARISTOCRAT	5¼	NOV	4	75.00
19½	GIANT YELLOWKNIFE	18¼	JAN	29	450.00
75½	HEWLETT PACKARD	84	OCT	21	262.50
14¾	HARMONY GOLD ADR	14¾	NOV	4	300.00
14¾	HARMONY GOLD ADR	14¾	FEB	10	425.00
17¾	HOUSTON OIL & MIN	17⅞	NOV	4	225.00
21	KLOOFGOLD ADR	21	FEB	10	537.50
10⅛	LTV CORP	10⅛	1 YEAR		212.50
27	PITTSTON CO.	27	NOV	4	325.00
12⅛	RANCHERS EXPLOR	12⅛	FEB	10	225.00
4	RAMADA INNS	4½	NOV	4	87.50
17¼	TESORO PETROLEUM	17¾	OCT	28	225.00
8⅜	TRANS WORLD AIR	8¾	NOV	4	87.50
31½	WESTERN DEEP ADR	31½	FEB	10	712.50
9⅛	WELKOM GOLD ADR	9⅛	FEB	10	275.00
5	WINNEBAGO	5¼	FEB	10	150.00
12¾	WESTINGHOUSE ELEC	13½	NOV	4	125.00

Members New York Stock Exchange, Inc.
and Other Principal Exchanges
Members of the Put and Call Dealers Association,
Members of the Chicago Board Option Exchange,
Prospectus Available on request

BLYTH EASTMAN DILLON & CO.
INCORPORATED
61 Broadway, New York 10006
Call Collect: (212) 943-4488

Everything in Puts & Calls

Figure 16–3 Puts and Calls Advertisement. *(Blyth Eastman Dillon & Co. Incorporated, New York)*

an option to sell at 19, while a bidder will take the option only if it is to sell at 18. The expiration date of the option is July 25 of the following year. The premium for this put is $337.50 or $3.375 per share. If the price of Reynolds should decrease to $13 per share, the shareholder–option buyer may "put" by requiring the option maker to purchase the 100 shares at the exercise price (we will use $18.50). The arithmetic would look like this:

$ 1,850.00	selling price of 100 shares
− 337.50	cost of put
1,512.50	realized with put
−1,300.00	realized without put
$ 212.50	net profit from put

The *put buyer* in this instance was attempting to *protect himself* from a *declining market.* The option maker received $337.50 for granting the option that required him to purchase 100 shares at $18.50 if called upon to do so. The new buyer had a net cost of $15.125 per share because of the premium received. If the market had not declined, the put buyer would not have required the maker to purchase, thereby allowing the maker to profit by the amount of the premium and causing the put buyer to lose his hedge.

Options exchanges There are now two organized options exchanges that feature the trading of options. These are the Chicago Board Options Exchange and the American Exchange. They feature standardization of option contracts, regular quotations of option transactions to stimulate a secondary market, and market makers, specialists who maintain a market in listed option contracts. The market makers provide a degree of liquidity in an option contract. They provide an option holder with the opportunity of selling his option before expiration date whenever the market price of the underlying stock is not heading for the anticipated rise. This benefit is readily available because there is an organized secondary market. The exchanges select specific common stocks to offer for option trading. They also offer four standardized exercise dates, the last business day of January, April, July, and October. Figure 16–4 illustrates options price quotations from the *Wall Street Journal.* Option prices are quoted in 1/16 of a dollar.

COMMODITIES

Commodities are basic raw materials such as foods, grains, oils, textiles, and metals. They are grown, mined, or fabricated and then purchased for current use by processors who use the commodities in their particular product and by wholesalers and dealers who resell them at a later date. These purchasers are representative of the buyer in the *cash* or *spot market.*

Contracts for future delivery have been developed because weather, strikes, governmental actions, and economic conditions can affect the supply and the price of commodities. Buyers and sellers who are producers, users, and dealers of commodities begin by hedging against future price uncertainties by purchasing or selling units of a commodity today for delivery in the future at stipulated prices. This procedure may be considered price insurance for these people. Commodity brokers become involved by arranging for speculators to buy future contracts in hopes of a price increase or sell in hopes of a decrease. As delivery time approaches, the speculator hopes to sell at a profit. Since he does not want physical possession of the commodity, he often takes a quick profit or loss well before the maturity

Chicago Board Options Exchange

Thursday, June 12, 1975

Closing prices of all options. Sales unit is 100 shares. Security description includes exercise price.

	— Jul —		— Oct —		— Jan —		Stock
Option & price	Vol.	Last	Vol.	Last	Vol.	Last	Close
Alcoa .. 40	13	3⅝	a	a	b	b	41⅝
Alcoa .. 45	44	1⅛	4	3⅜	5	5⅛	41⅝
Alcoa .. 50	9	⅜	9	2	a	a	41⅝
Am Tel 45	56	4¼	10	5¼	1	6⅜	48⅞
Am Tel 50	121	⅞	110	2	105	2¾	48⅞
Atl R .. 80	21	19⅝	12	22½	b	b	100
Atl R .. 90	325	10⅝	151	13⅛	7	16¾	100
Atl R ..100	b	b	142	7⅝	14	9⅛	100
Avon 30	43	13⅝	7	14¾	b	b	43⅜
Avon 35	37	8¾	9	10	b	b	43⅜
Avon 40	211	4¾	72	7	b	b	43⅜
Avon .. 45	268	2	91	4⅞	40	6¾	43⅜
Avon .. 50	558	⅞	137	2⅞	16	4⅝	43⅜
Beth S ..25	3	9	b	b	b	b	34
Beth S ..30	36	4⅝	23	6	b	b	34
Beth S ..35	180	1 3-16	101	2¾	24	3¾	34
Beth S ..40	82	⅜	107	1⅜	33	2¼	34
Bruns .. 10	39	4¾	12	5	b	b	14½
Bruns 15	203	⅝	173	1 11-16	76	2⅜	14½
Citicp .. 25	8	10	b	b	b	b	34½
Citicp .. 30	44	5⅜	3	6⅝	b	b	34½
Citicp .. 35	125	1½	71	3¾	18	5½	34½
Citicp .. 40	99	7-16	41	1⅞	18	3	34½
Delta .. 25	3	7⅞	a	a	b	b	32⅜
Delta .. 30	39	3¼	10	5⅜	b	b	32⅜
Delta .. 35	393	1 3-16	88	2⅞	47	4⅛	32⅜
Delta .. 40	396	⅜	85	1⅜	b	b	32⅜
Dow Ch 60	11	24	11	25	b	b	83⅞
Dow Ch 70	16	14¼	15	15¾	b	b	83⅞
Dow Ch 80	156	5¾	25	9⅛	9	12¾	83⅞
Dow Ch 90	172	1⅝	7	5	12	7⅝	83⅞
Eas Kd 60	1	41⅜	a	a	b	b	100
Eas Kd 70	3	31	a	a	b	b	100
Eas Kd 80	40	20¾	4	22½	b	b	100
Eas Kd 90	215	11	43	13¾	b	b	100
Eas Kd 100	575	4⅜	58	8½	32	11⅝	100
Exxon .. 60	1	30¼	b	b	b	b	89⅝
Exxon .. 70	38	19⅞	63	20¼	b	b	89⅝
Exxon ..80	374	10⅛	260	11⅜	15	12½	89⅝
Exxon .. 90	b	b	519	4½	43	6⅜	89⅝
F N M 15	65	2⅞	28	3¾	3	4½	17⅝
F N M 20	286	½	235	1¼	46	1 15-16	17⅝
Ford 30	30	6	b	b	b	b	35½
Ford 35	100	2¼	66	3⅜	67	5½	35½
Ford .. 40	166	½	76	1 15-16	25	3⅜	35½
G M 30	1	13¼	b	b	b	b	43⅜
G M 35	2	8½	a	a	b	b	43⅜
G M 40	65	4	26	6½	b	b	43⅜
G M 45	234	1¼	121	3⅝	82	4⅞	43⅜
Gen El . 30	2	15	b	b	b	b	45
Gen El 35	25	10½	2	11¾	b	b	45
Gen El 40	21	5¾	2	7¾	b	b	45
Gen El 45	57	2¼	26	4½	12	6½	45
Gen El 50	216	¾	95	2¼	31	3⅞	45
Glf Wn . 20	1	16½	b	b	b	b	36¼
Glf Wn 25	2	11¾	4	12½	b	b	36¼
Glf Wn 30	71	6⅝	25	8	b	b	36¼
Glf Wn 35	159	2⅝	42	4⅝	43	6	36¼
Gt Wst ..10	18	8¼	b	b	b	b	18¼

Figure 16–4 Chicago Board Options Exchange Price Quotations. *(Reprinted with permission of The Wall Street Journal, © Dow Jones & Company, Inc., 1975. All Rights Reserved.)*

date by selling to another speculator or to a commodity user or dealer.

The Futures Market

Contracts for future delivery of commodities are known as *futures*. Futures prices are quoted daily in the *Wall Street Journal*. Figure 16–5 shows the wide variety of commodities available for futures trading. The prices quoted are in cents and portions of cents per standard unit of measurement for the particular commodity. Corn, wheat, and other grains are priced by the bushel, feeds by the ton, fats by the pound, metals by the pound, foods by the pound or dozen, and animals by the hundredweight. Quotations show the price ranges for the day and the season and indicate the number of contracts sold for the day. Futures prices quote the month of delivery.

Commodities futures trading is subject to many limitations in order to control market pressures caused by over-speculation. Figure 16–6, a compilation of facts about futures trading, illustrates many of these regulations. The figure shows (1) commodity exchanges and trading hours; (2) trading units of the commodity, known as *contracts* (this is the minimum amount of a particular commodity that can be traded on a commodity exchange); (3) minimum quotable price fluctuations per unit and per contract to remind a trader of the unit-price movement for each commodity; (4) exchange commission charges for a "round turn" (a complete buy and sell transaction) on each of three to twenty-four contracts (one or two contract commissions are subject to an extra $5 charge); and (5) the daily trading limits of the commodity, the extent of daily price fluctuation allowed on the exchange to keep the commodity price from becoming overspeculative.

Qualitative Analysis of Commodities

Trading commodities involves a qualitative approach much the same as securities trading. You should have a background knowledge of all the factors that affect the market place, and you must also *keep abreast of current happenings*. Trading over relatively short periods of time is the key element in the commodity futures market. Quick responses to market prices are vital and must be based on knowledge.

Supply and demand factors Commodity futures prices are basically set by the laws of supply and demand. Agricultural commodities have more supply and demand variables than metals. Most commodity trading activity involves agricultural products; therefore, our discussion will center on them. For the sake of simplicity, we will assume that demand is relatively stable, with a small steady increase caused by population increases and new industrial uses. Supply would become the controlling factor for both spot prices and futures prices. Surpluses would cause lower prices, while shortages would raise prices. In short, the commodity will have price elasticity.

Commodity supply is computed on the basis of a crop year. Supply consists of the new crop, any old crop carryover (storage), and import/export programs. Obvious supply situations that affect new crops are usually well publicized. However, by the time most small investors discover the situation, the large speculators have already taken advantageous trading positions. Typical natural causes that could effectively change the commodity supply are: (1) good weather with bumper crops, (2) poor weather during the planting, growing, or harvest season, and (3) crop blight. Extensive research would be necessary to secure other detailed supply information.

Futures Prices

Friday, June 13, 1975

	Open	High	Low	Close	Change	Season's High	Season's Low
CHICAGO—WHEAT							
July	295¾	298½	293	298-297	+1½to½	509	293
Sept	300½	304½	298	303	+1¼	513	298
Dec	310	313	307½	312½-312	+1¾to1¼	523	307½
Mar 76	318	321½	316½	321½	+2½	392½	316½
May	321½	324½	320	324½	+2½	334	320
CORN							
July	276¼	278½	275¾	278-277¾	+¾to½	411	254¾
Sept	253	257½	252¼	257-256¾	+3¼to3	388½	246¼
Dec	237	242½	237	241½-242	+3¾to4¼	355	234
Mar 76	242¾	249	242¾	248	+4¼	358	239
May	247¾	253½	247¾	252½	+5	283	245
OATS							
July	146	147¼	144¾	147-146½	+¼to−¼	198½	123½
Sept	134½	136¼	133½	136-136¼	+1¼to1½	178	122¼
Dec	136	137¾	135	137¼-137	+¾to½	188	126½
Mar 76	137½	139½	137	139½	+1¼	160	136½
SOYBEANS							
July	500	511¾	497½	506½-508	+5¾to7¼	972½	490
Aug	489	496	487½	495½-495	+5to4½	961	482
Sept	481	488	479	485½-484	+3½to2	945	474
Nov	481	487	479	485-486	+3¼to4¼	869	476
Jan 76	488	493½	486	492½	+3¾	860	481
Mar	496	501	495	500-501	+2¾to3¾	620	491
May	502½	508½	501½	507	+3	579	498
July	509	513	509	512	+3	582	504
Aug	510	514	510	513	+3	546½	505
SOYBEAN OIL							
July	21.15	21.65	20.95	21.55 .45	+ .35to.25	45.12	20.85
Aug	19.90	20.40	19.75	20.25	+ .28	44.30	19.75
Sept	19.25	19.70	19.15	19.60	+ .40	43.70	19.15
Oct	18.60	19.05	18.40	19.05	+ .45	32.75	18.40
Dec	17.80	18.50	17.75	18.35	+ .43	30.90	17.75
Jan 76	17.60	18.20	17.55	18.00	+ .30	28.50	17.55
Mar	17.45	18.05	17.45	17.85	+ .25	24.50	17.45
May	17.40	17.80	17.35	17.70-.75	+ .20to.25	21.20	17.25
July	17.25	17.60	17.20	17.50-.55	+ .25to.30	20.70	16.90
Aug	17.10	17.40	17.10	17.30	+ .10	18.50	16.90
SOYBEAN MEAL							
July	122.50	123.00	122.10	122.50-.30	− .20to.40	212.50	112.00
Aug	123.50	124.20	123.30	123.50	− .30	212.00	115.00
Sept	125.00	125.00	124.50	124.00b	− .50	211.00	118.00
Oct	125.50	126.00	125.00	125.50	.....	170.00	121.10
Dec	127.50	128.00	126.70	127.50	....	166.00	123.00
Jan76	129.50	130.50	129.00	129.50b	− .50	169.00	124.00
Mar	131.50	133.30	131.50	132.00b	− .20	151.00	128.30
zMar	130.50	131.00	130.50	130.50b	....	135.00	128.00
z-New contract.							
ICED BROILERS							
June	48.25	48.85	48.25	48.65	+ .25	48.85	36.85
July	47.40	47.85	47.40	47.65	+ .40	47.85	37.05
Aug	45.55	45.80	45.50	45.75-.65	+ .35to.25	45.80	37.10
Sept	41.50	41.85	41.50	41.85	+ .25	42.50	35.75
Nov	37.60	38.00	37.60	37.90-.75	+ .40to.25	39.25	35.75
Jan 76	38.00	38.20	38.00	38.20	+ .25	38.30	36.95
Mar	38.00	38.00	38.00	38.00	....	38.00	37.80

	Open	High	Low	Close	Change	High	Low
Nov	58.15	58.45	58.10	58.35-.45	+ .25to.35	58.50	52.50
Dec	60.40	61.00	60.35	60.95-61.	+ .80to.85	61.00	54.50
Sales estimated at: 433 contracts.							
POTATOES (IDAHO RUSSET)							
May 76	9.50	9.62	9.50	9.61	+ .11	9.62	8.80
Sales: 15 contracts.							
FROZEN PORK BELLIES							
July	77.50	78.52	77.50	78.52-.40	+1.50to1.38	78.52	38.25
Aug	76.90	77.90	76.80	77.90 .75	+1.48to1.33	77.90	52.10
Feb 76	74.30	74.95	74.10	74.80-.95	+ .85to1.00	75.05	55.25
Mar	73.45	73.95	73.15	73.90	+ .88	74.05	58.20
May	72.50	73.25	72.50	73.20-.25	+ .83to.88	73.45	63.30
July	72.10	72.50	71.95	72.50	+ .48	73.00	68.80
Sales estimated at: 7,394 contracts.							
HOGS							
June	51.45	52.25	51.40	52.20-.25	+1.35to1.40	52.25	35.30
July	52.97	53.30	52.75	53.27-.20	+1.00to.93	53.30	36.72
Aug	51.50	51.80	51.22	51.72-.80	+ .85to.93	51.80	39.00
Oct	47.25	47.37	47.00	47.32-.25	+ .37to.27	47.80	38.70
Dec	47.35	47.45	47.15	47.35-.25	+ .50to.40	48.00	38.75
Feb 76	46.35	46.45	46.10	46.30	+ .23	46.45	38.30
Apr	43.10	43.25	42.95	42.97	− .03	43.50	38.00
June	43.37	43.55	43.30	43.40b	+ .05	43.70	42.75
Sales estimated at: 3,592 contracts.							
LUMBER							
July	147.50	148.00	145.00	145.50-146.	−2.1to1.6	168.00	111.00
Sept	156.50	157.00	154.50	155.20-.10	− .80to.90	164.90	127.50
Nov	155.10	155.20	152.70	153.30-.20	−2.0to2.1	161.20	140.00
Jan76	156.00	156.00	154.50	154.80b	−1.50	163.00	146.00
Mar	156.50	156.80	155.60	156.50b	....	156.80	154.50
Sales estimated at: 1,022 contracts.							
NEW YORK—SILVER							
June	448.00	448.00	446.10	446.10	−1.60	481.50	410.00
July	448.90	451.50	445.00	447.50	−1.70	659.40	400.00
Sept	455.70	457.80	452.00	454.10	−1.70	650.10	407.10
Dec	465.50	467.90	462.00	464.20	−1.70	568.00	417.00
Jan76	468.40	470.30	465.90	467.20	−1.70	572.00	419.00
Mar	475.00	475.00	473.20	473.80	−1.70	576.00	431.00
May	481.10	483.90	478.70	480.20	−1.80	529.00	432.00
July	488.50	488.50	486.50	486.20	−1.80	529.00	432.00
Sept	494.60	494.70	492.80	492.80	−2.00	519.40	475.00
Sales estimated at: 5,353 contracts.							
COPPER							
June	51.60	51.80	51.60	51.80	+ .30	59.70	51.10
July	51.80	52.10	51.70	51.90	+ .30	103.50	51.40
Sept	52.80	53.00	52.60	52.90	+ .40	76.00	52.30
Dec	54.20	54.50	54.10	54.40	+ .30	74.20	54.00
Jan76	55.00	55.00	54.80	54.90	+ .30	67.40	54.50
Mar	55.80	56.00	55.70	55.90	+ .30	68.30	55.50
May	56.60	57.00	56.60	56.90	+ .30	69.10	56.50
July	58.00	58.00	57.60	57.90	+ .30	59.90	57.50
Sales estimated at: 1,252 contracts.							

	Open	High	Low	Close	Change	High	Low
PLYWOOD							
July	137.30	138.80	136.30	138.00	+ .20	150.00	102.00
Sept	140.60	141.50	139.20	141.0-140.8	+.10 to-.10	151.50	104.50
Nov	142.00	142.80	141.00	142.70	+ .70	148.50	115.00
Jan76	143.00	143.90	142.70	143.50	+ .10	150.00	126.00
Mar	145.00	145.50	144.50	144.50	....	150.50	131.50
May	147.00	147.00	145.00	145.50	+ .50	147.00	138.00
CHICAGO—SILVER							
June	447.50	449.50	445.50	446.00	−3.00	653.00	395.00
July	446.00	450.00	446.00	448.00	−3.00	480.00	432.50
Aug	453.00	455.00	448.00	451.00-452.	−2.0to1.0	563.50	402.00
Oct	458.50	462.00	455.50	459.00	− .70	570.00	405.00
Dec	464.50	468.00	461.50	465.50-.80	unch to+.30	574.00	410.00
Feb76	473.00	475.00	469.50	472.50-473.	−.50tounch	509.50	428.00
Apr	479.00	481.50	473.50	479.00	− .50	516.00	432.00
June	485.50	488.00	479.00	486.00	.....	523.00	441.00
Aug	492.50	592.50	4855.0	492.00	− .50	523.00	473.30
KANSAS CITY—WHEAT							
July	305½	307	303¼	306½-307	−¼to+¼	509¾	303¼
Sept	311	312	308	312	+¾	489	308
Dec	317	319	315¼	319	+1½	409	315¼
Mar 76	326	326	324	325	−1	372½	322½
MINNEAPOLIS—WHEAT							
July	358	358	352½	354	−5	560	352½
Sept	343	343	340	343	−2	453	340
Dec	344	345	343	344	−1 ½	408	341½
WINNIPEG—RAPESEED (VANCOUVER)							
June	576	579¼	576	579b	+4½	974	524
Sept	556	560	551½	560b	+7	930	520
Nov	525	528	521	528b	+8	705	510
Jan 76	515	522	515	522b	+8	632	509¾
RYE							
July	217	217¼	215¾	216½	+1	364	185¾
Oct	214	214¼	212¾	213¾a	+¾	245	194
OATS							
July	162⅞	163	162¾	162⅞b	+⅛	197	140¼
Oct	150	150	149½	149¾b	−¼	182½	141
BARLEY							
July	234	234	233¾	233½b	−¾	325	211
Oct	208	208¾	208	208¾b	−¼	382	208
FLAXSEED							
July	755	780	755	780b	+30	1145	630
Oct	715	742	715	742b	+30	891	612
Nov	......	......	......	709b	+30	866	574
Dec	687½	687½	687½	687½	+30	790	574
CATTLE (CHICAGO MERCANTILE EXCHANGE)							
June	54.25	55.27	54.25	55.2-54.9	+1.35to1.05	55.27	35.17
Aug	48.80	49.40	48.80	49.20-.40	+ .70to.90	50.60	34.85
Oct	43.35	43.90	43.35	43.80-.90	+ .63to.73	43.90	34.27
Dec	41.60	41.95	41.60	41.90-.80	+ .35to.25	42.00	34.35
Feb 76	40.62	40.85	40.55	40.70-.55	+ .13to−.02	40.85	34.52
Apr	40.00	40.20	39.80	39.90	− .05	40.20	39.05
Sales estimated at: 13,487 contracts.							
FRESH EGGS							
June	44.50	44.80	44.25	44.80b	− .20	61.00	39.65
July	47.60	47.95	47.50	47.80a	+ .30	50.50	43.00
Aug	51.00	51.50	51.00	51.35	+ .75	52.20	46.20
Sept	57.90	58.25	57.70	58.05-.20	+ .50to.65	60.15	49.50
Oct	56.25	56.25	56.00	56.25	.....	56.75	51.00

	Open	High	Low	Close	Change	High	Low
SUGAR (WORLD CONTRACT)							
July	13.75	13.80	12.60	12.65-.75	− .80to.70	60.05	10.20
Sept	13.35	13.35	12.03	12.10-.25	− .90to.75	56.05	10.40
Oct	13.15	13.20	11.90	12.00-.10	− .80to.70	53.55	11.90
Mar 76	12.55	12.55	11.75	11.80-.90	− .43to.33	45.45	11.75
May	12.20	12.31	11.67	11.70-.85	− .41to.30	28.65	11.67
July	12.30	12.30	11.40	11.40-.45	− .60to.55	25.10	11.40
Sept	12.05	12.07	11.30	11.30-.35	− .55to.50	18.20	11.30
Oct	12.05	12.05	11.25	11.25-.30	− .50to.45	15.75	11.25
Sales estimated at: 6,439 contracts. Spot: 13.15n.							
COFFEE							
July	58.25	59.50	57.80	59.50-.40	+1.00to.96	66.55	47.00
Sept	58.60	59.95	58.45	59.90-.95	+1.05to1.10	63.55	48.30
Dec	59.10	60.24	58.60	60.05	+1.10	64.65	49.50
Mar 76	59.15	61.50	59.15	61.10-.50	+1.60to2.00	61.50	50.00
May	61.30	61.80	61.30	61.70	+2.00	61.80	51.80
Sales estimated at: 418 contracts.							
COCOA							
July	45.30	45.40	44.95	45.05	− .95	73.50	43.85
Sept	42.00	42.30	41.80	42.05	− .70	70.00	41.80
Dec	41.80	42.00	41.60	41.80	− .90	66.45	41.60
Mar 76	42.21	42.30	41.85	41.90	− .85	64.20	41.85
May	42.79	42.79	42.40	42.45	− .65	59.45	42.40
July	42.90	42.95	42.85	42.85	− .55	57.05	42.85
Sales estimated at: 1,362 contracts.							
WOOL FUTURES							
Dec	138.0	138.0	138.0	136.0b	−2.0	145.0	104.0
Mar76	138.0	138.0	138.0	138.0b	....	144.0	115.0
Spot: 134.0n.							
ORANGE JUICE (FROZEN CONCENTRATED)							
July	52.90	53.90	52.90	53.90	+1.00	61.90	48.20
Sept	54.80	56.00	54.80	56.00	+1.10	63.00	50.15
Nov	57.70	57.70	57.70	57.50b	+ .95	59.55	51.85
Jan 76	58.00	58.80	58.00	58.80	+1.20	64.50	52.90
Mar	60.50	60.75	60.50	60.20b	+1.00	60.75	53.90
July	62.00	62.25	62.00	62.25	+1.45	62.50	57.00
Sales estimated at: 150 contracts.							
COTTON							
July	44.45	44.57	44.37	44.42	− .25	64.00	38.02
Oct	45.75	45.96	45.75	45.80	− .23	60.50	9.95
Dec	46.55	46.65	46.50	46.60-.62	− .15to.13	61.50	40.80
Mar 76	47.35	47.55	47.35	47.50-.55	− .10to.05	56.10	42.00
Sales estimated at: 800 contracts.							
SILVER COIN FUTURES (IN DOLLARS)							
July	3135	3148	3129	3120a	−20	4730	2879
Oct	3200	3203	3185	3185	−23	4300	2965
Jan 76	3270	3270	3265	3253a	−23	4040	3020
July	3419	3419	3419	3389a	−23	3615	3125
Oct	3465	3465	3465	3457a	−21	3608	3375
Sales: 17 contracts.							
PLATINUM							
July	147.60	148.30	147.10	147.60a	− .30	325.50	141.50
Oct	150.70	151.80	150.20	150.80	− .20	253.00	144.30
Jan76	154.00	154.80	153.80	154.20a	− .40	244.50	149.00
Apr	157.50	157.50	157.00	157.50	....	211.00	151.50
July	161.30	161.30	160.90	160.40a	− .60	175.90	156.30
Oct	164.50	164.50	164.50	163.80a	− .20	169.00	162.50
Sales: 200 contracts.							
POTATOES (MAINE CONTRACT)							
Nov	6.10	6.18	5.78	5.78	− .22	6.18	4.15
Mar 76	7.20	7.25	6.80	6.92	− .14	7.27	5.00
Apr	7.90	8.00	7.80	7.80	+ .10	8.00	5.40
May	9.55	9.70	9.45	9.48	+ .05	9.70	5.92
Sales: 5,290 contracts.							
a-Asked. b Bid. n-Nominal.							

Figure 16–5 Commodity Futures Price Quotations. *(Reprinted with permission of The Wall Street Journal, © Dow Jones & Company, Inc., 1975. All Rights Reserved.)*

COMMODITY & EXCHANGE	Trading Hours (Local Time) Open AM	Close PM	CONTRACT UNIT	PRICE FLUCTUATIONS Minimum Move PER UNIT	PER CONTRACT	Round Turn Commission Domestic Non-Mbr	DAILY TRADING LIMITS (B)(C) (D) Above or below Previous Close +	Maximum Range	TRADING LIMIT NOTES
Boneless Beef (R) NYME	10:15	1:45	30,000 lbs	2¢ per cwt	$6.00	$45.00	$1.50+	$3.00	2 & 4 during del month.
Broilers, Iced - CBT	9:15	1:05	28,000 lbs	2 1/2¢ per lb / 100	$7.00	$45.00 (+50¢ fee)	2¢+	4¢	No limit in del. month after 1st notice day.
Cattle, Live (R) CME	9:05	12:45	40,000 lbs	2 1/2¢ per lb / 100	$10.00	$45.00	1 1/2¢	3¢	
Cattle, Western PCE (R)	7:05	11:30	50,000 lbs	2/100¢ per lb	$10.00	$51.00	1 1/2¢	3¢	
Citrus (FCOJ) (R) Citrus Assoc. of N.Y. Cotton Ex.	10:15	2:45	15,000 lbs	5/100¢ per lb	$7.50	$45.00	3¢	3¢	No limit in del. month on or after eighth day.
Cocoa N.Y. Cocoa Ex.	10:00	3:00	30,000 lbs	1/100¢ per lb	$3.00	$65.00	2¢	2¢	No limit in del. mo. on or after first notice day.
Coconut Oil (R) PCE	7:30	11:15	60,000 lbs	1/100¢ per lb	$6.00	$45.00	1¢	2¢	No limit after first notice day.
Coffee "C" N.Y. Cof & Sug Exchange	10:30	2:45	37,500 lbs	1/100¢ per lb	$3.75	$65.00 up to 49.99¢ lb	2¢	4¢	No limit in spot mo. in notice period.
Copper N.Y. Comex	9:50	2:00	25,000 lbs	10/100¢ per lb	$25.00	$45.00 plus 50¢ Ex. fee.	3¢	6¢	No limit on & after day prior to first notice day
Copper - IMM of CME	8:45	1:15	12,500 lbs	10/100¢ per lb	$12.50	$45.00	1/2¢	1¢	No limit last trdg day
Cotton (R) N.Y. Ctn Ex.	10:30	3:00	50,000 lbs	1/100¢ per lb	$5.00	*$55.00 up to 50¢ $65 over 50¢	2¢	4¢	No limit on and after first notice day.
Eggs, Fresh Shell (R) CME & Nest Run	9:20	1:00	22,500 doz	5/100¢ per doz	$11.25	$45.00	2¢+	4¢+	
Feeder Cattle (R) CME	9:05	12:45	42,000 lbs	$.00025 per lb	$10.50	$45.00	1 1/2¢	3¢	
Grains (R) CBT Corn, Wheat Soybeans Oats	9:30	1:15	5,000 bu	1/4¢ per bu	$12.50	$45.00 (+50¢ fee)	10¢ Corn 20¢ Wheat 20¢ Beans 6¢ Oats	20¢ 40¢ 40¢ 12¢	
Wheat (R) KC - MPLS Grain Ex	9:30	1:15	5,000 bu	1/8¢ per bu 1/4¢ (KC)	$6.25 $12.50	$45.00 KC Mpls	25¢ 20¢	50¢ KC 40¢ Mpls	
Wpg Cmdy Exch Flaxseed - Rapeseed Wheat, Oats Barley, Corn Rye	9:30	1:15	5,000 bu	1/4¢ per bu	$12.50	$45.00	30¢ Flax. 20¢ Rape. 10¢ Wheat 10¢ Barley 8¢ Oats 10¢ Rye	60¢ 40¢ 20¢ 20¢ 16¢ 20¢	
Gold CBT	8:45	1:30	3 kilograms (96.45 ozs.)	10¢ per oz	$9.64	$45.00 (+50¢ fee)	$10	$20	No limit in current mo during notice period.
Gold NY Comex	9:45	2:10	100 troy oz	10¢ per oz	$10.00	$45.00 (+50¢ fee)	$10	$20	"
Gold IMM of CME	8:45	1:30	100 troy oz	10¢ per oz	$10.00	$45.00	$10	$20	No limit last trdg day.
Gold NYME	9:25	2:30	1 kilogram 32.151 oz)	20¢ per oz	$6.40	$45.00	$10	$20	No limit in spot mo during del mo
Gold-Wpg Cmdy Ex Standard Contract Centum Contract	8:30	1:15	400 troy oz 100 troy oz	5¢ per oz or 10¢ at traders discretion	$20.00 $5.00	$80.00 $45.00	$10	$20	No limit in del. mo on last trdg day.

Figure 16–6 Commodity Futures Information. (*The information so provided herein is being made available through the courtesy of Merrill Lynch, Pierce, Fenner & Smith Inc., New York, N.Y. 10006 and is intended for educational purposes only. Said information should not be construed as accurate or complete in any respect whatever and, therefore, should not be relied upon as a basis for any investment decision.*)

COMMODITY & EXCHANGE	Trading Hours (Local Time) Open AM	Close PM	CONTRACT UNIT	PRICE FLUCTUATIONS Minimum Move PER UNIT	PER CONTRACT	Round Turn Commission Domestic Non-Mbr	DAILY TRADING LIMITS (B) Above or below Previous Close +	Maximum Range	TRADING LIMIT NOTES
Hogs, Live (R) CME	9:15	12:55	30,000 lbs	2 1/2¢ per lb / 100	$7.50	$45.00	1 1/2¢	3¢	
Lumber CME	9:00	1:05	100,000 bd ft	10¢ per MBF	$10.00	$45.00	$5	$10	
Lumber, Studs CBT	10:00	1:00	100,000 bd ft	10¢ per MBF	$10.00	$45.00	$5	$10	No limit on or after first notice day.
Milo - CME	9:30	1:15	400,000 lbs	.0025 per cwt	$10.00	$45.00	15¢	30¢	
Crude Oil Pet. Assoc of NYCE	9:50	2:20	5,000 barrels	1/10¢ per barrel	$5.00	$55.00	25¢	50¢	
Palm Oil PCE	7:20	11:20 AM	60,000 lbs	1/100¢ per lb	$6.00	$45.00	1¢	2¢	No limit in current mo during notice period.
Platinum NYME	9:45	2:10	50 troy oz	10¢ per oz	$5.00	$45.00	$10	$20	No limit last trdg day.
Plywood CBT	10:00	1:00	69,120 sq ft	10¢ per 1000 sq ft	$6.91	$45.00 (+50¢ fee)	$7	$14	No limit on or after 1st notice day.
Pork Bellies CME	9:10	1:00	36,000 lbs	.0025 per lb	$9.00	$45.00	$.015	$.030	
Potatoes, Idaho (R) CME	9:00	12:50	80,000 lbs	1¢ per 100 lbs	$8.00	$65.00	50¢+	$1	65¢ & $1.35 on last two days.
Potatoes (R) Maine (in 50 lb bags) NYME	9:45	1:30	50,000 lbs	1¢ per 100 lbs	$5.00	$45.00	50¢	$1	No limit on last trdg day.
Propane LPG Assoc of N.Y. Cotton Ex	9:45	2:35	100,000 gal	1/100¢ per gal	$10.00	$45.00	1¢	2¢	"
Rubber NY Comex	10:15	2:20	10 tons (22,040 lbs)	5/100¢ per lb	$11.02	$45.00 (+50¢ fee)	2¢	4¢	No limit in current mo. and during notice per.
Rubber NY Cocoa Ex	9:45	2:45	33,000 lbs	5/100¢ per lb	$16.50	$45.00	2¢	2¢	No limit in del mo in notice per.
Silver NY Comex	10:00	2:15	5,000 troy oz	10/100¢ per oz	$5.00	$45.00 (plus 50¢ ex fee)	20¢	40¢	No limit on or after day prior to 1st notice day.
Silver CBT	9:00	1:25	5,000 troy oz	10/100¢ per troy oz	$5.00	$45.00 (+50¢ fee)	20¢	40¢	No limit during notice period.
U.S. Silver Coins Canadian Silver Coins - IMM	8:50	1:20	$5,000 face value in 5 bags	$2 per bag	$10.00 per contract	$45.00	$150	$300	No limit last trdg day
Silver Coins NYME	9:35	2:15	$10,000 face value in 10 bags	$1 per bag	$10.00	$45.00	$150	$300	No limit on last trdg day.
Soybean Meal (R) CBT	9:30	1:15	100 tons (200,000 lbs)	10¢ per ton	$10.00	$45.00 (+50¢ fee)	$10	$20	No limit on and after 1st notice day.
Soybean Oil (R) CBT	9:30	1:15	60,000 lbs	1/100¢ per lb	$6.00	$45.00 (+50¢ fee)	1¢+	2¢	"
Sugar (Domestic) #10	10:00	2:50				$45.00	2¢	4¢	No limit last trdg day.
Sugar #12	10:00	2:55							
In bulk (World) #11 N.Y. Cof & Sug Ex	10:00	3:00	112,000 lbs	1/100¢ per lb	$11.20	$45.00 up to 5.49¢, $67.00 above 5.49¢	2¢	4¢	No limit on and after 1st bus. day of prior mo.
Wool, Grease (R) Wool Assoc of N.Y. Cotton Ex	10:00	2:30	6,000 lbs	1/10¢ per lb	$6.00	$55.00	5¢	10¢	"

Figure 16–6 (continued)

Government intervention in the commodities market occurs through agriculture price supports, acreage allowances, and import or export commitments. These activities are usually politically motivated. Trade and grower groups also affect supply by limiting, changing, or expanding production within certain parameters. These activities are usually profit motivated and may be caused by high production costs, projected livestock-feed demand ratios, and consumer and industrial demand forecasts.

Quantitative Analysis of Commodities

Quantitative analysis is usually called the technical approach to commodity trading. Technicians state that they use the quantitative approach because interpretations are not required. According to them, all qualitative factors are already included in the price.

Indexes The *Wall Street Journal* publishes a daily commodity index. It provides an indication of spot and futures trends by using weighted averages for a composite of commodities. Other indexes include the Commodity Research Bureau series of weekly futures indexes. Also, the Bureau of Labor Statistics provides a daily wholesale spot commodity price index of twenty-two commodities.

Charting Chartists construct graphs on the price movements of particular commodities. A vertical line representing the price range is drawn for each trading day. A horizontal line is drawn across the daily price range to indicate the day's close. A trendline from close to close can be drawn from the daily price movements. Figure 16–7 is a commercially prepared chart representing corn futures. Some chartists attempt to trade on reactions within a trend. Others attempt to forecast a topping or bottoming of a market by chart patterns. However, most chartists trade with, but slightly behind, the basic trend. Charts are the fastest and easiest way to determine past price performance. They are often considered price indicators, because if enough chartists interpret the charts in the same manner, their purchases will influence prices, thereby completing a self-fulfilling prophecy.

Moving averages A technician can verify a price trend by figuring moving averages. A moving average will always lag behind current prices, thereby offering some verification. The larger the number of days included in the average, the further the lag. A moving average is constructed by adding the sum of prices for the term of the average and dividing by the number of days. For example, a five-day moving average in December corn would be constructed in this manner (prices are rounded):

Date	Closing Price	Sum	5-day Moving Average
July 15	$295		
July 16	304		
July 17	300		
July 18	298		
July 19	308	1505	301.0

The moving average acts as a trendline, smoothing out the highs and lows of daily market fluctuations. It moves right along, following prices by adding the next day's close and dropping the first day in the average to keep it moving. For example, July 22 at $318 would be added, while July 15 would be dropped. The new five-day moving average would be 305.3.

Figure 16–7 Commodity Charts for Corn Futures.

Open Interest Another technical approach involves knowing what type of traders are in the market and what position they have taken. This information can be interpreted from the volume and open interest statistics published daily in the *Wall Street Journal.*

Open interest is simply the number of contracts that remain to be settled for a particular commodity in the futures market.

It reflects the positions of buyers and sellers who have not completed (closed) their contracts to buy or to sell. Whenever a buyer agrees to a contract to purchase a commodity at a future date, he has added to "open interest." Whenever a seller agrees to sell a future commodity without owning it, he has added to "open interest." Both of these traders must sell and buy respectively to "close their interest"; otherwise the buyer will eventually end up taking delivery, and the seller will be pressed to deliver something he does not have.

Open interest is said to be an indicator of the amount of professional trading taking place in the commodities market. A strong trader will take a position for a longer time and will not close his position against the first price change that takes place. You can be long or short in an open-interest position. If you do anything other than follow the trend as verified by open interest, you are taking an unjustifiable risk when you are not a sophisticated trader.

Spreads and straddles Sometimes called a straddle, a spread is the difference between two commodity prices. Traders use straddles to compensate for differences between a normal and abnormal market. Historically, all commodities have a differential between future and cash prices. Speculators trade on this difference. They can trade on spreads in the same commodity, in two different commodities, or the same commodity offered in two different markets.

Commodities Trading

In order to trade you must open an account. This entails having a good credit standing and substantial liquid assets. Brokerage houses have different minimum asset requirements. A somewhat standard requirement is $10,000 in liquid assets and a $50,000 net worth. A brokerage firm will also require that you maintain a capital deposit in your trading account of approximately $3,000. Your account will be a form of margin account without interest.

All trading in commodity futures is done on margin, with an extremely high leverage factor. As long as your position is following the price trend, your profits will increase by the leverage factor in each contract multiplied by the number of contracts you hold. As your position deteriorates, your losses will increase correspondingly. When you incur losses, your account will be subject to a margin call or even sold out if you fail to maintain the minimum margin.

The mechanics of a trade In futures trading, you assume one of three basic trading positions: (1) you *buy* a contract, which is to go *long*. This means you expect the future price of a particular commodity to rise—you are a *bull*; (2) you *sell* a contract, that is to go *short*. This means you expect the futures price to decline—you are a *bear*; (3) you *protect* a contract by a *stop-loss order* or by *closing* a contract. A stop-loss order is usually placed a few points above or below the current market to protect you from an adverse price fluctuation.

We will look at an example of long-position trade. Incidentally, statistics show that short-position traders make profits more consistently than those in long positions, probably because more small traders go long.

Assume that you purchase three contracts of December corn on July 15, at a price of $3.00 per bushel. Further assume that a 5 percent ($2,250) margin is required for the value of the contract bought. If you sold (closed) the contracts on July 24 at $3.38, your profits would be extremely large on a rather small investment.

Sell price per bushel	$3.38	
Buy price per bushel	3.00	
Profit per bushel	$ .38	
3 contracts @ 5,000 bu. each		$50,700
3 contracts @ 5,000 bu. each		45,000
profit		5,700
less commission		90
Net profit		$ 5,610

Every one-cent change in price creates a $50 fluctuation in the value of a corn contract. (See figure 16–7.)

Unfortunately, a commodity can go down as rapidly as it has gone up. For example, after watching the December corn futures rise, you plunge into the market on July 26, at $3.57. Your required margin was $2,677.50. The price goes up and then declines as the rains bring a better corn crop forecast. You "quickly" closed your position at $3.40 on August 5.

Buy price per bushel	$3.57	
Sell price per bushel	3.40	
Loss per bushel	$ .17	
3 contracts @ 5,000 bu. each		$53,550
3 contracts @ 5,000 bu. each		51,000
loss		(2,550)
plus commission		90
Net loss		($ 2,640)

Your broker probably required that you maintain a margin of 75 percent of the original requirement ($2,008.13 of $2,677.50). When the price dropped to $3.50 you received a margin call for at least $381 because you had lost $1,050, leaving your account with only $1,627.50. In practice, the broker would call for about $500 to protect himself even if you had a margin deposit of $3,000 as originally required. If you do not add the extra margin deposit, you must close. If you did not close voluntarily, the broker would have closed for you. As it was, you have lost $2,640, which is all but $360 of your original trading capital.

These situations can and do occur because of the volatility of commodities futures. A sophisticated trader would have allowed his profits to run in the first example. He would have protected himself by placing a stop order slightly below the current market price as long as the market was rising. In the second instance, the trader, once he placed the original long order for $3.57, would put a sell-stop order at $3.54 in case he guessed wrong about the market trend. Since the market did rise initially, he would also move the sell-stop upward.

Advisory services You must stay abreast of market happenings no matter which approach you use. It would probably be to your advantage to use an advisory service to assist you in selecting a position. You can check with your broker for advisory service suggestions. Your choice should be predicted on the service's results over the past year. A reliable service will provide you with its results over the last commodity year.

Summary

You should not risk the commodity market unless you have *money* to risk and *time* to research selected commodities. It might be well worth your while to try paper trading through one crop year before actually entering the market. If it appears that you know what you are doing, go to it! However, you must set certain rules for yourself: (1) Stick to your trading plan whether it is qualitative or quantitative. Do not let hunches sway you. (2) Be conservative; set a limit to the amount of capital you will risk in any one trade. Use stop-loss orders to protect the individual trade. Do not overtrade your margin, because you will defeat the risk limitation concept and may receive a margin call. (3) Diversify your position in the same or different commodity. Do not have all your eggs in one basket. Statistically you have a less than 1-in-2 chance of profit in any single commodity transaction. Therefore, you should assume that two contract positions will help your possibilities, providing that the positions are technically correct. (4) If your capital account allows it, add to your position in an identifiable trend, but only with sufficient stop orders to protect your profit.

A further cautionary note is needed for trading in gold, silver, and other precious metals. You should be aware of the difference between metal futures, coin trading, and mining and development stocks. Futures trading can be considered in the light of commodities trading. You may own coins (numismatics) either as collectibles or as a commodity. You will at least have coins to show for your investment money. Historically, coin values have increased over periods of time. Mining stocks are usually very speculative, especially if they involve extensive exploration and development. Whatever your interest in metals, prudent investment in anything requires thorough investigation before making a move.

FOREIGN INVESTMENT

Another investment medium for the sophisticated investor is the foreign markets, which present all the same investment opportunities that you have domestically, with a few modifications. Differences would include foreign-language difficulties, foreign currency exchange rates, different business customs, and government regulations, not to mention the possibility of unstable governments and the possibility of expropriation. If you do not understand the language, you put yourself at a great disadvantage. Even so, you can probably deal through translators, or possibly in English. However, the probability of error will increase.

Your choice of foreign investment will take one of these forms: (1) securities of American corporations with foreign holdings, (2) securities of foreign corporations, (3) ownership of foreign real estate or business ventures, (4) foreign exchange currency trading, (5) foreign government bonds, and (6) foreign bank savings deposits.

Foreign investment of any sort has more speculative features than domestic investment. This does not mean that you should immediately shun foreign investment. There are a number of advantages, not the least of which may be a business trip to a foreign country. Returns should be greater because the risk is inherently greater. For example, Mexican banks are currently offering twenty-four-month peso time deposits at 12.63 percent and dollar time deposits at 9.5 percent. Just proceed with caution. Investigate before plunging. Do not be emotionally led by the glamor of a foreign investment.

COLLECTIBLES

Collectibles are rather specialized "investments." Most people who own them started out gathering them for a hobby or for the intrinsic enjoyment of the article. Few people purchase these items strictly for investment, even though choice of a particular item may be dictated by its potential resale value. Art, memorabilia, antiques, jewelry, coins, and stamps are examples of what might be called collectibles.

These items should be considered consumer purchases unless you are an expert in the field. Use your regular budget to acquire them because they are not investments per se. Part of their value comes from public fickleness. What is currently popular goes up in price, but not necessarily in real value. At this writing, gold has declined in price on international exchanges and on the domestic coin market after making a spectacular climb. If you had bought at the height of this euphoria, you would now have about a 20 percent decline in value over your purchase price. Presumably you can hold onto this particular investment and it will again rise.

Collectibles should not be your first or second investment priority. Like some of the earlier mentioned speculative investments, they may be used to diversify your long-term portfolio. They have a certain advantage as physically attractive items that are enjoyable to own and *may* increase in value. As with any other investment, the amount of price appreciation will depend on the economy, inflation, and even more so, public infatuation with the collectible. Even the intrinsic value of a collectible is subject to interpretation about quality. You must have some knowledge of what you are purchasing, or you will have to rely on someone's advice.

For example, there are all levels of quality in diamonds. It takes an expert to judge their value. Furthermore, most of the increase in publicized value is at retail prices. Since there is no organized exchange, you will have to sell your diamonds back to a jeweler, who will invariably offer you his wholesale price. Insurance and possibly storage cost added to your original cost leave you with very little profit. This part of collecting is not publicized because it is not newsworthy. Dealers in collectibles also do not publicize the lack of a ready market, which would be detrimental to the "image" of the collectible. Finally, most collectibles do not provide current income. Unless you start a spare-time business out of your hobby, you must be content with a relatively long-range profit potential without liquidity.

YOUR OWN BUSINESS

At one time or another, almost everyone has considered going into business for himself. Quite a few people carry out their dream either by starting a sideline business while working for someone else, or they "go for broke." All too often the latter course prevails before they have a chance to really get started. Dun and Bradstreet estimates that for every 1,000 new businesses started each year, 970 operating businesses terminate operations. This does not mean that the closed business necessarily went broke. The real reasons why companies go out of business usually remain secret. No matter what the reason, few successful businesses would voluntarily close their doors.

Today there are more small businesses than at any time in the history of the United States. There are many reasons for this trend. Running a business is a way of life for many independent-minded people. Moreover, we have become a service-oriented society. And as big business gets bigger, it can no longer provide for small-volume products and services.

Advantages of Business Ownership

Perhaps the greatest of all the advantages in business ownership is the relative *freedom of opportunity* that allows an entrepreneur to develop his business in the manner that provides for his personal satisfaction. An owner's goal may be to make as much money as possible or to be as completely independent as possible.

The chance to make a profit and increase your assets is the usual reason for going into a part-time or a full-time business. Often you can increase your income because there are no definite salary limits that must follow company policy. Additional profits may become available to you after you pay expenses and draw your regular salary.

The desire to be your own boss often outweighs profit considerations. As *owner-manager,* you can meet challenges and develop new ideas. You are not subject to anyone else's authority. You can take whatever risks you feel are warranted. However, this does not necessarily mean complete freedom to do as you choose. There will be some restraints applied to your business operation by your customers, by government requirements, by employee needs, by suppliers of goods and services, by creditors, and by competitors. You can never operate in a vacuum.

Finally, a very important but unmeasurable advantage is a sense of *pride and self-satisfaction* that only comes from ownership. There is a natural tendency to work harder for gain when your entire effort benefits you. More often than not, a self-employed person will end up working harder for himself than he ever did for an employer. You may be your own toughest boss. Even if you seem to please your customers and others who would restrict your activities, you must still please yourself.

Disadvantages of Business Ownership

Every advantage has a disadvantage. First, you may not be your own boss, as described above. It depends on the type of business you are in and how many customers you need. You can be highly independent only if you do not care to be a successful or respected member of the community. Second, *general economic conditions* will affect your business just as much as any other. Failures always increase during periods of economic recession. Even if you do not go out of business, a recession will probably force you to operate on reduced income. Third, *lack of capital* is a perennial problem in small business. You may have very good ideas but very few dollars. Inevitably costs and expenses are greater than anticipated. Very few suppliers or banks will grant you a line of credit until you establish yourself. By then you may not need the funds because you have either generated capital in the business or have terminated operations.

Finally, there is the disadvantage of *sole responsibility.* All managerial successes and failures rest on you. These will affect your employees, creditors, and customers. You will have to be a well-rounded businessman capable of accomplishing the many specialized activities in any business operation. Eventually you can hire specialists, but at first you are both the owner and operator of your business.

Business Failure

The number one problem in small business operation is management, or the lack of it. You may have all the desire in the world, but it will not make a successful enterprise unless you know how to manage. Studies of the reasons for business failures point to managerial ineptitude. If the reason for failure is controllable, it is a management problem. We will discuss management in greater detail later in the chapter.

Reasons for business failures Over 50 percent of all businesses terminate within their first five years of operation. Most failures can be traced to lack of managerial expertise. Before going into business, use this failure checklist to see how you and your proposed business measure up:

1. Lack of experience
2. Lack of money
3. Competition
4. Wrong location
5. Unwise use of capital
6. Poor inventory control
7. Raiding the cash reserves

Types of Business Opportunities

Small business opportunities abound for the well-qualified individual. Again, a unique combination of drive, education, experience, managerial ability, and financial capability are needed to be well qualified. If you fit this description, you can find opportunity in almost any of the manufacturing, wholesale, retail, and service areas. They all have large numbers of small businesses.

Large companies operate best in high volume, highly technical enterprises that require large amounts of capital. Therefore, opportunities for small business tend to be available whenever any of the following situations prevail: (1) personal services are required; (2) the market for the product or service is mainly local; (3) there is a need for custom or low-volume products and services; and (4) innovative products and unique services are performed.

Legal Structure of Business

Before starting in business you must consider the different legal frameworks available for business enterprises. The three most important forms of legal organizations are sole proprietorships, partnerships, and corporations. All have advantages and disadvantages. You must decide which of these best suits your personal and operational needs.

Sole proprietorship This is the simplest form of organization. It is organized, operated, and owned by one individual. A sole proprietor has title to all the assets of the business. He is also responsible for all the claims (liabilities) against the business. The advantage of a sole proprietorship is complete ownership with the profits, responsibilities, and independence that go with it. The disadvantages tend to be the lack of continuity in the business in case of the owner's death, inability to raise large sums of capital, and complete vulnerability of the owner's personal assets to pay business debts.

Partnership A partnership is a voluntary association of two or more persons as co-owners to carry on a business for profit. It allows a pooling of capital and talent by the business partners. Any person capable of contracting may form a partnership without formal documentation. However, it is wise to consult an attorney to draw up formal articles of partnership because of the many possible areas of dissension that could arise whenever two or more people attempt to work and profit together. For instance, in the absence of specific agreements, common law recognizes an equal sharing of profits and losses by all partners.

The major advantages of partnerships are potentially larger sums of capital, increased potential for business loans, and the greater likelihood of specialized or balanced business talents. The major disadvantages lie in automatic termination of the partnership by death, incapacity, or withdrawal of any of the partners and the possibility of dissension because of more than one owner. Furthermore, all partners are fully liable for the business debts of the partnership even if they individually exercise good faith and care in performing their particular duties.

Corporate organization A corporation is a legal entity that is authorized to sue and be sued, hold and sell property, and engage in business activities stipulated in its state-issued charter. Corporations have three main advantages: continuous life, easier access to capital, and separate liability. A corporation has a continuing life, separate from that of its owners. A corporation can obtain large amounts of capital by issuing shares of stock and/or borrowing money in various ways. The corporation has sole liability for its own debts. This has a great appeal for owners, since their personal assets cannot be claimed to settle business debts, as is the case in the other forms of business organization. Directors and company officers are agents for the corporation binding it to contracts.

The main disadvantage of the corporate form of organization is the double taxation feature. As legal entities, corporations pay income tax to federal, state, and local authorities. Then the shareholders must include corporate dividends in their personal income-tax returns. This disadvantage is obviously outweighed by ease of obtaining business capital, the profitability provided by volume operations, the limited liability of owners, and the ease of liquidating an owner's investment.

Going into Business

There are two ways to go into business for yourself. You may *buy an established business* or you may *start a new business*. Purchasing a successful small business at a reasonable price is less risky than starting from scratch. It is also the most common method of going into business. Many people attempt to follow both methods by *obtaining a franchise.*

Buying an Existing Business

You will deal either with a business opportunity broker or with an owner directly when purchasing an existing business. Business brokers operate in much the same fashion as real estate brokers. The advantages of using a business broker are the same as for using a realtor. Available opportunities are often advertised in the classified ads of local papers. A purchase of an existing business will save you much time and effort and possibly be less expensive than start-up costs of a new enterprise. You purchase an existing name, clientele, inventory, and sometimes operating personnel. This eliminates much, but not all, of the risk of a new enterprise. You may inherit a number of problems: the prior owner may have been a poor manager; his clientele may be leaving him; the inventory may be outdated; his reputation may be tarnished; or his employees may be ill trained and ill motivated.

Evaluating the existing business The purchase price is the final determinant in your evaluation. Is it worth it? Before you can answer that question, you must evaluate many other factors:

1. The reason for selling. Sellers often indicate ill health or retirement as their reason for selling. What made them ill or want to retire?
2. Past profitability. This information is available from the financial statements of the business and federal and state income-tax returns.

3. Asset valuation. Current and fixed assets should be examined and compared to book value. Inventory should be accurately stated and should be salable. Accounts receivable should be checked for age and collectibility. Buildings and equipment must be in good repair and reflect proper depreciation.
4. Future profitability. Usually forecasts of future profits based on the books are not particularly accurate. At this point you must consider the three prior factors and then add your own managerial abilities. Will you do a better or worse job than the seller?

Obtaining a Franchise

Franchising is popularly considered the answer to the problem of whether to buy an existing business or to start from scratch. You do a little of both in franchising. It is a system of distributing brand-name or trademarked goods and services through independently owned outlets. A franchise is a contractual agreement allowing a franchisee to offer standardized trademarked products and services for resale.

Initial and annual fees are paid by the franchisee for the right to use the insignia and name of the franchisor. Franchise advantages include the right to receive varying amounts of assistance and expertise in merchandising and operational management. Supplies and goods for resale are usually made available at volume prices.

There are franchises available for nearly every type of endeavor where small business predominates. The *Directory of Franchising Organizations* and the *Franchise Journal* are annual publications that provide a comprehensive listing of available franchise opportunities.

Franchise agreements When a contract is preprinted by one party, it becomes obvious who has the greatest bargaining power. Extreme care must be exercised by a potential franchise owner before signing an agreement. He should consider such factors as the reputation of the franchisor and the quality and acceptance of the franchise product or service. Consult an attorney before signing any franchise agreement.

Having a franchise agreement does not automatically solve all of your business problems. It is no guarantee of success, especially in a new franchising scheme. Well-established franchises in certain fields cost over $100,000. You must decide if the cost and franchise requirements are worth the profit potential. You still have the alternative of starting your own business.

Planning a New Business

Starting a new business involves more time, effort, and risk than purchasing an existing business or securing a franchise. It may well be worth the effort because the business will truly be yours. Hopefully you will not make mistakes. You will be able to select your own business name, location, and equipment; to plan a proper layout, select your own products and inventory; and to determine your own operating policies. You will not have commitments and liabilities left by the previous owner. Sometimes you do not have a choice between buying into or starting your own business. There may not be an available existing business or franchise. For that matter, you may have an unusual idea that requires a pioneer effort.

Opening a competitive business Competition may be the lifeblood of business, but it can also be very expensive and unwise for the small businessman: You must be able to forecast accurately the possibility of success when opening a business similar to or identical with competitors. You must determine if there is really a need for your business. There may be a need under two conditions: (1) an expanding market is creating a greater demand than can be adequately filled by existing enterprises; and (2) present businesses are inefficiently managed.

Opening a unique business A new business may be truly unique or only partly original. It is extremely rare to find a completely new product or service, but if it is new, you must first decide if a demand can be created for the product or service. Then you must figure a way to profit from the pioneer effort. Often a new product can be tied in with a standard service, or a new service can be rendered with an established product. Creative thinking can lead to a new business. For example, the expansion of a hobby can lead to a part-time or full-time business. It is also well worth capitalizing on trends and consumer fads. Sometimes new opportunities occur because the demographic composition of a trading area changes over the years.

Operating the Business

Each type of business activity has its own special operating problems. Persons without experience in the industry can easily fail by making wrong operating decisions. This is why experience should accompany education in any small business venture. However, there are a number of problems common to all business. Some of these are best learned through experience; others can be learned by a little reading, some research, and lots of good advice. When operating your own business, be prepared to learn about and become involved in such activities as (1) insurance requirements; (2) employee recruitment, selection, training, promotions, wages, and benefits; (3) purchasing policies; (4) inventory or production control; (5) cost control; (6) marketing strategy, including pricing, advertising, sales promotion, sales credit, and market penetration, and (7) local, state, and federal government regulations and taxes.

The owner of any business needs expertise in two areas to help with all these problems. He must have the ability to understand and perform managerial functions and have the ability to read and comprehend financial statements. In addition, he must have certain personal characteristics that will be helpful to him.

Functions of management General experience and education are very useful; however, there are five functions of management that must be performed in the formation and operation of a business: planning, organizing, staffing, directing, and controlling. As a business becomes larger and more complex, these functions become more specialized. However, every person in a management position carries out these functions to some degree:

1. Planning. Provides for the short and long range goals of the business enterprise. The manager sets timing and resource objectives.
2. Organizing. Provides for the coordination of personnel, equipment, and finance necessary to reach enterprise goals effectively.
3. Staffing. Provides for selection of the right persons in the right jobs. Proper personnel selection should provide a balancing of talents and specialties.
4. Directing. Provides day-to-day supervision of business activities. Operational decision making and an understanding of human relations are important responsibilities.
5. Controlling. Provides for follow-up of financial and operational results. Verifies that the operation adhered to the plan in a successful manner.

The higher you are in the business hierarchy, the more likely it is that your management functions will be planning, organizing, and controlling. Lower-level supervision tends to focus on staffing, directing, and controlling.

Financial statements The second major area of expertise is financial analysis. An accounting background would be ideal for any owner, but at the least, a businessman should have an understanding of financial statements. We have already looked into financial analysis in chapter 13, so we will not do so again, but remember that the balance sheet, income statement, and reconciliation of net worth are like road maps. They show you where you have been; they show you where you are; and they offer advice on how to get to where you want to go. Figure 16–8 illustrates a composite financial statement required by Bank of America as part of a business loan application.

Full Appraisal

You should consider both the financial and nonfinancial advantages and disadvantages of owning an independent business. Make a realistic appraisal of your personal qualifications and managerial abilities. Consider the amount of capital available through personal, partner, shareholder, or debt financing. Check the type of business opportunities available. Investigate the competitive situation. Remember the reasons why businesses fail.

Investment in your own business may provide you with a higher rate of return than you could get elsewhere. The value of your time and services may be greater in self-employment than in working for others. However, the opposite may be just as true. You may be able to earn more if your funds were invested elsewhere or if you worked for someone else. You have to make the decision.

Vocabulary and Concepts

Call	Option
Collectibles	Partnership
Commodities	Proprietorship
Foreign exchange	Put
Franchise	Treasury bills
Futures	Treasury bonds
Municipal securities	Treasury notes

Questions for Discussion

1. Explain the difference between marketable and nonmarketable government securities. What are Treasury bills, notes, and bonds?
2. Why are municipal securities usually offered at relatively low interest rates?
3. Describe the advantages and disadvantages of a stock option contract.
4. Why is there a commodity futures market? Is this a speculative investment? Explain.
5. What is a moving average? Why are they used in commodity futures trading?
6. When purchasing a franchise, what should you look for?
7. Enumerate and describe the various types of foreign investment available.
8. What are the general advantages and disadvantages of "investing in collectibles"?
9. Describe the advantages and disadvantages of owning your own business.
10. What two possible choices must you consider before you open your own business? Which method of opening a business would you suggest? Why?

Projects

1. Visit a business opportunity broker. Find out the pertinent facts about the purchase of an existing business of your choice.

An example of how your own financial statement will look on paper.

FINANCIAL STATEMENT

INDIVIDUAL, PARTNERSHIP, OR CORPORATION

FINANCIAL STATEMENT OF

RECEIVED AT ______ BRANCH

NAME ______

BUSINESS ______

ADDRESS ______

AT CLOSE OF BUSINESS ______ 19 ___

To **Bank of America**
NATIONAL TRUST AND SAVINGS ASSOCIATION

The undersigned, for the purpose of procuring and establishing credit from time to time with you and to induce you to permit the undersigned to become indebted to you on notes, endorsements, guarantees, overdrafts or otherwise, furnishes the following (or in lieu thereof the attached) which is the most recent statement prepared by or for the undersigned as being a full, true and correct statement of the financial condition of the undersigned on the date indicated, and agrees to notify you immediately of the extent and character of any material change in said financial condition, and also agrees that if the undersigned, or any endorser or guarantor of any of the obligations of the undersigned, at any time fails in business or becomes insolvent, or commits an act of bankruptcy, or dies, or if a writ of attachment, garnishment, execution or other legal process be issued against property of the undersigned or if any assessment for taxes against the undersigned, other than taxes on real property, is made by the federal or state government or any department thereof, or if any of the representations made below prove to be untrue, or if the undersigned fails to notify you of any material change as above agreed, or if such change occurs, or if the business, or any interest therein, of the undersigned is sold, then and in such case, all of the obligations of the undersigned to you or held by you shall immediately become due and payable, without demand or notice. This statement shall be construed by you to be a continuing statement of the condition of the undersigned, and a new and original statement of all assets and liabilities upon each and every transaction in and by which the undersigned hereafter becomes indebted to you, until the undersigned advises in writing to the contrary.

ASSETS	DOLLARS	CENTS
Cash In ______ (NAME OF BANK)		
Cash on Hand		
Notes Receivable and Trade Acceptance (Includes $ ______ Past Due)		
Accounts Receivable—$ ______ Less Reserves $ ______		
Customer's . . . (Includes $ ______ Past Due)		
Merchandise—Finished—How Valued		
Merchandise—Unfinished—How Valued		
Merchandise—Raw Material—How Valued		
Supplies on Hand		
Stocks and Bonds—Listed (See Schedule B)		
TOTAL CURRENT ASSETS		
Real Estate—Less Depreciation of: $ ______ Net (See Schedule A)		
Machinery and Fixtures— Less Depreciation of: $ ______ Net		
Automobiles and Trucks— Less Depreciation of: $ ______ Net		
Stocks and Bonds—Unlisted (See Schedule B)		
Due from Partners, Employes, Relatives, Officers, Stockholders or Allied Companies		
Cash Surrender Value of Life Insurance		
Other Assets (Describe)		
TOTAL		

LIABILITIES	DOLLARS	CENTS
Notes Payable to Banks		
Notes Payable and Trade Acceptances for Merchandise		
Notes Payable to Others		
Accounts Payable (Includes $ ______ Past Due)		
Due to Partners, Employes, Relatives, Officers, Stockholders or Allied Companies		
Security Agreements and Contracts Payable (Describe Monthly Payments) . . . . . $		
Federal and State Income Tax		
Accrued Liabilities (Interest, Wages, Taxes, Etc.)		
Portion of Long Term Debt Due Within One Year		
TOTAL CURRENT LIABILITIES		
Liens on Real Estate (See Schedule A) $		
Less Current Portion Included Above $ ______ Net		
Capital Stock—Preferred		
Capital Stock—Common		
Surplus—Paid In		
Surplus—Earned and Undivided Profits		
Net Worth (If Not Incorporated)		
TOTAL		

PROFIT AND LOSS STATEMENT FOR THE PERIOD FROM ______ TO ______

Net Sales (After Returned Sales and Allowances)			
Cost of Sales:			
Beginning Inventory			
Purchases (or cost of goods mfd)			
TOTAL			
Less: Closing Inventory			
Gross Profit on Sales			
Operating Expenses:			
Salaries—Officers or Partners			
Salaries and Wages—Other			
Rent			
Depreciation			
Bad Debts			
Advertising			
Interest			
Taxes—Other Than Income			
Insurance			
Other Expenses			
Net Profit from Operations			
Other Income			
Less Other Expense			
Net Profit Before Income Tax			
Federal and State Income Tax			
Net Profit or Loss			
(To Net Worth or Earned Surplus)			

CR-1 3-64 (REV.)

RECONCILEMENT OF NET WORTH OR EARNED SURPLUS

Net Worth or Earned Surplus at Beginning of Period			
Add Net Profit or Deduct Net Loss			
Total			
Other Additions (Describe)			
Total			
Less: Withdrawals or Dividends			
Other Deductions (Explain)			
Total Deductions			
Net Worth or Capital Funds on This Financial Statement			

CONTINGENT LIABILITIES (NOT INCLUDED ABOVE)

There are no lease liabilities in existence nor are there encumbered assets securing leases, except as listed in attached schedule.

As Guarantor or Endorser or under agreements to purchase or service indebtedness			
Accounts, Notes, or Trade Acceptances Discounted or Pledged			
Surety On Bonds or Other Contingent Liability			
Letters of Credit			
Judgments Unsatisfied or Suits Pending			
Lease Liabilities			
Merchandise Commitments and Unfinished Contracts or Merchandise Held On Consignment From Others			
Unsatisfied Tax Liens or Notices From the Federal or State Governments of Intention to Assess Such Liens			

DETAIL OF INVENTORY

Is Inventory Figure Actual or Estimated? ______

By Whom Taken or Estimated ______ When? ______

Buy Principally From ______

Average Terms of Purchase ______ Sale ______

Time of Year Inventory Maximum ______ Minimum ______

Figure 16–8 Composite Financial Statement. *(Bank of America N.T. & S.A., San Francisco)*

Compare the promised rate of return with the average for that particular type of business.

2. Choose an option to buy or sell on the Chicago Board Options Exchange. Determine the profit or loss on the exercise of the option.
3. Choose to "invest" in a collectible that is interesting to you. Investigate the acquisition and storage costs. Find out how much it costs to liquidate your collection and to whom the sale will generally be made. Is it a better investment than the more traditional investment opportunities?

Case Problem

Bart Baker feels he is well on his way to becoming economically well off. He would like to apply leverage to increase his investment capital of $2,000. He is unsure whether to try stock options or the commodity futures market. He does not really understand the mechanics of either. Explain both alternatives by projecting a call and a particular commodity future that are due to mature in about three months. Does he have sufficient capital to speculate in the option and commodity that you have chosen?

index

A

B

C

G

H

R

S

T

U

V

W

Y